SIXTH EDITION

The Principles of Learning and Behavior

Michael Domjan

University of Texas at Austin

with contributions by
James W. Grau
Texas A & M University

Workbook by
Mark A. Krause
Southern Oregon University

 **WADSWORTH**
CENGAGE Learning™

Australia • Brazil • Japan • Korea • Mexico • Singapore • Spain • United Kingdom • United States

WADSWORTH
CENGAGE Learning

The Principles of Learning and Behavior, 6th Edition

Michael Domjan

Psychology Editor: Jon-David Hague

Assistant Editor: Rebecca Rosenberg

Editorial Assistant: Kelly Miller

Media Editor: Rachel Guzman

Marketing Manager: Tierra Morgan

Marketing Coordinator: Molly Felz

Marketing Communications Manager: Talia Wise

Content Project Manager: Charlene M. Carpentier

Creative Director: Rob Hugel

Art Director: Vernon Boes

Print Buyer: Linda Hsu

Rights Acquisitions Account Manager, Text: Bob Kauser

Rights Acquisitions Account Manager, Image: Robyn Young

Production Service: Elm Street Publishing Services

Text Designer: Lisa Henry

Photo Researcher: PrePress PMG

Cover Designer: Denise Davidson

Cover Image: Gerry Ellis/Globio

Compositor: Integra Software Services Pvt. Ltd.

For product information and technology assistance, contact us at **Cengage Learning Customer & Sales Support, 1-800-354-9706**

For permission to use material from this text or product, submit all requests online at **www.cengage.com/permissions**.

Further permissions questions can be e-mailed to **permissionrequest@cengage.com**.

Library of Congress Control Number: 2008941714

International Student Edition
ISBN-13: 978-0-495-80461-1
ISBN-10: 0-495-80461-4

Wadsworth
10 Davis Drive
Belmont, CA 94002-3098
USA

Cengage Learning is a leading provider of customized learning solutions with office locations around the globe, including Singapore, the United Kingdom, Australia, Mexico, Brazil, and Japan. Locate your local office at **www.cengage.com/international.**

Cengage Learning products are represented in Canada by Nelson Education, Ltd.

To learn more about Wadsworth, visit **www.cengage.com/Wadsworth**
Purchase any of our products at your local college store or at our preferred online store **www.ichapters.com.**

Printed in Canada
1 2 3 4 5 6 7 13 12 11 10 09

to Deborah

BRIEF CONTENTS

CONTENTS

9 Extinction of Conditioned Behavior   299

10 Aversive Control: Avoidance and Punishment   333

11 Comparative Cognition I: Memory Mechanisms 375

12 Comparative Cognition II: Special Topics 419

PREFACE

This edition of *The Principles of Learning and Behavior* is something of a personal and professional landmark. When I signed the original contract for the book in 1979, I thought I would be lucky to complete the first edition and had no idea that the book would remain a staple in the field for 30 years. Since its first publication, the book has served to introduce students to behavioral mechanisms of learning in the United States, Canada, Colombia, Chile, Turkey, Spain, and other European countries. Some of those students have become professors in their own right and have used later editions of the book in their own teaching.

Originally, I had three basic goals in writing the book. The first was to share with students all of the new ideas and findings that I considered so exciting in the area of conditioning and learning. The second was to integrate behavioral learning phenomena with how behavior systems have been shaped by evolution. This second goal provided the rationale for including *behavior* in the title of the book. The third goal was to provide an eclectic and balanced presentation of the field that was respectful of both the Pavlovian associationist tradition and the Skinnerian behavior-analytic tradition. These three goals have continued to motivate successive editions of the book.

Some books do not change much from one edition to another. That has not been the case with this book. In the first edition, I struggled to get all the facts right and to present them in a coherent fashion. I am still eager to get all the facts right, but I no longer find that task much of a struggle. Instead, the primary challenge is to incorporate new experimental findings and approaches. In the 2nd and 3rd editions, I simply added newly published results. Later editions involved substantial reorganizations of various parts of the book, with older material being deleted in favor of new information. That twofold process of updating and pruning is very much evident in the 6th edition. I had to decide not only what to add but what to remove. My apologies to investigators who may find their favorite experiment no longer cited in the book.

A major benefit of the revisions that I have undertaken is that successive editions of the book reflect how the field of learning has evolved in the past 30 years. One of my professorial colleagues recently remarked that he was highly familiar with learning theory because he knew all about Tolman, Guthrie, and Hull. He should read this new edition, as Tolman and Guthrie do not appear, and Hull is only mentioned briefly in favor of more contemporary research. That is not to say that I have ignored historical antecedents; I have not. However, I have ignored the learning theory debates that preoccupied psychologists for much of the twentieth century.

The field of conditioning and learning continues to evolve in significant ways. In the 5th edition, I commented on the great advances that were taking place in studies of the neural mechanisms of learning. Research on the neurobiology of learning continues to be a major area of investigation. My focus all along has been on behavioral mechanisms of learning because the significance of neurobiological processes ultimately rests with how those processes contribute to overt behavior. However, neurobiological findings are mentioned in the text more frequently now, and I am indebted again to Professor James Grau for providing summaries of key neuroscience topics in specially highlighted boxes.

Another major new direction that is evident in the field of learning is the emphasis encouraged by the National Institutes of Health to make the research more directly relevant to human clinical problems. This emphasis on translational research has stimulated a great deal of work on extinction, memory, and drug addiction. I have incorporated many of these new findings and have emphasized applications of the basic research findings to human situations throughout the book.

Significant progress has also been made in recent years in better understanding the habitual character of much of human behavior, the role of habituation processes in human food intake and obesity, and the evolutionary roots of important cognitive processes. These developments are reflected in major changes in many of the chapters.

Another major development in the field is that the basic behavioral principles that are described in this book are being utilized by a much broader range of scientists than at any previous period in the last 30 years. To update earlier editions of the book, I just needed to review recent reports in five specialty journals (*Journal of Experimental Psychology: Animal Behavior Processes, Learning & Behavior, The Journal of the Experimental Analysis of Behavior, Learning and Motivation,* and *The Quarterly Journal of Experimental Psychology*). These focal journals remain important sources of information on behavioral mechanisms of conditioning and learning. But, this time many of the new references I cited appeared in 78 other journals. Interesting new information on learning now appears in journals on addiction, health psychology, consulting and clinical psychology, psychiatry, neuroscience, cognitive science, evolution, animal behavior, and other areas.

Identifying relevant sources that appear in a diverse range of journals is made possible by the search engines of the new information age. The new information age has also altered the way in which books are produced. The first edition of this book was published by Brooks/Cole. The company flew me out to their offices in Pacific Grove, CA. I met briefly with the President and then had more extensive discussions with the Psychology Editor and various members of the production staff. Brooks/Cole subsequently merged with Wadsworth, which was purchased by Thomson Learning, which then sold its textbook publishing operations to Cengage. When I started the 6th edition, Cengage did not have a Psychology Editor, and I subsequently learned that the design and some aspects of the production of the book had been outsourced to a company in India. At first I was skeptical about how all this would work out, but I have been pleasantly surprised and pleased by the remarkable efficiency and professionalism of all of the people involved with the 6th edition, including Menaka Gupta and the new Psychology Editor, Jon-David Hague. I am grateful to them all for their help. I would also like to thank Professor Mark Krause for providing updates to the workbook exercises at the back of the book.

Successive editions of this book have also marked important transitions in my personal life. I was hard at work on the 1st edition when my son, Paul, was born. He will be 30 years old when the 6th edition appears. My daughter, Katherine, was born shortly before the 2nd edition appeared, and my son, Xavier, was born shortly after the 2nd edition. This book is dedicated to my wife, Deborah. Deborah and I have seven children, four grandchildren, two dogs, and a cat. They all provide lots of opportunities to observe and to experience learning every day.

Michael Domjan
Austin, Texas

MICHAEL DOMJAN is a Professor of Psychology at the University of Texas at Austin, where he has taught learning to undergraduate and graduate students since 1973. He also served as Department Chair from 1999–2005 and was the Founding Director of the Imaging Research Center from 2005–2008. Professor Domjan is noted for his functional approach to classical conditioning, which he has pursued in studies of sexual conditioning and taste aversion learning. His research was selected for a MERIT Award by the National Institutes of Mental Health as well as a Golden Fleece Award by United States Senator William Proxmire. He served as Editor of the *Journal of Experimental Psychology: Animal Behavior Processes* for six years and was recipient of the G. Stanley Hall Award from the American Psychological Association (APA). He is a past President of the Pavlovian Society and also served as President of the Division of Behavioral Neuroscience and Comparative Psychology of APA.

1

Introduction

CHAPTER PREVIEW

The goal of Chapter 1 is to introduce the reader to behavioral studies of learning. I begin by characterizing behavioral studies of learning and describing how these are related to cognition and the conscious control of behavior. I then describe the historical antecedents of key concepts in modern learning theory. This is followed by a discussion of the origins of contemporary experimental research in studies of the evolution of intelligence, functional neurology, and animal models of human behavior. I also discuss the implications of contemporary research for the development of memory-enhancing drugs and the construction of artificial intelligent systems or robots. I then provide a detailed definition of learning and discuss how learning can be examined at different levels of analysis. Methodological features of studies of learning are described in the next section. Because numerous experiments on learning have been performed with nonhuman animals, I conclude the chapter by discussing the rationale for the use of nonhuman animals in research, with comments about the public debate about animal research.

People have always been interested in understanding behavior, be it their own or the behavior of others. This interest is more than idle curiosity. Our quality of life depends on our actions and the actions of others. Any systematic effort to understand behavior must include consideration of what we learn and how we learn it. Numerous aspects of the behavior of both human and nonhuman animals are the results of learning. We learn to read, to write, and to count. We learn to walk down stairs without falling, to open doors, to ride a bicycle, and to swim. We also learn when to relax and when to become anxious. We learn what foods we are likely to enjoy and what foods will make us sick. We also learn the numerous subtle gestures that are involved in effective social interactions. Life is filled with activities and experiences that are shaped by what we have learned.

Learning is one of the biological processes that facilitate adaptation to one's environment. The integrity of life depends on successfully accomplishing a number of biological functions such as respiration, digestion, and resisting disease. Physiological systems have evolved to accomplish these tasks. However, for many species, finely tuned physiological processes do not take care of all of the adaptive functions that are required, and even those that are fairly efficient are improved by learning (Domjan, 2005). For example, reproduction, which is central to the survival of a species, is significantly improved by learning.

Animals, including people, have to learn to find new food sources when old ones become unavailable or when they move to a new area. They also have to find new shelter when storms destroy their old ones, as happened during Hurricane Katrina. Accomplishing these tasks obviously requires motor behavior, such as walking and manipulating objects. These tasks also require the ability to predict important events in the environment, such as when and where food will be available. All these things involve learning. Animals learn to go to a new water hole when their old one dries up and they learn to anticipate new sources of danger. These learned adjustments to the environment are as important as physiological processes such as respiration and digestion.

It is common to think about learning as involving the acquisition of new behavior. Indeed, learning is required before someone can read, ride a bicycle, or play a musical instrument. However, learning can just as well consist of the decrease or loss of a previously common response. A child, for example, may learn to not cross the street when the traffic light is red, to not grab food from someone else's plate, and to not yell and shout when someone is trying to take a nap. Learning to *withhold* responses is just as important as learning to *make* responses.

When considering learning, we are likely to think about forms of learning that require special training, such as the learning that takes place in schools and colleges. Solving calculus problems or completing a triple somersault when diving requires special instruction. However, we also learn all kinds of things without an expert teacher or coach during the course of routine interactions with our social and physical environment. Children learn how to open doors and windows, what to do when the phone rings, when to avoid a hot stove, and when to duck so as not to get hit by a flying ball. College students learn how to find their way around campus, how to avoid heartburn from cafeteria food, and how to predict when a roommate will stay out late at night, all without special instruction.

In the coming chapters, I will describe research on the basic principles of learning and behavior. We will focus on basic types of learning and behavior that are fundamental to life but, like breathing, are often ignored. These pervasive and basic forms of learning are a normal (and often essential) part of daily life, even though they rarely command our attention. I will describe the learning of relationships between events in the environment, the learning of motor movements, and the learning of emotional reactions to stimuli. These forms of learning are investigated in experiments that involve conditioning or "training" procedures of various sorts. However, these forms of learning occur in the lives of human and nonhuman animals without explicit or organized instruction or schooling.

Much of the research that I will describe is in the behaviorist tradition of psychology that emphasizes analyzing behavior in terms of its antecedent stimuli and consequences. Conscious reflection and reasoning are deliberately left out of this analysis. I will describe automatic **procedural learning** that does not require awareness (e.g., Lieberman, Sunnucks, & Kirk, 1998; Smith et al., 2005) rather than **declarative** or **episodic learning** that is more accessible to conscious report. One might argue that this restriction leaves out many interesting aspects of human behavior. However, social psychologists who have been examining these issues empirically have concluded that many important aspects of human behavior occur without awareness. Gosling, John, Craik, and Robins (1998), for example, found that people are relatively inaccurate in reporting about their own behavior (see also Stone et al., 2000). Wegner (2002) summarized his research on the experience of conscious intent in a book whose title, *The illusion of conscious will,* says it all. Bargh and Chartrand (1999) similarly concluded that "most of a person's everyday life is determined not by their conscious intentions and deliberate choices but by mental processes that are put into motion by features of the environment and that operate outside of conscious awareness and guidance (p. 462)" (See also Bargh & Morsella, 2008.)

The following chapters will describe how features of the environment gain the capacity to trigger our behavior whether we like it or not. This line of research has its origins in what has been called behavioral psychology. During the last quarter of the twentieth century, behavioral psychology was overshadowed by "the cognitive revolution." However, the cognitive revolution did not eliminate the taste aversions that children learn when they get chemotherapy, it did not reduce the cravings that drug addicts experience when they see their friends getting high, and it did not stop the proverbial Pavlovian dog from salivating when it encountered a signal for food. Cognitive science did not grow by taking over the basic learning phenomena that are the focus of this book. Rather, it grew by extending psychology into new areas of research, such as attention, problem solving, and knowledge representation. For example, in one prominent contemporary textbook on cognition (Anderson, 2005), classical and instrumental conditioning are not even mentioned. However, as important as are the new topics of cognitive psychology, they do not tell us how good and bad habits and emotions are acquired or how they may be effectively modified.

Basic behavioral processes remain important in the lives of organisms even as we learn more about other aspects of psychology. In fact, there is a major resurgence of interest in the basic behavioral mechanisms. This resurgence of interest is fueled by the growing appreciation of the limited role of consciousness in behavior (e.g., Pockett, Banks, & Gallagher, 2006) and the recognition that much of what takes us through the day involves habitual responses that we spend little time thinking about (Wood, & Neal, 2007). We don't think about how we brush our teeth, dry ourselves after a shower, put on our clothes, or chew our food. All of these are learned responses. Contemporary interest in behavior theory is also fueled by the tremendous growth of interest in the neural mechanisms of learning (Fanselow & Poulos, 2005). Animals interact with their environment through their actions. Therefore, behavioral phenomena provide the gold standard for assessing the functional significance of neural mechanisms. Behavioral models of conditioning and learning are also fundamental to the understanding of recalcitrant clinical problems such as pathological fears and phobias (Craske, Hermans, & Vansteenwegen, 2006), and drug addiction (Hyman, 2005; Hyman, Malenka, & Nestler, 2006; Olmstead, 2006). As Wiers and Stacy (2006) pointed out, "The problem, often, is not that substance abusers do not understand that the disadvantages of continued use outweigh the advantages; rather, they have difficulty resisting their automatically triggered impulses to use their substance of abuse" (p. 292). This book deals with how such behavioral impulses are learned.

HISTORICAL ANTECEDENTS

Theoretical approaches to the study of learning have their roots in the philosophy of René Descartes (see Figure 1.1). Before Descartes, most people thought of human behavior as entirely determined by conscious intent and free will. People's actions were not considered to be controlled by external stimuli or mechanistic natural laws. What someone did was presumed to be the result of his or her will or deliberate intent. Descartes took exception to this view of human nature because he recognized that many things people do are automatic reactions to external stimuli. However, he was not prepared to entirely abandon the idea of free will and conscious control. He therefore formulated a dualistic view of human behavior known as Cartesian **dualism.**

According to Cartesian dualism, there are two classes of human behavior: involuntary and voluntary. Descartes proposed that involuntary behavior consists of automatic reactions to external stimuli and is mediated by a special mechanism called a **reflex.** Voluntary behavior, by contrast, does not have to be triggered by external stimuli and occurs because of the person's conscious intent to act in that particular manner.

The details of Descartes' dualistic view of human behavior are diagrammed in Figure 1.2. Let us first consider the mechanisms of involuntary, or reflexive,

Library of Congress Prints and Photographs Division [LC-USZ62-61365]

FIGURE **1.1**

René Descartes (1596–1650)

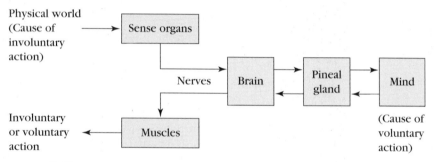

Physical world
(Cause of
involuntary
action)

Sense organs

Nerves

Brain

Pineal
gland

Mind

Involuntary
or voluntary
action

Muscles

(Cause of
voluntary
action)

FIGURE **1.2**

Diagram of Cartesian dualism. Events in the physical world are detected by sense organs. From here the information is transmitted to the brain. The brain is connected to the mind by way of the pineal gland. Involuntary action is produced by a reflex arc that involves messages sent first from the sense organs to the brain and then from the brain to the muscles. Voluntary action is initiated by the mind, with messages sent to the brain and then the muscles.

behavior. Stimuli in the environment are detected by the person's sense organs. The sensory information is then relayed to the brain through nerves. From the brain, the impetus for action is sent through nerves to the muscles that create the involuntary response. Thus, sensory input is *reflected* in response output. Hence, Descartes called involuntary behavior *reflexive*.

Several aspects of this system are noteworthy. Stimuli in the external environment are assumed to be the cause of all involuntary behavior. These stimuli produce involuntary responses by way of a neural circuit that includes the brain. However, Descartes assumed that only one set of nerves was involved. According to Descartes the same nerves transmitted information from the sense organs to the brain and from the brain down to the muscles. He believed this circuit permitted rapid reactions to external stimuli; for example, quick withdrawal of one's finger from a hot stove.

Descartes assumed that the involuntary mechanism of behavior was the only one available to animals other than humans. According to this view, all of nonhuman animal behavior occurs as reflex responses to external stimuli. Thus, Descartes believed that nonhuman animals lacked free will and were incapable of voluntary, conscious action. He considered free will and voluntary behavior to be uniquely human attributes. This superiority of humans over other animals existed because only human beings were thought to have a mind, or soul.

The mind was assumed to be a nonphysical entity. Descartes believed that the mind was connected to the physical body by way of the pineal gland, near the brain. Because of this connection, the mind could be aware of and keep track of involuntary behavior. Through this mechanism, the mind could also initiate voluntary actions. Because voluntary behavior was initiated in the mind, it could occur independently of external stimulation.

The mind-body dualism introduced by Descartes stimulated two intellectual traditions. One, mentalism, was concerned with the contents and workings of the mind, while the other, reflexology, was concerned with the mechanisms of reflexive behavior. These two intellectual traditions form the foundations of the modern study of learning.

Historical Developments in the Study of the Mind

Philosophers concerned with the mind were interested in what was in the mind and how the mind works. These questions are similar to those that preoccupy present day cognitive psychologists. Because Descartes thought the mind was connected to the brain by way of the pineal gland, he believed that some of the contents of the mind came from sense experiences. However, he also believed that the mind contained ideas that were innate and existed in all human beings independent of personal experience. For example, he believed that all humans were born with the concept of God, the concept of self, and certain fundamental axioms of geometry, such as the fact that the shortest distance between two points is a straight line. The philosophical approach that assumes we are born with innate ideas about certain things is called **nativism.**

Some philosophers after Descartes took issue with the nativist position. In particular, the British philosopher John Locke (1632–1704) believed that all the ideas people had were acquired directly or indirectly through experiences after birth. He believed that human beings were born without any preconceptions about the world. According to Locke, the mind started out as a clean slate (*tabula rasa*, in Latin), to be gradually filled with ideas and information as the person had various sense experiences. This philosophical approach to the contents of the mind is called **empiricism.** Empiricism was accepted by a group of British philosophers who lived from the seventeenth to the nineteenth centuries and who came to be known as the *British empiricists*.

The nativist and empiricist philosophers disagreed not only about what the mind was assumed to contain, but also on how the mind was assumed to operate. Descartes believed that the mind did not function in a predictable and orderly manner, according to strict rules or laws that one could identify. One of the first to propose an alternative to this position was the British philosopher Thomas Hobbes (1588–1679). Hobbes accepted the distinction between voluntary and involuntary behavior stated by Descartes and also accepted the notion that voluntary behavior was controlled by the mind. However, unlike Descartes, he believed that the mind operated just as predictably and lawfully as a reflex. More specifically, he proposed that voluntary behavior was governed by the principle of **hedonism.** According to this principle, people do things in the pursuit of pleasure and the avoidance of pain. Hobbes was not concerned with whether the pursuit of pleasure and the avoidance of pain were laudable or desirable. For Hobbes, hedonism was simply a fact of life. As we will see, the notion that behavior is controlled by positive and negative consequences has remained with us in one form or another to the present day.

According to the British empiricists, another important aspect of how the mind works involved the concept of **association.** Recall that empiricism assumes that all ideas originate from sense experiences. But how do our experiences of various colors, shapes, odors, and sounds allow us to arrive at more complex ideas? Consider, for example, the concept of a car. If someone says the word *car*, you have an idea of what the thing looks like, what it is used for, and how you might feel if you sat in it. Where do all these ideas come from given just the sound of the letters *c*, *a*, and *r*? The British empiricists proposed that simple sensations were combined into more complex ideas by associations. Because you have heard the word *car* when you saw a car, considered using one to get to work, or sat in one, connections or associations became established between the word *car* and these other attributes of cars. Once the associations are established, the word *car* will activate memories of the other aspects of cars that you have experienced. The British empiricists considered such associations to be the building blocks of mental activity. Therefore, they devoted considerable effort to characterizing the rules of associations.

Rules of Associations

The British empiricists accepted two sets of rules for the establishment of associations: one primary and the other secondary. The primary rules were originally set forth by the ancient Greek philosopher Aristotle. He proposed three principles for the establishment of associations: 1) contiguity, 2) similarity, and 3) contrast. Of these, the contiguity principle has been the most prominent in studies of associations and continues to play an important role in contemporary work. It states that if two events repeatedly occur together in space or time, they will become associated. For example, if you encounter the smell of tomato sauce with spaghetti often enough, your memory of spaghetti will be activated by the smell of tomato sauce by itself. The similarity and contrast principles state that two things will become associated if they are similar in some respect (i.e., both are red) or have some contrasting characteristics (i.e., one might be strikingly tall and the other strikingly short). Similarity as a basis for the formation of associations has been confirmed by modern studies of learning (e.g., Rescorla & Furrow, 1977). However, there is no contemporary evidence that making one stimulus strikingly different from another (contrast) facilitates the formation of an association between them.

Various secondary laws of associations were set forth by a number of empiricist philosophers, among them, Thomas Brown (1778–1820). Brown proposed that a number of factors influence the formation of associations between two sensations. These include the intensity of the sensations, and how frequently or recently the sensations occurred together. In addition, the formation of an association between two events was considered to depend on the number of other associations in which each event was already involved, and the similarity of these past associations to the current one being formed.

The British empiricists discussed rules of association as a part of their philosophical discourse. They did not perform experiments to determine whether or not the rules were valid, nor did they attempt to determine the circumstances in which one rule was more important than another. Empirical investigation of the mechanisms of associations did not begin until the pioneering work of the nineteenth-century German psychologist Hermann Ebbinghaus (1850–1909).

To study how associations are formed, Ebbinghaus invented **nonsense syllables.** Nonsense syllables are three-letter combinations (*bap*, for example), devoid of any meaning that might influence how someone might react to them. Ebbinghaus used himself as the experimental subject. He studied lists of nonsense syllables and measured his ability to remember them under various experimental conditions. This general method enabled him to answer such questions as how the strength of an association improved with increased training, whether nonsense syllables that appeared close together in a list were associated more strongly with one another than syllables that were farther apart, and whether a syllable became more strongly associated with the next one on the list than with the preceding one. Many of the issues that were addressed by the British empiricists and Ebbinghaus have their counterparts in modern studies of learning and memory.

Historical Developments in the Study of Reflexes

Descartes made a very significant contribution to the understanding of behavior when he formulated the concept of the reflex. The basic idea that behavior can reflect a triggering stimulus remains an important building block of behavior theory. However, Descartes was mistaken in his beliefs about the details of reflex action. He believed that sensory messages going from sense organs to the brain and motor messages going from the brain to the muscles traveled along the same nerves. He thought that nerves were hollow tubes, and neural transmission involved gases called *animal spirits*. The animal spirits, released by the pineal gland, were assumed to flow through the neural tubes and enter the muscles, causing them to swell and create movement. Finally, Descartes considered all reflexive movements to be innate and to be fixed by the anatomy of the nervous system. Over the course of several hundred years, all of these ideas about reflexes were demonstrated to be incorrect.

Charles Bell (1774–1842) in England and Francois Magendie (1783–1855) in France showed that separate nerves are involved in the transmission of sensory information from sense organs to the central nervous system and motor information from the central nervous system to muscles. If a sensory nerve is cut, the animal remains capable of muscle movements; if a motor nerve is cut, the animal remains capable of registering sensory information.

The idea that animal spirits are involved in neural transmission was also disproved after the death of Descartes. In 1669, John Swammerdam (1637–1680) showed that mechanical irritation of a nerve was sufficient to produce a muscle contraction. Thus, infusion of animal spirits from the pineal gland was not necessary. In other studies, Francis Glisson (1597–1677) demonstrated that muscle contractions were not produced by swelling due to the infusion of a gas, as Descartes had postulated.

Descartes and most philosophers after him assumed that reflexes were responsible only for simple reactions to stimuli. The energy in a stimulus was thought to be translated directly into the energy of the elicited response by the neural connections. The more intense the stimulus was, the more vigorous the resulting response would be. This simple view of reflexes is consistent with many causal observations. If you touch a stove, for example, the hotter the stove, the more quickly you withdraw your finger. However, some reflexes are much more complicated.

The physiological processes responsible for reflex behavior became better understood in the nineteenth century, and that understanding stimulated broader conceptions of reflex action. Two Russian physiologists, I. M. Sechenov (1829–1905) and Ivan Pavlov (1849–1936), were primarily responsible for these

SOVFOTO

FIGURE **1.3**

I. M. Sechenov (1829–1905)

developments. Sechenov proposed that stimuli did not always elicit reflex responses directly. Rather, in some cases a stimulus could release a response from inhibition. Where a stimulus released a response from inhibition, the vigor of the response would not depend on the intensity of the stimulus. This simple idea opened up all sorts of new possibilities.

If the vigor of an elicited response does not invariably depend on the intensity of its triggering stimulus, it would be possible for a very faint stimulus to produce a large response. Small pieces of dust in the nose, for example, can cause a vigorous sneeze. Sechenov took advantage of this type of mechanism to provide a reflex model of voluntary behavior. He suggested that complex forms of behavior (actions or thoughts) that occurred in the absence of an obvious eliciting stimulus were in fact reflexive responses. It is just that, in these cases, the eliciting stimuli are so faint that we do not notice them. Thus, according to Sechenov, voluntary behavior and thoughts are actually elicited by inconspicuous, faint stimuli.

Sechenov's ideas about voluntary behavior greatly extended the use of reflex mechanisms to explain a variety of aspects of behavior. However, his ideas were philosophical extrapolations from the actual research results he obtained. In addition, Sechenov did not address the question of how reflex mechanisms can account for the fact that behavior is not fixed and invariant throughout an organism's lifetime, but can be altered by experience. From the time of Descartes, reflex responses were considered to be innate and fixed by the connections of the nervous system. Reflexes were thought to depend on a prewired neural circuit connecting the sense organs to the relevant muscles. According to this view, a given stimulus could be expected to elicit the same response throughout an organism's life. Although this is true in some cases, there are also many examples in which responses to stimuli change as a result of experience. Explanation of such cases by reflex processes had to await the experimental and theoretical work of Ivan Pavlov.

Pavlov showed experimentally that not all reflexes are innate. New reflexes to stimuli can be established through mechanisms of association. Thus, Pavlov's role in the history of the study of reflexes is comparable to the role of Ebbinghaus in the study of the mind. Both were concerned with establishing the laws of associations through empirical research. However, Pavlov did this in the physiological tradition of reflexology rather than in the mentalistic tradition.

Much of modern behavior theory has been built on the reflex concept of stimulus-response, or S-R unit, and the concept associations. S-R units and associations continue to play prominent roles in contemporary behavior theory. However, these basic concepts have been elaborated and challenged over the years. As I will describe in later chapters, in addition to S-R units or connections, modern studies of learning have also demonstrated the existence of stimulus-stimulus (S-S) connection and modulatory, or hierarchical, associative structures (Schmajuk & Holland, 1998). Quantitative descriptions of learned behavior that do not employ associations have gained favor in some quarters (e.g., Gallistel & Gibbon, 2000, 2001; Leslie, 2001) and have been emphasized by contemporary scientists working in the Skinnerian tradition of behavioral analysis (e.g., Staddon, 2001). However, associative analyses continue to dominate behavior theory and provide the conceptual cornerstone for much of the research on the neural mechanisms of learning.

THE DAWN OF THE MODERN ERA

Experimental studies of basic principles of learning often are conducted with nonhuman animals and in the tradition of reflexology. Research in animal learning came to be pursued with great vigor starting a little more than a hundred years ago. Impetus for the research came from three primary sources (see Domjan, 1987). The first of these was interest in comparative cognition and the evolution of the mind. The second was interest in how the nervous system works (functional neurology), and the third was interest in developing animal models to study certain aspects of human behavior. As we will see in the ensuing chapters, comparative cognition, functional neurology, and animal models of human behavior continue to dominate contemporary research in learning.

Comparative Cognition and the Evolution of Intelligence

Interest in comparative cognition and the evolution of the mind was sparked by the writings of Charles Darwin (see Figure 1.4) who took Descartes' ideas about human nature one step further. Descartes started chipping away at the age-old notion that human beings have a unique and privileged position in the animal kingdom by proposing that at least some aspects of human behavior (their reflexes) were animal-like. However, Descartes preserved some privilege for human beings by assuming that humans (and only humans) have a mind.

Darwin attacked this last vestige of privilege. In his second major work, *The Descent of Man and Selection in Relation to Sex*, Darwin argued that "man is descended from some lower form, notwithstanding that connecting-links have not hitherto been discovered" (Darwin, 1897, p. 146). In claiming continuity from nonhuman to human animals, Darwin attempted to characterize not only the evolution of physical traits, but also the evolution of psychological or mental abilities. He argued that the human mind is a product of evolution. In making this claim, Darwin did not deny that human beings had such mental abilities such as the capacity for wonder, curiosity, imitation,

Philip Gendreau/Bettmann/CORBIS

FIGURE **1.4**

Charles Darwin (1809–1882)

attention, memory, reasoning, and aesthetic sensibility. Rather, he suggested that nonhuman animals also had these abilities. For example, he maintained that nonhuman animals were capable even of belief in spiritual agencies (Darwin, 1897, p. 95).

Darwin collected anecdotal evidence of various forms of intelligent behavior in animals in an effort to support his claims. Although the evidence was not compelling by modern standards, the research question was. Ever since, investigators have been captivated by the possibility of tracing the evolution of intelligence by studying the abilities of various species of animals.

Before one can investigate the evolution of intelligence in a systematic fashion, one must have a criterion for identifying intelligent behavior in animals. A highly influential proposal for a criterion was offered by George Romanes, in his book *Animal Intelligence* (Romanes, 1882). Romanes suggested that intelligence be identified by determining whether an animal learns "to make new adjustments, or to modify old ones, in accordance with the results of its own individual experience" (p. 4). Thus, Romanes defined intelligence in terms of the ability to learn. This definition was widely accepted by comparative psychologists at the end of the nineteenth and the start of the twentieth century and served to make the study of animal learning the key to obtaining information about the evolution of intelligence.

Only a subset of research on the mechanisms of animal learning has been concerned with the evolution of intelligence. Nevertheless, the cognitive abilities of nonhuman animals continue to fascinate both the lay public and the scientific community. In contemporary science, these issues are covered under the topic of "comparative cognition" or "comparative psychology" (e.g., Papini, 2008; Shettleworth, 1998). However, the connection to historical concerns is still evident, as in the title of a recent major text, *Comparative cognition: Experimental explorations of animal intelligence* (Wasserman & Zentall, 2006). We will discuss the results of contemporary research on comparative cognition in many chapters of this text, but especially in Chapters 11 and 12.

Functional Neurology

The modern era in the study of learning processes was also greatly stimulated by efforts to use studies of learning in nonhuman animals to gain insights into how the nervous system works. This line of research was initiated by the Russian physiologist Pavlov, quite independently of the work of Darwin, Romanes, and others interested in comparative cognition.

While still a medical student, Pavlov became committed to the principle of **nervism**. According to nervism, all key physiological functions are governed by the nervous system. Armed with this principle, Pavlov devoted his life to documenting how the nervous system controlled various aspects of physiology. Much of his work was devoted to identifying the neural mechanisms of digestion.

For many years, Pavlov's research progressed according to plan. But, in 1902, two British investigators, Bayliss and Starling, published results showing that the pancreas, an important digestive organ, was partially under hormonal rather than neural control. Some time later, Pavlov's friend and biographer noted that these novel findings produced a crisis in the laboratory because they "shook the very foundation of the teachings of the exclusive nervous regulation of the secretory activity of the digestive glands" (Babkin, 1949, p. 228).

The evidence of hormonal control of the pancreas presented Pavlov with a dilemma. If he continued his investigations of digestion, he would have to abandon his interest in the nervous system. On the other hand, if he maintained his commitment to nervism, he would have to stop studying digestive physiology. Nervism won out. In an effort to continue studying the nervous system, Pavlov changed from studying digestive physiology to studying the conditioning of reflexes. Thus, Pavlov regarded his studies of conditioning (which is a form of learning) as a way to obtain information about the functions of the nervous system: how the nervous system works. Pavlov's claim that studies of learning tell us about the functions of the nervous system is well accepted by contemporary neuroscientists. Kandel, for example, has commented that "the central tenet of modern neural science is that all behavior is a reflection of brain function" (Kandel, Schwartz, & Jessell, 1991, p. 3).

The behavioral psychologist is like a driver who tries to find out about an experimental car by taking it out for a test drive instead of first looking under the hood. By driving the car, a driver can learn a great deal about how it functions. He or she can discover its acceleration, its top speed, the quality of its ride, its turning radius, and how quickly it comes to a stop. Driving the car will not reveal how these various functions are accomplished, but it will reveal the major functional characteristics of the internal machinery of the car.

Knowledge of the functional characteristics of a car can, in turn, provide clues about its internal machinery. For example, if the car accelerates sluggishly and never reaches high speeds, chances are it is not powered by a rocket engine. If the car only goes forward when facing downhill, it is probably propelled by gravity rather than by an engine. On the other hand, if the car cannot be made to come to a stop quickly, it may not have brakes.

In a similar manner, behavioral studies of learning can provide clues about the machinery of the nervous system. Such studies tell us about the kinds of plasticity the nervous system can exhibit, the conditions under which learning can take place, how long learned responses persist, and the circumstances under which learned information is accessible or inaccessible. By detailing the functions of the nervous system, behavioral studies of learning define the features or functions that have to be explained by neurophysiological investigations.

Animal Models of Human Behavior

The third major impetus for the modern era in the study of animal learning was the belief that research with nonhuman animals can provide information that may help us better understand human behavior. Animal models of human behavior are of more recent origin than comparative cognition or functional neurology. The approach was systematized by Dollard and Miller and their collaborators (Dollard, Miller, Doob, Mowrer, & Sears, 1939; Miller & Dollard, 1941), and developed further by B. F. Skinner (1953).

Drawing inferences about human behavior on the basis of research with other animal species can be hazardous and controversial. The inferences are hazardous if they are unwarranted; they are controversial if the rationale for the model system approach is poorly understood. Model systems have been developed based on research with a variety of species, including several species of primates, pigeons, rats, and mice.

In generalizing from research with rats and pigeons to human behavior, one does not make the assumption that rats and pigeons are just like people. Animal models are used as we use other types of models. Architects, pharmacologists, medical scientists, and designers of automobiles all rely on models, which are often strikingly different from the real thing. Architects, for example, make small-scale models of buildings they are designing. Obviously, such models are not the same as a real building. The models are much smaller, made of cardboard and small pieces of wood instead of bricks and mortar, and they support little weight.

As Overmier (1999) pointed out, "Models are basic and powerful tools in science." Models are commonly used because they permit investigation of certain aspects of what they represent under conditions that are *simpler, more easily controlled,* and *less expensive.* With the use of a model, an architect can study the design of the exterior of a planned building without the expense of actual construction. The model can be used to determine what the building will look like from various vantage points and how it will appear relative to other nearby buildings. Studying a model in a design studio is much simpler than studying an actual building on a busy street corner. Factors that may get in the way of getting a good view, such as other buildings, traffic, and power lines, can be controlled and minimized in a model.

In a comparable fashion, a car designer can study the wind resistance of various design features of a new automobile with the use of a model in the form of a computer program. The program can be used to determine how the addition of spoilers or changes in the shape of the car will change its wind resistance. The computer model bears little resemblance to a real car. It has no tires or engine and cannot be driven. However, the model permits testing the wind resistance of a car design under conditions that are much simpler, better controlled, and less expensive than if the actual car were built and driven down the highway under various conditions.

Considering all the differences between a model and the real thing, what makes models valid for studying something? For a model to be valid, it must be comparable to its target referent in terms of the feature or function under study. This is called the *relevant feature* or *relevant function.* If the model of a building is used to study the building's exterior appearance, then all the exterior dimensions of the model must be proportional to the corresponding dimensions of the planned building. Other features of the model, such as its structural elements, are irrelevant. In contrast, if the model is used to study how well the building would withstand an earthquake, then its structural elements (beams and how they are connected) would be critical.

In a similar manner, the only thing relevant in a computer model of car wind resistance is that the computer program provides calculations for wind resistance that match the results obtained with real cars that are driven through real air. No other feature is relevant; therefore, the fact that the computer program lacks an engine or rubber tires is of no consequence.

The rationale and strategies associated with using nonhuman animals as models for human behavior are similar to those pertaining to models in other areas of inquiry. Animal models permit investigating problems that are difficult, if not impossible, to study directly with people. A model permits the research to be carried out under circumstances that are simpler, better controlled, and less expensive. Furthermore, the validity of animal models is based on the same criterion as the validity of other types of models. The important thing is similarity between the animal model and human behavior in *relevant features* for the problem at hand. As Schuster pointed out, "The demonstration that animals would self-administer many drugs of abuse led to a major reformulation of the conceptual framework of the problem of drug addiction" (Schuster, 1999, p. xiii). The fact that the animals had long tails and walked on four legs instead of two was entirely irrelevant to the issue.

The critical task in constructing a successful animal model is to identify the relevant similarity between the animal model and the human behavior of interest. The relevant similarity concerns the causal factors that are responsible for particular forms of behavior (Overmier, 1999). We can gain insights into human behavior based on the study of nonhuman animals if the causal relations in the two species are similar. Because animal models are often used to push back the frontiers of knowledge, the correspondence between the animal findings and human behavior always must be carefully verified by empirical data. This interaction between animal and human research continues to make important contributions to our understanding of human behavior (e.g., Branch & Hackenberg, 1998; Delgado, Olsson, & Phelps, 2006; Gosling, 2001), and has also informed our understanding of the behavior of nonhuman animals (e.g., Escobar, Matute, & Miller, 2001; Miller & Matute, 1996).

Applications of learning principles got a special boost in the 1960s with the accelerated development of behavior therapy. As O'Donohue commented, "the model of moving from the learning laboratory to the clinic proved to be an extraordinarily rich paradigm. In the 1960s, numerous learning principles were shown to be relevant to clinical practice. Learning research quickly proved to be a productive source of ideas for developing treatments or etiological accounts of many problems" (1998, p. 4). This fervor was tempered during subsequent developments of cognitive behavior therapy. However, recent advances in learning theory have encouraged a return to learning explanations of important human problems such as panic disorder (Bouton, Mineka, & Barlow, 2001).

In the upcoming chapters, I will describe animal models of love and attachment, drug tolerance and addiction, food-aversion learning, learning of fears and phobias, and stress and coping, among others. Animal models have also led to the development of numerous procedures now commonly employed with people, such as biofeedback, programmed instruction, exposure therapy, token economies, and other techniques of behavior modification. I will provide examples of such applications at relevant points in the text. (For additional examples, see Carroll & Overmier, 2001; Haug & Whalen, 1999; Higgins, Heil, & Lussier, 2004; and Higgins, Silverman, & Heil, 2008.)

Animal Models and Drug Development

Whether we visit a doctor because we have a physical or psychiatric illness, we are likely to leave with a prescription to alleviate our symptoms. Pharmaceutical companies are eager to bring new drugs to the market and to develop drugs for symptoms that were previously handled in other ways (e.g., erectile dysfunction). Drug development is not possible without animal models. The animal learning paradigms described in this text are especially important for developing new drugs to enhance learning and cognition. As people live longer, cognitive decline with aging is becoming more prevalent, as is the demand for drugs to slow that decline. Animal models of learning and memory are playing a central role in the development of these new drugs. Animal models are also important for the development of antianxiety medications and drugs that facilitate the progress of behavior and cognitive therapy (e.g., Davis et al., 2005; Gold, 2008; Richardson, Ledgerwood, & Cranney, 2004). Another important area of research is evaluation of the potential for drug abuse associated with new medications for pain relief and other medical problems (e.g., Ator & Griffiths, 2003). Experiments with animals that evaluate drug abuse potential are advisable before these drugs are distributed for human use. Many of these experiments employ methods described in this book.

Animal Models and Machine Learning

Animal models of learning and behavior are also of considerable relevance to robotics and intelligent artificial systems (machine learning). Robots are machines that are able to perform particular functions or tasks. The goal in robotics is to make the machines as "smart" as possible. Just as Romanes defined "intelligence" in terms of the ability to learn, contemporary roboticists view the ability to remember and learn from experience an important feature of smart, artificial systems. Information about the characteristics and mechanisms of such learning may be gleaned from studies of learning in nonhuman animals (e.g., Gnadt & Grossberg, 2007; Schaal, et al., 2004). Associative mechanisms are frequently used in artificial intelligent systems to enable the response of those systems to be altered by experience. One prominent approach called "reinforcement learning" (Sutton & Barto, 1998; Prescott, Bryson, & Seth, 2007) tackles many of the same issues that arise in studies of instrumental conditioning, which we will discuss starting in Chapter 5.

THE DEFINITION OF LEARNING

Learning is such a common human experience that people rarely reflect on exactly what it means to say that something has been learned. A universally accepted definition of learning does not exist. However, many important aspects of learning are captured in the statement:

> *Learning is an enduring change in the mechanisms of behavior involving specific stimuli and/or responses that results from prior experience with those or similar stimuli and responses.*

This definition has many important consequences for the study of learning. These implications are spelled out in the following sections.

The Learning-Performance Distinction

Whenever we see evidence of learning, we see the emergence of a change in behavior: the performance of a new response or the suppression of a response that occurred previously. A child becomes skilled in snapping the buckles of her sandals or becomes more patient in waiting for the popcorn to cook in the microwave oven. Such changes in behavior are the only way we can tell whether or not learning has occurred. However, notice that the preceding definition attributes learning to a change in the *mechanisms of behavior,* not to a change in behavior directly.

Why should we define learning in terms of a change in the mechanisms of behavior? The main reason is that behavior is determined by many factors in addition to learning. Consider, for example, eating. Whether you eat something depends on how hungry you are, how much effort is required to obtain the food, how much you like the food, and whether you know where to find food. Of all these factors, only the last one necessarily involves learning.

Performance refers to all of the actions of an organism at a particular time. Whether an animal does something or not (its performance) depends on many things. Even the occurrence of a simple response such as jumping into a swimming pool is multiply determined. Whether you jump depends on the availability, depth, temperature of the water, physical ability to spring away from the side of the pool, and so forth. Therefore, a change in performance cannot be automatically considered to reflect learning.

Learning is defined in terms of a change in the mechanisms of behavior to emphasize the distinction between learning and performance. The behavior of an organism (its performance) is used to provide evidence of learning. However, because performance is determined by many factors in addition to learning, one must be very careful in deciding whether a particular aspect of performance does or does not reflect learning. Sometimes evidence of learning cannot be obtained until special test procedures are introduced. Children, for example, learn a great deal about driving a car just by watching others drive, but this learning is not apparent until they are permitted behind the steering wheel. In other cases, a change in behavior is readily observed but cannot be attributed to learning because it does not last long enough or result from experience with specific environmental events.

Learning and Other Sources of Behavior Change

Several mechanisms produce changes in behavior that are too short–lasting to be considered instances of learning. One such process is **fatigue**. Physical exertion may result in a gradual reduction in the vigor of a response because the individual becomes tired. This type of change is produced by experience. However, it is not considered an instance of learning, because the decline in responding disappears if the individual is allowed to rest for a while.

Behavior also may be temporarily altered by a *change in stimulus conditions.* If the house lights in a movie theater suddenly come on in the middle of the show, the behavior of the audience is likely to change dramatically. However, this is not an instance of learning, because the audience is likely to return to watching the movie when the house lights are turned off again.

Other short-term changes in behavior that are not considered learning involve *alterations in the physiological or motivational state* of the organism.

Hunger and thirst induce responses that are not observed at other times. Changes in the level of sex hormones cause changes in responsiveness to sexual stimuli. Short-lasting behavioral effects may also accompany the administration of psychoactive drugs.

In some cases persistent changes in behavior occur, but without the type of experience with environmental events that satisfies the definition of learning. The most obvious example of this is **maturation.** A child cannot get something from a high shelf until he grows tall enough. However, the change in behavior in this case is not an instance of learning because it occurs with the mere passage of time. The child does not have to be trained to reach high places as he becomes taller. Maturation can also result in the disappearance of certain responses. For example, shortly after birth, touching an infant's feet results in foot movements that resemble walking, and stroking the bottom of the foot causes the toes to fan out. Both of these reflexes disappear as the infant gets older.

Generally, the distinction between learning and maturation is based on the importance of special experiences in producing the behavior change of interest. However, the distinction is blurred in cases where environmental stimulation is necessary for maturational development. Experiments with cats, for example, have shown that the visual system will not develop sufficiently to permit perception of horizontal lines unless the cats were exposed to such stimuli early in life (e.g., Blakemore & Cooper, 1970). The appearance of sexual behavior at puberty also depends on developmental experience. In particular, successful sexual behavior requires experience with playmates before puberty (e.g., Harlow, 1969).

Learning and Levels of Analysis

Because of its critical importance in everyday life, learning is being studied at many different levels of analysis (Byrne, 2008). Some of these are illustrated in Figure 1.5. Our emphasis will be on analyses of learning at the level

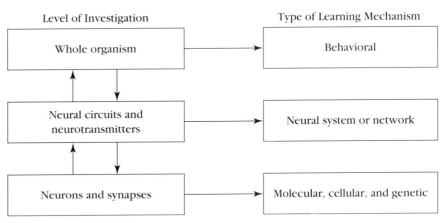

FIGURE **1.5**

Levels of analysis of learning. Learning mechanisms may be investigated at the organism level, at the level of neural circuits and transmitter systems, and at the level of nerve cells or neurons.

of behavior. The behavioral level of analysis is rooted in the conviction that the function of learning is to facilitate an organism's interactions with its environment. We interact with our environment primarily through our actions. Therefore, the behavioral level of analysis occupies a cardinal position.

Much research on learning these days is also being conducted at the level of neural mechanisms. This interest has been stimulated by tremendous methodological and technical advances that permit scientists to directly examine biological processes that previously were only hypothetical possibilities. The neural mechanisms involved in learning may be examined at the *systems level* that is concerned with how neural circuits and neurotransmitter systems are organized to produce learned responses. Neural mechanisms may also be examined at the level of individual neurons and synapses, with an emphasis on *molecular* and *cellular* mechanisms, including *genetic* mechanisms. Advances in the neural mechanisms of learning at several levels of analysis are described in boxes that appear throughout the text.

Periodically, we will also describe changes in learning that occur as a function of age. These are referred to as *developmental* changes. It is also useful to consider the *adaptive significance* of learning. Conceptually, adaptive significance refers to the contribution of a process to evolution. Practically, the basic measure of adaptive significance is how successful an organism is in reproducing and leaving healthy offspring behind. Most scientists would agree that learning mechanisms evolved because they increase reproductive fitness. The contribution of learning to reproductive fitness is often indirect. By learning to find food more efficiently, for example, an organism may live longer and have more offspring. However, studies of sexual conditioning have shown that learning can also facilitate the physiological and behavioral processes involved in reproduction and directly increase fertility (Matthews et al., 2007; Hollis et al., 1997).

METHODOLOGICAL ASPECTS OF THE STUDY OF LEARNING

There are two prominent methodological features of studies of learning. The first of these is a direct consequence of the definition of learning and involves the exclusive use of experimental—as contrasted with observational—research methods. The phenomena of learning simply cannot be investigated without the use of an experimental methodology. The second methodological feature is reliance on a general-process approach. Reliance on a general-process approach is more a matter of intellectual style than a matter of necessity.

Learning as an Experimental Science

Studies of learning focus on identifying how prior experience causes long-term changes in behavior. At the behavioral level, this boils down to identifying the critical components of training or conditioning protocols. The emphasis on identifying causal variables necessitates an experimental approach.

Consider the following example. Mary goes into a dark room. She quickly turns on a switch near the door and the lights in the room go on.

Can you conclude that turning on the switch "caused" the lights to go on? Not from the information provided. Perhaps the lights were on an automatic timer and would have come on without Mary's actions. Alternatively, the door may have had a built-in switch that turned on the lights after a slight delay. Or, there may have been a motion detector in the room that activated the lights.

How could you determine that manipulation of the wall switch caused the lights to go on? You would have to test various scenarios to prove the causal model. For example, you might ask Mary to enter the room again, but ask her not to turn on the wall switch. If the lights did not go on under these circumstances, certain causal hypotheses could be rejected. You could conclude that the lights were not turned on by a motion detector or by a switch built into the door. As this simple example illustrates, an experiment has to be conducted in which the presumed cause is removed in order to identify a cause. The results obtained with and without the presumed cause can then be compared.

In the study of learning, the behavior of living organisms is of interest, not the behavior of lights. But, scientists have to proceed in a similar fashion. They have to conduct experiments in which behavior is observed with and without the presumed cause. The most basic question is to identify whether a training procedure produces a particular type of learning effect. To answer this question, individuals who previously received the training procedure have to be compared to individuals who did not receive that training. This requires experimentally varying the presence and absence of the training experience. Because of this, *learning can be investigated only with experimental techniques*. This makes the study of learning primarily a laboratory science.

The necessity of using experimental techniques to investigate learning is not adequately appreciated by allied scientists. Many aspects of behavior can be studied with observational procedures that do not involve experimental manipulations of the presumed causes of the behavior. For example, observational studies can provide a great deal of information about whether and how animals set up territories, the manner in which they defend those territories, the activities involved in the courtship and sexual behavior of a species, the ways in which animals raise their offspring, and the changes in the activities of the offspring as they mature.

Fascinating information has been obtained with observational techniques that involve minimal intrusion into the ongoing activities of the animals. Unfortunately, learning cannot be studied that way. To be sure that the changes in behavior are not due to changes in motivation, sensory development, hormonal fluctuations, or other possible non-learning mechanisms, it is necessary to conduct experiments in which the presumed training experiences are systematically manipulated. The basic learning experiment compares two groups of subjects (see Figure 1.6). The experimental group receives the training procedure of interest, and how this procedure changes behavior is measured. The performance of the experimental group is compared to a control group that does not receive the training procedure but is otherwise treated in a similar fashion. Learning is presumed to have taken place if the experimental group responds differently from the control group. A similar rationale can be used to study learning in a single individual provided that one can be certain that the behavior is stable in the absence of a training intervention.

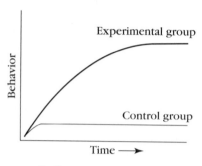
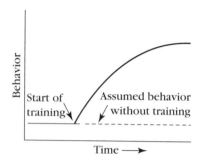

· FIGURE **1.6**

Two versions of the fundamental learning experiment. In the left panel, two groups of individuals are compared. The training procedure is provided for participants in the experimental group, but not for participants in the control group. In the right panel, a single individual is observed before and during training. The individual's behavior during training is compared to what we assume its behavior would have been without training.

The General-Process Approach to the Study of Learning

The second prominent methodological feature of studies of learning is the use of a general-process approach. In adopting a general-process approach, investigators of animal learning are following a long-standing tradition in science.

Elements of the General-Process Approach

The most obvious feature of nature is its diversity. Consider, for example, the splendid variety of minerals that exist in the world. Some are soft, some are hard, some are brilliant in appearance, others are dull, and so on. Plants and animals also exist in many different shapes and sizes. Dynamic properties of objects are diverse. Some things float up, whereas others rapidly drop to the ground; some remain still; others remain in motion.

In studying nature, one can either focus on differences or try to ignore the differences and search for commonalities. Scientists ranging from physicists to chemists, from biologists to psychologists, have all elected to search for commonalities. Rather than being overwhelmed by the tremendous diversity in nature, scientists have opted to look for uniformities. They have attempted to formulate *general laws* with which to organize and explain the diversity of events in the universe. Investigators of animal learning have followed this well-established tradition.

Whether or not general laws are discovered often depends on the level of analysis that is pursued. The diversity of the phenomena scientists try to understand and organize makes it difficult to formulate general laws at the level of the observed phenomena. It is difficult, for example, to discover the general laws that govern chemical reactions by simply documenting the nature of the chemicals involved in various reactions. Similarly, it is difficult to explain the diversity of species in the world by cataloging the features of various animals. Major progress in science comes from analyzing phenomena at a more elemental or molecular level. For example, by the nineteenth century, chemists knew many specific facts about what would happen when various chemicals were combined. However, a general account of chemical reactions had to await the development of the periodic table of the elements, which organized chemical elements in terms of their constituent atomic components.

Investigators of conditioning and learning have been committed to the general-process approach from the inception of this field of psychology. They have focused on the commonalities of various instances of learning and have assumed that learning phenomena are products of elemental processes that operate in much the same way in different learning situations.

The commitment to a general-process approach guided Pavlov's work on functional neurology and conditioning. Commitment to a general-process approach to the study of learning is also evident in the writings of early comparative psychologists. For example, Darwin (1897) emphasized commonalities among species in cognitive functions: "My object...is to show that there is no fundamental difference between man and the higher mammals in their mental faculties" (p. 66). At the start of the twentieth century, Jacques Loeb (1900) pointed out that commonalities occur at the level of elemental processes: "Psychic phenomena...appear, invariably, as a function of an elemental process, namely the activity of associative memory" (p. 213). Another prominent comparative psychologist of the time, C. Lloyd Morgan, stated that elementary laws of association "are, we believe, universal laws" (Morgan, 1903, p. 219).

The assumption that "universal" elemental laws of association are responsible for learning phenomena does not deny the diversity of stimuli that different animals may learn about, the diversity of responses they may learn to perform, and species differences in rates of learning. The generality is assumed to exist in the rules or processes of learning, not in the contents or speed of learning. This idea was clearly expressed nearly a century ago by Edward Thorndike, one of the first prominent American psychologists who studied learning:

> Formally, the crab, fish, turtle, dog, cat, monkey, and baby have very similar intellects and characters. All are systems of connections subject to change by the laws of exercise and effect. The differences are: first, in the concrete particular connections, in what stimulates the animal to response, what responses it makes, which stimulus connects with what response, and second, in the degree of ability to learn. (Thorndike, 1911, p. 280)

What an animal can learn (the stimuli, responses, and stimulus-response connections it learns about) varies from one species to another. Animals also differ in how fast they learn—in the degree of ability to learn. However, Thorndike assumed that the rules of learning were universal. We no longer share Thorndike's view that these universal rules of learning are the "laws of exercise and effect." However, contemporary scientists continue to adhere to the idea that universal rules of learning exist. The job of the learning psychologist is to discover those universal laws. (More about the work of Thorndike will follow in Chapter 5.)

Methodological Implications of the General-Process Approach

If we assume that universal rules of learning exist, then we should be able to discover those rules in any situation in which learning occurs. Thus, an important methodological implication of the general-process approach is that general rules of learning may be discovered by studying any species or

Robert W. Allan, Lafayette College

FIGURE **1.7**

A pigeon in a standard Skinner box. Three circular disks, arranged at eye level, are available for the bird to peck. Access to food is provided in the hopper below.

response system that exhibits learning. This implication has encouraged scientists to study learning in a small number of experimental situations. Investigators have converged on a few standard, or conventional, experimental paradigms. Most studies of learning are conducted in one of these paradigms. Figure 1.7, for example, shows an example of a pigeon in a standard Skinner box. I will describe other examples of standard experimental paradigms as I introduce various learning phenomena in future chapters.

Conventional experimental paradigms have been fine tuned over the years to fit well with the behavioral predispositions of the research animals. Because of these improvements, conventional experimental preparations permit laboratory study of reasonably naturalistic responses (Timberlake, 1990).

Proof of the Generality of Learning Phenomena

The generality of learning processes is not proven by adopting a general-process approach. Assuming the existence of common elemental learning processes is not the same as empirically demonstrating those commonalities. Direct empirical verification of the existence of common learning processes in a variety of situations remains necessary in effort to build a truly general account of how learning occurs.

The available evidence suggests that elementary principles of learning of the sort that will be described in this text have considerable generality (Papini, 2008). Most research on animal learning has been performed with pigeons, rats, and (to a much lesser extent) rabbits and monkeys. Similar forms of learning have been found with fish, hamsters, cats, dogs, human beings, dolphins, and sea lions. In addition, some of the principles of learning observed with these vertebrate species also have been demonstrated in *newts* (Ellins, Cramer, & Martin, 1982); *fruit flies* (Cadieu, Ghadraoui, & Cadieu, 2000; Davis, 1996; Holliday & Hirsch, 1986); *honeybees* (Bitterman, 1988, 1996); *terrestrial mollusks* (Sahley, Rudy, & Gelperin, 1981; Ungless, 1998); *wasps* (Kaiser & De Jong, 1995), and various *marine mollusks* (Carew, Hawkins, & Kandel, 1983; Colwill, Goodrum, & Martin, 1997; Farley & Alkon, 1980; Rogers, Schiller, & Matzel, 1996; Susswein & Schwarz, 1983).

Examples of learning in diverse species provide support for the general-process approach. However, the evidence should be interpreted cautiously. With the exception of the extensive program of research on learning in honeybees conducted by Bitterman and his associates, the various invertebrate species in the studies I cited have been tested on a limited range of learning phenomena, and we do not know whether their learning was mediated by the same mechanisms that are responsible for analogous instances of learning in vertebrate species.

USE OF NONHUMAN ANIMALS IN RESEARCH ON LEARNING

Although the principles described in this book apply to people, many of the experiments we will be considering have been conducted with nonhuman animals. Numerous types of animals have been used. Many of the studies have been conducted with pigeons and laboratory rats and mice for both theoretical and methodological reasons.

Rationale for the Use of Nonhuman Animals in Research on Learning

As I have argued, experimental methods are needed to investigate learning phenomena. Experimental methods make it possible to attribute the acquisition of new behaviors to particular previous experiences. Such experimental control of past experience cannot always be achieved with the same degree of precision in studies with human participants as in studies with laboratory animals. With laboratory animals, scientists can study how strong emotional reactions are learned and how learning is involved in acquiring food, avoiding pain or distress, or finding potential sexual partners. With people, investigators are limited to trying to modify maladaptive emotional responses after such responses have been already acquired. However, even the development of successful therapeutic procedures for the treatment of maladaptive emotional responses has required knowledge of how such emotional responses are learned in the first place—knowledge that required studies with laboratory animals.

Knowledge of the evolution and biological bases of learning also cannot be obtained without the use of nonhuman animals in research. How cognition and intelligence evolved is one of the fundamental questions about human nature. The answer to this question will shape our view of human nature, just as knowledge of the solar system has shaped our view of the place of mother Earth in the universe. As I have discussed, investigation of the evolution of cognition and intelligence rests heavily on studies of learning in nonhuman animals.

Knowledge of the neurobiological bases of learning may not change our views of human nature, but it is apt to yield important dividends in the treatment of learning and memory disorders. Such knowledge also rests heavily on research with laboratory animals. The kind of detailed investigations that are necessary to unravel how the nervous system learns and remembers simply cannot be conducted with people. Studying the neurobiological bases of learning first requires documenting the nature of learning processes at the behavioral level. Therefore, behavioral studies of learning in animals are a necessary prerequisite to any animal research on the biological bases of learning.

Laboratory animals also provide important conceptual advantages over people for studying learning processes. The processes of learning may be simpler in animals reared under controlled laboratory conditions than in people, whose backgrounds are more varied and often poorly documented. The behavior of nonhuman animals is not complicated by linguistic processes that have a prominent role in certain kinds of human behavior. Another important advantage is that demand characteristics are not involved in research with laboratory animals. In research with people, one has to make sure that the actions of the participants are not governed by their efforts to please, or displease, the experimenter. Such factors are not likely to determine what rats and pigeons do in an experiment.

Laboratory Animals and Normal Behavior

Some have suggested that domesticated strains of laboratory animals may not provide useful information because such animals have degenerated as a result of many generations of inbreeding and long periods of captivity (e.g., Lockard, 1968). However, this notion is probably mistaken. In an interesting test, Boice (1977) took five male and five female albino rats of a highly inbred laboratory stock and housed them in an outdoor pen in Missouri without artificial shelter. All ten rats survived the first winter with temperatures as low as –22°F. The animals reproduced normally and reached a stable population of about 50 members. Only three of the rats died before showing signs of old age during the two-year study period. Given the extreme climatic conditions, this level of survival is remarkable. Furthermore, the behavior of these domesticated rats in the outdoors was very similar to the behavior of wild rats observed in similar circumstances.

The results I will describe in this text should not be discounted simply because many of the experiments were conducted with domesticated animals. In fact, it may be suggested that laboratory animals are preferable in research to their wild counterparts. After all, most human beings live in what are largely "artificial" environments. Therefore, research may prove most relevant to human behavior if the research is carried out with domesticated animals that live in artificial laboratory situations. As Boice (1973) commented, "The domesticated rat may be a good model for domestic man" (p. 227).

Public Debate About Research with Nonhuman Animals

There has been much public debate about the pros and cons of research with nonhuman animals. Part of the debate has centered on the humane treatment of animals. Other aspects of the debate have centered on what constitutes ethical treatment of animals, whether human beings have the right to benefit at the expense of animals, and possible alternatives to research with nonhuman animals.

The Humane Treatment of Laboratory Animals

Concern for the welfare of laboratory animals has resulted in the adoption of strict federal standards for animal housing and for the supervision of animal research. Some argue that these rules are needed because without them, scientists would disregard the welfare of the animals in their zeal to obtain research data. However, this argument ignores the fact that good science requires good animal care. Scientists, especially those studying behavior, must be concerned about the welfare of their research subjects. Information about normal learning and behavior cannot be obtained from diseased or disturbed animals. Investigators of animal learning must ensure the welfare of their subjects if they are to obtain useful scientific data.

Learning experiments sometimes involve discomfort. However, every effort is made to minimize the degree of discomfort. In studies of food reinforcement, for example, animals are food deprived before each experimental session to ensure their interest in food. However, the hunger imposed is no more severe than the hunger animals are likely to encounter in the wild, and often it is less severe (Poling, Nickel, & Alling, 1990).

The investigation of certain forms of learning and behavior require the administration of aversive stimulation. Important topics, such as punishment or the learning of fear and anxiety, cannot be studied without some discomfort to the participants. However, even in such cases, efforts are made to keep the discomfort to a minimum.

What Constitutes the Ethical Treatment of Animals?

Although making sure that animals serving in experiments are comfortable is in the best interests of the animals as well as the research, formulating general ethical principles is difficult. Animal rights cannot be identified in the way we identify human rights (Lansdell, 1988), and animals seem to have different rights under different circumstances.

Currently, substantial efforts are made to house laboratory animals in conditions that promote their health and comfort. However, a laboratory mouse or rat loses the protection afforded by federal standards when it escapes from the laboratory and takes up residence in the walls of the building (Herzog, 1988). The trapping and extermination of rodents in buildings is a common practice that has not been the subject of either public debate or restrictive federal regulation. Mites, fleas, and ticks are also animals, but we do not tolerate them in our hair or on our pets. Which species have the right to life, and under what circumstances do they have that right? Such questions defy simple answers.

Assuming that a species deserves treatment that meets government mandated standards, what should those standards be? Appropriate treatment of laboratory animals is sometimes described as being "humane treatment." However, we have to be careful not to take this term literally. "Humane treatment" means treating someone as we would treat a human being. It is important to keep in mind that rats and other laboratory animals are not human beings. Rats prefer to live in dark burrows made of dirt that they never clean. People, in contrast, prefer to live in well illuminated and frequently cleaned rooms. Laboratories typically have rats in well-lit rooms that are frequently cleaned. One cannot help but wonder whether these housing standards were dictated more by considering human rather than rat comfort.

Should Human Beings Benefit From the Use of Animals?

Part of the public debate about animal rights has been fueled by the argument that human beings have no right to benefit at the expense of animals; humans have no right to *exploit* animals. This argument goes far beyond issues concerning the use of animals in research. Therefore, I will not discuss the argument in detail here, except to point out that far fewer animals are used in research than are used for food, clothing, and recreation (hunting and fishing). In addition, a comprehensive count of human exploitation of animals has to include disruptions of habitats that occur whenever we build roads, housing developments, and factories. We should also add the millions of animals that are killed by insecticides and other pest-control efforts in agriculture and elsewhere.

Alternatives to Research with Animals

Increased awareness of ethical issues involved in the use of nonhuman animals in research has encouraged a search for alternative techniques. Some years ago, Russell and Burch (1959) formulated the "three Rs" for animal research: *replacement* of animals with other testing techniques, *reducing* the number of animals used with statistical techniques, and *refining* the experimental procedures to cause less suffering. Replacement strategies have been successful in the cosmetic industry and in the manufacture of certain vaccines and hormones (Murkerjee, 1997). However, as Gallup and Suarez (1985) pointed out, good research on learning processes cannot be conducted without experiments on live organisms, be they animal or human. Some alternatives that have been proposed have been the following.

1. *Observational techniques.* As I discussed earlier, learning processes cannot be investigated with unobtrusive observational techniques. Experimental manipulation of past experience is necessary in studies of learning. Therefore, field observations of undisturbed animals cannot yield information about the mechanisms of learning.
2. *Plants.* Learning cannot be investigated in plants because plants lack a nervous system, which is required for learning.
3. *Tissue cultures.* Although tissue cultures may reveal the operation of cellular processes, how these cellular processes operate in an intact organism can be discovered only by studying the intact organism. Furthermore, a search for cellular mechanisms of learning first requires characterizing learning at the behavioral level.
4. *Computer simulations.* Writing a computer program to simulate a natural phenomenon requires a great deal of knowledge about the phenomenon. In the case of learning, programmers would have to have precise and detailed information about the nature of learning phenomena and the mechanisms and factors that determine learning before they could create a successful computer simulation. The absence of such knowledge necessitates experimental research with live organisms. Thus, experimen-

tal research with live organisms is a prerequisite for effective computer simulations. For that reason, computer simulations cannot be used in place of experimental research.

Computer simulations serve many useful functions in science. Simulations are effective in showing us the implications of the experimental observations that have been already obtained, or showing the implications of various theoretical assumptions. They can help identify gaps in knowledge and can suggest important future lines of research. However, they cannot be used to generate new, previously unknown facts about behavior. That can only be done by studying live organisms.

Earlier in this chapter, we described a computer simulation to measure the wind resistance of various automobile designs. Why is it possible to construct a computer program to study wind resistance, but it is not possible to construct one to study learning processes? The critical difference is that we know a lot more about wind resistance than we know about learning. Wind resistance is determined by the laws of mechanics: laws that have been thoroughly explored since the days of Sir Isaac Newton. Application of those laws to wind resistance has received special attention in recent years, as aerodynamics has become an important factor in the design of cars.

Designing automobiles with low wind resistance is an engineering task. It involves the application of existing knowledge, rather than the discovery of new knowledge and new principles. Research on animal learning involves the discovery of new facts and new principles. It is science, not engineering. As Conn and Parker (1998) pointed out, "Scientists depend on computers for processing data that we already possess, but can't use them to explore the unknown in the quest for new information."

SAMPLE QUESTIONS

1. Describe how historical developments in the study of the mind contributed to the contemporary study of learning.
2. Describe Descartes' conception of the reflex and how the concept of the reflex has changed since his time.
3. Describe the rationale for using animal models to study human behavior.
4. Describe the definition of learning and how learning is distinguished from other forms of behavior change.
5. Describe why learning can only be studied by using experimental methods.
6. Describe several alternatives to the use of animals in research and describe their advantages and disadvantages.

KEY TERMS

association A connection or linkage between the representations of two events (two stimuli or a stimulus and a response) so that the occurrence of one of the events activates the representation of the other.

declarative or episodic learning Learning about a specific event or fact, usually accessible to consciousness.

dualism The view of behavior according to which actions can be separated into two categories: voluntary behavior controlled by the mind, and involuntary behavior controlled by reflex mechanisms.

empiricism A philosophy according to which all ideas in the mind arise from experience.

fatigue A temporary decrease in behavior caused by repeated or excessive use of the muscles involved in the behavior.

hedonism The philosophy proposed by Hobbes according to which the actions of organisms are determined entirely by the pursuit of pleasure and the avoidance of pain.

learning An enduring change in the mechanisms of behavior involving specific stimuli and/or responses that results from prior experience with similar stimuli and responses.

maturation A change in behavior caused by physical or physiological development of the organism in the absence of experience with particular environmental events.

nativism A philosophy according to which human beings are born with innate ideas.

nervism The philosophical position adopted by Pavlov that all behavioral and physiological processes are regulated by the nervous system.

nonsense syllable A three-letter combination (two consonants separated by a vowel) that has no meaning.

performance An organism's activities at a particular time.

procedural learning Learning ways of doing things rather than learning about specific events. Procedural learning is typically not governed by conscious controlled processes.

reflex A mechanism that enables a specific environmental event to elicit a specific response.

2

Elicited Behavior, Habituation, and Sensitization

CHAPTER PREVIEW

Chapter 2 begins the discussion of contemporary principles of learning and behavior with a description of modern research on elicited behavior—behavior that occurs in reaction to specific environmental stimuli. Many of the things we do are elicited by discrete stimuli, including some of the most extensively investigated forms of behavior. Elicited responses range from simple reflexes to more complex behavior sequences and complex emotional responses and goal-directed behavior. Interestingly, simple reflexive responses can be involved in the coordination of elaborate social interactions. Elicited responses are also involved in two of the most basic and common forms of behavioral change: habituation and sensitization. Habituation and sensitization are important to understand because they are potentially involved in all learning procedures. They modulate simple elicited responses like the eyeblink response and are also involved in the regulation of complex emotions and motivated behavior like drug addiction.

Is behavior totally flexible or is it subject to constraints set by the organism's genetic history? This is an age-old question that has taken different forms during the course of intellectual history. One form of this question was the debate between the nativist position of René Descartes and the empiricist position of John Locke that was described in Chapter 1. Locke favored the view that experience and learning can shape behavior in virtually any direction. Descartes believed in innate contents of the mind, which in modern parlance suggests that the impact of learning is constrained by pre-existing behavior tendencies. The nativist/empiricist debate continues to this date (Pinker, 2002). The consensus emerging from modern behavioral neuroscience is that the nativists were closer to the truth than the empiricists. Behavior is not infinitely flexible, to move in any direction that a trainer may push it. Rather, organisms are born with pre-existing behavior systems and tendencies that set limits on how learning occurs and what the impact of learning can be.

The nativist position on learning was described elegantly by an analogy offered by Rachlin (1976), who compared learning to sculpting a wooden statue. The sculptor begins with a piece of wood that has little resemblance to a statue. As the carving proceeds, the piece of wood comes to look more and more like the final product. But, the process is not without limitation since the sculptor has to take into account the direction and density of the wood grain and any knots the wood may have. Wood carving is most successful if it is in harmony with the pre-existing structure of the wood. In a similar fashion, learning is most successful if it takes into account the pre-existing behavior structures of the organism. This chapter describes the most prominent of these pre-existing behavior structures.

THE NATURE OF ELICITED BEHAVIOR

All animals, whether they are single-celled paramecia or complex human beings, react to events in their environment. If something moves in the periphery of your vision, you are likely to turn your head in that direction. A particle of food in the mouth elicits salivation. Exposure to a bright light causes the pupils of the eyes to constrict. Touching a hot surface elicits a quick withdrawal response. Irritation of the respiratory passages causes sneezing and coughing. These and similar examples illustrate that much behavior occurs in response to stimuli. It is elicited.

Elicited behavior has been the subject of extensive investigation. Many of the chapters of this text deal, in one way or another, with responses to stimuli. We begin our discussion of elicited behavior by describing its simplest form: reflexive behavior.

The Concept of the Reflex

A light puff of air directed at the cornea makes the eye blink. A tap just below the knee causes the leg to kick. A loud noise causes a startle reaction. These are all examples of reflexes. A reflex involves two closely related events: an *eliciting stimulus* and a *corresponding response*. Furthermore, the stimulus and response are linked. Presentation of the stimulus is followed by the response, and the response rarely occurs in the absence of the stimulus. For example, dust in the nasal passages elicits sneezing, which does not occur in the absence of nasal irritation.

The specificity of the relation between a stimulus and its accompanying reflex response is a consequence of the organization of the nervous system. In vertebrates (including humans), simple reflexes are typically mediated by three neurons, as illustrated in Figure 2.1. The environmental stimulus for a

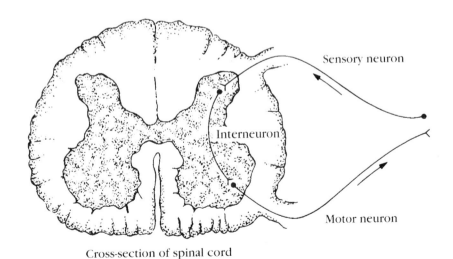

Cross-section of spinal cord

FIGURE **2.1**

Neural organization of simple reflexes. The environmental stimulus for a reflex activates a sensory neuron, which transmits the sensory message to the spinal cord. Here, the neural impulses are relayed to an interneuron, which in turn relays the impulses to the motor neuron. The motor neuron activates muscles involved in movement.

reflex activates a **sensory neuron** (also called **afferent neuron**), which transmits the sensory message to the spinal cord. Here, the neural impulses are relayed to the **motor neuron** (also called **efferent neuron**), which activates the muscles involved in the reflex response. However, sensory and motor neurons rarely communicate directly. Rather, the impulses from one to the other are relayed through at least one **interneuron**. The neural circuitry ensures that particular sensory neurons are connected to a corresponding set of motor neurons. Because of this restricted "wiring," a particular reflex response is elicited only by a restricted set of stimuli. The afferent neuron, interneuron, and efferent neuron together constitute the **reflex arc**.

The reflex arc in vertebrates represents the fewest neural connections necessary for reflex action. However, additional neural structures also may be involved in the elicitation of reflexes. For example, the sensory messages may be relayed to the brain, which in turn may modify the reflex reaction in various ways. I will discuss such effects later in the chapter. For now, it is sufficient to keep in mind that the occurrence of even simple reflexes can be influenced by higher nervous system activity.

Most reflexes contribute to the well-being of the organism in obvious ways. For example, in many animals, painful stimulation of one limb causes withdrawal, or flexion, of that limb and extension of the opposite limb (Hart, 1973). If a dog, for example, stubs a toe while walking, it will automatically withdraw that leg and simultaneously extend the opposite leg. This combination of responses removes the first leg from the source of pain and at the same time allows the animal to maintain balance.

Reflexes constitute much of the behavioral repertoire of newborn infants. If you touch an infant's cheek with your finger, the baby will reflexively turn her head in that direction, with the result that your finger will fall in the baby's mouth. This head-turning reflex probably evolved to facilitate finding the nipple. The sensation of an object in the mouth causes

FIGURE **2.2**

How dogs maintain balance. Painful simulation of one limb of a dog causes withdrawal (flexion) of that limb and extension of the opposite limb. (From "Reflexive Behavior," by B. L. Hart in G. Bermant [Ed.], 1973, *Perspectives in Animal Behavior*. Copyright © 1973 by Scott, Foresman. Reprinted by permission.)

reflexive sucking. The more closely the object resembles a nipple, the more vigorously the baby will suck.

Another important reflex, the *respiratory occlusion reflex,* is stimulated by a reduction of air flow to the baby, which can be caused by a cloth covering the baby's face, or by the accumulation of mucus in the nasal passages. In response to the reduced air flow, the baby's first reaction is to pull her head back. If this does not remove the eliciting stimulus, the baby will move her hands in a face-wiping motion. If this also fails to remove the eliciting stimulus, the baby will begin to cry. Crying involves vigorous expulsion of air, which may be sufficient to remove whatever was obstructing the air passages.

The respiratory occlusion reflex is obviously essential for survival. If the baby does not get enough air, he or she may suffocate. A problem arises, however, when the respiratory occlusion reflex is triggered during nursing. While nursing, the baby can get air only through the nose. If the mother presses the baby too close to the breast during feeding so that the baby's nostrils are covered by the breast, the respiratory occlusion reflex will be triggered. The baby will attempt to pull her head back from the nipple, may move her hands in a face-wiping motion that pushes away the nipple, and may begin to cry. Successful nursing requires a bit of experience. The mother and child have to adjust their positions so that nursing can progress without stimulation of the respiratory occlusion reflex (Gunther, 1961). (See Figure 2.3.)

Interestingly, successful nursing involves reflex responses not only on the part of the infant, but also on the part of the mother. The availability of milk in the breast is determined by the milk-letdown reflex. During early stages of nursing, the milk-letdown reflex is triggered by the infant's suckling behavior. However, after extensive nursing experience, the milk-letdown reflex can be

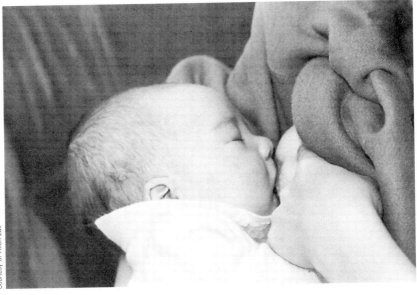

Courtesy of Allen Zak

FIGURE **2.3**

Suckling in infants. Suckling is one of the most prominent reflexes in infants.

also stimulated by cues that reliably predict the infant's suckling, such as the time of day or the infant's crying when he or she is hungry. Thus, successful nursing involves an exquisite coordination of reflex activity on the part of both the infant and the mother.

Modal Action Patterns

Simple reflex responses, such as pupillary constriction to a bright light and startle reactions to a brief loud noise, are evident in many species. By contrast, other forms of elicited behavior occur in just one species or in a small group of related species. For example, sucking in response to an object placed in the mouth is a characteristic of mammalian infants. Herring-gull chicks are just as dependent on parental feeding, but their feeding behavior is very different. When a parent gull returns to the nest from a foraging trip, the chicks peck at the tip of the parent's bill (see Figure 2.4). This causes the parent to regurgitate. As the chicks continue to peck, they manage to get the parent's regurgitated food, and this provides their nourishment.

Response sequences, such as those involved in infant feeding, that are typical of a particular species are referred to as **modal action patterns (MAPs)** (Baerends, 1988). Species-typical modal action patterns have been identified in many aspects of animal behavior, including sexual behavior, territorial defense, aggression, and prey capture. Ring doves, for example, begin their sexual behavior with a courtship interaction that culminates in the selection of a nest site and the cooperative construction of the nest by the male and female. By contrast, in the three-spined stickleback, a species of small fish, the male first establishes a territory and constructs a nest. Females that enter the territory after the nest has been built are then courted and induced to lay their eggs in the nest. Once a female has deposited her eggs, she is chased away, leaving the male stickleback to care for and defend the eggs until the offspring hatch.

Courtesy of G. P. Baerends

G. P. Baerends

FIGURE **2.4**

Feeding of herring-gull chicks. The chicks peck a red patch near the tip of the parent's bill, causing the parent to regurgitate food for them.

An important feature of modal action patterns is that the threshold for eliciting such activities varies (Camhi, 1984; Baerends, 1988). The same stimulus can have widely different effects depending on the physiological state of the animal and its recent actions. A male stickleback, for example, will not court a female who is ready to lay eggs until he has completed building his nest. And, after the female has deposited her eggs, the male will chase her away rather than court her as he did earlier. Furthermore, these sexual and territorial responses will only occur when environmental cues induce physiological changes that are characteristic of the breeding season in both males and females.

Modal action patterns were initially identified by ethologists, scientists interested in the study of the evolution of behavior. Early ethologists, such as Lorenz and Tinbergen, referred to species-specific action patterns as *fixed action patterns* to emphasize that the activities occurred pretty much the same way in all members of a species. However, subsequent detailed observations indicated that action patterns are not performed in exactly the same fashion each time. They are not strictly "fixed." Because of this variability, the term *modal action pattern* is preferred now (Baerends, 1988).

Eliciting Stimuli for Modal Action Patterns

The eliciting stimulus is fairly easy to identify in the case of simple reflexes, such as the startle response to a brief loud noise. The stimulus responsible for a modal action pattern can be more difficult to isolate if the response occurs in the course of complex social interactions. For example, let us consider again the feeding of a herring-gull chick. To get fed, the chick has to peck the parent's beak to stimulate the parent to regurgitate. But, exactly what stimulates the chick's pecking response?

Pecking by the chicks may be elicited by the color, shape, or length of the parent's bill, the noises the parent makes, the head movements of the parent, or some other stimulus. To isolate which of these stimuli elicits pecking, Tinbergen and Perdeck (1950) tested chicks with various artificial models instead of live adult gulls. From this research, they concluded that a model had to have several characteristics to strongly elicit pecking. It had to be a long, thin, moving object that was pointed downward and had a contrasting red patch near the tip. These experiments suggest that the yellow color of the adult's bill, the shape and coloration of its head, and the noises it makes are all not required for eliciting pecking in the gull chicks. The specific features that were found to be required to elicit the pecking behavior are called, collectively, the **sign stimulus**, or **releasing stimulus**, for this behavior. Once a sign stimulus has been identified, it can be exaggerated to elicit an especially vigorous response. Such an exaggerated sign stimulus is called a **supernormal stimulus**.

Although sign stimuli were originally identified in studies with nonhuman subjects, sign stimuli also play a major role in the control of human behavior. Following a major disaster, post-traumatic stress disorder (PTSD) and fear and anxiety attendant to trauma are frequently in the news. Better understanding of PTSD requires knowledge about how people react to danger and how they learn from those experiences (Kirmayer, Lemelson, & Barad, 2007).

Responding effectively to danger has been critical in the evolutionary history of all animals, including human beings. Individuals who did not respond effectively to danger succumbed to the assault and did not pass their genes on to future generations. Therefore, traumatic events have come to elicit strong defensive modal action patterns. Vestiges of this evolutionary history are evident in laboratory studies showing that both children and adults detect snakes faster than flowers, frogs, or other nonthreatening stimuli (e.g., LoBue & DeLoache, 2008). Early components of the defensive action pattern include the eyeblink reflex and the startle response. Because of their importance in defensive behavior, we will discuss these reflexes later in this chapter as well as in subsequent chapters.

Sign stimuli and supernormal stimuli also have a major role in social and sexual behavior. Copulatory behavior involves a complex sequence of motor responses that have to be elaborately coordinated with the behavior of one's sexual partner. The modal action patterns involved in sexual arousal and copulatory behavior are elicited by visual, olfactory, tactile, and other types of sign stimuli that vary among different species. Visual, tactile, and olfactory stimuli are all important in human social and sexual interactions. The cosmetic and perfume industries are in business because they take advantage of the sign stimuli that elicit human social attraction and affiliation, and enhance these stimuli. Women put rouge on their lips rather than on their ears because only rouge on the lips enhances the natural sign stimulus for human social attraction. Plastic surgery to enhance the breasts and lips are also effective because they enhance naturally occurring sign stimuli for human social behavior.

The studies of learning that we will be describing in this book are based primarily on modal action patterns involved in eating, drinking, sexual behavior, and defensive behavior.

The Sequential Organization of Behavior

Responses do not occur in isolation of one another. Rather, individual actions are organized into functionally effective behavior sequences. To obtain food, for example, a squirrel first has to look around for potential food sources, such as a pecan tree with nuts. It then has to climb the tree and reach one of the nuts. After obtaining the nut, it has to crack the shell, extract the meat, and chew and swallow it. All motivated behavior, whether it is foraging for

---

BOX **2.1**

The Learning of Instinct

Because modal action patterns occur in a similar fashion among members of a given species, they include activities that are informally characterized as *instinctive*. Instinctive behavior is considered primarily to reflect an individual's genetic history, leading to the impression that modal action patterns are not the product of learning and experi-

ence. However, the fact that all members of a species exhibit similar forms of behavior does not necessarily mean that the behavior was not learned through experience. As Tinbergen (1951) recognized many years ago, similar behavior on the part of all members of a species may reflect similar learning experiences. In a more recent expression of this

sentiment, Baerends (1988) wrote that "learning processes in many variations are tools, so to speak, that can be used in the building of some segments in the species-specific behavior organization" (p. 801). Thus, learning can be involved in what we commonly refer to as *instinctive* behaviors (Domjan, 2005; Hailman, 1967).

food, finding a potential mate, defending a territory, or feeding one's young, involves systematically organized sequences of actions. Ethologists called early components of a behavior sequence **appetitive behavior** and the end components **consummatory behavior** (Craig, 1918). The term *consummatory* was meant to convey the idea of *consummation* or *completion* of a species' typical response sequence. In contrast, appetitive responses occur early in a behavior sequence and serve to bring the organism into contact with the stimuli that will release the consummatory behavior.

Chewing and swallowing are responses that complete activities involved in foraging for food. Hitting and biting an opponent are actions that consummate defensive behavior. Copulatory responses serve to complete the sexual behavior sequence. In general, consummatory responses are highly stereotyped species' typical behaviors that have specific eliciting or releasing stimuli. In contrast, appetitive behaviors are less stereotyped and can take a variety of different forms depending on the situation (Tinbergen, 1951). In getting to a pecan tree, for example, a squirrel can run up one side or the other or jump from a neighboring tree. These are all possible appetitive responses leading up to actually eating the pecan nut. However, once the squirrel is ready to put the pecan meat in its mouth, the chewing and swallowing responses that it makes are fairly stereotyped.

As is evident from the varieties of ethnic cuisine, people of different cultures have many different ways of preparing food (appetitive behavior), but they all pretty much chew and swallow the same way (consummatory behavior). Actions that are considered to be rude and threatening (appetitive defensive responses) also differ from one culture to another. But, people hit and hurt one another (consummatory defensive behavior) in much the same way regardless of culture. Consummatory responses tend to be species-typical modal action patterns. In contrast, appetitive behaviors are more variable and more apt to be shaped by learning.

The sequential organization of naturally occurring behavior is of considerable importance to scientists interested in understanding how behavior is altered by learning because learning effects often depend on which component of the behavior sequence is being modified. As I will describe in later chapters, the outcomes of Pavlovian and instrumental conditioning depend on how these learning procedures modify the natural sequence of an organism's behavior. Learning theorists are becoming increasingly aware of the importance of considering natural behavior sequences, and have expanded on the appetitive and consummatory distinction made by early ethologists (Domjan, 1997; Fanselow, 1997; Timberlake, 1994, 2001).

In considering how animals obtain food, for example, it is now common to characterize the foraging response sequence as starting with a **general search mode**, followed by a **focal search mode**, and ending with a **food handling and ingestion mode**. Thus, in modern learning theory, the appetitive response category has been subdivided into general search and focal search categories (e.g., Timberlake, 2001). General search responses occur when the subject does not yet know where to look for food. Before a squirrel has identified a pecan tree, it will move around looking for potential sources of food. General search responses are not spatially localized. Once the squirrel has found a pecan tree, however, it will switch to the focal search mode and begin to search for pecans only in that tree. Thus, focal search behavior is characterized by considerable spatial specificity. Focal search behavior yields to food handling and ingestion (consummatory behavior) once a pecan nut has been obtained.

EFFECTS OF REPEATED STIMULATION

A common assumption is that an elicited response, particularly a simple reflex response, will automatically occur the same way every time the eliciting stimulus is presented. This is exactly what Descartes thought. In his view, reflexive behavior was unintelligent in the sense that it was automatic and invariant. According to the reflex mechanism Descartes proposed, each occurrence of the eliciting stimulus would produce the same reflex reaction because the energy of the eliciting stimulus was transferred to the motor response through a direct physical connection. If elicited behavior occurred the same way every time, it would be of limited interest, particularly for investigators of learning.

Contrary to Descartes, elicited behavior is not invariant. In fact, one of the most impressive features of elicited behavior is its plasticity. Even simple elicited responses do not occur the same way each time. Alterations in the nature of elicited behavior often occur simply as a result of repeated presentations of the eliciting stimulus. The following examples illustrate such results.

Salivation and Hedonic Ratings of Taste in People

The taste of food elicits salivation as a reflex response. This occurs as easily in people as in Pavlov's dogs. In one study, salivation was measured in eight women in response to the taste of either lemon juice or lime juice (Epstein, Rodefer, Wisniewski, & Caggiula, 1992). A small amount of one of the flavors (.03 ml) was placed on the participant's tongue on each of 10 trials. The participant was asked to rate how much she liked the taste on each trial, and salivation to each taste presentation was also measured. The results are summarized in Figure 2.5.

Salivation in response to the taste increased slightly from Trial 1 to Trial 2, but from Trial 2 to Trial 10, responding systematically decreased. A similar decrease was observed in hedonic ratings of the taste. Thus, as the taste stimulus was repeated 10 times, it became less effective in eliciting both salivation and hedonic responses. On Trial 11, the flavor of the taste was changed (to lime for participants that had been exposed to lemon, and to lemon for participants that had been previously exposed to lime). This produced a dramatic recovery in both the salivary reflex and the hedonic rating. (For similar results in a study with children, see Epstein et al., 2003.)

The results presented in Figure 2.5 are relatively simple but tell us a number of important things about the plasticity of elicited behavior. First, and most obviously, they tell us that elicited behavior is not invariant across repetitions of the eliciting stimulus. Both salivation and hedonic ratings decreased with repeated trials. In the case of salivation, the ultimate decline in responding was preceded by a brief increase from Trial 1 to Trial 2. The decline in responding that occurs with repeated presentation of a stimulus is called a **habituation effect.** Habituation is a prominent feature of elicited behavior that is evident in virtually all species and situations (Beck & Rankin, 1997).

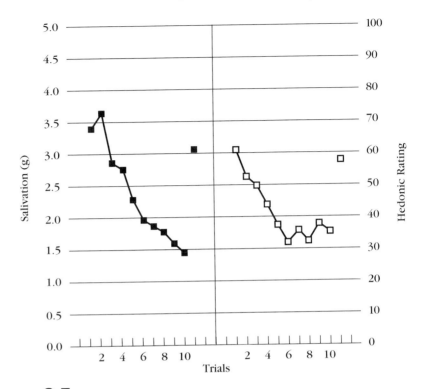

FIGURE **2.5**

Salivation and ratings of pleasantness in response to a taste stimulus (lime or lemon) repeatedly presented to women on Trials 1–10. The alternate taste was presented on Trial 11, causing a substantial recovery in responding. (After Epstein, Rodefer, Wisniewski & Caggiula, 1992).

Another prominent feature of the results presented in Figure 2.5 is that the decrease in responding was specific to the habituated stimulus. Individuals habituated to the taste of lemon showed invigorated responding when tested with the taste of lime at the end of the experiment (and vice versa). Thus, habituation was stimulus specific.

The stimulus specificity of habituation tells us that the subjects in this experiment could tell the difference between lemon and lime. That might not be an impressive finding, since we could have just as well asked the participants to tell us whether they could tell the difference between the two flavors. However, the stimulus specificity of habituation provides a powerful behavioral assay with individuals, such as infants, who cannot talk.

Although this was a rather simple experiment, it has interesting implications for how to present and prepare food. Chefs who expect to charge hefty prices for a gourmet dinner cannot afford to have people get bored with what they are eating within 10 bites, as occurred in this experiment. How, then, can such a habituation effect be avoided? The solution is to prepare and present food so that each bite provides a different flavor. The ingredients in a meal should not be mixed together into a homogeneous mass. Different ingredients should be kept separate to avoid having successive bites all taste the same. On the other hand, if the goal is to reduce eating (as in a weight loss program), then variation in flavors should be discouraged. It is hard to resist going back to a buffet table given the variety of flavors that are offered, but rejecting a second helping of mashed potatoes is easy if the second helping tastes the same as the first. (For a study of the relation between habituation to taste and obesity, see Epstein et al., 2008.)

Another major variable that influences the rate of taste habituation is attention to the taste stimulus. In a fascinating study, children were tested for habituation to a taste stimulus while they were working on a problem that required their close attention. In another condition, either no distracting task was given or the task was so easy that it did not require much attention. Interestingly, if the children's attention was diverted from the taste presentations, they showed much less habituation to the flavor (Epstein et al., 2005). This is a very important finding because it helps us understand why food tastes better and why people eat more if they are having dinner with friends or while watching TV. Having attention directed to non-food cues keeps the food from losing its flavor through habituation.

Visual Attention in Human Infants

Human infants have a lot to learn about the world. One way they obtain information is by looking at things. Visual cues elicit a looking response, which can be measured by how long the infant keeps his or her eyes on one object before shifting gaze elsewhere (see Figure 2.6).

In one study of visual attention (Bashinski, Werner, & Rudy, 1985; see also Kaplan, Werner, & Rudy, 1990), four-month-old infants were assigned to one of two groups, and each group was tested with a different visual stimulus. The stimuli are shown in the right panel of Figure 2.7. Both were check-

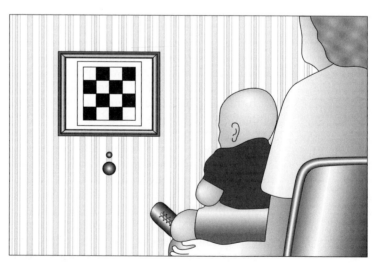

FIGURE **2.6**

Experimental setup for the study of visual attention in infants. The infant is seated in front of a screen that is used to present various visual stimuli. How long the infant looks at the display before diverting his gaze elsewhere is measured in each trial.

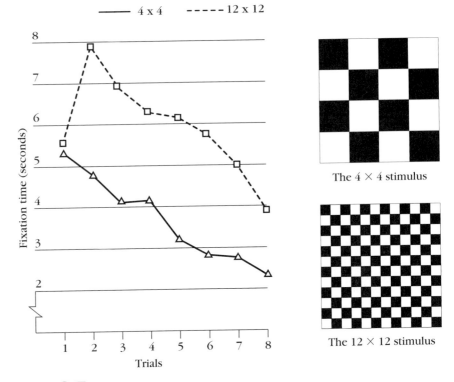

FIGURE **2.7**

Time infants spent looking at a visual stimulus during successive trials. For one group, the stimulus consisted of a 4 x 4 checkerboard pattern. For a second group, the stimulus consisted of a 12 x 12 checkerboard pattern. The stimuli are illustrated to the right of the results. (From "Determinants of Infant Visual Attention: Evidence for a Two-Process Theory," by H. Bashinski, J. Werner, and J. Rudy, *Journal of Experimental Child Psychology, 39,* pp. 580–598. Copyright © 1985 by Academic Press. Reprinted by permission of Elsevier.)

erboard patterns, but one had four squares on each side (the 4 x 4 stimulus) whereas the other had 12 squares on each side (the 12 x 12 stimulus). Each stimulus presentation lasted 10 seconds, and the stimuli were presented eight times at 10 second intervals.

Both stimuli elicited visual attention initially, with the babies spending an average of about 5.5 seconds looking at the stimuli. With repeated presentations of the 4 x 4 stimulus, visual attention progressively decreased, showing a habituation effect. By contrast, the 12 x 12 stimulus produced an initial sensitization effect, evident in increased looking during the second trial as compared to the first. But, after that, visual attention to the 12 x 12 stimulus also habituated.

This relatively simple experiment tells us a great deal about both visual attention, and habituation and sensitization. The results show that visual attention elicited by a novel stimulus changes as babies gain familiarity with the stimulus. The nature of the change is determined by the nature of the stimulus. With a relatively simple 4 x 4 pattern, only a progressive habituation effect occurs. With a more complex 12 x 12 pattern, a transient sensitization occurs, followed by habituation. Thus, whether or not sensitization is observed depends on the complexity of the stimulus. With both stimuli, the infants eventually showed less interest as they became more familiar with the stimulus. It may be too harsh to say that familiarity bred contempt, but familiarity certainly did not elicit much interest. Interest in what appeared on the screen would have recovered if a new or different stimulus had been presented after familiarization with the first one.

Infants cannot tell us in words how they view or think about things. Scientists are therefore forced to use behavioral techniques to study infant perception and cognition. The visual attention task can provide information about visual acuity. For example, from the data in Figure 2.7, we may conclude that these infants were able to distinguish the two different checkerboard patterns. This type of habituation procedure has also been used to study a wide range of other, more complicated questions about infant cognition and perception. One recent study, for example, examined the way 3.5 month old infants perceive human faces.

Faces provide a great deal of information that is critical in interpersonal interactions. People are experts at recognizing and remembering faces, but they show better discrimination if the faces are of their own race than if the faces are from individuals of a different race. This effect is known as the *other race effect*. Hayden et al. (2007) sought to determine whether the other-race effect occurs in 3.5 month old infants. Two groups of Caucasian infants were tested using the visual habituation task. One group was shown a Caucasian face on successive trials until their attentional response decreased at least 50% of its initial level. The second group of infants received the same kind of procedure, but for them an Asian face was shown on each trial. Thus, during this phase, one group became familiar with a face of their own race (Caucasian), while the second group became familiar with a face of the alternate race (Asian).

The investigators then asked whether a small change in the familiar face would be detectable for the infants. To answer this question, a special test was conducted. The test involved presenting two faces. One of the two faces was the same as what the infants had seen before, and therefore was not expected to elicit much looking behavior. In contrast, the second face was created by morphing a familiar face with a face of the alternate race. The resultant image was 70% like the familiar face and 30% like the alternate race. If the infants could detect this small change in features, they were expected to show more looking behavior to the new face.

The results are shown in Figure 2.8. Infants who were familiarized with Caucasian faces showed the expected results. They increased their looking time when the new face was presented that had some features from the alternate race. This result did not occur with the infants who were familiarized with Asian faces. They did not increase their looking when a new face was introduced. The authors interpreted this result as showing that the infants were more skilled at detecting small changes in facial features when those changes were variations in their own race (Caucasian) than when those variations were in the features of another race (Asian). Thus, these findings suggest that the other-race effect occurs in infants as young as 3.5 months of age.

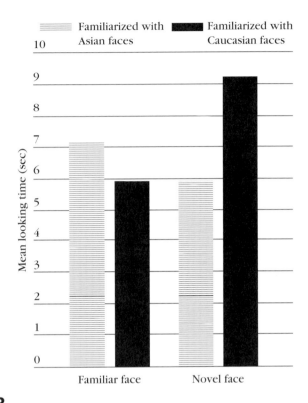

FIGURE **2.8**

The other-race effect in Caucasian infants. After having been habituated to either a Caucasian or an Asian face, infants were tested with a familiar face and a novel one that had 30% features from the alternate race. (Based on Hayden et al., 2007.)

The visual attention paradigm has become a prominent tool in the study of infant perception as well as more complex forms of cognition. For example, it has been used to study whether infants are capable of rudimentary mathematical operations, reasoning about the laws of the physical world, and discrimination between drawings of objects that are physically possible vs. ones that are physically not possible (Baillargeon, 2008; McCrink & Wynn, 2007; Shuwairi, Albert, & Johnson, 2007). Some of this type of research has been called into serious question by those who emphasize that habituation of visual attention in infants and recovery from habituation reflect perceptual properties of the stimuli rather than their meaning within the knowledge structure of the infant (Schöner & Thelen, 2006). Regardless of how this controversy is resolved, there is no doubt that the visual attention paradigm has provided a wealth of information about infant cognition at ages that long precede the acquisition of language. This is just one example of how the behavioral techniques described in this book can be used to examine cognition in nonverbal organisms.

The Startle Response

As I mentioned earlier, the startle response is part of an organism's defensive reaction to potential or actual attack. If someone unexpectedly blows a fog horn behind your back, you are likely to jump. This is the startle response. It consists of a sudden jump and tensing of the muscles of the upper part of the body, usually involving the raising of the shoulders. It also includes blinking of the eyes. The startle reaction can be measured by placing the subject on a surface that measures sudden movements. The startle response has been investigated extensively because of its role in fear and defensive behavior. Scientists interested in the neurobiology of fear, and the development of drugs that help alleviate fear, have often used the startle response as their behavioral anchor. Some of these studies have been conducted with primates, but in most of the studies, laboratory rats have been used as subjects.

Figure 2.9 shows a diagram of a *stabilimeter chamber* used to measure the startle response in rats. The chamber rests on pressure sensors. When startled, the rat jumps and thereby jiggles the chamber. These movements are measured by the pressure sensors under the chamber and are used as indicators of the vigor of the startle reaction.

The startle reaction can be elicited in rats by a variety of stimuli, including brief loud tones and bright lights. In one experiment (Leaton, 1976), the startle stimulus was a high pitched, loud tone presented for two seconds. The animals were first allowed to get used to the experimental chamber without any tone presentations. Each rat then received a single tone presentation once a day for 11 days. In the next phase of the experiment the tones were presented much more frequently (every three seconds) for a total of 300 trials.

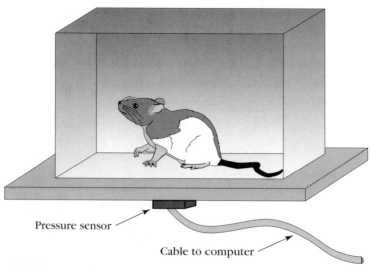

Pressure sensor

Cable to computer

FIGURE **2.9**

Stabilimeter apparatus to measure the startle response of rats. A small chamber rests on pressure censors. Sudden movements of the rat are detected by the pressure sensors and recorded on a computer.

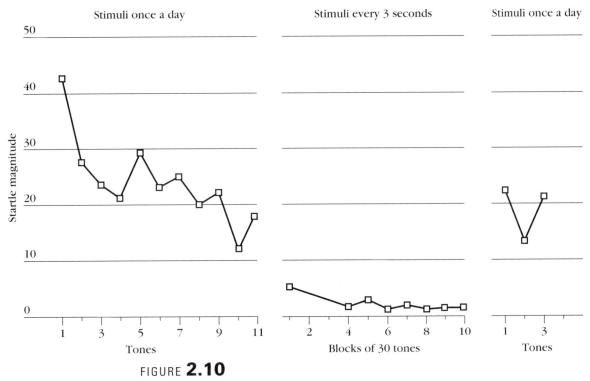

FIGURE **2.10**

Startle response of rats to a tone presented once a day in Phase 1, every three seconds in Phase 2, and once a day in Phase 3. (From "Long-Term Retention of the Habituation of Lick Suppression and Startle Response Produced by a Single Auditory Stiumuls," by R. N. Leaton, 1976, *Journal of Experimental Psychology: Animal Behavior Processes, 2,* pp. 248–259. Copyright © 1976 by the American Psychological Association. Reprinted by permission.)

Finally, the animals were given a single tone presentation on each of the next three days as in the beginning of the experiment.

Figure 2.10 shows the results. The most intense startle reaction was observed the first time the tone was presented. Progressively less intense reactions occurred during the next 10 days. Because the animals received only one tone presentation every 24 hours in this phase, the progressive decrements in responding indicated that the habituating effects of the stimulus presentations persisted throughout the 11-day period. It is worth noting, though, that this long-term habituation did not result in complete loss of the startle reflex. Even on the 11th day, the animals still reacted a little.

By contrast, startle reactions quickly ceased when the tone presentations occurred every three seconds in Phase 2 of the experiment. However, this dramatic loss of responsiveness was only temporary. In Phase 3 of the experiment, when trials were again administered just once each day, the startle response recovered to the level of the 11th day of the experiment. This recovery, known as **spontaneous recovery**, occurred simply because the tone had not been presented for a long time (24 hours).

This experiment illustrates that two different forms of habituation occur depending on the frequency of the stimulus presentations. If the stimuli are presented widely spaced in time, a long-term habituation effect occurs, which persists for 24 hours or longer. In contrast, if the stimuli are presented very closely in time (every three seconds in this experiment), a short-term habituation effect occurs. The short-term habituation effect is identified by spontaneous recovery of responding if a period without stimulation is introduced.

Repeated presentations of a stimulus do not always result in both long-term and short-term habituation effects. With the spinal leg-flexion reflex in cats, for example, only the short-term habituation effect is observed (Thompson & Spencer, 1966). In such cases, spontaneous recovery completely restores the animal's reaction to the eliciting stimulus if a long enough period of rest is permitted after habituation. By contrast, spontaneous recovery is never complete in situations that also involve long-term habituation, as in Leaton's experiment (see also Beck & Rankin, 1997; Pedreira et al., 1998; Staddon & Higa, 1996). As Figure 2.10 indicates, the startle response was restored to some extent in the last phase of the experiment, but the animals did not react as vigorously to the tone as they had the first time it was presented.

Sensitization and the Modulation of Elicited Behavior

Consider your reaction when someone walks up behind you and taps you on the shoulder. If you are in a supermarket, you will be mildly startled and will turn toward the side where you were tapped. Orienting toward a tactile stimulus is a common elicited response. In our evolutionary past, being touched could mean that we were about to be attacked by a predator, which is something that you wouldn't want to ignore. Being tapped on the shoulder is not a big deal if you are in a supermarket. However, if you are walking in a dark alley at night in a dangerous part of town, being tapped on the shoulder could be a very scary experience and will no doubt elicit a much more vigorous reaction. Generally speaking, if you are already aroused, the same eliciting stimulus will trigger a much stronger reaction. This is called a **sensitization effect.**

It is easier to study sensitization of the startle response in the laboratory than in a dark alley. In a classic study, Davis (1974), examined sensitization of the startle response of rats to a brief (90-millisecond) loud tone (110 decibels [dB], 4,000 cycles per second [cps]). Two groups of subjects were tested. Each group received 100 trials presented at 30 second intervals. In addition, a noise generator provided background noise that sounded something like water running from a faucet. For one group, the background noise was relatively quiet (60 dB); for the other, the background noise was rather loud (80 dB), but of lower intensity than the brief startle-eliciting tone.

The results of the experiment are shown in Figure 2.11. As in the other examples I described, repeated presentations of the eliciting stimulus (the 4,000 cps tone) did not always produce the same response. For rats tested in the presence of the soft background noise (60 dB), repetitions of the tone resulted in progressively weaker startle reactions. By contrast, when the background noise was loud (80 dB), repetitions of the tone elicited more vigorous startle reactions. This reflects a gradual build-up of sensitization created by the loud noise.

Reflex responses are sensitized when the subject becomes aroused for some reason. Arousal intensifies our experiences, whether those experiences

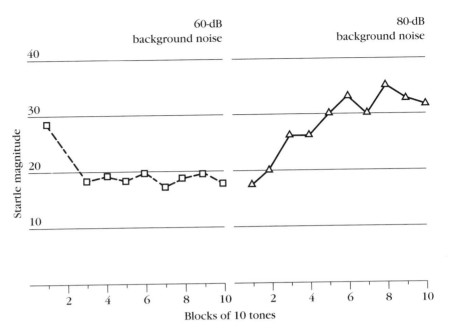

FIGURE **2.11**

Magnitude of the startle response of rats to successive presentations of a tone with background noise of 60 and 80 dB. (From "Sensitization of the Rat Startle Response by Noise," by M. Davis, 1974, *Journal of Comparative and Physiological Psychology, 87,* pp. 571–581. Copyright © 1974 by the American Psychological Association. Reprinted by permission.)

are pleasant or unpleasant. As is well-known in the live entertainment industry, introducing loud noise is a relatively simple way to create arousal. Live performances of rock bands are so loud that band members suffer hearing loss if they don't wear earplugs. The music does not have to be so loud for everyone to hear it. The main purpose of the high volume is to create arousal and excitement. Turning a knob on an amplifier is a simple way to increase excitement. Making something loud is a common device for increasing the enjoyment of movies, circus acts, car races, and football games, and is effective because of the phenomenon of sensitization.

Sensitization also plays a major role in sexual behavior. A major component of sexual behavior involves reacting to tactile cues. Consider the tactile cues of a caress or a kiss. The reaction to the same physical caress or kiss is totally different if you are touching your grandmother than if you are touching your boyfriend or girlfriend. The difference reflects sensitization and arousal. In a recent study of this issue, heterosexual males were tested for their sensitivity to a tactile stimulus presented to the right index finger (Jiao, Knight, Weerakoon, & Turman, 2007) before and after watching an erotic movie that was intended to increase their sexual arousal. Tactile sensitivity was significantly increased by the erotic movie. Watching a non-erotic movie did not produce this effect.

Sensitization has been examined most extensively in the defensive behavior system. Numerous studies have shown that fear potentiates the startle response (Davis, 1977). Startle can be measured using a stabilimeter like that shown in Figure 2.9, which measures the reaction of the entire body. A simpler procedure, particularly with human participants, is to measure the eyeblink response (Norrholm et al., 2006). The eyeblink is an early component of the startle response and can be elicited in people by directing a brief puff of air towards the eye.

In one study, using the eyeblink startle measure (Bradley, Moulder, & Lang, 2005), college students served as participants and were shown examples of pleasant and unpleasant pictures. To induce fear, one group of students was told that they could get shocked at some point when they saw the pleasant pictures but not when they saw the unpleasant pictures. The second group of participants received shock threat associated with the unpleasant pictures, but not the pleasant pictures. Shock was never delivered to any of the participants, but to make the threat credible, they were fitted with shock electrodes. To measure fear potentiated startle, the magnitude of the eyeblink response to a puff of air was measured during presentation of the pictures.

The results are shown in Figure 2.12. Let us first consider the startle reaction during presentations of the pleasant pictures. If the pleasant pictures were associated with shock threat, the eyeblink response was substantially greater than if the pictures were safe. This represents the fear-potentiated startle effect. The results with the unpleasant pictures were a bit different. With the unpleasant pictures, the startle response was elevated whether or not the pictures were associated with the threat of shock. This suggests that the unpleasant pictures were sufficiently discomforting to sensitize the defensive blink response independent of any shock threat.

Adaptiveness and Pervasiveness of Habituation and Sensitization

Organisms are constantly being bombarded by a host of stimuli. Consider the act of sitting at your desk. Even such a simple situation involves a

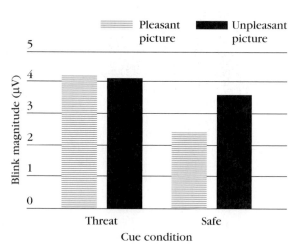

FIGURE **2.12**

Magnitude of the eyeblink response of college students to pleasant and unpleasant pictures that signaled shock or were safe. (Based on Bradley, Moulder, & Lang, 2005.)

myriad of sensations. You are exposed to the color, texture, and brightness of the paint on the walls; the sounds of the air-conditioning system; noises from other rooms; odors in the air; the color and texture of the desk; the tactile sensations of the chair against your legs, seat, and back; and so on. If you were to respond to all of these stimuli, your behavior would be disorganized and chaotic. Habituation and sensitization effects help sort out what stimuli to ignore and what to respond to. Habituation and sensitization effects are the end products of processes that help prioritize and focus behavior in the buzzing and booming world of stimuli that organisms live in.

There are numerous instances of habituation and sensitization in common human experience (Simons, 1996). Consider a grandfather clock. Most people who own such a clock do not notice each time it chimes. They have completely habituated to the clock's sounds. In fact, they are more likely to notice when the clock misses a scheduled chime. In a sense, this is unfortunate because they may have purchased the clock for the reason that they liked its sound. Similarly, people who live on a busy street or near a railroad track may become entirely habituated to the noises that frequently intrude their homes. Visitors who have not become familiarized with such sounds are much more likely to react and be bothered by them.

Driving a car involves exposure to a large array of complex visual and auditory stimuli. In becoming an experienced driver, a person habituates to the numerous stimuli that are irrelevant to driving, such as details of the color and texture of the road, the kind of telephone poles that line the sides of the highway, tactile sensations of the steering wheel, and routine noises from the engine. Habituation to irrelevant cues is particularly prominent during long driving trips. If you are driving continuously for several hours, you are likely to become oblivious to all kinds of stimuli that are irrelevant to keeping the car on the road. If you then come across an accident or arrive in a new town, you are likely to "wake up" and again pay attention to various things that you had been ignoring. Passing a bad accident or coming to a new town is arousing and sensitizes orienting responses that were previously habituated.

Habituation also determines how much we enjoy something. In his book, *Stumbling on happiness*, Daniel Gilbert noted that "Among life's cruelest truths is this one: Wonderful things are especially wonderful the first time they happen, but their wonderfulness wanes with repetition" (p. 130). He went on to write, "When we have an experience—hearing a particular sonata, making love with a particular person, watching the sun set from a particular window with a particular person—on successive occasions, we quickly begin to adapt to it, and the experience yields less pleasure each time" (p. 130).

Habituation and sensitization effects can occur in any situation that involves repeated exposures to a stimulus. Therefore, an appreciation of habituation and sensitization effects is critical for studies of learning. As I will describe in Chapter 3, habituation and sensitization are of primary concern in the design of control procedures for Pavlovian conditioning. Habituation and sensitization also play a role in operant conditioning (McSweeney, Hinson, & Cannon, 1996).

Habituation versus Sensory Adaptation and Response Fatigue

The key characteristic of habituation effects is a decline in the response that was initially elicited by a stimulus. However, not all instances in which repetitions of a stimulus result in a response decline represent habituation. To understand alternative sources of response decrement, we need to return to the concept of a reflex. A reflex consists of three components. First, a stimulus activates one of the sense organs, such as the eyes or ears. This generates sensory neural impulses that are relayed to the central nervous system (spinal cord and brain). The second component involves relay of the sensory messages through interneurons to motor nerves. Finally, the neural impulses in motor nerves, in turn, activate the muscles that create the observed response.

Given the three components of a reflex, there are several reasons why an elicited response may fail to occur (see Figure 2.13). The response will not be observed if for some reason the sense organs become temporarily insensitive to stimulation. A person may be temporarily blinded by a bright light, for example, or suffer a temporary hearing loss because of exposure to loud noise. Such decreases in sensitivity are called **sensory adaptation** and are different from habituation. The response also will not occur if the muscles involved become incapacitated by **fatigue**. Sensory adaptation and response fatigue are impediments to responding that are produced outside the nervous system in sense organs and muscles. Therefore, they are distinguished from habituation.

Habituation and sensitization are assumed to involve neurophysiological changes that hinder or facilitate the transmission of neural impulses from sensory to motor neurons. In habituation, the organism ceases to respond to a stimulus even though it remains fully capable of sensing the stimulus and making the muscle movements required for the response. The response fails because changes in the nervous system block the relay of sensory neural impulses to the motor neurons.

In studies of habituation, sensory adaptation is ruled out by evidence that *habituation is response specific*. An organism may stop responding to a stimulus in one aspect of its behavior while continuing to respond to the stimulus in other ways. When a teacher makes an announcement while you are concentrating on taking a test, you may look up from your test at first, but only

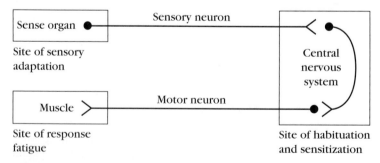

FIGURE **2.13**

Diagram of a simple reflex. Sensory adaptation occurs in the sense organs, and response fatigue occurs in effector muscles. In contrast, habituation and sensitization occur in the nervous system.

briefly. However, you will continue to listen to the announcement until it is over. Thus, your orienting response habituates quickly, but other attentional responses to the stimulus persist.

Response fatigue as a cause of habituation is ruled out by evidence that *habituation is stimulus specific*. A habituated response will quickly recover when a new stimulus is introduced. This was illustrated in the taste habituation study summarized in Figure 2.5. After the salivary and hedonic responses had habituated during the first 10 trials, presentation of the alternate taste in Trial 11 resulted in a recovery of both response measures. In an analogous fashion, after your orienting response to a teacher's announcement has habituated, you are likely to look up again if the teacher mentions your name. Thus, a new stimulus will elicit the previously habituated orienting response, indicating that failure of the response was not due to response fatigue.

THE DUAL-PROCESS THEORY OF HABITUATION AND SENSITIZATION

Habituation and sensitization effects are changes in behavior or performance. These are outward behavioral manifestations or results of stimulus presentations. What factors are responsible for such changes? To answer this question we have to shift our level of analysis from behavior to presumed underlying process or theory. Habituation effects can be satisfactorily explained by a single-factor theory that characterizes how repetitions of a stimulus change the efficacy of that stimulus (e.g., Schöner & Thelen, 2006). However, a second factor has to be introduced to explain why responding is enhanced under conditions of arousal. The dominant theory of habituation and sensitization remains the dual-process theory of Groves and Thompson (1970).

The dual-process theory assumes that different types of underlying neural processes are responsible for increases and decreases in responsiveness to stimulation. One neural process produces decreases in responsiveness. This is called the **habituation process**. Another process produces increases in responsiveness. This is called the **sensitization process**. The habituation and sensitization processes are not mutually exclusive. Rather, both may be activated at the same time. The behavioral outcome of these underlying processes depends on which process is stronger. Thus, habituation and sensitization processes compete for control of behavior.

It is unfortunate that the underlying processes that suppress and facilitate responding are called habituation and sensitization. One may be tempted to think that decreased responding or a habituation effect is a direct reflection of the habituation process, and that increased responding or a sensitization effect is a direct reflection of the sensitization process. In fact, both habituation and sensitization effects are the sum, or net, result of both habituation and sensitization processes. Whether the net result is an increase or a decrease in behavior depends on which underlying process is stronger in a particular situation. The distinction between *effects* and *processes* in habituation and sensitization is analogous to the distinction between *performance* and *learning* discussed in Chapter 1. Effects refer to observable behavior and processes refer to underlying mechanisms.

On the basis of neurophysiological research, Groves and Thompson (1970) suggested that habituation and sensitization processes occur in different parts of the nervous system (see also Thompson et al., 1973). Habituation processes are assumed to occur in what is called the **S-R system.** This system consists of the shortest neural path that connects the sense organs activated by the eliciting stimulus and the muscles involved in making the elicited response. The S-R system may be viewed as the reflex arc. Each presentation of an eliciting stimulus activates the S-R system and causes some build-up of habituation.

Sensitization processes are assumed to occur in what is called the **state system.** This system consists of other parts of the nervous system that determine the organism's general level of responsiveness or readiness to respond. In contrast to the S-R system, which is activated every time an eliciting stimulus is presented, only arousing events activate the state system. The state system is relatively quiescent during sleep, for example. Drugs, such as stimulants or depressants, may alter the functioning of the state system and thereby change responsiveness. The state system is also altered by emotional experiences. For example, the heightened reactivity that accompanies fear is caused by activation of the state system.

In summary, the state system determines the organism's general readiness to respond, whereas the S-R system enables the animal to make the specific response that is elicited by the stimulus of interest. The level of response a particular stimulus elicits depends on the combined actions of the S-R and state systems.

Applications of the Dual-Process Theory

The examples of habituation and sensitization (illustrated in the experimental evidence I previously reviewed) can be easily interpreted in terms of the dual-process theory. Repeated exposure to the 4 x 4 checkerboard pattern produced a decrement in visual orientation in infants (Figure 2.7). This presumably occurred because the 4 x 4 stimulus did not create much arousal. Rather, the 4 x 4 stimulus activated primarily the S-R system, and hence activated primarily the habituation process. The more complex 12 x 12 checkerboard pattern produced a greater level of arousal. It presumably activated not only the S-R system but also the state system. The activation of the state system resulted in the increment in visual attention that occurred after the first presentation of the 12 x 12 pattern. However, the arousal or sensitization process was not strong enough to entirely counteract the effects of habituation. As a result, after a few trials visual attention also declined in response to the 12 x 12 stimulus. (For an alternative interpretation of the 12 x 12 data, see Schöner & Thelen, 2006.)

A different type of application of the dual-process theory is required for the habituation and sensitization effects we noted in the startle reaction of rats (Figure 2.11). When the rats were tested with a relatively quiet background noise (60 dB), there was little to arouse them. Therefore, we can assume that the experimental procedures did not produce changes in the state system. Repeated presentations of the startle-eliciting tone merely activated the S-R system, which resulted in habituation of the startle response.

The opposite outcome occurred when the animals were tested in the presence of a loud background noise (80 dB). In this case, stronger startle reactions occurred to successive presentations of the tone. Because the identical tone was used for both groups, the difference in the results cannot be attributed to the tone. Rather, one must assume that the loud background noise increased arousal or readiness to respond in the second group. This sensitization of the state system was presumably responsible for increasing the startle reaction to the tone in the second group.

Implications of the Dual-Process Theory

The preceding interpretations of habituation and sensitization effects illustrate several important features of the dual-process theory. *The S-R system is activated every time a stimulus elicits a response* because it is the neural circuit that conducts impulses from sensory input to response output. Activation of the S-R system and its attendant habituating influence are universal features of elicited behavior. By contrast, *the state system becomes involved only in special circumstances*. Some extraneous event, such as intense background noise, may increase the individual's alertness and sensitize the state system. Alternatively, the state system may be sensitized by the repeated presentations of the test stimulus itself if that stimulus is sufficiently intense or excitatory (a 12 x 12 checkerboard pattern, as compared with a 4 x 4 pattern). If the arousing stimulus is repeated soon enough so that the second presentation occurs while the organism remains sensitized from the preceding trial, an increase in responding will be observed.

Both the habituation process and the sensitization process are expected to decay with the passage of time without stimulation. Thus, one would expect to see *spontaneous recovery* from both processes. The loss of the habituation process with time results in recovery, or increase, in the elicited behavior to baseline levels (hence the term spontaneous *recovery)*. In contrast, the temporal decay of the sensitization process results in a decrease of the elicited behavior down to its normal non-aroused level.

Because habituation resides in the S-R circuit, the dual-process theory predicts that *habituation will be stimulus specific*. If following habituation training the eliciting stimulus is changed, the new stimulus will elicit a nonhabituated response because it activates a different S–R circuit. We saw this outcome in the experiment on habituation of salivation and hedonic ratings to a taste (see Figure 2.5). After the salivary and emotional responses to one taste stimulus (e.g., lime) had substantially habituated (Trials 1-10), the responses showed total recovery when a different taste (lemon) was presented (Trial 11). The stimulus specificity of habituation also forms the basis for all of the studies of infant cognition that employ the visual attention paradigm (see Figure 2.8). Similar effects occur in common experience. For example, after you have become completely habituated to the chimes of your grandfather clock, your attention to the clock is likely to become entirely restored if the clock malfunctions and makes a new sound.

Unlike habituation, sensitization is not highly stimulus-specific. If an animal becomes aroused or sensitized for some reason, its reactivity will increase to a range of cues. For example, pain induced by foot-shock increases the reactivity of laboratory rats to both auditory and visual cues. Similarly, feelings of sickness or malaise increase the reactivity of rats to a wide range of novel tastes. However, shock-induced sensitization appears to be limited to exteroceptive cues and illness-induced sensitization is limited to gustatory stimuli (Miller & Domjan, 1981). Cutaneous pain and internal malaise seem to activate separate sensitization systems.

The dual-process theory of habituation and sensitization has been very influential (e.g., Barry, 2004; Pilz & Schnitzler, 1996), although it has not been successful in explaining all habituation and sensitization effects (e.g., Bee,

2001). One of the important contributions of the theory has been the assumption that elicited behavior can be strongly influenced by neurophysiological events that take place outside the reflex arc that is directly involved in a particular elicited response. The basic idea that certain parts of the nervous system serve to modulate S-R systems that are more directly involved in elicited behavior has been substantiated in numerous studies of habituation and sensitization (e.g., Borszcz, Cranney, & Leaton, 1989; Davis, 1997; Falls & Davis, 1994; Frankland & Yeomans, 1995; Lipp, Sheridan, & Siddle, 1994). (For a detailed discussion of other theories of habituation, see Stephenson & Siddle, 1983; Schöner & Thelen, 2006.)

BOX **2.2**

Learning in an Invertebrate

How does the brain acquire, store, and retrieve information? To answer this question, we need to know how neurons operate and how neural circuits are modified by experience. Studying these issues requires that we delve into the neural machinery to record and manipulate its operations. Naturally, people are not keen on volunteering for such experiments. Therefore, such research has to be conducted on other species.

Much can be learned from the vertebrates (rats, rabbits) that are typically used in behavioral studies of learning. Yet, at a neural level, even a rat poses technical challenge for a neurobiologist. Therefore, neurobiologists have focused on creatures with simpler nervous systems. Invertebrates are attractive because some of their neurons are very large, and they have far simpler nervous systems. Using this approach, Eric Kandel and his colleagues have uncovered the mechanisms that mediate some basic learning processes in the marine snail, *Aplysia*. Here, I provide an overview of the mechanisms that underlie habituation and sensitization (for a recent review, see Hawkins, Kandel, & Bailey, 2006).

Aplysia have two wing-like flaps (the parapodium) on their back (dorsal) surface. These flaps cover the gill and other components of the respiratory apparatus (see Figure 2.14A). The gill lies under a mantle shelf and a siphon helps to circulate water across the gill. In the relaxed state, the gill is extended (left side of Figure 2.14A), maximizing chemical exchange across its surface. It is a fragile organ that must be protected. For this reason, nature has given *Aplysia* a protective gill-withdrawal reflex. This reflex can be elicited by a light touch applied to the siphon, or mantle. In the laboratory, the reflex is often elicited by a water jet produced from a Water Pik. While the mechanisms that underlie this reflex can be studied in the intact organism, it is often easier to study the underlying system after the essential components have been removed and placed in a nutrient bath that sustains the tissue.

With this simple preparation, it is an easy matter to demonstrate both habituation and sensitization (see Figure 2.14B). Habituation can be produced by repeatedly applying the tactile stimulus to the siphon.

With continued exposure, the magnitude of the gill-withdrawal reflex becomes smaller (habituates). Interestingly, this experience has no effect on the magnitude of the gill-withdrawal elicited by touching the mantle shelf. Conversely, if we repeatedly touch the mantle, the withdrawal response observed habituates without affecting the response elicited by touching the siphon. A modification in one stimulus-response (S-R) pathway has no effect on the response vigor in the other.

In vertebrates, a painful shock engages a mechanism that generally sensitizes behavior, augmenting a variety of response systems including those that generate a startle response (Davis, 1989). A similar effect can be demonstrated in *Aplysia*. If a shock stimulus is applied to the tail, it sensitizes the gill-withdrawal response elicited by touching the mantle or siphon (Walters, 1994). Notice that this is a general effect that augments behavioral reactivity in both the mantle and siphon circuits.

The essential neural components that underlie gill-withdrawal in response to a siphon touch are illustrated in Figure 2.14C. A similar

(continued)

BOX **2.2** (continued)

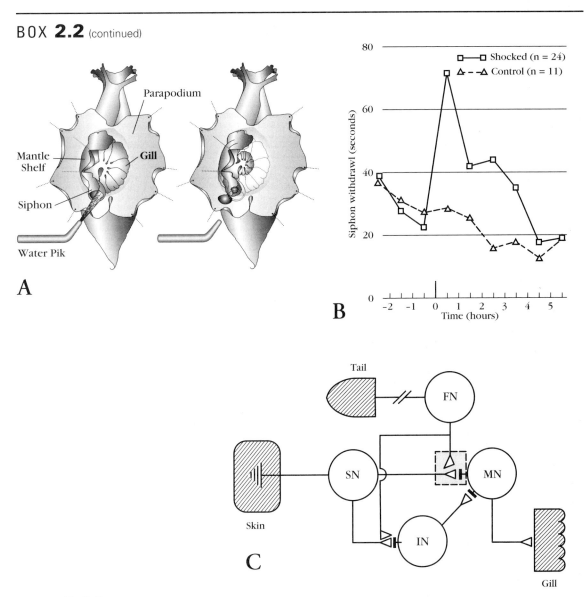

FIGURE **2.14**

(A) The gill-withdrawal reflex in *Aplysia*. A touch applied to the siphon or mantle causes the gill to retract (right). (Adapted from Kandel, 1976.) (B) Habituation and sensitization of the gill-withdrawal reflex. Repeated application of a tactile stimulus causes the withdrawal response to habituate (dashed line). A brief shock (applied at time 0) sensitizes the response (solid line). (Adapted from Kandel & Schwartz, 1982.) (C) The neural circuit that mediates habituation and sensitization. (Adapted from Dudai, 1989.)

diagram could be drawn for the neurons that underlie the gill-withdrawal elicited by touching the mantle.

Touching the siphon skin engages a mechanical receptor that is coupled to a sensory neuron (SN).

Just one receptor is illustrated here, but additional receptors and neurons innervate adjoining regions of

(continued)

BOX **2.2** (continued)

the siphon skin. The degree to which a particular receptor is engaged will depend on its proximity to the locus of stimulation, being greatest at the center of stimulation and weakening as distance increases. This yields the neural equivalent to a generalization gradient, with the maximum activity being produced by the neuron that provides the primary innervation for the receptive field stimulated.

The mechanical receptors that detect a touch engage a response within the dendrites of the sensory neuron (SN). This neural response is conveyed to the cell body (soma) and down a neural projection, the axon, to the motor neuron (MN). The sensory neuron is the presynaptic cell. The motor neuron is the postsynaptic cell. The motor neuron is engaged by the release of a chemical (neurotransmitter) from the sensory neuron. The motor neuron, in turn, carries the signal to the muscles that produce the gill-withdrawal response. Here, the release of neurotransmitter activates muscle fibers that cause the gill to retract.

The sensory neuron also engages other cells, interneurons that contribute to the performance of the gill-withdrawal response. However, because an understanding of the basic mechanisms that underlie learning does not hinge on their function, we will pay little attention to the interneurons engaged by the sensory neuron. We cannot, however, ignore another class of interneurons, those engaged by applying a shock to the tail. A tailshock engages neurons that activate an interneuron called the facilitory interneuron (FI). As shown in the figure, the facilitory interneuron impinges upon the end of the presynaptic, sensory, neuron. In more technical terms, the facilitory interneuron presynaptically innervates the sensory neuron. Because of this, the facilitory interneuron can alter the operation of the sensory neuron.

The magnitude of the gill-withdrawal response depends on the amount of neurotransmitter released from the motor neurons. The more that is released, the stronger is the response. Similarly, the probability that a response will be engaged in the motor neuron, and the number of motor neurons that are engaged, depends on the amount of neurotransmitter released from the sensory neuron. Increasing the amount released will usually enhance the motor neuron response and the gill-withdrawal response.

Research has shown that with repeated stimulations of the sensory neuron, there is no change in the action potential generated within the sensory neuron, but less transmitter is released, producing the behavioral phenomenon of habituation.

Sensitization, in contrast, engages the facilitory interneuron, which produces a change within the sensory neuron that causes it to release more neurotransmitter. Because more transmitter is released, the motor neurons are engaged to a greater extent, and the gill-withdrawal response is more vigorous. Thus, behavioral sensitization occurs, in part, because tailshock augments the release of neurotransmitter from the sensory neuron. In addition, recent work has shown that changes in the postsynaptic cell, analogous to the phenomenon of long-term potentiation described in Box 11.1, contribute to sensitization (Glanzman, 2006).

J. W. Grau

EXTENSIONS TO EMOTIONS AND MOTIVATED BEHAVIOR

To this point, our discussion of changes produced by repetitions of an eliciting stimulus has been limited to relatively simple responses. However, stimuli may also evoke complex emotions such as love, fear, euphoria, terror, or satisfaction. I have already described habituation of an emotional response to repeated presentations of a taste (Figure 2.5). The concepts of habituation and sensitization also have been extended to changes in more complex emotions (Solomon & Corbit, 1974) and various forms of motivated behavior including feeding, drinking, exploration, aggression, courtship, and sexual behavior (McSweeney & Swindell, 1999). An area of special interest is drug addiction (e.g., Baker et al., 2004; Baker, Brandon,

& Chassin, 2004; Ettenberg, 2004; Koob, et al., 1997; Koob & Le Moal, 2008; Robinson & Berridge, 2003).

Emotional Reactions and Their Aftereffects

In their landmark review of examples of emotional responses to various stimuli, including drugs, Solomon and Corbit (1974) noticed a couple of striking features. First, intense emotional reactions are often biphasic. One emotion occurs during the eliciting stimulus, and the opposite emotion is observed when the stimulus is terminated. Consider, for example, the psychoactive effects of alcohol. Someone who is drinking beer or wine becomes mellow and relaxed as they are drinking. These feelings, which are generally pleasant, reflect the primary sedative effects of alcohol. In contrast, something quite different occurs after a night of drinking. Once the sedative effects of alcohol have dissipated, the person is likely to become irritable and may experience headaches and nausea. The pleasant sedative effects of alcohol give way to the unpleasant sensations of a hangover. Both the primary direct effects of the drug and the hangover are dependent on dosage. The more you drink, the more sedated, or drunk, you become, and the more intense the hangover is afterward. Similar bi-phasic responses are observed with other drugs. With amphetamine, for example, the presence of the drug creates feelings of euphoria, a sense of well-being, self-confidence, wakefulness, and a sense of control. After the drug has worn off, the person is likely to feel tired, depressed, and drowsy.

Courtesy Donald A. Dewsbury

R. L. Solomon

Another common characteristic of emotional reactions is that they change with experience. The primary reaction becomes weaker and the after-reaction becomes stronger. Habitual drinkers are not as debilitated by a few beers as someone drinking for the first time. However, habitual drinkers experience more severe withdrawal symptoms if they quit drinking.

Habituation of a primary drug reaction is called **drug tolerance**. Drug tolerance refers to a decline in the effectiveness of a drug with repeated exposures. Habitual users of all psychoactive drugs (e.g., alcohol, nicotine, heroin, caffeine, sleeping pills, anti-anxiety drugs) are not as greatly affected by the presence of the drug as first-time users. A strong vodka tonic that would make a casual drinker a bit tipsy is not likely to have any effect on a frequent drinker. (We will revisit the role of opponent processes in drug tolerance in Chapter 4.)

Because of the development of tolerance, habitual drug users sometimes do not enjoy taking the drug as much as naive users. People who smoke frequently, for example, do not derive much enjoyment from doing so. Accompanying this decline in the primary drug reaction is a growth in the opponent after-reaction. Accordingly, habitual drug users experience much more severe hangovers when the drug wears off than naive users. A habitual smoker who has gone a long time without a cigarette will experience headaches, irritability, anxiety, tension, and general dissatisfaction. A heavy drinker who stops consuming alcohol is likely to experience hallucinations, memory loss, psychomotor agitation, delirium tremens, and other physiological disturbances. For a habitual user of amphetamine, the fatigue and depression that characterize the opponent aftereffect may be so severe as to cause suicide.

Solomon and Corbit (1974) noted that similar patterns of emotional reaction occur with other emotion arousing stimuli. Consider, for example, love and attachment. Newlyweds are usually very excited about each other and are very affectionate whenever they are together. This primary emotional reaction habituates as the years go by. Gradually, the couple settles into a comfortable mode of interaction that lacks the excitement of the honeymoon. However, this habituation of the primary emotional reaction is accompanied by a strengthening of the affective after-reaction. Couples who have been together for many years become more intensely unhappy if they are separated by death or disease. After partners have been together for several decades, the death of one may cause an intense grief reaction in the survivor. This strong affective after-reaction is remarkable, considering that by this stage in their relationship the couple may have entirely ceased to show any overt signs of affection.

The Opponent Process Theory of Motivation

The above examples illustrate three common characteristics of emotional reactions: 1) Emotional reactions are biphasic; a primary reaction is followed by an opposite after-reaction. 2) The primary reaction becomes weaker with repeated stimulations. 3) The weakening of the primary reaction with repeated exposure is accompanied by a strengthening of the after-reaction. These characteristics were identified some time ago and led to the formulation of the *opponent process theory of motivation* (Solomon & Corbit, 1973, 1974).

The opponent process theory assumes that neurophysiological mechanisms involved in emotional behavior serve to maintain emotional stability. Thus, the opponent process theory is a *homeostatic* theory. It is built on the premise that an important function of mechanisms that control emotions is to keep us on an even keel and minimize the highs and lows. The concept of homeostasis was originally introduced to explain the stability of our internal physiology, such as body temperature. Since then, the concept has also become important in the analysis of behavior. (I will discuss other types of homeostatic theories in later chapters.)

How might physiological mechanisms maintain emotional stability and keep us from getting too excited? Maintaining any system in a neutral or stable state requires that a disturbance that moves the system in one direction be met by an opposing force that counteracts the disturbance. Consider, for example, trying to keep a seesaw level. If something pushes one end of the seesaw down, the other end will go up. To keep the seesaw level, a force pushing one end down has to be met by an opposing force on the other side.

The idea of opponent forces serving to maintain a stable state is central to the opponent process theory of motivation. The theory assumes that an emotion-arousing stimulus pushes a person's emotional state away from neutrality. This shift away from emotional neutrality is assumed to trigger an opponent process that counteracts the shift. The patterns of emotional behavior observed initially and after extensive experience with a stimulus are the net results of the direct effects of an emotion arousing stimulus and the opponent process that is activated to counteract this direct effect.

The presentation of an emotion-arousing stimulus initially elicits what is called the **primary process,** or *a* **process,** which is responsible for the quality of the emotional state (e.g., happiness) that occurs in the presence of the stimulus. The primary, or *a* process, is assumed to elicit, in turn, an **opponent process,** or *b* **process,** that generates the opposite emotional reaction (e.g., irritability and dysphoria). Because the opponent process is activated by the primary reaction, it lags behind the primary emotional disturbance.

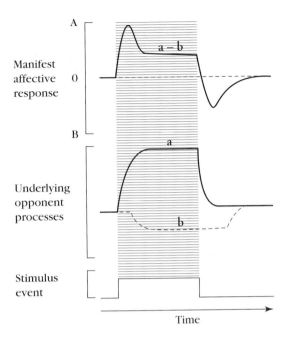

FIGURE **2.15**

Opponent process mechanism during the initial presentation of an emotion arousing stimulus. The observed emotional reactions are represented in the top panel. The underlying opponent processes are represented in the bottom panel. Notice that the *b* process starts a bit after the onset of the *a* process. In addition, the *b* process ends much later than the *a* process. This last feature allows the opponent emotions to dominate after the end of the stimulus. (From "An Opponent Process Theory of Motivation: I. The Temporal Dynamics of Affect," by R. L. Solomon and J. D. Corbit, 1974, *Psychological Review, 81,* pp. 119–145. Copyright © 1974 by the American Psychological Association. Reprinted by permission.)

Opponent Mechanisms During Initial Stimulus Exposure

Figure 2.15 shows how the primary and opponent processes determine the initial responses of an organism to an emotion arousing stimulus. The underlying primary and opponent processes are represented in the bottom of the figure. The net effects of these processes (the observed emotional reactions) are represented in the top panel. When the stimulus is first presented, the *a* process occurs unopposed by the *b* process. This permits the primary emotional reaction to reach its peak quickly. The *b* process then becomes activated and begins to oppose the *a* process. However, the *b* process is not strong enough to entirely counteract the primary emotional response, and the primary emotional response persists during the eliciting stimulus. When the stimulus is withdrawn, the *a* process quickly stops, but the *b* process lingers for awhile. At this point the *b* process has nothing to oppose. Therefore, emotional responses characteristic of the opponent process become evident for the first time.

Opponent Mechanisms After Extensive Stimulus Exposure

Figure 2.16 shows how the primary and opponent processes operate after extensive exposure to a stimulus. As I noted earlier, a highly familiar stimulus

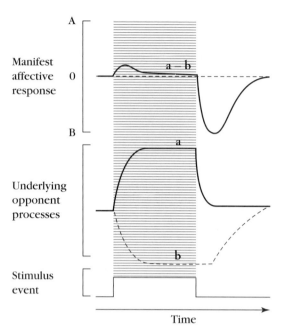

FIGURE **2.16**

Opponent process mechanism that produces the affective changes to a habituated stimulus. The observed emotional reactions are represented in the top panel. The underlying opponent processes are represented in the bottom panel. Notice that the *b* process starts promptly after the onset of the *a* process and is much stronger than in Figure 2.15. In addition, the *b* process ends much later than the *a* process. Because of these changes in the *b* process, the primary emotional response is nearly invisible during the stimulus, but the affective after-reaction is very strong. (From "An Opponent Process Theory of Motivation: I. The Temporal Dynamics of Affect," by R. L. Solomon and J. D. Corbit, 1974, *Psychological Review, 81,* pp. 119–145. Copyright © 1974 by the American Psychological Association. Reprinted by permission.)

does not elicit strong emotional reactions, but the affective after-reaction tends to be much stronger. The opponent process theory explains this outcome by assuming that the *b* process becomes strengthened with repeated use. It becomes activated sooner after the onset of the stimulus, its maximum intensity becomes greater, and it becomes slower to decay when the stimulus ceases. Because of these changes, the primary emotional responses are more effectively counteracted by the opponent process with repeated presentations of the eliciting stimulus. An associated consequence of the growth of the opponent process is that the affective after-reaction becomes stronger when the stimulus is withdrawn (see Figure 2.16).

Opponent Aftereffects and Motivation

If the primary pleasurable effects of a psychoactive drug are gone for habitual users, why do they continue taking the drug? Why are they addicted? The opponent process theory suggests that drug addiction is mainly an attempt to reduce the aversiveness of the affective after-reaction to the drugs such as the bad hangovers, the amphetamine "crashes," and the irritability that comes from not having the usual cigarette. Based on their extensive review of research on emotion and cognition, Baker et al. (2004) proposed an affective processing model of drug addiction that is built on opponent process concepts and concludes that "addicted drug users sustain their drug use largely to manage their misery" (p. 34) (see also Baker, Brandon, & Chassin, 2004; Ettenberg, 2004).

The opponent process interpretation of drug addiction as escape from the misery of withdrawal is also supported by a large body of neuroscience evidence. In their recent review of this evidence, Koob and Le Moal (2008) concluded that extensive drug use results in reduced activity in brain circuits associated with reward and strengthening of opponent neural mechanisms referred to as the *anti-reward* circuit. Drug seeking behavior is reinforced largely by the fact that drug intake reduces activity in the anti-reward circuit. As they pointed out, "the combination of decreases in reward neurotransmitter function and recruitment of anti-reward systems provides a powerful source of negative reinforcement that contributes to compulsive drug-seeking behavior and addiction" (p. 38). Thus, drug addicts are not "trapped" by the pleasure they derive from the drug (since activity in the reward circuit is reduced by chronic drug intake). Rather, they take the drug to reduce withdrawal pains. (For an alternative perspective, see Robinson & Berridge, 2003.)

CONCLUDING COMMENTS

The quality of life and survival itself depends on an intricate coordination of behavior with the complexities of the environment. Elicited behavior represents one of the fundamental ways in which the behavior of all animals, from single-celled organisms to people, is adjusted to environmental events.

Elicited behavior takes many forms, ranging from simple reflexes mediated by just three neurons to complex emotional reactions. Although elicited behavior occurs as a reaction to a stimulus, it is not rigid and invariant. In fact, one of its hallmark features is that elicited behavior is altered by experience. If an eliciting stimulus does not arouse the organism, repeated presentations of the stimulus will evoke progressively weaker responses (a habituation effect). If the organism is in a state of arousal, the elicited response will be enhanced (a sensitization effect).

Repeated presentations of an eliciting stimulus produce changes in simple responses as well as in more complex emotional reactions. Organisms tend to minimize changes in emotional state caused by external stimuli. According to the opponent process theory of motivation, emotional responses stimulated by an environmental event are counteracted by an opposing process in the organism. If the original elicited emotion is rewarding, the opponent process will activate anti-reward circuits and create an aversive state. The compensatory, or opponent, process is assumed to become stronger each time it is activated. Drug addiction involves efforts to minimize the aversive nature of the opponent or anti-reward processes attendant to repeated drug intake.

Habituation, sensitization, and changes in the strength of opponent processes are the simplest mechanisms, whereby organisms adjust their reactions to environmental events on the basis of past experience.

SAMPLE QUESTIONS

1. Describe how elicited behavior can be involved in complex social interactions, like breast feeding.
2. Describe sign stimuli involved in the control of human behavior.
3. Compare and contrast appetitive and consummatory behavior, and describe how these are related to general search, focal search, and food handling.
4. Describe components of the startle response and how the startle response may undergo sensitization.
5. Describe the distinction between habituation, sensory adaptation, and fatigue.
6. Describe the two processes of the dual-process theory of habituation and sensitization and the differences between these processes.
7. Describe how habituation and sensitization are involved in emotion regulation and drug addiction.

KEY TERMS

a **process** Same as *primary process* in the opponent process theory of motivation.

afferent neuron A neuron that transmits messages from sense organs to the central nervous system. Also called *sensory neuron.*

appetitive behavior Behavior that occurs early in a natural behavior sequence and serves to bring the organism in contact with a releasing stimulus. (See also *general search mode* and *focal search mode.*)

b **process** Same as *opponent process* in the opponent process theory of motivation.

consummatory behavior Behavior that serves to bring a natural sequence of behavior to consummation or completion. Consummatory responses are usually species-typical modal action patterns. (See also *food handling mode.*)

drug tolerance Reduction in the effectiveness of a drug as a result of repeated use of the drug.

efferent neuron A neuron that transmits impulses to muscles. Also called a *motor neuron.*

fatigue A temporary decrease in behavior caused by repeated or excessive use of the muscles involved in the behavior.

focal search mode The second component of the feeding behavior sequence following general search, in which the organism engages in behavior focused on a particular location or stimulus that is indicative of the presence of food. Focal search is a form of appetitive behavior that is more closely related to food than general search.

food handling mode The last component of the feeding behavior sequence, in which the organism handles and consumes the food. This is similar to what ethologists referred to as *consummatory behavior.*

general search mode The earliest component of the feeding behavior sequence, in which the organism engages in nondirected locomotor behavior. General search is a form of appetitive behavior.

habituation effect A progressive decrease in the vigor of elicited behavior that may occur with repeated presentations of the eliciting stimulus.

habituation process A neural mechanism activated by repetitions of a stimulus that reduces the magnitude of responses elicited by that stimulus.

interneuron A neuron in the spinal cord that transmits impulses from afferent (or sensory) to efferent (or motor) neurons.

modal action pattern (MAP) A response pattern exhibited by most, if not all, members of a species in much the same way. Modal action patterns are used as basic units of behavior in ethological investigations of behavior.

motor neuron Same as *efferent neuron*.

opponent process A compensatory mechanism that occurs in response to the primary process elicited by biologically significant events. The opponent process causes physiological and behavioral changes that are the opposite of those caused by the primary process. Also called the *b* process.

primary process The first process that is elicited by a biologically significant stimulus. Also called the *a* process.

reflex arc Neural structures consisting of the afferent (sensory) neuron, interneuron, and efferent (motor) neuron, that enable a stimulus to elicit a reflex response.

releasing stimulus Same as *sign stimulus*.

sensitization effect An increase in the vigor of elicited behavior that may result from repeated presentations of the eliciting stimulus or from exposure to strong extraneous stimulus.

sensitization process A neural mechanism that increases the magnitude of responses elicited by a stimulus.

sensory adaptation A temporary reduction in the sensitivity of sense organs caused by repeated or excessive stimulation.

sensory neuron Same as *afferent neuron*.

sign stimulus A specific feature of an object or animal that elicits a modal action pattern in another organism. Also called *releasing stimulus*.

spontaneous recovery Recovery of a response produced by a period of rest after habituation or extinction. (Extinction is discussed in Chapter 9.)

S-R system The shortest neural pathway that connects the sense organs stimulated by an eliciting stimulus and the muscles involved in making the elicited response.

state system Neural structures that determine the general level of responsiveness, or readiness to respond, of the organism.

supernormal stimulus An artificially enlarged or exaggerated sign stimulus that elicits an unusually vigorous response.

3

Classical Conditioning: Foundations

The Early Years of Classical Conditioning
The Discoveries of Vul'fson and Snarskii
The Classical Conditioning Paradigm

Experimental Situations
Fear Conditioning
Eyeblink Conditioning
Sign Tracking
Learning What Tastes Good or Bad

Excitatory Pavlovian Conditioning Procedures
Common Pavlovian Conditioning
   Procedures
Measuring Conditioned Responses
Control Procedures for Classical
   Conditioning
Effectiveness of Common Conditioning
   Procedures

Inhibitory Pavlovian Conditioning
Procedures for Inhibitory Conditioning
Measuring Conditioned Inhibition

Prevalence of Classical Conditioning

Concluding Comments

SAMPLE QUESTIONS
KEY TERMS

CHAPTER PREVIEW

Chapter 3 provides an introduction to another basic form of learning, namely classical conditioning. Investigations of classical conditioning began with the work of Pavlov, who studied how dogs learn to anticipate food. Since then, the research has been extended to a variety of other organisms and response systems. Some classical conditioning procedures establish an excitatory association between two stimuli and serve to activate behavior. Other procedures promote learning to inhibit the operation of excitatory associations. I will describe both excitatory and inhibitory conditioning procedures, and discuss how these are involved in various important life experiences.

In the preceding chapter, I described how environmental events can elicit behavior and how such elicited behavior can be modified by sensitization and habituation. These relatively simple processes help to bring the behavior of organisms in tune with their environment. However, if human and nonhuman animals only had the behavioral mechanisms described in Chapter 2, they would remain rather limited in the kinds of things they could do. For the most part, habituation and sensitization involve learning about just one stimulus. However, events in the world do not occur in isolation. Rather, much of our experience consists of predictable and organized sequences of stimuli. Every significant event (e.g., a hug from a friend) is preceded by other events (your friend approaching with extended arms) that are part of what leads to the target outcome.

Cause and effect relationships in the world ensure that certain things occur in combination with others. Your car's engine does not run unless the ignition has been turned on; you cannot walk through a doorway unless the door was first opened; it does not rain unless there are clouds in the sky. Social institutions and customs also ensure that events occur in a predictable order. Classes are scheduled at predictable times; people are predictably better dressed at church than at a picnic; a person who smiles is more likely to act in a friendly manner than one who frowns. Learning to predict events in the environment and learning what stimuli tend to occur together are important for aligning behavior with the environment. Imagine how much trouble you would have if you could not predict how long it takes to make coffee, when stores are likely to be open, or whether your key will work to unlock your apartment.

The simplest mechanism whereby organisms learn about relations between one event and another is classical conditioning. Classical conditioning enables human and nonhuman animals to take advantage of the orderly sequence of events in their environment to then take appropriate action in anticipation of what is about to happen. For example, classical conditioning is the process whereby we learn to predict when and what we might eat, when we are likely to face danger, and when we are likely to be safe. It is also integrally involved in the learning of new emotional reactions (e.g., fear or pleasure) to stimuli that have become associated with a significant event.

THE EARLY YEARS OF CLASSICAL CONDITIONING

Systematic studies of classical conditioning began with the work of the great Russian physiologist Pavlov (see Box 3.1). Classical conditioning was also independently discovered by Edwin Twitmyer in a PhD dissertation submitted to the University of Pennsylvania in 1902 (see Twitmyer, 1974). Twitmyer repeatedly tested the knee-jerk reflex of college students by sounding a bell 0.5 seconds before hitting the patellar tendon just below the knee cap. After several trials of this sort, the bell was sufficient to elicit the knee-jerk reflex in some of the students. However, Twitmyer did not explore the broader implications of his discoveries, and his findings did not attract much attention.

Pavlov's studies of classical conditioning were an extension of his research on the processes of digestion. Pavlov made major advances in the study of digestion by developing surgical techniques that enabled dogs to survive for many years with artificial fistulae that permitted the collection of various digestive juices. With the use of a stomach fistula, for example, Pavlov was able to collect stomach secretions in dogs that otherwise lived normally. Technicians in the laboratory soon discovered that the dogs secreted stomach juices in response to the sight of food, or even just upon seeing the person who usually fed them. The laboratory produced considerable quantities of stomach juice in this manner and sold the excess to the general public. The popularity of this juice as a remedy for various stomach ailments helped to supplement the income of the laboratory.

Assistants in the laboratory referred to stomach secretions elicited by food-related stimuli as *psychic secretions* because they seemed to be a response to the expectation or thought of food. However, the phenomenon of

BOX **3.1**

Ivan P. Pavlov: Biographical Sketch

Born in 1849 into the family of a priest in Russia, Pavlov dedicated his life to scholarship and discovery. He received his early education in a local theological seminary and planned a career of religious service. However, his interests soon changed, and when he was 21, he entered the University of St. Petersburg, where his studies focused on chemistry and animal physiology. After obtaining the equivalent of a bachelor's degree, he went to the Imperial Medico-Surgical Academy in 1875 to further his education in physiology. Eight years later, he received his doctoral degree for his research on the efferent nerves of the heart and then began investigating various aspects of digestive physiology. In 1888 he discovered the nerves that stimulate the digestive secretions of the pancreas—a finding that initiated a series of experiments for which Pavlov was awarded the Nobel Prize in Physiology in 1904.

Pavlov did a great deal of original research while a graduate student, as well as after obtaining his doctoral degree. However, he did not have a faculty position or his own laboratory until 1890, when he was appointed professor of pharmacology at the St. Petersburg Military Medical Academy. In 1895 he became professor of physiology at the same institution. Pavlov remained active in the laboratory until close to his death in 1936. In fact, much of the research for which he is famous today was performed after he received the Nobel Prize.

psychic secretions generated little scientific interest until Pavlov recognized that it could be used to study the mechanisms of association learning and could inform us about the functions of the nervous system (Pavlov, 1927). Thus, as many great scientists, Pavlov's contributions were important not just because he discovered something new, but because he figured out how to place the discovery into a compelling conceptual framework.

The Discoveries of Vul'fson and Snarskii

The first systematic studies of classical conditioning were performed by S. G. Vul'fson and A. T. Snarskii in Pavlov's laboratory (Boakes, 1984; Todes, 1997). Both of these students focused on the salivary glands, which are the first digestive glands involved in the breakdown of food. Some of the salivary glands are rather large and have ducts that are accessible and can be easily externalized with a fistula (see Figure 3.1). Vul'fson studied salivary responses to various substances placed in the mouth: dry food, wet food, sour water, and sand, for example. After the dogs had these substances placed in the mouth repeatedly, the mere sight of the substances was enough to make them salivate.

Whereas Vul'fson used naturally occurring substances in his studies, Snarskii extended these observations to artificial substances. In one experiment, Snarskii first gave his dogs sour water (such as strong lemon juice) that was artificially colored black. After several encounters with the black sour water, the dogs also salivated to plain black water or to the sight of a bottle containing a black liquid.

The substances tested by Vul'fson and Snarskii could be identified at a distance by sight. The substances also produced distinctive texture and taste sensations in the mouth. Such sensations are called *orosensory stimuli*. The first time that sand was placed in a dog's mouth, only the feeling of the sand in the mouth elicited salivation. However, after sand had been placed in the

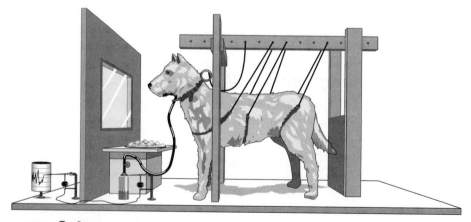

FIGURE **3.1**

Diagram of the Pavlovian salivary conditioning preparation. A cannula attached to the animal's salivary duct conducts drops of saliva to a data-recording device. (From "The Method of Pavlov in Animal Psychology," by R. M. Yerkes and S. Morgulis, 1909, *Psychological Bulletic, 6,* pp. 257–273.)

mouth several times, the sight of sand (its visual features) also came to elicit salivation. Presumably the dog learned to associate the visual features of the sand with its orosensory features. The association of one feature of an object with another is called **object learning**.

To study the mechanisms of associative learning, the stimuli to be associated have to be manipulated independently of one another. This is difficult to do when the two stimuli are properties of the same object. Therefore, in later studies of conditioning, Pavlov used procedures in which the stimuli to be associated came from different sources. This led to the experimental methods that continue to dominate studies of classical conditioning to the present day. However, contemporary studies are no longer conducted with dogs.

The Classical Conditioning Paradigm

Pavlov's basic procedure for the study of conditioned salivation is familiar to many. The procedure involves two stimuli. One of these is a tone or a light that does not elicit salivation at the outset of the experiment. The other stimulus is food or the taste of a sour solution placed in the mouth. In contrast to the light or tone, the food or sour taste elicits vigorous salivation even the first time it is presented.

Pavlov referred to the tone or light as the **conditional stimulus** because the effectiveness of this stimulus in eliciting salivation depended on (or was *conditional* on) pairing it several times with the presentation of food. By contrast, the food or sour-taste was called the **unconditional stimulus** because its effectiveness in eliciting salivation did not depend on any prior training. The salivation that eventually came to be elicited by the tone or light was called the **conditional response**, and the salivation that was always elicited by the food or sour taste was called the **unconditional response**. Thus, stimuli and responses whose properties did not depend on prior training were called *unconditional,* and stimuli and responses whose properties emerged only after training were called *conditional*.

In the first English translation of Pavlov's writings, the term uncondition*al* was erroneously translated as uncondition*ed,* and the term condition*al* was translated as condition*ed*. The -ed suffix was used exclusively in English writings for many years. However, the term condition*ed* does not capture Pavlov's original meaning of "dependent on" as accurately as the term condition*al* (Gantt, 1966).

Because the terms conditioned and unconditioned stimulus and conditioned and unconditioned response are used frequently in discussions of classical conditioning, they are often abbreviated. Conditioned stimulus and conditioned response are abbreviated **CS** and **CR**, respectively. Unconditioned stimulus and unconditioned response are abbreviated **US** and **UR**, respectively.

EXPERIMENTAL SITUATIONS

Classical conditioning has been investigated in a variety of situations and species (e.g., Domjan, 2005; Hollis, 1997; Turkkan, 1989). Pavlov did most of his experiments with dogs using the salivary-fistula technique. Most contemporary experiments on Pavlovian conditioning are carried out with domesticated rats, rabbits, and pigeons using procedures developed by North American scientists during the second half of the twentieth century.

Fear Conditioning

Following the early work of Watson and Rayner (1920/2000), a major focus of investigators of Pavlovian conditioning has been the conditioning of emotional reactions. Watson and Rayner believed that infants are at first limited in their emotional reactivity. They assumed that "there must be some simple method by means of which the range of stimuli which can call out these emotions and their compounds is greatly increased. (p. 313)" That simple method was Pavlovian conditioning. In a famous demonstration, Watson and Rayner conditioned a fear response in a nine-month-old infant, Albert, to the presence of a docile white laboratory rat.

There was hardly anything that Albert was afraid of. However, after testing a variety of stimuli, Watson and Rayner found that little Albert reacted with alarm when he heard the loud noise of a steel bar being hit by a hammer behind his head. Watson and Rayner then used this unconditioned alarming stimulus to condition fear to a white rat. Each conditioning trial consisted of presenting the rat to Albert and then striking the steel bar. At first Albert reached out to the rat when it was presented to him. But, after just two conditioning trials, he became reluctant to touch the rat. After five additional conditioning trials, Albert showed strong fear responses to the rat. He whimpered or cried, leaned as far away from the rat as he could, and sometimes fell over and moved away on all fours. Significantly, these fear responses were not evident when Albert was presented with his toy blocks. However, the conditioned fear did generalize to other furry things (a rabbit, a fur coat, cotton wool, a dog, and a Santa Claus mask).

Fear and anxiety are the sources of considerable human discomfort, and if sufficiently severe, they can lead to serious psychological and behavioral problems. There is considerable interest in how fear and anxiety are acquired, what the neural mechanisms of fear are, and how fear may be attenuated with pharmacological and behavioral treatments (e.g., Craske, Hermans, & Vansteenwegen, 2006; Kirmayer, Lemelson, & Barad, 2007). Many of these questions cannot be addressed experimentally using human subjects (at least not initially). Therefore, most of the research on fear conditioning has been conducted with laboratory rats and mice. The aversive US in these studies is a brief electric shock delivered through a metal grid floor. Shock is used because it can be regulated with great precision and its intensity can be adjusted so as to cause no physical harm. It is aversive primarily because it is startling, unlike anything the animal has encountered before. The CS may be a discrete stimulus (like a tone or a light), or the contextual cues of the place where the aversive stimulus is encountered.

Unlike little Albert who showed signs of fear by whimpering and crying, rats show their fear by freezing. Freezing is a species typical defense response that occurs in a variety of species in response to the anticipation of aversive stimulation (see Chapter 10). Freezing probably evolved as a defensive behavior because animals that are motionless are not easily seen by their predators. For example, a deer that is standing still in the woods is difficult to see because its coloration blends well with the colors of bark and leaves. However, as soon as the deer starts moving, you can tell where it is.

Freezing is defined as immobility of the body (except for breathing) and the absence of movement of the whiskers associated with sniffing (Bouton & Bolles, 1980). Direct measurement of freezing as an index of conditioned fear has become popular, especially in neurobiological studies of fear (e.g., Fendt & Fanselow, 1999; Quinn & Fanselow, 2006). However, investigators also use two different indirect measures of immobility. Both involve the suppression of ongoing behavior and are therefore referred to as **conditioned suppression** procedures. In one case, the ongoing behavior that is measured is licking a drinking spout that contains water. The animals are slightly water deprived and therefore lick readily when placed in an experimental chamber. If a fear CS (e.g., tone) is presented, their licking behavior is suppressed and they take longer to make a specified number of licks. The latency to complete a certain number of licks is measured as the behavioral index of conditioned fear. The **lick-suppression procedure** was devised more than 40 years ago (e.g., Leaf & Muller, 1965) but remains popular in contemporary research (e.g., Urcelay & Miller, 2008a).

Another prominent technique for the indirect measurement of conditioned fear is the **conditioned emotional response** procedure (**CER**) devised by Estes and Skinner (1941). In this procedure, rats are first trained to press a response lever for food reward in a small experimental chamber (Figure 3.2A). This lever press activity provides the behavioral baseline for measurement of fear. Once the rats are lever pressing at a steady rate, fear conditioning is introduced, consisting of a tone or light paired with a brief shock. As the participants acquire the conditioned fear, they come to suppress their lever pressing during the CS (Kamin, 1965).

To measure the suppression of lever pressing, a suppression ratio is calculated. The ratio compares the number of lever presses that occur during the CS with the number that occur during a comparable baseline period before the CS is presented (the pre-CS period). The specific formula is as follows:

$$\text{Suppression Ratio} = \text{CS responding} \div (\text{CS responding} + \text{pre-CS responding}) \quad (3.1)$$

Notice that the *suppression ratio* has a value of zero if the rat suppresses lever pressing completely during the CS, because in this case, the numerator of the formula is zero. At the other extreme, if the rat does not alter its rate of lever pressing at all when the CS is presented, the ratio has a value of 0.5. For example, let us assume that the CS is presented for two minutes and that in a typical two minute period the rat makes 30 responses. If the CS does not disrupt lever pressing, the animal will make 30 responses during the CS, so that the numerator of the ratio will be 30. The denominator will be 30 (CS responses) + 30 (pre-CS responses), or 60. Therefore, the ratio will be 30÷60 or 0.5. Decreasing values of the ratio from 0.5 to 0 indicate greater degrees of response suppression, or conditioned fear. Thus, the scale is inverse. Greater disruptions of lever pressing are represented by lower values of the suppression ratio.

Figure 3.2B shows sample results of a conditioned suppression experiment with rats. Two conditioning trials were conducted on each of five days of training. Very little suppression occurred the first time the CS was presented, and not much acquisition of suppression was evident during the first day of training. However, a substantial increase in suppression occurred from the last trial on Day 1 (Trial 2) to the first trial on Day 2 (Trial 3). With continued training, responding gradually became more and more suppressed, until an asymptotic suppression ratio of about 0.2 was achieved.

Interpreting conditioned suppression data can be confusing because the scale is inverse. Keep in mind that a suppression ratio of 0 indicates zero responding during the CS, which represents the greatest possible suppression of

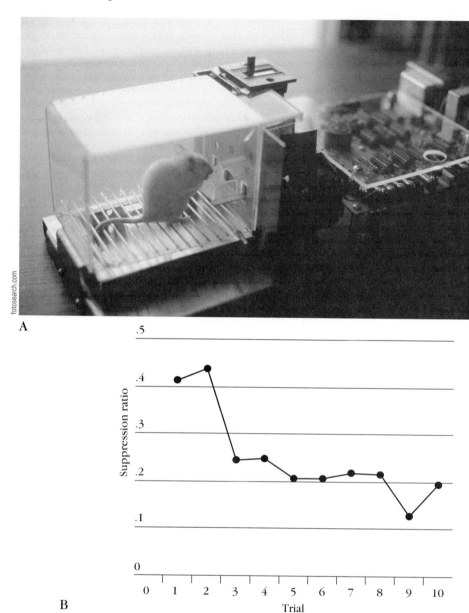

A

B

<figure>

FIGURE **3.2**

(A) Rat lever pressing for food in a conditioning chamber that also permits the presentation of an auditory cue as the CS and brief shock as the US. (B) Acquisition of conditioned suppression to a clicker CS paired with shock. Two conditioning trials were conducted each day for five days. Suppression ratios closer to zero indicate greater degrees of suppression of lever pressing during the CS and greater conditioned fear. (Based on Waddell, Morris, & Bouton, 2006.)

lever pressing. The smaller the suppression ratio, the more motionless the animal is, because the CS elicits more conditioned fear.

The conditioned suppression procedure has also been adapted for experiments with human subjects. In that case, the behavioral baseline is provided by playing a video game (e.g., Arcediano, Ortega, & Matute, 1996; Nelson & del Camen Sanjuan, 2006).

Eyeblink Conditioning

As I mentioned in Chapter 2, the eyeblink reflex is an early component of the startle response and occurs in a variety of species. To get someone to blink, all you have to do is clap your hands or blow a puff of air toward the eyes. If the air puff is preceded by a brief tone, the person will learn to blink when the tone comes on, in anticipation of the air puff.

Because of its simplicity, eyeblink conditioning was extensively investigated in studies with human participants early in the development of learning theory (see Hilgard & Marquis, 1940; Kimble, 1961). Eyeblink conditioning continues to be a very active area of research because it provides a powerful tool for the study of problems in development, aging, and Alzheimer's disease (Freeman & Nicholson, 2004; Woodruff-Pak, 2001; Woodruff-Pak et al., 2007). Eyeblink conditioning also has been used extensively in studies of the neurobiology of learning. This knowledge has in turn made eyeblink conditioning useful in studies of autism, fetal alcohol syndrome, and obsessive compulsive disorder (Steinmetz, Tracy, & Green, 2001).

A study of eyeblink conditioning in five-month-old infants (Ivkovich, Collins, Eckerman, Krasnegor, & Stanton, 1999) illustrates the technique. The CS was a 1,000 cps tone presented for 750 milliseconds, and the US was a gentle puff of air delivered to the right eye through a plastic tube. Each infant sat on a parent's lap facing a platform with brightly colored objects that maintained the infant's attention during the experimental sessions. Eyeblinks were recorded by video cameras. For one group of infants, the CS always ended with the puff of air, and these conditioning trials occurred an average of 12 seconds apart. The second group received the same number and distribution of CS and US presentations, but for them, the CSs and USs were spaced four to eight seconds apart in an explicitly unpaired fashion. Thus, the second group served as a control. Each participant received two training sessions, one week apart.

The results of the experiment are presented in Figure 3.3 in terms of the percentage of trials on which the subjects blinked during the CS. The rate of eyeblinks for the two groups did not differ statistically during the first experimental session. However, the paired group responded to the CS at a significantly higher rate from the beginning of the second session. This experiment illustrates a number of important points about learning. First, it shows that classical conditioning requires the pairing of a CS and US. Responding to the CS did not develop in the unpaired control group. Second, the learning was not observable at first. The infants in the paired group did not respond much in the first session, but they were starting to learn that the CS was related to the US. This learning was clearly evident when the subjects were returned to the experimental situation for a second session.

Recent interest in eyeblink conditioning in humans stems from the fact that substantial progress has been made in understanding the neurobiological substrates of this type of learning. Neurobiological investigations of eyeblink conditioning

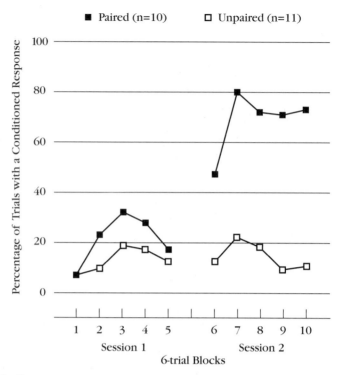

■ Paired (n=10)　　□ Unpaired (n=11)

FIGURE **3.3**

Eyeblink conditioning in five-month-old infants. For the infants in the paired group, a tone CS ended in a gentle puff of air to the eye. For the infants in the unpaired group, the tone and air puff never occurred together. (Adapted from D. Ivlovich, K. L. Collins, C. O. Eckerman, N. A. Krasnegor, and M. E. Stanton (1999). Classical delay eyeblink conditioning in four and five month old human infants. *Psychological Science*, 10, Figure 1, p. 6. Adapted with permission from Blackwell Publishing.)

I. Gormezano

have been conducted primarily in studies with domesticated rabbits. The rabbit eyeblink preparation was developed by Gormezano (see Gormezano, 1966; Gormezano, Kehoe, & Marshall, 1983). Domesticated rabbits are ideal for this type of research because they are sedentary and rarely blink in the absence of an air puff or irritation of the eye. In an eyeblink conditioning experiment, the rabbit is placed in an enclosure and attached to equipment that enables measurement of the blink response. The US to elicit blinking is provided by a small puff of air or mild irritation of the skin below the eye with a brief (0.1 second) electrical current. The CS may be a light, a tone, or a mild vibration of the animal's abdomen.

In the typical conditioning experiment, the CS is presented for half a second and is followed immediately by delivery of the US. The US elicits a rapid and vigorous eyelid closure. As the CS is repeatedly paired with the US, the eyeblink response is also made with the CS. Investigators record the percentage of trials in which a conditioned blink response is observed. Rabbit eyeblink conditioning is relatively slow, requiring several hundred trials for substantial levels of conditioned responding.

BOX **3.2**

Eyeblink Conditioning and the Search for the Engram

When an organism learns something, the results of this learning must be stored within the brain. Somehow, the network of neurons that makes up our central nervous system is able to encode the relationship between biologically significant events and use this information to guide the selection of responses the subject will perform. This biological memory is known as an *engram*. The traditional view is that the engram for a discrete CR is stored in localized regions of the brain. This raises a basic question in neurobiology: Where is the engram located?

This question has been pursued for nearly four decades by Richard Thompson and his collaborators (for recent reviews see Fanselow & Poulos, 2005; Steinmetz, Gluck, & Solomon, 2001; Thompson, 2005). Thompson recognized that locating the engram would require a well defined behavioral system in which both the conditions for learning and the motor output were precisely specified. These considerations led him to study the mechanisms that underlie eyeblink conditioning. In the eyeblink conditioning situation, a CS (e.g., a tone) is repeatedly paired with an air puff to the eye (the US) and acquires the ability to elicit a defensive eyeblink response. To pursue his neurobiological investigations, Thompson studied eyeblink conditioning in rabbits.

The search for the engram began with the hippocampus. Studies of humans with damage to this region revealed that the ability to consciously remember a recent event requires that the hippocampus remain intact. In animal subjects, small electrodes were lowered into the hippocampus and

neural activity was recorded during eyeblink conditioning. These studies revealed that cells in this region reflect the learning of a CS-US association. However, to the surprise of many investigators, removing the hippocampus did not eliminate the animal's ability to acquire and retain a conditioned eyeblink response. In fact, removing all of the brain structures above the midbrain (see Figure 3.4A) had little effect on eyeblink conditioning with a delayed conditioning procedure. This suggests that the essential circuitry for eyeblink conditioning lies within the lower neural structures of the brainstem and cerebellum. Subsequent experiments clearly showed that the acquisition of a well timed conditioned eyeblink response depends on a neural circuit that lies within the cerebellum (Ohyama, Nores, Morphy, & Mauk, 2003; Steinmetz et al., 2001).

The UR elicited by an air puff to the eye is mediated by neurons that project to a region of the brainstem known as the trigeminal nucleus (see Figure 3.4B). From there, neurons travel along two routes, either directly or through the reticular formation, to the cranial motor nucleus where the behavioral output is organized. Three basic techniques were used to define this pathway. The first involved electrophysiological recordings to verify that neurons in this neural circuit are engaged in response to the US. The second technique involved inactivating the neural circuit, either permanently (by killing the cells) or temporarily (by means of a drug or cooling), to show that the circuit plays an essential role in the eyeblink UR. If the circuit is necessary, disrupting its function

should eliminate the behavioral output. Finally, the circuit was artificially stimulated to show that activity in this circuit is sufficient to produce the behavioral response.

The same techniques (electrical recording, inactivation, and stimulation) have been used to define the neural pathway that mediates the acquisition and performance of the CR. As illustrated in Figure 3.4B, the CS input travels to a region of the brainstem known as the *pontine nucleus*. From there, it is carried by mossy fibers that convey the signal to the cerebellum. The US signal is carried into the cerebellum through the climbing fibers. These two signals meet in the cerebellar cortex where coincident activity brings about a synaptic modification that alters the neural output from the cerebellum. In essence, the climbing fibers act as teachers, selecting a subset of connections to be modified. This change defines the stimulus properties (the characteristics of the CS) that engage a discrete motor output. This output is mediated by neurons that project from the interpositus nucleus to the red nucleus, and finally, to the cranial motor nucleus.

As an eyeblink CR is acquired, conditioned activity develops within the interpositus nucleus. Neurons from the interpositus nucleus project back to the US pathway and inhibit the US signal within the inferior olive. This provides a form of negative feedback that decreases the effectiveness of the US. Many researchers believe that phenomena such as blocking and overshadowing occur because a predicted CS is less effective. In the eyeblink paradigm, this might occur

(continued)

BOX **3.2** (continued)

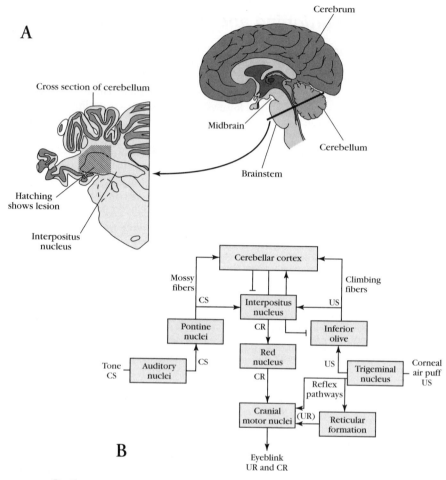

A

Cerebrum

Cross section of cerebellum

Midbrain

Cerebellum

Brainstem

Hatching shows lesion

Interpositus nucleus

Cerebellar cortex

Mossy fibers

Climbing fibers

CS

Interpositus nucleus

US

Pontine nuclei

CR

Inferior olive

Red nucleus

US

Tone CS

Auditory nuclei

CS

CR

Trigeminal nucleus

Corneal air puff US

Reflex pathways

Cranial motor nuclei

(UR)

Reticular formation

B

Eyeblink UR and CR

FIGURE **3.4**

(A) The cerebellum lies at the back of brain, beneath the lobes of the cerebrum. (B) A block diagram of the brain circuitry required for eyelid conditioning. (Adapted from Thompson, 1993.)

because the US input is inhibited within the inferior olive. Consistent with that prediction, Kim et al. (1998) showed that eliminating this source of inhibition eliminated the blocking effect.

Earlier we noted that the hippocampus is not needed for simple delayed conditioning. It is, however, required for more complex forms of learning. An example is provided by trace conditioning, in which a temporal delay is inserted between the end of the CS and the start of the US. A normal animal can readily acquire a conditioned eyeblink to a CS that ends 0.5 seconds before the US. However, it cannot span this gap if the hippocampus is removed. A similar pattern of results is observed in amnesic patients who have damage to the hippocampus (Clark & Squire, 1998). These patients cannot consciously remember the CS-US relation. In the absence of this explicit memory, they fail to learn with a trace conditioning procedure. Learning in the delayed procedure is not affected, even though the patient cannot consciously remember the CS-US relation from one session to the next. Interestingly, disrupting conscious awareness in a normal subject undermines the appreciation of the CS-US relation with the trace procedure. Again, subjects who cannot explicitly report the relation, fail to learn.

J. W. Grau

Sign Tracking

Pavlov's research concentrated on salivation and other highly reflexive responses. This encouraged the belief that classical conditioning occurs only in reflex response systems. In recent years, however, such a restrictive view of Pavlovian conditioning has been abandoned (e.g., Hollis, 1997). One experimental paradigm that has contributed significantly to modern conceptions of Pavlovian conditioning is the **sign tracking**, or **autoshaping**, paradigm (Hearst, 1975; Hearst & Jenkins, 1974; Locurto, Terrace, & Gibbon, 1981).

Animals tend to approach and contact stimuli that signal the availability of food. In the natural environment, the availability of food can be predicted by some aspect of the food itself, such as its appearance at a distance. For a hawk, the sight and noises of a mouse some distance away are cues indicating the possibility of a meal. By approaching and contacting these cues, the hawk can end up with a meal.

Sign tracking is investigated in the laboratory by presenting a discrete, localized visual stimulus just before each delivery of a small amount of food. The first experiment of this sort was performed by Brown and Jenkins (1968) with pigeons. The pigeons were placed in an experimental chamber that had a small circular key that could be illuminated and that the pigeons could peck. Periodically, the birds were given access to food for a few seconds. The key light was illuminated for 8 seconds immediately before each food delivery.

The birds did not have to do anything for the food to be delivered. Since they were hungry, one might predict that when they saw the key light, they would go to the food dish and wait for the food that was coming. Interestingly, that is not what happened. Instead of using the key light to tell them when they should go to the food dish, the pigeons started pecking the key itself. This behavior was remarkable because it was not required to gain access to the food. Presenting the keylight at random times or unpaired with food does not lead to pecking (e.g., Gamzu & Williams, 1971, 1973).

Since its discovery, many experiments have been done on sign tracking in a variety of species, including chicks, quail, goldfish, lizards, rats, rhesus monkeys, squirrel monkeys, and human adults and children (see Tomie, Brooks, & Zito, 1989). Research is also underway to develop sign tracking as a model system for studying the role of incentive motivation in drug addiction (e.g., Flagel, Akil, & Robinson, 2008).

The tracking of signals for food is dramatically illustrated by instances in which the signal is located far away from the food cup. In the first such experiment (see Hearst & Jenkins, 1974), the food cup was located about three feet (90 cm) from the key light. Nevertheless, the pigeons went to the key light rather than the food cup when the CS was presented. Burns and Domjan (2000) extended this "long-box" procedure in sexual conditioning with male quail. Domesticated quail, which copulate readily in captivity, were used in the experiment. The CS was a wood block lowered from the ceiling 30 seconds before a female copulation partner was released. The unusual feature of the experiment was that the CS and the female were presented at opposite ends of an eight foot long chamber (see Figure 3.5). Despite this long distance, the birds approached the CS rather than the location of the female before the female was released. Association of the CS with sexual reinforcement made it such an attractive stimulus that the birds were drawn to it nearly eight feet away, even

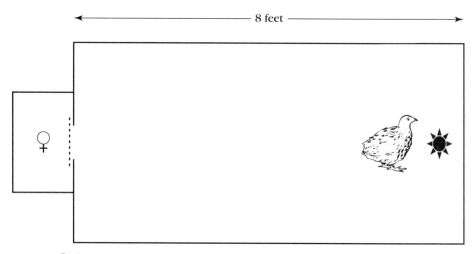

FIGURE **3.5**

Test of sign tracking in sexual conditioning of male domesticated quail. The CS was presented at one end of an eight foot long chamber before the release of a female from the other end. In spite of this distance, the male birds went to the CS when it appeared. (Based on Burns & Domjan, 2000.)

though approaching the CS took them away from where their sexual partner would appear on each trial.

Sign tracking occurs only in situations where the CS is localized and therefore can be approached and tracked. In one study, the CS was provided by diffuse spatial and contextual cues of the chamber in which pigeons were given food periodically. With the diffuse contextual cues, the learning of an association was evident in an increase in general activity, rather than in a specific approach response (Rescorla, Durlach, & Grau, 1985). In another experiment (conducted with laboratory rats), a localized light and a sound were compared as conditioned stimuli for food (Cleland & Davey, 1983). Only the light CS generated sign tracking behavior. The auditory CS elicited approach to the food cup rather than approach to the sound source. These experiments illustrate that for sign tracking to occur, the CS has to be of the proper modality and configuration.

Learning What Tastes Good or Bad

The normal course of eating provides numerous opportunities for the learning of associations. Rozin and Zellner (1985) concluded a review of the role of Pavlovian conditioning in the foods people come to like or dislike with the comment that "Pavlovian conditioning is alive and well, in the flavor-flavor associations of the billions of meals eaten each day...in the associations of foods and offensive objects, and in the associations of foods with some of their consequences" (p. 199).

A conditioned taste aversion is learned if ingestion of a novel flavor is followed by an aversive consequence such as indigestion or food poisoning. In contrast, a taste preference may be learned if a flavor is paired with nutritional repletion or other positive consequences (e.g., Capaldi, Hunter, & Lyn, 1997; Ramirez, 1997). The learning of taste-aversions and taste-preferences has been investigated extensively in various animal species (Reilly & Schachtman, 2008; Riley & Freeman, 2008; Pérez, Fanizza, & Sclafani, 1999; Sclafani, 1997). A growing body of evidence indicates that many human taste aversions are also the result of Pavlovian conditioning (Scalera, 2002). Much of this evidence has been provided by questionnaire studies (Logue, Ophir, & Strauss, 1981; Logue, 1985, 1988a). People report having acquired at least one food aversion during their lives. The typical aversion learning experience involves eating a distinctively flavored food and then getting sick. Such a flavor-illness experience can produce a conditioned food aversion in just one trial, and the learning can occur even if the illness is delayed several hours after ingestion of the food. Another interesting finding is that in about 20% of the cases, the individuals were certain that their illness was not caused by the food they ate. Nevertheless, they learned an aversion to the food. This indicates that food aversion learning can be independent of rational thought processes and can go against a person's conclusions about the causes of their illness.

Questionnaire studies can provide provocative data, but systematic experimental research is required to isolate the mechanism of learning. Experimental studies of taste-aversion learning have been conducted with people in situations where they encounter illness during the course of medical treatment. Chemotherapy for cancer is one such situation. Chemotherapy often causes nausea as a side effect. Both child and adult cancer patients have been shown to acquire aversions to foods eaten before a chemotherapy session (Bernstein, 1978, 1991; Bernstein & Webster, 1980; Carrell, Cannon, Best, & Stone, 1986). Such conditioned aversions may contribute to the lack of appetite that is a common side-effect of chemotherapy. (For laboratory studies on the role of nausea in the conditioning of taste aversions, see Parker, 2003.)

Conditioned food aversions also may contribute to the suppression of food intake or anorexia observed in other clinical situations (Bernstein & Borson, 1986; Scalera & Bavieri, 2008). The anorexia that accompanies the growth of some tumors may result from food-aversion learning. Animal research indicates that the growth of tumors can result in the conditioning of aversions to food ingested during the disease. Food-aversion learning may also contribute to anorexia nervosa, a disorder characterized by severe and chronic weight loss. Suggestive evidence indicates that people suffering from anorexia nervosa experience digestive disorders that may increase their likelihood of learning food aversions. Increased susceptibility to food-aversion learning may also contribute to loss of appetite seen in people suffering from severe depression.

Many of our ideas about food-aversion learning in people have their roots in research with laboratory animals. In the typical procedure, the subjects receive a distinctively flavored food or drink and are then made to feel sick by the injection of a drug or exposure to radiation. As a result of the taste-illness pairing, the animals acquire an aversion to the taste and suppress their subsequent intake of that flavor (Reilly & Schachtman, 2008).

Taste-aversion learning is a result of the pairing of a CS (in this case, a taste) and a US (drug injection or radiation exposure) in much the same manner as in other examples of classical conditioning, and follows standard rules of learning in many respects (e.g., Domjan, 1980, 1983). However, it also has

J. Garcia

some special features. First, strong taste aversions can be learned with just one pairing of the flavor and illness. Although one-trial learning also occurs in fear conditioning, such rapid learning is rarely observed in eyeblink conditioning, salivary conditioning, or sign tracking.

The second unique feature of taste-aversion learning is that it occurs even if the illness does not occur until several hours after exposure to the novel taste (Garcia, Ervin, & Koelling, 1966; Revusky & Garcia, 1970). Dangerous substances in food often do not have their poisonous effects until the food has been digested, absorbed in the blood stream, and distributed to various body tissues. This process takes time. *Long-delay learning* of taste aversions probably evolved to enable human and other animals to avoid poisonous foods that have delayed ill effects.

Long-delay taste-aversion learning was reported in an early study by Smith and Roll (1967). Laboratory rats were first adapted to a water deprivation schedule so that they would readily drink when a water bottle was placed on their cage. On the conditioning day, the water was flavored with the artificial sweetener saccharin (to make a 0.1% saccharin solution). At various times after the saccharin presentation ranging from 0 to 24 hours, different groups of rats were exposed to radiation from an X-ray machine to induce illness. Control groups of rats were also taken to the X-ray machine but were not irradiated. They were called the sham-irradiated groups. Starting a day after the radiation or sham treatment, each rat was given a choice of the saccharin solution or plain water to drink for two days.

The preference of each group of rats for the saccharin solution is shown in Figure 3.6. Animals exposed to radiation within six hours after tasting the

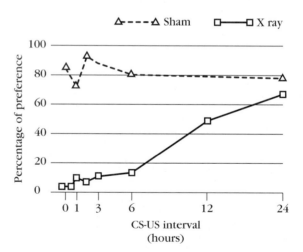

FIGURE **3.6**

Mean percent preference for the saccharin CS flavor during a test session conducted after the CS flavor was paired with X irradiation (the US) or sham exposure. Percent preference is the percentage of the participant's total fluid intake (saccharin solution plus water) that consisted of the saccharin solution. During conditioning, the interval between exposure to the CS and the US ranged from 0 to 24 hours for different groups of rats. (From "Trace Conditioning with X-rays as an Aversive Stimulus," by J. C. Smith and D. L. Roll, *Psychonomic Science*, 1967, 9, pp. 11–12. Copyright © 1967 by Psychonomic Society. Reprinted by permission.)

saccharin solution showed a profound aversion to the saccharin flavor in the postconditioning test. They drank less than 20% of their total fluid intake from the saccharin drinking tube. Much less of an aversion was evident in animals irradiated 12 hours after the saccharin exposure, and hardly any aversion was observed in rats irradiated 24 hours after the taste exposure. In contrast to this gradient of saccharin avoidance observed in the irradiated rats, all the sham-irradiated groups strongly preferred the saccharin solution. They drank more than 70% of their total fluid intake from the saccharin drinking tube.

A flavor can also be made unpalatable by pairing it with another taste that is already disliked. In an analogous fashion, the pairing of a neutral flavor with a taste that is already liked will make that flavor preferable. For example, in a recent study with undergraduate students, Dickinson and Brown (2007) used banana and vanilla as neutral flavors. To induce a flavor aversion or preference, the undergraduates received these flavors mixed with a bitter substance (to condition an aversion) or sugar (to condition a preference). In subsequent tests with the CS flavors, subjects reported increased liking of the flavor that had been paired with sugar and decreased liking of the flavor that had been paired with the bitter taste. In another study, coffee drinkers reported increased liking of a flavor that was paired with the taste of coffee (Yeomans, Durlach, & Tinley, 2005).

These examples of how people learn to like or dislike initially neutral flavors is part of the general phenomenon of **evaluative conditioning** (De Houwer, Thomas, & Baeyens, 2001). In evaluative conditioning, our evaluation or liking of a stimulus changes by virtue of having that stimulus associated with something we already like or dislike. Evaluative conditioning is used extensively in the advertising industry. The product the advertiser is trying to sell is presented with things people already like in an effort to induce a preference for the product.

EXCITATORY PAVLOVIAN CONDITIONING PROCEDURES

What we have been discussing so far are instances of excitatory Pavlovian conditioning. In excitatory conditioning, organisms learn an association between the conditioned and unconditioned stimuli. As a result of this association, presentation of the CS activates behavioral and neural activity related to the US in the absence of the actual presentation of the US. Thus, dogs come to salivate in response to the sight of sand or colored water, pigeons learn to approach and peck a key light that is followed by food, rats learn to freeze to a sound that precedes foot shock, babies learn to blink in response to a tone that precedes a puff of air, and people learn to avoid a flavor that is followed by illness.

Common Pavlovian Conditioning Procedures

One of the major factors that determines the course of classical conditioning is the relative timing of the CS and the US. In most conditioning situations, seemingly small and trivial variations in how a CS is paired with a US can have profound effects on how vigorously the CR occurs, and when the CR occurs.

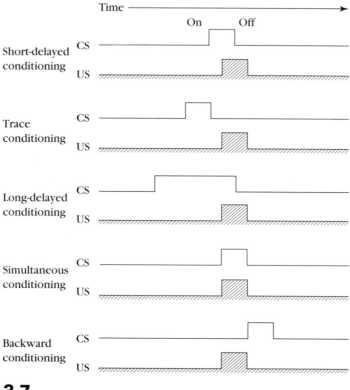

FIGURE **3.7**

Five common classical conditioning procedures.

Five common classical conditioning procedures are illustrated in Figure 3.7. The horizontal distance in each diagram represents the passage of time; vertical displacements represent when a stimulus begins and ends. Each configuration of CS and US represents a single **conditioning trial.**

In a typical classical conditioning experiment, CS-US episodes are repeated a number of times during an experimental *session.* The time from the end of one conditioning trial to the start of the next trial is called the **intertrial interval.** By contrast, the time from the start of the CS to the start of the US within a conditioning trial is called the **interstimulus interval** or **CS-US interval.** For conditioned responding to develop, it is advisable to make the interstimulus interval much shorter than the intertrial interval (e.g., Sunsay & Bouton, 2008). In many experiments the interstimulus interval is less than 1 minute, whereas the intertrial interval may be 5 minutes or more. (A more detailed discussion of these parameters is provided in Chapter 4.)

1. *Short-delayed conditioning.* The most frequently used procedure for Pavlovian conditioning involves delaying the start of the US slightly after the start of the CS on each trial. This procedure is called **short-delayed conditioning.** The critical feature of short-delayed conditioning is that the CS

starts each trial and the US is presented after a brief (less than one minute) delay. The CS may continue during the US or end when the US begins.

2. *Trace conditioning.* The **trace conditioning** procedure is similar to the short-delayed procedure in that the CS is presented first and is followed by the US. However, in trace conditioning, the US is not presented until some time after the CS has ended. This leaves a gap between the CS and US. The gap is called the **trace interval.**

3. *Long-delayed conditioning.* The long-delayed conditioning procedure is also similar to the short-delayed conditioning in that the CS starts before the US. However, in this case the US is delayed much longer (5-10 minutes) than in the short-delay procedure. Importantly, the long-delayed procedure does not include a trace interval. The CS lasts until the US begins.

4. *Simultaneous conditioning.* Perhaps the most obvious way to expose subjects to a CS and a US is to present the two stimuli at the same time. This procedure is called **simultaneous conditioning.** The critical feature of simultaneous conditioning is that the conditioned and unconditioned stimuli are presented concurrently.

5. *Backward conditioning.* The last procedure depicted in Figure 3.7 differs from the others in that the US occurs shortly *before*, rather than after, the CS. This technique is called **backward conditioning** because the CS and US are presented in a "backward" order compared to the other procedures.

Measuring Conditioned Responses

Pavlov and others after him have conducted systematic investigations of procedures like those depicted in Figure 3.7 to find out how the conditioning of a CS depends on the temporal relation between CS and US presentations. To make comparisons among the various procedures, one has to use a method for measuring conditioning that is equally applicable to all the procedures. This is typically done with the use of a **test trial.** A test trial consists of presenting the CS by itself (without the US). Responses elicited by the CS can then be observed without contamination from responses elicited by the US. Such CS-alone test trials can be introduced periodically during the course of training to track the progress of learning.

Behavior during the CS can be quantified in several ways. One aspect of conditioned behavior is how much of it occurs. This is called the **magnitude** of the CR. Pavlov, for example, measured the number of drops of saliva that were elicited by a CS. Other examples of the magnitude of CRs are the amount of response suppression that occurs in the CER procedure (see Figure 3.2) and the degree of depressed flavor preference that is observed in taste-aversion learning (see Figure 3.6).

The vigor of responding can also be measured by how often the CS elicits a CR. For example, we can measure the percentage of trials on which a CR is elicited by the CS. This measure is frequently used in studies of eyeblink conditioning (see Figure 3.3) and reflects the likelihood, or **probability** of responding.

A third aspect of conditioned responding is how soon the CR occurs after presentation of the CS. This measure of the vigor of conditioned behavior is called the **latency** of the CR. Latency is the amount of time that elapses between the start of the CS and the occurrence of the CR.

In the delayed and trace-conditioning procedures, the CS occurs by itself at the start of each trial (see Figure 3.7). Any conditioned behavior that occurs during this initial CS-alone period is uncontaminated by behavior elicited by the US and therefore can be used as a measure of learning. In contrast, responding during the CS in simultaneous and backward conditioning trials is bound to be contaminated by responding to the US or the recent presentation of the US. Therefore, test trials are critical for assessing learning in simultaneous and backward conditioning.

Control Procedures for Classical Conditioning

Devising an effective test trial is not enough to obtain conclusive evidence of classical conditioning. As I noted in Chapter 1, learning is an inference about the causes of behavior based on a comparison of at least two conditions. To be certain that a conditioning procedure is responsible for certain changes in behavior, those changes must be compared to the effects of a control procedure. What should the control procedure be? In studies of habituation and sensitization, we were interested only in the effects of prior exposure to a stimulus. Therefore, the comparison or control procedure was rather simple: it consisted of no prior stimulus exposure. In studies of classical conditioning, our interest is in how conditioned and unconditioned stimuli become associated. Concluding that an association has been established requires more carefully designed control procedures.

An association between a CS and a US implies that the two events have become connected in some way. After an association has been established, the CS is able to activate processes related to the US. An association requires more than just familiarity with the CS and US. It presumably depends on having the two stimuli experienced in connection with each other. Therefore, to conclude that an *association* has been established, one has to make sure that the observed change in behavior could not have been produced by prior separate presentations of the CS or the US.

As I described in Chapter 2, increased responding to a stimulus can be a result of sensitization, which is not an associative process. Presentations of an arousing stimulus, such as food to a hungry animal, can increase the behavior elicited by a more innocuous stimulus, such as a tone, without an association having been established between the two stimuli. Increases in responding observed with repeated CS-US pairings can sometimes result from exposure to just the US. If exposure to just the US produces increased responding to a previously ineffective stimulus, this is called **pseudo-conditioning.** Control procedures are required to determine whether responses that develop to a CS represent a genuine CS-US association, or just pseudo-conditioning.

Investigators have debated the proper control procedure for classical conditioning at length. Ideally, a control procedure should have the same number and distribution of CS and US presentations as the experimental procedure, but with the CSs and USs arranged so that they do not become associated. One possibility is to present the US periodically during both the CS and the intertrial interval, making sure that the probability of the US is the same during the intertrial interval as it is during the CS. Such a procedure is called a **random control procedure.** In a random control procedure, the CS does not signal an increase or change in the probability that the US will occur. The random control was promising when it was first proposed (Rescorla, 1967b), but it has not turned out to be a useful control procedure for classical conditioning. Evidence from a variety of sources indicates that having the same probability of US presentations during the CS and the intertrial interval does not prevent the development of conditioned responding (Kirkpatrick & Church, 2004; Papini & Bitterman, 1990; Rescorla, 2000a; Williams, Lawson, Cook, & Johns, 2008).

A more successful control procedure involves presenting the conditioned and unconditioned stimuli on separate trials. Such a procedure is called the **explicitly unpaired control**. In the explicitly unpaired control, the CS and US are presented far enough apart to prevent their association. How much time has to elapse between them depends on the response system. In taste-aversion learning, much longer separation is necessary between the CS and US than in other forms of conditioning. In one variation of the explicitly unpaired control, only CSs are presented during one session and only USs are presented during a second session.

Effectiveness of Common Conditioning Procedures

There has been considerable interest in determining which of the procedures depicted in Figure 3.7 produces the strongest evidence of learning. The outcome of many early studies of the five conditioning procedures depicted in Figure 3.7 can be summarized by focusing on the interval between the start of the CS and the start of the US: the *interstimulus interval* or *CS-US interval*. Generally, little conditioned responding was observed in simultaneous conditioning procedures, where the CS-US interval was zero (e.g., Bitterman, 1964; Smith, Coleman, & Gormezano, 1969). Delaying the presentation of the US just a bit after the CS often facilitated conditioned responding. However, this facilitation was fairly limited (Ost & Lauer, 1965; Schneiderman & Gormezano, 1964). If the CS-US interval was increased further, conditioned responding declined, as is illustrated in Figure 3.8. Even in the taste-aversion conditioning procedure, where learning is possible with CS-US intervals of an hour or two, conditioned responding declines as the CS-US interval is increased (see Figure 3.6).

Trace conditioning procedures are interesting because they can have the same CS-US interval as delayed conditioning procedures. However, in trace procedures the CS is turned off a short time before the US occurs, resulting in a *trace interval*. Traditionally, trace conditioning has been considered to be less effective than delayed conditioning (Ellison, 1964; Kamin, 1965), because of the trace interval (Kaplan & Hearst, 1982; Rescorla, 1982). As with delayed conditioning, however, less conditioned responding is evident with a trace procedure if the interval between the CS and US is increased (Kehoe, Cool, & Gormezano, 1991).

The above findings encouraged the conclusion that conditioning is most effective when the CS is a good signal for the impending delivery of the US. The signal value of the CS is best in the short-delayed procedure, where the US occurs shortly after the onset of the CS. The CS becomes a less effective signal for the impending delivery of the US as the CS-US interval is increased. The CS is also a poor predictor of the US in simultaneous and trace procedures. In simultaneous conditioning, the US occurs at the same time as the CS and is therefore not signaled by the CS. In trace conditioning, the CS is

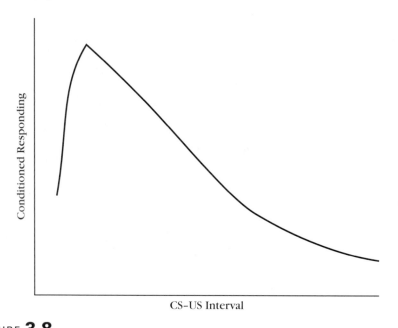

FIGURE **3.8**

Traditional effects of the CS-US interval on the vigor of Pavlovian conditioned responding. (Idealized data.)

followed by the trace interval rather than the US. Hence the trace interval is the best predictor of the US.

The one procedure whose results were difficult to interpret in terms of CS signal value was backward conditioning. Backward conditioning produced mixed results. Some investigators observed excitatory responding with backward pairings of a CS and US (e.g., Ayres, Haddad, & Albert, 1987; Spetch, Wilkie, & Pinel, 1981). Others reported primarily inhibition of conditioned responding with backward conditioning (e.g., Maier, Rapaport, & Wheatley, 1976; Siegel & Domjan, 1971; see also Chang, Blaisdell, & Miller, 2003). To make matters even more confusing, in a rather remarkable experiment, Tait and Saladin (1986) found both excitatory and inhibitory conditioning effects resulting from the same backward conditioning procedure (see also, McNish, Betts, Brandon, & Wagner, 1997).

The simple assumption that CS signal value determines whether a procedure will produce conditioned responding clearly cannot explain the complexity of findings that have been obtained in backward conditioning. The idea that there is a unitary hypothetical construct such as signal value or associative strength that varies as a function of the CS-US interval has also been challenged by the results of more recent experiments that have employed more sophisticated and diverse measures of learning. These studies have documented that delayed, simultaneous, trace, and backward conditioning can all produce strong learning and vigorous conditioned responding (e.g., Albert & Ayres, 1997; Akins & Domjan, 1996; Marchand & Kamper, 2000; Romaniuk & Williams, 2000; Schreurs, 1998; Williams & Hurlburt,

2000). However, different behavioral processes are engaged by these variations in procedure, and the learning that occurs is mediated by different neural circuits (e.g., Han et al., 2003; Kalmbach, et al., 2008; Waddell, Morris, & Bouton, 2006). In a study of fear conditioning (Esmorís-Arranz, Pardo-Vázquez, & Vázquez-Garcia, 2003), with a short-delayed procedure, the CS came to elicit conditioned freezing, but with a simultaneous procedure, the CR was movement away from the CS, or escape. As I will describe in greater detail in Chapter 4, the nature of the CR also varies between short-delayed and long-delayed conditioning procedures.

An important reason why animals come to perform different responses with different procedures is that instead of learning just a CS-US association, participants also learn *when* the US occurs in relation to the CS (Balsam, Drew, & Yang, 2001; Balsam & Gallistel, in press; Ohyama & Mauk, 2001). For example, in a recent study (Williams et al., 2008), rats received a pellet of food either 30 seconds or 90 seconds after the onset of an auditory CS. The investigators monitored when the rat poked its head into the food cup as a measure of conditioned behavior. Food-cup entries peaked at the scheduled time of food delivery: 30 or 90 seconds after the onset of the CS. The view that classical conditioning involves not only learning what to expect but when to expect it is called the **temporal coding hypothesis** (Amundson & Miller, 2008; Barnet, Cole, & Miller, 1997; Brown, Hemmes, & de Vaca, 1997; Cole, Barnet, & Miller, 1995; Savastano & Miller, 1998). I will revisit this issue in Chapter 4.

INHIBITORY PAVLOVIAN CONDITIONING

So far I have been discussing Pavlovian conditioning in terms of learning to predict when a significant event or US will occur. But, there is another type of Pavlovian conditioning, **inhibitory conditioning**, in which you learn to predict the *absence* of the US. Why would you want to predict the absence of something?

Consider being in an environment where bad things happen to you without warning. Civilians in a war zone can encounter road-side bombs or suicide bombers without much warning. A child in an abusive home also experiences unpredictable aversive events (yelling, slamming doors, and getting hit) for no particular reason. Getting pushed and shoved in a crowd also involves danger that arises without much warning and independent of what you might be doing. Research with laboratory animals has shown that exposure to unpredictable aversive stimulation is highly aversive and results in stomach ulcers and other physiological symptoms of stress. If one has to be exposed to aversive stimulation, predictable or signaled aversive stimuli are preferable to unpredictable aversive stimulation (Mineka & Henderson, 1985).

The benefit of predictability is evident even in the case of a panic attack. A panic attack is a sudden sense of fear or discomfort, accompanied by physical symptoms (e.g., heart palpitations) and a sense of impending doom. If such attacks are fairly frequent and become the source of considerable anxiety, the individual is said to suffer from panic disorder. At some point in their lives, 3.5% of the population has panic disorder (Kessler et al., 1994). Sometimes individuals with panic disorder are able to predict the onset of a panic attack. At other times, they may experience an attack without warning. In a study of individuals who experienced both predictable and unpredictable panic attacks,

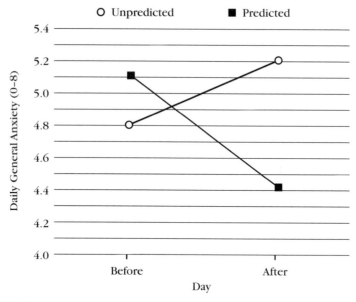

FIGURE **3.9**

Ratings of general anxiety in individuals with panic disorder before and after predicted and unpredicted panic attacks. (From M. G. Craske, D. Glover, and J. DeCola (1995). Predicted versus unpredicted panic attacks: Acute versus general distress. *Journal of Abnormal Psychology*, 104, Figure 1, p. 219. Copyright © 1995 by the American Psychological Association. Reprinted with permission.)

Craske, Glover, and DeCola (1995) measured the general anxiety of the participants before and after each type of attack. The results are summarized in Figure 3.9. Before the attack, anxiety ratings were similar whether the attack was predictable or not. Interestingly, however, anxiety significantly increased after an unpredicted panic attack and decreased after a predicted attack. Such results indicate that the anxiety that is generated by the experience of panic attacks occurs primarily because of the unpredictability of the attacks.

The ability to predict bad things is very helpful because it also enables you to predict when bad things will not happen. Consistent with this reasoning, many effective stress-reduction techniques, such as relaxation training or meditation, involve creating a predictable period of safety or a time when you can be certain that nothing bad will happen. Stress management consultants recognize that it is impossible to eliminate aversive events from one's life altogether. For example, a teacher supervising a playground with pre-school children is bound to encounter the unexpected stress of a child falling or hitting another child. One cannot prevent accidents or avoid having children hurt each other. However, introducing even short periods of predictable safety (e.g., by allowing the teacher to take a break) can substantially reduce stress. That is where conditioned inhibition comes in. A conditioned inhibitor is a signal for the absence of the US.

Although Pavlov discovered inhibitory conditioning early in the twentieth century, this type of learning did not command the serious attention of psychologists until decades later (Boakes & Halliday, 1972; Rescorla, 1969b; Savastano, Cole, Barnet, & Miller, 1999; Williams, Overmier, & LoLordo, 1992). I will describe two major procedures used to produce conditioned inhibition and the special tests that are necessary to detect and measure conditioned inhibition.

Procedures for Inhibitory Conditioning

Unlike excitatory conditioning, which can proceed without special preconditions, conditioned inhibition has an important prerequisite. For the absence of a US to be a significant event, the US has to occur periodically in the situation. There are many signals for the absence of events in our daily lives. Signs such as "Closed," "Out of Order," and "No Entry" are all of this type. However, these signs provide meaningful information and influence what we do only if they indicate the absence of something we otherwise expect to see. For example, if we encounter the sign "Out of Gas" at a service station, we may become frustrated and disappointed. The sign "Out of Gas" provides important information here because we expect service stations to have fuel. The same sign does not tell us anything of interest if it is in the window of a lumber yard, and it is not likely to discourage us from going to buy lumber. This illustrates the general rule that inhibitory conditioning and inhibitory control of behavior occur only if there is an excitatory context for the US in question (e.g., Chang, Blaisdell, & Miller, 2003; LoLordo & Fairless, 1985). This principle makes inhibitory conditioning very different from excitatory conditioning which has no such prerequisites.

Pavlov's Procedure for Conditioned Inhibition

Pavlov recognized the importance of an excitatory context for the conditioning of inhibition and was careful to provide such a context in his standard inhibitory training procedure (Pavlov, 1927). The procedure he used, diagrammed in Figure 3.10, involves two conditioned stimuli and two kinds of conditioning trials, one for excitatory conditioning and the other for inhibitory conditioning. The US is presented on excitatory conditioning trials (Trial Type A in Figure 3.10), and whenever the US occurs, it is announced by a stimulus labeled CS+ (e.g., a tone). Because of its pairings with the US, the CS+ becomes a signal for the US and can then provide the excitatory context for the development of conditioned inhibition.

During inhibitory conditioning trials (Trial Type B in Figure 3.10), the CS+ is presented together with the second stimulus called the CS– (e.g., a light), and the US does not occur. Thus, the CS– is presented in the excitatory context provided by the CS+ but the CS– is not paired with the US. This makes the CS– a conditioned inhibitor. During the course of training, A-type and B-type trials are alternated randomly. As the participant receives repeated trials of CS+ followed by the US and CS+/CS– followed by no US, the CS– gradually acquires inhibitory properties. (For recent studies with Pavlov's conditioned inhibition procedure, see Campolattaro, Schnitker, & Freeman, 2008; Urcelay & Miller, 2008a).

Pavlov's conditioned inhibition procedure is analogous to a situation in which something is introduced that prevents an outcome that would occur otherwise. A red traffic light at a busy intersection is a signal for potential

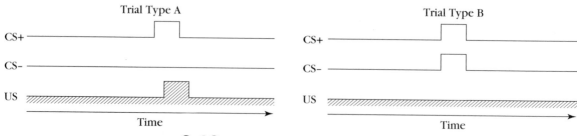

FIGURE **3.10**

Pavlov's procedure for conditioned inhibition. On some trials (Type A), the CS+ is paired with the US. On other trials (Type B), the CS+ is presented with the CS– and the US is omitted. The procedure is effective in conditioning inhibitory properties to the CS–.

danger because running the light could get you into an accident. However, if a police officer indicates that you should cross the intersection despite the red light (perhaps because the traffic light is malfunctioning), you will probably not have an accident. Here the red light is the CS+ and the gestures of the officer constitute the CS–. The gestures inhibit, or block, your hesitation to cross the intersection because of the red light.

A CS– acts as a safety signal in the context of danger. Children who are afraid will take refuge in the arms of a parent because the parent serves as a safety signal. Adults who are anxious also use safety signals to reduce or inhibit their fear or anxiety. People rely on prayer, a friend, a therapist, or a comforting food at times of stress (Barlow, 1988). These work in part because we have learned that bad things don't happen in their presence.

Negative CS-US Contingency or Correlation

Another common procedure for producing conditioned inhibition does not involve an explicit excitatory stimulus or CS+. Rather, it involves just a CS– that is negatively correlated with the US. A negative correlation or contingency means that the US is less likely to occur after the CS than at other times. Thus, the CS signals a reduction in the probability that the US will occur. A sample arrangement that meets this requirement is diagrammed in Figure 3.11. The US is periodically presented by itself. However, each occurrence of the CS is followed by the predictable absence of the US for a while.

Consider a child who periodically gets picked on by his classmates when the teacher is out of the room. This is like periodically receiving an aversive stimulus or US. When the teacher returns, the child can be sure he will not be bothered. Thus, the teacher serves as a CS– that signals a period free from harassment, or the absence of the US.

Conditioned inhibition is reliably observed in procedures in which the only explicit CS is negatively correlated with the US (Rescorla, 1969a). What provides the excitatory context for this inhibition? In this case, the environmental cues of the experimental chamber provide the excitatory context (Dweck & Wagner, 1970). Because the US occurs periodically in the experimental situation, the contextual cues of the experimental chamber acquire excitatory properties. This in turn permits the acquisition of inhibitory properties

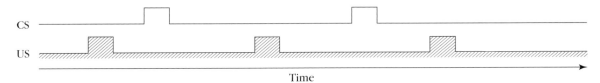

FIGURE **3.11**

A negative CS-US contingency procedure for conditioning inhibitory properties to the CS. Notice that the CS is always followed by a period without the US.

by the CS. (For a recent study on the role context in inhibitory conditioning, see Chang, Blaisdell, & Miller, 2003).

In a negative CS-US contingency procedure, the aversive US may occur shortly after the CS occasionally but it is much more likely to occur in the absence of the CS; that is what defines the negative CS-US contingency. However, even in the absence of the CS, the exact timing of the US cannot be predicted precisely because the US occurs at various times probabilistically. This is in contrast to Pavlov's procedure for conditioned inhibition. In Pavlov's procedure, the US always occurs at the end of the CS+ and does not occur when the CS– is presented together with the CS+. Since Pavlov's procedure permits predicting the exact timing of the US, it also permits predicting exactly when the US will *not* occur. The US will not occur at the end of CS+ if the CS+ is presented with the CS–. Tests of temporal learning have shown that in Pavlov's procedure for conditioned inhibition participants learn exactly when the US will be omitted (Denniston, Blaisdell, & Miller, 2004; Williams, Johns, & Brindas, 2008).

Measuring Conditioned Inhibition

How are conditioned inhibitory processes manifested in behavior? For conditioned excitation, the answer to this type of question is straightforward. Conditioned excitatory stimuli come to elicit new responses such as salivation, approach, or eye blinking, depending on what the US was. One might expect that conditioned inhibitory stimuli would elicit the opposites of these reactions—namely, suppression of salivation, approach, or eye blinking—but how are we to measure such response opposites?

Bi-Directional Response Systems

Identification of opposing response tendencies is easy with response systems that can change in opposite directions from baseline or normal performance. Heart rate, respiration, and temperature can all increase or decrease from a baseline level. Certain behavioral responses are also bi-directional. For example, animals can either approach or withdraw from a stimulus or drink more or less of a flavored solution. In these cases, conditioned excitation results in a change in behavior in one direction and conditioned inhibition results in a change in behavior in the opposite direction.

Unfortunately, many responses are not bi-directional. Consider freezing or response suppression as a measure of conditioned fear. A conditioned excitatory stimulus will elicit freezing, but a conditioned inhibitor will not produce activity above normal levels. A similar problem arises in eyeblink conditioning. A CS+ will elicit increased blinking, but the inhibitory effects of a CS– are difficult to detect because the baseline rate of blinking is low to begin with. It is hard to see inhibition of blinking below an already low baseline. Because of these limitations, conditioned inhibition is typically measured indirectly using the compound stimulus test and the retardation of acquisition test.

The Compound-Stimulus, or Summation, Test

The **compound-stimulus** (or **summation**) **test** was particularly popular with Pavlov and remains one of the most widely accepted procedures for the measurement of conditioned inhibition. The test is based on the simple idea that conditioned inhibition counteracts or inhibits conditioned excitation. Therefore, to observe conditioned inhibition, one has to measure how the presentation of a CS– disrupts or suppresses responding that would normally be elicited by a CS+.

A particularly well controlled demonstration of conditioned inhibition using the compound-stimulus or summation test was reported by Cole, Barnet, and Miller (1997). The experiment was conducted using the lick-suppression procedure with laboratory rats. The subjects received inhibitory conditioning in which the presentation of a flashing light by itself always ended in a brief shock (A+), and the presentation of an auditory cue (X) together with the light ended without shock (AX–). Thus, Pavlov's procedure for conditioned inhibition was used and X was predicted to become an inhibitor of fear. A total of 28 A+ trials and 56 AX– trials were conducted over 7 sessions. The participants also received training with another auditory stimulus (B) in a different experimental chamber, and this stimulus always ended in the brief shock (B+). The intent of these procedures was to establish conditioned excitation to A and B and conditioned inhibition to X.

Cole et al. then asked whether the presumed inhibitor X would suppress responding to the excitatory stimuli A and B. The results of those tests are summarized in Figure 3.12. How long the participants took to accumulate five seconds of uninterrupted drinking was measured. Notice that when the excitatory stimuli, A and B, were presented by themselves, the rats required substantial amounts of time to complete the five second drinking criterion. In contrast, when the excitatory stimuli were presented together with the conditioned inhibitor (AX and BX tests), the drinking requirement was completed much faster. Thus, presenting stimulus X with A and B reduced the drinking suppression that occurred when A and B were presented by themselves. X inhibited conditioned fear elicited by A and B.

Figure 3.12 includes another test condition, stimulus B, tested with another auditory cue, Y. Stimulus Y was not previously conditioned as an inhibitor and was presented to be sure that introducing a new stimulus with stimulus B would not cause disruption of the conditioned fear response. As Figure 3.12 illustrates, no such disruption occurred with stimulus Y. Thus, the inhibition of conditioned fear was limited to the stimulus (X) that received conditioned inhibition training. Another important aspect of these results is that X was able to inhibit conditioned fear not only to the exciter with which it was trained (A) but also to another exciter (B) that had never been presented with X during training.

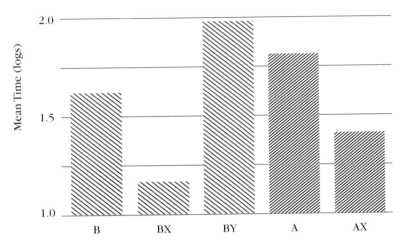

FIGURE **3.12**

Compound-stimulus test of inhibition in a lick suppression experiment. Stimuli A and B were conditioned as excitatory stimuli by being presented alone with shock (A+ and B+). Stimulus X was conditioned as an inhibitor by being presented with stimulus A without shock (AX–). Stimulus Y was a control stimulus that had not participated in either excitatory or inhibitory conditioning. A was a flashing light. B, X, and Y were auditory cues (a clicker, white noise, and a buzzer, counterbalanced across participants.) A, and AX were tested in the original training context. B, BX, and BY were tested in a different context. (From Cole, R. P., Barnet, R. C., & Miller, R. R. (1997). An evaluation of conditioned inhibition as defined by Rescorla's two-testing strategy in *Learning and Motivation*, Volume 28, 333, copyright 1997, Elsevier Science (USA). Reprinted by permission of Elsevier.)

The compound-stimulus test for conditioned inhibition indicates that the presentation of a conditioned inhibitor or safety signal can reduce the stressful effects of an aversive experience. This prediction was tested with patients who were prone to experience panic attacks (Carter, Hollon, Carson, & Shelton, 1995). Panic attack patients were invited to the laboratory and accompanied by someone with whom they felt safe. Panic was experimentally induced in the participants by having them inhale a mixture of gas containing elevated levels of carbon dioxide. The participants were then asked to report on their perceived levels of anxiety and catastrophic ideation triggered by the carbon dioxide exposure. The experimental manipulation was the presence of another person with whom the participants felt safe (the conditioned inhibitor). Half the participants were allowed to have their trusted acquaintance in the room with them during the experiment, whereas the remaining participants took part in the experiment alone. The results indicated that the presence of a safe acquaintance reduced the anxiety and catastrophic ideation associated with the panic attack. These results explain why children are less fearful during a medical examination if they are accompanied by a trusted parent or guardian. (For a review of panic disorder including the role of learning, see Craske & Waters, 2005.)

The Retardation of Acquisition Test

Another frequently used indirect test of conditioned inhibition is the **retardation of acquisition test** (Rescorla, 1969b). The rationale for this test is straightforward. If a stimulus actively inhibits a particular response, then it should be especially difficult to condition that stimulus to elicit the behavior. In other words, the rate of excitatory conditioning should be retarded if the CS is a conditioned inhibitor. This prediction was tested by Cole et al. (1997) in an experiment very similar to their summation test study described above.

After the same kind of inhibitory conditioning that produced the results summarized in Figure 3.12, Cole et al. took stimulus X (which had been conditioned as an inhibitor) and stimulus Y (which had not been used in a conditioning procedure before) and conducted a retardation of acquisition test by pairing each stimulus with shock on three occasions. (Three acquisition trials were sufficient since conditioned fear is learned faster than the inhibition of fear.) After the three acquisition trials, each stimulus was tested to see which would cause greater suppression of drinking. The results are presented in Figure 3.13. The time to complete five seconds of drinking took much longer in the presence of the control stimulus Y than in the presence of stimulus X, which had previously been trained as a conditioned inhibitor. Thus, the initial inhibitory training of X retarded its acquisition of excitatory conditioned fear properties.

Conditioned inhibition can be difficult to distinguish from other behavioral processes. Therefore, the best strategy is to use more than one test and be sure that all of the results point to the same conclusion. Rescorla (1969b) advocated using both the compound stimulus test and the retardation of acquisition test. This dual test strategy has remained popular ever since (Campolattaro, Schnitker, & Freeman, 2008; Savastano et al., 1999; Williams et al., 1992).

PREVALENCE OF CLASSICAL CONDITIONING

Classical conditioning is typically investigated in laboratory situations. However, we do not have to know much about classical conditioning to realize that it also occurs in a wide range of situations outside the laboratory. Classical conditioning is most likely to develop when one event reliably precedes another in a short-delayed CS-US pairing. This occurs in many aspects of life. As I mentioned at the beginning of the chapter, stimuli in the environment occur in an orderly temporal sequence, largely because of the physical constraints of causation. Some events simply cannot happen before other things have occurred. Eggs won't be hard boiled until they have been put in boiling water. Social institutions and customs also ensure that things happen in a predictable order. Whenever one stimulus reliably precedes another, classical conditioning may take place.

One area of research that has been of particular interest is how people come to judge one event as the cause of another. In studies of human causal judgment, participants are exposed to repeated occurrences of two events (pictures of a blooming flower and a watering can briefly presented on a computer screen) in

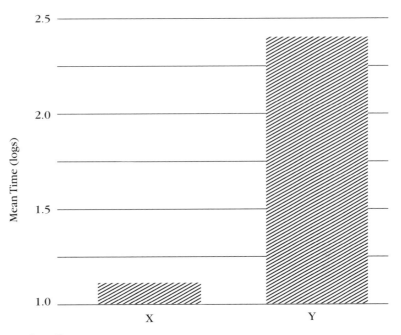

FIGURE **3.13**

Effects of a retardation of acquisition test of inhibition in a lick suppression experiment after the same kind of inhibitory conditioning as was conducted to produce the results presented in Figure 3.12. Stimulus X was previously conditioned as an inhibitory stimulus, and stimulus Y previously received no training. (From Cole, R. P., Barnet, R. C., & Miller, R. R. (1997). An evaluation of conditioned inhibition as defined by Rescorla's two-test strategy in *Learning and Motivation,* Volume 28, 333, copyright 1997, Elsevier Science (USA). Reprinted by permission of Elsevier.)

various temporal arrangements. In one condition, for example, the watering can may always occur before the flower; in another it may occur at random times relative to the flower. After observing numerous appearances of both objects, the subjects are asked to indicate their judgment about the strength of causal relation between them. Studies of human causal judgment are analogous to studies of Pavlovian conditioning in that both involve repeated experiences with two events and responses based on the extent to which those two events become linked to each other. Given this correspondence, one might suspect that there is considerable commonality in the outcomes of causal judgment and Pavlovian conditioning experiments. That prediction has been supported in numerous studies, suggesting that Pavlovian associative mechanisms are not limited to Pavlov's dogs, but may play a role in the numerous judgments of causality we all make during the course of our daily lives (see Allan, 2005).

As I described earlier in the chapter, Pavlovian conditioning can result in the conditioning of food preferences and aversions. It can also result in the acquisition of fear. Conditioned fear responses have been of special interest because they may contribute significantly to anxiety disorders, phobias, and panic disorder (Bouton, 2001; Bouton, Mineka, & Barlow, 2001; Craske, Hermans, & Vansteenwegen, 2006). As I will discuss further in Chapter 4, Pavlovian conditioning is also involved in drug tolerance and addiction. Cues that reliably accompany drug administration can come to elicit drug-related responses through conditioning. In discussing this type of learning among crack addicts, Dr. Scott Lukas of McLean Hospital in Massachusetts described the effects of drug-conditioned stimuli by saying that "These cues turn on crack-related memories, and addicts respond like Pavlov's dogs" (*Newsweek*, February 12, 2001, p. 40).

Pavlovian conditioning is also involved in infant and maternal responses in nursing. Suckling involves mutual stimulation for the infant and the mother. To successfully nurse, the mother has to hold the baby in a particular position, which provides special tactile stimuli for both the infant and the mother. The tactile stimuli experienced by the infant may become conditioned to elicit orientation and suckling responses on the part of the baby (Blass, Ganchrow, & Steiner, 1984). The tactile stimuli experienced by the mother may also become conditioned, in this case to elicit the milk let-down response of the mother in anticipation of having the infant suckle. Mothers who nurse their babies frequently experience the milk let-down reflex when the baby cries or when the usual time for breast-feeding arrives. All these stimuli (special tactile cues, the baby's crying, and the time of normal feedings) reliably precede suckling by the infant. Therefore, they can become conditioned by the suckling stimulation and come to elicit milk secretion as a CR. The anticipatory conditioned orientation and suckling responses and the anticipatory conditioned milk let-down response make the nursing experience more successful for both the baby and the mother.

Pavlovian conditioning is also important in sexual situations. Although clinical observations indicate that human sexual behavior can be shaped by learning experiences (Akins, 2004), the most systematic evidence of sexual conditioning has been obtained in studies with laboratory animals (Pfaus, Kippin, & Centeno, 2001; Woodson, 2002). In these studies, males typically serve as participants, and the US is provided either by the sight of a sexually receptive female, or by physical access to a female (Domjan, 1998). Subjects come to approach stimuli that signal the availability of a sexual partner (Burns & Domjan, 1996; Hollis, Cadieux, & Colbert, 1989). The presentation of a sexual CS also facilitates various aspects of reproductive behavior. Studies with rats, quail, and fish have shown that after exposure to a sexual CS, males are quicker to perform copulatory responses (Zamble, Hadad, Mitchell, & Cutmore, 1985), compete more successfully with other males for access to a female (Gutiérrez & Domjan, 1996), show more courtship behavior (Hollis, Cadieux, & Colbert, 1989), release greater quantities of sperm (Domjan, Blesbois, & Williams, 1998), and show increased levels of testosterone and leuteinizing hormone (Graham & Desjardins, 1980).

Although the preceding studies of sexual conditioning are noteworthy, the ultimate payoff for sexual behavior is the number of offspring that are produced. Hollis, Pharr, Dumas, Britton, and Field (1997) were the first to show (in a fish species) that the presentation of a Pavlovian CS+ before a sexual encounter greatly increased the numbers of offspring that resulted from the reproductive behavior. This effect of Pavlovian conditioning on increased fertility has since been also demonstrated in quail (Adkins-Regan & MacKillop, 2003; Mahometa & Domjan, 2005). In a recent study, Pavlovian conditioning

Courtesy of Donald A. Dewsbury

K. L. Hollis

also influenced the outcome of sperm competition in domesticated quail (Matthews, Domjan, Ramsey, & Crews, 2007). To observe sperm competition, two male quail were permitted to copulate with the same female. A copulatory interaction in quail can fertilize as many as 10 of the eggs the female produces after the sexual encounter. If two males copulate with the same female in succession, the male whose copulation is signaled by a Pavlovian CS+ sires significantly more of the resulting offspring. This is a very important finding because it shows that "learning and individual experience can bias genetic transmission and the evolutionary changes that result from sexual competition" (Matthews et al., 2007, p. 762).

CONCLUDING COMMENTS

Chapter 3 continued the discussion of elicited behavior by turning attention from habituation and sensitization to classical conditioning. Classical conditioning is a bit more complex in that it involves associatively-mediated elicited behavior. In fact, classical conditioning is one of the major techniques for investigating how associations are learned. As we have seen, classical conditioning may be involved in many different important aspects of behavior. Depending on the procedure used, the learning may occur quickly or slowly. With some procedures, excitatory responses are learned; with other procedures, the organism learns to inhibit an excitatory response tendency. Excitatory and inhibitory conditioning occur in many aspects of common experience and serve to help us cope with significant biological events (unconditioned stimuli).

SAMPLE QUESTIONS

1. Describe similarities and differences between habituation, sensitization, and classical conditioning.
2. What is object learning, and how is it similar or different from conventional classical conditioning?
3. What is the most effective procedure for excitatory conditioning and how is it different from other possibilities?
4. What is a control procedure for excitatory conditioning and what processes is the control procedure intended to rule out?
5. Are conditioned excitation and conditioned inhibition related? If so, how are they related?
6. Describe procedures for conditioning and measuring conditioned inhibition.
7. Describe four reasons why classical conditioning is of interest to psychologists.

KEY TERMS

autoshaping Same as *sign tracking*.

backward conditioning A procedure in which the conditioned stimulus is presented shortly after the unconditioned stimulus on each trial.

compound-stimulus test A test procedure that identifies a stimulus as a conditioned inhibitor if that stimulus reduces the responding elicited by a conditioned excitatory stimulus. Also called *summation test*.

conditional or conditioned response (CR) The response that comes to be made to the conditioned stimulus as a result of classical conditioning.

conditional or conditioned stimulus (CS) A stimulus that does not elicit a particular response initially, but comes to do so as a result of becoming associated with an unconditioned stimulus.

conditioned emotional response (CER) Suppression of positively reinforced instrumental behavior (e.g., lever pressing for food pellets) caused by the presentation of a stimulus that has become associated with an aversive stimulus. Also called *conditioned suppression.*

conditioned suppression Same as *conditioned emotional response.*

conditioning trial A training episode involving presentation of a conditioned stimulus with (or without) an unconditioned stimulus.

CS-US interval Same as *interstimulus interval.*

evaluative conditioning Changing the hedonic value or liking of an initially neutral stimulus by having that stimulus associated with something that is already liked or disliked.

explicitly unpaired control A procedure in which both conditioned and unconditioned stimuli are presented, but with sufficient time between them so that they do not become associated with each other.

inhibitory conditioning A type of classical conditioning in which the conditioned stimulus becomes a signal for the absence of the unconditioned stimulus.

interstimulus interval The amount of time that elapses between presentations of the conditioned stimulus (CS) and the unconditioned stimulus (US) during a classical conditioning trial. Also called the *CS-US interval.*

intertrial interval The amount of time that elapses between two successive trials.

latency The time elapsed between a stimulus (or the start of a trial) and the response that is made to the stimulus.

lick-suppression procedure Similar to the conditioned emotional response (CER), or conditioned suppression procedure. However, instead of lever pressing for food serving as the behavior that is suppressed by conditioned fear, the baseline is licking a water spout by thirsty rats. The presentation of a fear-conditioned CS slows down the rate of drinking.

magnitude of a response A measure of the size, vigor, or extent of a response.

object learning Learning associations between different stimulus elements of an object.

probability of a response The likelihood of making the response, usually represented in terms of the percentage of trials on which the response occurs.

pseudo-conditioning Increased responding that may occur to a stimulus whose presentations are intermixed with presentations of an unconditioned stimulus (US) in the absence of the establishment of an association between the stimulus and the US.

random control procedure A procedure in which the conditioned and unconditioned stimuli are presented at random times with respect to each other.

retardation of acquisition test A test procedure that identifies a stimulus as a conditioned inhibitor if that stimulus is slower to acquire excitatory properties than a comparison stimulus.

short-delayed conditioning A classical conditioning procedure in which the conditioned stimulus is initiated shortly before the unconditioned stimulus on each conditioning trial.

sign tracking Movement toward and possibly contact with a stimulus that signals the availability of a positive reinforcer, such as food. Also called *autoshaping*.

simultaneous conditioning A classical conditioning procedure in which the conditioned stimulus and the unconditioned stimulus are presented simultaneously on each conditioning trial.

summation test Same as *compound-stimulus test*.

temporal coding hypothesis The idea that Pavlovian conditioning procedures lead not only to learning that the US happens but exactly when it occurs in relation to the CS. The CS comes to represent (or code) the timing of the US.

test trial A trial in which the conditioned stimulus is presented without the unconditioned stimulus. This allows measurement of the conditioned response in the absence of the unconditioned response.

trace conditioning A classical conditioning procedure in which the unconditioned stimulus is presented after the conditioned stimulus has been terminated for a short period.

trace interval The interval between the end of the conditioned stimulus and the start of the unconditioned stimulus in trace-conditioning trials.

unconditional or unconditioned response (UR) A response that occurs to a stimulus without the necessity of prior training.

unconditional or unconditioned stimulus (US) A stimulus that elicits a particular response without the necessity of prior training.

Classical Conditioning: Mechanisms

CHAPTER PREVIEW

Chapter 4 continues the discussion of classical conditioning, focusing on the mechanisms and outcomes of this type of learning. The discussion is organized around three key issues. First, I will describe features of stimuli that determine their effectiveness as conditioned and unconditioned stimuli. Then, I will discuss factors that determine the types of responses that come to be made to conditioned stimuli. In the third and final section of the chapter, I will discuss the mechanisms of learning involved in the development of conditioned responding. Much of this discussion will deal with how associations are established and expressed. However, I will also comment on efforts to develop non-associative models of conditioning.

WHAT MAKES EFFECTIVE CONDITIONED AND UNCONDITIONED STIMULI?

This is perhaps the most basic question one can ask about classical conditioning. What makes stimuli effective as conditioned and unconditioned stimuli was originally addressed by Pavlov and continues to attract the attention of contemporary researchers.

Initial Responses to the Stimuli

Pavlov addressed the effectiveness criteria for conditioned and unconditioned stimuli in his definitions of the terms *conditioned* and *unconditioned*. According to these definitions, the CS does not elicit the conditioned response initially, but comes to do so as a result of becoming associated with the US. By contrast, the US is effective in eliciting the target response from the outset without any special training.

Pavlov's definitions were stated in terms of the elicitation of the response to be conditioned. Because of this, identifying potential CSs and USs requires comparing the responses elicited by each stimulus before conditioning. Such a comparison makes the identification of CSs and USs *relative*. A particular event may serve as a CS relative to one stimulus, and as a US relative to another.

Consider, for example, a palatable saccharin solution for thirsty rats. The taste of saccharin may serve as a CS in a taste-aversion conditioning procedure, with illness as the US. In this case, conditioning trials consist of exposure to the saccharin flavor followed by a drug that induces illness, and the participant acquires an aversion to the saccharin solution.

The same saccharin solution may also serve as a US in a sign-tracking experiment, for example. The conditioning trials in this case would involve presenting a signal light (the CS) just before each presentation of a small amount of saccharin in a cup (the US). After a number of trials of this sort, the animals would begin to approach the light CS. Thus, whether the saccharin solution is considered a US or a CS depends on its relation to other stimuli in the situation.

Novelty of Conditioned and Unconditioned Stimuli

As we saw in studies of habituation, the behavioral impact of a stimulus depends on its novelty. Highly familiar stimuli do not elicit as vigorous reactions as do novel stimuli. Novelty is also important in classical conditioning. If either the conditioned or the unconditioned stimulus is highly familiar, learning proceeds more slowly than if the CS and US are novel.

Latent Inhibition or CS Preexposure

Numerous studies have shown that if a stimulus is highly familiar, it will not be as readily associated with a US as a novel stimulus. This phenomenon is called the **latent-inhibition effect**, or **CS-preexposure effect** (Hall, 1991; Lubow, 1989). Experiments on the latent-inhibition effect involve two phases. Subjects are first given repeated presentations of the CS by itself. This is called the preexposure phase because it comes before the Pavlovian conditioning trials. CS preexposure makes the CS highly familiar and of no particular significance because at this point the CS is presented alone and without consequence. After the preexposure phase, the CS is paired with a US using conventional classical conditioning procedures. The common result is that subjects are slower to acquire responding because of the CS preexposure. Thus, CS preexposure inhibits or disrupts learning. The effect is called *latent inhibition* to distinguish it from the conditioned inhibition I described in Chapter 3.

Latent inhibition is similar to habituation. Both phenomena serve to limit processing and attention to stimuli that are presented by themselves and are therefore inconsequential. Habituation serves to bias elicited behavior in favor of novel stimuli; latent inhibition serves to bias learning in favor of novel stimuli. As Lubow and Gewirtz (1995) noted, latent inhibition "promotes the stimulus selectivity required for rapid learning" (p. 87).

Although it was originally discovered in studies with sheep (Lubow & Moore, 1959), the latent-inhibition effect has become of great interest in analyses of human behavior. Latent-inhibition experiments with human participants have used a video game paradigm (e.g., Nelson & Sanjuan, 2006) and a target detection task (Lubow & Kaplan, 2005). With both procedures, preexposure to a signal reduces the subsequent rate of learning about that stimulus. The dominant interpretation of these findings is that CS preexposure reduces attention to the CS, and that in turn disrupts subsequent learning about this stimulus.

Because latent inhibition involves attentional mechanisms, it has been implicated in diseases such as schizophrenia that include deficits in attention. Latent inhibition is reduced in acute schizophrenic patients who recently started medication and is also attenuated in normal individuals who are high on the schizotypal personality scale. Given the involvement of the neurotransmitter dopamine in schizophrenia, it is not surprising that latent inhibition is reduced by dopamine receptor agonists and enhanced by dopamine receptor antagonists (see review by Lubow & Kaplan, 2005).

The US Preexposure Effect

Experiments on the importance of US novelty are similar in design to CS-preexposure experiments. Subjects are first given repeated exposures to the US presented by itself. The US is then paired with a CS, and the progress of learning is monitored. Subjects familiarized with a US before its pairings with a CS are slower to develop conditioned responding to the CS than participants for whom the US is novel during the CS-US pairings. This result is called the **US-preexposure effect** (Randich & LoLordo, 1979; Saladin et al., 1989).

Analyses of the US preexposure effect have emphasized an *associative interference* mechanism (e.g., Hall, 2008). According to this account, the presentations of the US during the preexposure-phase conditions cues related to the US administrations. These may be the contextual cues of the situation in which the US is presented. If the US is a drug, the cues related to injecting the drug can become conditioned during the preexposure phase. The presence of these cues during the subsequent conditioning phase disrupts subsequent learning. I will have more to say about this interference mechanism later in the chapter when I describe the blocking effect.

CS and US Intensity and Salience

Another important stimulus variable for classical conditioning is the intensity of the conditioned and unconditioned stimuli. Most biological and physiological effects of stimulation are related to the intensity of the stimulus input. This is also true of Pavlovian conditioning. More vigorous conditioned responding occurs when more intense conditioned and unconditioned stimuli are used (e.g., Bevins, McPhee, Rauhut, & Ayres, 1997; Kamin, 1965; Ploog & Zeigler, 1996; Scavio & Gormezano, 1974).

Stimulus intensity is one factor that contributes to what is more generally called **stimulus salience**. The term *salience* is not well defined, but it roughly corresponds to *significance,* or *noticeability*. Theories of learning typically assume that learning will occur more rapidly with more salient stimuli (e.g., McLaren & Mackintosh, 2000; Pearce & Hall, 1980). One can make a stimulus more salient or significant by making it more intense and hence, more attention-getting. One can also make a stimulus more salient by making it more relevant to the biological needs of the organism. For example, animals become more attentive to the taste of salt if they suffer a nutritional salt deficiency (Krieckhaus, & Wolf, 1968). Consistent with this outcome, Sawa, Nakajima, and Imada, (1999) found that sodium deficient rats learn stronger aversions to the taste of salt than nondeficient control subjects.

Another way to increase the salience of a CS is to make it more similar to the kinds of stimuli an animal is likely to encounter in its natural environment. Studies of sexual conditioning with domesticated quail provide a good example. In the typical experiment, access to a female quail serves as the sexual reinforcer, or US for a male subject, and this sexual opportunity is signaled by the presentation of a CS. The CS can be an arbitrary cue such as a light or a terrycloth object. Alternatively, the CS can be made more natural or salient by adding partial cues of a female (see Figure 4.1). Studies have shown that if a naturalistic CS is used in sexual conditioning, the learning proceeds more rapidly, more components of sexual behavior become conditioning, and the

FIGURE **4.1**

CS objects used as signals for copulatory opportunity in studies of sexual conditioning with male quail. The object on the left is arbitrary and made entirely of terrycloth. The object on the right includes limited female cues provided by the head and some neck feathers from a taxidermically prepared female bird. (From Cusato & Domjan, 1998).

learning is not as easily disrupted by increasing the CS-US interval (Domjan, Cusato, & Krause, 2004). A naturalistic CS also facilitates learning if the US is food (Cusato & Domjan, 2000).

CS-US Relevance, or Belongingness

Another variable that governs the rate of classical conditioning is the extent to which the CS is relevant to or *belongs with* the US. The importance of stimulus relevance was first clearly demonstrated in a classic experiment by Garcia and Koelling (1966). The investigators compared learning about peripheral pain (induced by foot-shock) and learning about illness (induced by irradiation or a drug injection) in a study conducted with laboratory rats.

In their natural environment, rats are likely to get sick after eating a poisonous food. In contrast, they are likely to encounter peripheral pain after being chased and bitten by a predator that they can hear and see. To represent food-related cues, Garcia and Koelling used a flavored solution of water as the CS; to represent predator-related cues, they used an audiovisual CS.

The experiment, diagrammed in Figure 4.2, involved having the rats drink from a drinking tube before administration of one of the unconditioned stimuli. The drinking tube was filled with water flavored either salty or sweet. In addition, each lick on the tube activated a brief audiovisual stimulus (a click and a flash of light). Thus, the rats encountered the taste and audiovisual stimuli at the same time. After exposure to these conditioned stimuli, the animals either received a brief shock through the grid floor or were made sick.

Because the unconditioned stimuli used were aversive, the rats were expected to learn an aversion of some kind. The investigators measured the response of the animals to the taste and audiovisual CSs presented individually after conditioning. During tests of the taste CS, the water was flavored as before, but now licks did not activate the audiovisual cue. During tests of the audiovisual CS, the water was unflavored, but the audiovisual cue was briefly turned on each time the animal licked the spout. The degree of conditioned

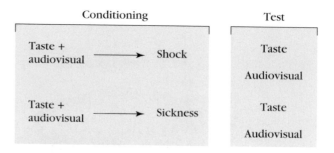

FIGURE **4.2**

Diagram of Garcia and Koelling's (1966) experiment. A compound taste-audiovisual stimulus was first paired with either shock or sickness for separate groups of laboratory rats. The subjects were then tested with the taste and audiovisual stimuli separately.

aversion to the taste or audiovisual CS was inferred from the suppression of drinking.

The results of the experiment are summarized in Figure 4.3. Animals conditioned with shock subsequently suppressed their drinking much more when tested with the audiovisual stimulus than when tested with the taste CS. The opposite result occurred for animals that had been conditioned with sickness. These rats suppressed their drinking much more when the taste CS was presented than when drinking produced the audiovisual stimulus.

Garcia and Koelling's experiment demonstrates the principle of CS-US relevance, or belongingness. Learning depended on the relevance of the CS to the US that was employed. Taste became readily associated with illness, and audiovisual cues became readily associated with peripheral pain. Rapid learning occurred only if the CS was combined with the appropriate US. The audiovisual CS was not generally more effective than the taste CS. Rather, the audiovisual CS was more effective only when shock served as the US. Correspondingly, the shock US was not generally more effective than the sickness US. Rather, shock conditioned stronger aversions than sickness only when the audiovisual cue served as the CS.

The CS-US relevance effect obtained by Garcia and Koelling was not readily accepted at first. However, numerous subsequent studies have confirmed the original findings (e.g., Domjan, 1983; Rescorla, 2008). The selective-association effect occurs even in rats one day after birth (Gemberling & Domjan, 1982). This observation indicates that extensive experience with tastes and sickness (or audiovisual cues and peripheral pain) is not necessary for the stimulus-relevance effect. Rather, the phenomenon appears to reflect a genetic predisposition for the selective learning of certain combinations of conditioned and unconditioned stimuli. (For evidence of stimulus relevance in human food aversion learning, see Logue et al., 1981; Pelchat & Rozin, 1982.)

Stimulus-relevance effects have been documented in other situations as well. For example, experiments have shown that pigeons associate visual cues with food much more easily than they associate auditory cues with food. By contrast, if the conditioning situation involves shock, auditory

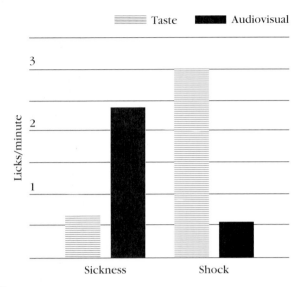

FIGURE **4.3**

Results of Garcia and Koelling's (1966) experiment. Rats conditioned with sickness learned a stronger aversion to taste than to audiovisual cues. By contrast, rats conditioned with shock learned a stronger aversion to audiovisual than to taste cues. (Adapted from Garcia and Koelling, 1966).

cues are more effective as the CS than visual cues (e.g., LoLordo, Jacobs, & Foree, 1982; Kelley, 1986). Analogous effects have been found with rats. For example, in a recent study learning with cocaine as the appetitive US was compared to learning with shock as the aversive US (Weiss et al., 2003). The cocaine US was more effective in conditioning a CS light, whereas shock was more effective in conditioning a CS tone. Taken together, these results indicate that visual cues are relevant to learning about biologically significant positive or pleasant events and auditory cues are relevant to learning about negative or aversive events (see also Weiss, Panlillo, & Schindler, 1993a, b).

Stimulus-relevance effects are also prominent in the acquisition of fear in primates (Öhman & Mineka, 2001; Mineka & Öhman, 2002). Experiments with both rhesus monkeys and people have shown that fear conditioning progresses more rapidly with fear-relevant cues (the sight of a snake) than with fear irrelevant cues (the sight of a flower or mushroom). However, this difference is not observed if an appetitive US is used. This selective advantage of snake stimuli in fear conditioning does not require conscious awareness (Öhman & Soares, 1998) and seems to reflect an evolutionary adaptation to rapidly detect biologically dangerous stimuli and acquire fear to such cues. In a recent study, for example, children as young as three years of age were able to detect pictures of snakes faster than pictures of flowers or frogs (LoBue & DeLoache, 2008). As Mineka and Öhman (2002) pointed out, "fear conditioning occurs most readily in situations that provide recurrent survival threats in mammalian evolution" (p. 928).

Learning Without an Unconditioned Stimulus

So far, we have been discussing classical conditioning in situations that include an US: a stimulus that has behavioral impact unconditionally or without prior training. If Pavlovian conditioning were only applicable to situations that involve a US, it would be somewhat limited. It would only occur if you received food, shock, or had sex. How about the rest of time, when you are not eating or having sex? As it turns out, Pavlovian conditioning can also take place in situations where you do not encounter a US. There are two different forms of classical conditioning without a US. One is *higher-order conditioning* and the other is *sensory preconditioning*.

Higher-Order Conditioning

Irrational fears often develop through **higher-order conditioning**. For example, Wolpe (1990) described the case of a lady who initially developed a fear of crowds. For her, being in a crowd was a CS that elicited conditioned fear. How this fear was originally learned is unknown. Perhaps she was pushed and shoved in a crowd (CS) and suffered an injury (the US). To avoid arousing her fear, the lady would go to the movies only in the daytime when few people were present. On one such visit, the theater suddenly became crowded with students. The lady became extremely upset by this, and came to associate cues of the movie theater with crowds. Thus, one CS (crowds) had conditioned fear to another (the movie theater) that previously elicited no fear. The remarkable aspect of this transfer of fear is that the lady never experienced bodily injury or an aversive US in the movie theater. In that sense, this was an irrational fear.

As this case study illustrates, higher-order conditioning occurs in two phases. During the first phase a cue (call it CS_1) is paired with a US often enough to condition a strong response to CS_1. In the above case study, the stimuli of crowds constituted CS_1. Once CS_1 elicited the conditioned response, pairing CS_1 with a new stimulus CS_2 (cues of the movie theater) was able to condition CS_2 to also elicit the conditioned response. The conditioning of CS_2 occurred in the absence of the US. Figure 4.4 summarizes these stages of learning that result in higher-order conditioning.

As the term "higher order" implies, conditioning may be considered to operate at different levels. In the preceding example, the experience of crowds (CS_1) paired with injury (US) is *first-order conditioning*. Pairings of CS_2 (movie theaters) with CS_1 (crowds) is *second-order conditioning*. If after becoming conditioned, CS_2 were used to condition yet another stimulus, CS_3, that would be *third-order conditioning*.

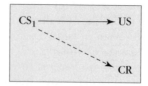 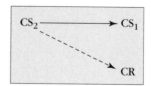

FIGURE **4.4**

Procedure for higher-order conditioning. CS_1 is first paired with the US and comes to elicit the conditioned response. A new stimulus (CS_2) is then paired with CS_1 and also comes to elicit the conditioned response.

The procedure for second-order conditioning shown in Figure 4.4 is similar to the standard procedure for inhibitory conditioning that was described in Chapter 3 (see Figure 3.10). In both cases, one conditioned stimulus (CS_1 or the CS^+) is paired with the US ($CS_1 \rightarrow US$ or $CS^+ \rightarrow US$), and a second CS (CS_2 or CS^-) is paired with the first one without the unconditioned stimulus ($CS_1/CS_2 \rightarrow noUS$ or $CS^+/CS^- \rightarrow noUS$). Why does such a procedure produce conditioned inhibition in some cases, and excitatory second-order conditioning under other circumstances? One important factor appears to be the number of non-US trials. With a few nonreinforced trials, second-order excitatory conditioning occurs. With extensive training, conditioned inhibition develops (Yin, Barnet, & Miller, 1994). Another important variable is whether the first- and second-order stimuli are presented simultaneously or one after the other. Simultaneous compounds favor the development of conditioned inhibition (Stout, Escobar, & Miller, 2004; see also, Wheeler, Sherwood, & Holland, 2008).

Although there is no doubt that second-order conditioning is a robust phenomenon (e.g., Rescorla, 1980; Winterbauer & Balleine, 2005), little research has been done to evaluate the mechanisms of third- and higher orders of conditioning. However, even the existence of second-order conditioning is of considerable significance because it greatly increases the range of situations in which classical conditioning can take place. With higher order conditioning, classical conditioning can occur without a primary US. The only requirement is that a previously conditioned stimulus be available.

Many instances of conditioning in human experience involve higher-order conditioning. For example, money is a powerful conditioned stimulus (CS_1) for human behavior because of its association with candy, toys, movies, and other things money can buy. A child may become fond of his uncle (CS_2) if the uncle gives him some money on each visit. The positive conditioned emotional response to the uncle develops because the child comes to associate the uncle with money, in a case of second-order conditioning.

Sensory Preconditioning

Associations can also be learned between two stimuli, each of which elicits only a mild orienting response before conditioning. Consider, for example, two flavors (i.e., vanilla and cinnamon) that you often encounter together in pastries without ill effects. Because of these pairings, the vanilla and cinnamon flavors may become associated with one another. What would happen if you then acquired an aversion to cinnamon through food poisoning or illness? Chances are your acquired aversion to cinnamon would lead you to also reject things with the taste of vanilla because of the prior association of vanilla with cinnamon. This is an example of **sensory preconditioning.**

As with higher-order conditioning, sensory preconditioning involves a two-stage process (see Figure 4.5). The cinnamon and vanilla flavors become associated with one another in the first phase when there is no US. Let's call these stimuli CS_1 and CS_2. The association between CS_1 and CS_2 that is established during the sensory preconditioning phase is usually not evident in any behavioral responses because neither CS has been paired with a US yet, and therefore, there is no reason to respond.

FIGURE **4.5**

Procedure for sensory preconditioning. First, CS_2 is paired with CS_1 without a US in the situation. Then, CS_1 is paired with a US and comes to elicit a conditioned response (CR). In a later test session, CS_2 is also found to elicit the CR, even though CS_2 was never paired with the US.

During the second phase, the cinnamon flavor (CS_1) is paired with illness (the US) and a conditioned aversion (the CR) develops to CS_1. Once this first-order conditioning has been completed, the subjects are tested with CS_2 and now show an aversion to CS_2 for the first time. The response to CS_2 is noteworthy because CS_2 was never directly paired with a US. (For examples of sensory preconditioning, see Berridge & Schulkin, 1989; Leising, Sawa, & Blaisdell, 2007; Ward-Robinson & Hall, 1996, 1998.)

Sensory preconditioning and higher-order conditioning help us make sense of things we seem to like or dislike for no apparent reason. What we mean by "no apparent reason" is that these stimuli were not directly associated with a positive or aversive US. In such cases, the conditioned preference or aversion probably developed through sensory preconditioning or higher-order conditioning.

WHAT DETERMINES THE NATURE OF THE CONDITIONED RESPONSE?

In the present and preceding chapter, I described numerous examples of classical conditioning. In each of these examples, conditioning was identified by the development of new responses to the conditioned stimulus. I described a variety of responses that can become conditioned, including salivation, eye blinking, fear, locomotor approach and withdrawal, and aversion responses. However, so far I have not addressed directly why one set of responses becomes conditioned in one situation and other responses are learned in other circumstances.

The Stimulus-Substitution Model

The first and most enduring explanation for the nature of the conditioned response is Pavlov's **stimulus-substitution** model. According to this model, the association of the CS with the US turns the conditioned stimulus into a surrogate US. The conditioned stimulus comes to function much like the US did previously. Thus, the CS is assumed to activate neural circuits previously activated only by the US and elicit responses similar to the US.

Pavlov suggested that conditioning results in the establishment of new functional neural pathways (see Figure 4.6). During the course of repeated pairings of the conditioned and unconditioned stimuli, a new connection

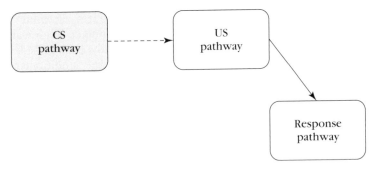

FIGURE **4.6**

Diagram of Pavlov's stimulus substitution model. The solid arrow indicates preexisting neural connections. The dashed arrow indicates neural connections established by conditioning. Because of these new functional connections, the CS comes to elicit responses previously elicited by the US.

develops between the neural circuits previously activated by the CS and the circuits previously activated only by the US. Once this new connection has been established, presentation of the CS results in activation of the US circuits, which in turn generate behavior similar to the UR. Therefore, according to Pavlov's model, conditioning makes the CS a *substitute* for the US.

The US as a Determining Factor for the CR

Different unconditioned stimuli elicit different URs. Food elicits salivation and approach; shock elicits aversion and withdrawal. If conditioning turns a CS into a surrogate US, CSs conditioned with different USs should elicit different types of conditioned responses. This prediction clearly matches experimental observations. Animals learn to salivate when conditioned with food, and to blink when conditioned with a puff of air to the eye. Salivation is not conditioned in eyeblink experiments, and eyeblink responses are not conditioned in salivary-conditioning experiments.

Evidence that the nature of the conditioned response depends on the US is also available from more subtle comparisons. In one famous experiment, for example, Jenkins and Moore (1973) compared Pavlovian conditioning in pigeons with food versus water as the US. A pigeon eating grain makes rapid, hard pecking movements directed at the grain with its beak open just before contact with the piece of grain. (In fact, the beak opening is related to the size of the grain about to be pecked.) By contrast, a pigeon drinks by lowering its beak into the water with the beak mostly closed. Once the beak is under water, it opens periodically to permit the bird to suck up the water (Klein, LaMon, & Zeigler, 1983). Thus, the URs of eating and drinking differ in both speed and form. Jenkins and Moore were interested in whether responses conditioned with food and water would differ in a corresponding fashion.

The CS was illumination of a pecking key for eight seconds. The CS was paired with either the presentation of grain or access to water. Conditioning resulted in pecking of the key light in both cases. However, the form of the conditioned response differed depending on the US. When food was the US, the pigeons pecked the key light as if eating: the pecks were rapid with the beak open at the moment of contact. With water as the US, the pecking movements were slower, made with the beak closed, and were often accompanied by swallowing. Thus, the form of the conditioned response resembled the form of the UR (see also Allan & Zeigler, 1994; Ploog & Zeigler, 1996; Ploog, 2001; Spetch, Wilkie, & Skelton, 1981; Stanhope, 1992). Similar findings have been obtained with food pellets and milk as unconditioned stimuli with laboratory rats (Davey & Cleland, 1982; Davey, Phillips, & Cleland 1981).

Learning and Homeostasis: A Special Case of Stimulus Substitution

Proper functioning of the body requires that certain physiological parameters, such as blood sugar, blood oxygen, and temperature, be maintained within acceptable limits. For example, having a body temperature of 98.6°F is so critical that substantial deviations from that value are considered symptoms of illness. The concept of **homeostasis** was introduced by Walter Cannon to refer to physiological mechanisms that serve to maintain the stability of critical physiological functions.

How is a desired or homeostatic level achieved and defended against challenges? I previously described the concept of homeostasis in discussions of the opponent process theory of motivation in Chapter 2. As I noted there, maintaining any system within a desirable range requires that a disturbance that moves the system in one direction be met by opponent processes that counteract the disturbance. Thus, achieving homeostasis requires that a challenge to the homeostatic level trigger a compensatory reaction that will neutralize the disturbance. In warm-blooded animals, for example, any lowering of body temperature caused by exposure to cold reflexively triggers compensatory reactions that help to conserve and increase temperature. These compensatory reactions include peripheral vasoconstriction and shivering. The system operates through a *negative feedback loop*. A drop in body temperature is detected and this serves as a stimulus to activate compensatory responses.

Walter Cannon lived from 1871 to 1945 and met Pavlov in 1923 when Pavlov visited the United States. The two of them had considerable respect for each other's work. However, it wasn't until more than half a century after both of them had passed away that Cannon's concept of homeostasis became integrated with studies of Pavlovian conditioning (Dworkin, 1993; Siegel, 2008). Homeostatic mechanisms as conceived by Cannon operated by negative feedback, like a thermostat on a heater. The thermostat turns on the heater only after a drop in temperature has been detected. This is rather inefficient because it allows the system to cool before the correction is activated. Imagine how much more efficient a thermostat would be if it could anticipate when the system would get cold.

Dworkin (1993) pointed out that challenges to homeostasis can be corrected more effectively if those challenges are anticipated. Pavlovian conditioning provides the means for such feed-forward anticipation. Warm-blooded animals learn about cues that signal when they will get cold. This in turn enables them to make feed-forward compensatory adjustments in anticipation of the cold and thereby avoid suffering a drop in body temperature (Riccio, MacArdy, & Kissinger, 1991). In this situation the conditioned

Courtesy of Donald A. Dewsbury

S. Siegel

response to a physiological challenge is the same as the reflexive compensatory response to the challenge. Thus, the conditioned response is the same as the UR, but the UR is a compensatory reaction to the physiological disturbance.

Conditioned homeostatic responses have been examined most extensively in studies of how organisms respond to the administration of a psychoactive drug (Poulos & Cappell, 1991; Siegel, 2005; Siegel & Allan, 1998). (For a general review of conditioned homeostatic mechanisms, see Siegel, 2008; for studies of Pavlovian feed-forward mechanisms in the control of social behavior, see Domjan, Cusato, & Villarreal, 2000.) Drugs often cause physiological challenges to homeostasis that trigger unconditioned compensatory reactions. Cues that become associated with the drug-induced physiological challenge can come to activate these compensatory reactions as anticipatory or feed-forward conditioned responses.

It has been recognized for a long time that the administration of a drug constitutes a conditioning trial in which cues related to drug administration are paired with the pharmacological effects of the drug. Caffeine, for example, is a commonly used drug, whose pharmacological effects are typically preceded by the smell and taste of coffee. Thus, the taste and smell of coffee can serve as conditioned stimuli that are predictive of the physiological effects of caffeine (e.g., Flaten & Blumenthal, 1999). Studies of drug conditioning have been conducted with a wide range of pharmacological agents, including alcohol, heroin, morphine, and cocaine, and there has been considerable interest in how Pavlovian conditioning may contribute to drug tolerance, drug craving, and drug addiction (Baker & Tiffany, 1985; Siegel, 1999, 2005; Siegel & Ramos, 2002).

In a study of naturally-acquired drug-conditioned responses, Ehrman, Robbins, Childress, and O'Brien (1992) tested men with a history of free-basing and smoking cocaine (but no history of heroin use). A control group that never used cocaine or heroin also provided data. The participants were observed under three test conditions. In one test, cues related to cocaine use were presented. The participants listened to an audio tape of people talking about their experiences free-basing and smoking cocaine, watched a video tape of people buying and using cocaine, and were asked to go through the motions of free-basing and smoking. In another test, cues related to heroin use were presented in the same manner as the cocaine stimuli. Finally, in the third test, control stimuli unrelated to drug use were presented. During each test, physiological responses and self-reports of feelings were recorded.

Both the physiological measures and self-reports of mood provided evidence that cocaine-related stimuli elicited conditioned responses. Figure 4.7 shows the results of measures of heart rate. Cocaine users exposed to cocaine-related stimuli experienced a significant increase in heart rate during the test. Furthermore, this increased heart rate was specific to the cocaine-related stimuli. The heart rate of cocaine users did not change in response to heroin-related stimuli or nondrug stimuli. The increased heart rate response was also specific to the cocaine users. Participants in the control group did not show elevations in heart rate in any of the test.

Participants with a history of cocaine use also reported feelings of cocaine craving and withdrawal elicited by the cocaine-related stimuli. They did not report these emotions in response to the heroin-related or nondrug stimuli. Feelings of cocaine craving and withdrawal were also not reported by participants in the control group. Thus, the results suggest that cocaine users

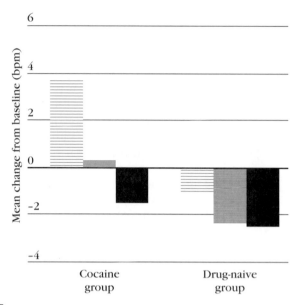

FIGURE **4.7**

Mean change in heart rate from baseline levels for men with a history of cocaine use and a drug-naïve control group during tests involving exposure to cocaine related stimuli (light bars), heroin related stimuli (medium bars), or nondrug stimuli (dark bars). (From "Conditioned Reponses to Cocaine-Related Stimuli in Cocaine Abuse Patients," by R. N. Ehrman, S. J. Robbins, A. R. Childress, and C. P. O'Brien, 1992, *Psychopharmacology*, *107*, pp. 523–529. Copyright © 1992 by Springer-Verlag. Reprinted by permission.)

acquired both conditioned physiological and emotional responses to cocaine-related stimuli during the course of their drug use.

In a more recent study, cocaine-related stimuli were presented to people who were dependent on crack cocaine using virtual-reality technology (Saladin, Brady, Graap, & Rothbaum, 2004). The drug-related scenes (soliciting and smoking crack, and being high on crack) elicited strong craving and desire among the participants. Interestingly, the drug-related cues also resulted in lower ratings of well-being and happiness, indicating the drug cues were activating emotions opposite to the direct effects of cocaine.

These results indicate that environmental cues conditioned by psychoactive drugs can elicit craving emotions related to the drug US. Such anticipatory conditioned responses can be also elicited by the initial effects of a drug experience (Siegel et al., 2000). For drug addicts, the beginnings of a buzz or high are typically followed by substantial additional drug intake and a more intense high. Therefore, the early weak drug effect can serve as a CS signaling additional drug intake and can elicit drug cravings and other drug conditioned reactions. In this case the CS is an internal sensation or *introceptive cue*. The conditioned craving elicited by a small dose of the drug makes it difficult for addicts to use drugs in moderation. That is why abstinence is their best hope for controlling cravings. (For a recent study involving conditioning the introceptive cues of nicotine, see Murray & Bevins, 2007.)

The Conditioning Model of Drug Tolerance

The role of Pavlovian conditioning has been examined extensively in relation to the development of **drug tolerance,** which typically accompanies drug addiction. Tolerance to a drug is said to develop when repeated administrations of the drug have progressively less effect. Because of this, increasing doses are required to produce the same drug effect. Traditionally, drug tolerance has been considered to result from pharmacological processes. However, there is also substantial evidence that drug tolerance can result from Pavlovian conditioning of homeostatic compensatory processes. This view, developed by Shepard Siegel and others, is known as the conditioning model of drug tolerance.

The conditioning model assumes that each drug-taking episode is a conditioning trial and is built on the idea of learned homeostasis. According to this idea, the administration of a psychoactive drug causes physiological changes that disrupt homeostasis. Those physiological changes in turn trigger unconditioned compensatory adjustments to counteract the disturbance. Through Pavlovian conditioning, stimuli that accompany the drug administration become conditioned to elicit these compensatory adjustments. Because the conditioned responses counteract the drug effects, the impact of the drug is reduced, resulting in the phenomenon of drug tolerance (see Figure 4.8).

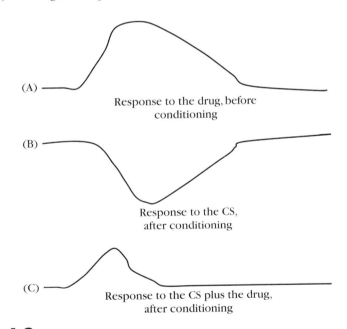

(A) Response to the drug, before conditioning

(B) Response to the CS, after conditioning

(C) Response to the CS plus the drug, after conditioning

FIGURE **4.8**

Illustration of the conditioning model of drug tolerance. The magnitude of a drug reaction is illustrated by deviation from the horizontal level. (A) Primary reaction to the drug before conditioning, illustrating the initial effects of the drug (without any homeostatic adjustments). (B) The homeostatic compensatory drug reaction that becomes conditioned to the drug-predictive CS after repeated drug administrations. (C) The net attenuated drug response that is observed when the drug is administered with the drug-conditioned CS. This net attenuated drug response illustrates the phenomenon of drug tolerance.

BOX **4.1**

Drug "Overdose" Caused by the Absence of Drug-Conditioned Stimuli

According to the conditioning model of drug tolerance, the impact of a drug will be reduced if the drug is consumed in the presence of cues that were previously conditioned to elicit **conditioned compensatory responses.** Consider a heroin addict who usually shoots up in the same place, perhaps with the same friends. That place and company will become conditioned to elicit physiological reactions that reduce the effects of the heroin, forcing the addict to inject higher doses to get the same effect. As long as the ad-dict shoots up in his usual place and with his usual friends, he is pro-tected from the full effects of the increased heroin dosage by the conditioned compensatory re-sponses. But, what will happen if he visits a new part of town and shoots up with newly found friends? In that case, the familiar CSs will be absent, as will the protective conditioned compensa-tory responses. Therefore, the ad-dict will get the full impact of the heroin he is using, and may suffer an "overdose." I put the word "overdose" in quotation marks because the problem is not that too high a dose of heroin was con-sumed, but that the drug was taken in the absence of the usual CS. Without the CS, a dose of heroin that the addict never had trouble with might kill him on this occa-sion. Evidence for this interpreta-tion has been obtained in both experimental research with labo-ratory animals, and with human cases of drug overdose (Siegel, Baptista, Kim, McDonald, & Weise-Kelly, 2000).

The conditioning model of drug tolerance attributes tolerance to compensatory responses conditioned to environmental stimuli paired with drug administration. A key prediction of the model is that drug tolerance will be reduced if participants receive the drug under novel circumstances or in the absence of the usual drug-predictive cues. The model also suggests that various factors (such as CS preexposure) that attenuate the development of conditioned responding will also attenuate the development of drug tolerance. These and other predictions of the conditioning model have been confirmed by Siegel and his colleagues, as well as by numerous other investigative teams in laboratory studies with opiates (i.e., morphine and heroin), alcohol, scopolamine, benzodiazepines, and amphet-amine (see reviews by Siegel, 1999, 2005, 2008; Siegel & Allan, 1998; Stewart & Eikelboom, 1987).

The CS as a Determinant of the Form of the CR

Our discussion thus far has considered how the form of the conditioned re-sponse is determined by the US. However, the US is not the only important fac-tor. The form of the CR is also influenced by the nature of the CS. This was first demonstrated in a striking experiment by Timberlake and Grant (1975).

Timberlake and Grant investigated classical conditioning in rats with food as the US. However, instead of a conventional light or tone, the CS was the presentation of another rat just before food delivery. One side of the ex-perimental chamber was equipped with a sliding platform that could be moved in and out of the chamber through a flap door (see Figure 4.9). A live rat was gently restrained on the platform. Ten seconds before each delivery of food, the platform was moved into the experimental chamber, thereby trans-porting the stimulus rat through the flap door.

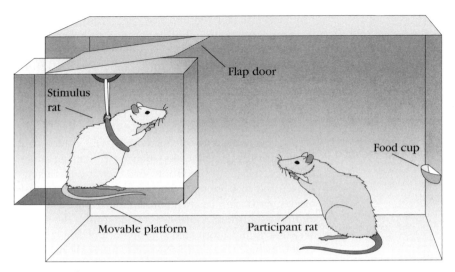

FIGURE **4.9**

Diagram of the experiment by Timberlake and Grant (1975). The CS for food was presentation of a stimulus rat on a movable platform through a flap door on one side of the experimental chamber.

The stimulus-substitution model predicts that CS-US pairings will generate responses to the CS that are similar to responses elicited by the food US. Since the food US elicited gnawing and biting, these responses were also expected to be elicited by the CS. Contrary to this prediction, the CS did not elicit gnawing and biting. Rather, as the CS rat was repeatedly paired with food, it came to elicit social affiliate responses (orientation, approach, sniffing, and social contacts). Such responses did not develop if the CS rat was not paired with food or was presented at times unrelated to food.

The outcome of this experiment does not support any model that explains the form of the conditioned response solely in terms of the US that is used. The conditioned social responses that were elicited by the CS rat were no doubt determined by having another rat serve as the CS. Other kinds of food-conditioned stimuli elicit different conditioned responses. For example, Peterson, Ackil, Frommer, and Hearst (1972) inserted an illuminated response lever into the experimental chamber immediately before presenting food to rats. With the protruding metal lever as the CS, the conditioned responses were "almost exclusively oral and consisted mainly of licking...and gnawing" (p. 1010). (For other investigations of how the CS determines the nature of the conditioned response, see Domjan, Cusato & Krause, 2004; Godsil & Fanselow, 2004; Holland, 1984; Kim, Rivers, Bevins, & Ayres, 1996; Sigmundi & Bolles, 1983).

Conditioned Responding and Behavior Systems

The approaches to the form of the conditioned response that I have been discussing so far have their intellectual roots in Pavlov's physiological model systems approach to the study of learning. In this approach, one or two responses are isolated and investigated in detail to provide information about learning. This approach is continuing to provide rich dividends in new knowledge. However, it is also becoming evident that this single-response approach provides an incomplete picture. Holland (1984), for example, has commented that the understanding of conditioned behavior will ultimately require "knowledge of the normal functions of behavior systems engaged by the various CSs, the natural, unlearned organization within those systems, and the ontogeny of those systems" (p. 164).

Different systems of behavior have evolved to enable animals to accomplish various critical tasks such as procuring and eating food, defending a territory, avoiding predation, producing and raising offspring, and so on. As I discussed in Chapter 2, each behavior system consists of a series of response modes, each with its own controlling stimuli and responses, arranged spatially and/or temporally. Consider, for example, the sexual behavior of male quail. When sexually motivated, the male will engage in a general search response which brings it into an area where a female may be located. Once he is in the female's territory, the male will engage in a more focal search response to actually locate her. Finally, once he finds her, the male will engage in courtship and copulatory responses. This sequence is illustrated in Figure 4.10.

Behavior systems theory assumes that the presentation of a US in a Pavlovian conditioning procedure activates the behavior system relevant to that US. Food-unconditioned stimuli activate the foraging and feeding system. A sexual US, by contrast, will activate the sexual behavior system. Classical conditioning procedures involve superimposing a CS-US relationship on the behavioral system activated by the US. As a conditioned stimulus becomes associated with the US, it becomes integrated into the behavioral system and comes to elicit component responses of that system. Thus, food-conditioned stimuli come to elicit components of the feeding system, and sexual-conditioned stimuli come to elicit components of the sexual behavior system.

An especially provocative prediction of behavior systems theory is that the form of the CR will depend on the CS-US interval that is used. The CS-US interval is assumed to determine where the CS becomes incorporated into the sequence of responses that makes up the behavior system.

Consider what might happen if a Pavlovian conditioning procedure were superimposed on the sexual behavior system. In the sexual conditioning of

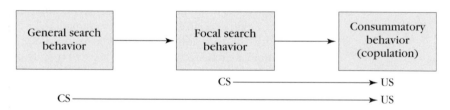

FIGURE **4.10**

Sequence of responses, starting with general search and ending with copulatory behavior that characterize the sexual behavior system. A conditioning procedure is superimposed on the behavior system. The CS-US interval determines where the CS becomes incorporated into the behavioral sequence.

Courtesy of C. K. Akins

C. K. Akins

male quail, the presence of a female copulation partner is the US. The presence of the female activates the courtship and copulatory responses that characterize the end of the sexual behavior sequence. With a short CS-US interval, the CS occurs shortly before the female is available. If the CS becomes incorporated into the behavior system at this point, the CS should elicit focal search behavior: the male should approach and remain near the CS. The CR should be different if a long CS-US interval is used. In this case (see Figure 4.10), the CS should become incorporated into an earlier portion of the behavior system and elicit general search rather than focal search behavior. General search behavior should be manifest in increased nondirected locomotor behavior.

The above predictions were tested in an experiment conducted with domesticated quail (Akins, 2000). Akins used a large rectangular experimental chamber. During each conditioning trial, a small visual CS was presented at one end either one minute before the male birds received access to a female, or 20 minutes before the release of the female. Control groups were exposed to the CS and US in an unpaired fashion. To detect focal search behavior, Akins measured how much time the males spent close to the conditioned stimulus. To detect general search behavior, she measured pacing between one half of the experimental chamber and the other.

The results of the focal search and general search CR measures are presented in Figure 4.11. With a one minute CS-US interval, the conditioning procedure produced significant focal search, but not general search behavior. In contrast, with the 20 minute CS-US interval, conditioning produced significant general search but not focal search responding. These results are precisely what are predicted by behavior systems theory. According to behavior systems theory, the CS does not come to either substitute for or compensate

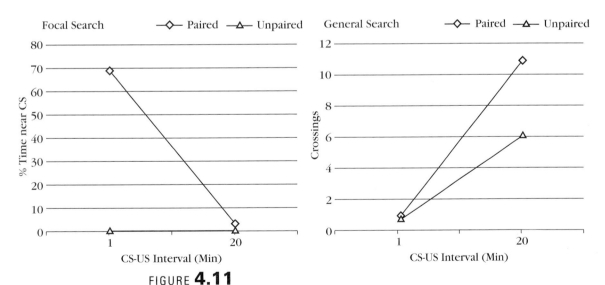

FIGURE 4.11

Effects of the CS-US interval on the conditioning of focal search and general search responses in male domesticated quail. When the CS-US interval was one minute, conditioning resulted in increased focal search behavior. When the CS-US interval was 20 minutes, conditioning resulted in increased general search behavior. (Adapted from Akins, 2000.)

for the US. Rather, it comes to substitute for a stimulus in the behavior system at a point that is determined by the CS-US interval. (For related studies, see Delamater & Holland, 2008; Waddell, Morris, & Bouton, 2006; Silva & Timberlake, 1997.)

Behavior-systems theory has been developed most extensively by William Timberlake (Timberlake, 2001; Timberlake & Lucas, 1989) and is consistent with much of what we know about the nature of classically conditioned behavioral responses. The theory is clearly consistent with the fact that the form of conditioned responses is determined by the nature of the US, since different USs activate different behavior systems. The theory is also consistent with the fact that the form of CR is determined by the nature of the CS. Certain types of stimuli are more effective in eliciting particular component responses of a behavior system than other types of stimuli. Therefore, the nature of the CS is expected to determine how the CS becomes incorporated into the behavior system. Finally, the behavior-systems theory makes unique predictions about differences in conditioned behavior as a function of the CS-US interval and other procedural parameters (e.g., Esmorís-Arranz, Pardo-Vázquez, & Vázquez-Garcia, 2003).

S-R versus S-S Learning

So far I have been discussing various accounts of the nature of conditioned behavior without saying much about how a CS produces responding. Let's turn to that question next.

Historically, conditioned behavior was viewed as a response elicited directly by the CS. According to this idea, conditioning establishes a new *stimulus-response*, or S-R connection between the CS and the CR. An important alternative view is that subjects learn a new *stimulus-stimulus* or S-S connection between the CS and the US. According to this interpretation, participants respond to the CS not because it elicits a CR directly, but because the CS activates a representation or memory of the US. Conditioned responding is assumed to reflect the status of the US representation that is activated by the CS.

How might we decide between these two interpretations? A popular research method that has been used to decide between S-R and S-S learning involves the technique of **US devaluation**. This technique has been used to answer many major questions in behavior theory. (I will describe applications of it in instrumental conditioning in Chapter 7.) Therefore, it is important to understand its rationale.

The basic strategy of a US devaluation experiment is illustrated in Figure 4.12. Holland and Rescorla (1975), for example, first conditioned two groups of mildly food-deprived rats by repeatedly pairing a tone with pellets of food. This initial phase of the experiment was assumed to establish an association between the tone CS and the food US, as well as to get the rats to form a representation of the food that was used. Conditioned responding was evident in increased activity elicited by the tone.

In the next phase of the experiment, the experimental group received a treatment designed to make the US less valuable to them. This US devaluation was accomplished by giving the participants sufficient free food to completely satisfy their hunger. If you are fully satiated, food is not as valuable to you as when you are hungry. Thus, food satiation reduces the value of food and thus devalues the US representation. The deprivation state of the control group

R. A. Rescorla

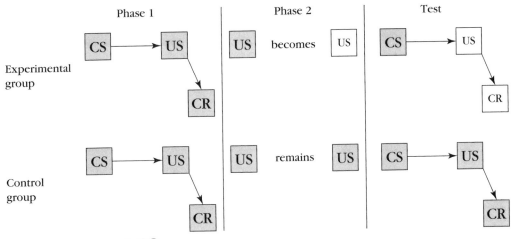

FIGURE **4.12**

Basic strategy and rationale involved in US-devaluation experiments. In Phase 1 the experimental and control groups receive conventional conditioning to establish an association between the CS and the US and to lead the participants to form a representation of the US. In Phase 2 the US representation is devalued for the experimental group but remains unchanged for the control group. If the CR is elicited by way of the US representation, devaluation of the US representation should reduce responding to the CS.

was not changed in Phase 2, and therefore the US representation was assumed to remain intact for them (see Figure 4.12). Both groups then received a series of test trials with the tone CS. During these tests, the experimental group showed significantly less conditioned responding than the control group. These results are indicative of S-S learning rather than S-R learning.

If conditioning had established a new S-R connection between the CS and CR, the CR would have been elicited whenever the CS occurred, regardless of the value of the food. That did not happen. Rather, conditioning resulted in an association between the CS and a representation of the US (S-S learning). Presentation of the CS activated the US representation, and the CR depended on the current status of that US representation.

Evidence of S-S learning is available from a variety of classical conditioning situations (e.g., Cleland & Davey, 1982; Colwill & Motzkin, 1994; Delamater, Campese, LoLordo, & Sclafani, 2006; Dwyer, 2005; Kraemer, Hoffmann, Randall, & Spear, 1992; Hilliard, Domjan, Nguyen, & Cusato, 1998). However, not all instances of classical conditioning involve S-S learning. In some cases, the participants appear to learn a direct S-R association between the CS and the CR. I will have more to say about S-R learning in Chapter 7.

HOW DO CONDITIONED AND UNCONDITIONED STIMULI BECOME ASSOCIATED?

I have described numerous situations in which classical conditioning occurs and discussed various factors that determine what responses result from this learning. However, I have yet to address in detail the critical issue of how conditioned and unconditioned stimuli become associated. What are the mechanisms of learning, the underlying processes that are activated by conditioning procedures to produce learning? This question has been the subject of intense scholarly work. The evolution of theories of classical conditioning continues today, as investigators strive to formulate comprehensive theories that can embrace all of the diverse findings of research in Pavlovian conditioning. (For reviews, see Pearce & Bouton, 2001; Mowrer & Klein, 2001; Pelley, 2004; Vogel, Castro, & Saavedra, 2004; Wasserman & Miller, 1997.)

The Blocking Effect

The modern era in theories of Pavlovian conditioning got underway about 40 years ago with the discovery of several provocative phenomena that stimulated the application of information processing ideas to the analysis of classical conditioning (e.g., Rescorla, 1967b, 1969a; Wagner, Logan, Haberlandt, & Price, 1968). One of the most prominent of these phenomena was the **blocking effect**.

To get an intuitive sense of the blocking effect, consider the following scenario. Each Sunday afternoon, you visit your grandmother who always serves bread pudding that slightly disagrees with you. Not wanting to upset her, you politely eat the pudding during each visit, and consequently acquire an aversion to bread pudding. One of the visits falls on a holiday, and to make the occasion a bit more festive, your grandmother makes a special sauce to serve with the bread pudding. You politely eat the bread pudding with the sauce, and as usual you get a bit sick to your stomach. Will you now develop an aversion to the sauce? Probably not. Knowing that bread pudding disagrees with you, you probably will attribute your illness to the proven culprit and not learn to dislike the special sauce.

The above example illustrates the basic sequence of events that produces the blocking effect (see Figure 4.13). Two conditioned stimuli are employed (in the above example these were the taste of the bread pudding and the taste of the special sauce). In Phase 1, the experimental group receives repeated pairings of one of the stimuli (A) with the US. This phase of training is continued until a strong CR develops to Stimulus A. In the next phase of the experiment, Stimulus B is presented together with Stimulus A, and paired

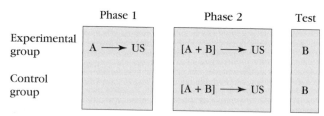

FIGURE **4.13**

Diagram of the blocking procedure. During Phase 1, Stimulus A is conditioned with the US in the experimental group, while the control group receives Stimulus A presented unpaired with the US. During Phase 2, both experimental and control groups receive conditioning trials in which Stimulus A is presented simultaneously with Stimulus B and paired with the US. A later test of Stimulus B alone shows that less conditioned responding occurs to Stimulus B in the experimental group than in the control group.

with the US. After several such conditioning trials, Stimulus B is presented alone in a test trial to see if it also elicits the CR. Interestingly, very little responding occurs to Stimulus B even though B was repeatedly paired with the US during Phase 2.

The control group in the blocking design receives the same kind of conditioning trials with Stimulus B as the experimental group, as indicated in Phase 2 of Figure 4.13. That is, for the control group, Stimulus B is also presented simultaneously with Stimulus A during its conditioning trials. However, for the control group, Stimulus A is not conditioned prior to these compound-stimulus trials. Rather, during Phase 1, the control group receives presentations of Stimulus A and the US in an unpaired fashion. In many replications of this design, Stimulus B invariably produces less conditioned responding in the experimental group than in the control group. (For a more detailed discussion of controls for blocking, see Taylor, Joseph, Balsam, & Bitterman, 2008.)

The blocking effect was initially investigated using the conditioned suppression technique with rats (Kamin, 1968, 1969). Subsequently, however, the phenomenon has been demonstrated in various other conditioning preparations with both human participants and laboratory animals (e.g., Bradfield & McNally, 2008; Holland & Kenmuir, 2005; Mitchell, Lovibond, Minard, & Lavis, 2006). College students served in one study employing a video game version of the conditioned suppression procedure (Arcediano, Matute, & Miller, 1997). The task was a variation on a video game that required the students to repeatedly fire a laser gun to prevent invading Martians from landing. To create conditioned suppression of this behavior, periodically an anti-laser shield was activated during which Martians would land in large numbers if the subject continued to shoot. The presence of the anti-laser shield permitting Martians to land was the US.

L. J. Kamin

For participants in the blocking group, in Phase 1 of the experiment presentations of the US were signaled by a visual CS that consisted of a change in the color of the background of the computer screen. As Phase 1 progressed, the students came to suppress their shooting of the laser gun during the visual CS. In Phase 2, this visual CS was presented together with an auditory CS (a complex tone), and this stimulus compound ended with the US. Participants in the control group received similar training, but for them the light CS was unpaired with the US in Phase 1. Blocking was assessed after Phase 2 by measuring conditioned suppression to the tone CS. The blocking group showed significantly less suppression to the tone CS than the control group. Thus, as anticipated, the presence of a pre-trained visual CS in Phase 2 blocked the acquisition of conditioned suppression to the tone CS. (For other human studies of blocking, see Crookes & Moran, 2003; Kruschke, Kappenman, & Hetrick, 2005.)

Since the time of Aristotle, temporal contiguity has been considered the primary means by which stimuli become associated. The blocking effect has become a landmark phenomenon in classical conditioning because it called into question the assumption that temporal contiguity is sufficient for learning. The blocking effect clearly shows that pairings of a CS with a US are not enough for conditioned responding to develop. During Phase 2 of the blocking experiment, CS_B is paired with the US in an identical fashion for the experimental and the control groups. Nevertheless, CS_B comes to elicit vigorous conditioned responding only in the control group.

BOX **4.2**

The Picture-Word Problem in Teaching Reading: A Form of Blocking

Early instruction in reading often involves showing children a written word, along with a picture of what that word represents. Thus, two stimuli are presented together. The children have already learned what the picture is called (e.g., a horse). Therefore, the two stimuli in the picture-word compound include one that is already known (the picture) and one that is not (the word). This makes the picture-word compound much like the compound stimulus in a blocking experiment: a known stimulus is presented along with a new one the child does not know yet. Research on the blocking effect predicts that the presence of the previously learned picture

should disrupt learning about the word. Singh and Solman (1990) found that this is indeed the case with picture-word compounds in a study of reading with mentally retarded students.

The children were taught to read words such as *knife, lemon, radio, stamp,* and *chalk.* Some of the words were taught using a variation of the blocking design in which the picture of the object was presented first and the child was asked to name it. The picture was then presented together with its written word, and the child was asked, "What is that word?" In other conditions, the words were presented without their corre-

sponding pictures. All eight participants showed the slowest learning for the words that were taught with the corresponding pictures present. By contrast, six of the eight children showed the fastest learning of the words that were taught without their corresponding pictures. (The remaining two participants learned most rapidly with a modified procedure.) These results suggest that processes akin to blocking may occur in learning to read. The results also suggest that pictorial prompts should be used with caution in reading instruction because they may disrupt rather than facilitate learning (see also Didden, Prinsen, & Sigafoos, 2000).

Why does the presence of the previously-conditioned Stimulus A block the acquisition of responding to the added cue B? Kamin, the originator of the blocking effect, explained the phenomenon by proposing that a US has to be surprising to be effective in producing learning. If the US is signaled by a previously conditioned stimulus (A), it will not be surprising. Kamin reasoned that if the US is not surprising, it will not startle the animal and stimulate the *mental effort* needed for the formation of an association. Unexpected events are events to which the organism has not yet adjusted. Therefore, unexpected events activate processes leading to new learning. To be effective, the US has to be unexpected or surprising.

The basic idea that learning occurs when the environment changes and the subject is surprised by outcomes remains a fundamental concept in learning theory. For example, in a recent Bayesian analysis of learning, the authors noted that "Change increases uncertainty, and speeds subsequent learning, by making old evidence less relevant to the present circumstances" (Courville, Daw, & Touretzky, 2006).

The Rescorla-Wagner Model

The idea that the effectiveness of a US is determined by how surprising it is forms the basis of a formal mathematical model of conditioning by Robert Rescorla and Allan Wagner (Rescorla & Wagner, 1972; Wagner & Rescorla, 1972). With the use of this model, investigators could extend the implications of the concept of US surprise to a wide variety of conditioning phenomena. The Rescorla-Wagner model has become a reference point for all subsequent

A. R. Wagner

learning theories and continues to be used in a variety of areas of psychology (Siegel & Allen, 1996).

What does it mean to say that something is surprising? How might we measure the level of surprise of a US? By definition, *an event is surprising if it is different from what is expected.* If you expect a small gift for your birthday and get a car, you will be very surprised. This is analogous to an unexpectedly large US. Correspondingly, if you expect a car and receive a box of candy, you will also be surprised. This is analogous to an unexpectedly small US. According to the Rescorla-Wagner model, an unexpectedly large US is the basis for excitatory conditioning or increases in associative value, and an unexpectedly small US (or the absence of the US) is the basis for inhibitory conditioning or decreases in associative value.

Rescorla and Wagner assumed that the level of surprise, and hence the effectiveness of a US, depends on how different the US is from what the individual expects. Furthermore, they assumed that expectation of the US is related to the conditioned or associative properties of the stimuli that precede the US. Strong conditioned responding indicates strong expectation that the US will occur; weak conditioned responding indicates a low expectation of the US.

These ideas can be expressed mathematically by using λ to represent the US that is received on a give trial and V to represent the associative value of the stimuli that precede the US. The level of surprise of the US will then be $(\lambda - V)$, or the difference between what occurs (λ) and what is expected (V). At the start of conditioning trials, what is expected (V) will be much smaller than what occurs (λ) and the amount of surprise $(\lambda - V)$ will be large. As learning proceeds, expectations (V) will come in line with what occurs (λ), and the surprise term $(\lambda - V)$ will get smaller and smaller. As learning progresses, V grows to match λ. At the limit or asymptote of learning, $V = \lambda$ and the surprise term $(\lambda - V)$ is equal to zero. These changes are illustrated in Figure 4.14.

Learning on a given conditioning trial is the change in the associative value of a stimulus. That change can be represented as ΔV. The idea that learning depends on the level of surprise of the US can be expressed as follows,

$$\Delta V = k(\lambda - V), \qquad (4.1)$$

where k is a constant related to the salience of the CS and US. This is the fundamental equation of the Rescorla-Wagner model.

Application of the Rescorla-Wagner Equation to the Blocking Effect

The basic ideas of the Rescorla–Wagner model clearly predict the blocking effect. In applying the model, it is important to keep in mind that expectations of the US are based on all of the cues available to the organism during the conditioning trial. As was presented in Figure 4.13, the experimental group in the blocking design first receives extensive conditioning of Stimulus A so that it acquires a perfect expectation that the US will occur whenever it encounters Stimulus A. Therefore, by the end of Phase 1, V_A will be equal to the asymptote of learning or, $V_A = \lambda$.

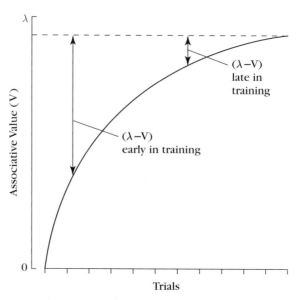

FIGURE 4.14

Growth of associative value (V) during the course of conditioning until the asymptote of learning (λ) is reached. Note that the measure of surprise (λ–V) is much larger early in training than late in training.

In Phase 2, Stimulus B is presented together with Stimulus A, and the two CSs are followed by the US. To predict what will be learned about Stimulus B, the basic Rescorla-Wagner equation has to be applied to Stimulus B: $\Delta V_B = k(\lambda - V)$. In carrying out this calculation, keep in mind that V refers to all of the stimuli present on a trial. In Phase 2, there two cues: A and B. Therefore, $V = V_A + V_B$. Because of its Phase 1 training, $V_A = \lambda$ at the start of Phase 2. In contrast, V_B starts out at zero. Therefore, at the start of Phase 2, $V_A + V_B$ is equal to $\lambda + 0$, or λ. Substituting this value into the equation for ΔV_B gives a value for ΔV_B of $k(\lambda - \lambda)$, or $k(0)$, which is equal to zero. This indicates that Stimulus B will not acquire associative value in Phase 2. Thus, the conditioning of Stimulus B will be blocked.

Loss of Associative Value Despite Pairings with the US

The Rescorla-Wagner model is consistent with fundamental facts of classical conditioning, such as acquisition and the blocking effect. However, much of the importance of the model has come from its unusual predictions. One unusual prediction is that the conditioned properties of stimuli can decrease despite continued pairings with the US. How might this happen? Stimuli are predicted to lose associative value if they are presented together on a conditioning trial after having been trained separately. Such an experiment is outlined in Figure 4.15.

Figure 4.15 shows a three phase experiment. In Phase 1, Stimuli A and B are paired with the same US (e.g., 1 pellet of food) on separate trials. This continues until both stimulus A and stimulus B predict perfectly the 1-food pellet US. Thus, at the end of Phase 1, V_A and V_B each equal λ. Phase 2 is

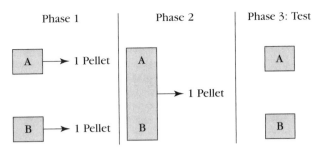

FIGURE **4.15**

Diagram of the overexpectation experiment. In Phase 1, Stimuli A and B are separately conditioned to asymptote with a 1-pellet US. In Phase 2, an overexpectation is created by presenting A and B simultaneously and pairing the compound stimulus with a 1-pellet US. In Phase 3, A and B are tested individually and found to have lost associative value because of the overexpectation in Phase 2.

then initiated. In Phase 2, Stimuli A and B are presented simultaneously for the first time, and this stimulus compound is followed by the usual single food pellet. The question is what happens to the conditioned properties of Stimuli A and B as a result of the Phase 2 training?

Note that the same US that was used in Phase 1 continues to be presented in Phase 2. Given that there is no change in the US, informal reflection suggests that the conditioned properties of Stimuli A and B should also remain unchanged. In contrast to this common sense prediction, the Rescorla-Wagner model predicts that the conditioned properties of the individual Stimuli A and B will decrease in Phase 2.

As a result of training in Phase 1, Stimuli A and B both come to predict the 1-food pellet US ($V_A = \lambda$; $V_B = \lambda$). When Stimuli A and B are presented simultaneously for the first time, in Phase 2, the expectations based on the individual stimuli are assumed to add together, with the result that two food pellets are predicted as the US rather than one ($V_{A+B} = V_A + V_B = 2\lambda$). This is an overexpectation because the US remains only one food pellet. Thus, there is a discrepancy between what is expected (two pellets) and what occurs (one pellet). At the start of Phase 2, the participants find the US surprisingly small. To align their expectations of the US with what actually occurs in Phase 2, the participants have to decrease their expectancy of the US based on Stimuli A and B. Thus, Stimuli A and B are predicted to lose associative value despite continued presentations of the same US. The loss in associative value will continue until the sum of the expectancies based on A and B equals one food pellet. The predicted loss of the CR to the individual Stimuli A and B in this type of procedure is highly counterintuitive, but has been verified experimentally (e.g., Kehoe & White, 2004; Khallad & Moore, 1996; Lattal & Nakajima, 1998; Rescorla, 1999b).

Conditioned Inhibition

How does the Rescorla-Wagner model explain the development of conditioned inhibition? Consider, for example, Pavlov's procedure for inhibitory conditioning (see Figure 3.9). This procedure involves two kinds of trials: one in which the US is presented (reinforced trials), and one in which the US is omitted (nonreinforced trials). On reinforced trials, a conditioned excitatory stimulus (CS+) is presented and paired with the US. On nonreinforced trials, the CS+ is presented together with the conditioned inhibitory stimulus CS−, and the compound is not followed by the US.

Application of the Rescorla-Wagner model to such a procedure requires considering reinforced and nonreinforced trials separately. To accurately anticipate the US on reinforced trials, the CS+ has to gain excitatory properties. The development of such conditioned excitation is illustrated in the left-hand panel of Figure 4.16. Excitatory conditioning involves the acquisition of positive associative value and ceases once the organism predicts the US perfectly on each reinforced trial.

What happens on nonreinforced trials? On these trials, both the CS+ and CS− occur. Once the CS+ has acquired some degree of conditioned excitation (because of its presentation on reinforced trials), the organism will expect the US whenever the CS+ occurs, including on nonreinforced trials. However, the US does not happen on nonreinforced trials. Therefore, this is a case of over-expectation, similar to the example illustrated in Figure 4.15. To accurately predict the absence of the US on nonreinforced trials, the associative value of the CS+ and the value of the CS− have to sum to zero (the value represented by no US). How can this be achieved? Given the positive associative value of the CS+, the only way to achieve a net zero expectation of the US on nonreinforced trials is to make the associative value of the CS− negative. Hence, the Rescorla-Wagner model explains conditioned inhibition by assuming that the CS− acquires negative associative value (see the left-hand panel of Figure 4.16).

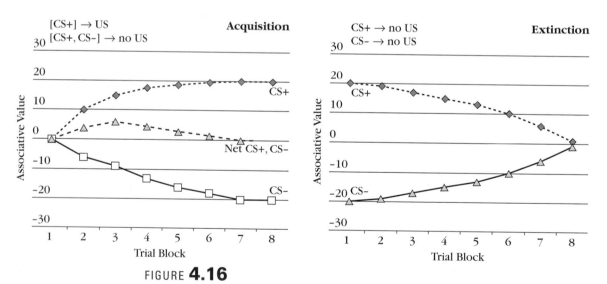

FIGURE **4.16**

Left Panel: Acquisition of conditioned excitation to CS+ and conditioned inhibition to CS−. The *Net* curve is the associative value of the CS+ and CS− presented simultaneously. Right Panel: Predicted extinction of excitation to CS+ and inhibition to CS− when these cues are presented repeatedly without the US, according to the Rescorla-Wagner model.

Extinction of Excitation and Inhibition

In an extinction procedure, the CS is presented repeatedly without the US. I will discuss extinction more in-depth in Chapter 9. Let us consider, however, predictions of the Rescorla-Wagner model for extinction. These predictions are illustrated in the right-hand panel of Figure 4.16. If a CS has acquired excitatory properties (see CS+ in Figure 4.16), there will be an over-expectation of the US the first time the CS+ is presented by itself in extinction. With continued CS-alone trials, the expectation elicited by the CS+ will be gradually aligned with the absence of the US by gradual reduction of the associative value of the CS+ to zero.

The Rescorla-Wagner model predicts an analogous scenario for extinction of conditioned inhibition. At the start of extinction, the CS– has negative associative value. This may be thought of as creating an underprediction of the US: the organism predicts less than the zero US that occurs on extinction trials. To align expectations with the absence of the US, the negative associative value of the CS– is gradually lost and the CS– ends up with zero associative strength.

Problems with the Rescorla-Wagner Model

The Rescorla-Wagner model stimulated a great deal of research and led to the discovery of many new and important phenomena in classical conditioning (Siegel & Allan, 1996). Not unexpectedly, however, the model has also encountered a growing number of difficulties (see Miller, Barnet, & Grahame, 1995).

One of the difficulties with the model that became evident early on is that its analysis of the extinction of conditioned inhibition is not correct. As indicated in Figure 4.16, the model predicts that repeated presentations of a conditioned inhibitor (CS–) by itself will lead to loss of conditioned inhibition. However, this does not occur (Zimmer-Hart & Rescorla, 1974; Witcher & Ayres, 1984). In fact, some investigators have found that repeated nonreinforcement of a CS– can enhance its conditioned inhibitory properties (e.g., DeVito & Fowler, 1987; Hallam, Grahame, Harris, & Miller, 1992). Curiously, an effective procedure for reducing the conditioned inhibitory properties of a CS– does not involve presenting the CS– at all. Rather, it involves extinguishing the excitatory properties of the CS+ with which the CS– was presented during inhibitory training (Best et al., 1985; Lysle & Fowler, 1985). (For a more complete discussion of procedures for extinguishing conditioned inhibition, see Fowler, Lysle, & DeVito., 1991.)

Another difficulty is that the Rescorla-Wagner model views extinction as the reverse of acquisition, or the return of the associative value of a CS to zero. However, as I will discuss in Chapter 9, a growing body of evidence indicates that extinction should not be viewed as simply the reverse of acquisition. Rather extinction appears to involve the learning of a new relationship between the CS and the US (namely that the US no longer follows the CS).

Another puzzling finding that has been difficult to incorporate into the Rescorla-Wagner model is that under certain conditions, the same CS may have both excitatory and inhibitory properties (Barnet & Miller, 1996; Matzel, Gladstein, & Miller, 1988; McNish, Betts, Brandon, & Wagner, 1997; Robbins, 1990; Tait & Saladin, 1986; Williams & Overmier, 1988). The Rescorla-Wagner model allows for conditioned stimuli to have only one associative value at a given time. That value can be excitatory or inhibitory, but not both.

The Rescorla-Wagner model also has difficulty explaining some unusual findings obtained in taste and odor aversion learning. These experiments employed a two-phase procedure very similar to the blocking design (Figure 4.13). In Phase 1, laboratory rats received one CS (taste or odor) paired with illness to condition an aversion to that stimulus. In Phase 2, this previously-conditioned stimulus was presented simultaneously with a new stimulus, and the compound was paired with illness. The CS added in Phase 2 was a novel odor for the taste-conditioned subjects and a novel taste for the odor-conditioned subjects. Thus, Phase 2 involved conditioning two CSs presented together, one component of which had been previously conditioned. Based on the blocking effect, one would expect that the presence of the previously-conditioned CS would interfere with the conditioning of the CS that was added in Phase 2. However, just the opposite result has been found: an **augmentation**, or **contra-blocking**, effect (Batson & Batsell, 2000; Batsell, Paschall, Gleason, & Batson, 2001; see also Batsell & Paschall, 2008). Instead of disrupting conditioning of the added CS in Phase 2, the previously conditioned stimulus augmented, or facilitated, the conditioning of the added CS. The augmentation, or contra-blocking, effect is one of a growing list of phenomena in which the presence of one stimulus facilitates responding to another simultaneously present CS, probably through a within-compound association between the two cues.

Other Models of Classical Conditioning

Devising a comprehensive theory of classical conditioning is a formidable challenge. Given the nearly 100 years of research on classical conditioning, a comprehensive theory must account for many diverse findings. No theory available today has been entirely successful in accomplishing that. Nevertheless, interesting new ideas about classical conditioning continue to be proposed and examined. Some of these proposals supplement the Rescorla-Wagner model. Others are incompatible with the Rescorla-Wagner model and move the theoretical debate in dramatically new directions.

Attentional Models of Conditioning

In the Rescorla-Wagner model, how much is learned on a conditioning trial depends on the effectiveness of the US. North American psychologists have favored theories of learning that focus on changes in US effectiveness. In contrast, British psychologists have approached phenomena, such as the blocking effect, by postulating changes in how well the CS commands the participant's attention. The general assumption is that for conditioning to occur, participants have to pay attention to the CS. Procedures that disrupt attention to the CS are expected to also disrupt learning (Mackintosh, 1975; McLaren & Mackintosh, 2000; Pearce & Hall, 1980).

Attentional theories differ in their assumptions about what determines the salience or noticeability of the CS on a given trial. Pearce and Hall (1980), for example, assume that the amount of attention an animal devotes to the CS on a given trial is determined by how surprising the US was on the preceding trial (see also Hall, Kaye, & Pearce, 1985; McLaren & Mackintosh, 2000).

N. J. Mackintosh

Animals have a lot to learn if the US was surprising to them on the preceding trial. Therefore, under these conditions they pay closer attention to that CS on the next trial. In contrast, if a CS was followed by an expected US, the participants pay less attention to that CS on the next trial. An expected US is assumed to decrease the salience or attention commanded by the CS.

An important feature of attentional theories is that they assume that the level of surprise of the US on a given trial alters the degree of attention commanded by the CS on future trials. For example, if Trial 10 ends in a surprising US, that will increase attention to the CS on Trial 11. Thus, US surprise is assumed to have only a *prospective*, or *proactive*, influence on attention and conditioning. This is an important contrast to US-reduction models like the Rescorla-Wagner model, in which the level of surprise of the US on a given trial determines what is learned on that same trial.

The assumption that the US on a given trial influences what is learned on the next trial has permitted attentional models to explain certain findings (e.g., Mackintosh, Bygrave, & Picton, 1977). However, that assumption has made it difficult for the models to explain other results. In particular, the models cannot explain blocking that occurs on the first trial of Phase 2 of the blocking experiment (e.g., Azorlosa & Cicala, 1986; Balaz, Kasprow, & Miller, 1982; Dickinson, Nicholas, & Mackintosh, 1983; Gillan & Domjan, 1977). The presence of the previously-conditioned CS_A in Phase 2 makes the US unsurprising, but that reduces attention to CS_B only on the second and subsequent trials of Phase 2. Thus, CS_B should command full attention on the first trial of Phase 2, and learning about CS_B should proceed normally on Trial 1. However, that does not occur. The conditioning of CS_B can be blocked by CS_A even on the first trial of Phase 2. (For a recent powerful attentional theory of learned performance, see Schmajuk & Larrauri, 2006. For an empirical study of the role of attention in learning with measures of eyetracking, see Kruschke, Kappenman, & Hetrick, 2005.)

Temporal Factors and Conditioned Responding

Neither the Rescorla-Wagner model nor CS modification models were designed to explain the effects of time in conditioning. However, time is obviously a critical factor. One important temporal variable is the CS-US interval. As I noted in Chapter 3, in many learning situations conditioned responding is inversely related to the CS-US interval or CS duration. Beyond an optimal point, procedures with longer CS-US intervals produce less responding (see Figure 3.7). This relation appears to be a characteristic primarily of responses closely related to the US (such as focal search). If behaviors that are ordinarily farther removed from the US are measured (such as general search), responding is greater with procedures that involve longer CS-US intervals (see Figure 4.11). Both types of findings illustrate that the duration of the CS is an important factor in conditioning.

The generally accepted view now is that in a Pavlovian procedure, participants learn not only that a CS is paired with a US, but when that US will occur (e.g., Balsam, Drew, & Yang, 2001; Balsam & Gallistel, in press; Ohyama & Mauk, 2001). Williams et al. (2008), for example, concluded on the basis of their results that learning *when* the US occurs trumps learning *whether* it occurs.

P. D. Balsam

The idea that participants learn about the point in time when the US occurs is called *temporal coding*. The *temporal coding hypothesis* states that participants learn when the US occurs in relation to a CS and use this information in blocking, second-order conditioning, and other paradigms in which what is learned in one phase of training influences what is learned in a subsequent phase. Numerous studies have upheld interesting predictions of the temporal coding hypothesis (e.g., Amundson & Miller, 2008; Barnet, Cole, & Miller, 1997; Brown, Hemmes, & de Vaca, 1997; Cole, Barnet, & Miller, 1995; Savastano & Miller, 1998).

Another important temporal variable is the interval between successive trials. Generally, more conditioned responding is observed with procedures in which trials are spaced farther apart (e.g., Sunsay & Bouton, 2008). In addition, the intertrial interval and the CS duration (or CS-US interval) sometimes act in combination to determine responding. Numerous studies have shown that the critical factor is the relative duration of these two temporal intervals rather than the absolute value of either one by itself (Gibbon & Balsam, 1981; Gallistel & Gibbon, 2000). A particularly clear example of this relationship was reported by Holland (2000).

Courtesy of J. Gibbon

J. Gibbon

Holland's experiment was conducted with laboratory rats. Food was presented periodically in a cup as the US, and presentations of the food were signaled by a CS that was white noise. Initially the rats only went to the food cup when the food was delivered. However, as conditioning proceeded, they started going to the food cup as soon as they heard the noise CS. Thus, nosing of the food cup served as the anticipatory CR. Each group was conditioned with one of two CS durations, either 10 seconds or 20 seconds, and one of six intertrial intervals (ranging from 15 seconds to 960 seconds). Each procedure could be characterized in terms of the ratio of the intertrial interval (I) and the CS duration, which Holland called the trial duration (T). The results of the experiment are summarized in Figure 4.17. Time spent nosing the food cup during the CS is shown as a function of the relative value of the intertrial interval (I) and the trial duration (T) for each group. Notice that conditioned responding was directly related to the I/T ratio. At each I/T ratio, the groups that received the 10 second CS responded similarly to those that received the 20 second CS. (For other studies of the role of the I/T ratio in conditioning, see Balsam, Fairhurst, & Gallistel, 2006; Burns & Domjan, 2001; Kirkpatrick & Church, 2000; Lattal, 1999.)

Courtesy of M. Burns

M. Burns

Various interpretations have been offered for why conditioned responding is so strongly determined by the I/T ratio. An early explanation, *the relative-waiting-time hypothesis* assumes that a CS is informative about the occurrence of the US only if one has to spend less time waiting for the US when the CS is present than in the experimental situation irrespective of the CS (Jenkins, Barnes, & Barrera, 1981; see also scalar expectancy theory, Gibbon & Balsam 1981). With a low I/T ratio, the CS waiting time is similar to the context waiting time. In this case, the CS provides little new information about when the US will occur, and not much conditioned responding will develop. In contrast, with a high I/T ratio, the CS waiting time is much shorter than the context waiting time. This makes the CS highly informative about when the US will occur, and conditioned responding will be more vigorous.

These ideas have been elaborated in a comprehensive theory of temporal factors and conditioning called *rate estimation theory* (Gallistel & Gibbon,

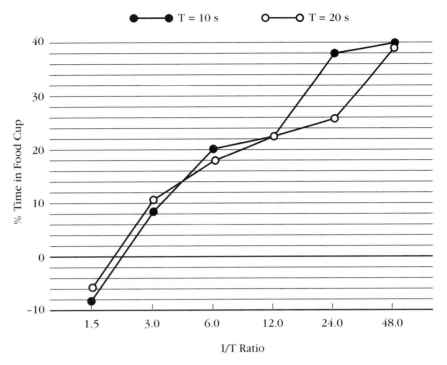

FIGURE **4.17**

Percent time rats spent nosing the food cup during an auditory CS in conditioning
with either a 10 second or a 20 second trial duration (T) and various intertrial intervals
(I) that created I/T ratios ranging from 1.5 to 48.0. Data are shown in relation to responding
during baseline periods when the CS was absent. (From "Trial and Intertribal Durations in
Appetitive Conditioning in Rats," by P. C. Holland, 2000, *Animal Learning & Behavior,
Vol. 28,* Figure 2, p. 125. Copyright 2000 Psychonomic Society, Inc. Reprinted with
permission.)

2000). Rate estimation theory (RET) has been rather controversial because it
is a nonassociative theory. It attempts to explain all conditioning phenomena
without relying on the idea that an association becomes established between a
CS and a US. Rather, according to rate estimation theory, conditioned responding reflects the participant's estimates of the rate of US presentations
during the CS and the rate of US presentations in the absence of the CS.

Rate estimation theory can be debated on both formal and empirical
grounds. Formally it ignores all of the neurophysiological data on associative
learning. It also imposes an unrealistic computational burden for animals in
complex natural environments. Estimating rates of US presentations during
and between CSs may be feasible in simple laboratory situations that involve
repetitions of one or two CSs and one US. But, outside the laboratory human
and nonhuman animals have to cope with numerous CSs and USs, and keeping track of all of those reinforcement rates would be a far greater computational burden than relying on associations. Empirically, rate estimation theory
has generated some predictions that have been confirmed (e.g., Gottlieb,
2008). But, rate estimation theory is inconsistent with a growing body of

experimental literature (e.g., Domjan, 2003; Gottlieb, 2004; Sunsay & Bouton, 2008; Williams et al., 2008).

The Comparator Hypothesis

Courtesy of R. R. Miller

R. R. Miller

The relative-waiting-time hypothesis and related theories were developed to explain the effects of temporal factors in excitatory conditioning. One of their important contributions was to emphasize that conditioned responding depends not only on what happens during the CS, but also on what happens in other aspects of the experimental situation. The idea that both of these factors influence learned performance is also central to the **comparator hypothesis** and its successors developed by Ralph R. Miller and his collaborators (Denniston, Savastano, & Miller, 2001; Miller & Matzel, 1988; Stout & Miller, 2007).

The comparator hypothesis was motivated by an interesting set of findings known as *revaluation effects*. Consider, for example, the blocking phenomenon (see Figure 4.13). Participants first receive a phase of training in which CS_A is paired with the US. CS_A is then presented simultaneously with CS_B and this stimulus compound is paired with the US. Subsequent tests of CS_B by itself show little responding to CS_B. As I explained, the Rescorla-Wagner model interprets the blocking effect as a failure of learning to CS_B. The presence of CS_A blocks the conditioning of CS_B.

The comparator hypothesis takes a different approach. It assumes that what is blocked is responding to CS_B. If that is true, then responding to CS_B should become evident if the block is removed somehow. How might that be accomplished? As it turns out, one way to remove the block to CS_B is to eliminate responding to CS_A by presenting it repeatedly without the US. A number of studies have shown that such extinction of CS_A following the blocking procedure unmasks conditioned responding to CS_B (e.g., Blaisdell, Gunther, & Miller, 1999). This is called a *revaluation effect* because it involves changing the conditioned value of a stimulus (CS_A) that was present during the training of the target stimulus CS_B. The unmasking of responding to CS_B shows that blocking did not prevent the conditioning of CS_B but disrupted the performance of the response to CS_B.

Inspired by revaluation effects, the comparator hypothesis is a theory of performance rather than learning. It assumes that conditioned responding depends not only on associations between a target CS and the US, but also on associations that may be learned between the US and other stimuli that are present when the target CS is being conditioned. These other stimuli are called the *comparator* cues and can include the experimental context. In the blocking experiment, the target stimulus is CS_B and the comparator cue that is present during the conditioning of this target is CS_A.

Another key assumption of the comparator hypothesis is that it only allows for the formation of excitatory associations with the US. Whether conditioned responding reflects excitation or inhibition is assumed to be determined by the relative strengths of excitation conditioned to the target CS as compared to the excitatory value of the comparator stimuli that were present with the target CS during training.

The comparator process is represented by the balance in Figure 4.18. As Figure 4.18 illustrates, a comparison is made between the excitatory value of

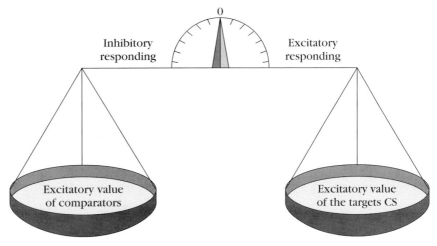

FIGURE **4.18**

Illustration of the comparator hypothesis. Whether the target CS elicits inhibitory or excitatory responding depends on whether the balance tips to the left or the right. If the excitatory value of the target CS is greater than the excitatory value of the comparator cues present during training of the target, the balance tips to the right, in favor of excitatory responding. As the associative value of the comparator stimuli increases, the balance becomes less favorable for excitatory responding and may tip to the left, in favor of inhibitory responding.

the target CS and the excitatory value of the comparator cues that are present during the training of the target CS. If the excitatory value of the target CS exceeds the excitatory value of the comparator cues, the balance of the comparison will be tipped in favor of excitatory responding to the target. As the excitatory value of the comparator cues becomes stronger, the balance of the comparison will become less favorable for excitatory responding. In fact, if the excitatory value of the comparator cues becomes sufficiently strong, the balance will be tipped in favor of inhibitory responding to the target CS.

Unlike the relative waiting-time hypothesis or RET, the comparator hypothesis emphasizes associations rather than time. It assumes that organisms learn three associations during the course of conditioning. These are illustrated in Figure 4.19. The first association (Link 1 in the Fig. 4.19) is between the target CS (X) and the US. The second association (Link 2) is between the target CS (X) and the comparator cues. Finally, there is an association between the comparator stimuli and the US (Link 3). With all three of these links in place, once the CS is presented, it activates the US representation directly (through Link 1) and indirectly (through Links 2 and 3). A comparison of the direct and indirect activations determines the degree of excitatory or inhibitory responding that occurs (for further elaboration, see Stout & Miller, 2007).

An important corollary to the comparator hypothesis is that the comparison of CS-US and comparator-US associations is made at the time of testing for conditioned responding. Because of this assumption, the comparator hypothesis makes the unusual prediction that extinction of comparator-US association following training of a target CS will enhance responding to that

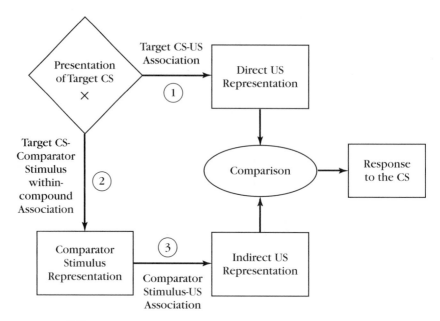

FIGURE **4.19**

The associative structure of the comparator hypothesis. The target CS is represented as X. Excitatory associations result in activation of the US representation, either directly by the target (Link 1) or indirectly (through Links 2 and 3). (From Friedman, et al. (1998). *Journal of Experimental Psychology: Animal Behavior Processes,* 2, p. 454. Copyright © 1998 by the American psychological Association. Reprinted with permission.)

target CS. It is through this mechanism that the comparator hypothesis is able to predict that extinction of CS_A will unmask conditioned responding to CS_B in the blocking procedure. (For additional examples of such revaluation effects, see Stout & Miller, 2007; Urcelay & Miller, 2008.)

The comparator hypothesis has also been tested in studies of conditioned inhibition. In a conditioned inhibition procedure (e.g., see Figure 4.16), the target is the CS–. During conditioned inhibition training, the CS– is presented together with a CS+ that provides the excitatory context for the learning of inhibition. Thus, the comparator stimulus is the CS+. Consider the comparator balance presented in Figure 4.18. According to this balance, inhibitory responding will occur to the target (CS–) because it has less excitatory power than its comparator (the CS+). Thus, the comparator hypothesis attributes inhibitory responding to situations in which the association of the target CS with the US is weaker than the association of the comparator cues with the US. Interestingly, conditioned inhibition is not viewed as the result of negative associative value, but as the result of the balance of the comparison tipping away from the target and in favor of the comparator stimulus. An interesting implication of the theory is that extinction of the comparator CS+ following inhibitory conditioning will reduce inhibitory responding. As I noted earlier in the discussion of the extinction of conditioned inhibition, this unusual prediction has been confirmed (Best et al., 1985; Lysle & Fowler, 1985).

Overview of Theoretical Alternatives

The Rescorla-Wagner model ushered in an exciting new era for learning theory that has generated many new ideas in the last 40 years. Although it failed to address a number of important issues, it has continued to be the standard against which subsequent theories are measured. Older attentional models attempted to address the same wide range of phenomena as the Rescorla-Wagner model, but also had difficulties. More recent models have emphasized different aspects of classical conditioning. The relative-waiting-time hypothesis addresses phenomena involving the temporal distribution of conditioned and unconditioned stimuli, although its successor (rate estimation theory) is much more far reaching. The comparator hypothesis is very ambitious and describes a wide range of effects involving interactions between various types of learning experiences, but it is a theory of performance rather than learning, and therefore it does not provide an explanation of how associations are acquired. As Stout and Miller (2007) pointed out, "acquired performance arises from an intricate interplay of many memories" (p. 779). Future theoretical developments will no doubt tell us more about how temporal factors determine learned behavior and how such behavior depends not only on associations of cues with USs, but with other stimuli that are encountered at the same time.

CONCLUDING COMMENTS

Initially, some psychologists regarded classical conditioning as a relatively simple and primitive type of learning that is involved in the regulation only of glandular and visceral responses, such as salivation. The establishment of CS-US associations was assumed to occur fairly automatically with the pairing of a CS and a US. Given the simple and automatic nature of the conditioning, it was not viewed as important in explaining the complexity and richness of human experience. Clearly, this view of classical conditioning is no longer tenable.

The research reviewed in Chapters 3 and 4 has shown that classical conditioning involves numerous complex processes and is involved in the control of a wide variety of responses, including emotional behavior and approach and withdrawal responses. The learning does not occur automatically with the pairing of a CS with a US. Rather, it depends on the organism's prior experience with each of these stimuli, the presence of other stimuli during the conditioning trial, and the extent to which the CS and US are relevant to each other. Furthermore, the processes of classical conditioning are not limited to CS-US pairings. Learned associations can occur between two biologically weak stimuli (sensory preconditioning), or in the absence of a US (higher-order conditioning).

Given these and other complexities of classical conditioning processes, it is a mistake to disregard classical conditioning in attempts to explain complex forms of behavior. The richness of classical conditioning mechanisms makes them relevant to the richness and complexity of human experience.

SAMPLE QUESTIONS

1. What, if any, limits are there on the kinds of stimuli that can serve as conditioned and unconditioned stimuli in Pavlovian conditioning?
2. How can Pavlovian conditioning mechanisms explain drug tolerance and what are some of the implications of these mechanisms?
3. How can you distinguish between S-R and S-S learning experimentally?
4. Describe the basic idea of the Rescorla-Wagner model. What aspect of the model allows it to explain the blocking effect and make some unusual predictions?
5. In what respects are attentional theories of learning different from other theories?
6. What is the basic assumption of rate estimation theory?
7. How does the comparator hypothesis explain the blocking effect?

KEY TERMS

augmentation Facilitation of the conditioning of a novel stimulus because of the presence of a previously conditioned stimulus. Also called the *contra-blocking effect.*

blocking effect Interference with the conditioning of a novel stimulus because of the presence of a previously conditioned stimulus.

comparator hypothesis The idea that conditioned responding depends on a comparison between the associative strength of the conditioned stimulus (CS) and the associative strength of other cues present during training of the target CS.

conditioned compensatory-response A conditioned response opposite in form to the reaction elicited by the US and which therefore compensates for this reaction.

contra-blocking effect Same as *augmentation.*

CS-preexposure effect Interference with conditioning produced by repeated exposures to the CS before the conditioning trials. Also called *latent-inhibition effect.*

drug tolerance Reduction in the effectiveness of a drug as a result of repeated use of the drug.

higher-order conditioning A procedure in which a previously conditioned stimulus (CS_1) is used to condition a new stimulus (CS_2).

homeostasis A concept introduced by Walter Cannon to refer to physiological mechanisms that serve to maintain critical aspects of physiology (such as blood sugar level and temperature) within acceptable limits. The homeostatic level is achieved by the operation of negative feedback and feed forward mechanisms that serve to counteract the effects of challenges to the homeostatic level.

latent-inhibition effect Same as *CS-preexposure effect.*

relative-waiting-time hypothesis The idea that conditioned responding depends on how long the organism has to wait for the US in the presence of the CS, as compared to how long the organism has to wait for the US in the experimental situation irrespective of the CS.

stimulus-response (S-R) learning The learning of an association between a stimulus and a response, with the result that the stimulus comes to elicit the response.

stimulus-stimulus (S-S) learning The learning of an association between two stimuli, with the result that exposure to one of the stimuli comes to activate a representation, or "mental image," of the other stimulus.

sensory preconditioning A procedure in which one biologically weak stimulus (CS_2) is repeatedly paired with another biologically weak stimulus (CS_1). Then, CS_1 is conditioned with an unconditioned stimulus. In a later test trial, CS_2 also will elicit the conditioned response, even though CS_2 was never directly paired with the US.

stimulus salience The significance or noticeability of a stimulus. Generally, conditioning proceeds more rapidly with more salient conditioned and unconditioned stimuli.

stimulus substitution The theoretical idea that as a result of classical conditioning participants come to respond to the CS in much the same way that they respond to the US.

US-preexposure effect Interference with conditioning produced by repeated exposures to the unconditioned stimulus before the conditioning trials.

US devaluation Reduction in the attractiveness of an unconditioned stimulus, usually achieved by aversion conditioning or satiation.

Instrumental Conditioning: Foundations

5

CHAPTER PREVIEW

This chapter begins our discussion of instrumental conditioning and goal-directed behavior. This is the type of conditioning that is involved in training a quarterback to throw a touchdown or a child to skip rope. In this type of conditioning, obtaining a goal or reinforcer depends on the prior occurrence of a designated response. I will first describe the origins of research on instrumental conditioning and the investigative methods used in contemporary research. This discussion lays the groundwork for the following section in which the four basic types of instrumental conditioning procedures are described. I will conclude the chapter with a discussion of three fundamental elements of the instrumental conditioning paradigm: the instrumental response, the reinforcer or goal event, and the relation between the instrumental response and the goal event.

In the preceding chapters, I discussed various aspects of how responses are elicited by discrete stimuli. Studies of habituation, sensitization, and classical conditioning are all concerned with analyses of the mechanisms of elicited behavior. Because of this emphasis, the procedures used in experiments on habituation, sensitization, and classical conditioning do not require the participant to make a particular response to obtain food or other USs or CSs. Classical conditioning reflects how organisms adjust to events in their environment that they cannot directly control. In the present chapter, we turn to the analysis of learning situations in which the stimuli an organism encounters are a direct result of its behavior. Such behavior is commonly referred to as *goal-directed* or *instrumental*, because responding is necessary to produce a desired environmental outcome.

By studying hard, a student can earn a better grade in a class; by turning the car key in the ignition, a driver can start the engine; by putting a coin in a vending machine, a child can obtain a piece of candy. In all these instances, some aspect of the individual's behavior is instrumental in producing a significant stimulus or outcome. Furthermore, the behavior occurs because similar actions produced the same type of outcome in the past. Students would not study if doing so did not yield better grades; drivers would not turn the ignition key if this did not start the engine; and children would not put coins in a vending machine if they did not get candy in return. Behavior that occurs because it was previously instrumental in producing certain consequences is called **instrumental behavior.**

The fact that the consequences of an action can determine whether you make that response again is obvious to everyone. If you happen to find a dollar bill when you glance down, you will keep looking at the ground as you walk. How such consequences influence future behavior is not so readily apparent. Many of the upcoming chapters of this book are devoted to the mechanisms responsible for the control of behavior by its consequences. In the present chapter, I will describe some of the history, basic techniques, procedures, and issues in the experimental analysis of instrumental, or goal-directed, behavior.

How might one investigate instrumental behavior? One way would be to go to the natural environment and look for examples. However, this approach is not likely to lead to definitive results because factors responsible for goal-directed behavior are difficult to isolate without experimental manipulation. Consider, for example, a dog sitting comfortably in its yard. When an intruder approaches, the dog starts to bark vigorously, and the intruder goes away. Because the dog's barking has a clear consequence (departure of the intruder), we may conclude that the dog barked in order to produce this consequence—that barking was goal directed. However, an equally likely possibility is that barking was elicited by the novelty of the intruder and persisted as long as the eliciting stimulus was present. The response consequence (departure of the intruder) may have been incidental to the dog's barking. Deciding between such alternatives is difficult without experimental manipulations of the relation between barking and its consequences. (For an experimental analysis of a similar situation in a fish species, see Losey & Sevenster, 1995.)

EARLY INVESTIGATIONS OF INSTRUMENTAL CONDITIONING

Laboratory and theoretical analyses of instrumental conditioning began in earnest with the work of the American psychologist E. L. Thorndike. Thorndike's original intent was to study animal intelligence (Thorndike, 1898, 1911; for more recent commentaries, see Catania, 1999; Dewsbury, 1998; Lattal, 1998). As I noted in Chapter 1, the publication of Darwin's theory of evolution stimulated people to speculate about the extent to which human intellectual capacities were present in animals. Thorndike pursued this question through empirical research. He devised a series of puzzle boxes for his experiments. His training procedure consisted of placing a hungry animal (cat, dog, or chicken) in the puzzle box with some food left outside in plain view of the animal. The task for the animal was to learn how to get out of the box and obtain the food.

Different puzzle boxes required different responses to get out. Some were easier than others. Figure 5.1 illustrates two of the easier puzzle boxes. In Box A, the required response was to pull a ring to release a latch that blocked the door on the outside. In Box I, the required response was to push down a lever, which released a latch. Initially, the subjects were slow to make the correct response, but with continued practice on the task, their latencies became shorter and shorter. Figure 5.2 shows the latencies of a cat to get out of Box A on successive trials. The cat took 160 sec to get out of Box A on the first trial. Its shortest latency later on was six seconds (Chance, 1999).

Thorndike's careful empirical approach was a significant advance in the study of animal intelligence. Another important contribution was Thorndike's strict avoidance of anthropomorphic interpretations of the behavior he observed. Although he titled his treatise *animal intelligence,* to Thorndike many aspects of behavior seemed rather unintelligent. He did not think that his subjects got faster in escaping from a puzzle box because they gained insight into the task or figured out how the release mechanism was designed.

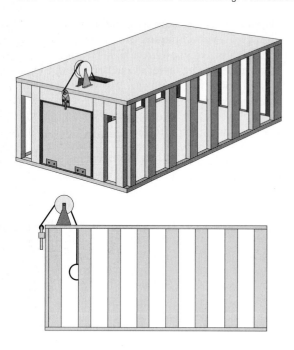

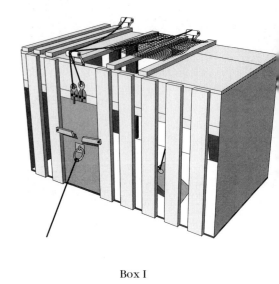

Box I

Box A

FIGURE **5.1**

Two of Thorndike's puzzle boxes, A and I. In Box A, the participant had to pull a loop to release the door. In Box I, pressing down on a lever released a latch on the other side. *Left:* From Chance, P. (1999). Thorndike's puzzle boxes and the origins of the experimental analysis of behavior. *Journal of the Experimental Analysis of Behaviour,* 72, 433–440. Copyright 1999 by the Society for the Experimental Analysis of Behaviour, Inc. Reprinted with permission. *Right:* Thorndike (1898) *Animal Intelligence Experimental Studies.*

Rather, he interpreted the results of his studies as reflecting the learning of an S-R association. When a cat was initially placed in a box, it displayed a variety of responses typical of a confined animal. Eventually, some of these responses resulted in opening the door. Thorndike believed that such successful escapes led to the learning of an association between the stimuli of being in the puzzle box and the escape response. As the association, or connection, between the box cues and the successful response became stronger, the animal came to make that response more quickly. The consequence of the successful response strengthened the association between the box stimuli and that response.

On the basis of his research, Thorndike formulated the **law of effect.** The law of effect states that if a response in the presence of a stimulus is followed by a *satisfying event,* the association between the stimulus (S) and the response (R) is strengthened. If the response is followed by an *annoying event,* the S-R association is weakened. It is important to stress here that, according to the law of effect, what is learned is an association between the response and the stimuli present at the time of the response. Notice that the conse-

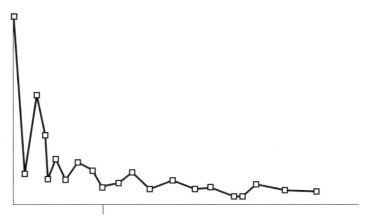

FIGURE **5.2**

Latencies to escape from Box A during successive trials. The longest latency was 160 seconds; the shortest was six seconds. (Notice that the axes are not labeled, as in Thorndike's original report.)

quence of the response is not one of the elements in the association. The satisfying or annoying consequence simply serves to strengthen or weaken the association between the preceding stimulus and response. Thorndike's law of effect involves *S-R learning*. This form of learning has remained of interest in the last hundred years since Thorndike's proposal and is currently entertained by contemporary neuroscientists as the basis for the compulsive nature of drug addiction (Everitt & Robbins, 2005).

BOX **5.1**

E.L. Thorndike: Biographical Sketch

Edward Lee Thorndike was born in 1874 and died in 1949. As an undergraduate at Wesleyan University, he became interested in the work of William James, who was then at Harvard. Thorndike himself entered Harvard as a graduate student in 1895. During his stay he began his research on instrumental behavior, at first using chicks. Since there was no laboratory space in the psychology department at the university, he set up his project in William James' cellar. Soon after that, he was offered a fellowship at Columbia University. This time, his laboratory was located in the attic of psychologist James Cattell.

Thorndike received his PhD from Columbia in 1898, for his work entitled "Animal Intelligence: An Experimental Analysis of Associative Processes in Animals." This included the famous puzzle-box experiments. After a short stint at Western Reserve University in Cleveland, Thorndike returned to Columbia, where he served as professor of educational psychology in the Teachers College for many years. Among other things, he worked to apply to children the principles of trial-and-error learning he had uncovered with animals. He also became interested in psychological testing and became a leader in this newly formed field. By the time of his retirement, he had written 507 scholarly works (without a computer word processor), including about 50 books (Cumming, 1999). Several years before his death, Thorndike returned to Harvard as the William James Lecturer: a fitting honor considering the origins of his interests in psychology.

MODERN APPROACHES TO THE STUDY OF INSTRUMENTAL CONDITIONING

Thorndike used fifteen different puzzle boxes in his investigations. Each box required different manipulations for the cat to get out. As more scientists became involved in studying instrumental learning, the range of tasks they used became smaller. A few of these became "standard" and have been used repeatedly to facilitate comparison of results obtained in different laboratories.

Discrete-Trial Procedures

Discrete-trial procedures are similar to the method Thorndike used in that each training trial ends with removal of the animal from the apparatus, and the instrumental response is performed only once during each trial. Discrete-trial investigations of instrumental behavior are often conducted in some type of maze. The use of mazes in investigations of learning was introduced at the turn of the twentieth century by the American psychologist W. S. Small (1899, 1900). Small was interested in studying rats and was encouraged to use a maze by an article he read in *Scientific American*, describing the complex system of underground burrows that kangaroo rats build in their natural habitat. Small reasoned that a maze would take advantage of the rats' "propensity for small winding passages."

Figure 5.3 shows two mazes frequently used in contemporary research. The runway, or straight-alley, maze contains a start box at one end and a goal box at the other. The rat is placed in the start box at the beginning of

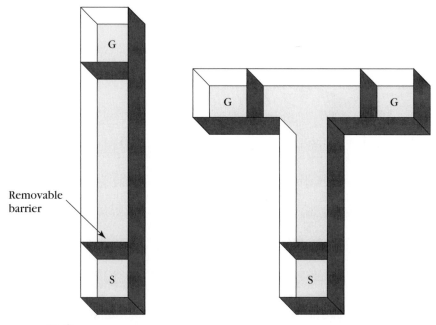

Removable barrier

FIGURE **5.3**

Top view of a runway and a T-maze. S is the start box; G is the goal box.

each trial. The movable barrier separating the start box from the main section of the runway is then lifted. The rat is allowed to make its way down the runway until it reaches the goal box, which usually contains a reinforcer, such as food or water.

Another maze that has been used in many experiments is the T maze, shown on the right in Figure 5.3. The T maze consists of a start box and alleys arranged in the shape of a T. A goal box is located at the end of each arm of the T. Because it has two choice arms, the T maze can be used to study more complex questions. For example, the two arms of the maze can be distinguished by lining the walls with either light or dark panels, and the experiment can be set up so that the light arm of the T maze is always the one that ends with a pellet of food. With this arrangement, one can study how subjects learn to use environmental cues to tell them which way to turn or which of two response alternatives to perform.

Behavior in a maze can be quantified by measuring how fast the animal gets from the start box to the goal box. This is called the **running speed.** The running speed typically increases with repeated training trials. Another common measure of behavior in runways is the **latency.** The latency of the running response is the time it takes the animal to leave the start box and begin moving down the alley. Typically, latencies become shorter as training progresses. In a T maze, one can also measure the percentage of correct choices that end with food.

Free-Operant Procedures

In a runway or a T maze, after reaching the goal box, the animal is removed from the apparatus for a while before being returned to the start box for its next trial. Thus, the animal has limited opportunities to respond, and those opportunities are scheduled by the experimenter. By contrast, **free-operant procedures** allow the animal to repeat the instrumental response without constraint over and over again. The free-operant method was invented by B. F. Skinner (1938) to study behavior in a more continuous manner than is possible with mazes.

Skinner (Figure 5.4) was interested in analyzing in the laboratory of a form of behavior that would be representative of all naturally occurring ongoing activity. However, he recognized that before behavior can be experimentally analyzed, a measurable unit of behavior must be defined. Casual observation suggests that ongoing behavior is continuous; one activity leads to another. Behavior does not fall neatly into units, as do molecules of a chemical solution. Skinner proposed the concept of the operant as a way of dividing behavior into meaningful measurable units.

Figure 5.5 shows a typical Skinner box used to study free-operant behavior in rats. (A Skinner box used to study pecking in pigeons is presented in Figure 1.7). The box is a small chamber that contains a lever that the rat can push down repeatedly. The chamber also has a mechanism that can deliver a reinforcer, such as food or water. In the simplest experiment, a hungry rat is placed in the chamber. The lever is electronically connected to the food-delivery system. When the rat depresses the lever, a pellet of food automatically falls into the food cup.

An **operant response,** such as the lever press, is defined in terms of the effect that it has on the environment. Activities that have the same environmental effect are considered to be instances of the same operant response. The critical thing is

Bettmann/CORBIS

FIGURE **5.4**

B. F. Skinner (1904–1990)

Photo Researchers, Inc.

FIGURE **5.5**

A Skinner box equipped with a response lever and a food-delivery device. Electronic equipment is used to program procedures and record responses automatically.

not the muscles involved in performing the behavior, but the way in which the behavior *operates* on the environment. For example, the lever-press operant is typically defined as sufficient depression of the lever to activate the recording sensor. The rat may press the lever with its right paw, its left paw, or its tail. These different muscle responses constitute the same operant if they all depress the lever the required amount. Various ways of pressing the lever are assumed to be functionally equivalent because they all have the same effect on the environment: namely, activation of the recording sensor.

We perform numerous operants during the course of our daily lives. If we are interested in opening a door, it does not matter whether we use our right hand or left hand to turn the door knob. The operational outcome (opening the door) is the critical measure of success. Similarly, in basketball or baseball, it's the operational outcome that counts—getting the ball in the basket or hitting the ball into the outfield—rather than the way the task is accomplished. With operational definition of behavioral success, one does not need judges to assess whether the behavior has been successfully accomplished. The environmental outcome keeps the score. If the ball went into the basket, that's all that counts. Whether it went in directly or bounced on the rim is irrelevant. This contrasts with figure skating, gymnastics, and ballroom dancing in which the way something is performed is just as important as is the environmental impact of the behavior. Getting a ball into the basket is an operant behavior. Performing a graceful dismount from the parallel bars is not. However, any response that is required to produce a desired consequence is an *instrumental response,* since it is "instrumental" in producing a particular outcome.

Magazine Training and Shaping

When children first attempt to toss a basketball in a basket, they are not very successful. Many attempts end with the ball bouncing off the backboard or not even landing near the basket. Similarly, a rat placed in a Skinner box will not press the lever that produces a pellet of food right away. Successful training of an operant or instrumental response often requires lots of practice and a carefully designed series of training steps that move the student from the status of a novice to that of an expert. This is clearly the case with something like championship figure skating that requires hours of daily practice under the careful supervision of an expert coach. Most parents do not spend a great deal of money hiring the right coach to teach a child basketball. However, even there, the child moves through a series of training steps that may start with a small ball and a Fisher Price® basketball set that is much lower than the standard and is easier to reach. The training basket is also adjustable so that it can be gradually raised as the child becomes more proficient.

There are also preliminary steps for establishing lever-press responding in a laboratory rat. First, the rat has to learn when food is available in the food cup. This involves classical conditioning: the sound of the food-delivery device is repeatedly paired with the delivery of a food pellet into the cup. The food-delivery device is called the *food magazine*. After enough pairings of the sound of the food magazine with food delivery, the sound comes to elicit a sign tracking response: the animal goes to the food cup and picks up the food pellet. This preliminary phase of conditioning is called **magazine training.**

After magazine training, the rat is ready to learn the required operant response. At this point food is given if the rat does anything remotely related to pressing the lever. For example, at first the rat may be given a food pellet each time it gets up on its hind legs anywhere in the experimental chamber. Once the rearing response has been established, the food pellet may be given only if the rat makes the rearing response over the response lever. Rearing in other parts of the chamber would no longer be reinforced. Once rearing over the lever has been established, the food pellet may be given only if the rat actually depresses the lever. Such a sequence of training steps is called **shaping.**

As the preceding examples show, the shaping of a new operant response requires training components or approximations to the final behavior. Whether you are trying to teach a child to throw a ball into a basket, or a rat to press a response lever, at first only crude approximations of the final performance are required for reinforcement. Once the child becomes proficient at throwing the ball into a basket placed at shoulder height, the height of the basket can be gradually raised. As the shaping process progresses, more and more is required, until the reinforcer is only given if the final target response is made.

Successful shaping of behavior involves three components. First, you have to clearly define the final response you wish for the subject to perform. Second, you have to clearly assess the starting level of performance, no matter how far it is from the final response you are interested in. Third, you have to divide the progression from the starting point to the final target response into appropriate training steps or successive approximations. The successive approximations are your training plan. The execution of the training plan involves two complementary tactics: *reinforcement of successive approximations* to the final behavior and *nonreinforcement of earlier response forms.*

Although the principles involved in shaping behavior are reasonably well understood, their application can be tricky. If the shaping steps are too far apart, or you spend too much time on one particular shaping step, progress may not be satisfactory. Sports coaches, piano teachers, driver's education instructors, and others involved in the training of instrumental behavior are all aware of how tricky it can be to design the most effective training steps or successive approximations. The same principles of shaping are involved in training a child to put on her socks or to drink from a cup without spilling, but the training in those cases is less formally organized. (For a study of shaping drug abstinence behavior in cocaine users, see Preston, Umbricht, Wong, & Epstein, 2001.)

Shaping and New Behavior

Shaping procedures are often used to generate new behavior, but exactly how new are those responses? Consider, for example, a rat's lever-press response. To press the bar, the rat has to approach the bar, stop in front of it, raise its front paws, and then bring the paws down on the bar with sufficient force to push it down. All of these response components are things the rat is likely to have done at one time or another in other situations (while exploring its cage, interacting with another rat, or handling pieces of food). In teaching the rat to press the bar, we are not teaching new response components. Rather, we are teaching the rat how to combine familiar responses into a new activity. Instrumental conditioning often involves the construction, or synthesis, of a new behavioral unit from preexisting response components that already occur in the subject's repertoire (Balsam, Deich, Ohyama, & Stokes, 1998; Reid, Chadwick, Dunham, & Miller, 2001; Schwartz, 1981).

Instrumental conditioning can also be used to produce responses unlike anything the subject ever did before. Consider, for example, throwing a football 60 yards down the field. It takes more than putting familiar behavioral components together to achieve such a feat. The force, speed, and coordination involved in throwing a football 60 yards is unlike anything an untrained individual might do. It is an entirely new response. Expert performance in sports, in playing a musical instrument, or in ballet all involves such novel response forms. Such novel responses are also created by shaping.

The creation of new responses by shaping depends on the inherent variability of behavior. If a particular shaping step requires a quarterback trainee to throw a football 30 yards, and he meets this criterion on most trials, this will not be achieved by a series of 30 yard throws. On average, the throws may be 30 yards, but from one attempt to the next, the trainee is likely to throw the ball 25, 32, 29, or 34 yards. Each throw is likely to be somewhat different. This variability permits the coach to set the next successive approximation at 34 yards. With that new target, the trainee will start to make longer throws, and the new distribution of responses will center around 34 yards. Each throw will again be different, but more of the throws will now be 34 yards and longer. The shift of the distribution to longer throws will permit the coach to again raise the response criterion, perhaps to 38 yards this time. With gradual iterations of this process, the trainee will make longer and longer throws, achieving distances that he would never perform otherwise. Thus, a shaping process takes advantage of the variability of behavior and thereby generates responses that are entirely new in the trainee's repertoire. That is how spectacular new feats of performance are learned in sports, ballet, or playing a musical instrument. (For laboratory studies of shaping, see Deich, Allan, & Zeigler, 1988; and Stokes, Mechner, & Balsam, 1999.)

Response Rate as a Measure of Operant Behavior

In contrast to discrete-trial techniques for studying instrumental behavior, free-operant methods permit continuous observation of behavior over long

Ryan Remiorz/AP Photo

FIGURE **5.6**

Shaping is required to learn special skills.

periods. With continuous opportunity to respond, the organism rather than the experimenter determines the frequency of its instrumental response. Hence, free-operant techniques provide a special opportunity to observe changes in the likelihood of behavior over time.

How might we take advantage of this opportunity and measure the probability of an operant response? Measures of response latency and speed that are commonly used in discrete-trial procedures do not characterize the likelihood of repetitions of a response. Skinner proposed that the *rate of occurrence* of operant behavior (e.g., frequency of the response per minute) be used as a measure of response probability. Highly likely responses occur frequently and have a high rate. In contrast, unlikely responses occur seldomly and have a low rate. Response rate has become the primary measure in studies that employ free-operant procedures.

INSTRUMENTAL CONDITIONING PROCEDURES

In all instrumental conditioning situations, the participant makes a response and thereby produces an outcome. Paying the boy next door for mowing the lawn, yelling at a cat for getting on the kitchen counter, closing a window to prevent the rain from coming in, and revoking a teenager's driving privileges for staying out late are all forms of instrumental conditioning. Two of these examples involve pleasant events (getting paid, driving a car), whereas the other two involve unpleasant stimuli (the sound of yelling and rain coming in the window). A pleasant outcome is technically called an **appetitive stimulus.** An unpleasant outcome is technically called an **aversive stimulus.** The instrumental response may produce the stimulus, as when mowing the lawn results in getting paid. Alternatively, the instrumental response may turn off or eliminate a stimulus, as in closing a window to stop the incoming rain. Whether the result of a conditioning procedure is an increase or a decrease in the rate of responding depends both on the nature of the outcome and whether the response produces or eliminates the stimulus. The primary instrumental conditioning procedures are described in Table 5.1.

TABLE **5.1**
Types of Instrumental Conditioning Procedures

Name of Procedure	Response-Outcome Contingency	Result of Procedure
Positive Reinforcement	*Positive:* Response produces an appetitive stimulus	*Reinforcement* or increase in response rate
Punishment (Positive Punishment)	*Positive:* Response produces an aversive stimulus	*Punishment* or decrease in response rate
Negative Reinforcement (Escape or Avoidance)	*Negative:* Response eliminates or prevents the occurrence of an aversive stimulus	*Reinforcement* or increase in response rate
Omission Training (DRO)	*Negative:* Response eliminates or prevents the occurrence of an appetitive stimulus	*Punishment* or decrease in response rate

Positive Reinforcement

A father gives his daughter a cookie when she puts her toys away; a teacher praises a student when the student hands in a good report; an employee receives a bonus check when he performs well on the job. These are all examples of **positive reinforcement.** Positive reinforcement is a procedure in which the instrumental response produces an appetitive stimulus. If the response occurs, the appetitive stimulus is presented; if the response does not occur, the appetitive stimulus is not presented. Thus, there is a positive contingency between the instrumental response and the appetitive stimulus. Positive reinforcement procedures produce an increase in the rate of responding. Requiring a hungry rat to press a response lever to obtain a food pellet is a common laboratory example of positive reinforcement.

Punishment

A mother reprimands her child for running into the street; your boss criticizes you for being late to a meeting; a teacher gives you a failing grade for answering too many test questions incorrectly. These are examples of **punishment.** In a punishment procedure, the instrumental response produces an unpleasant, or aversive, stimulus. There is a positive contingency between the instrumental response and the stimulus outcome (the response produces the outcome), but the outcome is an aversive stimulus. Effective punishment procedures produce a decline in the instrumental response.

Negative Reinforcement

Opening an umbrella to stop the rain from getting you wet, rolling up your car window to reduce the wind that is blowing in, and putting on your sunglasses to shield you from the brightness of the summer sun are all examples of **negative reinforcement.** In all of these cases, the instrumental response turns off an aversive stimulus. Hence there is a *negative contingency* between the instrumental response and the aversive stimulus. Negative reinforcement procedures increase the instrumental response. You are more likely to open an umbrella if it stops you from getting wet when it is raining.

People tend to confuse negative reinforcement and punishment. An aversive stimulus is used in both procedures. However, the relation of the instrumental response to the aversive stimulus is drastically different. In punishment procedures, the instrumental response produces the aversive stimulus, and there is a positive contingency between the instrumental response and the aversive stimulus. By contrast, in negative reinforcement, the response terminates the aversive stimulus and there is a negative response-outcome contingency. This difference in the contingencies produces very different outcomes. The instrumental response is decreased by punishment and increased by negative reinforcement.

Omission Training

Omission training is being used when a child is told to go to her room after doing something bad. The child does not receive an aversive stimulus when she is told to go to her room. There is nothing aversive about the child's room. Rather, by sending the child to the room, the parent is withdrawing sources of positive reinforcement, such as playing with friends or watching television. Suspending someone's driver's license for drunken driving also constitutes **omission training** (withdrawal of the pleasure and privilege of driving). In omission training, the instrumental response prevents the delivery of a pleasant or appetitive stimulus. Thus, this type of procedure also involves a negative contingency between the response and an environmental event. Omission training is often a preferred method of discouraging human behavior because, unlike punishment, it does not involve delivering an aversive stimulus. (For a recent laboratory study of omission training, see Sanabria, Sitomer, & Killeen, 2006.)

Omission-training procedures are also called **differential reinforcement of other behavior (DRO)**. This term highlights the fact that in omission training, the individual periodically receives the appetitive stimulus provided he is engaged in behavior other than the response specified by the procedure. Making the target response results in omission of the reward that would have been delivered had the individual performed some *other* behavior. Thus, omission training involves the reinforcement of *other* behavior.

BOX **5.2**

Differential Reinforcement of Other Behavior as Treatment for Self-Injurious Behavior and Other Behavior Problems

Self-injurious behavior is a problematic habit that is evident in some individuals with developmental disabilities. Bridget was a 50-year-old woman with profound mental retardation whose self-injurious behavior was hitting her body and head, and banging her head against furniture, walls, and floors. Preliminary assessments indicated that her head banging was maintained by the attention she received from others when she banged her head against a hard surface. To discourage the self-injurious behavior, an omission training procedure, or DRO, was put into place (Lindberg, Iwata, Kahng, DeLeon, 1999). The training procedures were implemented in 15 minute sessions. During the omission training phase, Bridget was ignored when she banged her head against a hard surface but received attention periodically if she was not head bang-

ing. The attention consisted of the therapist talking to Bridget for three to five seconds and occasionally stroking her arm or back.

The results of the study are presented in Figure 5.7. During the first 19 sessions, when Bridget received attention for her self-injurious behavior, the rate of head banging fluctuated around six responses per minute. The first phase of DRO training (sessions 20–24) resulted in a rapid decline in head banging. The self-injurious behavior returned during sessions 25–31, when the baseline condition was reintroduced. DRO training was resumed in session 32 and remained in effect for the remainder of the study. The significant outcome of the study was that self-injurious behavior decreased significantly during the DRO sessions.

The study with Bridget illustrates several behavioral principles

that are also evident in other situations. One general principle is that attention is a very powerful reinforcer for human behavior. People do all sorts of things to attract attention. As with Bridget, even responses that are injurious to the individual can develop if these responses are positively reinforced by attention. Unfortunately, some responses are difficult to ignore, but in attending to them, one may be providing positive reinforcement. A child misbehaving in a store or restaurant is difficult to ignore, but paying attention to the child may serve to encourage the misbehavior. Many forms of disruptive behavior develop because of the attention that such behavior attracts. As with Bridget, the best therapy is to ignore the disruptive behavior and pay attention when the child is doing something else. However, deliberately reinforcing other behavior is

(continued)

BOX **5.2** (continued)

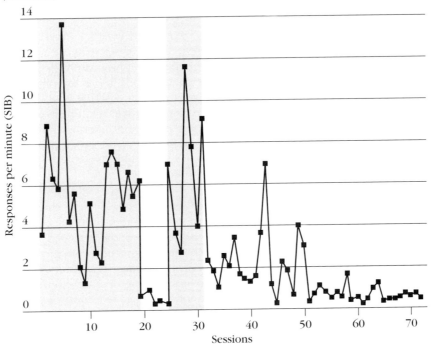

FIGURE **5.7**

Rate of Bridget's self-injurious behavior during baseline sessions (1–19, and 25–31) and during sessions in which a DRO contingency was in effect (20–24, and 32–72). (From Lindberg et al., 1999.)

not easy to do and requires conscious effort and discipline on the part of the parent or teacher.

No one questions the need for such conscious effort in training complex responses in animals. As Amy Sutherland (2008) pointed out, animal "trainers did not get a sea lion to salute by nagging. Nor did they teach a baboon to flip by carping, nor an elephant to paint by pointing out everything the elephant did wrong.... Progressive animal trainers reward the behavior they want and, equally importantly, ignore the behavior they don't" (p. 59). In her engaging book, *What Shamu taught me about life,* *love, and marriage,* Amy Sutherland went on to argue that one can profitably use the same principles to achieve better results with one's spouse by not nagging them about leaving their dirty socks on the floor but by providing attention and social reinforcement for responses other than the offending habits.

FUNDAMENTAL ELEMENTS OF INSTRUMENTAL CONDITIONING

As we will see in the coming chapters, analysis of instrumental conditioning involves numerous factors and variables. However, the essence of instrumental behavior is that it is controlled by its consequences. Thus, instrumental conditioning fundamentally involves three elements: the instrumental response, the outcome of the response (the reinforcer), and the relation or contingency between the response and the outcome. In the remainder of this chapter, I will describe how each of these elements influences the course of instrumental conditioning.

The Instrumental Response

The outcome of instrumental conditioning procedures depends in part on the nature of the response being conditioned. Some responses are more easily modified than others. In Chapter 10 I will describe how the nature of the response influences the outcome of negative reinforcement (**avoidance**) and punishment procedures. The present section describes how the nature of the response determines the results of positive reinforcement procedures.

Behavioral Variability versus Stereotypy

Thorndike described instrumental behavior as involving the *stamping in* of an S-R association. Skinner wrote about behavior being *reinforced*, or strengthened. Both of these pioneers emphasized that reinforcement increases the likelihood that the instrumental response will be repeated in the future. This emphasis encouraged the belief that instrumental conditioning produces repetitions of the same response, that it produces uniformity or stereotypy in behavior. Increasingly stereotyped responding does develop if that is allowed or required by the instrumental conditioning procedure (e.g., Pisacreta, 1982; Schwartz, 1980, 1985, 1988). However, that does not mean that instrumental conditioning cannot also be used to produce creative or variable responses.

Courtesy of A. Neuringer

A. Neuringer

We are accustomed to thinking about the requirement for reinforcement being an observable action, such as movement of an individual's leg, torso, or hand. Interestingly, however, the criteria for reinforcement can also be defined in terms of more abstract dimensions of behavior, such as its novelty. The behavior required for reinforcement can be defined as doing something new, something unlike what the participant did on the preceding four or five trials (Neuringer, 2004). To satisfy this requirement, the participant has to perform differently on each trial. In such a procedure, *response variability* is the basis for instrumental reinforcement.

In a classic study of the instrumental conditioning of response variability (Page & Neuringer, 1985), pigeons had to peck two response keys eight times to obtain food. The eight pecks could be distributed between the two keys in any manner. All the pecks could be on the left or the right key, or the pigeons could alternate between the keys in various ways (e.g., two pecks on the left, followed by one on the right, one on the left, three on the right, and one on the left). However, to obtain food on a given trial, the sequence of left-right pecks had to be different from the pattern of left-right pecks the bird made on the preceding 50 trials. Thus, the pigeons had to generate novel patterns of left-right pecks and not repeat any pattern for 50 trials. In a control condition, food was provided at the same frequency for eight pecks, but now the sequence of right and left pecks did not matter. The pigeons did not have to generate novel response sequences in the control condition.

Sample results of the experiment are presented in Figure 5.8 in terms of the percentage of response sequences performed during each session that was different from each other. Results for the first and last five days are presented separately for each group. About 50% of the response sequences performed

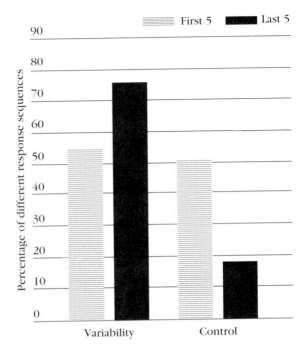

FIGURE **5.8**

Percentage of novel left-right response sequences pigeons performed when variability in response sequences was required for food reinforcement (left) and when food reinforcement was provided regardless of the response sequence performed (right). Data are shown for the first five and last five sessions of each procedure. (From "Variability as an Operant," by S. Page and A. Neuringer, 1985, *Journal of Experimental Psychology: Animal Behavior Process*, 11, 249–452. Copyright © 1985 by the American Psychological Association. Reprinted with permission.)

were different from each other during the first five sessions for each group. When the instrumental conditioning procedure required response variability, variability in responding increased to about 75% by the last five days of training. By contrast, in the control condition, when the pigeons were reinforced regardless of the sequence of left-right pecks they made, variability in performed sequences dropped to less than 20% by the last five days of the experiment.

This study illustrates two interesting facts about instrumental conditioning. First, it shows that variability in responding can be increased by reinforcement. Thus, response variability can be established as an operant (see also Machado, 1989, 1992; Maes, 2003; Morgan & Neuringer, 1990; Wagner & Neuringer, 2006). The results also show that in the absence of explicit reinforcement of variability, responding becomes more stereotyped with continued instrumental conditioning. Pigeons in the control condition decreased the range of different response sequences they performed as training progressed. Thus, Thorndike and Skinner were correct in saying that responding becomes more stereotyped with continued instrumental conditioning. However, this is not an inevitable result and only occurs if there is no requirement to vary the behavior from trial to trial.

BOX **5.3**

Detrimental Effects of Reward: More Myth than Reality

Reinforcement procedures have become commonplace in educational settings as a way to encourage students to read and do their assignments. However, some have been concerned that reinforcement may actually undermine a child's intrinsic interest and willingness to perform a task once the reinforcement procedure is removed. Similar concerns have been expressed about possible detrimental effects of reinforcement on creativity or originality. Extensive research on these questions has produced inconsistent results. However, more recent meta-analyses of the results of numerous studies indicated that under most circumstances, reinforcement does not reduce intrinsic motivation or performance (Cameron, Banko, & Pierce, 2001; Cameron & Pierce, 1994). Research with children also indicated that reinforcement makes children respond with less originality only under limited circumstances (see Eisenberger & Cameron, 1996; Eisenberger & Shanock, 2003). As in experiments with pigeons and laboratory rats, reinforcement can increase or decrease originality, depending on the criterion for reinforcement. If highly original responding is required to obtain reinforcement, originality increases, provided that the reinforcer is not so salient as to distract the participant from the task. (For a more general discussion of creativity, see Stokes, 2006.)

Relevance or Belongingness in Instrumental Conditioning

As the preceding section showed, instrumental conditioning can act on response components or on abstract dimensions of behavior, such as variability. How far do these principles extend? Are there any limits on the types of new behavioral units or response dimensions that may be modified by instrumental conditioning? A growing body of evidence indicates that there are important limitations.

In Chapter 4, I described how classical conditioning occurs at different rates depending on which combination of conditioned and unconditioned stimulus is used. Rats readily learn to associate tastes with sickness, for example, whereas associations between tastes and shock are not so easily learned. For conditioning to occur rapidly, the CS has to belong with the US, or be relevant to it. Analogous belongingness and relevance relations occur in instrumental conditioning. As Jozefowiez and Staddon (2008) recently commented, "a behavior cannot be reinforced by a reinforcer if it is not naturally linked to that reinforcer in the repertoire of the animal" (p. 78).

This type of natural linkage was first observed by Thorndike. In many of his puzzle-box experiments, the cat had to manipulate a latch or string to escape from the box. However, Thorndike also tried to get cats to scratch or yawn to be let out of a puzzle box. The cats could learn to make these responses. However, interestingly, the form of the responses changed as training proceeded. At first, the cat would scratch itself vigorously to be let out of the box. On later trials, it would only make *aborted* scratching movements. It might put its leg to its body but would not make a true scratch response. Similar results were obtained in attempts to condition yawning. As training progressed, the animal would open its mouth, but it would not give a bona fide yawn.

Thorndike used the term **belongingness** to explain the failures to train scratching and yawning. According to this concept, certain responses naturally *belong with* the reinforcer because of the animal's evolutionary history. Operating a latch and pulling a string are manipulatory responses that are naturally related to release from confinement. By contrast, scratching and yawning characteristically do not help animals escape from confinement and therefore do not *belong with* release from a puzzle box.

The concept of belongingness in instrumental conditioning is nicely illustrated by a more recent study involving a small fish species, the three-spined stickleback (*Gasterosteus aculeatus*). During the mating season each spring, male sticklebacks establish territories in which they court females but chase away and fight other males. Sevenster (1973) used the presentation of another male or a female as a reinforcer in instrumental conditioning of male sticklebacks. One group of fish was required to bite a rod to obtain access to the reinforcer. When the reinforcer was another male, biting behavior increased; access to another male was an effective reinforcer for the biting response. By contrast, biting did not increase when it was reinforced with the presentation of a female fish. However, the presentation of a female was an effective reinforcer for other responses, such as swimming through a ring. Biting belongs with territorial defense and can be reinforced by the presentation of a potentially rival male. By contrast, biting does not *belong with* presentation of a female, which typically elicits courtship rather than aggression.

M. Breland-Bailey

Thorndike's difficulties in conditioning scratching and yawning did not have much impact on behavior theory until additional examples of misbehavior were documented by Breland and Breland (1961). The Brelands set up a business to train animals to perform entertaining response chains for displays used in amusement parks and zoos. During the course of this work, they observed dramatic behavior changes that were not consistent with the reinforcement procedures they were using. For example, they described a raccoon that was reinforced for picking up a coin and depositing it in a coin bank.

> We started out by reinforcing him for picking up a single coin. Then the metal container was introduced, with the requirement that he drop the coin into the container. Here we ran into the first bit of difficulty: he seemed to have a great deal of trouble letting go of the coin. He would rub it up against the inside of the container, pull it back out, and clutch it firmly for several seconds. However, he would finally turn it loose and receive his food reinforcement. Then the final contingency: we [required] that he pick up [two] coins and put them in the container.
>
> Now the raccoon really had problems (and so did we). Not only could he not let go of the coins, but he spent seconds, even minutes, rubbing them together (in a most miserly fashion), and dipping them into the container. He carried on this behavior to such an extent that the practical application we had in mind—a display featuring a raccoon putting money in a piggy bank— simply was not feasible. The rubbing behavior became worse and worse as time went on, in spite of nonreinforcement (p. 682).
>
> From "The Misbehavior of Organisms," by K. Breland and M Breland, 1961. In *American Psychologist, 16,* 682.

The Brelands had similar difficulties with other species. Pigs, for example, also could not learn to put coins in a piggy bank. After initial training, they began rooting the coins along the ground. The Brelands called the development of such responses **instinctive drift.** As the term implies, the extra responses that developed in these food reinforcement situations were activities the animals instinctively perform when obtaining food. Pigs root along the ground in connection with feeding, and raccoons rub and dunk food-related

Raccoons are adept at doing some things, like tearing up a package, but it is difficult to condition them to drop coins into a container for food reinforcement.

objects. These natural food-related responses were apparently very strong and competed with the responses required by the training procedures. The Brelands emphasized that such instinctive response tendencies have to be taken into account in the analysis of behavior.

Behavior Systems and Constraints on Instrumental Conditioning

The response limitations on instrumental conditioning described above are consistent with behavior systems theory. I previously described this theory in Chapter 4, in discussions of the nature of the conditioned response (see Timberlake, 2001; Timberlake & Lucas, 1989). According to behavior systems theory, when an animal is food deprived and is in a situation where it might encounter food, its feeding system becomes activated, and it begins to engage in foraging and other food-related activities. An instrumental conditioning procedure is superimposed on this behavior system. The effectiveness of the procedure in increasing an instrumental response will depend on the compatibility of that response with the preexisting organization of the feeding system. Furthermore, the nature of other responses that emerge during the course of training (or instinctive drift) will depend on the behavioral components of the feeding system that become activated by the instrumental conditioning procedure.

According to the behavior systems approach, we should be able to predict which responses will increase with food reinforcement by studying what animals do when their feeding system is activated in the absence of instrumental conditioning. This prediction has been confirmed. In a study of hamsters, Shettleworth (1975) found that food deprivation decreases the probability of self-care responses, such as face washing and scratching, but increases the

S. J. Shettleworth

probability of environment-directed activities, such as digging, scratching at a wall (scrabbling), and rearing on the hind legs. These results suggest that self-care responses (face washing and scratching) are not part of the feeding system activated by hunger, whereas digging, scrabbling, and rearing are. Given these findings, behavior systems theory predicts that food reinforcement should produce increases in digging, scrabbling, and rearing, but not increases in face washing and scratching. This pattern of results is precisely what has been observed in studies of instrumental conditioning (Shettleworth, 1975). Thus, the susceptibility of various responses to food reinforcement can be predicted from how those responses are altered by food deprivation, which presumably reflects their compatibility with the feeding system.

As we saw in Chapter 4, another way to diagnose whether a response is a part of a behavior system is to perform a classical conditioning experiment. Through classical conditioning, a CS comes to elicit components of the behavior system activated by the US. If *instinctive drift* reflects responses of the behavior system, responses akin to instinctive drift should be evident in a classical conditioning experiment. Timberlake and his associates (see Timberlake, 1983; Timberlake, Wahl, & King, 1982) tested this prediction with rats in a modification of the coin-handling studies conducted by Breland and Breland.

Instead of a coin, the apparatus used by Timberlake, Wahl, and King (1982) delivered a ball bearing into the experimental chamber at the start of each trial. The floor of the chamber was tilted so that the ball bearing would roll from one end of the chamber to the other and exit through a hole. In one experimental condition, the rats were required to make contact with the ball bearing to obtain food. A second condition was a classical conditioning procedure: food was provided after the ball bearing rolled across the chamber whether or not the rat touched it. Consistent with the behavior systems view, in both procedures the rats came to touch and extensively handle the ball bearing instead of letting it roll into the hole. Some animals picked up the bearing, put it in their mouth, carried it to the other end of the chamber, and sat and chewed it. These responses resemble the *instinctive drift* observed by the Brelands. The results indicate that touching and handling the ball bearing are manifestations of the feeding behavior system in rats. Instinctive drift represents the intrusion of responses appropriate to the behavior system activated during the course of instrumental conditioning. (For a recent review of response constraints on instrumental conditioning, see Domjan, 2008.)

The Instrumental Reinforcer

Several aspects of a reinforcer determine its effects on the learning and performance of instrumental behavior. I will first consider the direct effects of the quantity and quality of a reinforcer on instrumental behavior. I will then discuss how responding to a particular reward amount and type depends on the organism's past experience with other reinforcers.

Quantity and Quality of the Reinforcer

The quantity and quality of a reinforcer are obvious variables that would be expected to determine the effectiveness of positive reinforcement. This is certainly true at the extreme. If a reinforcer is very small and of poor quality, it will not be effective in increasing instrumental responding. Indeed, studies conducted in straight alley runways generally show faster running with larger and more palatable reinforcers (see Mackintosh, 1974, for a review). However, the results are more complicated in free-operant situations. Consider, for example, a rat that gets a week's supply of food after making one lever-press response. Such a large reinforcer is not likely to encourage frequent lever pressing. The effects of the quality and quantity of reinforcement often depend on factors such as how many responses are required for each reinforcer.

One of the participants in a recent study of the effects of amount of reinforcement was Chad, a 5 year-old boy (Trosclair-Lasserre et al., 2008). Although he was diagnosed with autism, he could communicate effectively using speech. Preliminary assessment indicated that social attention was an effective reinforcer for Chad. Attention consisted of praise, tickles, hugs, songs, stories, and interactive games. The instrumental response was pressing a button long enough to produce an audible click. Reinforcer magnitude was manipulated by providing different durations of attention (10, 105, or 120 seconds). Preliminary testing established that Chad preferred reinforcers of 120 seconds over reinforcers of just 10 seconds.

A progressive ratio schedule of reinforcement was used to evaluate the effects of reinforcer magnitude on instrumental responding. I will describe schedules of reinforcement in greater detail in Chapter 6. For now, it is sufficient to note that in a progressive ratio schedule the participant has to make increasing numbers of responses to obtain the reinforcer. At the start of each session Chad had to make just one button press to get reinforced, but as the session went on, the number of button presses required for each reinforcer progressively increased (hence the name *progressive ratio* schedule). The response requirement was raised from 1 press to 2, 5, 10, 20, 30, and finally 40 presses per reinforcer.

The results of the experiment are presented in Figure 5.9 in terms of the number of times Chad obtained each reinforcer as a function of how many times he had to press the button. As expected, increasing the number

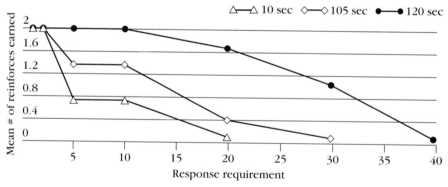

FIGURE **5.9**

Average number of reinforcers earned by Chad per session as the response requirement was increased from 1 to 40. (The maximum possible was 2 reinforcers per session at each response requirement.) Notice that responding was maintained much more effectively in the face of increasing response requirements when the reinforcer was 120 seconds long. (From Trosclair-Lasserre et al. (2008), Figure 3, page 215.)

of presses required resulted in fewer reinforcers earned for all three reinforcer magnitudes. Increasing the response requirement from 1 to 20 responses produced a rapid drop in numbers of reinforcers earned if the reinforcer was 10 seconds. Less of a drop was evident if the reinforcer was 105 seconds. When the reinforcer was 120 seconds, not much of a decrease was evident until the response requirement was raised to 30 or 40 button presses for each reinforcer. Thus, the longer reinforcer was much more effective in maintaining instrumental responding.

The magnitude of the reinforcer has also been found to be a major factor in voucher programs for the reinforcement of abstinence in the treatment of substance use disorder. Individuals who are addicted to cocaine, methamphetamine, opiates, or other drugs have been treated successfully in programs based on the principles of instrumental conditioning (Higgins, Silverman, & Heil, 2008). The target response in these programs is absence from drug use as verified by drug tests conducted two or three times per week. Reinforcement is provided in the form of vouchers that can be exchanged for money. A recent meta-analysis of studies on the success of voucher reinforcement programs indicated that the magnitude of the reinforcer contributed significantly to abstinence (Lussier et al., 2006). Studies in which individuals could earn upwards of $10 per day for remaining drug free, showed greater success in encouraging abstinence than those in which smaller payments were used. Providing reinforcement soon after the evidence of abstinence was also important. Getting paid right after the drug test was more effective than getting paid one or two days later. I will have more to say about the importance of immediate reinforcement later in this chapter.

Shifts in Reinforcer Quality or Quantity

The effectiveness of a reinforcer depends not only on its quality and quantity but also on what the subject received previously. If a teenager receives an allowance of $25 per week, a decrease to $10 may be a great disappointment. But, if she never got used to receiving $25 per week, an allowance of $10 might seem OK. As this example suggests, the effectiveness of a reinforcer depends not only on its own properties, but also on how that reinforcer compares with others the individual has experienced in the recent past.

We saw in Chapter 4 that the effectiveness of a US in classical conditioning depends on how the US compares with the individual's expectations based on prior experience. This idea serves as the foundation of the Rescorla-Wagner model. If the US is larger (or more intense) than expected, it will support excitatory conditioning. By contrast, if it is smaller (or weaker) than expected, the US will support inhibitory conditioning. Analogous effects occur in instrumental conditioning. Numerous studies have shown that the effects of a particular amount and type of reinforcer depend on the quantity and quality of the reinforcers the individual experienced previously (for a comprehensive review, see Flaherty, 1996). Speaking loosely, a large reward is treated as especially good after reinforcement with a small reward, and a small reward is treated as especially poor after reinforcement with a large reward.

Effects of a shift in the quantity of reward were first described by Crespi (1942). The basic results are also nicely illustrated by an experiment by Mellgren (1972) conducted with four groups of rats in a runway apparatus. During Phase

Courtesy of Donald A. Dewsbury

C. F. Flaherty

1, two of the groups received a small reward (S: 2 food pellets) each time they reached the end of the runway. The other two groups received a large reward (L: 22 pellets) for each trip down the runway. (Delivery of the food was always delayed for 20 seconds after the rats reached the end of the runway so that they would not run at their maximum speed.) After 11 trials of training in Phase 1, one group of rats with each reward quantity was shifted to the alternate quantity. Thus, some rats were shifted from the small to the large reward (S-L), and others were shifted from the large to the small reward (L-S). The remaining two groups continued to receive the same amount of reward in Phase 2 as they got in Phase 1. (These groups were designated as L-L and S-S.)

Figure 5.10 summarizes the results. At the end of Phase 1, the animals that received the large reward ran slightly, but not significantly, faster than the rats that received the small reward. For groups that continued to receive the same amount of reward in Phase 2 as in Phase 1 (groups L-L and S-S),

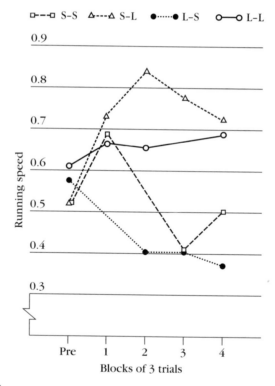

FIGURE **5.10**

Running speeds of four groups of rats in blocks of 3 trials. Block "Pre" represents running speeds at the end of Phase 1. Blocks 1–4 represent running speeds in Phase 2. At the start of Phase 2, groups S-L and L-S experienced a shift in amount of reward from small to large and large to small, respectively. Groups S-S and L-L received small and large rewards, respectively, throughout the experiment. (From "Positive and Negative Contrasts Effects Using Delayed Reinforcements," by R. L. Mellgren, 1972, *Learning and Motivation, 3*, p. 185–193. Copyright © 1972 by Academic Press. Reprinted by permission of Elsevier.)

instrumental performance did not change much during Phase 2. By contrast, significant deviations from these baselines of running were observed in groups that received shifts in reward magnitude. Rats that were shifted from the large to the small reward (group L-S) rapidly decreased their running speeds and rats that were shifted from the small to the large reward (group S-L) soon increased their running speeds.

The most significant finding was that following a shift in reward magnitude, running speed was not entirely determined by the new reward magnitude. Rather, response to the new reward was enhanced by previous experience with a contrasting reward magnitude. Rats that were shifted from a small to a large reward (group S-L) ran faster for the large reward than rats that always received the large reward (group L-L). Correspondingly, animals that were shifted from a large to a small reward (group L-S) ran slower for the small reward than animals that always received the small reward (group S-S).

The results Mellgren obtained illustrate the phenomena of successive positive and negative contrast. **Positive contrast** refers to elevated responding for a favorable reward resulting from prior experience with a less attractive outcome. More informally, the favorable reward looks especially good to individuals who experienced a worse outcome previously. **Negative contrast** refers to depressed responding for a small reward because of prior experience with a better outcome. In this case, the small reward looks especially bad to individuals who experienced a better reward previously.

Recent research shows that the phenomenon of behavioral contrast may explain a long-standing paradox in the drug abuse literature. The paradox arises from two seemingly conflicting findings. The first is that drugs of abuse, like cocaine, will support the conditioning of a place preference in laboratory animals. Rats given cocaine in a distinctive chamber will choose that area over a place where they did not get cocaine. This suggests that cocaine is reinforcing. The conflicting finding is that rats given a saccharin solution to drink before receiving cocaine come to suppress their saccharin intake. Thus, cocaine can condition a taste aversion even though it appears to be reinforcing in place preference conditioning. Grigson and her colleagues have conducted a series of studies that suggest that the saccharin aversion conditioned by cocaine reflects an anticipatory contrast effect (Grigson et al., 2008). Because cocaine is so highly reinforcing and occurs after exposure to saccharin, the saccharin flavor loses its hedonic value in anticipation of the much greater hedonic value of cocaine. This type of negative contrast may explain why individuals addicted to cocaine derive little satisfaction from conventional reinforcers (a tasty meal) that others enjoy on a daily basis.

Courtesy of Donald A. Dewsbury

R. L. Mellgren

The Response-Reinforcer Relation

The hallmark of instrumental behavior is that it produces and is controlled by its consequences. In some cases, there is a strong relation between what a person does and what is the consequence that follows. If you put a dollar into a soda machine, you will get a can of soda. As long as the machine is working, you will get your can of soda every time you put in the required money. In other cases, there is no relation between behavior and an outcome. You may wear your lucky hat to a test and get a good grade, but the grade would not be causally related to what you were wearing. The relation between behavior and its consequences can also be probabilistic. For example, you might have to call several times before you get to talk to your friend on the phone.

Human and other animals perform a continual stream of responses and encounter all kinds of environmental events. You are always doing something, even if it is just sitting around, and things are continually happening in your environment. Some of the things you do have consequences; others don't. It makes no sense to work hard to make the sun rise each morning, because that will happen anyway. Instead, you should devote your energy to fixing breakfast or working for a paycheck: things that do not happen without your effort. To be efficient, you have to know when you have to do something to obtain a reinforcer and when the reinforcer is likely to be delivered independent of your actions. Efficient instrumental behavior requires sensitivity to the response-reinforcer relation.

There are actually two types of relationships between a response and a reinforcer. One is the **temporal relation.** The temporal relation refers to the time between the response and the reinforcer. A special case of the temporal relation is **temporal contiguity.** Temporal contiguity refers to the delivery of the reinforcer immediately after the response. The second type of relation between a response and the reinforcer is the *causal relation* or **response-reinforcer contingency.** The response-reinforcer contingency refers to the extent to which the instrumental response is necessary and sufficient for the occurrence of the reinforcer.

Temporal and causal factors are independent of each other. A strong temporal relation does not require a strong causal relation, and vice versa. For example, there is strong causal relation between submitting an application for admission to college and getting accepted. (If you don't apply, you cannot be admitted.) However, the temporal relation between applying and getting admitted is weak. You may not hear about the acceptance for weeks (or months) after submitting your application.

Effects of the Temporal Relation

Both conventional wisdom and experimental evidence tell us that immediate reinforcement is preferable to delayed reinforcement (Williams, 2001). In addition, since the early work of Grice (1948), learning psychologists have correctly emphasized that instrumental conditioning requires providing the reinforcer immediately after the occurrence of the instrumental response. Grice reported that instrumental learning can be disrupted by delays as short as 0.5 seconds. More recent research has indicated that instrumental conditioning is possible with delays as long as 30 seconds (Critchfield & Lattal, 1993; Lattal & Gleeson, 1990; Lattal & Metzger, 1994; Sutphin, Byrnne, & Poling, 1998; Williams & Lattal, 1999). However, the fact remains that immediate reinforcement is much more effective.

The effects of delayed reinforcement on learning to press a response lever in laboratory rats is shown in Figure 5.11 (Dickinson, Watt, & Griffiths, 1992). Each time the rats pressed the lever, a food pellet was set up to be delivered after a fixed delay. For some subjects, the delay was short (2–4 seconds). For others the delay was considerable (64 seconds). If the subject pressed the lever again during the delay interval, the new response resulted in

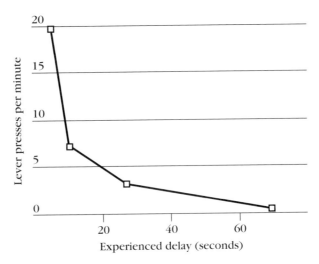

FIGURE **5.11**

Effects of delay of reinforcement on acquisition of lever pressing in rats. (From "Free-Operant Acquisition with Delayed Reinforcement," by A. Dickinson, A. Watt, and W. J. H. Griffiths, 1992, *The Quarterly Journal of Experimental Psychology*, 45B, pp. 241–258. Copyright © 1992 by The Experimental Psychology Society. Reprinted by permission.)

another food pellet after the specified delay. (In other studies, such *extra* responses are programmed to reset the delay interval.) Figure 5.11 shows response rates as a function of the mean delay of reinforcement experienced by each group. Responding dropped off fairly rapidly with increases in the delay of reinforcement. No learning was evident with a 64 second delay of reinforcement in this experiment.

Why is instrumental conditioning so sensitive to a delay of reinforcement? There are several contributing factors. One stems from the fact that a delay makes it difficult to figure out which response deserves the credit for the reinforcer that is delivered. As I pointed out earlier, behavior is an ongoing, continual stream of activities. When reinforcement is delayed after performance of a specified response, R1, the participant does not stop doing things. After performing R1, the participant may perform R2, R3, R4, and so on. If the reinforcer is set up by R1 but not delivered until some time later, the reinforcer may occur immediately after some other response, let's say R6. To associate R1 with the reinforcer, the participant has to have some way to distinguish R1 from the other responses it performs during the delay interval.

There are a couple of ways to overcome this problem. The first technique, used by animal trainers and coaches for centuries, is to provide a secondary or conditioned reinforcer immediately after the instrumental response, even if the primary reinforcer cannot occur until some time later. A **secondary, or conditioned, reinforcer** is a conditioned stimulus that was previously associated with the reinforcer. Verbal prompts in coaching, such as "good," "keep going," and "that's the way" are conditioned reinforcers that can provide immediate reinforcement for appropriate behavior. Effective coaches and animal trainers are constantly providing such immediate verbal feedback or conditioned reinforcement. Conditioned reinforcers can serve to bridge a delay between the

D. A. Lieberman

instrumental response and delivery of the primary reinforcer (Cronin, 1980; Winter & Perkins, 1982; Williams, 1991).

Another technique that facilitates learning with delayed reinforcement is to *mark* the target instrumental response in some way to make it distinguishable from the other activities of the organism. Marking can be accomplished by introducing a brief light or noise after the target response or by picking up the subject and moving it to a holding box for the delay interval. The effectiveness of a **marking procedure** was first demonstrated by David Lieberman and his colleagues (Lieberman, McIntosh, & Thomas, 1979) and has since been replicated in other studies (e.g., Lieberman, Davidson, & Thomas, 1985; Lieberman & Thomas, 1986; Thomas & Lieberman, 1990; Urcuioli & Kasprow, 1988).

In a variation of the marking procedure, Williams (1999) compared the learning of a lever-press response in three groups of rats. For each group, the food reinforcer was delayed 30 seconds after a press of the response lever. (Any additional lever presses during the delay interval were ignored.) The no-signal group received this procedure without a marking stimulus. For the marking group, a light was presented for 5 seconds right after each lever press. For a third group of subjects (called the *blocking* group), the five second light was presented at the end of the delay interval, just before food delivery.

Results of the experiment are shown in Figure 5.12. Rats in the no-signal group showed little responding during the first three blocks of two trials and only achieved modest levels of lever pressing after that. In contrast, the marking group showed much more robust learning. Clearly, introducing a brief light right after each lever-press response substantially facilitated learning with the 30 second delay of reinforcement. Placing the light at the end of the interval, just before food, had the opposite effect. Subjects in the blocking group never learned the lever-press response. For those subjects, the light became associated with the food, and this classical conditioning blocked the conditioning of the instrumental response. This interference effect is related to the blocking effect that I discussed in Chapter 4 (see Williams, 2001, for a more detailed discussion).

The Response-Reinforcer Contingency

As I noted earlier, the response-reinforcer contingency refers to the extent to which the delivery of the reinforcer depends on the prior occurrence of the instrumental response. In studies of delay of reinforcement, there is a perfect causal relation between the response and the reinforcer but learning is disrupted. This shows that a perfect causal relation between the response and the reinforcer is not sufficient to produce vigorous instrumental responding. Even with a perfect causal relation, conditioning does not occur if reinforcement is delayed too long. Such data encouraged early investigators to conclude that response-reinforcer contiguity, rather than contingency, was the critical factor producing instrumental learning. However, this view has turned out to be incorrect. The response-reinforcer contingency is also important.

Skinner's Superstition Experiment

A landmark experiment in the debate about the role of contiguity versus contingency in instrumental learning was Skinner's superstition experiment (Skinner, 1948). Skinner placed pigeons in separate experimental chambers

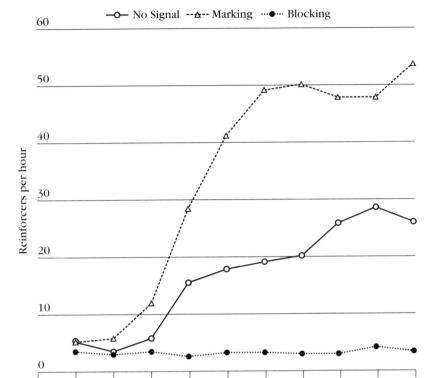

FIGURE **5.12**

Acquisition of lever pressing in rats with a 30 second delay of reinforcement.
For the marking group, a light was presented for five seconds at the beginning of the delay interval, right after the instrumental response. For the blocking group, the light was introduced at the end of the delay interval, just before the delivery of food. (From Williams, 1999.)

and set the equipment to deliver a bit of food every 15 seconds irrespective of what the pigeons were doing. The birds were not required to peck a key or perform any other particular response to get the food. After some time, Skinner returned to see what his birds were doing. He described some of what he saw as follows:

> In six out of eight cases the resulting responses were so clearly defined that two observers could agree perfectly in counting instances. One bird was conditioned to turn counterclockwise about the cage, making two or three turns between reinforcements. Another repeatedly thrust its head into one of the upper corners of the cage. A third developed a "tossing" response, as if placing its head beneath an invisible bar and lifting it repeatedly. (p. 168)

The pigeons appeared to be responding as if their behavior controlled the delivery of the reinforcer when, in fact, food was provided independently of behavior. Accordingly, Skinner called this **superstitious behavior.**

Skinner's explanation of superstitious behavior rests on the idea of **accidental**, or **adventitious, reinforcement.** Adventitious reinforcement refers to the accidental pairing of a response with delivery of the reinforcer. Animals are always doing something, even if no particular responses are required to obtain food. Skinner suggested that whatever response a subject happened to make just before it got free food became strengthened and subsequently increased in frequency because of adventitious reinforcement. One accidental pairing of a response with food increases the chance that the same response will occur just before the next delivery of the food. A second accidental response-reinforcer pairing further increases the probability of the response. In this way, each accidental pairing helps to strengthen a particular response. After a while, the response will occur frequently enough to be identified as superstitious behavior.

Skinner's interpretation of his experiment was appealing and consistent with views of reinforcement that were widely held at the time. Impressed by studies of delay of reinforcement, theoreticians thought that temporal contiguity was the main factor responsible for learning. Skinner's experiment appeared to support this view and suggested that a positive response-reinforcer contingency is not necessary for instrumental conditioning.

Reinterpretation of the Superstition Experiment

Courtesy of Donald A. Dewsbury

J. E. R. Staddon

Skinner's bold claim that response-reinforcer contiguity rather than contingency is most important for instrumental conditioning was challenged by subsequent empirical evidence. In a landmark study, Staddon and Simmelhag (1971) attempted to replicate Skinner's experiment. However, Staddon and Simmelhag made more extensive and systematic observations. They defined and measured the occurrence of many responses, such as orienting to the food hopper, pecking the response key, wing flapping, turning in quarter circles, and preening. They then recorded the frequency of each response according to when it occurred during the interval between successive free deliveries of food.

Figure 5.13 shows the data obtained by Staddon and Simmelhag for several responses for one pigeon. Clearly, some of the responses occurred predominantly toward the end of the interval between successive reinforcers. For example, R1 and R7 (orienting to the food magazine and pecking at something on the magazine wall) were much more likely to occur at the end of the food-food interval than at other times. Staddon and Simmelhag called these **terminal responses.** Other activities increased in frequency after the delivery of food and then decreased as the time for the next food delivery drew closer. The pigeons were most likely to engage in R8 and R4 (moving along the magazine wall and making a quarter turn) somewhere near the middle of the interval between food deliveries. These activities were called **interim responses.**

Which actions were terminal responses and which were interim responses did not vary much from one pigeon to another. Furthermore, Staddon and Simmelhag failed to find evidence for accidental reinforcement effects. Responses did not always increase in frequency merely because they occurred coincidentally with food delivery. Food delivery appeared to influence only the strength of terminal responses, even in the initial phases of training.

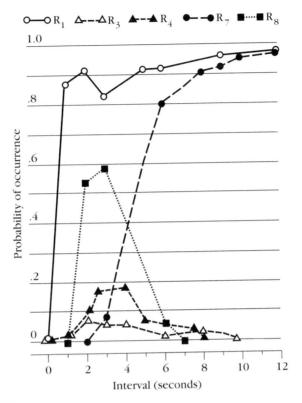

FIGURE **5.13**

Probability of several responses as a function of time between successive deliveries of a food reinforcer. R1 (orienting toward the food magazine wall) and R7 (pecking at something on the magazine wall) are terminal responses, having their highest probabilities at the end of the interval between food deliveries. R3 (pecking at something on the floor), R4 (a quarter turn), and R8 (moving along the magazine wall) are interim responses, having their highest probabilities somewhere near the middle of the interval between food deliveries. (From "The 'Superstition' Experiment: A Reexamination of Its Implications for the Principles of Adaptive Behavior," by J. E. R. Staddon and V. L. Simmelhag, 1971. *Psychological Review 78*, pp. 3–43. Copyright © 1971 by the American Psychological Association. Reprinted by permission.)

Subsequent research has provided much additional evidence that periodic presentations of a reinforcer produce behavioral regularities, with certain responses predominating late in the interval between successive food presentations and other responses predominating earlier in the food-food interval (Anderson & Shettleworth, 1977; Innis, Simmelhag-Grant, & Staddon, 1983; Silva & Timberlake, 1998). It is not clear why Skinner failed to observe such regularities in his experiment. One possibility is that he focused on different aspects of the behavior of different birds in an effort to document that each bird responded in a unique fashion. For example, he may have focused on the terminal response of one bird and interim responses in other birds. Subsequent investigators have also noted some variations in behavior between individuals but have emphasized what are even more striking similarities among animals that are given food periodically, independent of their behavior.

Explanation of the Periodicity of Interim and Terminal Responses

What is responsible for the development of similar terminal and interim responses in animals exposed to the same schedule of response-independent food presentations? Staddon and Simmelhag (1971) suggested that terminal responses are species typical responses that reflect the anticipation of food as time draws closer to the next food presentation. By contrast, they viewed interim responses as reflecting other sources of motivation that become prominent early in the interfood interval, when food presentation is unlikely.

Numerous subsequent studies have examined the behavior of various species of animals in situations where the likelihood of encountering food is systematically varied. These studies have led to reinterpretation of Staddon and Simmelhag's results in the more comprehensive theoretical framework of behavior systems theory. I previously described how behavior systems theory deals with response constraints on instrumental conditioning. The theory can also explain results such as those of Staddon and Simmelhag (1971) that result from periodic deliveries of food independent of behavior.

The critical idea is that periodic deliveries of food activate the feeding system and its preorganized species-typical foraging and feeding responses. Different behaviors occur depending on when food was last delivered and when food is going to occur again. Just after the delivery of food, the organism is assumed to display *post-food focal search* responses that involve activities near the food cup. In the middle of the interval between food deliveries (when the subjects are least likely to get food), *general search* responses are evident that take the subject away from the food cup. As the time for the next food delivery approaches, the subject exhibits *focal search* responses that are again concentrated near the food cup. In Figure 5.13, the terminal responses, R1 and R7 were distributed in time in the manner expected of focal search behavior, and R4 and R8 were distributed in the manner expected of general search responses. (For studies examining these issues in greater detail, see Timberlake & Lucas, 1985; Silva & Timberlake, 1998.)

Consistent with behavior systems theory, the distribution of activities that develops with periodic deliveries of a reinforcer depend on the nature of that reinforcer. For example, different patterns of behavior develop with food versus water presentations (Innis, Simmelhag-Grant, & Staddon, 1983; Papadouka & Matthews, 1995; Reberg, Innis, Mann, & Eizenga, 1978; Timberlake & Lucas, 1991), presumably because food and water activate different foraging patterns.

Effects of the Controllability of Reinforcers

A strong contingency between an instrumental response and a reinforcer essentially means that the response controls the reinforcer. With a strong contingency, whether the reinforcer occurs depends on whether the instrumental response has occurred. Studies of the effects of control over reinforcers have provided the most extensive body of evidence on the sensitivity of behavior to response-reinforcer contingencies. Some of these studies have

S. F. Maier

involved positive reinforcement (e.g., Job, 2002). However, most of the research has focused on the effects of control over aversive stimulation (see reviews by LoLordo & Taylor, 2001; Overmier & LoLordo, 1998; Maier & Jackson, 1979; Peterson, Maier, & Seligman, 1993).

Contemporary research on this problem originated with the pioneering studies of Seligman, Overmier, and Maier (Overmier & Seligman, 1967; Seligman & Maier, 1967), who investigated the effects of exposure to uncontrollable shock on subsequent escape-avoidance learning in dogs. The major finding was that exposure to uncontrollable shock disrupted subsequent learning. This phenomenon has come to be called the **learned-helplessness effect.**

The learned helplessness effect continues to be the focus of a great deal of research, but dogs are no longer used in the experiments. Instead, most of the research is conducted with laboratory rats and mice and human participants. The research requires exposing animals to stressful events, and some may find the research objectionable because of that. However, this line of work has turned out to be highly informative about the mechanisms of stress and coping at the behavioral, hormonal, and neurophysiological levels. The research has been especially informative about depression and has been used in the testing and development of antidepressant medications. As Henkel et al. (2002) noted, "the learned helplessness paradigm is still considered to be one of the better animal models of depression" (p. 243).

The Triadic Design

Learned-helplessness experiments are usually conducted using the *triadic design* presented in Table 5.2. The design involves two phases: an exposure phase and a conditioning phase. During the exposure phase, one group of rats (E, for *e*scape) is exposed to periodic shocks that can be terminated by performing an escape response (e.g., rotating a small wheel or tumbler). Each subject in the second group (Y, for *y*oked) is yoked to an animal in Group E and receives the same duration and distribution of shocks as its Group E partner. However, animals in Group Y cannot do anything to turn off the shocks. The third group (R, for *r*estricted) receives no shocks during the exposure phase but is restricted to the apparatus for as long as the other groups. During the conditioning phase, all three groups receive escape-avoidance training. This is usually conducted in a shuttle apparatus that has two adjacent compartments (see Figure 10.4). The animals have to go back and forth between the two compartments to avoid shock (or escape any shocks that they did not avoid).

TABLE **5.2**
The Triadic Design Used in Studies of the Learned-Helplessness Effect

Group	Exposure Phase	Conditioning Phase	Result
Group E	Escapable shock	Escape-avoidance training	Rapid-avoidance learning
Group Y	Yoked inescapable shock	Escape-avoidance training	Slow-avoidance learning
Group R	Restricted to apparatus	Escape-avoidance training	Rapid-avoidance learning

The remarkable finding in experiments on the learned-helplessness effect is that the effects of aversive stimulation during the exposure phase depend on whether or not shock is escapable. Exposure to uncontrollable shock (Group Y) produces a severe disruption in subsequent escape-avoidance learning. In the conditioning phase of the experiment, Group Y typically shows much poorer escape-avoidance performance than both Group E and Group R. By contrast, little or no deleterious effects are observed after exposure to escapable shock. In fact, Group E often learns the subsequent escape-avoidance task as rapidly as Group R, which received no shock during the exposure phase. Similar detrimental effects of exposure to yoked inescapable shock have been reported on subsequent responding for food reinforcement (e.g., Rosellini & DeCola, 1981; Rosellini, DeCola, & Shapiro, 1982; see also DeCola & Rosellini, 1990).

The fact that Group Y shows a deficit in subsequent learning in comparison to Group E indicates that the animals are sensitive to the procedural differences between escapable and yoked inescapable shock. The primary procedural difference between Groups E and Y is the presence of a response-reinforcer contingency for Group E but not for Group Y. Therefore, the difference in the rate of learning between these two groups shows that the animals are sensitive to the response-reinforcer contingency.

The Learned-Helplessness Hypothesis

The first major explanation of studies employing the triadic design—the **learned-helplessness hypothesis**—was based on the conclusion that animals can perceive the contingency between their behavior and the delivery of a reinforcer (Maier & Seligman, 1976; Maier, Seligman, & Solomon, 1969). The learned-helplessness hypothesis assumes that during exposure to uncontrollable shocks, animals learn that the shocks are independent of their behavior: that there is nothing they can do to control the shocks. Furthermore, they come to expect that reinforcers will continue to be independent of their behavior in the future. This expectation of future lack of control undermines their ability to learn a new instrumental response. The learning deficit occurs for two reasons. First, the expectation of lack of control reduces the motivation of the subjects to perform an instrumental response. Second, even if they make the response and get reinforced in the conditioning phase, the previously learned expectation of lack of control makes it more difficult for the subjects to learn that their behavior is now effective in producing reinforcement.

It is important to distinguish the learned helplessness *hypothesis* from the learned helplessness *effect*. The learned-helplessness effect is the pattern of results obtained with the triadic design (poorer learning in Group Y than in Groups E and R). The learned-helplessness effect has been replicated in numerous studies and is a well established finding. By contrast, the learned-helplessness hypothesis, or interpretation, has been a provocative and controversial explanation of the learned-helplessness effect since its introduction (see LoLordo & Taylor, 2001; Overmier & LoLordo, 1998).

Courtesy of M. E. P. Seligman

M. E. P. Seligman

Activity Deficits

Early in the history of research on the learned-helplessness effect, investigators became concerned that the learning deficit observed in Group Y

BOX **5.4**

Human Extensions of Animal Research on the Controllability of Reinforcers

The fact that a history of lack of control over reinforcers can severely disrupt subsequent instrumental performance has important implications for human behavior. The concept of helplessness has been extended and elaborated to a variety of areas of human concern, including aging, athletic performance, chronic pain, academic achievement, susceptibility to heart attacks, and victimization and bereavement (see Garber & Seligman, 1980;

Overmier, 2002; Peterson, Maier, & Seligman, 1993). Perhaps the most prominent area to which the concept of helplessness has been applied is depression (Abramson, Metalsky, & Alloy, 1989; Henkel et al., 2002; Peterson & Seligman, 1984).

Animal research on uncontrollability and unpredictability has also been used to gain insights into human post-traumatic stress disorder (Foa, Zinbarg, & Rothbaum, 1992). Victims of assault or combat

stress have symptoms that correspond to the effects of chronic uncontrollable and unpredictable shock in animals. Recognition of these similarities promises to provide new insights into the origin and treatment of post-traumatic stress disorder. Animal models of helplessness have also contributed to the understanding of the long-term effects of sexual abuse and revictimization (Marx, Heidt, & Gold, 2005).

Courtesy of N. K. Dess

N. K. Dess

was a result of these animals learning to be inactive in response to shock during the exposure phase. Although it is unlikely that learned inactivity can explain all instances of the learned helplessness effect (Jackson, Alexander, & Maier, 1980; Rosellini et al., 1984), concern about learned inactivity has persisted. For example, Shors (2006) found that exposure to inescapable shock disrupts the escape learning of rats in a shuttle box but facilitates eyeblink conditioning. Based on these results, Shors suggested that helplessness effects are most likely to be observed in tasks that require movement.

Stimulus Relations in Escape Conditioning

The interpretations of the learned helplessness effect I described so far have focused on the harmful effects of exposure to inescapable shock. However, an equally important question is why exposure to *escapable* shock is not nearly as bad (Minor, Dess, & Overmier, 1991). What is it about the ability to make an escape response that makes exposure to shock less debilitating? This question has stimulated a closer look at what happens when animals are permitted to escape shock in the exposure phase of the triadic design.

The defining feature of **escape** behavior is that the instrumental response results in the termination of an aversive stimulus. The act of performing a skeletal response provides sensory feedback stimuli. For example, you can feel that you are raising your hand even if your eyes are closed. Because of the response feedback cues, you don't have to see your arm go up to know that you are raising your arm. Making an escape response such as pressing a lever similarly results in internal sensations or response feedback cues. These are illustrated in Figure 5.14. Some of the response-produced stimuli are experienced at the start of the escape response, just before the shock is turned

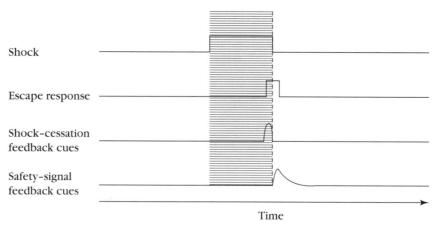

FIGURE **5.14**

Stimulus relations in an escape-conditioning trial. Shock-cessation feedback cues are experienced at the start of the escape response, just before the termination of shock. Safety-signal feedback cues are experienced just after the termination of shock, at the start of the intertrial interval.

off. These are called *shock-cessation feedback cues.* Other response-produced stimuli are experienced as the animal completes the response, just after the shock has been turned off at the start of the intertrial interval. These are called *safety-signal feedback cues.*

At first, investigations of stimulus factors involved with escapable shock centered on the possible significance of safety-signal feedback cues. Safety-signal feedback cues are reliably followed by the intertrial interval, and hence by the absence of shock. Therefore, such feedback cues can become conditioned inhibitors of fear and limit or inhibit fear elicited by contextual cues of the experimental chamber. (I discussed the development of conditioned inhibition in Chapter 3.) No such safety signals exist for animals given yoked, inescapable shock, because for them, shocks and shock-free periods are not predictable. Therefore, contextual cues of the chamber in which shocks are delivered are more likely to become conditioned to elicit fear with inescapable shock.

These considerations have encouraged analyzing the triadic design in terms of group differences in signals for safety rather than in terms of differences in whether shock is escapable or not. In an experiment conducted by Jackson and Minor (1988), for example, one group of rats received the usual inescapable shocks in the exposure phase of the triadic design. However, at the end of each shock presentation, the houselights were turned off for five seconds as a safety signal. The introduction of this safety signal entirely eliminated the disruptive effects of shock exposure on subsequent shuttle-escape learning. Another study (Minor, Trauner, Lee, & Dess, 1990) also employed inescapable shocks, but this time an auditory and visual cue was introduced

T. R. Minor

during the last three seconds of each shock presentation. This was intended to mimic shock cessation cues. The introduction of these shock cessation cues also largely eliminated the helplessness effect.

Focusing on stimulus factors in escape conditioning rather than on response-reinforcer contingencies has not yet yielded a comprehensive account of the results of all experiments with the triadic design. However, the available evidence indicates that significant differences in how animals cope with aversive stimulation can result from differences in the ability to predict when shocks will end and when a safe intertrial interval without shocks will begin. Learning to predict shock termination and shock absence can be just as important as being able to escape from shock. This is good news. We encounter many aversive events in life that we cannot control (e.g., the rising price of gas or a new demanding boss). Fortunately, controlling a stressful event need not be our only coping strategy. Learning to predict when we will encounter the stressful event (and when we will not encounter it) can be just as effective in reducing the harmful effects of stress.

BOX **5.5**

Helplessness within the Spinal Cord

If someone asked you where learning occurs, you would likely give a quick response accompanied by an expression of disbelief. Everyone knows that learning occurs within the brain. But what about the neural tissue that lies below the brain, the cylinder of axons and gray matter that is protected by the bones of the vertebrate column? Can it learn? Recent work suggests that neurons within this region are sensitive to environmental relations and can exhibit some simple forms of learning (Patterson & Grau, 2001).

The spinal cord is composed of two regions (see Figure 5.15). The inner region (the central gray) is made up of neurons that form a network that can modulate signals and organize some simple behaviors. The central gray is surrounded by a band of axons (the white matter) that carry neural signals up and down the spinal

J. W. Grau

cord, relaying information between the periphery and the brain. When an individual has an accident that causes paralysis below the waist (paraplegia), the loss of sensory and motor function is due to disruption in the relay cable formed by the axons of the white matter.

What many people do not realize is that spinal injury does not eliminate neural control of reflex responses. Below the point of injury, the neurons of the central gray retain the capacity to organize some simple behaviors. These spinal reflexes can be studied in nonhuman subjects by surgically cutting the spinal cord, disconnecting the lower region of the spinal cord (the lumbar-sacral region) from the brain. After the spinal injury, pressure applied to the rear paw will still elicit an upward movement of the paw (a flexion response). This protective reflex is designed to move the limb away from noxious stimuli that might cause damage to the skin. The reflex is mediated by neurons within the lumbosacral region of the spinal cord. The flexion response does not require the brain.

(continued)

BOX **5.5** (continued)

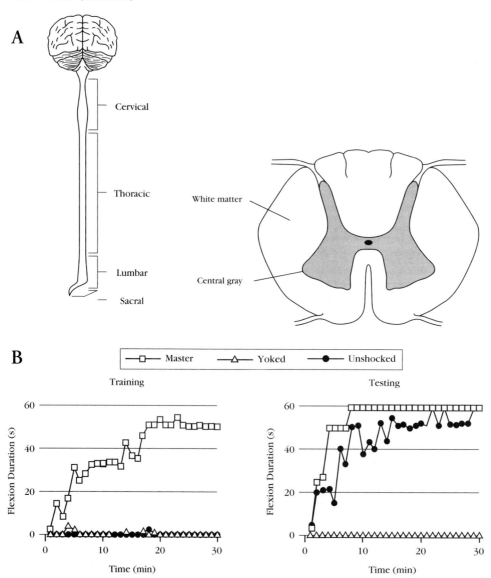

FIGURE **5.15**

(A) A cross-section of the spinal cord. The inner region (central gray) is composed of cell bodies, interneurons, and glia. It is surrounded by a band of axons (the white matter) that relay signals to and from the brain, segments of the cord, and the periphery. (B) Training with response-contingent shock. Master rats receive shock whenever one leg is extended. Even though the spinal cord has been surgically disconnected from the brain, they learn to hold their leg up (an increase in flexion duration) to minimize net shock exposure. Yoked rats, that receive the same amount of shock independent of leg position, fail to learn. (C) Learned helplessness after noncontingent shock. When all subjects are subsequently tested with response-contingent shock, master rats quickly re-learn the required response. Yoked rats, that had previously received shock independent of leg position, fail to learn. (Adapted from Grau & Joynes, 2001.)

(continued)

BOX **5.5** (continued)

Groves and Thompson showed some time ago that the vigor of a spinal reflex can change with experience. Repeated stimulation produces habituation while an intense stimulus can induce sensitization. These observations formed the cornerstone of the dual process theory of nonassociative learning that was described in Chapter 2 (Groves & Thompson, 1970).

More recently, Grau and his colleagues have shown that neurons within the spinal cord can also support a simple form of instrumental learning (reviewed in Grau et al., 2006). In these studies, the spinal cord was cut and subjects were trained using a shock that elicited a hind limb flexion response. One group (the master rats) received leg shock whenever the leg was extended. Subjects in a yoked group were experimentally coupled to the master subjects. Each time a master rat received shock, its yoked partner did too. Master rats quickly learned to hold their leg up, effectively minimizing net shock exposure (see Figure 5.15). In contrast, the yoked rats, that received shock independent of leg position, failed to learn. This difference between the master and yoked rats indicates that neurons within the spinal cord are sensitive to an instrumental (response-reinforcer) relation (for additional evidence, see Grau et al., 2006).

Master and yoked rats were then tested under common conditions with controllable shock. As you would expect, master rats learned faster than control subjects that previously had not received shock. In contrast, the yoked rats failed to learn. Their behavioral deficit resembles the phenomenon of learned helplessness (Maier & Seligman, 1976). Crown and Grau (2001) have gone on to show that prior exposure to controllable

shock has an immunizing effect that can protect the spinal cord from becoming helpless. Other experiments demonstrated that a combination of behavioral and drug treatments can restore the spinal cord's capacity for learning.

Across a range of behavioral manipulations, the spinal cord has yielded a pattern of results remarkably similar to those derived from brain-mediated behaviors. These results indicate that learning theorists have identified some very general principles of learning, principles that apply across a range of species (from *Aplysia* to humans) and across different levels of the neural axis (from spinal cord to forebrain). Of course, higher neural systems enable more complex functional capacity. However, there appear to be some core principles of neural plasticity that are evident in all learning situations. Some envision these primitives as a kind of biological alphabet that is used to assemble the functional systems that underlie learning (Hawkins & Kandel, 1984). A simple system like the spinal cord reveals the basic letters while a comparison to brain-mediated learning shows how this alphabet can be embellished and organized to produce more sophisticated learning systems. Because this approach seeks to describe the mechanisms that underlie learning at both a functional and neurobiological level, Grau and Joynes (2005) have labeled it neurofunctionalism (also see the Functional Neurology, Chapter 1).

Other researchers have shown that spinal cord neurons can support stepping behavior (Edgerton et al., 2004). In these studies, the spinal cord was cut and the animal's hind legs were sus-

pended over a treadmill. The movement of the treadmill against the paws engaged a neural circuit that organized stepping behavior. With experience, and some shaping of the response, an animal can recover the capacity to step over a range of treadmill speeds. Moreover, this system can be modified by experience. If an obstacle is placed in the path of the paw so that the paw hits it while the leg swings forward, the spinal cord will learn to lift the paw higher to minimize contact with the obstacle.

On the basis of these observations, Anton Wernig (Wernig, Muller, Nanassy, & Cagol, 1995) attempted to shape locomotive behavior in humans who were paraplegic. The participants were suspended over a treadmill and step training was conducted over a period of 12 weeks. Over the course of this experience, the spinal cord appeared to regain the capacity to organize stepping. The participants regained additional leg support and learned to engage the stepping circuit, allowing them to walk forward using a wheeled walker (rollator). The results were remarkable. At the start of training, 86% of the participants were confined to a wheelchair. By the end, 86% were able to move about using a walker, or rollator. Observations such as these have stimulated hope that behavioral training, coupled with neurobiological treatment, can help restore function after spinal injury. The aim of rehabilitative techniques is to retrain the injured system, using behavioral contingencies to promote adaptive functional outcomes. You should recognize that this is just another example of learning.

J. W. Grau

Contiguity and Contingency: Concluding Comments

As we have seen, organisms are sensitive to the contiguity as well as the contingency between an instrumental response and a reinforcer. Typically, these two aspects of the relation between response and reinforcer act jointly to produce learning (Davis & Platt, 1983). Both factors serve to focus the effects of reinforcement on the instrumental response. The causal relation, or contingency, ensures that the reinforcer is delivered only after occurrence of the specified instrumental response. The contiguity relation ensures that other activities do not intrude between the specified response and the reinforcer to interfere with conditioning of the target response.

SAMPLE QUESTIONS

1. Compare and contrast free-operant and discrete-trial methods for the study of instrumental behavior.
2. What are the similarities and differences between positive and negative reinforcement?
3. What is the current thinking about instrumental reinforcement and creativity, and what is the relevant experimental evidence?
4. What are the effects of a delay of reinforcement on instrumental learning and what causes these effects?
5. What was the purpose of Skinner's superstition experiment? What were the results, and how have those results been reinterpreted?
6. Describe alternative explanations of the learned helplessness effect.

KEY TERMS

accidental reinforcement An instance in which the delivery of a reinforcer happens to coincide with a particular response, even though that response was not responsible for the reinforcer presentation. Also called *adventitious reinforcement*.

adventitious reinforcement Same as accidental reinforcement.

appetitive stimulus A pleasant or satisfying stimulus that can be used to positively reinforce an instrumental response.

aversive stimulus An unpleasant or annoying stimulus than can be used to punish an instrumental response.

avoidance An instrumental conditioning procedure in which the instrumental response prevents the delivery of an aversive stimulus.

belongingness The theoretical idea, originally proposed by Thorndike, that an organism's evolutionary history makes certain responses fit or belong with certain reinforcers. Belongingness facilitates learning.

conditioned reinforcer A stimulus that becomes an effective reinforcer because of its association with a primary or unconditioned reinforcer. Also called *secondary reinforcer*.

contiguity The occurrence of two events, such as a response and a reinforcer, very close together in time. Also called *temporal contiguity*.

differential reinforcement of other behavior (DRO) An instrumental conditioning procedure in which a positive reinforcer is periodically delivered only if the participant does something other than the target response.

discrete-trial procedure A method of instrumental conditioning in which the participant can perform the instrumental response only during specified periods, usually determined either by placement of the participant in an experimental chamber, or by the presentation of a stimulus.

escape An instrumental conditioning procedure in which the instrumental response terminates an aversive stimulus. (See also *negative reinforcement.*)

free-operant procedure A method of instrumental conditioning that permits repeated performance of the instrumental response without intervention by the experimenter. (Compare with *discrete-trial procedure.*)

instinctive drift A gradual drift of instrumental behavior away from the responses required for reinforcement to species-typical, or instinctive, responses related to the reinforcer and to other stimuli in the experimental situation.

instrumental behavior An activity that occurs because it is effective in producing a particular consequence or reinforcer.

interim response A response that increases in frequency after the delivery of a periodic reinforcer, and then declines as time for the next reinforcer approaches.

latency The time between the start of a trial (or the start of a stimulus) and the instrumental response.

law of effect A rule for instrumental behavior, proposed by Thorndike, which states that if a response in the presence of a stimulus is followed by a satisfying event, the association between the stimulus and the response will be strengthened; if the response is followed by an annoying event, the association will be weakened.

learned-helplessness effect Interference with the learning of new instrumental responses as a result of exposure to inescapable and unavoidable aversive stimulation.

learned-helplessness hypothesis A theoretical idea that assumes that during exposure to inescapable and unavoidable aversive stimulation participants learn that their behavior does not control environmental events. This reduces motivation to respond and disrupts subsequent instrumental conditioning.

magazine training A preliminary stage of instrumental conditioning in which a stimulus is repeatedly paired with the reinforcer to enable the participant to learn to go and get the reinforcer when it is presented. The sound of the food-delivery device, for example, may be repeatedly paired with food so that the animal will learn to go to the food cup when food is delivered.

marking procedure A procedure in which the instrumental response is immediately followed by a distinctive event (the participant is picked up or a flash of light is presented) that makes the instrumental response more memorable and helps overcome the deleterious effects of delayed reinforcement.

negative contrast Less responding for a less desired or small reinforcer following previous experience with a more desired or large reinforcer than in the absence of such prior experience.

negative reinforcement An instrumental conditioning procedure in which there is a negative contingency between the instrumental response and an aversive stimulus. If the instrumental response is performed, the aversive stimulus is terminated or canceled; if the instrumental response is not performed, the aversive stimulus is presented.

omission training An instrumental conditioning procedure in which the instrumental response prevents the delivery of a reinforcing stimulus. (See also *differential reinforcement of other behavior.*)

operant response A response that is defined by the effect it produces in the environment. Examples include pressing a lever and opening a door. Any sequence of movements that depresses the lever or opens the door constitutes an instance of that particular operant.

positive contrast A greater response for a favorable or large reinforcer following previous experience with a less desired or small reinforcer, than in the absence of such prior experience.

positive reinforcement An instrumental conditioning procedure in which there is a positive contingency between the instrumental response and a reinforcing stimulus. If the participant performs the response, it receives the reinforcing stimulus; if the participant does not perform the response, it does not receive the reinforcing stimulus.

punishment An instrumental conditioning procedure in which there is a positive contingency between the instrumental response and an aversive stimulus. If the participant performs the instrumental response, it receives the aversive stimulus; if the participant does not perform the instrumental response, it does not receive the aversive stimulus.

response-reinforcer contingency The relation of a response to a reinforcer defined in terms of the probability of getting reinforced for making the response as compared to the probability of getting reinforced in the absence of the response.

running speed How fast (e.g., in feet per second) an animal moves down a runway.

secondary reinforcer Same as *conditioned reinforcer*.

shaping Reinforcement of successive approximations to a desired instrumental response.

superstitious behavior Behavior that increases in frequency because of accidental pairings of the delivery of a reinforcer with occurrences of the behavior.

temporal contiguity Same as *contiguity*.

temporal relation The time interval between an instrumental response and the reinforcer.

terminal response A response that is most likely at the end of the interval between successive reinforcements that are presented at fixed intervals.

6

Schedules of Reinforcement and Choice Behavior

CHAPTER PREVIEW

Instrumental responses rarely get reinforced each time they occur. This chapter continues our discussion of the importance of the response-reinforcer relation in instrumental behavior by describing the effects of intermittent schedules of reinforcement. A schedule of reinforcement is a program or rule that determines which occurrence of the instrumental response is followed by delivery of the reinforcer. Schedules of reinforcement are important because they determine the rate, pattern, and persistence of instrumental behavior. To begin, I will describe simple fixed and variable ratio and interval schedules, and the patterns of instrumental responding that are produced by these schedules. Then, I will describe how schedules of reinforcement can help us understand how organisms make choices between different response alternatives. Concurrent and concurrent-chain schedules of reinforcement are techniques that have been widely used to examine the mechanisms of choice in laboratory experiments. A particularly interesting form of choice is between modest short-term gains versus larger long-term gains, because these alternatives represent the dilemma of self control.

In describing various instrumental conditioning procedures in Chapter 5, I may have given the impression that every occurrence of the instrumental response invariably results in delivery of the reinforcer. Casual reflection suggests that such a perfect contingency between response and reinforcement is rare in the real world. You do not get a high grade on a test each time you study hard. You don't reach your girlfriend every time you dial her phone number, and inviting someone for dinner does not always result in a pleasant evening. In fact, in most cases the relation between instrumental responses and consequent reinforcement is rather complex. Laboratory investigations have been examining how these complex relations determine the rate and pattern of instrumental behavior.

A **schedule of reinforcement** is a program or rule that determines which occurrence of a response is followed by the reinforcer. There are an infinite number of ways that such a program could be set up. The delivery of a reinforcer could depend on the occurrence of a certain number of responses, the passage of time, the presence of certain stimuli, the occurrence of other responses, or any number of other factors. One might expect that cataloging the behavioral effects produced by the various possible schedules of reinforcement would be a difficult task. However, research so far has shown that the job is quite manageable. Reinforcement schedules that involve similar relations between responses and reinforcers usually produce similar patterns of behavior. The exact rate of responding may differ from one situation to another, but the pattern of behavior is highly predictable. This regularity has made the study of reinforcement schedules both interesting and very useful. Applications of reinforcement principles typically have a behavioral goal. Achieving that goal often requires adjusting the schedule of reinforcement to produce the desired outcome.

Schedules of reinforcement influence both how an instrumental response is learned and how it is then maintained by reinforcement. Traditionally, however, investigators of schedule effects have been concerned primarily with the maintenance of behavior. Thus, schedule effects are highly relevant to the motivation of behavior. Whether someone works hard (showing a high rate of responding) or is lazy (showing a low rate of responding) depends less on their personality than on the schedule of reinforcement that is in effect.

Schedules of reinforcement are important for managers who have to make sure their employees continue to perform a job after having learned it. Even public school teachers are often concerned with encouraging the occurrence of already learned responses rather than teaching new ones. Many students who do poorly in school know how to do their homework and how to study, but simply choose not to. Schedules of reinforcement can be used to motivate more frequent studying behavior.

Studies that focus on schedules of reinforcement have provided important information about the reinforcement process and have also provided "useful baselines for the study of other behavioral processes" (Lattal & Neef, 1996). The behavioral effects of drugs, brain lesions, or manipulations of neurotransmitter systems often depend on the schedule of reinforcement that is in effect during the behavioral testing. This makes the understanding of schedule performance critical to the study of a variety of other issues in behavior theory and behavioral neuroscience. Because of their pervasive importance, Zeiler (1984) called reinforcement schedules the *sleeping giant* in the analysis of behavior. We will try to wake up that giant in this chapter.

Laboratory studies of schedules of reinforcement are typically conducted using a Skinner box that has a clearly defined response that can occur repeatedly, so that changes in the rate of responding can be readily observed and analyzed (Ferster & Skinner, 1957). The manner in which the lever-press or key-peck response is initially shaped and conditioned is usually of little interest. Rather, the focus is on schedule factors that control the timing and repetitive performance of the instrumental behavior.

SIMPLE SCHEDULES OF INTERMITTENT REINFORCEMENT

Processes that organize and direct instrumental performance are activated in different ways by different schedules of reinforcement. I will begin with a discussion of *simple* schedules. In simple schedules, a single factor determines which occurrence of the instrumental response is reinforced.

Ratio Schedules

The defining characteristic of a **ratio schedule** is that reinforcement depends only on the number of responses the organism has performed. A ratio schedule requires merely counting the number of responses that have occurred, and delivering the reinforcer each time the required number is reached. If the required number is one, every occurrence of the instrumental response results in delivery of the reinforcer. Such a schedule is technically called **continuous reinforcement (CRF).**

Contingency management programs used in the treatment of drug abuse often employ a continuous reinforcement schedule. The clients are required to come to the clinic several times a week to be tested for drug use. If the test indicates that they have not used drugs since the last visit, they receive a voucher which can be exchanged for money. In an effective variation of this procedure, the amount of money paid is increased with successive drug-free tests and is reset to zero if the participant relapses (Roll & Newton, 2008).

Continuous reinforcement is not common outside the laboratory because the world is not perfect. Pushing an elevator button usually brings the elevator, but the elevator may malfunction, in which case nothing happens when you push the button. Turning on the hot-water faucet usually gets you hot water, but only if the water heater is working properly. Biting into a strawberry is usually reinforced by a good flavor, but not if the strawberry is rotten. Situations in which responding is reinforced only some of the time are said to involve **partial or intermittent reinforcement.**

Fixed-Ratio Schedule

Consider, for example, delivering the reinforcer after every tenth lever-press response in a study with laboratory rats. In such a schedule, there would be a fixed ratio between the number of responses the rat made and the number of reinforcers it got (ten responses per reinforcer). This makes the procedure a **fixed-ratio schedule.** More specifically, the procedure would be called a *fixed-ratio 10* or *FR 10*.

Fixed-ratio schedules are found in daily life wherever a fixed number of responses are always required for reinforcement. A newspaper delivery person is working on a fixed ratio schedule because he has a fixed number of houses on his route. Checking class attendance by reading the roll is on a fixed-ratio schedule, set by the number of students on the class roster. Making a phone call also involves a fixed-ratio schedule: you have to press a fixed number of digits on the keypad to complete each call.

A continuous reinforcement schedule is also a fixed-ratio schedule. Continuous reinforcement involves a fixed ratio of one response per reinforcer. On a continuous reinforcement schedule, organisms typically respond at a steady and moderate rate. Only brief and unpredictable pauses occur. On a CRF schedule, a pigeon, for example, will peck a key for food steadily at first and will slow down only as it gets full.

A very different pattern of responding occurs when a fixed-ratio schedule is in effect that requires more than one response. You are not likely to pause in the middle of dialing a phone number. However, you may take a while to start making the call. This is the typical pattern for fixed ratio schedules. There is a steady and high rate of responding once the behavior gets under way. But, there may be a pause before the start of the required number of responses. These features of responding are clearly evident in a **cumulative record** of the behavior.

A *cumulative record* is a special way of representing how a response is repeated over time. It shows the total (or cumulative) number of responses that

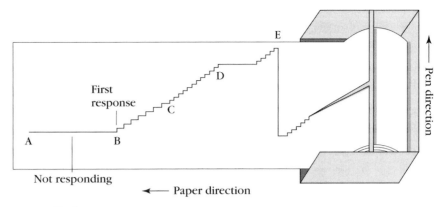

FIGURE **6.1**

The plotting of a cumulative record by a cumulative recorder for the continuous recording of behavior. The paper moves out of the machine toward the left at a constant speed. Each response causes the pen to move up the paper one step. No responses occurred between points A and B. A moderate rate of responding occurred between points B and C, and a rapid rate occurred between points C and D. At point E, the pen reset to the bottom of the page.

have occurred up to a particular point in time. In the days before computers became common, cumulative records were obtained with the use of a chart recorder (see Figure 6.1). The recorder consisted of a rotating drum that pulled paper out of the recorder at a constant speed. A pen rested on the surface of the paper. If no responses occurred, the pen remained at the same level and made a horizontal line as the paper came out of the machine. If the subject performed a lever-press response, the pen moved one step vertically on the paper. Since each lever-press response caused the pen to move one step up the paper, the total vertical distance traveled by the pen represented the cumulative (or total) number of responses the subject made. Because the paper came out of the recorder at a constant speed, the horizontal distance on the cumulative record provided a measure of how much time had elapsed in the session. The slope of the line made by the cumulative recorder represents the subject's *rate of responding*.

The cumulative record provides a complete visual representation of when and how frequently the subject responds during a session. In the record of Figure 6.1, for example, the subject did not perform the response between points A and B, and a slow rate of responding occurred between points B and C. Responses occurred more frequently between points C and D, but the subject paused at D. After responding resumed, the pen reached the top of the page (at point E) and reset to the bottom for additional responses.

Figure 6.2 shows the cumulative record of a pigeon whose responding had stabilized on a reinforcement schedule that required 120 pecks for each delivery of the reinforcer (an FR 120 schedule). Each food delivery is indicated by the small downward deflections of the recorder pen. The bird stopped responding after each food delivery, as would be expected. However, when it resumed pecking, it responded at a high and steady rate. The zero

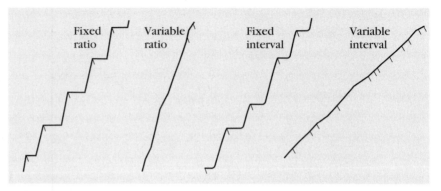

FIGURE **6.2**

Sample cumulative records of different pigeons pecking a response key on four simple schedules of food reinforcement: fixed ratio 120, variable ratio 360, fixed interval four minute, and variable interval two minute. (From *Schedules of Reinforcement*, by C.B. Ferster and B. F. Skinner, 1957, Appleton-Century-Crofts.)

rate of responding that occurs just after reinforcement is called the **post-reinforcement pause.** The high and steady rate of responding that completes each ratio requirement is called the **ratio run.**

If the ratio requirement is increased a little (e.g., from FR 120 to 150), the rate of responding during the ratio run may remain the same. However, with higher ratio requirements, longer post-reinforcement pauses tend to occur (e.g., Felton & Lyon, 1966; Williams, Saunders, & Perone, 2008). If the ratio requirement is suddenly increased a great deal (e.g., from FR 120 to FR 500), the animal is likely to pause periodically before the completion of the ratio requirement (e.g., Stafford & Branch, 1998). This effect is called **ratio strain.** In extreme cases, ratio strain may be so great that the animal stops responding altogether. In using ratio schedules, one must be careful not to raise the ratio requirement (or, more generally, the difficulty of a task) too quickly, or ratio strain may occur and the subject may give up altogether.

Although the pause that occurs before a ratio run in fixed-ratio schedules is historically called the *post-reinforcement pause,* research has shown that the length of the pause is controlled by the upcoming ratio requirement (e.g., Baron & Herpolsheimer, 1999; see also Wade-Galuska, Perone, & Wirth, 2005). Consider, for example, washing your car by hand rather than driving through a car wash. Washing your car by hand is a fixed-ratio task since it requires a set number of responses and a set amount of effort each time, as determined by the size of your car. If you procrastinate before starting to wash your car, it is because you are not quite ready to tackle the job, not because you are resting from the previous time you did the work. Thus, the *post-reinforcement pause* would be more correctly labeled the *pre-ratio pause.*

Variable-Ratio Schedule

In a fixed-ratio schedule, a predictable number of responses or effort is required for each reinforcer. This predictability can be disrupted by varying the number of responses required for reinforcement from one occasion to the next, which would be the case if you worked at a car wash where you had to work on cars of different sizes. Such a situation is still a ratio schedule because washing each car still depends on how many responses or effort you make. However, a different number of responses is required for the delivery of each reinforcer. Such a procedure is called a **variable-ratio schedule (VR)**. We may, for example, require a pigeon to make 10 responses to earn the first reinforcer, 13 to earn the second, 7 for the next one, and so on. The numerical value of a variable-ratio schedule indicates the average number of responses required per reinforcer. Thus, our procedure would be a variable-ratio 10 schedule (VR 10).

Variable-ratio schedules are found in daily life whenever an unpredictable amount of effort is required to obtain a reinforcer. For example, each time a custodian goes into a room on his rounds, he knows that some amount of cleaning will be necessary, but he does not know exactly how dirty the room will be. Gamblers playing a slot machine are also responding on a variable-ratio schedule. They have to play the machine to win. However, they never know how many plays will produce the winning combination. Variable-ratio schedules are also common in sports. A certain number of strokes are always required to finish a hole in golf. But, most players cannot be sure how many strokes they will need when they start.

Because the number of responses required for reinforcement is not predictable, predictable pauses in the rate of responding are less likely with variable-ratio schedules than with fixed-ratio schedules. Rather, organisms respond at a fairly steady rate on VR schedules. Figure 6.2 shows a cumulative record for a pigeon whose pecking behavior was maintained on a VR 360 schedule of reinforcement. Notice that even though on average the VR 360 schedule required many more pecks for each reinforcer than the FR 120 schedule shown in Figure 6.2, the VR 360 schedule maintained a much steadier pattern of responding.

Although post-reinforcement pauses can occur on variable-ratio schedules (see Blakely & Schlinger, 1988; Schlinger, Blakely, & Kaczor, 1990), such pauses are longer and more prominent with fixed-ratio schedules. The overall response rate on fixed- and variable-ratio schedules is similar provided that, on average, similar numbers of responses are required. However, the overall response rate tends to be distributed in a pause-run pattern with fixed-ratio schedules, whereas a steadier pattern of responding is observed with variable-ratio schedules (e.g., Crossman, Bonem, & Phelps, 1987). (For additional analyses of ratio schedules, see Bizo & Killeen, 1997.)

Interval Schedules

In ratio schedules, reinforcement depends only on the number of responses the subject has performed. In other situations, responses are reinforced only if the responses occur after a certain amount of time has passed. **Interval schedules** illustrate this type of situation.

Fixed-Interval Schedule

In a simple interval schedule, a response is reinforced only if it occurs more than a set amount of time after a reference point, the last delivery of the reinforcer or

BOX **6.1**

The Post-Reinforcement Pause and Procrastination

The post-reinforcement pause that occurs in fixed-ratio schedules in the laboratory is also evident in common human experience. As I noted earlier, the pause occurs because a predictably large number of responses are required to produce the next reward. Such procrastination is legendary in human behavior. Consider, for example, a semester in which you have several term papers to write. You are likely to work on one term paper at a time. However, when you have completed one paper, you probably will not start working on the next one right away. Rather, there will be a post-reinforcement pause. After completing a large project, people tend to take some time off before starting the next one. In fact, procrastination between tasks or before the start of a new job is the rule rather than the exception.

Laboratory results provide a suggestion for overcoming procrastination. Fixed-ratio-schedule performance in the laboratory indicates that once animals begin to respond on a ratio run, they respond at a high and steady rate until they complete the ratio requirement. This suggests that if somehow you got yourself to start on a job, chances are you will not find it difficult to keep going. Only the beginning is hard. One technique that works pretty well is to tell yourself that you will start by just doing a little bit of the job. If you are trying to write a paper, tell yourself that you will write only one paragraph to start with. You may find that once you have completed the first paragraph, it will be easier to write the second one, then the one after that, and so on. If you are procrastinating about spring cleaning, instead of thinking about doing the entire job, start with a small part of it, such as washing the kitchen floor. The rest will then come more easily.

the start of the trial. In a **fixed-interval schedule (FI),** the amount of time that has to pass before a response is reinforced, is constant from one trial to the next. Fixed-interval schedules are found in situations where a fixed amount of time is required to prepare or set up the reinforcer. A washing machine operates on a fixed interval schedule. A fixed amount of time is required to complete the wash cycle. No matter how many times you open the washing machine before the required time has passed, you will not be reinforced with clean clothes. Once the cycle is finished, the reinforcer becomes available, and you can take out your clean clothes any time after that.

Similar contingencies can be set up in the laboratory. Consider, for example, a fixed-interval 4-minute schedule (FI four min) for pecking in pigeons. A bird on this schedule would get reinforced for the first peck it made after four minutes have passed since the last food delivery (or the beginning of the schedule cycle). Because pecks made less than four minutes into the trial are never reinforced, participants learn to wait to respond until the end of the FI interval (see Figure 6.2). As the time for the availability of the next reinforcer draws closer, the response rate increases. This increase in response rate is evident as an acceleration in the cumulative record toward the end of the fixed interval. The pattern of responding that develops with fixed-interval reinforcement schedules is accordingly called the **fixed-interval scallop.**

Performance on an FI schedule reflects the subject's accuracy in telling time. (I will have more to say about the psychology of timing in Chapter 12.) If the subject were entirely incapable of telling time, it would be equally likely to respond at any point in the FI cycle. The post reinforcement pause and the subsequent acceleration towards the end of the interval reflects a rudimentary ability to tell time. How could this ability be improved? Common experience suggests that having a watch or clock of some sort makes it much easier to judge time intervals. The same thing happens with pigeons on an FI schedule. In one study, the clock consisted of a spot of light that grew as time passed during the FI cycle. Introduction of this clock stimulus increased the duration of the post-reinforcement pause and caused responding to shift closer to the end of the FI cycle (Ferster & Skinner, 1957).

It is important to realize that a fixed-interval schedule does not guarantee that the reinforcer will be provided at a certain point in time. Pigeons on an FI four min schedule do not automatically receive access to grain every four minutes. The interval determines only when the reinforcer *becomes available*, not when it is delivered. In order to receive the reinforcer after it has become available, the subject still has to make the instrumental response. (For reviews of fixed-interval timing and operant behavior, see Staddon & Cerutti, 2003; Jozefowiez & Staddon, 2008.)

The scheduling of tests in college courses has major similarities to the basic fixed-interval schedule. Usually there are only two or three tests, and the tests are evenly distributed during the term. The pattern of studying that such a schedule encourages is very similar to what is observed with an FI schedule in the laboratory. Students spend little effort studying at the beginning of the semester or just after the midterm exam. Rather, they begin to study a week or two before each exam, and the rate of studying rapidly increases as the day of the exam approaches. Interestingly, members of the United States Congress behave the same way, writing bills at much higher rates as the end of the congressional session approaches (Critchfield et al., 2003).

Variable-Interval Schedule

In fixed-interval schedules, responses are reinforced if they occur after a fixed amount of time has passed after the start of the trial or schedule cycle. Interval schedules also can be unpredictable. With a **variable-interval schedule (VI)**, responses are reinforced if they occur after a variable interval after the start of the trial or the schedule cycle.

Variable-interval schedules are found in situations where an unpredictable amount of time is required to prepare or set up the reinforcer. A mechanic who cannot tell you how long it will take to fix your car has imposed a variable-interval schedule on you. The car will not be ready for some time, during which attempts to get it will not be reinforced. How much time has to pass before the car will be ready is unpredictable. A sales clerk at a bakery is also on a VI schedule of reinforcement. Some time has to pass after waiting on a customer before another will enter the store to buy something. However, the interval between customers is unpredictable.

In a laboratory study, a VI schedule could be set up in which the first food pellet became available when at least one minute has passed since the beginning of the session, the second food pellet became available when at least three minutes have passed since the previous pellet, and the third reinforcer became available when at least two minutes have passed since the previous pellet. In this procedure, the average interval that has to pass before successive reinforcers become available is two minutes. Therefore, the procedure would be called a variable-interval two-minute schedule, or VI two min.

As in fixed-interval schedules, the subject has to perform the instrumental response to obtain the reinforcer. Reinforcers are not given for free. Rather, they are given if the individual responds after the variable interval has timed out. Like variable-ratio schedules, variable-interval schedules maintain steady and stable rates of responding without regular pauses (see Figure 6.2).

Interval Schedules and Limited Hold

In simple interval schedules, once the reinforcer becomes available, it remains available until the required response is made, no matter how long that may take. On an FI two minute schedule, for example, the reinforcer becomes available two minutes after the start of the schedule cycle. If the animal responds at exactly this time, it will be reinforced. If it waits and responds 90 minutes later, it will still get reinforced. Once the reinforcer has been set up, it remains available until the response occurs.

With interval schedules outside the laboratory, it is more common for reinforcers to become available for only limited periods. Consider, for example, a dormitory cafeteria. Meals are served only at fixed intervals. Therefore, going to the cafeteria is reinforced only after a certain amount of time has passed since the last meal. However, once a meal becomes available, you have a limited amount of time in which to get it. This kind of restriction on how long a reinforcer remains available is called a **limited hold**. Limited-hold restrictions can be added to both fixed-interval and variable-interval schedules.

Comparison of Ratio and Interval Schedules

There are striking similarities between the patterns of responding maintained by simple ratio and interval schedules. As we have seen, with both fixed-ratio and fixed-interval schedules, there is a post-reinforcement pause after each delivery of the reinforcer. In addition, both FR and FI schedules produce high rates of responding just before the delivery of the next reinforcer. By contrast, variable-ratio and variable-interval schedules both maintain steady rates of responding, without predictable pauses. Does this mean that interval and ratio schedules motivate behavior in the same way? Not at all! The surface similarities hide fundamental differences in the underlying motivational mechanisms of interval and ratio schedules.

Early evidence of fundamental differences between ratio and interval schedules was provided by an important experiment by Reynolds (1975). Reynolds compared the rate of key pecking in pigeons reinforced on variable-ratio and variable-interval schedules. Two pigeons were trained to peck the response key for food reinforcement. One of the birds was reinforced on a VR schedule. Therefore, for this bird the frequency of reinforcement was entirely determined by its rate of responding. The other bird was reinforced on a VI schedule. To make sure that the opportunities for reinforcement would be identical for the two birds, the VI schedule was controlled by the behavior of the bird reinforced on the VR schedule. Each time the VR pigeon was just one response short of the requirement for reinforcement on that trial, the experimenter ended the waiting time for the VI bird. With this arrangement, the next response made by each bird was reinforced. Thus, the frequency of reinforcement was virtually identical for the two animals.

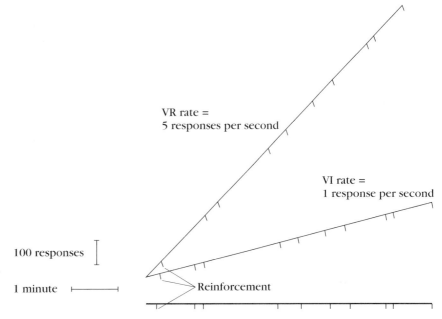

VR rate =
5 responses per second

VI rate =
1 response per second

100 responses

1 minute

Reinforcement

FIGURE **6.3**

Cumulative records for two pigeons, one reinforced on a variable ratio (VR) schedule and the other yoked to it on a variable interval (VI) schedule. Although the two pigeons received the same rate of reinforcement, the VR bird responded five times as fast as the VI bird. (From *A Primer of Operant Conditioning,* 2nd ed., by G. S. Reynolds. Copyright © 1975 by Scott Foresman. Reprinted by permission.)

Figure 6.3 shows the cumulative record of pecking exhibited by each bird. Even though the two pigeons received the same frequency and distribution of reinforcers, they behaved very differently. The pigeon reinforced on the VR schedule responded at a much higher rate than the pigeon reinforced on the VI schedule. The VR schedule motivated much more vigorous instrumental behavior. This basic finding has since been replicated in numerous studies and has stimulated lively theoretical analysis (e.g., Baum, 1993; Cole, 1994, 1999; Reed, 2007a, b).

Results similar to those Reynolds observed with pigeons also have been found with undergraduate students (e.g., Raia, Shillingford, Miller, & Baier, 2000). The task was akin to a video game. A target appeared on a computer screen and the students had to maneuver a spaceship and "fire" at the target with a joystick as the instrumental response. Following a direct hit of the target, the subjects received five cents. However, not every "hit" was reinforced. Which occurrence of the instrumental response was reinforced depended on the schedule of reinforcement programmed into the software. The students were assigned to pairs but each worked in a separate cubicle and didn't know that he or she had a partner. One member of each pair received reinforcement on a variable ratio schedule. The other member of the pair was reinforced on a variable interval schedule that was yoked to the VR schedule.

Thus, as in the pigeon experiment, reinforcers became available to both subjects at the same time, but one controlled access to the reinforcer through a VR schedule and the other did not.

Raia et al. (2000) studied the effects of response shaping, instructions, and the presence of a consummatory response on performance on the VR-VI yoking procedure. (The consummatory response was picking up the five cent reinforcer each time it was delivered and putting it into a piggy bank.) One set of conditions was quite similar to the pigeon studies: the students were shaped to make the instrumental response, they received minimal instructions, and they were required to make the consummatory response. Interestingly, under these conditions, the college students performed just like the pigeons. Higher rates of responding occurred for the individual of each pair who was reinforced on the variable-ratio schedule.

The higher response rates that occur on ratio as compared to interval schedules powerfully illustrate how schedules can alter the motivation for instrumental behavior. A simplistic theory might assume that rate of responding is just a function of how many reinforcers the participant earns. But, in the experiments described above, the rates of reinforcement were identical in the ratio and interval schedule conditions. Nevertheless, the ratio schedules produced much more behavior. This is important news if you are a manager trying to get the most effort from your employees. The reinforcer in an employment situation is provided by the wages individuals earn. The Reynolds experiment tells you us that you can get employees to work harder for the same pay if the wages are provided on a ratio rather than an interval schedule.

Why might ratio schedules produce higher rates of responding than interval schedules? Investigators have focused on two alternative explanations.

Reinforcement of IRTs

The first explanation of higher response rates on ratio schedules focuses on the spacing or interval between one response and the next. This interval is called the **inter-response time (IRT).** I noted in Chapter 5 that various features of behavior can be increased by reinforcement. The interval between successive responses is one such behavioral feature. If the subject is reinforced for a response that occurs shortly after the preceding one, then a short IRT is reinforced and short IRTs become more likely in the future. On the other hand, if the subject is reinforced for a response that ends a long IRT, then a long IRT is reinforced and long IRTs become more likely in the future. A subject that has mostly short inter-response times is responding at a high rate. By contrast, a subject that has mostly long inter-response times is responding at a low rate.

How do ratio and interval schedules determine the reinforcement of inter-response times? Consider a ratio schedule. With a ratio schedule there are no time constraints and the faster the participant completes the ratio requirement, the faster she will receive the reinforcer. Thus, a ratio schedule favors not waiting long between responses. It favors short inter-response times. Ratio schedules differentially reinforce short inter-response times.

In contrast, interval schedules provide little advantage for short inter-response times. In fact, interval schedules favor waiting longer between responses. Consider, for example, an FI two minute schedule of food reinforcement. Each food pellet becomes available two minutes after the last one was delivered. If the participant responds frequently before the food pellet is set up, those responses and short IRTs will not be reinforced. On the other hand, if the participant waits a long time between responses (emitting long IRTs), those responses are more likely to occur after the two minutes has timed out, and are more likely to be reinforced. Thus, interval schedules differentially reinforce long IRTs, and thus results in lower rates of responding than ratio schedules (Baum, 1993; Cole, 1994, 1999; Tanno & Sakagami, 2008).

Feedback Functions

The second major explanation of the higher response rates that are observed on ratio schedules focuses on the relationship between response rates and reinforcement rates calculated over an entire experimental session or an extended period of time (e.g., Reed, 2007a, b). This relationship is called the *feedback function* because reinforcement is considered to be the feedback or consequence of responding.

In the long run, what is the relationship between response rate and reinforcement rate on ratio schedules? The answer is pretty straightforward. Since the only requirement for reinforcement on a ratio schedule is making a certain number of responses, the faster the subject completes the ratio requirement, the faster it obtains the next reinforcer. Thus, response rate is directly related to reinforcement rate. The higher the response rate, the more reinforcers the subject will earn per hour and the higher its reinforcement rate will be. Furthermore, there is no limit to this increasing function. No matter how rapidly the subject responds, if it can increase its response rate even further, it will enjoy a corresponding increase in the rate of reinforcement. The feedback function for a ratio schedule is an increasing linear function and has no limit.

How about the feedback function for an interval schedule? Interval schedules place an upper limit on the number of reinforcers a subject can earn. On a VI two minute schedule, for example, if the subject obtains each reinforcer as soon as it becomes available, it can earn a maximum of 30 reinforcers per hour. Because each trial on an interval schedule begins with a period during which the reinforcer is not available, there is an upper limit to the number of reinforcers a subject can earn. On a VI two minute schedule, the limit is 30 reinforcers per hour. A subject cannot increase its reinforcement rate above 30 per hour no matter how much it increases its rate of responding.

Doctors, lawyers, and hair dressers in private practice are all paid on a ratio schedule with a linearly increasing feedback function. Their earnings depend on the number of clients or procedures they perform each day. The more procedures they perform, the more money they make and there is no limit to this relationship. No matter how much money they are making, if they can squeeze in another client, they can earn another fee. This is in contrast to salaried employees in a supermarket or the post office, who cannot increase their income as readily by increasing their efforts. Their only hope is that their diligence is recognized when employees are considered for a raise or promotion every six months. The wage scale for salaried employees has strong interval schedule components.

CHOICE BEHAVIOR: CONCURRENT SCHEDULES

The reinforcement schedules I described thus far were focused on a single response and reinforcement of that response. The simplicity of single-response situations facilitates scientific discovery, but experiments in which only one response is being measured ignore some of the richness and complexity of behavior. Even in a simple situation like a Skinner box, organisms engage in a variety of activities and are continually choosing among possible alternatives. A pigeon can peck the only response key in the box, or preen or move about the chamber. People are also constantly having to make choices about what to do. Should you go to the movies or stay at home and watch TV? If you stay at home, which show should you watch and should you watch it to the end or change the channel? Understanding the mechanisms of choice is fundamental to understanding behavior, since much of what we do is the result of choosing one activity over another.

Choice situations can be rather complicated. For example, a person may have a choice of 12 different activities (playing a video game, watching television, text messaging a friend, playing with the dog, and the like), each of which produces a different type of reinforcer according to a different reinforcement schedule. Analyzing all the factors that control someone's choices can be a formidable task, if not an impossible one. Therefore, psychologists have begun experimental investigations of the mechanisms of choice by studying simpler situations. The simplest choice situation is one which has two response alternatives, and each response is followed by a reinforcer according to its own schedule of reinforcement.

Numerous studies of choice have been conducted in Skinner boxes equipped with two pecking keys a pigeon could peck. In the typical experiment, responding on each key is reinforced on some schedule of reinforcement. The two schedules are in effect at the same time (or concurrently), and the subject is free to switch from one response key to the other. This type of procedure is called a **concurrent schedule.** Concurrent schedules allow for continuous measurement of choice because the organism is free to change back and forth between the response alternatives at any time.

Playing slot machines in a casino is on a concurrent schedule, with lots of response options. Each type of slot machine operates on a different schedule of reinforcement, and you can play any of the machines. Furthermore, you are at liberty to switch from one machine to another at any time. Closer to home, operating the remote control for your TV is also on a concurrent schedule. You can select any one of a number of channels to watch. Some channels are more interesting than others, which indicates that your watching behavior is reinforced on different schedules of reinforcement on different channels. As with the slot machines, you can change your selection at any time. Talking to various people at a party involves similar contingencies. You can talk to whomever you want and move to someone else if the conversation gets boring, indicting a reduced rate of reinforcement.

Figure 6.4 shows a laboratory example of a concurrent schedule. If the pigeon pecks the key on the left, it receives food according to a VI 60 second schedule. Pecks on the right key produce food according to an FR 10 schedule. The pigeon is free to peck on either side at any time. The point of the ex-

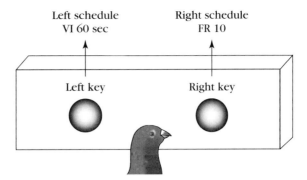

FIGURE **6.4**

Diagram of a concurrent schedule for pigeons. Pecks at the left key are reinforced according to a VI 60 second schedule of reinforcement. Pecks on the right key are reinforced according to an FR 10 schedule of reinforcement.

periment is to see how the pigeon distributes its pecks on the two keys and how the schedule of reinforcement on each key influences its choices.

Measures of Choice Behavior

The individual's choice in a concurrent schedule is reflected in the distribution of its behavior between the two response alternatives. This can be measured in several ways. One common technique is to calculate the *relative rate of responding* on each alternative. The relative rate of responding on the left key, for example, is calculated by dividing the rate of responding on the left by the total rate of responding (left key plus right key). To express this mathematically, let's designate B_L as pecking or behavior on the left, and B_R as behavior on the right. Then, the relative rate of responding on the left is:

$$\frac{B_L}{(B_L + B_R)} \tag{6.1}$$

If the pigeon pecks equally as often on the two response keys, this ratio will be 0.5. If the rate of responding on the left is greater than the rate of responding on the right, the ratio will be greater than 0.5. On the other hand, if the rate of responding on the left is less than the rate of responding on the right, the ratio will be less than 0.5. The relative rate of responding on the right (B_R) can be calculated in a comparable manner.

As you might suspect, how an organism distributes its behavior between the two response alternatives is greatly influenced by the reinforcement schedule in effect for each response. For example, if the same variable-interval reinforcement schedule is available for each response alternative, as in a concurrent VI 60 second VI 60 second procedure, the pigeon will peck the two keys equally often. The relative rate of responding for pecks on each side will be 0.5. This result is intuitively reasonable. If the pigeon spent all its time pecking on one side, it would miss reinforcers programmed on the other side. The bird can get more reinforcers by pecking on both sides. Since the VI schedule available on each side is the same, there is no advantage in responding more on one side than on the other.

By responding equally often on each side of a concurrent VI 60 second VI 60 second schedule, the pigeon will also earn reinforcers equally often on each side. The relative rate of reinforcement earned for each response alternative can be calculated in a manner comparable to the relative rate of response. Let's designate r_L as the rate of reinforcement on the left and r_R as the rate of reinforcement on the right. Then, the relative rate of reinforcement on the left will be r_L divided by the total rate of reinforcement (the sum of the rate of reward earned on the left and the rate of reward earned on the right). This is expressed in the formula:

$$\frac{r_L}{(r_L + r_R)} \tag{6.2}$$

where r_L and r_R represent the rates of reinforcement earned on each response alternative. On a concurrent VI 60 second VI 60 second schedule, the relative rate of reinforcement for each response alternative will be 0.5 because the subject earns rewards equally often on each side.

The Matching Law

As we have seen, with a concurrent VI 60 second VI 60 second schedule, both the relative rate of responding and the relative rate of reinforcement for each response alternative are 0.5. Thus, the relative rate of responding is equal to the relative rate of reinforcement. Will this equality also occur if the two response alternatives are not reinforced according to the same schedule? This important question was asked by Herrnstein (1961).

Herrnstein studied the distribution of responses on various concurrent VI-VI schedules in which the maximum total rate of reinforcement the pigeons could earn was fixed at 40 per hour. Depending on the exact value of each VI schedule, different proportions of the 40 reinforcers could be obtained by pecking the left and right keys. Consider, for example, a concurrent VI six minute VI two minute schedule. With such a schedule, a maximum of 10 reinforcers per hour could be obtained by responding on the VI six minute alternative, and a maximum of 30 reinforcers per hour could be obtained by responding on the VI two minute alternative.

There was no constraint on which side the pigeons could peck on the various concurrent VI-VI schedules Herrnstein tested. The pigeons could respond exclusively on one side or the other, or they could split their pecks between the two sides in various proportions. As it turned out, the pigeons distributed their responses in a highly predictable fashion. The results, summarized in Figure 6.5, indicate that the relative rate of responding on a given alternative was always very nearly equal to the relative rate of reinforcement earned on that alternative. If the pigeons earned a greater proportion of their reinforcers on the left, they made a correspondingly greater proportion of their responses on that side. The relative rate of responding on an alternative *matched* the relative rate of reinforcement on that alternative. Similar findings have been obtained in numerous other experiments, which encouraged Herrnstein to state the relation as a law of behavior, the **matching law.** (For an anthology of Herrnstein's papers on this topic, see Herrnstein, 1997. For a recent review of the matching law, see Jozefowiez, & Staddon, 2008.)

There are two common mathematical expressions of the matching law. In one formulation, rate of responding or behavior (B) and rate of reinforcement

Courtesy of Donald A. Dewsbury

R. J. Herrnstein

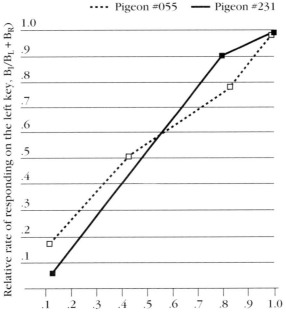

FIGURE **6.5**

Results of various concurrent VI VI schedules were tested with pigeons. Note that throughout the range of schedules, the relative rate of responding nearly equals (matches) the relative rate of reinforcement. (From "Relative and Absolute Strength of Response as a Function of Frequency of Reinforcement," by R. J. Herrnstein, 1961, *Journal of the Experimental Analysis of Behavior, 4*, pp. 267–272. Copyright © 1961 by the Society for the Experimental Analysis of Behavior, Inc. Reprinted by permission.)

(r) on one choice alternative are expressed as a proportion of total response and reinforcement rates, as follows:

$$\frac{B_L}{(B_L + B_R)} = \frac{r_L}{(r_L + r_R)} \tag{6.3}$$

As before, B_L and B_R in this equation represent the rates of behavior on the left and right keys, and r_L and r_R represent the rates of reinforcement earned on each response alternative.

The second formulation of the matching law is simpler but mathematically equivalent to equation 6.3. In the second version, the rates of responding and reinforcement on one alternative are expressed as a proportion of the rates of responding and reinforcement on the other alternative, as follows:

$$\frac{B_L}{B_R} = \frac{r_L}{r_R} \tag{6.4}$$

Both mathematical expressions of the matching law represent the same basic principle, namely that *relative rates of responding match relative rates of reinforcement.*

The matching law has had a profound impact on the way in which we think about instrumental behavior. The major insight provided by the matching law is that the rate of a particular response does not depend on the rate of reinforcement of that response alone. Whether a behavior occurs frequently or infrequently depends not only on its own schedule of reinforcement but also on the rates of reinforcement of other activities the individual may perform. A given simple reinforcement schedule that is highly effective in a reward-impoverished environment may have little impact if there are numerous alternative sources of reinforcement. Therefore, how we go about training and motivating a particular response (e.g., studying among high school students) has to take into account other activities and sources of reinforcement the individuals have at their disposal.

The importance of alternative sources of reinforcement has provided useful insights into problematic behaviors such as unprotected sex among teenagers, which results in unwanted pregnancies, abortions, and sexually transmitted diseases. Based on the concepts of the matching law, Bulow and Meller (1998) predicted that "adolescent girls who live in a reinforcement-barren environment are more likely to engage in sexual behaviors than those girls whose environments offer them a fuller array of reinforcement opportunities" (p. 586). To test this prediction, they administered a survey to adolescent girls that asked them about the things they found reinforcing and their sexual activities. From these data the investigators estimated the rates of sexual activity and contraceptive use and the rates of reinforcement derived from sexual and other activities. These data were then entered into the equations of the matching law. The results were impressive. The matching law predicted the frequency of sexual activity with an accuracy of 60%, and predicted contraceptive use with 67% accuracy. These findings suggest that efforts to reduce unprotected sex among teenagers have to consider not only their sexual activities but other things they may learn to enjoy (such as playing a sport or musical instrument).

Undermatching, Overmatching, and Response Bias

The matching law clearly indicates that choices are not made capriciously. Rather, choice is an orderly function of rates of reinforcement. Although the matching law has enjoyed considerable success and has guided much research over the past 40 years, relative rates of responding do not always match relative rates of reinforcement exactly. The precise characterization of the matching function is the subject of continuing research (e.g., Baum, 1979; Davison & McCarthy, 1988; McDowell, 2005).

Most instances in which choice behavior does not correspond perfectly to the matching relation can be accommodated by adding two parameters, b, and s, to equation 6.4. This generalized form of the matching law (Baum, 1974) is as follows:

$$B_L/B_R = b(r_L/r_R)^s \qquad (6.5)$$

The parameter s represents *sensitivity* of the choice behavior to the relative rates of reinforcement for the response alternatives. When perfect matching occurs, s is equal to 1. In that case, relative response rates are a direct function of relative rates of reinforcement. The most common deviation from perfect matching involves reduced sensitivity of the choice behavior to the relative rates of reinforcement. Such results are referred to as **undermatching**

W. M. Baum

and can be accommodated by equation 6.5 by making the exponent s less than one. Notice that if the exponent s is less than one, the value of the term representing relative reinforcer rates, (r_A/r_B), becomes smaller, indicating the reduced sensitivity to the relative rate of reinforcement.

Numerous variables have been found to influence the sensitivity parameter, including the species tested, effort or difficulty involved in switching from one alternative to the other, and the details of how the schedule alternatives are constructed. In general, undermatching is reduced if there is less reinforcement for switching from one response alternative to the other and if subjects have more extensive experience with the choice procedure (see Jozefowiez & Staddon, 2008).

The parameter b in equation 6.5 represents *response bias*. In Herrnstein's original experiment (and in most others that have followed), animals chose between two responses of the same type (pecking a response key), and each response was reinforced by the same type of reinforcer (brief access to food). Response bias influences choice when the response alternatives require different amounts of effort or if the reinforcer provided for one response is much more desirable than the reinforcer provided for the other response. A preference (or bias) for one response or one reinforcer over the other results in more responding on the preferred side and is represented by a higher value of the bias parameter b.

The Matching Law and Simple Reinforcement Schedules

If the matching law is a fundamental feature of behavior, then it should also characterize responding on simple schedules of reinforcement. But, in simple schedules, only one response manipulandum is provided. How can a law that describes choice among several alternatives be applied to a single response?

As Herrnstein (1970) pointed out, even single-response situations can be considered to involve a choice. The choice is between making the specified response (e.g., bar pressing or pecking a key) and engaging in other possible activities (grooming, walking around, pecking the floor, sniffing holes in the experimental chamber). On a simple schedule, the subject receives explicit reinforcement for making a specific operant response. In addition, it undoubtedly receives reinforcers for the other activities in which it may engage (some of these may be intrinsic rewards). Hence, the total reinforcement in a simple schedule experiment includes the programmed extrinsic rewards as well as other unprogrammed sources of reinforcement. These considerations enable the matching law to be applied to single-response reinforcement schedules.

Let us assume that B_X represents the rate of the specified or target operant response in the schedule, B_O represents the rate of the animal's other activities, r_X is the rate of the explicit programmed reinforcement, and r_O is the rate of the unprogrammed reinforcement for the other activities. With these values substituted into equation 6.3, the matching law for single-response situations can be stated as follows:

$$\frac{B_X}{(B_X + B_O)} = \frac{r_X}{(r_X + r_O)} \tag{6.6}$$

Solving this equation for B_X provides the following:

$$B_X = \frac{(B_X + B_O)r_X}{(r_X + r_O)} \tag{6.7}$$

This equation can be solved if one assumes that $(B_X + B_O)$ is equal to a constant irrespective of the reinforcer that is employed. If this constant is labeled k, equation 6.7 can be rewritten as:

$$B_X = \frac{k\, r_X}{(r_X + r_O)} \tag{6.8}$$

This equation predicts that the rate of responding (R_X) will be directly related to the rate of reinforcement for that response in a negatively accelerating fashion. Another implication of the equation, of particular clinical interest, is that the rate of the target response B_X will decline as one increases the rate of alternative sources of reinforcement (r_O). Thus, equation 6.8 provides two ways of changing the rate of a response: by changing its rate of reinforcement, or by changing the rate of other sources of reinforcement. (For recent applications of the generalized matching law to single response situations, see Dallery, Soto, & McDowell, 2005; McDowell, 2005.)

Mechanisms of the Matching Law

The matching law describes how organisms distribute their responses in a choice situation, but does not explain what mechanisms are responsible for this response distribution. It is a descriptive law of nature rather than a mechanistic

---

BOX **6.2**

The Matching Law and Complex Human Behavior

The matching law and its implications have been found to apply to a wide range of human behavior including social conversation (Borrero et al., 2007), courtship and mate selection (Takeuchi, 2006), and the choices that lead to substance abuse (e.g., Frisher & Beckett, 2006; Vuchinich & Tucker, 2006). In an interesting recent study, Vollmer and Bourret (2000) examined the choices that college basketball players made during the course of intercollegiate games. A basketball player can elect to shoot at the basket from an area close to the basket and thereby get two points, or he or she can elect to shoot from an area farther away and thereby get three points. Teams compile statistics on the number of two- and three-point shots attempted and made by individual players. These data provide information about the relative rates of selecting each response alternative. The team data also include information about the success of each attempt, and these data can be used to calculate the rate of reinforcement for each response alternative. Vollmer and Bourret examined the data for 13 players on the men's team and 13 players on the women's team of a large university, and found that the relative choice of the different types of shots was proportional to the relative rates of reinforcement for those shots. Thus, the choice behavior of these athletes during regular games followed the matching law.

The matching law also has been used to analyze the choice of plays in professional football games of the American National Football League (Reed, Critchfield, & Martins, 2006). Data on running plays versus passing plays were analyzed in terms of the number of yards that were gained as a consequence of each play. This way of looking at the game provided response rates (frequency of one or the other type of play) and reinforcement rates (yards gained). The generalized matching law accounted for 75% of the choice of plays. The sensitivity parameter showed that the relative frequency of passing versus running plays undermatched the relative yardage gained by these plays. Thus, the choice of plays did not take full advantage of the yardage gains that could have been obtained. The response bias parameter in the generalized matching law indicated that there was a significant bias in favor of running plays. Interestingly, teams whose play calling followed the matching law more closely had better win records than teams that significantly deviated from matching.

law. Factors that may be responsible for matching in choice situations have been the subject of continuing experimentation and theoretical debate (see Davison & McCarthy, 1988; Herrnstein, 1997; Jozefowiez, & Staddon, 2008).

The matching law is stated in terms of rates of responding and reinforcement averaged over the entire duration of experimental sessions. It ignores when individual responses are made. Some theories of matching are similar in that they ignore what might occur at the level of individual responses. Such explanations are called *molar theories*. Molar theories explain aggregates of responses. They deal with the overall distribution of responses and reinforcers in choice situations.

In contrast to molar theories, other explanations of the matching relation focus on what happens at the level of individual responses and view the matching relation as the net result of these individual choices. Such explanations are called *molecular theories*. I previously described molecular and molar explanations of why ratio schedules produce higher response rates than interval schedules. The explanation that emphasized the reinforcement of inter-response times was a molecular or local account. In contrast, the explanation that emphasized feedback functions of ratio and interval schedules was a molar theory. (For a detailed discussion of molecular versus molar approaches to the analysis of behavior, see Baum, 2002.)

Matching and Maximizing Rates of Reinforcement

The most extensively investigated explanations of choice behavior are based on the intuitively reasonable idea that organisms distribute their actions among response alternatives so as to receive the maximum amount of reinforcement possible in the situation. According to this idea, animals switch back and forth between response alternatives so as to receive as many reinforcers as they possibly can. The idea that organisms maximize reinforcement has been used to explain choice behavior at both molecular and molar levels of analysis.

Molecular Maximizing

According to molecular theories of maximizing, organisms always choose whichever response alternative is most likely to be reinforced at the time (Hinson & Staddon, 1983a, 1983b). Shimp (1966, 1969) proposed an early version of molecular matching. He suggested that when two schedules (A and B) are in effect simultaneously, the subject switches from schedule A to schedule B as the probability of reinforcement for schedule B increases. Consider, for example, a pigeon working on a concurrent VI-VI schedule. As the pigeon pecks Key A, the timer controlling reinforcement for Key B is still operating. The longer the pigeon stays on Key A, the greater will be the probability that the requisite interval for Key B has elapsed and the pigeon will be reinforced for pecking key B. By switching, the pigeon can pick up the reinforcer on Key B. Now, the longer it continues to peck Key B, the more likely Key A will become set for reinforcement. Shimp proposed that the matching relation is a byproduct of prudent switching when the probability of reinforcement on the alternative response key becomes greater than the probability of reinforcement on the current response key.

Detailed studies of the patterns of switching from one to another response alternative have not always supported the molecular maximizing

B. A. Williams

theory proposed by Shimp. In fact, some studies have shown that matching is possible in the absence of momentary maximizing (e.g., Nevin, 1979; Machado, 1994; Williams, 1991, 1992). However, subsequent approaches to molecular analyses of choice behavior have met with more success.

One approach has emphasized analyzing a two-alternative choice in terms of reinforcement for staying with a particular alternative and reinforcement for switching to the other option. For example, a situation in which a laboratory rat has two response levers available can be analyzed as involving four different options: staying on the right lever, switching from the right lever to the left one, staying on the left lever, and switching from the left lever to the right one. Each of these four options has its own reinforcement contingency by virtue of the schedule of reinforcement that is programmed on each lever. The relative distribution of right and left responses is presumed to depend on the relative rate of reinforcement for staying on each lever versus switching to the other one (MacDonall, 1999, 2000, 2005). (For other analyses of local reinforcement effects in choice, see Davison & Baum, 2003; Krägeloh, Davison, & Elliffee, 2005.)

Molar Maximizing

Molar theories of maximizing assume that organisms distribute their responses among various alternatives so as to maximize the amount of reinforcement they earn over the long run. What is long enough to be considered a *long run* is not clearly specified. However, in contrast to molecular theories, molar theories focus on aggregates of behavior over some period of time, usually the total duration of an experimental session, rather than on individual choice responses.

Molar maximizing theory was originally formulated to explain choice on concurrent schedules made up of ratio components. In concurrent ratio schedules, animals rarely switch back and forth between response alternatives. Rather, they respond exclusively on the ratio component that requires the fewest responses. On a concurrent FR 20-FR 10 schedule, for example, the organism is likely to respond only on the FR 10 alternative. In this way, it maximizes its rate of reinforcement with the least effort.

In many situations, molar maximizing accurately predicts the results of choice procedures. However, certain findings present difficulties for molar maximizing theories. One difficulty arises from the results of concurrent VI-VI schedules of reinforcement. On a concurrent VI-VI schedule, organisms can earn close to all of the available reinforcers on both schedules, provided they occasionally sample each alternative. Therefore, the total amount of reinforcement obtained on a concurrent VI-VI schedule can be close to the same despite wide variations in how responding is distributed between the two alternatives. The matching relation is only one of many different possibilities that yield close to maximal rates of reinforcement on concurrent VI-VI schedules.

Another challenge for molar matching is provided by results of studies in which there is a choice between a variable ratio and a variable interval schedule. On a variable-ratio schedule, the organism can obtain reinforcement at any time by making the required number of responses. By contrast, on a variable-interval schedule, the subject only has to respond occasionally to obtain close to the maximum number of reinforcers possible. Given these differences, for maximum return on a concurrent VR-VI schedule, subjects should concentrate their responses on the variable-ratio alternative and respond only occasionally on the variable-interval component. Evidence shows that animals do favor the VR component but not always as strongly as molar maximizing predicts (DeCarlo, 1985; Heyman & Herrnstein, 1986; see also Baum & Aparicio, 1999). Human participants also respond much more on the VI alternative than is prudent if they are trying to maximize their rate of reinforcement (Savastano & Fantino, 1994).

Courtesy of Donald A. Dewsbury

E. Fantino

Melioration

The third major mechanism of choice that I will describe, **melioration**, operates on a scale between molecular and molar mechanisms.

Many aspects of behavior are not optimal in the long run. People make choices that result in their being overweight, addicted to cigarettes or other drugs, or being without close friends. No one chooses these end points. As Herrnstein (1997) pointed out, "A person does not normally make a once-and-for-all decision to become an exercise junkie, a miser, a glutton, a profligate, or a gambler; rather he slips into the pattern through a myriad of innocent, or almost innocent choices, each of which carries little weight" (p. 285). It is these "innocent choices" that melioration is intended to characterize.

The term *melioration* refers to making something better. Notice that melioration does not refer to selecting the best alternative at the moment (molecular maximizing) or making something as good as it can be in the long run (molar maximizing). Rather, melioration refers to the more modest (or *innocent*) goal of just making the situation better. Better than what? Better than how that situation has been in the recent past. Thus, the benefits are assessed specific to a limited situation, not overall or in the long run.

An important term in translating these ideas to testable experimental predictions is the *local rate* of responding and reinforcement. *Local rates* are calculated only over the time period that a subject devotes to a particular choice alternative. For example, if the situation involves two options (A and B), the local rate of responding on A is calculated by dividing the frequency of responses on A by the time the subject devotes to responding on A. This contrasts with the *overall rate*, which is calculated dividing the frequency of responses on A by the entire duration of an experimental session.

The local rate of a response is always higher than its overall rate. If the subject responds 75 times in an hour on the left response key, the overall rate for response L will be 75/hour. However, those 75 responses might be made during just 20 minutes that the subjects spends on the left side, with the rest of the session being spent on the right key. Therefore, the local rate of response L will be 75/20 minutes, or 220/hour.

Melioration theory assumes that organisms change from one response alternative to another to improve on the local rate of reinforcement they are receiving (Herrnstein, 1997; Herrnstein & Vaughan, 1980; Vaughan, 1981, 1985). Adjustments in the distribution of behavior between alternatives are assumed to continue until the organism is obtaining the same local rate of reward on all alternatives. It can be shown mathematically that when subjects distribute their responses so as to obtain the same local rate of reinforcement on each response alternative, they are behaving in accordance with the matching law. Therefore, the mechanism of melioration results in matching. (For a human study of choice consistent with melioration, see Madden, Peden, & Yamaguchi, 2002.)

COMPLEX CHOICE

In a standard concurrent schedule of reinforcement, two (or more) response alternatives are available at the same time, and switching from one to the other can occur at any time. At a potluck dinner, for example, you can choose one or another dish to eat, and if you don't like what you are eating, you can switch at any time to something else. Similarly, you can visit one or another booth at a county fair and make a new selection at any time. That is not the case if you select a movie at a multiplex. Once you have paid your ticket and started watching the movie, you cannot change your mind and go see another one at any time. In that case choosing one alternative makes other alternatives unavailable for a period. To make another selection, you have to return to the ticket window, which is the choice point.

Many complex human decisions limit your options once you have made a choice. Should you go to college and get a degree in engineering or start a fulltime job without a college degree when you graduate from high school? It is difficult to switch back and forth between such alternatives. Furthermore, to make the decision, you need to consider long-range goals. A degree in engineering may enable you to get a higher paying job eventually, but it may require significant economic sacrifices initially. Getting a job without a college degree would enable you to make money sooner, but in the long run you would not be able to earn as much.

Important choices in life often involve a short-term small benefit versus a more delayed but larger benefit. This is fundamentally the problem of self control. People are said to lack self control if they choose a small short-term reward instead of waiting for a larger but bigger benefit. The student who talks with a friend instead of studying is selecting a small short-term reward over the more delayed, but larger reward of doing well on the test. The heroin addict who uses a friend's needle instead of getting a clean one is similarly selecting the smaller quicker reward, as is the drunk who elects to drive home now instead of waiting to sober up.

Concurrent-Chain Schedules

Obviously, we cannot conduct experiments that directly involve choosing between college and a job after high school, or driving while intoxicated versus waiting to sober up. However, simplified analogous questions can be posed in laboratory experiments. Numerous studies of this sort have been done with monkeys, pigeons, and rats, and these experiments have stimulated analogous studies with human subjects. The basic technique in this area of research is the **concurrent-chain schedule of reinforcement** (for recent examples, see Berg & Grace, 2006; Kyonka & Grace, 2008; Mazur, 2006).

We have all heard that *variety is the spice of life*. How could we determine whether this is really true? One implication may be that subjects will prefer a variable ratio schedule of reinforcement (which provides variety in the number of responses required for successive reinforcers) over a fixed-ratio schedule (which requires the same number of responses per reinforcer). A *concurrent-chain schedule* is ideal for answering such questions.

A concurrent-chain schedule of reinforcement involves two stages or links (see Figure 6.6). The first stage is called the *choice link*. In this link, the participant is allowed to choose between two schedule alternatives by making

Courtesy of Randolph Grace

R. C. Grace

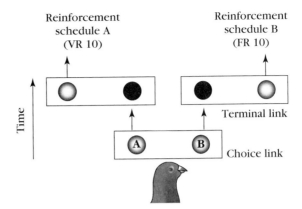

FIGURE **6.6**

Diagram of a concurrent-chain schedule. Pecking the left key in the choice link activates reinforcement schedule A in the terminal link. Pecking the right key in the choice activates reinforcement schedule B in the terminal link.

one of two responses. In the example diagrammed in Figure 6.6, the pigeon makes its choice by pecking either the left or the right response key. Pecking the left key produces alternative A, the opportunity to peck the left key for 10 minutes on a VR 10 schedule of reinforcement. If the pigeon pecks the right key in the choice link, it produces alternative B, which is the opportunity to peck the right key for 10 minutes on an FR 10 schedule. Responding on either key during the choice link does not yield food. The opportunity for reinforcement occurs only after the initial choice has been made and the pigeon has entered the *terminal link*. Another important feature of the concurrent-chain schedule is that once the participant has made a choice, it is stuck with that choice until the end of the terminal link of the schedule (10 minutes in our hypothetical example). Thus, concurrent-chain schedules involve *choice with commitment*.

The pattern of responding that occurs in the terminal component of a concurrent-chain schedule is characteristic of whatever schedule of reinforcement is in effect during that component. In our example, if the pigeon selected Alternative A, its pattern of pecking during the terminal component will be similar to the usual response pattern for a VR 10 schedule. If the pigeon selected Alternative B, its pattern of pecking during the terminal component will be characteristic of an FR 10 schedule.

Studies of this sort have shown that subjects prefer the variable-ratio alternative. In fact, pigeons favor the VR alternative even if it requires on average more responses per reinforcer than the FR alternative. Thus, variety is the spice of life on a concurrent-chain schedule. The preference for the VR schedule is driven by the fact that occasionally a VR schedule provides reinforcement for relatively few responses (Field, Tonneau, Ahearn, & Hineline, 1996). (For a more recent study of the preference for variability, see Andrzejewski, et al., 2005.)

As I noted, the consequence of responding during the initial (choice) link of a concurrent schedule is not the primarily reinforcer (food). Rather, it is entry into one of the terminal links, each of which is typically designated by a particular color on the pecking key. Thus, the immediate consequence of an initial-link response is a stimulus that is associated with the terminal link that was chosen. Since that stimulus is present when the primary reinforcer is provided, the terminal link stimulus becomes a *conditioned reinforcer*. Thus, one may regard a concurrent schedule as one in which the initial-link responses are reinforced by the presentation of a conditioned reinforcer. Differences in the value of the conditioned reinforcer will then determine the relative rate of each choice response in the initial link. Because of this, concurrent-chain schedules provide an important tool for the study of conditioned reinforcement (Goldshmidt, Lattal, & Fantino, 1998; Mazur, 1998; Savastano & Fantino, 1996; Williams, 1997).

Although many studies of concurrent-chain schedules represent efforts to determine how organisms select between different situations represented by the terminal links, the consensus of opinion is that choice behavior is governed by both the terminal link schedules and whatever schedule is in effect in the initial link. Several different models have been proposed to explain how variables related to the initial and terminal links act in concert to determine concurrent choice performance (for reviews, see Mazur, 2000; Jozefowiez & Staddon, 2008).

Studies of "Self Control"

Self control is often a matter of choosing a large delayed reward over an immediate small reward. For example, self control in eating involves selecting the large delayed reward of being thin over the immediate small reward of eating a piece of cake. When a piece of cake is in plain view, it is very difficult to choose the delayed reward; it is difficult to pass up the cake in favor of being thin. Self control is easier if the tempting alternative is not as readily available. It is easier to pass up a piece of cake if you are deciding on what to eat at the next meal or your next visit to a favorite restaurant. Based on these ideas, Rachlin and Green (1972) conducted a classic experiment on self control with pigeons.

The procedures used by Rachlin and Green are shown in Figure 6.7. In the terminal component of each procedure, responding was rewarded by either immediate access to a small amount of grain (Alternative A) or access to a large amount of grain that was delayed by four seconds (Alternative B). The pigeons could choose between these two alternatives by pecking either Key A or Key B during the initial component of the procedures.

The investigators tested choice behavior under two different conditions. In the *direct choice procedure,* the small immediate reward and the delayed large reward were available as soon as the pigeons pecked the corresponding choice key once. Under these conditions, the pigeons lacked self control. They predominantly selected the small immediate reward. In the *concurrent chain procedure,* the terminal components of the concurrent chain schedule were delayed after the pigeons made their initial choice. If a sufficient delay was imposed before the terminal components, the pigeons showed self control; they primarily selected the large delayed reward instead of the small more immediate reward (for more recent studies with rats and pigeons, see Green & Estle, 2003; Hackenberg & Vaidya, 2003).

The phenomenon of self control as illustrated by the Rachlin and Green experiment has stimulated much research and theorizing. Numerous investi-

L. Green

Large
reward

Small
reward

Delay

Direct-choice procedure
Pigeon chooses
immediate, small
reward

Time

Large
reward

Small
reward

Delay

A ● ● B

A B

Concurrent-chain procedure
Pigeon chooses the
schedule with the
delayed large reward

Time

FIGURE **6.7**

Diagram of the experiment by Rachlin and Green (1972) on self control. The direct-choice procedure is shown at the top; the concurrent-chain procedure, at the bottom.

Courtesy of A. W. Logue

A. W. Logue

gators have found, in agreement with Rachlin and Green, that preferences shift in favor of the delayed large reward as participants are required to wait longer to receive either reward after making their choice. If rewards are delivered shortly after a choice response, subjects generally favor the immediate small reward. The crossover in preference has been obtained in experiments with both people and laboratory animals, and thus represents a general property of choice behavior. (For applications of these concepts to university administrators, see Logue, 1998a; for more general reviews of self control, see Logue, 1995; Rachlin, 2000.)

Value-Discounting and Explanations of Self Control

Which would you prefer, $1,000 today or $1,000 next year? The answer is obvious. For most people, $1,000 today would be of much greater value. How about $1,000 next week, or next month? Most people would agree that the longer one has to wait for the $1,000, the less exciting is the prospect of getting the money. This illustrates a general principle that is the key to behavioral explanations of self control, namely that the value of a reinforcer is reduced by how long you have to wait to get it. The mathematical function

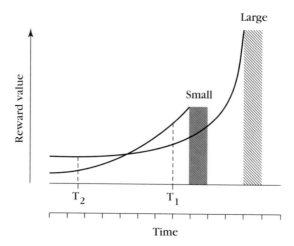

FIGURE 6.8

Hypothetical relations between reward value and waiting time to reward delivery for a small reward and a large reward presented some time later.

Courtesy of James E. Mazur

James E. Mazur

describing this decrease in value is called the **value-discounting function** (for a general discussion of discounting, see Rachlin, 2006). The exact mathematical form of the value discounting function has taken a bit of empirical effort to pin down. But, the current consensus is that the value of a reinforcer (V) is directly related to reward magnitude (M) and inversely related to reward delay (D), according to the formula:

$$V = M/(1 + KD) \tag{6.9}$$

where K is the discounting rate parameter (Mazur, 1987). Equation 6.9 is called the *hyperbolic decay function*. (For a generalized version of the hyperbolic decay function, see Grace, 1999.) According to this equation, if the reinforcer is delivered with no delay (D=0), the value of the reinforcer is directly related to its magnitude (larger reinforcers have larger values). The longer the reinforcer is delayed, the smaller is its value.

How can the discounting function explain the problem of self control, which involves a small reward available soon versus a large reward available after a longer delay? Consider Figure 6.8. Time in this figure is represented by distance on the horizontal axis, and reward value is represented by the vertical axis. The figure represents the value of a large and a small reward as a function of how long you have to wait to receive the reward. Two different points in time are identified, T_1 and T_2. The usual self control dilemma involves considering the reward values at T_1. At T_1 there is a very short wait for the small reward and a longer wait for the large reward. Waiting for each reward reduces its value. Because reward value decreases rapidly at first, given the delays involved at T_1, the value of the large reward is smaller than the value of the small reward. Hence, the model predicts that if the choice occurs at T_1, you will select the small reward (the impulsive option). However, the discounting functions cross over with further delays. The value of both rewards is less at T_2 than at T_1 because

T_2 involves longer delays. However, notice that at T_2 the value of the large reward is now greater than that of the small reward. Therefore, a choice at T_2 would have you select the large reward (the self control option).

The value discounting functions illustrated in Figure 6.8 predict the results of Rachlin and Green (1972) described above, as well as numerous other studies of self control. Increasing the delay to both the small and large reward makes it easier to exhibit self control because the value discounting functions of the two rewards cross over with longer delays, making the larger delayed reward more attractive.

Value Discounting Functions and Impulsivity in Human Behavior

Courtesy of T. S. Critchfield

T. S. Critchfield

As I noted above, the parameter K in equation 6.9 indicates how rapidly reward value declines as function of delay. The steeper a person's delay discounting function is, the more difficulty that person will have in exhibiting self control and the more impulsive that person might be. Consistent with these ideas, steeper reward-discounting functions have been found in studies of people who engage in binge drinking, in cigarette smokers, in individuals who are addicted to heroin, and in gamblers who also have a substance abuse problem. Young children also have steeper reward-discounting functions than college-aged adults, and college students who engage in unprotected sex have steeper discounting functions than those who use condoms (see review by Critchfield & Kollins, 2001). These studies show that the reward-discounting function measures an important feature of behavior that is relevant to self control in a broad range of situations.

A study by Madden, Petry, Badger, and Bickel (1997) illustrates how such experiments are conducted. They tested a group of heroin-dependent patients enrolled in a substance abuse program. A group of nondependent individuals matched for age, gender, education, and IQ served as the control group. In each trial, the participants were asked to choose between two hypothetical scenarios: getting $1,000 some time in the future, or a smaller amount of money right away. In different repetitions of the question, the $1,000 was to be received at different delays ranging from one week to 25 years. For each delay period, the magnitude of the smaller immediate alternative was varied across trials until the investigators determined how much money obtained immediately was as attractive as the $1,000 some time in the future. Using these data, Madden et al. (1997) were able to construct reward discount functions for both the heroin-dependent and control participants.

The results are summarized in Figure 6.9. Keep in mind that these are reward discount functions for hypothetical choices between different amounts of money to be received soon (T_1) or after a substantial delay (T_2). The results for the heroin addicts are presented in the left panel and the results for the control subjects appear in the right panel. The reward discount functions were much steeper for the heroin addicts. That is, for heroin-dependent participants, the value of money dropped very quickly if receipt of the money was to be delayed. Madden et al. (1997, p.261) speculated that because drug-dependent participants showed more rapid discounting of reward value, "heroin-addicted individuals may be more likely to engage in criminal and dangerous activities to obtain immediate rewards (e.g., theft, prostitution, drug sales)."

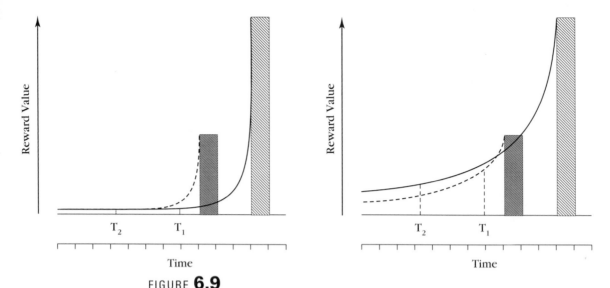

FIGURE **6.9**

Reward discount functions for a large and smaller monetary reward. The left panel shows the discount functions obtained with a group of heroin-dependent participants. The right panel shows data from a control group. (From "Impulsive and Self-Control Choices in Opioid-Dependent Patients and Non-Drug-Using Control Participants: Drug and Monetary Rewards," by G. J. Madden, N. M. Petry, G. J. Badger, and W. K. Bickel, 1997, *Experimental and Clinical Psychopharmacology, 5,* pp. 256–262. Reprinted by permission.)

Can Self Control Be Trained?

A person who cannot tolerate the waiting time required for large rewards has to forgo obtaining those reinforcers. Self control, or the preference for a large delayed reward over a small immediate reward, is often a sensible strategy. In fact, some have suggested that self control is a critical component of socialization and emotional adjustment. This raises an interesting question: Can self control be trained? Fortunately for society, the answer is yes.

Training people with delayed reward appears to have generalized effects in increasing their tolerance for delayed reward. In one study (Eisenberger & Adornetto, 1986), second- and third-grade students in a public elementary school were first tested for self control by being asked whether they wanted to get 2¢ immediately or 3¢ at the end of the day. Children who elected the immediate reward were given 2¢. For those who elected the delayed reward, 3¢ was placed in a cup to be given to the child later. The procedure was repeated eight times to complete the pretest. The children then received three sessions of training with either immediate or delayed reward.

During each training session, various problems were presented (counting objects on a card, memorizing pictures, and matching shapes). For half the students, correct responding was reinforced immediately with 2¢. For the remaining students, correct responses resulted in 3¢ being placed in a cup that was given to the child at the end of the day. After the third training session, preference for small immediate reward versus larger delayed reward was measured as in the pretest. Provided that the training tasks involved low effort, training with delayed reward increased preference for the larger delayed reward during the posttest. Thus, training with delayed reinforcement produced generalized self control. (For other approaches to increasing self control, see Logue, 1998b; Neef, Bicard, & Endo, 2001; Schweitzer & Sulzer-Azaroff, 1988.)

CONCLUDING COMMENTS

The basic principle of instrumental conditioning is very simple: reinforcement increases (and punishment decreases) the future probability of an instrumental response. However, as we have seen, the experimental analysis of instrumental behavior can be rather intricate. Many important aspects of instrumental behavior are determined by the schedule of reinforcement. There are numerous schedules that can be used to reinforce behavior. Reinforcement can depend on how many responses have occurred, responding after a certain amount of time, or a combination of these. Furthermore, more than one reinforcement schedule may be available to the organism at the same time. The pattern of instrumental behavior, as well as choices between various response alternatives, are strongly determined by the schedule of reinforcement that is in effect. These various findings have told us a great deal about how reinforcement controls behavior in a variety of circumstances, and have encouraged numerous powerful applications of reinforcement principles to human behavior.

SAMPLE QUESTIONS

1. Compare and contrast ratio and interval schedules in terms of how the contingencies of reinforcement are set up and the effects they have on the instrumental response.
2. Describe how response rate schedules are designed and what their effects are.
3. Describe the generalized matching law equation and explain each of its parameters.
4. Describe various theoretical explanations of the matching law.
5. How are concurrent-chain schedules different from concurrent schedules, and what kinds of research questions require the use of concurrent-chain schedules?
6. What is a reward discounting function and how is it related to the problem of self control?

KEY TERMS

concurrent-chain schedule of reinforcement A complex reinforcement procedure in which the participant is permitted to choose during the first link which of several simple reinforcement schedules will be in effect in the second link. Once a choice has been made, the rejected alternatives become unavailable until the start of the next trial.

concurrent schedule A complex reinforcement procedure in which the participant can choose any one of two or more simple reinforcement schedules that are available simultaneously. Concurrent schedules allow for the measurement of direct choice between simple schedule alternatives.

continuous reinforcement (CRF) A schedule of reinforcement in which every occurrence of the instrumental response produces the reinforcer.

cumulative record A graphical representation of how a response is repeated over time, with the passage of time represented by the horizontal distance (or x-axis), and the total or cumulative number of responses that have occurred up to a particular point in time represented by the vertical distance (or y-axis).

fixed-interval scallop The gradually increasing rate of responding that occurs between successive reinforcements on a fixed-interval schedule.

fixed-interval schedule (FI) A reinforcement schedule in which the reinforcer is delivered for the first response that occurs after a fixed amount of time following the last reinforcer or the beginning of the trial.

fixed-ratio schedule (FR) A reinforcement schedule in which a fixed number of responses must occur in order for the next response to be reinforced.

intermittent reinforcement A schedule of reinforcement in which only some of the occurrences of the instrumental response are reinforced. The instrumental response is reinforced occasionally, or intermittently. Also called *partial reinforcement.*

inter-response time (IRT) The interval between one response and the next. IRTs can be differentially reinforced in the same fashion as other aspects of behavior, such as response force or variability.

interval schedule A reinforcement schedule in which a response is reinforced only if it occurs after a set amount of time following the last reinforcer or start of the trial.

limited hold A restriction on how long a reinforcer remains available. In order for a response to be reinforced, it must occur before the end of the limited-hold period.

matching law A rule for instrumental behavior, proposed by R. J. Herrnstein, which states that the relative rate of responding on a particular response alternative equals the relative rate of reinforcement for that response alternative.

melioration A mechanism for achieving matching by responding so as to improve the local rates of reinforcement for response alternatives.

partial reinforcement Same as *intermittent reinforcement.*

post-reinforcement pause A pause in responding that typically occurs after the delivery of the reinforcer on fixed-ratio and fixed-interval schedules of reinforcement.

ratio run The high and invariant rate of responding observed after the postreinforcement pause on fixed-ratio schedules. The ratio run ends when the necessary number of responses have been performed, and the participant is reinforced.

ratio schedule A reinforcement schedule in which reinforcement depends only on the number of responses the participant performs, irrespective of when those responses occur.

ratio strain Disruption of responding that occurs when a fixed-ratio response requirement is increased too rapidly.

response-rate schedule A reinforcement schedule in which a response is reinforced depending on how soon that response is made after the previous occurrence of the behavior.

schedule of reinforcement A program, or rule, that determines how and when the occurrence of a response will be followed by the delivery of the reinforcer.

undermatching Less sensitivity to the relative rate of reinforcement than predicted by the matching law.

value discounting function The mathematical function that describes how reinforcer value decreases as a function of how long one has to wait for delivery of the reinforcer.

variable-interval schedule (VI) A reinforcement schedule in which reinforcement is provided for the first response that occurs after a variable amount of time from the last reinforcer or the start of the trial.

variable-ratio schedule (VR) A reinforcement schedule in which the number of responses necessary to produce reinforcement varies from trial to trial. The value of the schedule refers to the average number of responses needed for reinforcement.

7

Instrumental Conditioning: Motivational Mechanisms

CHAPTER PREVIEW

This chapter is devoted to a discussion of processes that motivate and direct instrumental behavior. Two distinctively different approaches have been pursued in an effort to understand why instrumental behavior occurs. The first of these is in the tradition of Thorndike and Pavlov and focuses on identifying the associative structure of instrumental conditioning. The associationist approach considers molecular mechanisms and is not concerned with the long-range goal or function of instrumental behavior. The second strategy is in the Skinnerian tradition and focuses on how behavior is regulated in the face of limitations or restrictions created by an instrumental conditioning procedure. Behavior regulation theories describe reinforcement effects within the broader context of an organism's behavioral repertoire, using concepts from several areas of inquiry, including behavioral economics and behavioral ecology. The behavioral regulation approach considers molar aspects of behavior and regards instrumental conditioning effects as manifestations of maximization or optimization processes. The associationist and behavior regulation approaches provide an exciting illustration of the sometimes turbulent course of scientific inquiry. Investigators studying the motivational substrates of instrumental behavior have moved boldly to explore radically new conceptions when older ideas did not meet the challenges posed by new empirical findings.

In Chapters 5 and 6, I defined instrumental behavior, pointed out how this type of learning is investigated, and described how instrumental behavior is influenced by various experimental manipulations, including schedules of reinforcement. Along the way, I did not say much about what motivates instrumental responding, perhaps because the answer seemed obvious. Informal reflection suggests that individuals perform instrumental responses because they are motivated to obtain the goal or reinforcer that results from the behavior. But what does it mean to be *motivated* to obtain the reinforcer? And, what is the full impact of setting up a situation so that the reinforcer is only accessible by making the required instrumental response? Answers to these questions have occupied scientists for more than a century and have encompassed some of the most important and interesting research in the analysis of behavior.

The motivation of instrumental behavior has been considered from two radically different perspectives. The first originated with Thorndike and involves analysis of the *associative structure of instrumental conditioning*. As this label implies, this approach relies heavily on the concept of associations and hence is compatible with the theoretical tradition of Pavlovian conditioning. In fact, much of the research relevant to the associative structure of instrumental conditioning was stimulated by efforts to identify the role of Pavlovian mechanisms in instrumental learning. In addition, some of the research methods that were developed to study Pavlovian conditioning were applied to the problem of instrumental learning.

The associative approach takes a molecular perspective. It focuses on individual responses and their specific stimulus antecedents and outcomes. To achieve this level of detail, the associative approach examines instrumental learning in isolated behavioral preparations, not unlike studying something in a test tube or a Petri dish. Because associations can be substantiated in the nervous system, the associative approach also provides a convenient framework for studying the neural mechanisms of instrumental conditioning (e.g., Balleine & Ostlund, 2007).

The second strategy for analyzing motivational processes in instrumental learning is *behavioral regulation*. This approach was developed within the Skinnerian tradition and involves considering instrumental conditioning within the broader context of the numerous activities that organisms are constantly doing. In particular, the behavioral regulation approach is concerned with how an instrumental conditioning procedure limits an organism's free flow of activities and the behavioral consequences of such constraints. Unlike the associative approach, behavioral regulation considers the motivation of instrumental behavior from a more molar perspective. It considers long-term goals and how organisms manage to achieve those goals within the context of all of their behavioral options. Thus, behavioral regulation theory views instrumental behavior from a more functional perspective. Because it takes a molar approach, behavioral regulation does not provide as convenient a framework for studying the neural mechanisms of instrumental learning.

To date, the associative and behavioral regulation approaches have proceeded pretty much independently of one another. Each approach has identified important issues, but it has become clear that neither can stand alone. The hope is that at some point, the molecular analyses of the associative approach will make sufficient contact with the more molar functional analyses of behavioral regulation to provide a comprehensive integrated account of the motivation of instrumental behavior.

THE ASSOCIATIVE STRUCTURE OF INSTRUMENTAL CONDITIONING

Edward Thorndike was the first to recognize that instrumental conditioning involves more than just a response and a reinforcer. The instrumental response occurs in the context of specific environmental stimuli. Turning the key in the ignition of your car occurs in the context of your sitting in the driver's seat and holding the key between your fingers. One can identify such environmental stimuli in any instrumental situation. Hence, there are three events to consider in an analysis of instrumental learning: the stimulus context (S), the instrumental response (R), and the response outcome (O), or reinforcer. Skinner also subscribed to the idea that there are three events to consider in an analysis of instrumental or operant conditioning. He described instrumental conditioning in terms of a *three-term contingency* involving S, R,

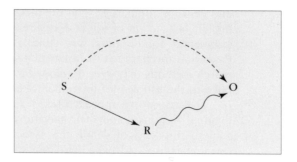

FIGURE **7.1**

Diagram of instrumental conditioning. The instrumental response (R) occurs in the presence of distinctive stimuli (S) and results in delivery of the reinforcer outcome (O). This allows for the establishment of several different types of associations.

and O. (For a more recent discussion, see Davison & Nevin, 1999.) The relation among these three terms is presented in Figure 7.1.

The S-R Association and the Law of Effect

The basic structure of an instrumental conditioning procedure permits the development of several different types of associations. The first of these was postulated by Thorndike and is an association between the contextual stimuli (S) and the instrumental response (R): the *S-R association*. Thorndike considered the S-R association to be the key to instrumental learning and central to his *Law of Effect*. According to the Law of Effect, instrumental conditioning involves the establishment of an S-R association between the instrumental response (R) and the contextual stimuli (S) that are present when the response is reinforced. The role of the reinforcer is to "stamp in" the S-R association. Thorndike thought that once established, this S-R association was solely responsible for the occurrence of the instrumental behavior. Thus, the basic impetus, or motivation, for the instrumental behavior was the activation of the S-R association by exposing the subject to contextual stimuli (S) in the presence of which the response was previously reinforced.

An important implication of the Law of Effect is that instrumental conditioning does not involve learning about the reinforcer (O) or the relation between the response and the reinforcing outcome (the R-O association). The Law of Effect assumes that the only role of the reinforcer is to strengthen the S-R association. The reinforcer itself is not a party or participant in this association.

Although the S-R mechanism of the Law of Effect was proposed about a hundred years ago, it fell into disfavor during the latter part of the twentieth century and became a victim of the *cognitive revolution* in psychology. Interestingly, however, there has been a resurgence of interest in S-R mechanisms in recent efforts to characterize habitual behavior in people. Habits are things we do automatically in the same way each time without thinking. Estimates are that habits constitute about 45% of human behavior. Wood and Neal (2007) recently proposed a new comprehensive model of human habits. Central to the model is the idea that habits "arise when people repeatedly use a particular behavioral means in particular contexts to pursue their goals. However, once acquired, habits are performed without mediation of a goal" (p. 844). Rather, the habitual response is an automatic reaction to the stimulus context in which the goal was previously obtained, similar to Thorndike's S-R association.

Thorndike's S-R association is also being seriously entertained as one of the mechanisms that may explain the habitual nature of drug addiction (e.g., Everitt & Robbins, 2005). In this model, procuring and taking a drug of abuse is viewed as instrumental behavior that is initially reinforced by the positive aspects of the drug experience. However, with repetitive use, taking the drug becomes habitual in the sense that it becomes an automatic reaction to contextual cues that elicit drug seeking behavior, without regard to its consequences. Compulsive eating, gambling, or infidelity can be thought of in the same way. What makes these behaviors compulsive is that the person "cannot help" doing them given the triggering contextual cues, even though the activities can have serious negative consequences. According to the S-R mechanism, those consequences are not relevant. To borrow terminology from Wood and Neal (2007), the S-R association "stipulates an outsourcing of behavioral control to contextual cues that were, in the past, contiguous with performance" (p. 844).

BOX **7.1**

The Role of Dopamine in Addiction and Reward

Drug addiction is a long-standing societal problem. What underlies compulsive drug use and why is it that individuals with a history of drug use are so prone to relapse? Answers to these questions require an understanding of how learning influences drug-taking behavior. It is now widely recognized that drugs of abuse usurp control over the neural circuitry that mediates learning about natural rewards, producing an artificial high that tricks the brain into following a path that leads to maladaptive consequences (for recent reviews, see Hyman, Malenka, & Nestler, 2006; Robinson & Berridge, 2003). Understanding how drugs exert their effects at a neurobiological level should help address the prob-

lem of drug addiction and shed light on the mechanisms that underlie learning about natural rewards.

Understanding addiction requires some background in psychopharmacology, the study of how drugs impact the nervous system to influence psychological/behavioral states. There are many ways that this can occur, but for present purposes we can focus on how drugs influence neural communication at the synapse. Neural signals within a neuron are encoded by changes in ionic concentrations that form an electrical impulse that travels down the neuron, from the dendrites to the axon. The tip of the axon (the synaptic bouton) adjoins the target cell, which (within the brain) is typically another neuron. The con-

nection between the cells is known as a synapse and the small gap that separates the cells is called the synaptic cleft (see Figure 7.2). When a neural impulse arrives at the synaptic bouton of the presynaptic cell, it initiates the release of a chemical (the neurotransmitter) that diffuses across the cleft and engages the recipient (postsynaptic) neuron by engaging a receptor that is specially designed to recognize this particular neurochemical. Some neurotransmitters (e.g., glutamate) excite the postsynaptic cell while others (e.g., GABA) have an inhibitory effect.

Drugs can influence synaptic communication in a number of ways. For example, an agonist can substitute for the endogenous (internally manufactured) drug, binding to

(continued)

BOX **7.1** (continued)

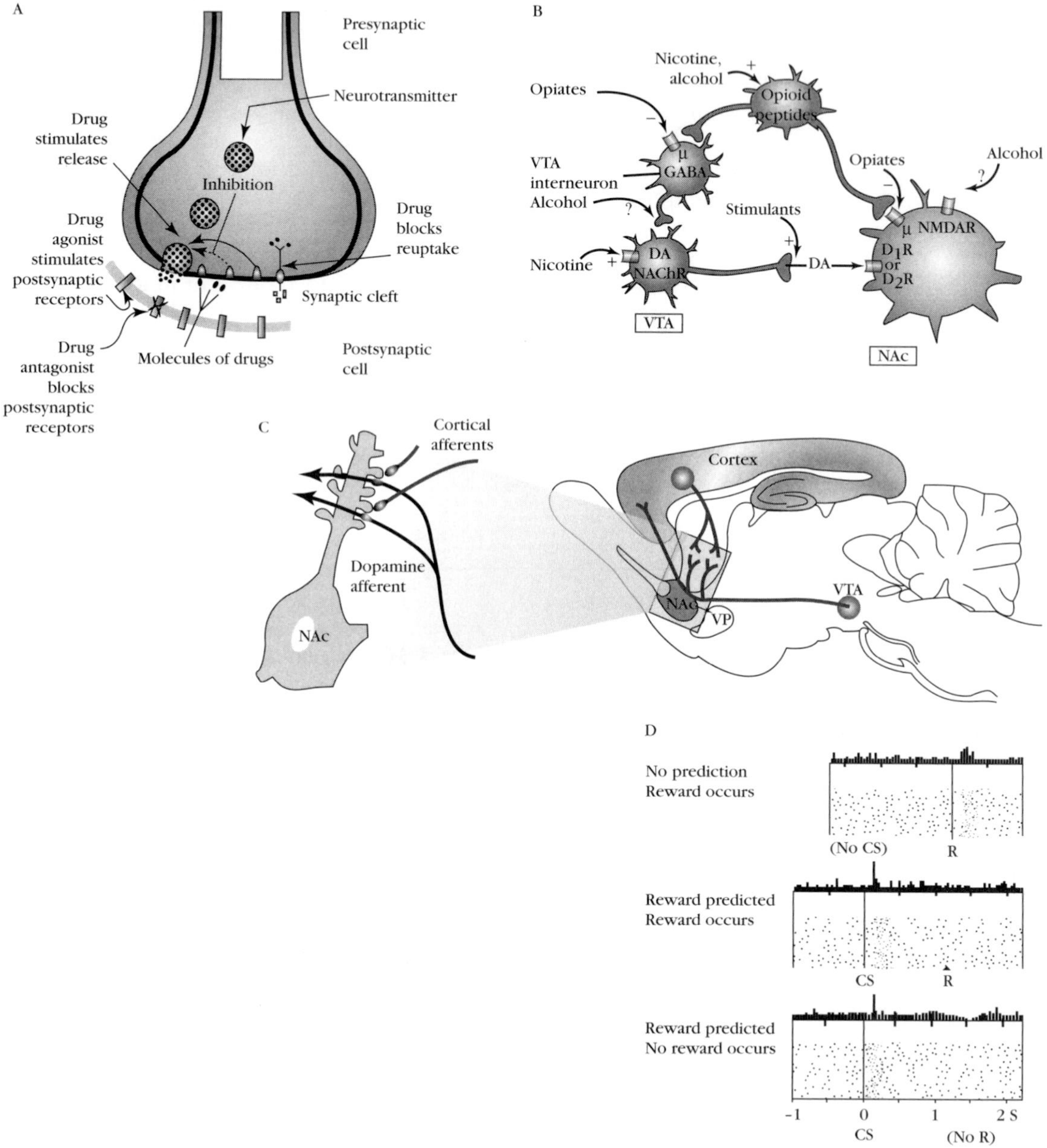

A

Presynaptic cell

Neurotransmitter

Drug stimulates release

Inhibition

Drug agonist stimulates postsynaptic receptors

Drug blocks reuptake

Synaptic cleft

Drug antagonist blocks postsynaptic receptors

Molecules of drugs

Postsynaptic cell

B

Nicotine, alcohol

Opiates

Opioid peptides

VTA interneuron
Alcohol

μ GABA

Opiates

Alcohol
?

Nicotine

DA NAChR

Stimulants

DA

μ NMDAR

D₁R or D₂R

VTA

NAc

C

Cortical afferents

Dopamine afferent

NAc

Cortex

NAc
VP

VTA

D

No prediction
Reward occurs

(No CS)   R

Reward predicted
Reward occurs

CS   R

Reward predicted
No reward occurs

-1   0   1   2 S
CS   (No R)

(continued)

BOX **7.1** (continued)

FIGURE **7.2**

(A) Neurotransmission at a synapse. Transmitter is packaged in vesicles and released from the presynpatic cell. The transmitter diffuses across the synaptic cleft and influences electrical activity in the postsynaptic cell by engaging specialized receptors. After release, the transmitters are reabsorbed into the presynpatic neuron (the process of reuptake). Drugs can affect neurochemical transmission by promoting neurotransmitter release or inhibiting reuptake. Drugs can also bind to the receptor on the postsynaptic cell to produce an effect similar to the neurotransmitter (agonist) or block its action (antagonist). (B) The addictive quality of many psychoactive drugs appears to be linked to their capacity to influence neural function within the nucleus accumbens. Neurons that release an opioid or dopamine directly impact neurons within the nucleus accumbens. The release of these neurochemicals is influenced by other psychoactive drugs, such as alcohol and nicotine (adapted from Hyman et al., 2006). (C) Dopaminergic neurons (right panel) from the ventral tegmental area (VTA) project through the nucleus accumbens (NAc) and synapse onto the dendrites of medium spiny neurons (left panel). These neurons also receive input from cortical neurons. Neurons from the nucleus accumbens project to the ventral pallidum (VP) (adapted from Hyman et al., 2006). (D) Neural activity in dopaminergic neurons within the ventral tegmental area. The speckled regions indicate neural spikes over time. Activity across many recordings is averaged (top) to produce the histograms depicted on the top of each panel. In the upper panel, the presentation of a reward (R) elicits a burst of activity. After subjects have learned that a conditioned stimulus (CS) predicts the reward (middle panel), the CS elicits activity while the expected reward has little effect. If the CS is presented and the reward is omitted (bottom panel), the no reward period (No R) is accompanied by an inhibition of neural activity (adapted from Schultz et al., 1997).

the receptor on the postsynaptic cell and producing a similar cellular effect. Conversely, drug antagonists bind to the receptor, but do not engage the same cellular consequences. Instead, the antagonist acts as a kind of roadblock that effectively prevents an agonist from having its usual effect on the postsynaptic cell. Drugs can also influence function in a less direct manner. For example, some drugs increase neurotransmitter availability by enhancing release or by blocking their reabsorption (reuptake) into the presynaptic neuron.

In general, drugs of abuse impact the nervous system by promoting the release of a particular neurotransmitter or by emulating its action. For

example, psychostimulants influence the neurotransmitter dopamine by blocking its reuptake (cocaine) or promoting its release (amphetamine). Opiates, such as morphine and heroin, have their effect by emulating endogenous opioids (endorphins) that engage the mu opioid receptor. Another common addictive substance, nicotine, engages acetylcholine receptors while sedatives (alcohol, valium) act, in part, through their impact on GABAergic neurons.

Drugs of abuse appear to promote addiction by influencing neurons within particular brain regions, such as the nucleus accumbens (Figure 7.2). Many of the neurons within this region have spiny dendritic fields

that allow for many synaptic contacts (Hyman et al., 2006). These medium spiny neurons receive input from neurons that release an endogenous opioid that engages the mu receptor. In addition, dopaminergic neurons project from a region of the midbrain (the ventral tegmental area) and innervate the spiny neurons as they pass through en route to other regions (e.g., the prefrontal cortex). Other psychoactive drugs influence the activity of neurons within the nucleus accumbens by modulating opioid/dopamine release, engaging receptors on the medium spiny neurons, or by influencing the inhibitory action of GABAergic neurons that regulate neural activity (Figure 7.2).

(continued)

BOX **7.1** (continued)

Neurons within the nucleus accumbens also receive input from other regions, such as the cortex. These neurons release the excitatory neurotransmitter glutamate. As discussed in Box 11.1, changes in how the postsynaptic cell responds to glutamate can produce a long-term modification (e.g., a long-term potentiation) in how a neural circuit operates: a physiological alteration that has been linked to learning and memory. Within the nucleus accumbens, cortical neurons that release glutamate provide a rich input to the nucleus accumbens, an input that is thought to carry information about the specific details of the sensory systems engaged. At the same time, dopaminergic input on to these neurons provides a diffuse input that can signal the motivational state of the organism. When paired, this dopaminergic input may help select the relevant pattern of glutamatergic input, acting as a kind of teacher that binds sensory attributes with reward value, thereby enhancing the motivational significance of these cues (Hyman et al., 2006).

When does the dopaminergic teacher instruct the nucleus accumbens to learn? To answer this question, researchers have examined neural activity in monkeys while they work for reward (e.g., a sip of fruit juice). Electrodes are lowered into the source of the dopaminergic input, neurons within the ventral tegmental area (Schultz, Daya, & Montaque, 1997). These neurons exhibit a low level of tonic activity (Figure 7.2). When the animal receives an unexpected reward, the neurons show a burst of firing. If the animal is then trained with signaled reward, the signal begins to elicit a burst of activity. The expected reward, itself, produces no effect. If, however, the expected reward is omitted, there is an inhibition of neural activity at the time of reward. What these observations suggest is that dopamine activity does not simply report whether or not a reward has occurred. Instead, dopamine activity seems to code the "reward prediction error"—the deviation between what the animal received and what it expected (Schultz, 2006):

Dopamine response = Reward occurred – Reward predicted

The notion that learning is a function of the discrepancy between what the animal received, and what it expected, parallels the learning rule posited by Rescorla and Wagner (1972). As discussed in Chapter 4, learning appears to occur when an event is unexpected. The best example of this is observed in the blocking paradigm, where one cue (represented symbolically with the letter A) is first paired with the unconditioned stimulus (US). After this association is well learned, a second cue (X) is added and the compound (AX) is paired with the US. Prior learning that A predicts the US blocks learning that X also predicts the US. This effect is also exhibited at a neural level by dopaminergic neurons within the ventral tegmentum. In this case, the originally paired cue (A) would drive a burst of dopamine activity, while the added cue (X) does not.

These observations suggest that abused drugs may encourage a cycle of dependency because they have a pharmacological advantage. For example, psychostimulants artificially drive dopaminergic activity, and in this way act as a kind of Trojan horse that fools the nervous system, producing a spike in dopamine activity that the brain interprets as a positive prediction error (Hyman et al., 2006). This reinforces new learning and links the sensory cues associated with drug administration to reward, giving them a motivational value that fuels the acquired drug craving (see Box 7.2).

J. W. Grau

Expectancy of Reward and the S-O Association

The idea that reward expectancy might motivate instrumental behavior was not considered seriously until about 40 years after the formulation of the Law of Effect. How might we capture the notion that subjects learn to expect the reinforcer during the course of instrumental conditioning? You come to expect that something important will happen when you encounter a stimulus that signals the significant event or allows you to predict that the event will occur. Pavlovian conditioning is the basic process of signal learning. Hence, one way to look for reward expectancy is to consider how Pavlovian processes may be involved in instrumental learning.

As Figure 7.1 illustrates, specification of an instrumental response ensures that the participant will always experience certain distinctive stimuli (S) in connection with making the response. These stimuli may involve the place where the response is to be performed, the texture of the object the participant is to manipulate, or distinctive olfactory or visual cues. Whatever the stimuli may be, reinforcement of the instrumental response will inevitably result in pairing these stimuli (S) with the reinforcer or response outcome (O). Such pairings provide the potential for classical conditioning and the establishment of an association between S and O. This S-O association is represented by the dashed line in Figure 7.1 and is one of the mechanisms of reward expectancy in instrumental conditioning.

One of the earliest and most influential accounts of the role of classical conditioning in instrumental behavior was offered by Clark Hull (1930, 1931) and later elaborated by Kenneth Spence (1956). Their proposal was that the instrumental response increases during the course of instrumental conditioning for two reasons. First, the presence of S comes to evoke the instrumental response directly through Thorndike's S-R association. Second, the instrumental response also comes to be made in response to an S-O association that creates the expectancy of reward. Exactly how the S-O association comes to motivate instrumental behavior has been the subject of considerable debate and experimental investigation. A particularly influential formulation was the *two-process theory* of Rescorla and Solomon (1967).

Two-Process Theory

The two-process theory assumes that there are two distinct types of learning: Pavlovian and instrumental conditioning. Nothing too radical there. The theory further assumes that these two learning processes are related in a special way. In particular, during the course of instrumental conditioning, the stimuli (S) in the presence of which the instrumental response is reinforced, become associated with the response outcome (O) through Pavlovian conditioning, and this results in an S-O association. Rescorla and Solomon assumed that the S-O association activates an emotional state which motivates the instrumental behavior. The emotional state is assumed to be either positive or negative, depending on whether the reinforcer is an appetitive or an aversive stimulus (e.g., food or shock). Thus, various appetitive reinforcers (e.g., food and water) are assumed to lead to a common positive emotional state and various aversive stimuli are assumed to lead to a common negative emotion.

How could we test the idea that an S-O association (and the expectancies or emotions that such an association activates) can motivate instrumental behavior? The basic experimental design for evaluating this idea is what has come to be called the *Pavlovian-Instrumental Transfer Test* in the behavioral neuroscience literature (Everitt & Robbins, 2005). The test involves three separate phases (see Table 7.1). In one phase, subjects receive standard instrumental conditioning (e.g., lever pressing is reinforced with food). In the next phase, they receive a pure Pavlovian conditioning procedure (the response lever is removed from the experimental chamber and a tone is paired with food). The critical transfer phase occurs in Phase 3, where the subjects are

TABLE **7.1**

Experimental Design for Pavlovian Instrumental Transfer Test

Phase 1	Phase 2	Transfer Test
Instrumental Conditioning	Pavlovian Conditioning	Present Pavlovian CS during performance of instrumental response
(Lever Press→Food)	(Tone→Food)	(Lever Press→Food; Tone vs. No Tone)

again permitted to perform the instrumental lever-press response, but now the Pavlovian CS is presented periodically. If a Pavlovian S-O association motivates instrumental behavior, then the rate of lever pressing should increase when the tone CS is presented. The experiment is called the Pavlovian Instrumental Transfer Test because it determines how an independently established Pavlovian CS transfers to influence or motivate instrumental responding.

Phase 1 can precede or follow Phase 2. The order is not critical. The two phases of training can also be conducted in different experimental chambers, provided the Pavlovian CS is portable so that it can be presented in the instrumental conditioning chamber during the transfer test while the subject is performing the instrumental response.

The two-process theory has stimulated a great deal of research using the Pavlovian instrumental transfer test. As predicted, the presentation of a Pavlovian CS for food increases the rate of instrumental responding for food (e.g., Estes, 1943, 1948; LoLordo, 1971; Lovibond, 1983). This presumably occurs because the positive emotion elicited by the CS+ for food summates with the appetitive motivation that is involved in lever pressing for food. The opposite outcome (a suppression of responding) is predicted if the Pavlovian CS elicits a negative emotion. I described such a result in Chapter 3 where I described the conditioned suppression procedure. In that case, the Pavlovian CS was paired with shock (coming to elicit the fear). Presentation of the CS+ for shock was then tested when subjects were lever pressing for food. The result was that the Pavlovian CS suppressed the instrumental lever-press behavior (Blackman, 1977; Davis, 1968; Lyon, 1968). According to two-process theory, conditioned suppression occurs because the CS+ for shock elicits an emotional state (fear) that is contrary to the positive emotion or expectancy (hope) that is established in instrumental conditioning with food. (For a more detailed discussion of other predictions of two-process theory, see Domjan, 1993.)

Response Interactions in Pavlovian Instrumental Transfer

Classically conditioned stimuli elicit not only emotional states, but also overt responses. Consequently, a classically conditioned stimulus may influence instrumental behavior through the overt responses it elicits. Consider a hypothetical situation in which the classically conditioned stimulus elicits sign tracking that moves the animal to the left side of the experimental chamber but the instrumental response is pressing a lever on the right side. In this case, presentation of the CS will decrease the instrumental response simply because the sign tracking behavior (going to the left) will interfere with being on the right to press the bar. An elicited emotional state is not necessary to understand such an outcome. An elicited emotional state is also unnecessary if the classically conditioned stimulus elicited overt responses (e.g., key pecking in pigeons) that were similar to the instrumental behavior (also key pecking). In this case, presentation of the CS would increase responding because responses elicited by the CS would be added to the responses the animal was performing to receive instrumental reinforcement.

Investigators have been very concerned with the possibility that the results of Pavlovian instrumental transfer experiments are due to the fact that Pavlovian CSs elicit overt responses that either interfere with or summate with the behavior required for instrumental reinforcement. A number of experimental strategies have been designed to rule out such response interactions (for a review, see Overmier & Lawry, 1979). These strategies generally have been successful in showing that many instances of Pavlovian instrumental transfer are not produced by interactions between overt responses. However, overt classically conditioned responses have been important in some cases (e.g., Karpicke, 1978; LoLordo, McMillan, & Riley, 1974; Schwartz, 1976).

Conditioned Emotional States or Reward-Specific Expectancies?

The two-process theory assumes that classical conditioning mediates instrumental behavior through the conditioning of positive or negative emotions depending on the emotional valence of the reinforcer. However, animals also acquire specific reward expectancies instead of just categorical positive or negative emotions during instrumental and classical conditioning (Peterson & Trapold, 1980).

In one study, for example, solid food pellets and a sugar solution were used as USs in a Pavlovian instrumental transfer test with rats (Kruse, Overmier, Konz, & Rokke, 1983). During the transfer phase, the CS+ for food pellets facilitated instrumental responding reinforced with pellets much more than instrumental behavior reinforced with the sugar solution. Correspondingly, a CS+ for sugar increased instrumental behavior reinforced with sugar more than instrumental behavior reinforced with food pellets. Thus, expectancies for specific rewards rather than a general positive emotional state determined the results in the transfer test.

This study and other similar experiments clearly indicate that under some circumstances, individuals acquire reinforcer-specific expectancies rather than the more general emotions during instrumental and classical conditioning. (For additional evidence of reinforcer-specific expectancies, see Estévez et al., 2001; Overmier & Linwick, 2001; Urcuioli, 2005.) Reinforcer-specific expectancy learning is a challenging alternative to the two-process theory. However, this alternative is also based on the assumption that instrumental conditioning involves the learning of an S-O association.

R-O and S(R-O) Relations in Instrumental Conditioning

So far we have considered two different associations that can motivate instrumental behavior, Thorndike's S-R association, and the S-O association, which activates a reward-specific expectancy or emotional state. However, for a couple of reasons, it would be odd to explain all of the motivation of

BOX **7.2**

Addiction: Liking, Wanting, and Hedonic Hot Spots

A central problem in addiction concerns the compulsion to take drugs, a compulsion that can fuel relapse in the face of clear knowledge that the drug has harmful effects. We all know the sad story of individuals enslaved by addiction, who know that continued use of alcohol will kill them, and yet they continue drinking. Even people who have been sober for years are prone to relapse. This is well recognized by Alcoholics Anonymous, which assumes that an individual is never completely cured and is forever prone to relapse.

Why is abstinence so difficult and what predisposes an addict to relapse? Anyone who has quit smoking can tell you that they are weakest, and most prone to relapse, when they are re-exposed to the cues associated with smoking. Individuals who have not smoked for months may experience an irresistible urge to smoke again if they enter a smoky bar. Observations of this sort suggest that cues associated with drug consumption acquire motivational significance and incentive value that can fuel drug craving. In the laboratory, the conditional control of drug reactivity is clearly evident in studies of drug-induced sensitization. For example, rats that repeatedly receive a psychostimulant (amphetamine or cocaine) exhibit a gradual increase in locomotor activity across days. Interestingly, this behavioral sensitization is context specific; rats only exhibit increased activity when tested in the presence of drug-paired cues (Robinson & Berridge, 2003).

Understanding how conditioning and hedonic value influence relapse has required further specification of the ways in which reward can impact psychological/behavioral systems. Abused drugs (e.g., heroin) and natural rewards (e.g., a sweet solution) engage a pleasant conscious experience, a hedonic state that Berridge and Robinson (2003) call *liking*. Interestingly, we behaviorally give away how much we like a sweet taste through our facial expression; across species, administration of a sweet taste elicits a stereotyped pattern of licking (tongue protrusions). Conversely, a bitter solution (tainted with quinine) elicits a gaping response indicative of dislike. What is of special interest is that these behavioral signs of hedonic value are modulated by psychoactive drugs. For example, pretreatment with an opioid agonist increases the liking response elicited by a sweet solution. Conversely, administration of an opioid antagonist reduces signs of liking (Berridge & Robinson, 2003).

In Box 7.1 we discussed how reward is related to neural activity in the nucleus accumbens. Given this, Berridge and colleagues explored whether a mu opioid receptor agonist (DAMGO) microinjected into the nucleus accumbens would affect the liking response elicited by a sweet solution (Pecina, Smith, & Berridge, 2006). They found that that DAMGO enhanced signs of liking, but only when the drug was applied within a small subregion (1 mm^3) of the nucleus accumbens (Figure 7.3), an area they called a *hedonic hot spot*. Outside this region, DAMGO could elicit eating (a behavioral sign of *want-ing*, discussed below), but not signs of *liking*.

A second hedonic hot spot has been discovered in an adjoining region of the brain, the ventral pallidum. Here too, local infusion of the opioid agonist enhances the liking response to a sweet solution (Figure 7.3). Further, electrophysiological recordings revealed that neurons in this region exhibit increased activity in response to a sweet solution (Tindell, Smith, Pecina, Berridge, & Aldridge, 2006), suggesting that these neurons are linked to hedonic value. Amazingly, the activity in these neurons can be shifted by physiological manipulations that alter the liking response. Normally, rats will exhibit a dislike response to an intensely salty solution. If, however, the subjects are physiologically deprived of salt, they exhibit a salt craving and behavioral signs that they now like very salty solutions. This is in turn accompanied by a shift in the activity of neurons in the ventral pallidum. Now, salty solutions that previously did not elicit neural activity within the ventral pallidum hedonic hot spot, elicit neural activity, as if the underlying neural code has been shifted.

For many years, researchers have assumed that dopamine release plays a key role in mediating pleasure. Given this, it was surprising that the complete destruction of dopaminergic neurons innervating the nucleus accumbens had no effect on opioid-induced liking (Berridge & Robinson, 2003). Conversely, liking reactions to sweet tastes are not elicited by manipulations that engage dopaminergic neurons.

(continued)

BOX **7.2** (continued)

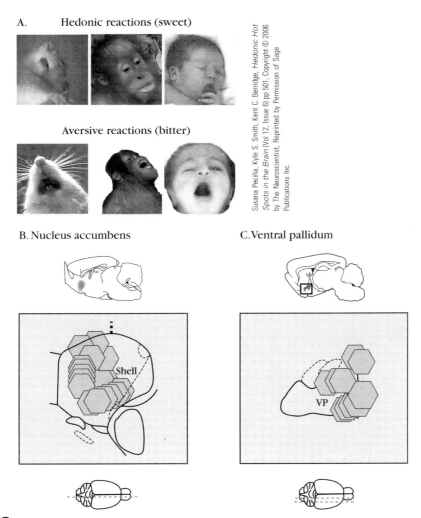

Susana Peciña, Kyle S. Smith, Kent C. Berridge. *Hedonic Hot Spots in the Brain* (Vol 12, Issue 6) pp 501. Copyright © 2006 by The Neuroscientist. Reprinted by Permission of Sage Publications Inc.

FIGURE **7.3**

(A) Across species, animals exhibit comparable reactions to sweet (top panels) and bitter tastes (bottom). (B) Administration of the mu opioid DAMGO into a small region of the nucleus accumbens shell amplifies *liking* reactions to a sweet taste (left panel). Administering DAMGO outside of this hedonic hot spot can elicit signs of *wanting* (e.g., food consumption) but not liking. A second hedonic hot spot exists in the adjoining ventral pallidum (right panel). (Adapted from Pecina et al., 2006.)

(continued)

BOX **7.2** (continued)

K. C. Berridge

T. E. Robinson

These observations suggest that dopamine activity is neither required (necessary) nor sufficient to generate liking. Yet, it was well known that manipulations that im-

pact dopaminergic neurons can dramatically affect drug-taking behavior (Koob, 1999; Hyman et al., 2006). For example, self administration of a psychostimulant is blocked by pretreatment with a dopamine antagonist or a physiological manipulation that destroys dopaminergic neurons in this region. Across a range of tasks, in the absence of dopamine, rats cannot use information about rewards to motivate goal-directed behavior; they cannot act on their preferences (Hyman et al., 2006).

Berridge and Robinson (2003) have suggested that manipulations of the dopamine system affect motivation because they impact a distinct quality of reward. Rather than influencing how much the animal consciously likes the reward, Berridge and Robinson propose that dopamine activity is coupled to an unconscious process that they call wanting. They see wanting as related to the underlying motivational value of the reward, encoding the degree to which the organism is driven to obtain and consume the reward independent of whether consumption engenders pleasure. From this perspective, opioids mi-

croinjected outside of the nucleus accumbens hot spot engender eating because they enhance wanting even though pleasure (liking) is not enhanced.

Berridge and Robinson (2003) also assume that cues paired with reward gain an incentive salience that drives a form of wanting. From their perspective, incentive salience transforms sensory signals of reward into attractive, desired goals. These cues act as motivational magnets that unconsciously pull the animal to approach the reward. In Box 7.1 we discussed how a positive prediction error engages dopamine activity and how this activity can act as a teacher, fostering the association of sensory cues with reward. From this view, dopamine activity within the nucleus accumbens binds the hedonic properties of a goal to motivation, driving the wanting that can fuel drug craving. The conditioned value of drug paired cues can be assessed using a Pavlovian-to-instrumental transfer test, and evidence suggests that this effect depends on dopamine activity.

J. W. Grau

instrumental behavior in terms of these two associations alone. First, notice that neither the S-R nor the S-O association involves a direct link between the response (R) and the reinforcer or outcome (O). This is counterintuitive. If you asked someone why he or she was performing an instrumental response, the reply would be that he or she expected the response (R) to result in the reinforcer (O). Intuition suggests that instrumental behavior involves R-O associations. You comb your hair because you expect that doing so will improve your appearance; you go to see a movie because you expect that watching the movie will be entertaining; and you open the refrigerator because you anticipate that doing so will enable you to get something to eat. Although our informal explanations of instrumental behavior emphasize R-O associations, such associations do not exist in two-process models.

Another peculiarity of the associative structure of instrumental conditioning assumed by two-process theories is that S is assumed to become associated directly with O on the assumption that the pairing of S with O is sufficient for the occurrence of classical conditioning. However, as we saw in Chapter 4, CS-US pairings are not sufficient for the development of Pavlovian associations. The CS must also provide information about the US, or in some way be related to the US. In an instrumental conditioning situation, the reinforcer (O) cannot be predicted from S alone. Rather O occurs if the individual makes response (R) in the presence of S. Thus, instrumental conditioning involves a conditional relation in which S is followed by O only if R occurs. This conditionality in the relation of S to O is ignored in two-process theories.

Evidence of R-O Associations

Courtesy of B. Balleine

B. Balleine

A number of investigators have suggested that instrumental conditioning leads to the learning of response-outcome associations (e.g., Bolles, 1972b; Mackintosh & Dickinson, 1979), and several different types of evidence support this possibility. A common technique involves devaluing the reinforcer after conditioning to see if this decreases the instrumental response (for reviews, see Colwill & Rescorla, 1986; Dickinson & Balleine, 1994; Ostlund, Winterbauer, & Balleine, 2008). This strategy is analogous to the strategy of US devaluation in studies of Pavlovian conditioning (see Chapter 4). In Pavlovian conditioning, US devaluation is used to determine whether the conditioned response is mediated by a CS-US association. If US devaluation after conditioning disrupts the CR, one may conclude that the CR was mediated by the CS-US association. In a corresponding fashion, reinforcer devaluation has been used to determine if an instrumental response is mediated by an association between the response and its reinforcer outcome.

In a definitive demonstration, Colwill and Rescorla (1986) first reinforced rats for pushing a vertical rod either to the right or the left. Responding in either direction was reinforced on a variable-interval one-minute schedule of reinforcement. Both response alternatives were always available during training sessions. The only difference was that responses in one direction were reinforced with food, pellets and responses in the opposite direction were always reinforced with a bit of sugar solution (sucrose).

After both responses had become well established, the rod was removed and the reinforcer devaluation procedure was conducted. One of the reinforcers (either food pellets or sugar solution) was periodically presented in the experimental chamber, followed by an injection of lithium chloride to condition an aversion to that reinforcer. After an aversion to the selected reinforcer had been conditioned, the vertical rod was returned, and the rats received a test, during which they were free to push the rod either to the left or to the right, but neither food nor sucrose was provided.

The results of the test are presented in Figure 7.4. The important finding was that the rats were less likely to make the response whose reinforcer had been made aversive by pairings with lithium chloride. For example, if sucrose was used to reinforce responses to the left and an aversion was then conditioned to sucrose, the rats were less likely to push the rod to the left than to the right.

Studies of reinforcer devaluation are conducted in a manner similar to the procedures used by Colwill and Rescorla (1986). An initial phase of

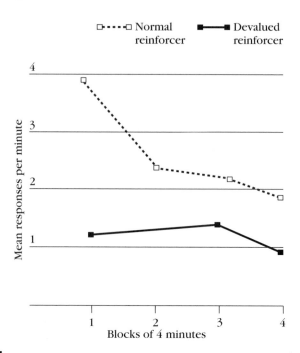

FIGURE 7.4

Effects of reinforcer devaluation on instrumental behavior. Devaluation of a reinforcer selectively reduces the response that was previously reinforced with that reinforcer. (From "Associative Structure in Instrumental Learning," by R. M. Colwill and R. A. Rescorla, in G. H. Bower [Ed.], 1986. *The Psychology of Learning and Motivation,* Vol. 20, pp. 55–104. Copyright © 1986 Academic Press. Reprinted by permission.)

instrumental conditioning is followed by a phase in which the reinforcer is devalued by pairing it with illness or by making the subject full so that it no longer feels like eating. The rate of the instrumental behavior is then measured in the absence of the reinforcer. However, there is another important step in the process. The subject has to experience the new value of the reinforcer. That is, the subject has to taste how bad the food became after it was paired with illness or how unpalatable the food is once the subject is no longer hungry. This is called *incentive learning.* Only if the subject has had a chance to learn what the new incentive value of the reinforcer is will its instrumental behavior be reduced (see Ostlund, Winterbauer, & Balleine, 2008, for a review).

The results presented in Figure 7.4 constitute particularly good evidence of R-O associations because alternative accounts are not tenable. For example, the selective response suppression illustrated in Figure 7.4 cannot be explained in terms of an S-O association. Pushing the vertical rod left or right occurred in the same experimental chamber, with the same manipulandum, and therefore in the presence of the same external stimuli (S). If devaluation of one of the reinforcers had altered the properties of S, that should have changed the two responses equally. That did not happen. Instead, devaluation of a reinforcer selectively depressed the particular response that had been trained with that reinforcer. This finding indicates that each response was associated separately with its own reinforcer. The participants learned separate R-O associations.

The results presented in Figure 7.4 also cannot be explained by S-R associations. S-R associations do not include the reinforcer. Therefore, devaluation of the reinforcer cannot alter behavior mediated by an S-R association. In fact, lack of sensitivity to reinforcer devaluation is often used as evidence for an S-R association (Everitt & Robbins, 2005). Instrumental behavior becomes habitual and insensitive to reinforcer devaluation if a single instrumental response is followed by the same outcome over an extended period of training (Dickinson et al., 1995). This effect of extended training is not observed if several instrumental responses are trained, each with its own reinforcer (Holland, 2004).

Hierarchical S(R-O) Relations

The evidence cited above clearly shows that organisms learn to associate an instrumental response with its outcome. However, R-O associations cannot act alone to produce instrumental behavior. As Mackintosh and Dickinson (1979) pointed out, the fact that the instrumental response activates an expectancy of the reinforcer is not sufficient to tell us what caused the response in the first place. An additional factor is required to activate the R-O association. One possibility is that the R-O association is activated by the stimuli (S) that are present when the response is reinforced. According to this view, S does not activate R directly, but rather it activates the R-O association. Stated informally, the subject comes to think of the R-O association when it encounters S, and that motivates it to make the instrumental response.

Skinner (1938) suggested many years ago that S, R, and O in instrumental conditioning are connected through a conditional S(R-O) relation. This suggestion was vigorously pursued at the end of the twentieth century. A variety of direct and indirect lines of evidence have been developed that point to the learning of S(R-O) relations in instrumental conditioning (Colwill & Rescorla, 1990; Davidson, Aparicio, & Rescorla 1988; Holman & Mackintosh, 1981; Goodall & Mackintosh, 1987; Rescorla, 1990a, 1990b). Most of these studies have involved rather complicated discrimination training procedures that are beyond the scope of the present discussion. (For an especially good example, see Colwill & Delamater, 1995, Experiment 2.)

BEHAVIORAL REGULATION

Although contemporary associative analyses of instrumental motivation go far beyond Thorndike's Law of Effect, they are a part of the Thorndikeian and Pavlovian tradition that views the world of behavior in terms of stimuli, responses, and associations. Behavioral regulation analyses are based on a radically different world view. Instead of considering instrumental conditioning in terms of the reinforcement of a response in the presence of certain stimuli, behavioral regulation focuses on how instrumental conditioning procedures put limitations on an organism's activities and cause redistributions of those activities.

Antecedents of Behavioral Regulation

Reinforcers were initially considered to be special kinds of stimuli. Thorndike, for example, characterized a reinforcer as a stimulus that produces a *satisfying state of affairs*. Various proposals were made about the special characteristics a stimulus must have to serve as a reinforcer. Although there were differences of opinion, for about a half a century after Thorndike's Law of Effect, theoreticians agreed that reinforcers were special stimuli that strengthened instrumental behavior.

Consummatory-Response Theory

The first challenge to the idea that reinforcers are stimuli came from Fred Sheffield and his colleagues, who formulated the **consummatory-response theory**. Many reinforcers, like food and water, elicit species-typical unconditioned responses, such as chewing, licking, and swallowing. The consummatory-response theory attributes reinforcement to these species typical behaviors. It asserts that species-typical consummatory responses (eating, drinking, and the like) are themselves the critical feature of reinforcers. In support of this idea, Sheffield, Roby, and Campbell (1954) showed that saccharin, an artificial sweetener, can serve as an effective reinforcer, even though it has no nutritive value and hence cannot satisfy a biological need. The reinforcing properties of artificial sweeteners now provide the foundations of a flourishing diet food industry. Apart from their commercial value, however, artificial sweeteners were important in advancing our thinking about instrumental motivation.

The consummatory-response theory was a radical innovation because it moved the search for reinforcers from special kinds of stimuli to special types of responses. Reinforcer responses were assumed to be special because they involved the consummation, or completion, of an instinctive behavior sequence. (See discussion of consummatory behavior in Chapter 2.) The theory assumed that consummatory responses (e.g., chewing and swallowing) are fundamentally different from various potential instrumental responses, such as running, jumping, or pressing a lever. David Premack took issue with this and suggested that reinforcer responses are special only because they are more likely to occur than the instrumental responses they follow.

The Premack Principle

Premack pointed out that responses involved with commonly used reinforcers involve activities that animals are highly likely to perform. In a food reinforcement experiment participants are typically food deprived and therefore are highly likely to engage in eating behavior. By contrast, instrumental responses are typically low-probability activities. An experimentally naive rat, for example, is much less likely to press a response lever than it is to eat. Premack (1965) proposed that this difference in response probabilities is critical for reinforcement. Formally, the **Premack principle** can be stated as follows:

> Given two responses of different likelihood, H and L, the opportunity to perform the higher probability response (H) after the lower probability response (L) will result in reinforcement of response L. (L→H reinforces L.) The opportunity to perform the lower probability response (L) after the higher probability response (H) will not result in reinforcement of response H. (H→L does not reinforce H.)

The Premack principle focuses on the difference in the likelihood of the instrumental and reinforcer responses. Therefore, it is also called the **differential probability principle.** Eating will reinforce bar pressing because eating is typically more likely than bar pressing. Beyond that, Premack's theory denies that there is anything special about a reinforcer.

Premack and his colleagues conducted many experiments to test his theory (see Premack, 1965). One of the early studies was conducted with young children. Premack first gave the children two response alternatives (eating candy and playing a pinball machine) and measured which response was more probable for each child. Some of the children preferred eating candy over playing pinball, while others preferred the pinball machine. In the second phase of the experiment (see Figure 7.5), the children were tested with one of two procedures. In one procedure, eating was specified as the reinforcing response, and playing pinball was the instrumental response. That is, the children had to play the pinball machine in order to get access to candy. Consistent with Premack's theory, only those children who preferred eating to playing pinball showed a reinforcement effect under these circumstances.

In another test, the roles of the two responses were reversed. Eating was the instrumental response, and playing pinball was the reinforcing response. The children had to eat candy to get access to the pinball machine. In this situation, only those children who preferred playing pinball to eating showed a reinforcement effect.

The power of the Premack principle is that potentially any high probability activity can be an effective reinforcer for a response that the subject is not inclined to perform. In laboratory rats, for example, drinking a drop of sucrose is a high probability response, and as one might predict, sucrose is effective in reinforcing lever-press responding. Running in a running wheel is also a high

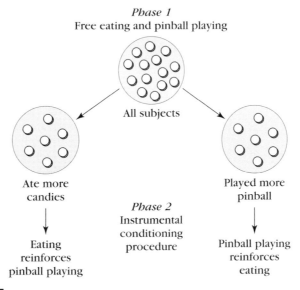

FIGURE **7.5**

Diagram of Premack's (1965) study.

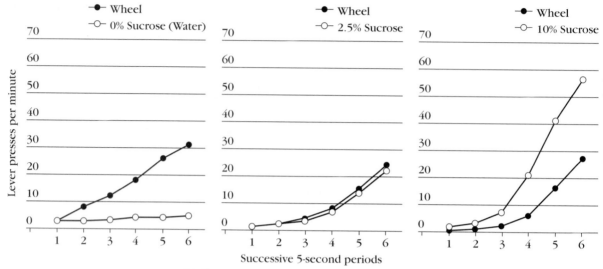

FIGURE **7.6**

Rate of lever pressing during successive five-minute periods of a fixed interval 30-second schedule reinforced with access to a running wheel or access to various concentrations of sucrose. (Based on Belke & Hancock, 2003.)

probability response in rats. Thus, one might predict that running would also effectively reinforce lever pressing. Numerous studies have confirmed this prediction. Belke and Hancock (2003), for example, compared lever pressing on a fixed-interval 30-second schedule, reinforced by either sucrose or the opportunity to run in a wheel for 15 seconds. In different phases of the experiment, the rats were tested with different concentrations of the sucrose reinforcer.

Lever pressing on the FI 30-second schedule is summarized in Figure 7.6 for the wheel-running reinforcer and for sucrose concentrations ranging from 0 to 10%. The data are presented in terms of the rate of lever pressing in successive five-second periods of the FI 30-second schedule. As expected with a fixed interval schedule, response rates increased closer to the end of the 30 second period. Wheel running as the reinforcer was just as effective as 2.5% sucrose. Wheel running was more effective than 0% sucrose, but at a sucrose concentration of 10%, responding for sucrose exceeded responding for running.

Applications of the Premack Principle

The Premack principle had an enduring impact in the design of reinforcement procedures used to help various clinical populations. In an early application, Mitchell and Stoffelmayr (1973) studied two hospitalized patients with chronic schizophrenia who refused all tangible reinforcers that were offered to them (candy, cigarettes, fruit, biscuits). The other patients on the ward participated in a work project that involved removing tightly wound copper wire from coils. The two participants in this study did not take part in the coil-stripping project and spent most of their time just sitting. Given this limited behavioral repertoire, what could be an effective reinforcer? The Premack principle suggests that the opportunity to sit should be a good reinforcer for these patients. To test this idea, the investigators gave the subjects a chance to sit down only if they worked a bit on the coil-stripping task.

Each participant was trained separately. At the start of each trial, they were asked or coaxed into standing. A piece of cable was then handed to them. If they made the required coil-stripping responses, they were permitted to sit for about 90 seconds, and then the next trial started. This procedure was highly successful. As long as the instrumental contingency was in effect, the two patients worked at a much higher rate than when they were simply told to participate in the coil-stripping project. Normal instructions and admonitions to participate in coil stripping were entirely ineffective, but taking advantage of the one high-probability response the participants had (sitting) worked very well.

Other interesting studies have been conducted with children with autism who engaged in unusual repetitive or stereotyped behaviors. One such behavior, called *delayed echolalia,* involves repeating words. For example, one autistic child was heard to say over and over again, "Ding! ding! ding! You win again," and "Match Game 83." Another form stereotyped behavior, *perseverative behavior,* involves persistent manipulation of an object. For example, the child may repeatedly handle only certain plastic toys.

The high probability of echolalia and perseverative behavior in children with autism suggests that these responses may be effectively used as reinforcers in treatment procedures. Charlop, Kurtz, and Casey (1990) compared the effectiveness of different forms of reinforcement in training various academic-related skills in several children with autism (see also Hanley, Iwata, Thompson, & Lindberg, 2000). The tasks included identifying which of several objects was the same or different from the one held up by the teacher, adding up coins, and correctly responding to sentences designed to teach receptive pronouns or prepositions. In one experimental condition, a preferred food (e.g., a small piece of chocolate, cereal, or a cookie) served as the reinforcer, in the absence of programmed food deprivation. In another condition, the opportunity to perform a stereotyped response for 3–5 seconds served as the reinforcer.

Some of the results of the study are illustrated in Figure 7.7. Each panel represents the data for a different student. Notice that in each case, the opportunity to engage in a prevalent stereotyped response resulted in better performance on the training tasks than food reinforcement. Delayed echolalia and perseverative behavior both served to increase task performance above what was observed with food reinforcement. These results indicate that high-probability responses can serve to reinforce lower probability responses, even if the reinforcer responses are not characteristic of normal behavior.

The Premack principle advanced our thinking about reinforcement in significant ways. It encouraged thinking about reinforcers as responses rather than as stimuli, and it greatly expanded the range of activities investigators started to use as reinforcers. With the Premack principle, any behavior could serve as a reinforcer provided that it was more likely than the instrumental response. Differential probability as the key to reinforcement paved the way for applications of reinforcement procedures to all sorts of human problems. However, problems with the measurement of response probability and a

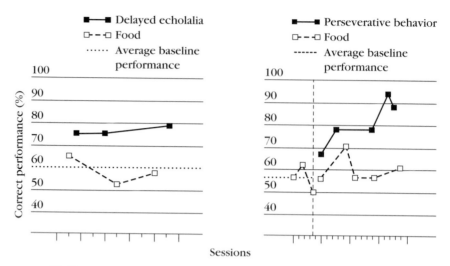

FIGURE 7.7

Task performance for two children with autism. One student's behavior was reinforced with food or the opportunity to engage in delayed echolalia. Another student's behavior was reinforced with food or the opportunity to engage in perseverative responding. (Responding during baseline periods was also reinforced with food.) (From "Using Aberrant Behaviors as Reinforcers for Autistic Children," by M. H. Charlop, P. F. Kurtz, & F. G. Casey, *Journal of Applied Behavior Analysis, 23,* pp. 163–181. Copyright © 1990 by the Society for the Experimental Analysis of Behavior, Inc. Reprinted by permission.)

closer look at instrumental conditioning procedures moved subsequent theoretical developments past the Premack principle.

The Response-Deprivation Hypothesis

In most instrumental conditioning procedures, the probability of the reinforcer activity is kept at a high level by restricting access to the reinforcer. Laboratory rats reinforced with food are typically not given food before the experimental session and receive a small pellet of food for each lever press response. These limitations on access to food (and eating) are very important. If we were to give the rat a full meal for one lever press, chances are it would not respond more than once or twice a day. Generally, restrictions on the opportunity to engage in the reinforcing response increase its effectiveness as a reinforcer.

Courtesy of W. Timberlake

W. Timberlake

Premack (1965) recognized the importance of restricting access to the reinforcer, but that was not the main idea behind his theory. By contrast, Timberlake and Allison (1974; see also Allison, 1993) abandoned the differential probability principle altogether and argued that restriction of the reinforcer activity was the critical factor for instrumental reinforcement. This proposal is called the **response-deprivation hypothesis** or the **disequilibrium model** (in applied research).

In particularly decisive tests of the response-deprivation hypothesis, several investigators found that even a low probability response can serve as a reinforcer, provided that participants are restricted from making this response (Timberlake & Allison, 1974; Eisenberger, Karpman, & Trattner, 1967). Johnson et al. (2003) tested this prediction in a classroom setting with students who had moderate to severe mental retardation. For each student, teachers identified things the students were not very likely to do. For example, filing cards and tracing letters were both low probability responses for Edgar, but tracing was the less likely of the two responses. Nevertheless, the opportunity to trace was an effective reinforcer for filing behavior, if access to tracing was restricted below baseline levels. This result is contrary to the Premack principle and shows that response deprivation is more basic to reinforcement effects than differential response probability.

The response-deprivation hypothesis provided a new principle for predicting what will serve as an effective reinforcer. It also provided a new procedure for creating reinforcers: restricting access to the reinforcer activity. It is interesting to note that some restriction is inherent to all instrumental conditioning procedures. All instrumental conditioning procedures require withholding the reinforcer until the specified instrumental response has been performed. The response-deprivation hypothesis points out that this defining feature of instrumental conditioning is critical for producing a reinforcement effect.

Traditional views of reinforcement assume that a reinforcer is something that exists independent of an instrumental conditioning procedure. Food, for example, was thought to be a reinforcer whether or not it was used in instrumental conditioning. The response-deprivation hypothesis makes explicit the radically different idea that a reinforcer is produced by the instrumental contingency itself. How instrumental contingencies create reinforcers and reinforcement effects has been developed further in behavioral regulation theories, which we will consider next.

Behavioral Regulation and the Behavioral Bliss Point

Regulation is a recurrent theme in behavior theory. I previously discussed regulatory processes in Chapter 2 in connection with the opponent-process theory of motivation, and in Chapter 4 in connection with the role of learning in physiological homeostasis. Physiological homeostasis refers to mechanisms that serve to maintain critical aspects of the body (such as blood sugar level and temperature) within acceptable limits. A shift away from the physiologically optimal or homeostatic level triggers changes that serve to return the system to the homeostatic level.

Behavioral regulation theories assume that analogous mechanisms exist with respect to behavior. Within the framework of behavioral regulation, organisms are presumed to have a preferred or optimal distribution of activities that they work to maintain in the face of challenges or disruptions. Behavioral regulation theories focus on the extent to which an instrumental response-reinforcer contingency disrupts behavioral stability and forces the individual away from its preferred or optimal distribution of activities (see Allison, 1983, 1989; Hanson & Timberlake, 1983; Tierney, 1995; Timberlake, 1980, 1984, 1995).

An individual has to eat, breathe, drink, keep warm, exercise, reproduce, care for its young, and so on. All these activities have to occur in particular proportions. You don't want to eat too much or too little, or exercise too much or too little. If the preferred or optimal balance of activities is upset,

J. Allison

behavior is assumed to change so as to correct the deviation from the homeo-static level. This basic assumption of behavioral regulation is fairly simple. However, as we will see, numerous factors (some of which are a bit compli-cated) can influence how organisms meet challenges to their preferred or opti-mal distribution of responses.

The Behavioral Bliss Point

Every situation provides various response opportunities. In an experimental chamber, for example, an animal may run in a wheel, drink, eat, scratch it-self, sniff holes, or manipulate a response lever. Behavioral regulation theory assumes that if organisms are free to distribute their responses among the available alternatives, they will do so in a way that is most comfortable, or in some sense *optimal,* for them. This response distribution defines the **behav-ioral bliss point.**

The particular distribution of activities that constitutes the bliss point will vary from one situation to another. For example, if the running wheel is made very difficult to turn or the participant is severely deprived of water, the relative likelihood of running and drinking will change. However, for a given circumstance, the behavioral bliss point, as revealed in unconstrained choices among response alternatives, is assumed to be stable across time.

The behavioral bliss point can be identified by the relative frequency of occurrence of all the responses of an organism in an unconstrained situation. To simplify analysis, let us focus on just two responses. Consider how a high school student may distribute her activities between studying and watching TV. Figure 7.8 represents time spent watching TV on the vertical axis and time spent studying on the horizontal axis. If no restrictions are placed on the student's behavior, she will probably spend a lot more time watching TV than studying. This is represented by the open circle in Figure 7.8 and is the *behavioral bliss point* in this situation. At the bliss point, the student watches TV for 60 minutes for every 15 minutes of studying.

Imposing an Instrumental Contingency

How would the introduction of an instrumental contingency between study-ing and watching TV disrupt the student's behavioral bliss? That depends on the nature of the contingency. Figure 7.8 shows a schedule line starting at the origin and increasing at a 45° angle. This line defines a schedule of reinforce-ment, according to which the student is allowed to watch TV for as long as she spent studying. If the student studies for 10 minutes, she will get to watch TV for 10 minutes; if she studies for an hour, she will get to watch TV for an hour. What might be the consequences of disrupting the free choice of study-ing and TV watching by imposing such a schedule constraint?

Behavioral-regulation theory states that organisms will defend against chal-lenges to the behavioral bliss point, just as physiological regulation involves de-fense against challenges to a physiological set point. However, the interesting thing is that the free-baseline behavioral bliss point usually cannot be reestab-lished after an instrumental contingency has been introduced. In our example, the behavioral bliss point was 60 minutes of watching TV and 15 minutes of studying. Once the instrumental contingency is imposed, there is no way the student can watch TV for 60 minutes and only study for 15 minutes. If she in-

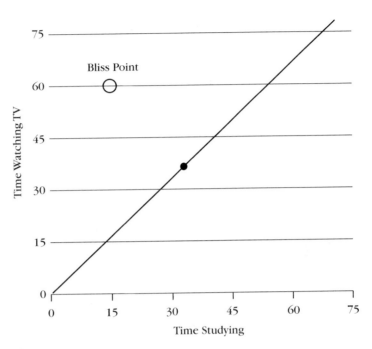

FIGURE **7.8**

Allocation of behavior between watching TV and studying. The open circle shows the optimal allocation, or behavioral bliss point, obtained when there are no constraints on either activity. The schedule line represents a schedule of reinforcement in which the student is required to study for the same amount of time that she gets to watch TV. Notice that once this schedule of reinforcement is imposed, it is no longer possible for the student to achieve the behavioral bliss point. The schedule deprives the student of access to the TV and forces or motivates and increase in studying.

sists on watching TV for 60 minutes, she will have to tolerate adding 45 min to her studying time. On the other hand, if the student insists on spending only the 15 minutes on her studies (as at the bliss point), she will have to make do with 45 minutes less than the optimal 60 minutes of TV watching. Defending the bliss amount of studying, or defending the bliss amount of TV watching both have their disadvantages. That is often the dilemma posed by an instrumental contingency. It does not permit getting back to the bliss point.

Although the instrumental contingency shown in Figure 7.8 makes it impossible to return to the behavioral bliss point, this does not mean that the bliss point becomes irrelevant. On the contrary, behavioral-regulation theory assumes that returning to the behavioral set point remains a goal of response allocation. When this goal cannot be reached, the redistribution of responses between the instrumental and contingent behaviors becomes a matter of compromise. The rate of one response is brought as close as possible to its preferred level without moving the other response too far away from its preferred level.

Staddon, for example, proposed a **minimum-deviation model** of behavioral regulation to solve the dilemma of schedule constraints (Staddon, 1983/2003). According to this model, introduction of a response-reinforcer contingency causes organisms to redistribute their behavior between the instrumental and contingent responses in a way that minimizes the total deviation of the two responses from the bliss point. The minimum deviation point is shown by the filled circle on the schedule line in Figure 7.8. For situations in which the free-baseline behavioral bliss point cannot be achieved, the minimum-deviation model provides one view of how organisms settle for the next best thing.

Explanation of Reinforcement Effects

How are reinforcement effects produced by behavioral regulation? Behavioral regulation involves the defense of a behavioral bliss point in the face of restrictions on responding imposed by a response-reinforcer contingency. As noted above, this defense may require settling for something that is close to but not exactly at the free-baseline bliss point. How do these mechanisms lead to increases in instrumental behavior in typical instrumental conditioning procedures?

A reinforcement effect is identified by an increase in the occurrence of an instrumental response above the level of that behavior in the absence of the response-reinforcer contingency. The schedule line shown in Figure 7.8 involves restricting access to TV watching below the level specified by the bliss point. To move towards the behavioral bliss point, the student has to increase her studying so as to gain more opportunity to watch TV. This is precisely what occurs in typical instrumental conditioning procedures. Access to the reinforcer is restricted; to gain more opportunity to engage in the reinforcer response, the individual has to perform more of the instrumental response. Thus, increased performance of the instrumental response (a reinforcement effect) results from behavioral-regulatory mechanisms that function to minimize deviations from the behavioral bliss point.

BOX **7.3**

The Bliss Point Approach and Behavior Therapy

Behavior regulation theories of reinforcement not only provide new insights into age-old theoretical issues concerning reinforcement, but also suggest alternative approaches to behavior therapy (Farmer-Dougan, 1998; Timberlake & Farmer-Dougan, 1991). The bliss-point approach, for example, forces us to consider the behavioral context in which an instrumental contingency is introduced.

Depending on that behavioral context, a reinforcement procedure may increase or decrease the target response. Thus, the bliss-point approach can provide insights into situations in which a reinforcement procedure produces an unexpected decrease in the instrumental response.

One area of behavior therapy in which reinforcement procedures are surprisingly ineffective is the use of parental social reinforcement to increase a child's prosocial behavior. A parent whose child frequently misbehaves is encouraged to provide more social reinforcement for positive behavior on the assumption that low rates of parental reinforcement are responsible for the child's misbehavior. Viken and McFall (1994) have pointed out that the common failure of such reinforcement procedures is pre-

(continued)

BOX **7.3** (continued)

dictable if we consider the behavioral bliss point of the child.

Figure 7.9 shows the behavioral space for parental social reinforcement and positive child behavior. The open circle represents the child's presumed bliss point. Left to his own devices, the child prefers a lot of social reinforcement while emitting few positive behaviors. The dashed line represents the low rate of parental reinforcement in effect before a therapeutic intervention. According to this schedule line, the child has to perform two positive responses to receive each social reinforcer from the parent. The filled point on the line indicates the equilibrium point, where positive responses by the child and social reinforcers earned are equally far from their respective bliss point values.

The therapeutic procedure involves increasing the rate of social reinforcement, let's say to a ratio of 1:1. This is illustrated by the solid line in Figure 7.9. Now the child receives one social reinforcer for each positive behavior. The equilibrium point is again illustrated by the filled data point. Notice that with the increased social reinforcement, the child can get more of the social reinforcers it wants without having to make more positive responses. In fact, the child can increase its rate of social reinforcement while performing fewer positive responses. No wonder, then, that the therapeutic reinforcement procedure does not increase the rate of positive responses. The unexpected result of increased social reinforcement illustrated in Figure 7.9 suggests that solutions to behavior problems require careful consideration of the relation between the new instrumental contingency and prior baseline conditions.

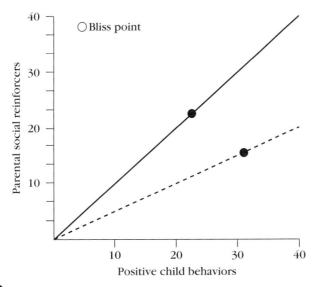

FIGURE **7.9**

Hypothetical data on parental social reinforcement and positive child behavior. The behavioral bliss point for the child is indicated by the open circle. The dashed line represents the rate of social reinforcement for positive behavior in effect prior to introduction of a treatment procedure. The solid line represents the rate of social reinforcement for positive behavior set up by the behavior therapy procedure. The solid point on each line represents the equilibrium point for each schedule.

Viewing Reinforcement Contingencies in a Broader Behavioral Context

The above explanation of how schedule constraints produce reinforcement effects considers only the instrumental and reinforcer responses (studying and watching TV). However, a student's environment most likely provides a much greater range of options. Instrumental contingencies do not occur in a behavioral vacuum. They occur in the context of a variety of responses and reinforcers the participant has available. Furthermore, that broader behavioral context can significantly influence how the person adjusts to a schedule constraint. For example, if the student enjoys listening to her iPod as much as watching TV, restrictions on access to the TV may not increase studying behavior. Rather, the student may switch to listening to her iPod, playing a video game, or hanging out with friends. Any of these options will undermine the instrumental contingency. The student could listen to her iPod or hang out with friends in place of watching TV without increasing her studying behavior.

This example illustrates that accurate prediction of the effects of an instrumental conditioning procedure requires considering the broader context of the organism's response options. Focusing on just the instrumental response and its antecedent and consequent stimuli (i.e., the associative structure of instrumental behavior) is not enough. The effect of a particular instrumental conditioning procedure may depend on what alternative sources of reinforcement are available to the organism, how those other reinforcers are related to the particular reinforcer involved in the instrumental contingency, and the costs of obtaining those alternative reinforcers. These issues have been systematically considered with the application of economic concepts to the problem of response allocation.

Economic Concepts and Response Allocation

The bliss-point approach redefined the fundamental issue in reinforcement. It shifted attention away from the notion that reinforcers are special stimuli that enter into special associative relations with the instrumental response and its antecedents. With the bliss-point approach, the fundamental question became, *How do the constraints of an instrumental conditioning procedure produce changes in behavior?*

Students who have studied economics may recognize a similarity here to problems addressed by economists. Economists, like psychologists, strive to understand changes in behavior in terms of preexisting preferences and restrictions on fulfilling those preferences. As Bickel, Green, and Vuchinich (1995) noted, "economics is the study of the allocation of behavior within a system of constraint" (p. 258). In the economic arena, the restrictions on behavior are imposed by our income and the price of the goods that we want to purchase. In instrumental conditioning situations, the restrictions are provided by the number of responses an organism is able to make (it's "income") and the number of responses required to obtain each reinforcer (the "price" of the reinforcer).

Psychologists have become interested in the similarities between economic restrictions in the marketplace and schedule constraints in instrumental conditioning. The analysis of behavior regulation in terms of economic concepts can be a bit complex. For the sake of simplicity, I will concentrate on the basic ideas that have had the most impact on understanding reinforcement. (For further details, see Allison, 1983, 1993; Green & Freed, 1998; Hursh & Silberberg, 2008; Lea, 1978; and Rachlin, 1989.)

Consumer Demand

Fundamental to the application of economic concepts to the problem of reinforcement is the relation between the price of a commodity and how much of it is purchased. This relation is called the **demand curve.** Figure 7.10 shows three examples of demand curves. Curve A illustrates a situation in which the consumption of a commodity is very easily influenced by its price. This is the case with candy. If the price of candy increases substantially, the amount purchased quickly drops. Other commodities are less responsive to price changes (Curve C in Figure 7.10). The purchase of gasoline, for example, is not as easily discouraged by increases in price. People continue to purchase gas for their cars even if the price increases, showing a small decline only at the highest prices.

The degree to which price influences consumption is called **elasticity of demand.** Demand for candy is highly elastic. The more candy costs, the less you will buy. In contrast, demand for gasoline is much less elastic. People continue to purchase gas even if the price increases a great deal.

The concept of consumer demand has been used to analyze a variety of major behavior problems including eating and drug abuse (e.g., Epstein, Leddy, Temple, & Faith, 2007). In a recent laboratory study, for example, children 10–12 years old increased their purchases of healthy foods as the price of unhealthy alternatives was increased (Epstein et al., 2006). The selection of healthy food also increased in a study of food choices in a restaurant when the healthy alternatives were reduced in price (Horgen & Brownell, 2002). Interestingly, a decrease in price was more effective in encouraging the selection of healthy foods than messages encouraging patrons to eat healthy.

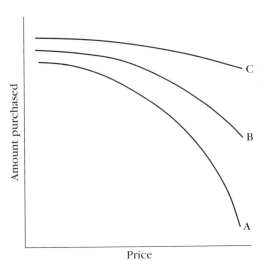

FIGURE **7.10**

Hypothetical consumer demand curves illustrating high sensitivity to price (Curve A), intermediate sensitivity (Curve B), and low sensitivity (Curve C).

The concept of consumer demand has been used to analyze instrumental behavior by considering the number of responses performed (or time spent responding) to be analogous to money and the reinforcer obtained to be analogous to the commodity that is purchased. The price of a reinforcer then is the time or number of responses required to obtain the reinforcer. Thus, the price of the reinforcer is determined by the schedule of reinforcement. The goal is to understand how instrumental responding (spending) is controlled by instrumental contingencies (prices).

Johnson and Bickel (2006) investigated the elasticity of demand for cigarettes and money in smokers with a mean age of 40 years old who were not trying to quit (see also Madden, Bickel, & Jacobs, 2000). The apparatus had three plungers the subjects could pull, each for a different reinforcer. The reinforcers were three puffs on a cigarette, 5¢, or 25¢. Only one of the plungers (and its assigned reinforcer) was available in a particular session. The response requirement for obtaining the reinforcer was gradually increased during each session. The ratio requirement started at an FR 3 and was then raised to FR 30, 60, 100, 300, 600, and eventually 6,000. The investigators wanted to determine at what point the participants would quit responding because the response requirement, or price, was too high. (None of the reinforcers could support responding on the FR 6,000 schedule.)

The results of the experiment are summarized in Figure 7.11. Data for the 5¢ reinforcer and the 25¢ reinforcer are presented in separate panels. Data for the cigarette reinforcer are replicated in both panels for comparison. The greatest elasticity of demand was evident for the 5¢ monetary reinforcer. Here, the number of reinforcers obtained started decreasing as soon as more than three responses were required to obtain the 5¢ and dropped quickly when 100 or more responses were required. With the 25¢ reinforcer, the demand curve did not start to decline until the response requirement exceeded FR 300. As might be expected, the participants were most resistant to increases in the price of puffs at a cigarette. When cigarette puffs served as the reinforcer, the number of reinforcers obtained did not start to decline until the response requirement

W. K. Bickel

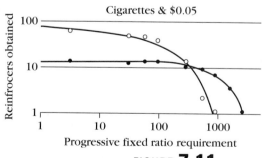
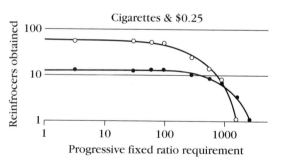

FIGURE **7.11**

Demand curves for cigarettes (solid circles) and money (open circles) with progressively larger fixed ratio requirements. The number of reinforcers obtained and the fixed ratio requirements are both presented on logarithmic scales. (Based on Johnson & Bickel, 2006.)

was raised above an FR 600. These results show that the participants were willing to make many more responses for puffs at a cigarette than they were willing to perform for the monetary rewards. No doubt the results would have been different if the experiment had been conducted with nonsmokers. (For reviews of behavioral economic approaches to drug abuse, see Higgins, Heil, & Lussier, 2004; and Murphy, Correla, & Barnett, 2007.)

Determinants of the Elasticity of Demand

The application of economic concepts to the analysis of instrumental conditioning would be of little value if the application did not provide new insights into the mechanisms of reinforcement. As it turns out, economic concepts have helped to identify three major factors that influence how schedule constraints shape the reallocation of behavior. Each of these factors determines the degree of elasticity of demand, or the extent to which increases in price cause a decrease in consumption.

1- Availability of Substitutes

Perhaps the most important factor that influences the elasticity of demand is the availability of alternative reinforcers that can serve as substitutes for the reinforcer of interest. Whether increases in the price of one item cause a decline in consumption depends on the availability (and price) of other goods that can be used in place of the original item. The availability of substitutes increases the sensitivity of the original item to higher prices.

Newspaper subscriptions in the United States have been steadily declining since news has become readily available on 24-hour cable channels and the internet. This basically reflects a price war since news obtained from cable channels and the internet is typically of lower marginal cost. The availability of substitutes is also influencing how often people go to the movies. Watching a movie on a rented DVD is a reasonable substitute for going to the theater, especially now that surround sound is readily available for home use. This means that increases in the price of movie tickets at the theater will encourage cost-conscious movie goers to wait for the release of the movie on DVD. In contrast, the amount of gasoline people buy is not as much influenced by price (especially in areas without mass transit), because at this point there are no readily available substitutes for gasoline to fuel a car.

Contemporary analyses of drug abuse are also cognizant of the importance of substitute reinforcers. Murphy, Correla, & Barnett (2007), for example, considered how one might reduce excessive alcohol intake among college students and concluded that "Behavioral economic theory predicts that college students' decisions about drinking are related to the relative availability and price of alcohol, the relative availability and price of substance-free alternative activities, and the extent to which reinforcement from delayed substance-free outcomes is devalued relative to the immediate reinforcement associated with drinking" (p. 2573).

Drug reinforcers can also serve as substitutes for other, more conventional reinforcers, such as food. This was examined by Foltin (1999) in an experiment conducted with baboons. The baboons had to press a response lever to obtain food pellets. As in Johnson and Bickel's study of cigarette smoking as a reinforcer, the price of the food pellets was varied by requiring different numbers of lever presses for each pellet (using fixed ratio schedules). Foltin was interested in whether food intake would decrease as the price of food was increased, and whether the availability of alternative reinforcers would influence this function. In different experimental conditions, responses on a second lever produced either nothing, a sugar solution, or solutions with different concentrations of cocaine. The availability of these alternative reinforcers always required two presses (FR 2) on the alternate lever. In general, the baboons obtained fewer food pellets as the behavioral price of food was increased. More interestingly, the availability of cocaine on the alternate response lever increased the elasticity of demand for food. This effect was particularly striking in Baboon 3.

The results for Baboon 3 are shown in Figure 7.12. Notice that for this subject, increasing the price of food had little effect if the alternate response lever produced either nothing or dextrose (a sugar solution). However, when the alternate response lever yielded cocaine, increases in the price of food resulted in a precipitous decline in food-reinforced responding. The largest ef-

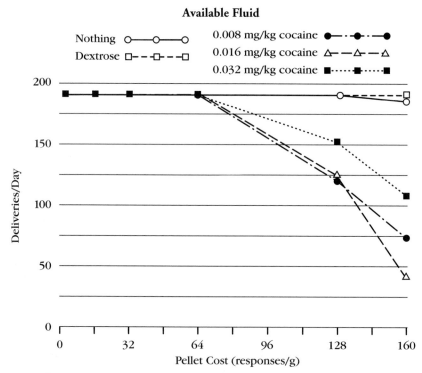

FIGURE **7.12**

Number of food pellets obtained as a function of increases in the response requirement for food for a baboon that could also press an alternate response lever that produced either nothing, a solution of dextrose (a type of sugar), or different concentrations of cocaine. Notice that the elasticity of demand for food dramatically changed with the availability of cocaine. (After Foltin, 1999.)

fect was obtained with the intermediate cocaine concentration. With this concentration, availability of cocaine on the alternative lever dramatically increased the elasticity of demand for food. This study shows a powerful example of substitutability on the elasticity of demand. In addition, it illustrates how the methodology provided by behavioral economic concepts can be used to identify substitutable reinforcers. For Baboon 3 an intermediate concentration of cocaine was an excellent substitute for food.

2- Price Range

Another important determinant of the elasticity of demand is the price range of the commodity. Generally, an increase in price has less of an effect at low prices than at high prices. Consider, for example, the cost of candy. A 10% increase in the price from 50¢ to 55¢ is not likely to discourage consumption. But if the candy costs $5.00, a 10% increase to $6.00 might well discourage purchases.

Price effects on elasticity of demand are evident in Figures 7.11 and 7.12. Notice that at low prices, there is little change in the number of reinforcers obtained as the price increases a bit. With a small increase in price at the low end of the price range, participants adjust by increasing the number of responses they perform to obtain the reinforcer. However, dramatic declines occur in the number of reinforcers obtained in the high range of prices. (For laboratory studies of price effects on obtaining food reinforcers, see Hursh et al., 1988; Foltin, 1991, 1994; and Sumpter, Temple, & Foster, 2004.)

3- Income Level

A third factor that determines elasticity of demand is the level of income. In general, the higher your income, the less deterred you will be by increases in price. This is also true for reinforcers obtained on schedules of reinforcement. In studies of instrumental conditioning, the number of responses or amount of time available for responding corresponds to income. These are resources an organism can use to respond to a schedule constraint. The more responses or time animals have available, the less their behavior is influenced by increases in the cost of the reinforcer (Silberberg, Warren-Bouton, & Asano, 1987; see also Hastjarjo & Silberberg, 1992; DeGrandpre, Bickel, Rizvi, & Hughes, 1993).

Income level also influences the choice of substitutes. In an interesting study of choice between healthy and unhealthy foods (Epstein et al., 2006), children 10–14 years old were tested at three different income levels ($1, $3, and $5). At the low income level, increases in the price of unhealthy foods (potato chips, cookies, pudding, cola) led to increased choice of the healthy alternatives (apples, pretzels, yogurt, milk). In contrast, at the high income level, the children continued to purchase the unhealthy, but preferred, foods as the price of these foods went up. This left them with less money to buy the lower priced, healthier substitutes. Thus, at the high income level, increases in the price of the unhealthy foods reduced the choice of substitutes.

Problems with Behavioral Regulation Approaches

Behavioral regulation theories have done much to change the way we think about reinforcement and instrumental conditioning. However, this approach is not without some difficulties. One problem concerns how the bliss point or preferred combination of activities is determined. Typically the bliss point is determined during a free-operant baseline period when there are no constraints on response choices. Choices observed during this baseline period are then used to predict performance after an instrumental conditioning procedure has been introduced. For such predictions to work, one has to assume that responses performed in the absence of experimenter-imposed constraints are basically the same as the responses that occur when an instrumental contingency is in effect. However, responses that occur during a free-operant baseline period do not always have the same value as responses that occur as a part of an arranged instrumental contingency (e.g., Allison, Buxton, & Moore, 1987). Doing something when there are no externally-imposed requirements (e.g., jogging for your own pleasure) appears to be different from doing the same thing when it is required by an instrumental contingency (e.g., jogging in a physical education class).

Another shortcoming is that behavioral regulation and economic approaches to instrumental behavior do not say much about how organisms manage to defend a preferred combination of goods or activities. Behavioral regulation and economic approaches are molar theories and therefore do not provide insights into the molecular processes that lead to the molar outcomes. As Killeen pointed out, economics "provides an approach to understanding the trade-offs animals make between alternate packages of goods," but it does not tell us the processes that are involved in making those trade-offs (Killeen, 1995, p. 426).

Contributions of Behavioral Regulation

The behavioral regulation approach emerged from the theoretical developments that originated with Premack and his differential probability principle. Although this line of theorizing encountered some serious difficulties, it has also made major contributions to how we think about the motivation of instrumental behavior (see Tierney, 1995). It is instructive to review some of these contributions.

1. Behavioral regulation and the Premack principle moved us away from thinking about reinforcers as special kinds of stimuli or as special kinds of responses. We are now encouraged to look for the causes of reinforcement in how instrumental contingencies constrain the free flow of behavior. Reinforcement effects are regarded as the consequences of schedule constraints on an organism's ongoing activities.

2. Instrumental conditioning procedures are no longer considered to "stamp in" or to strengthen instrumental behavior. Rather, instrumental conditioning is seen as creating a new distribution, or allocation, of responses. Typically, the reallocation of behavior involves an increase in the instrumental response and a decrease in the reinforcer response. These two changes are viewed as equally important features of the redistribution of behavior.

3. There is no fundamental distinction between instrumental and reinforcer responses. Reinforcer responses are not assumed to be more likely than instrumental responses. They are not assumed to provide any special physiological benefits or to have any inherent characteristics that make them different from instrumental responses. Rather, instrumental and reinforcer responses are distinguished only by the roles assigned to them by an instrumental conditioning procedure.

4. Behavioral regulation and behavioral economics embrace the assumption that organisms respond so as to maximize benefits. The idea of optimization or maximization is not original with behavioral regulation. We previously encountered the idea (maximizing rates of reinforcement) in discussions of concurrent schedules. The bliss point approach suggests that the optimal distribution of activities is determined not only by physiological needs, but also by the organism's ecological niche and natural or phylogenetically determined response tendencies. It is not always clear what is being maximized. In fact, studies of behavior can be used to identify what organisms value and work to conserve (Rachlin, 1995).

5. Behavioral regulation and behavioral economics have provided new and precise ways of describing constraints that various instrumental conditioning procedures impose on an organism's behavioral repertoire. More importantly, they have emphasized that instrumental behavior cannot be studied in a vacuum or behavioral test tube. Rather, all of the organism's response options at a given time must be considered as a system. Changes in one part of the system influence changes in other parts. Constraints imposed by instrumental procedures are more or less effective depending on the nature of the constraint, the availability of substitutes, and the organism's level of income.

CONCLUDING COMMENTS

Motivational processes in instrumental behavior have been addressed from two radically different perspectives and intellectual traditions, the associationist perspective rooted in Thorndike's Law of Effect and Pavlovian conditioning, and the behavioral regulation perspective rooted in Skinner's behavioral analysis. These two approaches differ in more ways than they are similar, making it difficult to imagine how they might be integrated. The fundamental concept in the associationist approach (the concept of an association) is entirely ignored in behavioral regulation. On the other hand, the critical concepts of behavioral regulation (bliss points, schedule constraints, response reallocations) have no correspondence in the associationist approach. Both approaches have contributed significantly to our understanding of the motivation of instrumental behavior. Therefore, neither approach can be ignored in favor of the other.

One way to think about the two approaches is that they involve different levels of analysis. The associationist approach involves the molecular level where the focus is on individual stimuli, responses, and their connections. In contrast, behavioral regulation operates at a molar level of aggregates of behavior and the broader behavioral context in which an instrumental contingency is introduced. Thus, the behavioral regulation approach makes better contact with the complexities of an organism's ecology.

Another way to think about the relation between the two approaches is that one is concerned with processes and the other is more concerned with functions or long-range goals. The associationist approach describes specific processes (S-R, S-O, R-O, and S(R-O) associations) that serve to generate and direct instrumental behavior but ignores the long-range *purpose*, or function, of instrumental learning. That is the purview of behavioral regulation and behavioral economics, which assumes that organisms work to defend an optimal distribution of activities. The defense of the behavioral bliss point is achieved through the molecular mechanisms of associations. (For a formal discussion of the relations between processes, ecology, and function, see Killeen, 1995.)

These alternative perspectives provide an exciting illustration of the nature of scientific inquiry. The inquiry has spanned intellectual developments from simple stimulus–response formulations to comprehensive considerations of how the organism's repertoire is constrained by instrumental contingencies, and how organisms solve complex ecological problems. This area in the study of conditioning and learning, perhaps more than any other, has moved boldly to explore radically new conceptions when older ideas did not meet the challenges posed by new empirical findings.

SAMPLE QUESTIONS

1. Describe what is an S-O association and what research tactic provides the best evidence for it.
2. What investigative techniques are used to provide evidence of R-O associations? Why is it not possible to explain instrumental behavior by assuming only R-O association learning?
3. How do studies of the associative structure of instrumental conditioning help in understanding the nature of drug addition?
4. Describe similarities and differences between the Premack principle and subsequent behavioral regulation theory.
5. What are the primary contributions of economic concepts to the understanding of the motivational bases of instrumental behavior?
6. What are the shortcomings of behavioral-regulation theory?
7. Describe implications of modern concepts of reinforcement for behavior therapy.

KEY TERMS

behavioral bliss point The preferred distribution of an organism's activities before an instrumental conditioning procedure is introduced that sets constraints and limitations on response allocation.

consummatory response theory A theory that assumes that species-typical consummatory responses (eating, drinking, and the like) are the critical features of reinforcers.

demand curve The relation between how much of a commodity is purchased and the price of the commodity.

differential probability principle A principle that assumes that reinforcement depends on how much more likely the organism is to perform the reinforcer response than the instrumental response before an instrumental conditioning procedure is introduced. The greater the differential probability of the reinforcer and instrumental responses during baseline conditions, the greater is the reinforcement effect of providing opportunity to engage in the reinforcer response after performance of the instrumental response. Also known as the *Premack principle*.

disequilibrium model Model used in applied behavioral analysis that assumes that reinforcement effects are produced by restricting access to the reinforcer response below the rate of this response during a nonconstrained free baseline period. (Similar to the *response deprivation hypothesis*.)

elasticity of demand The degree to which price influences the consumption or purchase of a commodity. If price has a large effect on consumption, elasticity of demand is high. If price has a small effect on consumption, elasticity of demand is low.

minimum-deviation model A model of instrumental behavior, according to which participants respond to a response-reinforcer contingency in a manner that gets them as close as possible to their behavioral bliss point.

Premack principle The same as *differential probability principle.*

response-deprivation hypothesis An explanation of reinforcement according to which restricting access to a response below its baseline rate of occurrence (response deprivation) is sufficient to make the opportunity to perform that response an effective positive reinforcer.

8

Stimulus Control of Behavior

Identification and Measurement of Stimulus Control
Differential Responding and Stimulus Discrimination
Stimulus Generalization
Stimulus Generalization Gradients as Measures of Stimulus Control

Stimulus and Response Factors in Stimulus Control
Sensory Capacity and Orientation
Relative Ease of Conditioning Various Stimuli
Type of Reinforcement
Type of Instrumental Response
Stimulus Elements versus Configural Cues in Compound Stimuli

Learning Factors in Stimulus Control
Stimulus Discrimination Training
Effects of Discrimination Training on Stimulus Control

Range of Possible Discriminative Stimuli
What Is Learned in Discrimination Training?
Interactions Between S+ and S–: Peak Shift Effect
Stimulus Equivalence Training

Contextual Cues and Conditional Relations
Control by Contextual Cues
Control by Conditional Relations

Concluding Comments

SAMPLE QUESTIONS
KEY TERMS

CHAPTER PREVIEW

This chapter is concerned with issues related to stimulus control. Although most of the chapter deals with the ways in which instrumental behavior comes under the control of particular stimuli that are present when the response is reinforced, the concepts are equally applicable to classical conditioning. The chapter begins with a definition of stimulus control and the basic concepts of stimulus discrimination and generalization. I then go on to discuss factors that determine the extent to which behavior comes to be restricted to particular stimuli. Along the way, I will describe special forms of stimulus control (intradimensional discrimination) and control by special categories of stimuli (compound stimuli and contextual cues). The chapter concludes with a discussion of the learning of conditional relations in both instrumental and classical conditioning.

As I pointed out in earlier chapters, both Thorndike and Skinner recognized that instrumental responses and reinforcers occur in the presence of particular stimuli. As I described in Chapter 7, research on the associative structure of instrumental conditioning emphasized that these stimuli can come to determine whether or not the instrumental response is performed. The importance of antecedent stimuli has been examined further in studies of the stimulus control of instrumental behavior, which is the topic of this chapter.

The stimulus control of instrumental behavior is evident in many aspects of life. Studying, for example, is under the strong control of school-related stimuli. College students who fall behind in their work may make determined resolutions to study a lot when they go home during the holidays. However, such good intentions are rarely carried out. The stimuli of the holidays are very different from the stimuli students experience when classes are in session. Because of that, the holiday stimuli do not engender effective studying behavior.

The proper fit between an instrumental response and the stimulus context in which the response is performed is so important that the failure of appropriate stimulus control is often considered abnormal. Getting undressed, for example, is acceptable instrumental behavior in the privacy of your bedroom. The same behavior on a public street will get you arrested. Staring at a television set is considered appropriate if the TV is turned on. Staring at a blank television screen may be a symptom of behavior pathology. If you respond in a loving manner to the presence of your spouse or other family members, your behavior is welcomed. The same behavior directed toward strangers is likely to be greeted with far less acceptance.

The stimulus control of behavior is an important aspect of how organisms adjust to their environment. The survival of animals (including human animals) depends on their ability to perform responses that are appropriate to their circumstances. With seasonal changes in food supply, for example, animals have to change how they forage for food. Within the same season, they have to respond one way in the presence of predators or intruders and in other ways in the absence of imminent danger. In a similar fashion, people are vigilant and alert when they are in a strange environment that might pose danger, but relax and let down their guard in the safety of their home. To effectively obtain comfort and avoid pain, we all have to behave in ways that are appropriate to our changing circumstances.

IDENTIFICATION AND MEASUREMENT OF STIMULUS CONTROL

To investigate the stimulus control of behavior, one first has to figure out how to identify and measure it. How can a researcher tell that an instrumental response has come under the control of certain stimuli?

Differential Responding and Stimulus Discrimination

Consider, for example, an experiment by Reynolds (1961). Two pigeons were reinforced on a variable-interval schedule for pecking a circular response key. Reinforcement for pecking was available whenever the response key was illuminated by a visual pattern consisting of a white triangle on a red background (see Figure 8.1). Thus the stimulus on the key had two components: the white triangle and the red color of the background. Reynolds was interested in which of these stimulus components gained control over the pecking behavior.

After the pigeons learned to peck steadily at the triangle on the red background, Reynolds measured the amount of pecking that occurred when only one of the stimuli was presented. On some of the test trials, the white triangle was projected on the response key without the red color. On other test trials, the red background color was projected on the response key without the white triangle.

The results are summarized in Figure 8.1. One of the pigeons pecked a great deal more when the response key was illuminated with the red light than when it was illuminated with the white triangle. This outcome shows that its pecking behavior was much more strongly controlled by the red color than by the white triangle. By contrast, the other pigeon pecked a great deal more when the white triangle was projected on the response key than when the key was illuminated by the red light. Thus, for the second bird, the pecking behavior was more strongly controlled by the triangle. (For a similar effect in pigeon search behavior, see Cheng & Spetch, 1995.)

This experiment illustrates several important ideas. First, it shows how to experimentally determine whether instrumental behavior has come under the control of a particular stimulus. *The stimulus control of instrumental behavior is demonstrated by variations in responding (differential responding) related to variations in stimuli.* If an organism responds one way in the presence of one stimulus and in a different way in the presence of another stimulus, its behavior has come under the control of those stimuli. Such differential responding was evident in the behavior of both pigeons Reynolds tested.

Differential responding to two stimuli also indicates that the pigeons were treating each stimulus as different from the other. This is called **stimulus discrimination.** *An organism is said to exhibit stimulus discrimination if it*

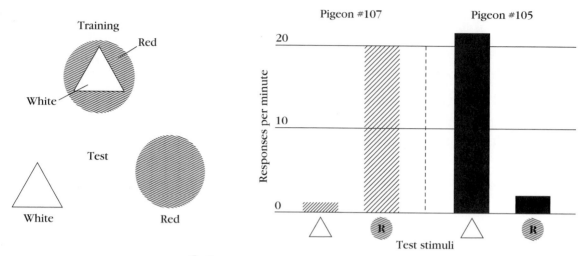

FIGURE **8.1**

Summary of procedure and results of an experiment by Reynolds (1961). Two pigeons were first reinforced for pecking whenever a compound stimulus consisting of a white triangle on a red background was projected on the response key. The rate of pecking was then observed with each pigeon when the white triangle and the red background stimuli were presented separately.

responds differently to two or more stimuli. Stimulus discrimination and stimulus control are two ways of considering the same phenomenon. One cannot have one without the other. If an organism does not discriminate between two stimuli, its behavior is not under the control of those cues.

Another interesting aspect of the results of Reynolds' experiment was that the pecking behavior of each bird came under the control of a different stimulus. The behavior of bird 107 came under the control of the red color, whereas the behavior of bird 105 came under the control of the triangle. The procedure used by Reynolds did not direct attention to one of the stimuli at the expense of the other. Therefore, it is not surprising that each bird came to respond to a different aspect of the situation. The experiment is comparable to showing a group of children a picture of a cowboy grooming a horse. Some of the children may focus on the cowboy; others may find the horse more interesting. In the absence of special procedures, one cannot always predict which of the various stimuli an organism experiences will gain control over its instrumental behavior.

Stimulus Generalization

Identifying and differentiating various stimuli is not a simple matter (Fetterman, 1996; Lea & Wills, 2008). Stimuli may be defined in all kinds of ways. Sometimes widely different objects or events are considered instances of the same stimulus because they all share the same function. A wheel, for example, may be small or large, spoked or not spoked, and made of wood, rubber, or metal, but it is still a wheel. By contrast, in other cases stimuli are identified and distinguished in terms of precise physical features, such as a specific wavelength or color of light. Artists and interior decorators make fine distinctions among different shades of green or red, for example, worrying about distinctions that are difficult to see for someone with a less well-trained eye.

Psychologists and physiologists have long been concerned with how organisms identify and distinguish different stimuli. In fact, some have suggested that this is the single most important question in psychology (Stevens, 1951). The problem is central to the analysis of stimulus control. As you will see, numerous factors are involved in the identification and differentiation of stimuli. Experimental analyses of the problem have depended mainly on the phenomenon of **stimulus generalization.** In a sense, stimulus generalization is the opposite of differential responding, or stimulus discrimination. *An organism is said to show stimulus generalization if it responds in a similar fashion to two or more stimuli.*

The phenomenon of stimulus generalization was first observed by Pavlov. He found that after one stimulus was used as a CS, his dogs would also make the conditioned response to other, similar stimuli. That is, they failed to respond differentially to stimuli that were similar to the original conditioned stimulus. Since then, stimulus generalization has been examined in a wide range of situations and species. In their review of work in this area, Ghirlanda and Enquist (2003) noted that "Empirical data gathered in about 100 years of research establish generalization as a fundamental behavioral phenomenon, whose basic characteristics appear universal" (p. 27).

In a landmark study of stimulus generalization in instrumental conditioning, Guttman and Kalish (1956) first reinforced pigeons on a variable-interval schedule for pecking a response key illuminated by a yellowish-orange light with a wavelength of 580 nanometers (nm). After training, the birds were tested with a variety of other colors presented in a random order without reinforcement, and the rate of responding in the presence of each color was recorded.

The results of the experiment are summarized in Figure 8.2. The highest rate of pecking occurred in response to the original 580-nm color. But, the birds also made substantial numbers of pecks when lights of 570-nm and 590-nm wavelengths were tested. This indicates that responding generalized to the 570-nm and 590-nm stimuli. However, as the color of the test stimuli became increasingly different from the color of the original training stimulus, progressively fewer responses occurred. The results showed a gradient of responding as a function of how similar each test stimulus was to the original training stimulus. This is an example of a **stimulus generalization gradient.**

Stimulus Generalization Gradients as Measures of Stimulus Control

Stimulus generalization gradients are an excellent way to measure stimulus control because they provide precise information about how sensitive the organism's behavior is to variations in a particular aspect of the environment (Honig & Urcuioli, 1981; Kehoe, 2008). With the use of stimulus generalization gradients, investigators can determine exactly how much a stimulus has to be changed to produce a change in behavior.

Consider, for example, the gradient in Figure 8.2. The pigeons responded much more when the original 580-nm training stimulus was presented than

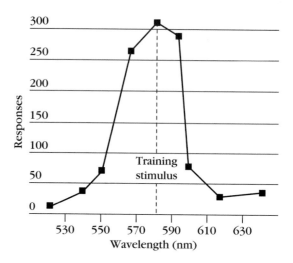

FIGURE **8.2**

Stimulus generalization gradient for pigeons that were trained to peck in the presence of a colored light of 580-nm wavelength and were then tested in the presence of other colors. (From "Discriminability and Stimulus Generalization," by N. Guttman and H. I. Kalish, 1956, *Journal of Experimental Psychology, 51,* pp. 79–88.)

when the response key was illuminated by lights whose wavelengths were 520, 540, 620, or 640 nm. Thus, differences in color controlled different levels of responding. However, this control was not very precise. Responding to the 580nm color generalized to the 570- and 590-nm stimuli. The wavelength of the 580nm training stimulus had to be changed by more than 10nm before a decrement in performance was observed. This aspect of the stimulus generalization gradient provides precise information about how large a variation in the stimulus is required for the pigeons to respond to the variation.

How do you suppose the pigeons would have responded if they had been color blind? In that case they could not have distinguished lights on the basis of color or wavelength. Therefore, they would have responded in much the same way regardless of what color was projected on the response key. Figure 8.3 presents hypothetical results of an experiment of this sort. If the pigeons did not respond on the basis of the color of the key light, similar high rates of responding would have occurred as different colors were projected on the key. Thus, the stimulus generalization gradient would have been flat.

A comparison of the results obtained by Guttman and Kalish and our hypothetical experiment with color-blind pigeons indicates that *the steepness of a stimulus generalization gradient provides a precise measure of the degree of stimulus control.* A steep generalization gradient (Figure 8.2) indicates good control of behavior by the stimulus dimension that is tested. In contrast, a flat generalization gradient (Figure 8.3) indicates poor stimulus control. The primary question in this area of behavior theory is what determines the degree of stimulus control that is obtained. The remainder of this chapter is devoted to answering that question.

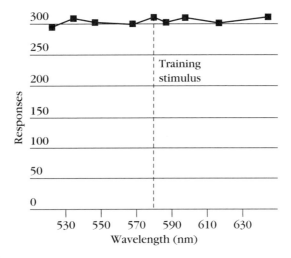

FIGURE **8.3**

Hypothetical stimulus generalization gradient for color-blind pigeons trained to peck in the presence of a colored light of 580nm wavelength and then tested in the presence of other colors.

BOX **8.1**

Generalization of Treatment Outcomes

Stimulus generalization is critical to the success of behavior therapy. Like other forms of therapy, behavior therapy is typically conducted in a distinctive environment (e.g., in a therapist's office). For the treatment to be maximally useful, what is learned during the treatment should generalize to other situations. An autistic child, for example, who is taught certain communicative responses in interactions with a particular therapist, should also exhibit those responses in interactions with other people. The following techniques have been proposed to facilitate generalization of treatment outcomes (e.g.,

Schreibman, Koegel, Charlop, & Egel, 1990; Stokes & Baer, 1977):

1. The treatment situation should be made as similar as possible to the natural environment of the client. Thus, if the natural environment provides reinforcement only intermittently, it is a good idea to reduce the frequency of reinforcement during treatment sessions as well. Another way to increase the similarity of the treatment procedure to the natural environment is to use the same reinforcers the client is likely

to encounter in the natural environment.

2. Generalization also may be increased by conducting the treatment procedure in new settings. This strategy is called *sequential modification*. After a behavior has been conditioned in one situation (a classroom), training is conducted in a new situation (the playground). If that does not result in sufficient generalization, training can be extended to a third environment (e.g., the school cafeteria).

3. Using numerous examples during training also facilitates

(continued)

BOX **8.1** (continued)

generalization. In trying to extinguish fear of elevators, for example, training should be conducted in many different types of elevators.

4. Generalization may be also encouraged by conditioning the new responses to stimuli that are common to various situations. Language provides effective mediating stimuli. Responses conditioned to verbal or instructional cues are likely to generalize to new situations in which those instructional stimuli are encountered.

5. Another approach is to make the training procedure indiscriminable or incidental to other activities. In one study (McGee, Krantz, & McClannahan, 1986), the investigators took advantage of the interest that autistic children showed in specific toys during a play session to teach the children how to read the names of the toys.

6. Finally, generalization outside a training situation is achieved if the training helps to bring the individual in contact with contingencies of reinforcement available in the natural environment (Baer & Wolf, 1970). Once a response is acquired through special training, the behavior often can be maintained by naturally available reinforcers. Reading, doing simple arithmetic, and riding a bicycle are all responses that are maintained by natural reinforcers once the responses have been acquired through special training.

An interesting recent study involved teaching four and five year old children safety skills to prevent playing with firearms (Jostad, Miltenberger, Kelso, & Knudson, 2008). During the training sessions, a disabled handgun was deliberately left in places where the children would find it. If the child found the firearm, he or she was instructed to not touch it and to report it to an adult. Praise and corrective feedback served as reinforcers. The unusual aspect of the study was that the training was conducted by children who were just a bit older (six and seven years old) than the research participants. This required training the peer trainers first.

The results were very encouraging. With many (but not all) of the participants, the safety behaviors generalized to new situations and were maintained as long as a year. The experiment was not designed to prove that peer trainers were critical in producing the generalized responding. However, accidents often occur when two or more children find and play with a firearm together. The fact that the safety training was conducted between one child and another should facilitate generalization of the safety behaviors to other situations in which two or more children find a gun.

STIMULUS AND RESPONSE FACTORS IN STIMULUS CONTROL

In the experiment by Reynolds (1961) described at the beginning of the chapter, pigeons pecked a response key that had a white triangle on a red background. Such a stimulus obviously has two features, the color of the background and the shape of the triangle. Perhaps less obvious is the fact that all stimulus situations can be analyzed in terms of multiple features. Even if the response key only had the red background, one could characterize it in terms of its brightness, shape, or location in the experimental chamber, in addition to its color.

Situations outside the laboratory are even more complex. During a football game, for example, cheering is reinforced by social approval if the people near you are all rooting for the same team as you are, and if your team is doing well. The cues that accompany appropriate cheering include your team making a good play on the field, the announcer describing the play, cheerleaders dancing exuberantly, and the people around you cheering.

The central issue in the analysis of the stimulus control is what determines which of the numerous features of a stimulus situation gains control over the instrumental behavior. Stimuli as complex as those found at a football game are difficult to analyze experimentally. Laboratory studies are typically conducted with stimuli that consist of more easily identified features. In the present section we will consider stimulus and response factors that determine which cues come to control behavior. In the following section we will consider learning factors.

Sensory Capacity and Orientation

The most obvious variable that determines whether a particular stimulus feature comes to control responding is the organism's sensory capacity and orientation. Sensory capacity and orientation determine which stimuli are included in an organism's sensory world. People, for example, cannot hear sounds with a pitch above about 20,000 cycles per second. Such stimuli are called *ultrasounds* because they are outside the range of human hearing. Other species, however, are able to hear ultrasounds. Dogs, for example, can hear whistles outside the range of human hearing and can be trained to respond to such sounds. Dogs are also much more sensitive to adors. These differences make the sensory world of dogs very different from ours.

Limitations on the stimuli that can come to control behavior are also set by whether the individual comes in contact with the stimulus. Consider, for example, a child's crib. Parents often place mobiles and other decorations on and around the crib to provide interesting stimuli for the child to look at. The crib shown in Figure 8.4 is decorated with such a mobile. The mobile consists of several animal figures (a giraffe, a seal, and a lion) made of thin needlework.

Which aspects of the mobile in the crib can potentially control the child's behavior? To answer this question, one first has to consider what the child sees about the mobile rather than what the mobile looks like to us. From the child's vantage point under the mobile, only the bottom edges of the animal figures are visible. The shapes of the animals and their surface decorations cannot be seen from below. Therefore, these other features are not likely to gain control of the child's looking behavior.

Because sensory capacity sets a limit on what stimuli can come to control behavior, studies of stimulus control are often used to determine what an organism is, or is not, able to perceive (Heffner, 1998; Kelber, Vorobyev, & Osorio, 2003). Consider, for example, the question: can horses see color? To answer that question, investigators used a training procedure in which horses had to select a colored stimulus over a gray one to obtain food reinforcement (Blackmore, Foster, Sumpter, & Temple, 2008). The colored and gray stimuli were projected on separate stimulus panels placed side by side on a table in front of the horse. There was a response lever in front of each stimulus panel that the horse could push with its head to register its choice on that trial. Several shades of gray were tested with several shades of red, green, yellow, and blue.

If the horses could not detect color, they could not consistently select the colored stimulus in such a choice task. However, all of the four horses in the experiment chose blue and yellow over gray more than 85% of the time. Three of the horses also did well on choices between green and gray. However,

Photo courtesy of the author

FIGURE **8.4**

An infant looking up at a mobile.

only one of the horses consistently selected the color when red was tested against gray. These results indicate that horses have good color vision over a large range of colors, but have some difficulty detecting red. (For a similar experiment with giant pandas, see Kelling et al., 2006.)

Studies of stimulus control also have been used to determine the visual and hearing thresholds of several species of pinniped (sea lions, harbor seals, and elephant seals) (Levenson & Schusterman, 1999; Kastak & Schusterman; 1998). The pinnipeds in these studies were first reinforced (with a piece of fish) for resting their chin on a piece of PVC pipe. This was done so that the head of the subjects would be in a standard position at the start of each trial. Trials then consisted of the presentation of a visual or auditory cue or no stimulus. In the presence of the target stimulus, the subject had to move its head to one side and press on a paddle or ball to obtain a piece of fish. Responses were not reinforced if the target stimulus was absent. After responding was established to a visual or auditory cue that was well above the subject's threshold, the intensity of the target stimulus was systematically varied to obtain estimates of the limits of visual and auditory sensitivity (see also Kastak, Schusterman, Southall, & Reichmuth, 1999).

Relative Ease of Conditioning Various Stimuli

Having the necessary sense organs and the appropriate sensory orientation does not guarantee that the organism's behavior will come under the control of a particular stimulus. Whether a stimulus comes to control behavior also depends on presence of other cues in the situation. In particular, how strongly organisms learn about one stimulus depends on how easily other cues in the situations can become conditioned. This phenomenon is called **overshadowing.** Overshadowing illustrates competition among stimuli for access to the processes of learning.

Consider, for example, trying to teach a child to read by having her follow along as you read a children's book that has a big picture and a short sentence on each page. Learning about pictures is easier than learning words. Therefore, the pictures may well overshadow the words. The child will quickly memorize the story based on the pictures rather than the words and will learning little about the words.

Pavlov (1927) was the first to observe that if two stimuli are presented at the same time, the presence of the more easily trained stimulus may hinder learning about the other one. In many of Pavlov's experiments, the two stimuli differed in intensity. Generally, the more intense stimulus became conditioned more rapidly and overshadowed learning about the weaker stimulus. Pavlov found that the weak stimulus could become conditioned (somewhat slowly) if it was presented by itself. However, less conditioning occurred if the weak stimulus was presented simultaneously with a more intense stimulus. (For more recent studies of overshadowing, see Jennings, Bonardi, & Kirkpatrick, 2007; Pearce et al., 2006; and Savastano, Arcediano, Stout, & Miller, 2003.)

Type of Reinforcement

The development of stimulus control also depends on the type of reinforcement that is used. Certain types of stimuli are more likely to gain control over the instrumental behavior in appetitive than in aversive situations. This relation has been extensively investigated in experiments with pigeons (see LoLordo, 1979).

In one study (Foree & LoLordo, 1973), two groups of pigeons were trained to press a foot treadle in the presence of a compound stimulus consisting of a red light and a tone whose pitch was 440 cycles per second. When the light/tone compound was absent, responses were not reinforced. For one group of pigeons, reinforcement for treadle pressing was provided by food. For the other group, treadle pressing was reinforced by the avoidance of shock. If the avoidance group pressed the treadle in the presence of the light/tone stimulus, no shock was delivered on that trial; if they failed to respond during the light/tone stimulus, a brief shock was periodically applied until a response occurred.

Both groups of pigeons learned to respond during the light/tone compound. Foree and LoLordo then sought to determine which of the two elements of the compound stimulus was primarily responsible for the treadle-press behavior. Test trials were conducted during which the light and tone stimuli were presented one at a time. The results are summarized in Figure 8.5.

Pigeons that were trained with food reinforcement responded much more when tested with the light stimulus alone than when tested with the tone alone. In fact, their rate of treadle pressing in response to the isolated presentation of the red light was nearly as high as when the light was presented simultaneously with the tone. Therefore, we can conclude that the behavior of these birds was nearly exclusively controlled by the red light.

Courtesy of Donald A. Dewsbury

V. M. LoLordo

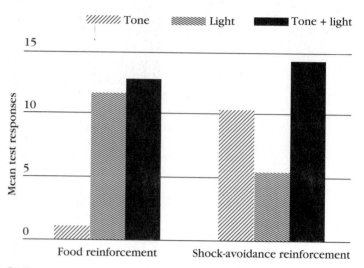

FIGURE **8.5**

Effects of type of reinforcement on stimulus control. A treadle-press response in pigeons was reinforced in the presence of a compound stimulus consisting of a tone and red light. With food reinforcement, the light gained much more control over the behavior than the tone. With shock-avoidance reinforcement, the tone gained more control over behavior than the light. (Adapted from Foree & LoLordo, 1973).

A contrasting pattern of results occurred with the pigeons that had been trained with shock avoidance reinforcement. These birds responded much more when tested with the tone alone than when tested with the light alone. Thus, with shock-avoidance reinforcement, the tone acquired more control over the treadle response than the red light (see also Kelley, 1986; Kraemer & Roberts, 1985; Schindler & Weiss, 1982).

The above findings indicate that stimulus control of instrumental behavior is determined in part by the type of reinforcement that is used. Subsequent research showed that the critical factor is whether the compound tone + light CS acquires positive or aversive properties (Weiss, Panlilio, & Schindler, 1993a, 1993b). Visual control predominates when the CS acquires positive or appetitive properties, and auditory control predominates when the CS acquires negative or aversive properties.

The dominance of visual control in appetitive situations and auditory control in aversive situations is probably related to the behavior systems that are activated in the two cases. A signal for food activates the feeding system. Food eaten by pigeons and rats is more likely to be identified by visual cues than by auditory cues. Therefore, activation of the feeding system is accompanied by increased attention to visual rather than auditory stimuli. In contrast, a signal for an aversive outcome activates the defensive behavior system. Responding to auditory cues may be particularly adaptive in avoiding danger.

Unfortunately, we do not know enough about the evolutionary history of pigeons or rats to be able to calculate the adaptive value of different types of stimulus control in feeding versus defensive behavior. We also do not know much about how stimulus control varies as a function of type of reinforcement in other species. Thus, this issue remains a fertile area for future research.

Type of Instrumental Response

Another factor that can determine which of several features of a compound stimulus gains control over behavior is the nature of the response required for reinforcement. The importance of the instrumental response for stimulus control was demonstrated in a classic experiment by Dobrzecka, Szwejkowska, and Konorski (1966). These investigators studied the control of instrumental behavior by auditory stimuli in dogs. The dogs were gently restrained in a harness, with a metronome placed in front of them and a buzzer placed behind them. The metronome and buzzer provided qualitatively different types of sounds: a periodic beat versus a continuous rattle. The two stimuli also differed in spatial location, one in front of the animal and the other behind it. The investigators were interested in which of these two features (sound quality or location) would come to control behavior.

Another important variable was the response required of the dogs. Two groups served in the experiment (see Figure 8.6). Group 1 received training in a right/left task. When the metronome sounded, dogs in Group 1 were reinforced for raising their right leg; when the buzzer sounded, they were reinforced for raising the left leg. Thus, the location of the response (right/left) was important for reinforcement in Group 1.

Group 2 received training on a go/no-go task. In this case, the dogs had to raise the right leg when the buzzer sounded and not raise the leg when the metronome sounded. Thus, the quality of the response (go/no-go) rather than its location was important for reinforcement for Group 2.

What aspect of the auditory cues (quality or location) gained control over the instrumental behavior in the two groups? To answer this question, the dogs were tested with the positions of the metronome and buzzer reversed. During these tests, the buzzer was placed in front of the animals and the metronome behind them (see Figure 8.6). This manipulation produced different results in the two groups.

Dogs trained on the right/left task (Group 1) responded mainly on the basis of the location of the auditory cues rather than their quality. They raised their right leg in response to sound from the front, regardless of whether the sound was made by the metronome or the buzzer. When the sound came from the back, they raised the left leg, again regardless of whether it was the metronome or the buzzer. Thus, with the left/right task, behavior was more strongly controlled by the location of the sounds than its quality.

The opposite outcome was observed in the dogs trained on the go/no-go task. These dogs responded more on the basis of the quality of the sound rather than its location. They raised a leg in response to the buzzer whether the sound came from the front or the back, and they did not raise a leg when the metronome was sounded, again irrespective of the location of the metronome.

These results indicate that responses that are differentiated by location (right/left) are more likely to come under the control of the spatial feature of auditory cues. By contrast, responses that are differentiated by quality (go/no-go) are more likely to come under the control of the quality of auditory cues. This phenomenon is called the *quality-location effect* and has been observed

Group 1
(right/left discrimination)

Group 2
(go/no-go discrimination)

Training

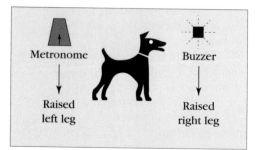

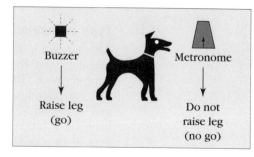

Testing

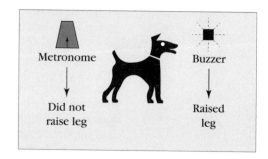

FIGURE **8.6**

Diagram of the experiment by Dobrzecka, Szwejkowska, and Konorski (1966). Dogs were trained on a left/right or go/no-go task (Groups 1 and 2, respectively) with auditory stimuli that differed both in location (in front or in back of the animals) and in quality (the sound of a buzzer or a metronome). During testing, the location of the two sounds was reversed. The results showed that the left/right differential response was controlled mainly by the location of the sounds, whereas the go/no-go differential response was controlled mainly by the quality of the sounds.

not only in dogs, but also pigeons, rats, chinchillas and opossum (Bowe, Miller, & Green, 1987; Neill & Harrison, 1987; Stasiak & Masterton, 1996). Although the effect is robust and evident in a variety of species, it is not an all-or-none phenomenon. With judicious placement of the sound sources, subjects can come to respond to location features in a go/no-go task (Neill & Harrison, 1987). (For another interesting phenomenon involving spatial features of stimuli and responses, see Urcuioli, 2008.)

Stimulus Elements versus Configural Cues in Compound Stimuli

So far I have assumed that organisms treat stimulus features as distinct and separate elements. Thus, in the quality-location effect, the quality and location of an auditory stimulus were considered to be separate features of the auditory cues. The assumption was that a particular stimulus feature (sound quality) was perceived the same way regardless of the status of the other feature (sound location). This way of thinking about a compound stimulus is known as the **stimulus element approach** and has been dominant in learning theory going back nearly 80 years. An important alternative assumes that organisms treat a compound stimulus as an integral whole that is not divided into parts or elements. This is called the **configural-cue approach**. Although the configural-cue approach also has deep roots (in Gestalt psychology), its prominence in behavior theory is of more recent vintage.

According to the configural-cue approach, individuals respond to a compound stimulus in terms of the unique configuration of its elements. It is assumed that the elements are not treated as separate entities. In fact, they may not even be identifiable when the stimulus compound is presented. In the configural-cue approach, stimulus elements are important, not because of their individuality, but because of the way they contribute to the entire configuration of stimulation provided by the compound.

The concept of a configural cue may be illustrated by considering the sound made by a symphony orchestra. The orchestral sound originates from the sounds of the individual instruments. However, the sound of the entire orchestra is very different from the sound of any of the individual instruments, some of which are difficult to identify when the entire orchestra is playing. We primarily hear the configuration of the sounds made by the individual instruments.

The configural-cue approach has been championed by John Pearce (Pearce, 1987, 1994, 2002), who showed that many learning phenomena are consistent with this framework. Let us consider, for example, the overshadowing effect (see Table 8.1). An overshadowing experiment involves two groups of subjects and two stimulus elements, one of low intensity (*a*) and the other of high intensity (*B*). For the overshadowing group, the two stimuli are presented together (*aB*) as a compound cue and paired with reinforcement during conditioning. For the control group, only the low intensity stimulus (*a*) is presented during conditioning. Tests are then conducted for each group with the weaker stimulus element (*a*) presented alone. These tests show less responding to *a* in the overshadowing group than in the control group. Thus, the presence of *B* during conditioning disrupts control of behavior by the weaker stimulus *a*.

According to the configural-cue approach, overshadowing reflects different degrees of generalization decrement from training to testing for the overshadowing and the control groups (Pearce, 1987). There is no generalization decrement for the control group when it is tested with the weak stimulus *a*, because that is the same as the stimulus it received during conditioning. In contrast, considerable generalization decrement occurs when the overshadowing group is tested with stimulus *a* after conditioning with the compound *aB*. For the overshadowing group, responding becomes conditioned to the *aB*

J. M. Pearce

TABLE **8.1**
Configural Explanation of Overshadowing

Group	Training stimuli	Test stimulus	Generalization from training to test
Overshadowing group	*aB*	*a*	Decrement
Control group	*a*	*a*	No decrement

compound, which is very different from *a* presented alone during testing. Therefore, responding conditioned to *aB* suffers considerable generalization decrement. According to the configural-cue approach, this greater generalization decrement is responsible for the overshadowing effect.

The configural-cue approach has enjoyed considerable success in generating new experiments and explaining the results of those experiments (see Pearce & Bouton, 2001, for a review). However, other findings have favored analyses of stimulus control in terms of stimulus elements (e.g., Myers, Vogel, Shin, & Wagner, 2001; Rescorla, 1997c, 1999a). What is required is a comprehensive theory that deals successfully with both types of results. Whether such a theory requires abandoning the fundamental concept of stimulus elements, remains a heatedly debated theoretical issue (Melchers, Shanks, & Lachnit, 2008; Wagner, 2003, 2008a; Wagner & Vogel, 2008).

LEARNING FACTORS IN STIMULUS CONTROL

The stimulus and response factors described in the preceding section set the preconditions for how human and nonhuman animals learn about the environmental stimuli they encounter. Stimulus and response factors are the starting points for stimulus control. However, the fact that certain stimuli can be perceived does not insure that those stimuli will come to control behavior. A child, for example, may see numerous Hondas and Toyotas, but may not be able to distinguish between them. A novice chess player may be able to look at two different patterns on a chess board without being able to identify which represents the more favorable configuration. Whether or not certain stimuli come to control behavior often depends on what the organism has learned about those stimuli, not just whether the stimuli can be detected.

The suggestion that experience with stimuli may determine the extent to which those stimuli come to control behavior originated in efforts to explain the phenomenon of stimulus generalization. As I noted earlier, stimulus generalization refers to the fact that a response conditioned to one stimulus will also occur when other stimuli similar to the original cue are presented. Pavlov suggested that stimulus generalization occurs because learning about a CS becomes transferred to other stimuli on the basis of the physical similarity of those test stimuli to the original CS.

In a spirited attack, Lashley and Wade (1946) took exception to Pavlov's proposal. They rejected the idea that stimulus generalization reflects the transfer of learning. Rather, they argued that stimulus generalization reflects the *absence* of learning. More specifically, they proposed that stimulus generalization occurs if organisms have not learned to distinguish differences among the stimuli. Lashley and Wade proposed that animals have to learn to treat stimuli as different from one another. Thus, in contrast to Pavlov, Lashley and Wade considered the shape of a stimulus generalization gradient to be determined primarily by the organism's previous learning experiences rather than by the physical properties of the stimuli tested.

Stimulus Discrimination Training

As it has turned out, Lashley and Wade were closer to the truth than Pavlov. Numerous studies have shown that stimulus control can be dramatically altered by learning experiences. Perhaps the most powerful procedure for bringing behavior under the control of a stimulus is **stimulus discrimination training** (see Kehoe, 2008, for a recent review). Stimulus discrimination training can be conducted using either classical conditioning or instrumental conditioning procedures. For example, Campolattaro, Schnitker, and Freeman (2008, Experiment 3) used a discrimination training procedure in eyeblink conditioning with laboratory rats. A low pitched tone (2000 cycles per second) and a high pitched tone (8000 cycles per second) served as the conditioned stimuli. Each session consisted of 100 trials. On half of the trials one of the tones (A+) was paired with the US. One the remaining trials, the other tone (B–) was presented without the US. The results are presented in Figure 8.7. Participants showed progressive increases in eyeblink responding to the A+ tone that was paired with the US. By the 15th session, the subjects responded to A+ more than 85% of the time. Responding to the B– also increased at first, but not as rapidly. Furthermore, after the 10th session, responding to the B– tone gradually declined. By the end of the experiment, the participants showed very nice differential responding to the two tones.

The results presented in Figure 8.7 are typical for discrimination training in which the reinforced (A+) and nonreinforced (B–) stimuli are of the same modality. The conditioned responding that develops to A+ generalizes to B– at first, but with further training responding to B– declines and a clear discrimination becomes evident. It is as if the participants confuse A+ and B– at first, but come to tell them apart with continued training. The same kind of thing happens when children are taught the names of different types of fruit. They may confuse oranges and tangerines at first, but with continued training they learn the distinction.

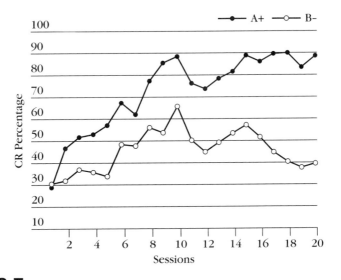

FIGURE **8.7**

Eyeblink conditioning in rats to a tone (A+) paired with the US and a different tone (B–) presented without the US. (Adapted from Campolattaro, Schnitker, & Freeman 2008.)

Stimulus discrimination training can also be conducted with instrumental conditioning procedures. This is the case when children are taught what to do at an intersection controlled by a traffic light. Crossing the street is reinforced with praise and encouragement when the traffic light is green but not when the light is red. The stimulus (the green light) that signals the availability of reinforcement for the instrumental response is technically called the S+ or S^D (pronounced "ess dee"). By contrast, the stimulus (the red light) that signals the lack of reinforcement for responding is called the S– or S$^\Delta$ (pronounced "ess delta").

As in Figure 8.7, initially a child may attempt to cross the street during both the S+ (green) and S– (red) lights. However, as training progresses, responding in the presence of the S+ persists and responding in the presence of the S– declines. The emergence of greater responding to the S+ than to the S– indicates differential responding to these stimuli. Thus, a **stimulus discrimination procedure** establishes control by the stimuli that signal when reinforcement is and is not available. Once the S+ and S– have gained control over the organism's behavior, they are called **discriminative stimuli.** The S+ is a discriminative stimulus for performing the instrumental response, and the S– is a discriminative stimulus for not performing the response. (For a recent laboratory example of discrimination training in instrumental conditioning, see Andrzejewski et al., 2007.)

In the discrimination procedures I described so far, the reinforced and non-reinforced stimuli (S+ and S–) were presented on separate trials. (Green and red traffic lights are never presented simultaneously at a street crossing.) Discrimination training can also be conducted with the S+ and S– stimuli presented at the same time next to each other, in a situation where the subject can respond to one or the other. Such a simultaneous discrimination procedure allows the subject to directly compare S+ and S– and makes discrimination training easier. For example, Huber, Apfalter, Steurer, & Prosssinger (2005) examined whether pigeons can learn to tell the difference between male and female faces that were presented with the people's hair masked out. As you might imagine, this is not an easy discrimination. However, the pigeons learned the discrimination in a few sessions if the male and female faces were presented at the same time, and the birds were reinforced for pecking one of the face categories. If the faces were presented on successive trials, the pigeons had a great deal more difficulty with the task.

An instrumental conditioning procedure in which responding is reinforced in the presence of one stimulus (the S+) and not reinforced in the presence of another cue (the S–) is a special case of a **multiple schedule of reinforcement.** In a multiple schedule, different schedules of reinforcement are in effect during different stimuli. For example, a VI schedule of reinforcement may be in effect when a light is turned on, and an FR schedule may be in effect when a tone is presented. With sufficient exposure to such a procedure, the pattern of responding during each stimulus will correspond to the schedule of reinforcement in effect during that stimulus. The participants will show a steady rate of responding during the VI stimulus and a stop-run pattern during the FR stimulus. (For a study of multiple-schedule performance with cocaine reinforcement, see Weiss et al., 2003.)

Stimulus discrimination and multiple schedules are common outside the laboratory. Nearly all reinforcement schedules that exist outside the laboratory are in effect only in the presence of particular stimuli. Playing a game yields reinforcement only in the presence of enjoyable or challenging partners. Driving rapidly is reinforced when you are on a freeway, but not when you are on a crowded city street. Loud and boisterous discussion with your friends is reinforced at a party. The same type of behavior is frowned upon during a church service. Eating with your fingers is reinforced at a picnic, but not when you are in a fine restaurant. Daily activities typically consist of going from one situation to another (to the kitchen, to the bus stop, to your office, to the grocery store, and so on), and each situation has its own schedule of reinforcement.

BOX **8.2**

Stimulus Control of Sleeping

Getting young children to go to sleep in the evening and remain asleep during the night can be difficult. Night wakings by young children can be stressful for parents and have been linked to increased maternal malaise, marital discord, and child abuse. Behavioral approaches to the treatment of night waking have stressed the concepts of stimulus control and extinction.

In the absence of special intervention, a child may wake up at night and cry or call a parent. The parent visits with the child and tries to put him or her back to sleep in either in the child's own bed or in the parent's bed, where the child eventually falls asleep. This scenario may serve to maintain the sleep disturbance in two ways. First, parental attention upon waking may serve to reinforce the child for waking up. Second, special efforts the parent makes to encourage the child to go back to sleep (e.g., taking the child into the parent's bed) may introduce special discriminative stimuli for getting back to sleep. In the absence of those cues, getting back to sleep may be especially difficult.

In a study of behavioral treatment of night waking in infants from 8–20 months old, France and Hudson (1990) gave parents the following instructions.

At bedtime, carry out the usual bedtime routine (story, song, etc.). Then place (*child's name*) in bed. Bid him or her "Good night" and immediately leave the room. Do not return unless absolutely necessary. If absolutely necessary, check your child (when illness or danger is suspected), but do so in silence and with a minimum of light. (p. 93)

This procedure was intended to minimize reinforcement of the child for waking up. The procedure was also intended to make the child's own bed in the absence of parental interaction, a discriminative stimulus for getting back to sleep should the child wake up at night. With the introduction of these procedures, all seven infants in the study were reported to decrease the number of times they woke up and cried or called for their parents during the night. Prior to introduction of the procedure, the mean number of

nightly awakenings was 3.3. After the treatment procedure, this declined to 0.8. These gains were maintained during follow-up tests conducted three months and two years later.

Insomnia is also a problem in middle age and among the elderly, many of whom take sleeping pills to manage the problem. However, studies have shown that stimulus control training can also solve their problem. Stimulus control training involves instructing the participants to use their bed only for sleeping. The participants are told not to watch TV, read, or listen to their iPod in bed. Rather, they are to use their bed only for sleeping. To further encourage an association of the bed with sleeping, participants are encouraged to reduce the time they spend in bed (so that more of their time in bed is spent sleeping). This type of stimulus control training and sleep restriction has been found to be as effective as taking sleeping pills, and may be more effective than other forms of cognitive behavior therapy (Harvey, Inglis, & Espie, 2002; Irwin, Cole, & Nicassio, 2006; Smith et al., 2002).

Effects of Discrimination Training on Stimulus Control

Discrimination training brings the instrumental response under the control of the S+ and S−. How precise is the control that S+ acquires over the instrumental behavior, and what factors determine the precision of the stimulus control that is achieved? To answer these questions, it is not enough to observe differential responding to S+ versus S−. One must also find out how steep the generalization gradient is when the participants are tested with stimuli that systematically vary from the S+. Another important question is which aspect of the discrimination training procedure is responsible for the type of stimulus generalization gradient that is obtained? These issues were first addressed in classic experiments by Jenkins and Harrison (1960, 1962).

Jenkins and Harrison examined how auditory stimuli that differ in pitch can come to control the pecking behavior of pigeons reinforced with food. As I discussed earlier in this chapter, when pigeons are reinforced with food, they tend to pay closer attention to visual than to auditory cues. However, as Jenkins and Harrison found out, with the proper training procedures, the behavior of pigeons can come under the control of auditory cues. They evaluated the effects of three different training procedures.

One group of pigeons received a training procedure in which a 1,000 cycle per second (cps) tone served as the S+ and the absence of the tone served as the S−. Pecking a response key was reinforced on a variable interval schedule on trials when the 1,000 cps tone was present and no reinforcement occurred on trials when the tone was off. A second group also received discrimination training. The 1,000 cps tone again served as the S+. However, for the second group the S− was a 950 cps tone. The third group of pigeons served as a control group and did not receive discrimination training. For them the 1,000 cps tone was continuously turned on, and they could always receive reinforcement for pecking during the experimental sessions.

Upon completion of the three different training procedures, each group was tested for pecking in the presence of tones of various frequencies to see how precisely pecking was controlled by pitch. Figure 8.8 shows the generalization gradients that were obtained. The control group, which had not received discrimination training, responded nearly equally in the presence of all of the test stimuli. The pitch of the tones did not control their behavior; they acted tone deaf. Each of the other two training procedures produced more stimulus control by pitch. The steepest generalization gradient, and hence the strongest stimulus control, was observed in birds that had been trained with the 1,000 cps tone as S+ and the 950 cps tone as S−. Pigeons that previously received discrimination training between the 1,000 cps tone (S+) and the absence of tones (S−) showed an intermediate degree of stimulus control by tonal frequency.

The Jenkins and Harrison experiment provided two important principles. First, they showed that discrimination training increases the stimulus control of instrumental behavior. Second, a particular stimulus dimension (such as tonal frequency) is most likely to gain control over responding if the S+ and S− differ along that stimulus dimension. The most precise control by tonal frequency was observed after discrimination training in which the S+ was a tone of one frequency (1,000 cps) and the S− was a tone of another frequency (950 cps). Discrimination training did not produce as strong control by pitch

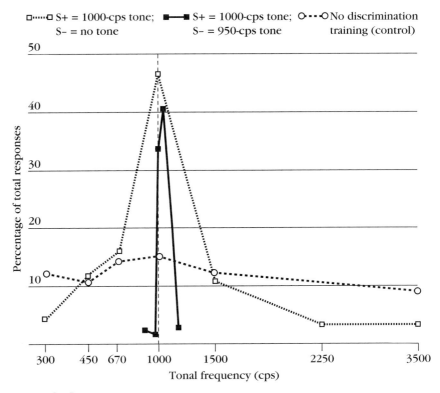

□⋯⋯□ S+ = 1000-cps tone;   ■——■ S+ = 1000-cps tone;   ○⋯○ No discrimination
S– = no tone   S– = 950-cps tone   training (control)

FIGURE **8.8**

Generalization gradients of response to tones of different frequencies after various types of training. One group received discrimination training in which a 1,000 cps tone served as the S+ and the absence of tones served as the S–. Another group received training in which a 1,000 cps tone served as the S+ and 950 cps tone served as the S–. The control group did not receive discrimination training before the generalization test. (From "Effects of Discrimination Training on Auditory Generalization," by H. M. Jenkins and R. H. Harrison, 1960, *Journal of Experimental Psychology, 59*, pp. 246–253; also from "Generalization Gradients of Inhibition Following Auditory Discrimination Learning," by H. M. Jenkins and R. H. Harrison, 1962, *Journal of Experimental Analysis of Behavior, 5*, pp. 435–441.

if the S+ was a 1,000 cps tone and the S– was the absence of tones. The discrimination between the presence and absence of the 1,000 cps tone could have been based on the loudness or timbre of the tone rather than its frequency. Hence tonal frequency did not gain as much control in this case. (For further discussion of these and related issues, see Balsam, 1988; Kehoe, 2008; and Lea & Wills, 2008.)

Range of Possible Discriminative Stimuli

Discrimination procedures can be used to bring an organism's instrumental behavior under the control of many different kinds of stimuli. A variety of species (rats, pigeons, carp, monkeys) have been shown to be able to discriminate between different types of music (Chase, 2001; D'Amato & Salmon,

1982). In other studies, pigeons learned to distinguish color slides of paintings by Monet from paintings of Picasso (Watanabe, Sakamoto, & Wakita, 1995), pictures of male versus female human faces (Huber et al. 2005), and pictures of male versus female pigeons (Nakamura, Ita, Croft & Westbrook, 2006). Stimulus discrimination procedures with laboratory rats and pigeons have also used discriminative stimuli consisting of internal cues related to level of hunger (Davidson, Flynn, & Jarrard, 1992), number of stimuli in a visual array (Emmerton & Renner, 2006), the relative frequency of events (Keen & Machado, 1999; Machado & Cevik, 1997), time of day (Budzynski & Bingman, 1999), and artificial and natural movement cues (Cook & Roberts, 2007; Mui et al., 2007).

Investigators have also been interested in studying whether animals can detect the internal sensations created by a drug state or withdrawal from an addictive drug. Internal sensations produced by a psychoactive drug (or other physiological manipulation such as food deprivation) are called *introceptive cues*. The detection of introceptive cues associated with drug withdrawal and the stimulus control that such cues may exert are prominent components of modern theories of drug addiction (Baker et al., 2004). Such theories gain substantial support from laboratory research on the stimulus control of instrumental behavior by drug-produced introceptive cues. Investigators in this area have inquired whether an organism can tell when it is under the influence of a sedative (pentobarbital), and whether other drugs (e.g., chlordiazepoxide, alcohol, and methamphetamine) produce sensations similar to those of pentobarbital. Discrimination training with drug stimuli and tests of stimulus generalization are used to provide answers to such questions (e.g., McMillan & Li, 1999, 2000; McMillan, Li, & Hardwick, 1997; Snodgrass & McMillan, 1996; Zarcone & Ator, 2000). Interestingly, this research has shown that the mechanisms of stimulus control by drug stimuli are remarkably similar to the mechanisms identified by Jenkins and Harrison (1960, 1962) for the control of key pecking by auditory cues in pigeons.

Schaal and his colleagues, for example, compared the extent of stimulus control by the introceptive cues of cocaine before and after discrimination training (Schaal, McDonald, Miller, & Reilly, 1996). Pigeons were reinforced for pecking a response key on a variable interval two-minute schedule of reinforcement. In the first phase of the experiment (no discrimination training), the birds were injected with 3.0 mg/kg of cocaine before each session. After responding stabilized, generalization tests were periodically interspersed between training sessions. During these tests, the subjects received no drug (saline) or various doses of cocaine ranging from 0.3 to 5.6 mg/kg. (Responding was not reinforced during the test sessions.) The results obtained with one of the birds (P1) are presented in the left side of Figure 8.9. Notice that the generalization gradient as a function of drug dose is fairly flat, indicative of weak stimulus control.

During the next phase of the experiment, a discrimination procedure was introduced. During this phase, some sessions were preceded with an injection of cocaine as before, and pecking was reinforced. In addition, the subjects also received sessions without the drug, during which pecking was not reinforced. Thus, the cocaine in the bird's system served as the S+. The subjects learned the discrimination, responding strongly during S+ sessions and much less during S– sessions. Once the discrimination was established, generalization tests were conducted as before. The results of those tests are shown in

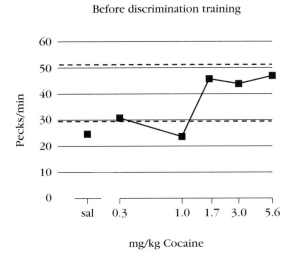

Before discrimination training   After discrimination training

FIGURE **8.9**

Responding as a function of cocaine dose for a pigeon before (left panel) and after (right panel) discrimination training in which 3.0 mg/kg of cocaine was present during S+ sessions and a saline injection (no drug) was give prior to S– sessions. (After Schaal, et al., 1996. Discrimination of methadone and cocaine by pigeons without explicit discrimination training. *Journal of the Experimental Analysis of Behavior, 66*, p. 199. Copyright 1996 by the Society for the Experimental Analysis of Behavior, Inc. Reprinted with permission.)

the right panel of Figure 8.9 for pigeon P1. Notice that now the generalization gradient is much steeper, indicating much stronger control by the internal drug stimuli. The greatest level of responding occurred when the pigeon was tested with the 3.0 mg/kg of cocaine that had been used during reinforced sessions. Virtually no responding occurred during sessions with no drug or with just 0.3 or 1.0 mg/kg of cocaine. Interestingly, responding also declined a bit when the test dose was 5.6 mg/kg, which exceeded the training dose. Thus, as was the case with stimulus control of behavior by tonal frequency (Figure 8.8), discrimination training increased stimulus control by the internal sensations created by cocaine.

The fact that stimulus discrimination procedures can be used to bring behavior under the control of a wide variety of stimuli makes these procedures powerful tools for the investigation of how animals process information. Some impressive results of this research will be presented in discussions of animal memory and cognition in Chapters 11 and 12.

What Is Learned in Discrimination Training?

Because of the profound effect that discrimination training has on stimulus control, investigators have been interested in what is learned during discrimination training. Consider the following relatively simple situation: Responses are reinforced whenever a red light is turned on (S+) and not reinforced whenever a loud tone is presented (S–). What strategies could a subject use to make sure that most of its responses were reinforced in this situation? One possibility is to learn to respond whenever the S+ is present and not respond otherwise. If an organism adopted this strategy, it would end up responding much more to S+ than to S– without having learned anything specific about S–. Another possibility is to learn to suppress responding during S– but respond whenever S– is absent. This strategy would also lead to more responding during S+ than S– but without learning anything specific about S+. A third possibility is to learn the significance of both S+ and S–, to learn both to respond to S+ and to suppress responding to S–.

Spence's Theory of Discrimination Learning

Coly Kent, 1961; Courtesy of Department of Psychology, University of Iowa

K. W. Spence

One of the first and most influential theories of discrimination learning was proposed by Kenneth Spence (1936). Although Spence's theory was proposed nearly 75 years ago, it remains influential in stimulating research (Lazareva et al., 2008; Pearce et al., 2008; Wagner, 2008b). The basic idea of Spence's theory of discrimination learning is based on the last of the possibilities described above. According to his theory, reinforcement of a response in the presence of the S+ conditions excitatory response tendencies to S+. By contrast, nonreinforcement of responding during S– conditions inhibitory properties to S– that serve to suppress the instrumental behavior. Differential responding to S+ and S– is assumed to reflect both the excitation of responding to S+ and the inhibition of responding to S–.

How can the excitation-inhibition theory of discrimination learning be experimentally evaluated? The mere observation that organisms respond more to S+ than to S– is not sufficient to prove that they have learned something about both of these stimuli. One possibility is to conduct tests of stimulus generalization with stimuli that vary systematically from S+ and S–. In theory such tests should reveal an **excitatory generalization gradient** around S+ and an **inhibitory generalization gradient** around S–. However, there are serious technical problems in isolating one type of generalization gradient from the other. (For a classic study in which these problems were successfully solved, see Honig, Boneau, Burstein, & Pennypacker, 1963. For a more recent comparison of excitatory and inhibitory generalization gradients, see Rescorla, 2006c.) Another approach is to determine whether an S– stimulus has active inhibitory properties following discrimination training.

In a study of cocaine self administration in laboratory rats, Kearns et al. (2005) employed a summation test to determine if an S– gains active inhibitory control over behavior following discrimination training. I previously discussed the summation test in Chapter 3 as a technique for measuring Pavlovian conditioned inhibition. Application of the test to evaluate inhibition following discrimination training rests on the same rationale. Basically, if S– acquires active inhibitory properties as a result of discrimination training, it should suppress responding that is otherwise elicited by an S+. Kearns et al. (2005) evaluated this prediction.

Laboratory rats were outfitted so that they could receive small doses of cocaine intravenously. The drug was delivered contingent on lever pressing on a variable-interval schedule. On reinforced trials lever pressing produced cocaine. These trials alternated with trials during which lever pressing was never reinforced. For the experimental group, the reinforced trials were signaled by a tone half the time and a clicker the remaining times. Thus, both the tone and the clicker became S+ stimuli. A light was always presented during trials when reinforcement was not available, making the light an S–. The procedures were similar for the control group, except an effort was made to avoid having the light become an S–. This was accomplished by presenting the light half the time with the clicker (when cocaine was available) and half the time during the nonreinforced trials (when cocaine was not available). Because the light occurred equally on reinforced and nonreinforced trials, it was not expected to acquire inhibitory properties.

The summation test was conducted after the subjects were well practiced on their procedures. In fact, the criterion for moving to the test phase was that lever-pressing during reinforced trials had to exceed lever pressing during the nonreinforced trials by a factor of seven. Two trials were conducted during the summation test. In one trial the tone was presented by itself. Since the tone was an S+ for both groups, both groups were expected to respond vigorously during the tone. During the second test, the tone was presented together with the light. Recall that the light was trained as an S– for the experimental group but not for the control group. Therefore, the light was expected to suppress responding only in the experimental group.

The results of the experiment are presented in Figure 8.10. As expected, both groups showed vigorous responding to the tone. Adding the light to the tone did not disrupt responding in the control group, but produced a profound suppression of lever pressing in the experimental group. Keep in mind that the test phase was the first time the light was presented at the same time as the tone. The suppression of responding evident in the experimental group shows that a stimulus that is a signal for nonreinforcement (S–) in a discrimination procedure acquires active inhibitory properties, as predicted by Spence.

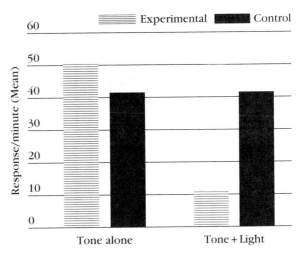

FIGURE **8.10**

Self administration of cocaine by rats during tone-alone and tone+light test trials. The experimental group previously received discrimination training in which the tone occurred only on reinforced trials (S+) and the light occurred only on nonreinforced trials (S–). The control group received similar prior training but for them the light occurred equally often on both reinforced and nonreinforced trials. (Based on Kearns et al., 2005.)

The above experiment by Kearns et al. (2005) is interesting not only because of its relevance to theories of discrimination training but also because it suggests a novel approach to the treatment of drug abuse. The emphasis in analyses of drug abuse has been on identifying and moderating factors that lead to drug self-administration. On the whole these involve various forms of excitatory conditioning. The study by Kearns et al. suggests that negative discriminative stimuli (S– cues) can exert a powerful inhibitory influence on drug seeking and drug self-administration behavior. Furthermore, this inhibitory influence transfers to counteract the excitatory effects of an S+ if the S– is presented at the same time as the S+. This suggests drug seeking can be reduced by inhibition even if excitatory processes remain in tact.

Interactions Between S+ and S–: Peak Shift Effect

So far I have described general characteristics of stimulus discrimination training under the assumption that what subjects learn about S+ is pretty much independent of what they learn about S–. This assumption is too simplistic. Learning is not so neatly compartmentalized. What you learn about S+ can influence your response to S– and vise versa. Such interactions are particularly likely if S+ and S– are related in some way.

S+ and S– may be related if they are similar except for one feature or attribute. This was the case in the Jenkins and Harrison experiment, whose results are presented in Figure 8.8. For one of the groups in that study, the S+ was a 1,000 cps tone and the S– was a 950 cps tone. Thus, the S+ and S– stimuli differed only slightly in pitch. A training procedure in which the S+ and S– differ only in terms of the value of one stimulus feature (in this case pitch) is called an **intradimensional discrimination**. The eyeblink stimulus discrimination procedure whose results are presented in Figure 8.7 was also an intradimensional discrimination. In that study, the CS+ and CS– stimuli were also tones differing in pitch (2,000 cps versus 8,000 cps).

Intradimensional discriminations are of particular interest because they are related to the issue of expert performance. Expert performance typically involves making subtle distinctions. Distinguishing stimuli that differ only in a single feature is more difficult than distinguishing stimuli that differ in many respects. It does not require much expertise to tell the difference between a compact car and a bus. In contrast, one has to be fairly sophisticated about cars to tell the difference between one version of the Honda Civic and another. The fewer distinguishing features there are between two stimuli, the more difficult it is to tell them apart, and the greater expertise is required to make the distinction. Two championship skaters may perform with equal skill as far as most people can tell, but expert judges are able to detect subtle but important distinctions that result in one performer getting higher marks than the other. Intradimensional discrimination requires detecting a single differentiating feature between S+ and S– and therefore is a form of expert performance.

Intradimensional discriminations are interesting because they can produce a counterintuitive phenomenon known as the **peak-shift effect**. This was demonstrated in a famous experiment by Hanson (1959). Hanson examined the effects of intradimensional discrimination training on the extent to which various colors controlled pecking behavior in pigeons. All the participants were reinforced for pecking in the presence of a light whose wavelength was 550 nanometers. Thus, the S+ was the same for all of the subjects. The groups differed in how similar the S– was to the S+ (how expert the pigeons had to become in telling the colors apart). One group received discrimination training in which the S– was a color of 590 nm wavelength, 40 nm away from the S+. For another group the wavelength of the S– was 555 nm, only 5 nm away from the S+. The performance of these pigeons was compared with the behavior of a control group that did not receive discrimination training but was also reinforced for pecking in the presence of the 550 nm stimulus. (Notice the similarity of this experiment to the study by Jenkins and Harrison. In both studies, the difficulty of the discrimination was varied across groups.)

After their contrasting training experiences, all of the birds were tested for their rate of pecking in the presence of test stimuli that varied in color. The results are shown in Figure 8.11. Let us consider first the performance of the control group that did not receive discrimination training. These animals responded most to the S+ stimulus, and responded progressively less as the color

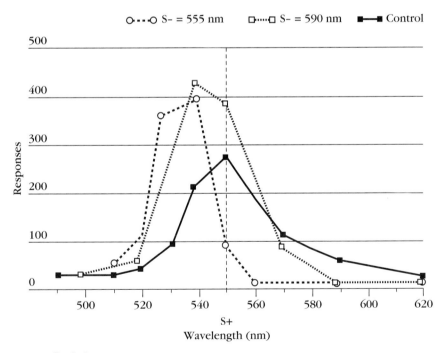

FIGURE **8.11**

Effects of intradimensional discrimination training on stimulus control. All three groups of pigeons were reinforced for pecking in the presence of 550-nm light (S+). One group received discrimination training in which the S– was a 590-nm light. For another group, the S– was a 555-nm light. The third group served as a control and did not receive discrimination training before the test for stimulus generalization. (From "Effects of Discrimination Training on Stimulus Generalization," by H. M. Hanson, 1959, *Journal of Experimental Psychology, 58,* pp. 321–333.)

of the test stimuli deviated from the color of S+. Thus, the control group showed a standard excitatory generalization gradient centered at the S+.

Different results were obtained after discrimination training with the 590-nm color as S–. These pigeons also responded at high rates to the 550-nm color that had served as the S+. However, they showed much more generalization of the pecking response to the 540-nm color. In fact, their rate of response was slightly higher to the 540-nm color than to the original 550-nm S+. This shift of the peak responding away from the original S+ was even more dramatic after discrimination training with the 555-nm color as S–. These birds showed much lower rates of responding to the original S+ (550 nm) than either of the other two groups. Furthermore, their highest response rates occurred to colors of 540- and 530-nm wavelength. This shift of the peak of the generalization gradient away from the original S+ is remarkable because in the earlier phase of discrimination training, responding was never reinforced in the presence of the 540-nm or 530-nm stimuli. Thus, the highest rates of pecking occurred to stimuli that had never even been presented during original training.

The shift of the peak of the generalization gradient away from the original S+ is called the **peak-shift effect.** Two features of the peak-shift effect evident in Figure 8.11 are important to note. First, the peak-shift effect is a result of intradimensional discrimination training. The control group, which did not receive intradimensional discrimination training, did not show the peak-shift effect. Second, the peak-shift effect was a function of the similarity of the S– to the S+ used in discrimination training. The biggest peak shift occurred after training in which the S– was very similar to the S+ (555 nm and 550 nm, respectively). Less of a peak shift occurred after discrimination training with more widely different colors (590 nm compared with 550 nm).

Similar results were evident in the Jenkins and Harrison experiment (see Figure 8.8). A small peak-shift effect was evident in subjects that received discrimination training with the 1,000 cps tone as S+ and the 950 cps tone as S–. Notice that for this group, the highest rate of responding occurred to a tonal frequency above 1000 cps. No peak shift occurred for subjects trained with the 1,000 cps tone as S+ and the absence of the tone as S–.

The peak-shift effect can result from any intradimensional discrimination, not just pitch and color. The S+ and S– may be lines of different orientations, tones of different loudness, temporal cues, spatial stimuli, or facial cues. Furthermore, the effect has been observed in a variety of species, including people (e.g., Bizo & McMahon, 2007; Cheng & Spetch, 2002; Moye & Thomas, 1982; Spetch, Chang, & Clifford, 2004; Russella & Kirkpatrick, 2007).

Spence's Explanation of Peak-Shift

The peak-shift effect is remarkable because it shows that the S+, or reinforced, stimulus is not necessarily the one that evokes the highest response rate. How can this be? Excitatory stimulus generalization gradients are supposed to peak at the S+. Can the peak-shift effect be explained in terms of excitation generalized around S+ and inhibition generalized around S–? In an ingenious analysis, Spence (1937) suggested that excitatory and inhibitory gradients may in fact produce the peak-shift phenomenon. His analysis is particularly remarkable because it was proposed more than 20 years before the peak-shift effect and gradients of excitation and inhibition were experimentally demonstrated.

Spence assumed that intradimensional discrimination training produces excitatory and inhibitory stimulus generalization gradients centered at S+ and S–, respectively, in the usual fashion. However, because the S+ and S– are similar in intradimensional discrimination tasks (e.g., both being colors), the generalization gradients of excitation and inhibition will overlap. Furthermore, the degree of overlap will depend on the degree of similarity between S+ and S–. Because of this overlap, generalized inhibition from S– will suppress responding to S+, resulting in a peak-shift effect. More inhibition from S– to S+ will occur if S– is closer to S+, and this will result in a greater peak-shift effect, just as Hanson found (see Figure 8.11).

Spence's theory of discrimination learning has been remarkably successful (e.g., Hearst, 1968, 1969; Klein & Rilling, 1974; Marsh, 1972), although the theory has not been able to explain some experimental results (e.g., Lazareva et al., 2008). Reflecting on the overall impact of Spence's theory, Pearce et al. (2008) recently noted that "The interaction between excitatory and inhibitory generalization gradients ... provides a useful framework for appreciating how animals solve discriminations between stimulus configurations." They went on to comment that "The study of discrimination learning represents one of psychology's more enduring theoretical endeavors. Spence's theory has already made a significant contribution to this endeavor, and it seems likely that it will continue to do so for many years to come" (p. 199).

Alternative Accounts of Peak-Shift

As I noted earlier, studies of stimulus control can tell us a great deal about how organisms (human and nonhuman) view the world. An important question that has been a source of debate for decades is whether we view stimuli in terms of their individual and absolute properties, or in terms of their relation to other stimuli that we experience (e.g., Köhler, 1939). The elemental versus configural analysis of control by stimulus compounds that I discussed earlier in this chapter is part of this long-standing debate. As with many such debates, evidence consistent with both the elemental and relational approaches is available, suggesting that both types of mechanisms can operate, perhaps under different circumstances (e.g., Hulse, Page, & Braaten, 1990).

Spence's model of discrimination learning is an absolute stimulus learning model. It predicts behavior based on the net excitatory properties of individual stimuli. The alternative approach assumes that organisms learn to respond to a stimulus based on the relation of that stimulus to other cues in the situation. For example, when presented with an S+ that is larger than the S–, the subject may respond to the S+ based on its relative size (in comparison to the S–) rather than in terms of its absolute size. An interesting prediction of this approach is that the shape of a generalization gradient will change as a function of the range of test stimuli that are presented during the generalization test session. These and other predictions of the relational approach have been confirmed in studies with both human and nonhuman subjects (e.g., Bizo & McMahon, 2007; Lazareva Miner, Wasserman, & Young 2008; Thomas, 1993).

Stimulus Equivalence Training

The peak-shift effect is a provocative and counterintuitive outcome of intradimensional discrimination training. However, as the studies of Jenkins and Harrison showed (see Figure 8.8), even with this effect, discrimination training dramatically increases the stimulus control of behavior. It limits the generalization of behavior from S+ to other cues and increases the steepness of generalization gradients. This raises a few questions: Are there learning procedures that have the opposite effect? Are there learning procedures that increase stimulus generalization? How might we construct such procedures?

In a discrimination procedure, stimuli are treated differently: they have different consequences. One stimulus is associated with reinforcement, whereas the other is not. This differential treatment or significance of the stimuli leads organisms to respond to them as distinct from each other. What would happen if two stimuli were treated in the same or equivalent fashion? Would such a procedure lead organisms to respond to the stimuli as similar or equivalent? The answer seems to be yes. Just as discrimination training encourages differential responding, equivalence training encourages generalized responding.

Several approaches are available to promote generalization rather than discrimination among stimuli. In Chapter 12, I will describe research on concept learning that involves learning to treat various physically different instances of a category in the same manner. For example, pigeons can be trained to respond in a similar fashion to different photographs, all of which include water in some form (ocean, lake, puddle, stream) (Herrnstein, Loveland, & Cable, 1976). The basic training strategy for categorization is to reinforce the same response (pecking a response key) in the presence of various pictures containing water, and to not reinforce that response when photographs without water appear. Herrnstein et al. trained such a discrimination using 500–700 photographs of various scenes in New England. Once the pigeons learned the water/no-water discrimination, their behavior generalized to novel photographs that had not been presented during training.

Investigators have also explored the possibility that **stimulus equivalence** between two different stimuli might be established by linking each of the distinct cues with a common third event. In an experiment by Honey and Hall (1989), for example, rats first received presentations of two different auditory cues, a noise and a clicker, paired with food. The common food outcome was expected to create functional equivalence between the noise and clicker stimuli. The control group also received presentations of the noise and the clicker, but for that group only the clicker was paired with food. Both groups then had the noise paired with mild foot shock, resulting in the conditioning of fear to the noise. The main question was whether this conditioned fear of the noise would generalize to the clicker. Significantly more generalization occurred in the equivalence trained animals than in the control group. The equivalence-trained group treated the clicker and noise as more similar than the control group.

In the above experiment, equivalence was established by associating the two physically different stimuli (noise and clicker) with a common reinforcer (food). The equivalence class in this case had two members (the noise and the clicker). A larger equivalence class could have been created by pairing additional cues with the common food outcome. The critical factor is to associate

TABLE **8.2**
Stimulus Equivalence Training with Common Responses

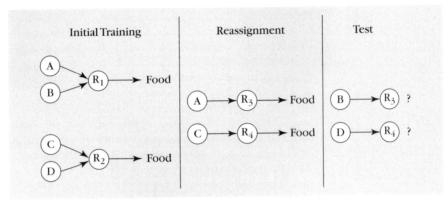

P. Urcuioli

all of the members of a stimulus set with a common event. The common event can be a reinforcer, like food, or it can be a common response or a common stimulus outcome (e.g., Delius, Jitsumori, & Siemann, 2000).

Table 8.2 illustrates the experimental design that is often used to train stimulus equivalence classes based on associating various cues with a common response (see Urcuioli, 2006, for a recent review). The letters A, B, C, and D represent four different sets of stimuli. For example, Set A may consist of four arbitrary designs, Set B may consist of four more arbitrary designs, and so on. During initial training, subjects are reinforcing for making one response (R_1) whenever stimuli from set A or B are presented. Making this common response presumably gets the subjects to treat the A and B stimuli as *equivalent*. A similar procedure is carried out with stimuli from sets C and D, but in that case the common reinforced response is R_2. Once subjects are well trained on the original discrimination problem (consistently making R_1 on A and B trials and R_2 on C and D trials), they are ready to move on to the reassignment phase of the experiment.

During the reassignment phase, the stimuli in Set A are trained with a new response R_3 and the stimuli in Set C are trained with a new response R_4. Notice that stimuli from sets B and D are not presented during the reassignment training phase. However, if stimuli in Set B became *equivalent* to those in Set A during original training, they should also come to elicit response R_3 after the reassignment training. Following the same reasoning, stimuli in Set D should come to elicit R_4 following the reassignment training of Set C. These predictions of stimulus equivalence are tested in the last phase of the experiment.

Experimental designs like that presented in Table 8.2 have been employed in numerous studies of stimulus equivalence training with both human and nonhuman subjects (e.g., Hall, 1991; Jitsumori, Shimada, & Inoue, 2006; Smeets, & Barnes-Holmes, 2005; Zentall & Smeets, 1996). The basic idea is that pairing different stimuli with the same outcome creates *functional equivalence* among those stimuli, with the result that subjects come to response to all of the cues in the equivalence class in a similar fashion.

A more formal definition of *equivalence class* has been proposed by Sidman and his colleagues (Sidman, 1990, 1994; 2000; Sidman & Tailby, 1982;

see also Tierney & Bracken, 1998). An equivalence class is said to exist if its members possess three mathematical properties: 1) reflexivity or sameness, 2) symmetry, and 3) transitivity. Consider, for example, an equivalence class consisting of three stimuli A, B, and C. *Reflexivity,* or sameness, refers to the relation A = A, B = B, and C = C. *Symmetry* is said to exist if a relationship is bidirectional. Thus, for example, if A leads to B (A→B), then symmetry requires that B leads to A (B→A). Finally, *transitivity* refers to the integration of two relationships into a third one. For example, given the relations A→B, and B→C, transitivity requires that A→C.

The concept of equivalence class has been particularly important in analyses of language. The word *apple,* for example, derives its meaning from the fact that the word is in an equivalence class that includes other items that we call *apple,* such as an actual apple and a photograph or drawing of an apple. These physically different stimuli have the property of reflexivity (apple = apple). They also have the property of symmetry. If you learned to say the word *apple* when you saw a picture of one, you will be able to pick out the picture if asked to identify what the word *apple* signifies. Finally, these items exhibit transitivity. If you learned that the word refers to the picture (A→B), and the picture refers to the physical apple object (B→C), you will be able to identify the apple object when given the word (A→C).

Generally, individuals with better verbal skills learn equivalence classes more easily, and the ability to use verbal labels facilitates equivalence class formation (e.g., Randell & Remington, 1999). However, language competence is not essential for the acquisition of stimulus equivalence classes (Carr, Wilkinson, Blackman, & McIlvane, 2000), and the use of verbal labels is not always helpful (e.g., Carr & Blackman, 2001). The ability to form equivalence classes is probably one of the components or prerequisites of verbal skill, but we still have much to discover about how such learning contributes to complex verbal repertoires.

CONTEXTUAL CUES AND CONDITIONAL RELATIONS

So far I have been discussing the control of behavior by discrete stimuli, such as a tone or a light, presented individually or in combination with one another. A stimulus is said to be *discrete* if it is presented for a brief period, has a clear beginning and end, and can be easily characterized. Although studies with discrete stimuli have provided much information about the stimulus control of instrumental behavior, such studies do not tell the whole story. A more comprehensive analysis of the stimuli organisms experience during the course of instrumental conditioning indicates that discrete discriminative stimuli occur in the presence of background contextual cues. The contextual cues may be visual, auditory, or olfactory features of the room or place where the discrete discriminative stimuli are presented. Recent research indicates that contextual cues can provide an important additional source of control of learned behavior.

Control by Contextual Cues

Several of the examples of stimulus control I described at the beginning of this chapter involved the control of behavior by contextual cues. It is easier to concentrate on studying when you are in the school library rather than at home during holidays because of contextual control of studying behavior by stimuli experienced in the library. Cheering at a football game but not during a church sermon also illustrates the power of contextual cues.

Contextual cues can come to control behavior in a variety of ways (see Balsam, 1985; Balsam & Tomie, 1985). In a study of sexual conditioning, for example, Akins (1998, Experiment 1), used contextual cues as a signal for sexual reinforcement, in much the same way that a discrete CS might be used. Male domesticated quail served as subjects, and the apparatus consisted of two large compartments that were distinctively different. One compartment had sand on the floor and the walls and ceiling were colored orange. The other compartment had a wire-mesh floor and walls and ceiling painted green. Before the start of the conditioning trials, the subjects were allowed to move back and forth between the two compartments during a 10-minute preference test to determine their baseline preference. The nonpreferred compartment was then designated as the CS. Conditioning trials consisted of placing the male subject in its CS context for five minutes, at which point a sexually receptive female was placed with them for another five minutes. Thus, these subjects received exposure to the CS context paired with the sexual US. Subjects in a control group received access to a female in their home cages two hours before being exposed to the CS context; for them, the CS and US were unpaired.

In addition to the preference test conducted before the start of conditioning, tests were conducted after the 5th and 10th conditioning trials. The results of these tests are presented in Figure 8.12. Notice that the paired and unpaired groups showed similar low preferences for the CS compartment at the outset of the experiment. This low preference persisted in the control group. In contrast, subjects that received the CS context paired with sexual reinforcement came to prefer that context. Thus, the association of contextual cues with sexual reinforcement increased preference for those cues.

Experiments like the one by Akins illustrate that contextual cues can come to control behavior if they serve as a signal for a US or a reinforcer. This methodology is common in studies of drug-conditioned place preference. The conditioned place preference technique is used to determine whether a drug has reinforcing effects. This question is particularly important in the development of new drugs because drugs that can condition a place preference have the potential of becoming drugs of abuse.

As in the study by Akins, the participants (usually laboratory rats or mice) in a conditioned place preference experiment are first familiarized with two distinct contexts. One of these is then designated as the conditioned stimulus and paired with the administration of the drug under evaluation. The subjects are then tested for their preference between the two contexts to see if they now prefer the drug-paired context (see Tzschentke, 2007, for a review). Studies of fear conditioning also often employ contextual cues as CSs (e.g., McNally & Westbrook, 2006). These types of experiments beg the question: Do contextual cues also come to control behavior when they do not signal reinforcement, when they are truly "background" stimuli that the organism is not specifically required to pay attention to? This is one of the fundamental questions in the stimulus control of instrumental behavior. Much work has been devoted to it, and the answer is clearly *yes*. Contextual cues do not have to signal reinforcement to gain control over behavior.

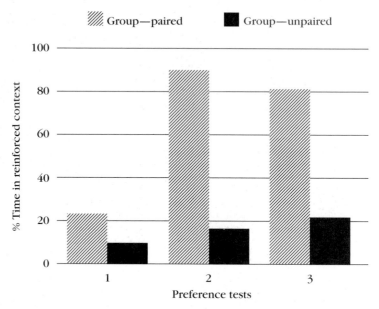

FIGURE **8.12**

Development of a preference for a distinctive context paired (or unpaired) with sexual reinforcement in male domesticated quail. Five conditioning trials were conducted between successive tests for the subjects in the paired group. (From "Context Excitation and Modulation of Conditioned Sexual Behavior," by C. K. Akins, *Animal Learning & Behavior, Vol. 26,* Figure 1, p. 419. Copyright 1998 Psychonomic Society, Inc. Reprinted with permission.)

A classic experiment by Thomas, McKelvie, and Mah (1985) illustrates control by contextual cues that are not correlated with the availability of reinforcement. Thomas et al. first trained pigeons on a line-orientation discrimination in which a vertical line (90°) served as the S+ and a horizontal line (0°) served as the S–. The pigeons were periodically reinforced with food for pecking on S+ trials and were not reinforced on S– trials. The training took place in a standard Skinner box (Context 1), but the availability of reinforcement was signaled by the line-orientation cues (90+/0–) rather than by contextual cues.

After the discrimination was well learned, the contextual cues of the experimental chamber were changed by altering both the lighting and the type of noise in the chamber. In the presence of these new contextual cues (Context 2), the discrimination training contingencies were reversed. Now, the horizontal line (0°) served as the S+ and the vertical line (90°) served as the S–. Notice that the pigeons were not specifically required to pay attention to the contextual cues. They were simply required to learn a new discrimination problem. (They could have learned this new problem had the contextual cues not been changed.)

After mastery of the reversal problem, the birds received generalization tests in which lines of various orientations between 0° and 90° were presented.

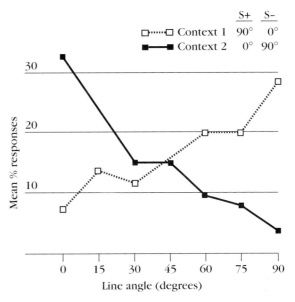

FIGURE **8.13**

Generalization gradients obtained with various line-angle stimuli following training in two different contexts. In Context 1, the 90° stimulus served as the S+ and the 0° stimulus served as the S–. In Context 2, the 0° stimulus served as the S+ and the 90° stimulus served as the S–. (From "Context as a Conditional Cue in Operant Discrimination Reversal Learning," by D. R. Thomas, A. R. McKelvie, & W. L. Mah, 1985, *Journal of Experimental Psychology: Animal Behavior Processes, 11*, pp. 317–330. Copyright © 1985 by the American Psychological Association. Reprinted by permission.)

One such generalization test was conducted in Context 1, and another was conducted in Context 2. The results of these tests are presented in Figure 8.13. Remarkably, the shape of the generalization gradient in each context was appropriate to the discrimination problem that was in effect in that context. Thus, in Context 1, the birds responded most to the 90° stimulus, which had served as the S+ in that context, and least to the 0° stimulus, which had served as the S–. The opposite pattern of results occurred in Context 2. Here, the pigeons responded most to the 0° stimulus and least to the 90° stimulus, appropriate to the reverse discrimination contingencies that had been in effect in Context 2. (For a similar result in human predictive learning, see Üngör and Lachnit, 2006.)

The findings presented in Figure 8.13 clearly illustrate that contextual cues can come to control instrumental behavior. The results also illustrate that contextual stimulus control can occur without one context being more strongly associated with reinforcement than another. In both Context 1 and Context 2, the pigeons received reinforced (S+) and nonreinforced (S–) trials. Therefore, one context could not have become a better signal for the availability of reinforcement than the other. (See also Hall & Honey, 1989; Honey, Willis, & Hall, 1990; Swartzentruber, 1993.)

How did Context 1 and Context 2 come to produce different types of responding? Since one context was not a better signal for reinforcement than the other, direct associations of each context with food cannot explain the results. A different kind of mechanism must have been involved. One possibility is that each context activated a different memory. Context 1 activated the memory of reinforcement with 90° and nonreinforcement with 0° (90+/0–). In contrast, Context 2 activated the memory of reinforcement with 0° and nonreinforcement with 90° (90–/0+). Instead of being associated with a particular stimulus, each context came to activate a different S+/S– contingency. The subjects learned a **conditional relation**: If Context 1, then 90+/0–; if Context 2, then 90–/0+. The relationship between the line orientations and reinforcement was conditional upon the context in which the subjects were located.

Control by Conditional Relations

In much of the book so far, I have emphasized relations that involved just two events: a CS and US, or a response and a reinforcer. Relations between two events are called *binary relations*. Under certain circumstances, the nature of a binary relation is determined by a third event, called a **modulator**. In the above experiment by Thomas et al. (1985), each context was a modulator. Whether or not a particular line-angle stimulus was associated with reinforcement depended on which contextual cues were present. The relation of a modulator to the binary relation that it signals is called a *conditional relation*. Numerous experiments have indicated that animals can learn to use modulators to tell when a particular binary relation is in effect (see reviews by Holland, 1984, 1992; Schmajuk, & Holland, 1998; Swartzentruber, 1995).

We have already encountered some conditional relations without having identified them as such. One example is instrumental stimulus discrimination training. In an instrumental discrimination procedure, the organism is reinforced for responding during S+ but is not reinforced during S–. The discriminative stimuli S+ and S– are modulators that signal the relation between the response and the reinforcer. One response-reinforcer relation exists during S+ (positive reinforcement), and a different relation exists during S– (nonreinforcement). Thus, instrumental discrimination procedures involve conditional control of the relation between the response and the reinforcer (Davidson, Aparicio, & Rescorla, 1988; Goodall & Mackintosh, 1987; Holman & Mackintosh, 1981; Jenkins, 1977; Skinner, 1938).

Conditional Control in Pavlovian Conditioning

Conditional relations have been extensively investigated using Pavlovian conditioning procedures. Classical conditioning typically involves a binary relation between a CS and a US. The CS may be a brief auditory cue (white noise), and the US may be food. A strong relation exists between the CS and US if the food is presented immediately after each occurrence of the CS but not at other times. How could conditional control be established over such a CS-US relation?

Establishing a conditional relation requires introducing a third event (the modulator) that indicates when presentation of the auditory CS will end in food. For example, a light could be introduced, in the presence of which the brief auditory CS would be followed by food. In the absence of the light, presentations of the auditory CS would be nonreinforced. This procedure is diagrammed

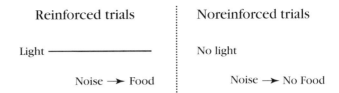

Reinforced trials   Noreinforced trials

Light ———————   No light

Noise � Food   Noise � No Food

FIGURE **8.14**

Procedure for establishing conditional stimulus control in classical conditioning. On reinforced trials, a light stimulus (modulator) is presented and the CS (noise) is paired with food. On nonreinforced trials, the modulator is absent and the CS (noise) is presented without food.

in Figure 8.14. As in instrumental discrimination procedures, both reinforced and nonreinforced trials are conducted. During reinforced trials, the light is turned on for 15 seconds. Ten seconds into the light, the noise CS is turned on for five seconds, and is immediately followed by the food US. During nonreinforced trials, the noise CS is presented by itself and does not end in food.

The procedure I just described is similar to one that was conducted by Fetsko, Stebbins, Gallagher, & Colwill (2005) in a study with inbred mice. (There is great interest in adapting conditioning techniques for use with mice so that problems of learning and memory can be studied in specially engineered genetic knockout mice.) A light was used as the modulator on reinforced trials, and the target CS was a five-second noise stimulus. Food was delivered into a food cup that was recessed in the wall of the experimental chamber. An infrared detector recorded each time a mouse poked its head into the food cup. As the noise CS became associated with food, the mice showed increased head poking into the food cup during the CS (in anticipation of the arrival of the food pellet). These anticipatory head pokes were measured as the conditioned response.

The results of the experiment are presented in Figure 8.15. The mice showed much more food-cup head entries during the noise CS when the CS was presented at the end of the light (L→N+) than on trials in which the noise CS was presented by itself (N–). The experiment also included trials with the light presented by itself (L–). The subjects also showed low levels of responding during those trials. These results show that the modulator (L) facilitated responding to the noise CS. This occurred even though the modulator did not elicit responding by itself. Just as a discriminative stimulus facilitates instrumental behavior, the modulator facilitated CS-elicited responding in the study by Fetsko et al.

Research on the modulation of conditioned responding in Pavlovian conditioning was pioneered by Peter Holland (Holland, 1985; Ross & Holland, 1981) and Robert Rescorla (Rescorla, 1985; Rescorla, Durlach, & Grau, 1985). Holland elected to call a Pavlovian modulator an *occasion setter*, because the modulator sets the occasion for reinforcement of the target CS. Rescorla elected to call a Pavlovian modulator a *facilitator*, because the modulator facilitates responding to the target CS. The terms **occasion setting** and **facilitation** have both been used in subsequent discussions of Pavlovian modulation.

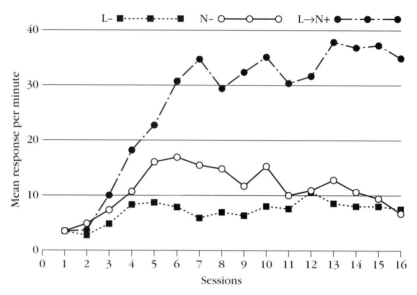

L– ■ ⋯ ■ ⋯ ■   N– ○——○——○   L→N+ ● ⋯ ● ⋯ ●

FIGURE **8.15**

Head entries into the food cup during a light and a noise stimulus when these stimuli were presented alone (L– and N–) without food and when the noise was presented at the end of the light stimulus and paired with food (L→N+). (From Fetsko, Stebbins, Gallagher, & Colwill, 2005.)

It is interesting to note that the procedure outlined in Figure 8.14 is the converse of the standard procedure for inhibitory conditioning (see Figure 3.9). To turn the procedure outlined in Figure 8.14 into one that will result in the conditioning of inhibitory properties to the noise, all one has to do is to reverse which type of trial has the light. Instead of presenting the light on reinforced trials, the light would be presented on nonreinforced trials in a conditioned inhibition procedure.

Presenting the light on nonreinforced trials would make the light a signal for nonreinforcement of the noise CS, and might make the light a conditioned inhibitor (see Chapter 3). This example shows that the procedure for inhibitory Pavlovian conditioning involves a conditional relation, just as positive occasion setting and facilitation procedures do. This argument also suggests that conditioned inhibition may be the conceptual opposite of facilitation or positive occasion setting rather than the opposite of conditioned excitation (Rescorla, 1987, 1988).

Distinction Between Excitation and Modulation

Occasion setting is an important aspect of classical conditioning not only because it illustrates that classical conditioning is subject to conditional control, but also because it appears to involve a new mechanism of learning. As discussed in Chapter 4, pairings of a CS with a US result in an association between the two events such that presentation of the CS comes to activate a representation of the US. This kind of learning is the conditioning of excitation to the CS. Modulation is different from conditioned excitation.

As the results presented in Figure 8.15 show, the light stimulus was effective in facilitating responding to the noise CS on L→N+ trials but the light itself did not elicit responding on L− trials (see also Bouton & Swartzentruber, 1986; Puente, Cannon, Best, & Carrell, 1988). This shows that a modulator need not have conditioned excitatory properties. In fact, conditioning excitatory properties to a stimulus does not make that stimulus function as a modulator (see Holland, 1985; Rescorla, 1985; but see Gewirtz, Brandon, & Wagner, 1998; Swartzentruber, 1997).

Additional evidence for a distinction between modulation and conditioned excitation is based on the effects of extinction procedures. *Extinction* refers to a procedure in which a previously conditioned stimulus is presented repeatedly but now without the US. I will describe extinction in greater detail in Chapter 9. The typical outcome of extinction is that conditioned responding declines. Interestingly, the same procedure (repeated nonreinforced stimulus presentations) carried out with an occasion setter often has no effect. Once a stimulus has become established to set the occasion for a CS-US relation, repeated presentations of the stimulus by itself usually do not reduce its ability to facilitate conditioned responding to the CS (e.g., Holland, 1989a; Rescorla, 1985).

The difference in the effects of an extinction procedure on conditioned excitatory stimuli and occasion setters is related to what is signaled. A conditioned excitatory stimulus signals the forthcoming presentation of the US. The absence of the US following presentation of the CS during extinction is a violation of that expectancy. Hence, the signal value of the CS has to be readjusted in extinction to bring it in line with the new reality. In contrast, an occasion setter signals a relation between a CS and a US. The absence of the US when the occasion setter is presented alone does not mean that the relation between the target CS and the US has changed. The information signaled by an occasion setter is not invalidated by presenting the modulator by itself during extinction. Therefore, the ability of the modulator to promote responding elicited by another CS remains intact during extinction. However, a modulator's effectiveness is reduced if the CS-US relation signaled by the modulator is altered (Rescorla, 1986).

Modulation versus Configural Conditioning

Not all conditional discrimination procedures of the type illustrated in Figure 8.14 result in the learning of a conditional relation between the stimuli involved. On reinforced trials in this procedure, a compound stimulus was presented consisting of the light and the noise CS. As I noted earlier, organisms can respond to a compound stimulus either in terms of the elements that make up the compound, or in terms of the unique stimulus configuration produced by the elements. For the light to serve as a signal that the noise will be paired with food, the light and noise cues have to be treated as independent events rather than as a combined configural cue (Holland, 1992).

To encourage organisms to treat stimulus compounds as consisting of independent elements, investigators have presented the elements one after the other, rather than simultaneously, in what is called a *serial compound*. On reinforced trials, the occasion setter is usually presented first, followed by the target CS and reinforcement. This is how the procedure in Figure 8.14 was designed. The light started 10 seconds before the noise on each reinforced trial. In many of his experiments on occasion setting, Holland has even inserted a five-second gap between the modulator and the target CS. Such procedures discourage the perception of a stimulus configuration based on the occasion setter and the target CS. Holland and his associates have reported that organisms respond to conditional discriminations involving serial compounds in terms of conditional relations. By contrast, if the modulator and the target CS are presented simultaneously, modulatory effects may not be observed (for example, Holland, 1986, 1989a, 1991; Ross & Holland, 1981).

CONCLUDING COMMENTS

Stimulus control refers to how precisely tuned an organism's behavior is to specific features of the environment. Therefore, issues concerning the stimulus control of behavior are critical for understanding how an organism interacts with its environment. Stimulus control is measured in terms of the steepness of generalization gradients. A steep generalization gradient indicates that small variations in a stimulus produce large differences in responding. Weaker stimulus control is indicated by flatter generalization gradients.

The degree of stimulus control is determined by numerous factors, including the sensory capacity and sensory orientation of the organism, the relative salience of other cues in the situations, the type of reinforcement used, and the type of response required for reinforcement. Importantly, stimulus control is also a function of learning. Discrimination training increases the stimulus control of behavior whether that training involves stimuli that differ in several respects (interdimensional discrimination) or stimuli that differ in only one respect (intradimensional discrimination). Intradimensional discrimination training produces more precise stimulus control and may lead to the counterintuitive outcome that peak responding is shifted away from the reinforced stimulus. The converse of discrimination training is equivalence training, which increases the generalization of behavior to a variety of physically different stimuli because all of those stimuli have similar functions.

Not only discrete stimuli, but also background contextual cues, can come to control behavior. Furthermore, stimulus control by contextual cues can develop even if attention to contextual cues is not required to optimize reinforcement. Finally, behavior can come under the control of conditional relations among stimuli.

SAMPLE QUESTIONS

1. Describe the relationship between stimulus discrimination and stimulus generalization.
2. Describe the phenomenon of overshadowing and describe how it may be explained by elemental and configural approaches to stimulus control.
3. Describe how the steepness of a generalization gradient may be altered by experience and learning.

4. Describe the difference between intradimensional- and interdimensional-discrimination training.
5. Describe the peak-shift effect and its determinants.
6. Compare and contrast conditioned excitation and modulatory or occasion setting properties of stimuli.

KEY TERMS

conditional relation A relation in which the significance of one stimulus or event depends on the status of another stimulus.

configural-cue approach An approach to the analysis of stimulus control which assumes that organisms respond to a compound stimulus as an integral whole rather than a collection of separate and independent stimulus elements. (Compare with *stimulus element approach*.)

discriminative stimulus A stimulus that controls the performance of instrumental behavior because it signals the availability (or nonavailability) of reinforcement.

excitatory generalization gradient A gradient of responding that is observed when organisms are tested with the S+ from a discrimination procedure and with stimuli that increasingly differ from the S+. Typically the highest level of responding occurs to stimuli similar to the S+; progressively less responding occurs to stimuli that increasingly differ from the S+. Thus, the gradient has an inverted-U shape.

facilitation A procedure in which one cue designates when another cue will be reinforced. Also called *occasion setting*.

inhibitory generalization gradient A gradient of responding observed when organisms are tested with the S– from a discrimination procedure and with stimuli that increasingly differ from the S–. The lowest level of responding occurs to stimuli similar to the S–; progressively more responding occurs to stimuli that increasingly differ from S–. Thus, the gradient has a U shape.

intradimensional discrimination A discrimination between stimuli that differ only in terms of the value of one stimulus feature, such as color, brightness, or pitch.

modulator A stimulus that signals the relation between two other events. The nature of a binary relation may be determined by a third event, called a *modulator*.

multiple schedule of reinforcement A procedure in which different reinforcement schedules are in effect in the presence of different stimuli presented in succession. Generally, each stimulus comes to evoke a pattern of responding that corresponds to whatever reinforcement schedule is in effect during that stimulus.

occasion setting Same as *facilitation*.

overshadowing Interference with the conditioning of a stimulus because of the simultaneous presence of another stimulus that is easier to condition.

peak-shift effect A displacement of the highest rate of responding in a stimulus generalization gradient away from the S+ in a direction opposite the S–.

stimulus discrimination Differential responding in the presence of two or more stimuli.

stimulus discrimination procedure (in classical conditioning) A classical conditioning procedure in which one stimulus (the CS+) is paired with the unconditioned stimulus on some trials and another stimulus (the CS–) is presented without the unconditioned stimulus on other trials. As a result of this procedure the CS+ comes to elicit a conditioned response and the CS– comes to inhibit this response.

stimulus discrimination procedure (in instrumental conditioning) A procedure in which reinforcement for responding is available whenever one stimulus (the S+, or S^D) is present and not available whenever another stimulus (the S−, or S$^\Delta$) is present.

stimulus–element approach An approach to the analysis of control by compound stimuli which assumes that participants respond to a compound stimulus in terms of the stimulus elements that make up the compound. (Compare with *configural–cue*.)

stimulus equivalence Responding to physically distinct stimuli as if they were the same because of common prior experiences with the stimuli.

stimulus generalization Responding to test stimuli that are different from the cues that were present during training.

stimulus generalization gradient A gradient of responding that is observed if participants are tested with stimuli that increasingly differ from the stimulus that was present during training. (See also *excitatory generalization gradient* and *inhibitory generalization gradient*.)

9

Extinction of Conditioned Behavior

CHAPTER PREVIEW

This chapter represents a departure from previous chapters in that for the first time, the focus of the discussion is on procedures that produce a decline in responding. Extinction can only be conducted after a response or association has been established using Pavlovian or instrumental conditioning. Often the goal is to reverse the effects of acquisition. However, a true reversal of acquisition is rarely achieved and may not be possible. The phenomena of spontaneous recovery, renewal, and reinstatement all attest to the fact that extinction does not erase what was learned originally. Additional evidence indicates that S-O and R-O associations survive extinction procedures. Rather than erasure of old learning, extinction seems to involve new learning of an inhibitory S-R association. The inhibition arises from the frustrative effects of the unexpected absence of reward. The frustration produced by non-reward is responsible for a number of paradoxical reward effects, including the partial reinforcement extinction effect. Intermittent or partial reinforcement permits organisms to learn about non-reward in ways that serve to immunize them against the effects of extinction. That kind of resistance to change is also the subject of studies of behavioral momentum that are described at the end of the chapter.

So far, our discussion of classical and instrumental conditioning has centered on various aspects of the acquisition and maintenance of new associations and new responses. Learning mechanisms are useful because the new responses that are acquired promote adjustments to a changing environment. But changes in the environment can also favor the loss of conditioned behavior as life circumstances change. Not many reinforcement schedules remain in effect forever. Responses that are successful at one point may cease to be effective later. Children are praised for drawing crude representations of people and objects in nursery school, but the same type of drawing is not rewarded if made by a high school student. Dating someone may be extremely pleasant and rewarding at first, but stops being reinforcing when that person falls in love with someone else.

Acquisition of conditioned behavior involves procedures in which a reinforcing outcome occurs. In Pavlovian conditioning, the outcome or unconditioned stimulus is presented as a consequence of a conditioned stimulus. In instrumental conditioning, the reinforcing outcome is presented as a consequence of the instrumental response. **Extinction** involves omitting the US, or reinforcer. In classical conditioning, extinction involves repeated presentations of the CS by itself. In instrumental conditioning, extinction involves no longer presenting the reinforcer as a consequence of the instrumental response. With both types of procedures conditioned responding declines. Thus, the behavior change that occurs in extinction is the reverse of what was observed in acquisition. Because of this, extinction appears to be the opposite of acquisition. Indeed, that is how extinction has been characterized in traditional theories of learning, such as the Rescorla-Wagner model (see Chapter 4). However, as the evidence described in the present chapter shows, this view of extinction is incorrect.

It is important to point out that the loss of conditioned behavior that occurs as a result of extinction is not the same as the loss of responding that may occur because of **forgetting**. Extinction is an active process produced by the unexpected absence of the US or the reinforcer. Forgetting, by contrast, is a decline in responding that may occur simply because of the passage of time and does not require non-reinforced encounters with the CS or the instrumental response.

Courtesy of M. Davis

M. Davis

Extinction is one of the most vigorous areas of research in learning today. Behavioral investigations of extinction are being pursued in both appetitive conditioning and aversive or fear conditioning paradigms (Bouton & Woods, 2008; Delamater, 2004; Rescorla, 2001a). Extinction is also being studied at the level of brain structures, neurotransmitter systems, and cellular and genetic mechanisms. Impressive progress is being made in the neuroscience and neurobiology of extinction, especially in the case of conditioned fear (e.g., Barad, 2006; Barad & Cain, 2007; Myers & Davis, 2007; Quirk, Milad, Santini & Lebrón, 2007). As Myers and Davis (2007) noted, "Because of the availability of intensively studied fear acquisition paradigms for which the underlying neural circuitry is well understood, the literature on fear extinction has expanded at an incredible rate" (p.143).

Extinction is also one of the hot areas for translational research that seeks to improve clinical practice based on laboratory findings (e.g., Bouton & Nelson, 1998; Vansteenwegen et al., 2006). Social phobia, fear of flying, claustrophobia, and other pathological fears and phobias are typically treated with some form of exposure therapy (Craske & Mystkowski, 2006). Exposure therapy is basically an extinction procedure in which participants are exposed to cues that elicit fear in the absence of the aversive US. Exposure to the actual fearful stimulus is the best way to conduct exposure therapy, but that is often not practical. Having clients imagine being in the fearful situation can be helpful. However, more vivid and realistic exposure is now possible with the use of virtual reality techniques (e.g., Rothbaum et al., 2000; Rothbaum et al., 2001). Exposure therapy is also employed in treating drug addiction, with the aim of extinguishing cues associated with drug taking behavior. More careful consideration of the relevant basic research literature promises to substantially improve the effectiveness of exposure therapy in this area (Conklin & Tiffany, 2002).

EFFECTS OF EXTINCTION PROCEDURES

What would you do if you unexpectedly did not succeed in opening the door to your apartment with your key? Chances are you would not give up after the first attempt, but would try several more times, perhaps jiggling the key in different ways each time. But, if none of those response variations worked, you would eventually quit trying. This illustrates two basic behavioral effects of extinction. The most obvious behavioral effect is that the target response decreases when the response no longer results in reinforcement. This is the primary behavioral effect of extinction and the outcome that has occupied most of the attention of scientists. Investigations of extinction have been concerned with how rapidly responding decreases and how long the response suppression lasts. If the key to your apartment no longer opens the door, you will give up trying. However, notice that before you give up entirely, you are likely to jiggle the key in various ways in an effort to make it work. This illustrates the second basic behavioral effect of extinction, namely that it increases response variability, at least at first.

The two basic behavioral effects of extinction are nicely illustrated in a study with laboratory rats (Neuringer, Kornell, & Olufs, 2001). Two groups served in the experiment. The apparatus and procedure were set up to facilitate the measurement of response variability. The experimental chamber had two response levers on one wall and a round response key on the opposite wall. During the reinforcement phase, the rats had to make three responses in a row to obtain a food pellet. For example, they could press the left lever three times (LLL), press each lever and the response key once (RLK), or press the left lever twice and the key once (LLK). One group of subjects was reinforced for varying its response sequences (Group Var). They got food on a trial only if the sequence of responses they made was different from what they did on earlier trials. Each subject in the second group was also required to make three responses to get reinforced, but for them, there was no requirement to vary how they accomplished that (Group Yoke). After responding was well established by the reinforcement contingencies in both groups, the subjects were shifted to an extinction procedure in which food was no longer provided no matter what the rats did.

Figure 9.1 shows the results of the experiment for the last four sessions of the reinforcement phase and the first four sessions of the extinction phase. The left panel represents the variability in the response sequences each group performed; the right panel represents their rates of responding. Notice that reinforcement produced the expected difference between the two groups in terms of the variability of their response sequences. Subjects reinforced for varying their responses (Group Var) showed much more variability than the subjects that did not have to vary their behavior (Group Yoke). The second group responded somewhat faster, perhaps because they did not have to move as frequently from one manipulandum to another.

Extinction produced a decline in the rate of responding in both groups (see right panel of Figure 9.1). Interestingly, this decline in responding occurred in the face of an increase in the variability of the response sequences the subjects performed (see left panel of Figure 9.1). Both groups showed a significant increase in the variability of the response sequences they performed during the extinction phase. The increase in response variability was evident during the first extinction session and increased during subsequent sessions. Thus, extinction produced a decline in the number of response sequences the subjects completed but it increased the variability of those sequences (see also Gharib, Derby, & Roberts, 2001).

Another interesting finding in this experiment was that the increase in response variability that occurred during extinction did not come at the expense of the subjects repeating response sequences that they had performed during the reinforcement phase. Response sequences that were highly likely to occur during the reinforcement phase continued to occur during extinction. But, these were supplemented by sequences that the participants had rarely tried previously. Thus, extinction decreased the rate of responding and increased response variabililty, but otherwise it did not alter the basic structure of the instrumental behavior (see also Machado & Cevik, 1998; Schwartz, 1981; for similar evidence in Pavlovian conditioning, see Ohyama, Gibbon, Deich, & Balsam, 1999).

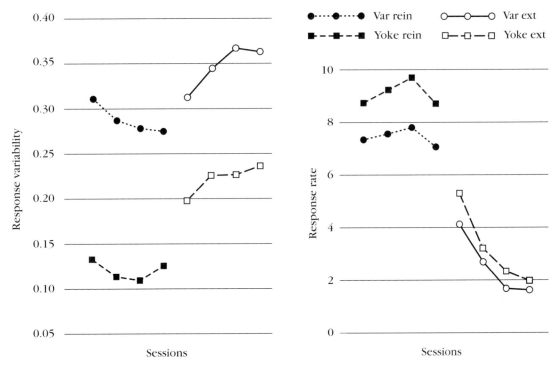

FIGURE **9.1**

Effects of extinction on response variability (left panel) and response rates (right panel) for rats that were required to perform variable response sequences for reinforcement (Var) or received reinforcement regardless of their response sequence (Yoke). The filled symbols represent the last four sessions of the reinforcement phase. The open symbols represent the first four sessions of the extinction phase. (Response variability was measured in terms of the probability of meeting the variability criterion. Response rate was measured in terms of the number of three-response sequences that were completed per minute.) (From Neuringer, et al. (2001). *Journal of Experimental Psychology: Animal Behavior Processes,* 27. Figure 4, p. 84. Copyright © 2001 by the American Psychology Association. Reprinted with permission.)

Courtesy of M. R. Papini

M. R. Papini

In addition to the behavioral effects illustrated in Figure 9.1, extinction procedures also often produce strong emotional effects (Amsel, 1992; Papini, 2003). If an organism has become accustomed to receiving reinforcement for a particular response, it may become upset when reinforcers are no longer delivered. The emotional reaction induced by withdrawal of an expected reinforcer is called **frustration**. Frustrative non-reward energizes behavior (Dudley & Papini, 1995, 1997; Thomas & Papini, 2001). Under certain conditions, frustration may be intense enough to induce aggression. When a vending machine breaks down and no longer delivers the expected candy bar, you are likely to become annoyed and may pound and kick the machine. If your partner takes you on a date every Saturday evening, you will surely be very upset if your partner calls one Saturday afternoon to unexpectedly cancel the date.

Frustrative aggression induced by extinction is dramatically demonstrated by experiments in which two animals (e.g., pigeons) are placed in the same Skinner box (Azrin, Hutchinson, & Hake, 1966). One of them is initially reinforced for pecking a response key, while the other animal is restrained in a corner of the experimental chamber. The key-pecking bird largely ignores the other one as long as pecking is reinforced with food. However, when extinction is introduced and reinforcement ceases, the previously rewarded animal is likely to attack its innocent partner. Aggression also occurs if a stuffed model instead of a real animal is placed in the Skinner box. Extinction-induced aggression has been observed in studies with pigeon, rats, and with people (e.g., Lewis, Alessandri, & Sullivan, 1990; Nation & Cooney, 1982; Tomie, Carelli, & Wagner, 1993) and can be a problem when extinction is used in behavior therapy (Lerman, Iwata, & Wallace, 1999).

BOX **9.1**

Consolidating (and Reconsolidating) Memories Requires Protein Synthesis

The process of forming a long-term memory is called **consolidation**. Research has shown that across a range of behavioral paradigms, memory consolidation depends on protein synthesis (for a recent review, see Hernandez & Abel, 2008). For example, as we saw in Chapter 3, pairing a tone with a mild electric shock endows the tone with the capacity to elicit conditioned freezing in laboratory rats, a Pavlovian conditioned response (CR) indicative of fear. Ordinarily conditioned freezing is remembered for months after training. If, however, subjects are given a drug that inhibits protein synthesis (e.g., anisomycin) prior to the tone-shock pairings, they don't remember the fear conditioning. They show amnesia. Further research has shown that the required protein synthesis occurs within the first hour or two of training; if protein synthesis is inhibited four to six hours after training, it has little effect on long-term memory (Figure 9.2). Similar effects have been obtained in other learning paradigms (Hernandez & Abel, 2008).

The fact that inhibiting protein synthesis six hours after training generally has little effect on long-term retention is important because drugs like anisomycin have a broad range of effects and impact cellular function throughout the body. These secondary effects of drug treatment could indirectly disrupt the expression of the conditioned response, leading us to mistakenly conclude that protein synthesis is needed for memory. Further, the physiological consequences of drug treatment could take a long time to decay and impact the expression of the CR at the time of testing. If either of these alternatives were operating, delaying the injection of anisomycin after training should (if anything) produce more memory loss, because such a delay decreases the interval between drug treatment and testing (Figure 9.2). However, the opposite is observed (Hernandez & Abel, 2008). Across a range of behavioral learning paradigms, administration of anisomycin soon after training disrupts the memory of conditioning while delayed drug treatment has little effect. This suggests that the drug has a temporally limited impact and disrupts memory by interfering with the mechanisms that underlie consolidation.

Researchers have also obtained evidence that anisomycin selectively impacts processes involved in learning and memory if the drug is injected specifically into regions of the brain known to mediate long-term retention of the CR. As described in Box 10.1, fear conditioning depends on the basolateral region of the amygdala. Microinjection of a protein synthesis inhibitor into the basolateral amygdala disrupts consolidation in the usual time-dependent manner (Schafe & LeDoux, 2000). That is, the greatest disruption occurs when the injection is given soon after training, and there is little effect if the injection occurs six hours later. Additional evidence that gene expression and protein synthesis is critical has been obtained using pharmacological/genetic techniques that target other components of translation/transcription processes (Hernandez & Abel, 2008).

Researchers have used these same manipulations to explore whether extinction requires protein synthesis and, in general, parallel

(continued)

BOX **9.1** (continued)

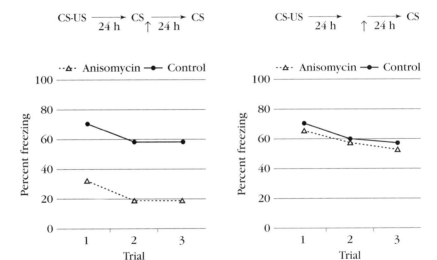

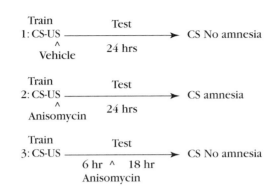

A

Train 1: CS-US ——————→ CS No amnesia
Test
Vehicle   24 hrs

Train 2: CS-US ——————→ CS amnesia
Test
Anisomycin   24 hrs

Train 3: CS-US ——————→ CS No amnesia
Test
6 hr ^ 18 hr
Anisomycin

B

CS-US ——→ CS ——→ CS
24 h   ↑ 24 h

CS-US ——→   CS
24 h   ↑ 24 h

Percent freezing

FIGURE **9.2**

(A) Subjects (1: vehicle control) that receive a conditioned stimulus (CS) paired with a unconditioned stimulus (US) exhibit a conditioned response to the CS when it is presented 24 hrs later. Subjects (2: immediate anisomycin) treated with the protein synthesis inhibitor anisomycin soon after training do not exhibit a conditioned response to the CS when it is presented 24 hrs later. If drug treatment is delayed for 6 hrs (3: delayed anisomycin), anisomycin has little effect. (B) The left panel illustrates conditioned freezing in rats that received a single presentation of the CS 24 hrs after training, followed by drug treatment. When the CS was presented the next day, rats that had received anisomycin exhibited amnesia. Drug treatment had no effect when the reminder CS was omitted (right panel). (Adapted from Nader et al., 2000.)

results have been obtained (Myers & Davis, 2007). Subjects that undergo extinction treatment in the presence of a protein synthesis inhibitor later exhibit a robust CR, as if the extinction treatment had not occurred. Here too, if the drug is administered hours after the extinction treatment, it generally has little effect.

(continued)

BOX **9.1** (continued)

Photo by Quentin Huys, courtesy of J. E. LeDoux

J. E. LeDoux

Interestingly, the non-reinforced presentation of a previously trained CS does not always weaken the CR. This effect was nicely illustrated by a series of experiments performed by LeDoux and his colleagues (Nader, Schafe, & LeDoux, 2000). Using a Pavlovian paradigm, rats received a single presentation of a tone paired with a mild shock. The next day, subjects were given a single exposure to the tone (Figure 9.2). Re-exposure to the previously trained cue activates the memory for the earlier training episode, and during this reminder, the memory may be in an especially labile state (making it sensitive to disruption). Supporting this, presenting an amnesia-inducing event (e.g., an electroconvulsive shock) soon after the reminder treatment undermines retention of the previously learned response (Misani, Miller, & Lewis, 1968). These results suggest that once a memory has been retrieved,

it has to be *reconsolidated* for subsequent retention. If this reconsolidation process is disrupted, the earlier memory may be erased.

LeDoux and his colleagues hypothesized that the process of reconsolidation depends on protein synthesis. To explore this possibility, they microinjected anisomycin into the basolateral amygdala immediately after subjects received the reminder cue (Figure 9.2). Other rats received the drug vehicle after the reminder cue, or received these drug treatments alone (without the reminder cue). The rats were then tested with the CS the next day. Subjects that had not received the reminder treatment exhibited a robust CR, whether or not they got anisomycin. In contrast, rats that received anisomycin after the reminder treatment exhibited a profound amnesia. This was not due to the presentation of the CS alone (extinction), because rats that received the reminder followed by the vehicle exhibited a normal CR. These observations suggest that re-exposure to the CS had indeed placed the memory in a labile state and that, during this period, the maintenance of the memory required a second round of protein synthesis.

Further work showed that reconsolidation is disrupted when the drug is given soon after training, but not when it's given six hours

later (Nader et al., 2000). In addition, drug treatment appears to only impact long-term retention. Inhibiting protein synthesis after the reminder treatment has no effect when subjects are tested four hours later (short-term retention).

Work on reconsolidation has raised a host of questions that continue to drive empirical studies (see Myers, & Davis, 2007; Quirk & Mueller, 2008; Routtenberg, 2008; Rudy, 2008). One basic issue concerns the relation between extinction and reconsolidation. On the face of it, both involve a common manipulation: the nonreinforced presentation of a previously trained cue. Why then does inhibiting protein synthesis in one case (extinction) help preserve the CR while in the other (reconsolidation) it has an amnesic effect? One obvious difference concerns the number of stimulus presentations. Reminder treatments typically involve only a few CS presentations whereas extinction requires extensive exposure to the CS alone. Other hotly debated issues concern the locus of the protein synthesis. Though many scientists assumed that this occurs within the cell body, recent research suggests that the dendrites contain the biological machinery needed to locally synthesize proteins. (For additional discussion of reconsolidation, see Chapter 11.)

J. W. Grau

EXTINCTION AND ORIGINAL LEARNING

Although extinction produces important behavioral and emotional effects, it does not reverse the effects of acquisition. Evidence that extinction does not erase what was originally learned has been obtained through a variety of different procedures (see Bouton & Woods, 2008). I will describe four lines of evidence that have attracted the most attention: studies of spontaneous recovery, renewal, reinstatement, and reinforcer devaluation.

Spontaneous Recovery

Extinction typically produces a decline in conditioned behavior, but this effect dissipates with time. If a rest period is introduced after extinction training, responding is observed to recover. Because nothing specific is done during the rest period to produce the recovery, the effect is called *spontaneous recovery*. I previously described spontaneous recovery in Chapter 2 in connection with habituation. There, the term referred to recovery from the effects of habituation training. Procedurally, spontaneous recovery from extinction is similar in that it is also produced by the introduction of a period of rest.

Spontaneous recovery was originally identified by Pavlov. However, the phenomenon has since been observed by numerous other investigators. Rescorla (2004a) characterized spontaneous recovery as "one of the basic phenomena of Pavlovian conditioning" (p. 501). The effect is illustrated by one of Rescorla's experiments in which original acquisition was conducted with two different unconditioned stimuli (sucrose and a solid food pellet) delivered into cups recessed in one wall of the experimental chamber (Rescorla, 1997a). Infrared detectors identified each time the rat poked its head into the food cups. The experimental chamber was normally dark. One of the unconditioned stimuli was signaled by a noise CS and the other was signaled by a light CS. As conditioning progressed, each CS quickly came to elicit the goal tracking conditioned response, with the two CSs eliciting similar levels of responding. The left panel of Figure 9.3 shows the progress of acquisition, with data for the two CSs averaged together.

Two extinction sessions (of 16 trials each) were then conducted with each CS, followed by a series of four test trials. The experimental manipulation of primary interest was the interval between the end of extinction training and the test trials. For one of the conditioned stimuli (S1), an eight-day period separated extinction and testing. In contrast, for the other stimulus (S2) the test trials were started immediately after extinction training. The middle panel shows that during the course of extinction, responding declined in a similar fashion for S1 and S2. Responding remained suppressed during the test trials conducted immediately afterward with S2. However, responding substantially recovered for S1, which was tested eight days after extinction training.

The recovery of responding observed to S1 represents *spontaneous recovery*. Notice that the recovery was not complete. At the end of the acquisition phase, the rate of head pokes into the food cup had been 15.6 responses/minute. During the first trial after the rest period, the mean response rate to S1 was about 6.2 responses/minute.

Spontaneous recovery is also a prominent phenomenon following extinction of instrumental behavior. Here again, the critical factor is introducing a period of rest between the end of extinction training and assessments of responding. The typical finding is that behavior that has become suppressed by extinction recovers with a period of rest. (For recent studies of spontaneous recovery, see Prados, Manteiga, & Sansa, 2003; Rescorla, 2006b, 2007b.)

Renewal of Original Excitatory Conditioning

Another strong piece of evidence that extinction does not result in permanent loss of conditioned behavior is the phenomenon of **renewal**, identified by

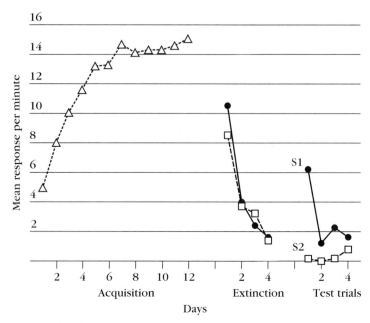

FIGURE **9.3**

Rate of rats poking their head into the food cup (goal tracking) for two different CSs. The left panel shows the original acquisition of responding to the two stimuli (averaged together) when each was paired with food. The middle panel shows loss of responding during the extinction phase. The final test trials were conducted right after extinction for S2 and eight days after extinction for S1. Note that the eight-day rest period resulted in a substantial recovery of the conditioned behavior. (From Rescorla, 2004a, p. 503.)

M. E. Bouton

Mark Bouton and his colleagues (see Bouton & Woods, 2008, for a recent review). Renewal refers to a recovery of acquisition performance when the contextual cues that were present during extinction are changed. The change can be a return to the context of original acquisition or a shift to a *neutral* context. Renewal has been of special interest for translational research because it suggests that clinical improvements that are achieved in the context of a therapist's office may not persist when the client returns home or goes to work of school.

The phenomenon of renewal was demonstrated in a classic study by Bouton and King (1983). The experiment employed the conditioned suppression procedure to study acquisition and extinction of conditioned fear in laboratory rats. To establish a baseline of activity that could be suppressed by fear, the rats were first conditioned to press a response lever for food reinforcement. Acquisition of fear was then accomplished by pairing a tone CS with foot shock. This fear conditioning occurred in one of two experimental chambers that provided distinctively different contextual cues. The context that was used for training was counterbalanced across subjects and designated as Context A. As expected, the tone-shock pairings resulted in a conditioned suppression of lever pressing during presentations of the tone. The subjects were then assigned to one of three groups for the extinction phase of the experiment.

Two of the groups received 20 extinction trials consisting of presentations of the tone CS without shock. For Group A these extinction trials occurred in the same context (A) as original fear conditioning. For Group B, extinction occurred in the alternate context (B). The third group (NE) did not receive extinction training and served as a control.

The results of the extinction trials are shown in the left side of Figure 9.4. Recall that in a conditioned suppression procedure, greater levels of conditioned fear are represented by smaller values of the suppression ratio (see Chapter 3). Groups A and B showed similarly strong levels of suppression to the tone at the start of the extinction trials. This shows that the fear that had been conditioned in Context A easily generalized when the tone was presented in Context B for Group B. As the tone was repeatedly presented during the extinction phase, conditioned suppression gradually dissipated, and did so in a similar fashion in the two contexts.

Following extinction in either Context A or B, all of the subjects received a series of test trials in Context A, where they had been trained originally. The results of these test trials are presented in the right panel of Figure 9.4.

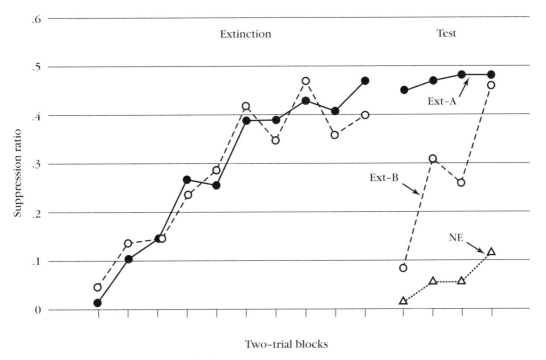

FIGURE 9.4

Demonstration of the renewal effect in conditioned suppression. All of the subjects first received pairings of a tone with foot shock in Context A (data not shown). Groups A and B then received extinction trials either in Context A or Context B. Group NE did not receive extinction. Test sessions were then conducted in Context A for all subjects. (From Bouton & King, 1983.)

Group NE, which did not receive extinction, showed the strongest degree of suppression to the tone during the test trials. In contrast, the least suppression was evident in Group A, which received extinction in the same context as the context of testing. Group B, which also received extinction (but in Context B), showed substantial levels of suppression when first returned to Context A. In fact, their conditioned fear during the first three test trials was substantially greater than what it had been at the end of the extinction phase. Thus, conditioned fear was *renewed* when Group B was removed from the extinction context (B) and returned to the context of original training (A).

The difference in the degree of conditioned fear in Groups A and B evident during the test sessions is significant because these two groups showed similar losses of conditioned fear during the extinction phase. The fact that conditioned fear was renewed in Group B indicates that the loss of suppression evident during the extinction phase for this group did not reflect the unlearning of the conditioned fear response.

Since its original demonstration, the renewal effect has been observed in a variety of learning situations with both human and nonhuman subjects (for recent examples, see Bailey & Westbrook, 2008; Pineño & Miller, 2004; Rescorla, 2007a). Interestingly, the phenomenon is evident not just with external contextual cues, but with contextual cues created by drug states (e.g., Bouton, Kenney, & Rosengard, 1990; Cunningham, 1979). Renewal can also occur if the subject is removed from the context of extinction to an alternate context, which is not the context of original acquisition (Bouton & Ricker, 1994). However, this type of renewal is not as robust as the renewal that occurs when the context of original acquisition is reinstated.

A simple and rather uninteresting explanation of the renewal effect is that it is due to excitatory properties conditioned to the renewal context. Because the US was presented in Context A during acquisition, Context A presumably acquired excitatory properties. These excitatory properties could summate with residual excitation remaining to the CS at the end of extinction training. The result would be greater responding to the CS in Context A than in Context B. A number of control experiments, however, have ruled out this kind of simple summation explanation of the renewal effect. In one study (Harris et al., 2000, Experiment 1), for example, original acquisition with two different conditioned stimuli was conducted in Context C. One CS was then extinguished in Context A and the other was extinguished in Context B. Subsequent tests revealed that responding to the CS extinguished in Context A was renewed if this CS was tested in Context B. This outcome cannot be attributed to possible excitatory properties of the Context B because the US was never presented in Context B (see also Bouton & Ricker, 1994).

The preponderance of evidence indicates that the renewal effect occurs because the memory of extinction is specific to the cues that were present during the extinction phase. Therefore, a shift away from the context of extinction disrupts retrieval of the memory of extinction, with the result that extinction performance is lost. But, why should this restore behavior characteristic of original acquisition? To account for that, one has to make the added assumption that original acquisition performance generalizes from one context to another more easily than extinction performance does. This is indeed the case. Consider, for example, the results summarized in Figure 9.4. Acquisition for all subjects occurred in Context A. One of the groups was then shifted to Context B for extinction. Figure 9.4 shows that these subjects performed the same way during the extinction phase as subjects that remained in context A during extinction. Thus, a shift in context did not disrupt the originally acquired conditioned suppression.

Why is it that original acquisition is less disrupted (if at all) by a change in context when extinction performance is highly context specific? Bouton (1993, 1994) has suggested that contextual cues serve to disambiguate the significance of a conditioned stimulus. This function is similar to the function of semantic context in disambiguating the meaning of a word. Consider the word *cut*. *Cut* could refer to the physical procedure of creating two pieces, as in "The chef cut the carrots." Alternatively, it could refer to dropping a player from a team, as in "Johnny was cut from the team after the first game." The meaning of the word *cut* depends on the semantic context. A CS that has undergone excitatory conditioning and then extinction also has an ambiguous meaning in that the CS could signify that shock is about to occur (acquisition) or that shock won't occur (extinction). This ambiguity allows the CS to come under contextual control more easily. After just acquisition training, the CS is not ambiguous because it only signifies one thing (shock will occur). Therefore, such a CS is not as susceptible to contextual control.

The renewal effect has important implications for behavior therapy, and unfortunately these implications are rather troubling. It suggests that even if a therapeutic procedure is effective in extinguishing a pathological fear or phobia in the relative safety of a therapist's office, the conditioned fear may easily return when the client encounters the fear CS in a different context. Equally problematic is the fact that the effects of excitatory conditioning readily generalize from one context to another (e.g., the left panel of Figure 9.4). Thus, if you acquire a pathological fear in one situation, the fear is likely to plague you in a variety of other contexts. But, if you overcome your fear, that benefit will not generalize as readily to new situations. Thus the problems created by conditioning will have much more widespread effects than the solutions or remedies for those problems. (For a review of renewal following exposure therapy for fear, see Vansteenwegen et al., 2006).

Troubled by the above dilemma, investigators have explored ways to reduce the renewal effect. One procedure that shows promise is to conduct extinction in a variety of different contexts. Extinction performance is less context specific if extinction training (or exposure therapy) is carried out in several different contexts (Chelonis, Calton, Hart, & Schachtman, 1999; Gunther, Denniston, & Miller, 1998; Vansteenwegen et al., 2007). Other techniques for reducing the renewal effect involve conditioned inhibition training, differential conditioning, and presenting the CS explicitly unpaired with the US (Rauhut, Thomas, & Ayres, 2001). (For further discussion of the implications of the renewal effect for behavior therapy, see Bouton & Nelson, 1998.)

Reinstatement of Conditioned Excitation

Another procedure that serves to restore responding to an extinguished conditioned stimulus is called **reinstatement**. Reinstatement refers to the recovery of conditioned behavior produced by exposures to the unconditioned stimulus. Consider, for example, learning an aversion to fish because you got sick after eating fish on a trip. Your aversion is then extinguished by nibbling on fish without getting sick on a number of occasions. In fact, you may learn to enjoy eating fish again because of this extinction experience. The phenomenon of reinstatement suggests that if you were to become sick again for some reason, your aversion to fish would return even if your illness had nothing to do with eating this particular food. (For an analogous study with laboratory rats, see Schachtman, Brown, & Miller, 1985.)

As with renewal, reinstatement is a challenging phenomenon for behavior therapy. Consider, for example, a client who suffers from anxiety and fear of intimacy acquired during the course of being raised by an abusive parent. Extensive therapy may be successful in providing relief from these symptoms. However, the phenomenon of reinstatement suggests that the fear and anxiety may return full blown if the client experiences an abusive encounter later in life. Because of reinstatement, responses that are successfully extinguished during the course of therapeutic intervention can reoccur if the individual is exposed to the unconditioned stimulus again.

Although reinstatement was originally discovered in studies with laboratory rats (Rescorla & Heth, 1975), the phenomenon has since been documented in human fear conditioning (Vansteenwegen et al., 2006). In one study, Yale undergraduates served as participants (LaBar & Phelps, 2005). The CS was a blue square presented on a computer screen for four seconds. On each acquisition trial, the CS ended with a one-second burst of very loud pulsating noise (the US). Conditioned fear was measured in terms of increased skin conductance (produced by mild sweating). Subjects received four acquisition trials followed by eight extinction trials. Four reinstatement noise bursts were then presented either in the same test room or in a different room. After this, all of the students were tested for fear of the CS in the original training context.

The results of the experiment are presented in Figure 9.5. Skin conductance increased during the course of fear conditioning and decreased during extinction. Subsequent US presentations in the same room resulted in recovery of the extinguished skin conductance response. US presentations in a different room did not produce this recovery. Thus, the reinstatement effect was context specific. (For reinstatement of human conditioned fear in fear-potentiated startle, see Norrholm et al., 2006.)

The context specificity of reinstatement raises the possibility that reinstatement is a result of context conditioning. The US presentations that occur during the reinstatement phase can result in conditioning of the contextual cues of the experimental situation. That context conditioning could then summate with any excitation remaining to the CS at the end of extinction to produce the reinstatement of conditioned responding. This may be why presentations of the US in a different context do not produce reinstatement.

A great deal of research has been done on the reinstatement effect in the past twenty years (see Bouton, 1993, 1994; Bouton & Nelson, 1998; Bouton & Wood, 2008). The results have indicated that context conditioning is important, but not because it permits summation of excitation. Rather, as was the case with renewal, the role of context is to disambiguate the significance of a stimulus that has a mixed history of conditioning and extinction. Context has relatively little effect on stimuli that do not have a history of extinction.

These conclusions are supported by the results of an early study by Bouton (1984). The experiment was conducted in the conditioned suppression

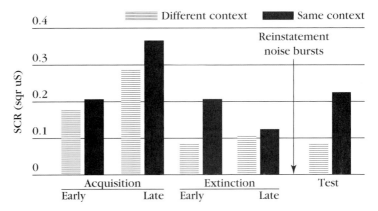

FIGURE **9.5**

Fear conditioning in human subjects as measured by increased skin conductance. All participants received acquisition followed by extinction, reinstatement USs, and tests of responding to the CS. The reinstatement USs were presented in either the same or a different context than the rest of the experiment. (Based on LaBar & Phelps, 2005.)

preparation with rats. The procedure is summarized in Table 9.1. For half the subjects, reinstatement was conducted after conditioning a CS with a weak shock that produced only moderate levels of conditioned fear. The remaining subjects were initially conditioned with a strong shock that produced more fear, but these subjects also received a phase of extinction so that they ended up with the same level of fear as the first set of rats. The reinstatement procedure was then conducted. Reinstatement consisted of four unsignaled shocks delivered either in the context of testing or in a different context. All of the subjects then received four test trials with the CS. The results of these tests are presented in Figure 9.6.

For subjects that were conditioned with the weak shock and did not receive extinction (left side of Figure 9.6), it did not make any difference whether the reinstatement shocks occurred in the test context (shock same) or elsewhere (shock different). This outcome shows that contextual conditioning did not summate with the suppression elicited by the target CS. In contrast, for subjects

TABLE **9.1**

Effects of Reinstatement After Acquisition Alone or After Both Acquisition and Extinction (Bouton, 1984)

Phase 1	Phase 2	Reinstatement	Test
CS → Weak Shock	No treatment	Shock Same	CS
CS → Weak Shock	No treatment	Shock Different	CS
CS → Strong Shock	Extinction	Shock Same	CS
CS → Strong Shock	Extinction	Shock Different	CS

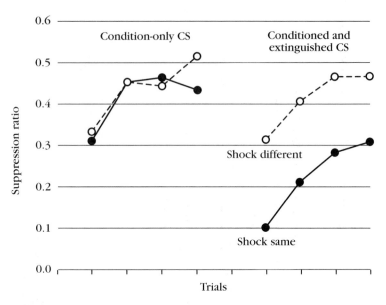

FIGURE **9.6**

Demonstration of reinstatement of conditioned suppression. Four reinstatement shocks were delivered either in the training and test context (shock same) or in a different context (shock different) after just excitatory conditioning (conditioned only CS) or after conditioning and extinction (conditioned and extinguished CS). (From Bouton, M. E. and Nelson, J. B. (1998). The role of context in classical conditioning: Some implications for behavior therapy. In William O'Donohue, ed., *Learning and Behavior Therapy*, pp. 59–84, Fig. 4–3; published by Allyn & Bacon, Boston, MA. © 1998 by Pearson Education. Reprinted by permission of the publisher.)

that received extinction (right side of Figure 9.6), reinstatement shocks given in the same context as testing produced significantly more response suppression than shocks given in a different context. This outcome shows that context conditioning facilitates the reinstatement effect.

Results such as those presented in Figure 9.6 have encouraged Bouton to think about reinstatement as a form of renewal. According to this interpretation, conditioned contextual cues provide some of the contextual cues for excitatory responding under ordinary circumstances. These contextual cues become extinguished when the CS is presented by itself during extinction. Reinstatement US presentations in the test context serve to restore the excitatory properties of the contextual cues and thereby enable those cues to be more effective in reactivating the memory of the original acquisition training.

Retention of Knowledge of the Reinforcer

As we have seen, extinction does not erase what was originally learned because conditioned behavior can be restored through spontaneous recovery, renewal, and reinstatement. The next question I turn to is how much of original learning is retained despite extinction? Is information about the specific nature of the reinforcer retained during the course of repeated extinction trials? How can we answer this question?

As I discussed in Chapters 4 and 7, a powerful technique for determining whether conditioned behavior reflects knowledge about the reinforcer is to test the effects of reinforcer devaluation. If conditioned behavior reflects an S-O or R-O association, devaluation of the reinforcer should produce a decrement in responding. We can determine whether extinction eliminates S-O and R-O associations by seeing if reinforcer devaluation also suppresses conditioned responding after extinction. But, there is a small technical problem. Following extinction, responding may be so close to zero that additional suppression caused by reinforcer devaluation cannot be detected. To get around this difficulty, investigators typically retrain the CS or response with a new reinforcer, just to create a response baseline high enough for the devaluation test.

A variety of experiments have been conducted based on the above rationale. These experiments have shown that S-O associations are not lost during Pavlovian extinction (Delamater, 1996; Rescorla, 1996a, 2001a). Thus, an extinguished CS continues to activate a representation of the US. Information about the reinforcer is also not lost during the course of extinction of an instrumental response. Rescorla (1993a), for example, has commented that "R-O associations, once trained, are relatively impervious to modification" (p. 244). (For related studies, see Rescorla, 1992, 1993b, 1996b; 2001a.)

Another line of evidence that also indicates that knowledge of the reinforcer is not lost during the course of extinction comes from tests of the specificity of reinstatement. The design of a recent study employing this strategy is presented in Table 9.2 (Ostlund & Balleine, 2007). Rats were trained in an experimental chamber that had two response levers. Pressing one of the levers produced a pellet of food; pressing the other lever produced a few drops of a sugar solution. The two responses were trained in separate 30-minute sessions each day, with each response reinforced according to a VR 20 schedule of reinforcement with its assigned reinforcer. During the next session, extinction was in effect for both responses for 15 minutes. Responding on both levers declined rapidly during this extinction phase. One of the reinforcers (either a food pellet or sugar water) was then presented once and responding was monitored for the next three minutes.

The results of the experiment are summarized in Figure 9.7. Presentation of a reinforcer after extinction produced a selective recovery of lever pressing. Much more responding occurred on the lever whose associated reinforcer had been used for the reinstatement procedure. The food pellet selectively increased responding on the lever that previously produced food and the sugar water selectively increased responding on the lever that previously produced a few drops of sugar water. These results indicate that the extinction procedure did not erase knowledge of which reinforcer had been used with which response during original training.

TABLE **9.2**
Selective Reinstatement of Instrumental Behavior

Training	Extinction	Reinstatement	Test
R1 → O1	R1	O1	R1
and	and	or	vs.
R2 → O2	R2	O2	R2

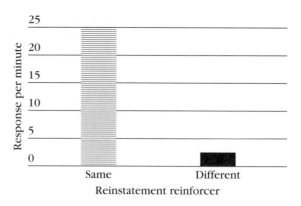

FIGURE **9.7**

Reinstatement of lever pressing depending on whether the reinstatment reinforcer was the same or different from the reinforcer originally used to train the response. (Based on Ostlund & Balleine, 2007.)

ENHANCING EXTINCTION

The mounting evidence that extinction does not erase much of what was originally learned is bad news for various forms of exposure therapy whose goal is to eliminate pathological fear, phobias, and bad habits. Can the impact of extinction be increased so as to make such procedures more effective? This question is increasingly commanding the attention of scientists doing translational research in this area. The focus on this question is one of the major new areas of research in learning theory. We don't have many answers yet and some of the new findings have been inconsistent. But, there are some clues that suggest ways exposure therapy may be enhanced.

Number and Spacing of Extinction Trials

Perhaps the simplest way to increase the impact of extinction is to conduct more extinction trials. The use of larger numbers of extinction trials produces a more profound decrease in conditioned responding. This outcome has been found in a variety of learning situations including eyeblink conditioning, taste-aversion learning, and context conditioning (e.g., Brooks, Bowker, Anderson, & Palmatier, 2003; Leung et al., 2007; Weidemann & Kehoe, 2003).

Another way to increase the effects of extinction is to conduct extinction trials spaced close together in time (massed) rather than spread out (massed). Using a fear conditioning procedure with mice, for example, Cain, Blouin and Barad (2003) found greater loss of fear with massed extinction trials than with spaced trials, and this difference persisted when the subjects were tested the next day. Unfortunately, it is not clear at this point whether similar effects occur in appetitive conditioning (Moody, Sunsay, & Bouton, 2006). What seems clear is that massed extinction trials produce a more rapid decrement in responding within a session. However, sometimes this is just a temporary performance effect, with responding substantially recovering between sessions.

Reducing Spontaneous Recovery

Another approach to increasing the impact of extinction procedures is to find ways to reduce spontaneous recovery. Several investigators have explored that possibility. Studies of spontaneous recovery introduce a period of rest after extinction and then test for recovery. One way to substantially reduce spontaneous recovery is to repeat periods of rest and testing. Less and less recovery occurs with successive cycles of rest and testing (Rescorla, 2004a). Another factor that influences the degree of spontaneous recovery is the interval between initial training and extinction. However, the effects of this manipulation have been inconsistent across experiments. Myers, Ressler, and Davis (2006) reported that fear extinction conducted 24–72 hours after fear acquisition showed the usual spontaneous recovery, renewal, and reinstatement effects. However, if extinction was conducted 10–60 minutes after fear acquisition, these recovery effects were not observed. Thus, the effects of extinction in fear conditioning were more permanent if extinction was conducted right after acquisition.

A contrasting pattern of results was obtained by Rescorla (2004b) in extinction of appetitive conditioning. In those experiments, increasing the interval between training and extinction reduced the degree of spontaneous recovery that occurred. There are numerous procedural differences between the experiments by Myers et al. (2006) and those by Rescorla (2004b). In addition to using different motivational systems (fear conditioning vs. appetitive conditioning), the two studies employed different experimental designs. Myers et al. used a between-subjects design whereas Rescorla used a within-subjects design. It will be interesting to see which of these variables turns out to be responsible for the contrasting findings that were obtained.

Yet another way to reduce spontaneous recovery is to introduce cues associated with extinction. Just as returning a subject to the context of acquisition causes renewal of conditioned responding, introducing stimuli that were present during extinction can reactivate extinction performance. Investigators have found that introducing cues that were present during extinction training can attenuate spontaneous recovery and enhance extinction performance in taste aversion learning (Brooks, Palmatier, Garcia, & Johnson, 1999) as well as in appetitive conditioning preparations (Brooks, 2000; Brooks & Bouton, 1993).

Reducing Renewal

Another strategy for increasing the impact of extinction training is to reduce the renewal effect. As you may recall, renewal refers to recovery of the extinguished response when subjects are moved out of the extinguished context (either to a new context or back to the context of acquisition). This problematic recovery of the extinguished response can be attenuated by conducting extinction in several different contexts (Chelonis et al., 1999; Gunther, Denniston, & Miller, 1998; Vansteenwegen et al., 2007). Evidently, conducting extinction in several different contexts helps to increase stimulus generalization of extinction performance, so as to reduce renewal when subjects are shifted out of the extinction context. However, this outcome is not always observed. Therefore, this is another area that will require additional research to sort out (Bouton et al., 2006).

Another strategy is to present reminder cues of extinction in the renewal context. As I described earlier, the introduction of extinction cues can reduce spontaneous recovery (see above). Extinction cues may similarly reduce the renewal effect by reactivating extinction performance in the renewal context. This prediction has been confirmed in studies of appetitive conditioning with rats (Brooks & Bouton, 1994). Encouraging results were also found in a study of exposure therapy with people who were afraid of spiders (Mystkowski, Craske, Echiverri, & Labus, 2006). Participants who were instructed to mentally recall the treatment context showed less fear of spiders in a novel situation than participants who did not engage in the reminder exercise. This tactic can be applied more broadly to increase generalization of treatment outcomes by encouraging clients to carry a card, repeat a short phrase, or call a help line whenever they are concerned about relapsing, to remind them of the therapeutic context.

Compounding Extinction Stimuli

Yet another interesting approach to enhancing extinction involves presenting two stimuli at the same time that are both undergoing extinction. In fact, recent research has shown that presenting two extinguished stimuli at the same time can deepen the extinction of those cues (Rescorla, 2006a; Thomas & Ayres, 2004). Consider, for example, the experiment outlined in Table 9.3. The table outlines an instrumental conditioning experiment (Rescorla, 2006a, Experiment 3) in which rats were first conditioned to press a response lever during each of three different discriminative stimuli, a light (L) and a noise and a tone stimulus (X and Y). During initial acquisition training lever pressing during these stimuli was reinforced on a VI 30-second schedule with food. Lever pressing was not reinforced when these stimuli were absent (between trials).

Following acquisition, the light, tone, and noise stimuli were each presented repeatedly by themselves with lever presses no longer reinforced. Responding during each of these cues declined to close to zero. However, some sub-threshold tendency to respond may have remained. Compound extinction trials were introduced to evaluate that possibility. During this second extinction phase, the light was presented simultaneously with one of the auditory cues (X). The other auditory cue, Y, continued to be presented alone without reinforcement, as a control. The effects of compound extinction were evaluated at the end of the experiment by testing responding during X and Y, each presented by itself.

Figure 9.8 shows rates of responding at the end of the first phase of extinction, the compound extinction trials, and during the final test trials.

TABLE **9.3**
Test of Compounding Extinction Stimuli

Acquisition	Element extinction	Compound extinction	Test
L+	L−	LX−	X
and	and	and	and
X+	X−	Y−	Y
and	and		
Y+	Y−		

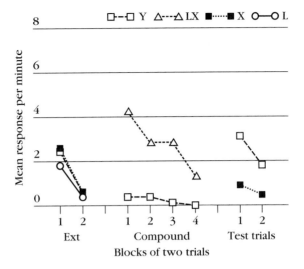

FIGURE **9.8**

Discriminative lever pressing in the presence of a light (L) and two auditory cues (a tone and a noise stimulus counterbalanced as X and Y) at the end of a series of extinction trials with each stimulus presented by itself, during a compound extinction phase in which L was presented simultaneously with X, and during a test phase conducted six days later. (Based on Rescorla, 2006a, Figure 3, page 139.)

Responding was close to zero by the end of the first extinction phase. However, presenting L in compound with X (LX) during the next extinction phase resulted in a substantial elevation of responding. This represents summation of subthreshold responding that remained to the L and X stimuli despite their individual extinction treatments (Reberg, 1972). No such elevation was evident with control stimulus Y, which was presented by itself during the compound extinction phase.

The data of greatest interest were obtained during the final tests with X and Y. This final test was conducted six days after the end of the compound extinction phase. The six-day rest period caused substantial spontaneous recovery of responding to Y. However, no such recovery occurred to stimulus X. This outcome shows that the compound extinction trials deepened the extinction of stimulus X. Other experiments have shown that this deepening of extinction also reduces the reinstatement effect and slows the rate of reacquisition of an extinguished stimulus (Rescorla, 2006a; see also Thomas & Ayres, 2004).

The fact that compounding two extinction cues deepens the extinction of the individual stimuli suggests that extinction operates at least in part by an error-correction process like the Rescorla-Wagner model. As I described in Chapter 4, according to the Rescorla-Wagner model, associative values are adjusted if the outcome of a trial is contrary to what is expected. Original acquisition creates an expectation that the US will occur. This expectation is violated when the US is omitted in extinction, and that *error* is corrected by reduced responding on subsequent extinction trials. Compounding two conditioned stimuli increases the resulting *error* when the trial ends without a reinforcer. This induces a larger correction and greater reduction of responding.

The above reasoning predicts an entirely different outcome if an extinction cue is compounded with a conditioned inhibitor during extinction training. In that case, there should be an interference rather than a facilitation of the extinction process. Recall that a conditioned inhibitor is a signal for the absence of a US. In the fear system, a conditioned inhibitor is a safety signal indicating that the aversive US will not occur. If such a safety signal is compounded with a fear stimulus during extinction, the absence of the US will be fully predicted by the safety signal. Therefore, there won't be any error to encourage learning that the fear stimulus no longer ends in shock. Thus, the safety signal will block extinction of the fear stimulus. This prediction has been confirmed in laboratory studies with rats and pigeons (Thomas & Ayres, 2004; Rescorla, 2003) as well as in human clinical research (e.g., Schmidt et al., 2006).

WHAT IS LEARNED IN EXTINCTION?

Studies of spontaneous recovery, renewal, reinstatement, and knowledge of the reinforcer after extinction all indicate that extinction does not involve *un-learning* and leaves response-outcome (R-O) and stimulus-outcome (S-O) associations pretty much intact. In Chapter 4, I reviewed evidence indicating that S-O associations (or CS-US associations) have a major role in Pavlovian conditioning. In Chapter 7, I discussed the importance of S-O and R-O associations in instrumental conditioning. The importance of S-O and R-O associations for conditioned responding and their survival through a series of extinction trials creates a dilemma for theories of extinction. If these associations remain intact, what produces the response decrement? This question remains the topic of continuing debate and empirical study (Bouton & Woods, 2008; Delamater, 2004). A fully satisfactory answer is not available yet, but investigators are considering the importance of inhibitory S-R associations motivated by the unexpected absence of the reinforcer in extinction.

Inhibitory S-R Associations

An associative analysis has relatively few candidates. Learning could involve S-O, R-O or S-R associations. Since extinction seems to leave S-O and R-O associations intact, investigators have turned to changes in S-R mechanisms to explain extinction performance. They have come to the conclusion that nonreinforcement produces an inhibitory S-R association. That is, nonreinforcement of a response in the presence of a specific stimulus produces an inhibitory S-R association that serves to suppress that response whenever S is present. Consistent with the renewal effect, this hypothesis predicts that the effects of extinction will be highly specific to the context in which the response was extinguished.

Why should nonreinforcement produce an inhibitory S-R association? In answering this question, it is important to keep in mind that extinction involves a special type of nonreinforcement. It involves nonreinforcement after a history of conditioning with repeated presentations of the reinforcer. Nonreinforcement without such a prior history is not extinction, but more akin to habituation. This is an important distinction because the effects of nonreinforcement depend critically on the subject's prior history. If your partner

TABLE **9.4**

Development of an Inhibitory S-R Association in Instrumental Extinction
(Rescorla 1993a, Experiment 3)

Phase 1	Phase 2	Extinction	Test
N: Rc → P	R1 → P	N: R1–	N: R1 vs. R2
L: Rc → P	R2 → P	L: R2–	L: R1 vs. R2

N and L were noise and light discriminative stimuli. Rc was a common response (nose poking) for all subjects, P represents the food pellet reinforcer, R1 and R2 were lever press and chain pull, counterbalanced across subjects.

never made you coffee in the morning, you would not be disappointed if the coffee is not ready when you got up. If you never received an allowance, you would not be disappointed when you didn't get one. It is only the omission of an expected reward that creates disappointment or frustration. These emotional effects are presumed to play a critical role in the behavioral decline that occurs during extinction.

As I mentioned at the outset of the chapter, extinction involves both behavioral and emotional effects. The emotional effects stem from the frustration that is triggered when an expected reinforcer is not forthcoming. Nonreinforcement in the face of the expectation of reward is assumed to trigger an unconditioned aversive frustrative reaction (Amsel, 1958; Papini, 2003). This aversive emotion serves to discourage responding during the course of extinction through the establishment of an inhibitory S-R association (Rescorla, 2001a).

The establishment of an inhibitory S-R association during the course of extinction is illustrated by an experiment whose procedures are outlined in Table 9.4. Laboratory rats first received discrimination training in which a common response (poking the nose into a hole) was reinforced with food pellets whenever a light or noise stimulus (L or N) was present. This training was conducted so that nonreinforcement in the presence of L or N would elicit frustration when extinction was introduced. The targets of extinction were a lever press and a chain pull response (designated as R1 and R2, counterbalanced across subjects). R1 and R2 were first reinforced, again with food pellets. Notice that the reinforcement of R1 and R2 did not occur in the presence of the light and noise stimuli. Therefore, this reinforcement training was not expected to establish any S-R associations involving the light and noise stimuli.

Extinction was conducted in the third phase and consisted of presentations of L and N (to create the expectancy of reward) with either R1 or R2 available but nonreinforced. The extinction phase presumably established inhibitory S-R associations involving L-R1 and N-R2. The presence of these associations was tested by giving subjects a choice of R1 and R2 in the presence of the L and N stimuli. If an inhibitory L-R1 association was established during extinction, the subjects were predicted to make fewer R1 than R2 responses when tested with L. In a corresponding fashion, they were expected to make fewer R2 than R1 responses when tested with N. Notice that this differential response outcome cannot be explained in terms of changes in R-O or S-O associations because such changes should have influenced R1 and R2 equally.

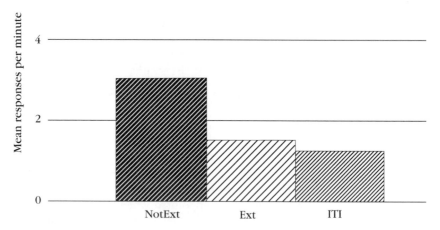

FIGURE **9.9**

Demonstration that extinction involves the acquisition of an inhibitory S-R association that is specific to the stimulus in the presence of which the response is nonreinforced (see procedure summarized in Table 9.4). A particular response occurred less often during the stimulus with which the response had been extinguished (Ext) than during an alternative stimulus (NotExt). (From "Inhibitory Associations between S and R in Extinction," by R. A. Rescorla, *Animal Learning & Behavior,* Vol. 21, Figure 7, p. 333. Copyright 1993 Psychonomic Society, Inc. Reprinted by permission.)

The results of the experiment are presented in Figure 9.9. Responding is shown for the intertrial interval (ITI) and in the presence of the stimulus (L or N) with which the response had been extinguished or not. Responding during the stimulus with which the response had been extinguished was significantly less than responding during the alternate stimulus. Furthermore, the extinction stimulus produced responding not significantly higher than what occurred during the intertrial interval. These results indicate that the extinction procedure produced an inhibitory S-R association that was specific to a particular stimulus and response. (For related studies, see Rescorla, 1997.)

Paradoxical Reward Effects

If the decline in responding in extinction is due to the frustrative effects of an unexpected absence of reinforcement, then one would expect more rapid extinction following training that establishes greater expectations of reward. This is indeed the case and has led to a number of paradoxical effects. For example, the more training that is provided with reinforcement, the stronger will be the expectancy of reward, and therefore the stronger will be the frustration that occurs when extinction is introduced. That in turn should produce more rapid extinction. This prediction has been confirmed and is called the **overtraining extinction effect** (Ishida & Papini, 1997; Senkowski, 1978; Theios & Brelsford, 1964).

The overtraining extinction effect is paradoxical because it represents fewer responses in extinction after more extensive reinforcement training. Casually thinking, one might believe that more extensive training should create a stronger response that would be more resistant to extinction. But, in fact, the opposite is the case, especially when training involves continuous rather than intermittent reinforcement.

Another paradoxical reward effect that reflects similar mechanisms is the **magnitude reinforcement extinction effect.** This phenomenon refers to the fact that responding declines more rapidly in extinction following reinforcement with a larger reinforcer (Hulse, 1958; Wagner, 1961) and is also readily accounted for in terms of the frustrative effects of nonreward. Nonreinforcement is apt to be more frustrating if the individual has come to expect a large reward than if the individual expects a small reward. Consider the following scenarios. In one you receive $100/month from your parents to help with incidental expenses at college. In the other, you get only $20/month. In both cases your parents stop the payments when you drop out of school for a semester. This nonreinforcement will be more aversive if you had come to expect the larger monthly allowance.

The most extensively investigated paradoxical reward effect is the **partial reinforcement extinction effect.** A key factor that determines the magnitude of both the behavioral and emotional effects of an extinction procedure is the schedule of reinforcement that is in effect before the extinction procedure is introduced. Various subtle features of reinforcement schedules can influence the rate extinction. However, the most important variable is whether the instrumental response was reinforced every time it occurred (**continuous reinforcement**) or only some of the times it occurred (*intermittent,* or *partial, reinforcement*). Extinction is much slower and involves fewer frustration reactions if partial reinforcement rather than continuous reinforcement was in effect before the introduction extinction. This phenomenon is called the *partial reinforcement extinction effect (PREE).*

Courtesy of A. Amsel

A. Amsel

In one interesting study, the emergence of the PREE during the course of postnatal development was examined with infant rats serving as subjects (Chen & Amsel, 1980). The rat pups were permitted to run or crawl down an alley for a chance to suckle and obtain milk as the reinforcer. Some pups were reinforced each time (continuous reinforcement), whereas others were reinforced only some of the time (partial reinforcement). Following training, all of the pups were tested under conditions of extinction. The experiment was repeated with rat pups of two different ages. In one replication, the experiment began when the pups were 10 days of age. In another, the experiment began when the subjects were 12 days old, just two days later. The results are presented in Figure 9.10.

All of the pups acquired the runway response. As might be expected, the 12-day-old pups ran faster than the 10-day-old pups, but the 10-day-old pups also increased their running speeds with training. This increase was due to instrumental reinforcement rather than to getting older, because when extinction was introduced, all of the subjects slowed down. However, a difference in extinction between continuous reinforcement and partial reinforcement only developed for the pups that began the experiment at 12 days of age. Thus, the PREE was evident in 12-day-old rat pups, but not in 10-day old pups. On the basis of a variety of different lines of evidence, Amsel (1992)

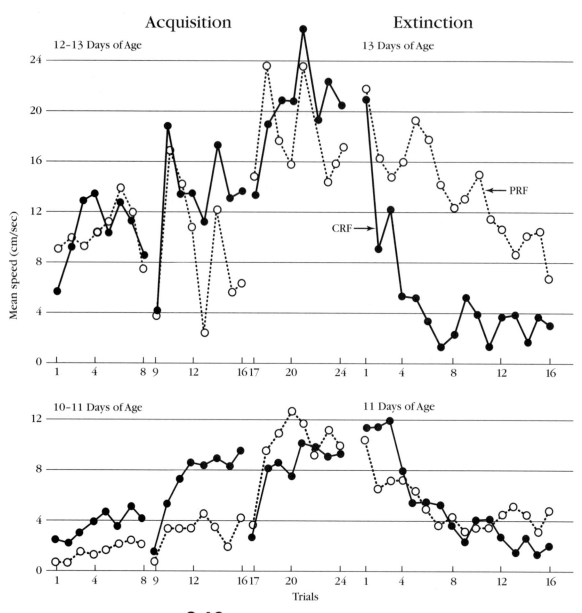

FIGURE **9.10**

Emergence of the partial reinforcement extinction effect between the 10th and 12th day of life in infant rat pups. During acquisition, the pups were reinforced with a chance to suckle milk after running down an alley on either a continuous or a partial reinforcement schedule. Extinction was introduced after three sessions of reinforcement training. (From "Learned Persistence at 11–12 Days but not at 10–11 Days in Infant Rats," by J. S Chen & A. Amsel, in *Developmental Psychobiology, Vol. 13*, Figure 1, p. 484. © 1980 John Wiley & Sons, Inc. Reprinted by permission of John Wiley & Sons, Inc.)

concluded that this developmental difference in the emergence of the PREE is related to the rapid maturation of the hippocampus during this stage of life in rat pups.

The persistence in responding that is created by **intermittent reinforcement** can be remarkable. Habitual gamblers are at the mercy of intermittent reinforcement. Occasional winnings encourage them to continue gambling during long strings of losses. Intermittent reinforcement can also have undesirable consequences in parenting. Consider, for example, a child riding in a grocery cart while the parent is shopping. The child asks the parent to buy a piece of candy for him. The parent says no. The child asks over and over, and then begins to throw a temper tantrum because the parent continues to say no. At this point, the parent is likely to give in to avoid public embarrassment. By finally getting the candy, the parent will have provided intermittent reinforcement for the repeated demands. The parent will also have reinforced the tantrum behavior. The intermittent reinforcement of the requests for candy will make the child very persistent (and obnoxious) in asking for candy during future shopping trips.

Although most studies of the partial reinforcement extinction effect have employed instrumental conditioning procedures, the PREE has been also demonstrated in Pavlovian conditioning (for recent examples, see Haselgrove, Aydin, & Pearce, 2004; Rescorla, 1999c). In early studies, the PREE was found only in studies that compared the effects of continuous and partial reinforcement training in different groups of subjects. However, later studies have demonstrated that the PREE can also occur in the same subjects if they experience continuous reinforcement in the presence of one set of cues and intermittent reinforcement in the presence of other stimuli (e.g., Nevin & Grace, 2005; Rescorla, 1999c; Svartdal, 2000).

Mechanisms of the Partial-Reinforcement Extinction Effect

Perhaps the most obvious explanation of the PREE is that the introduction of extinction is easier to detect after continuous reinforcement than after partial reinforcement. If you don't get reinforced after each response during training, you may not immediately notice when reinforcers are omitted altogether in extinction. The absence of reinforcement is presumably much easier to detect after continuous reinforcement. This explanation of the partial-reinforcement extinction effect is called the **discrimination hypothesis.**

Although the discrimination hypothesis is plausible, the partial reinforcement extinction effect is not so simple. In an ingenious test of the hypothesis, Jenkins (1962) and Theios (1962) first trained one group of animals with partial reinforcement and another with continuous reinforcement. Both groups then received a phase of continuous reinforcement before extinction was introduced. Because the extinction procedure was introduced immediately after continuous reinforcement training for both groups, extinction should have been equally noticeable or discriminable for both. Nevertheless, Jenkins and Theios found that the subjects that initially received partial reinforcement training responded more in extinction. These results indicate that the response persistence produced by partial reinforcement does not come from greater difficulty in detecting the start of extinction. Rather, subjects learn something long lasting from partial reinforcement that is carried over even if they subsequently receive continuous reinforcement. Partial reinforcement seems to teach subjects to not give up in the face of failure, and this learned persistence is retained even if subjects experience an unbroken string of successes.

What do subjects learn during partial reinforcement that makes them more persistent in the face of a run of bad luck or failure? Hundreds of experiments have been performed in attempts to answer this question. These studies indicate that partial reinforcement promotes persistence in two different ways. One explanation, **frustration theory**, is based on what subjects learn about the emotional effects of nonreward during partial reinforcement training. The other explanation, **sequential theory**, is based on what subjects learn about the memory of nonreward.

Frustration Theory

Frustration theory was developed by Abram Amsel (e.g., 1958, 1962, 1967, 1992; see also Papini, 2003). According to frustration theory, persistence in extinction results from learning something paradoxical, namely to continue responding when you expect to be nonreinforced or frustrated. This learning occurs in stages. Intermittent reinforcement involves both rewarded and nonrewarded trials. Rewarded trials lead individuals to expect reinforcement and nonrewarded trials lead them to expect the absence of reward. Consequently, intermittent reinforcement initially leads to the learning of two competing expectations. These two competing expectations lead to conflicting behaviors: the expectation of reward encourages subjects to respond, and the anticipation of nonreinforcement discourages responding. However, as training continues, this conflict is resolved in favor of responding.

The resolution of the conflict occurs because reinforcement is not predictable in the typical partial reinforcement schedule. Therefore, the instrumental response ends up being reinforced some of the times when the subject expects nonreward. Because of such experiences, the instrumental response becomes conditioned to the expectation of nonreward. According to frustration theory, this is the key to persistent responding in extinction. With sufficient training, *intermittent reinforcement results in learning to make the instrumental response when the subject expects nonreward*. Once the response has become conditioned to the expectation of nonreward, responding persists when extinction is introduced. By contrast, there is nothing about the experience of continuous reinforcement that encourages subjects to respond when they expect nonreward. Therefore, continuous reinforcement does not produce persistence in extinction.

Sequential Theory

The major alternative to frustration theory, sequential theory, was proposed by Capaldi (e.g., 1967, 1971) and is stated in terms memory concepts. It assumes that subjects can remember whether or not they were reinforced for performing the instrumental response in the recent past. They remember both recent rewarded and nonrewarded trials. The theory assumes further that during intermittent reinforcement training, the memory of nonreward becomes a cue for performing the instrumental response. Precisely how this happens depends on the sequence of rewarded (R) and nonrewarded (N) trials that are administered. That is why the theory is labeled *sequential*.

Courtesy of E. J. Capaldi

E. J. Capaldi

Consider the following sequence of trials: RNN<u>R</u>RN<u>R</u>. In this sequence the subject is rewarded on the first trial, not rewarded on the next two trials, then rewarded twice, then not rewarded, and then rewarded again. The fourth and last trials are critical in this schedule and are therefore underlined. On the fourth trial, the subject is reinforced after receiving nonreward on the preceding two trials. Because of this, the memory of two nonrewarded trials becomes a cue for responding. Responding in the face of the memory of non-reward is again reinforced on the last trial. Here, the animal is reinforced for responding during the memory of one nonreinforced trials. With enough experiences of this type, the subject learns to respond whenever it remembers not having been reinforced on the preceding trials. This learning creates persistence of the instrumental response in extinction. (For studies of this mechanism, see Capaldi, Alptekin, & Birmingham, 1996; Capaldi, Alptekin, Miller, & Barry, 1992; Haggbloom et al., 1990.)

Some have regarded frustration theory and sequential theory as competing explanations of the partial-reinforcement extinction effect. However, since the two mechanisms were originally proposed, a large and impressive body of evidence has been obtained in support of each theory. Therefore, it is unlikely that one theory is correct and the other is wrong. A better way to think about them is that the two theories point out different ways in which partial reinforcement can promote responding during extinction. Memory mechanisms may make more of a contribution when training trials are scheduled close together and it is easier to remember what happened on the preceding trial. In contrast, the emotional learning described by frustration theory is less sensitive to intertrial intervals and thus provides a better explanation of the PREE when widely spaced training trials are used.

All of the studies I have described in this section have involved appetitive conditioning because most of the experiments focusing on emotional effects of extinction and the learning of inhibitory S-R associations have been conducted in appetitive conditioning situations. However, one can construct analogous arguments and mechanisms for extinction in aversive situations. There, the unexpected omission of the aversive reinforcer should result in relief, and learning supported by such relief should lead to the inhibition of fear. Application of these ideas to aversive situations is a wide open area for investigation.

RESISTANCE TO CHANGE AND BEHAVIORAL MOMENTUM

Another way to think about response persistence in extinction is that it represents resistance to the change in reinforcement contingencies that occurs when the extinction procedure is introduced (Nevin & Grace, 2005). Nevin and Grace have thought about resistance to change more broadly and have proposed the concept of **behavioral momentum** to characterize the susceptibility of behavior to disruptions (Grace & Nevin, 2004; Nevin, 1992; Nevin & Grace, 2000). The term *behavioral momentum* is based on an analogy to physical momentum in Newtonian physics. The momentum of a physical object is the product of its weight (or mass) and its speed. A fast moving bullet and a slow moving freight train both have a great deal of momentum. The bullet is light but moves very fast. A freight train moves much slower but is much heavier. In both cases the product of weight × speed is large, indicating great momentum. Their great momentum makes both the bullet and the train hard to stop and resistant to change. By analogy (fleshed out by mathematical equations), the behavioral momentum hypothesis states that behavior that has a great deal of momentum will also be hard to "stop" or disrupt by various manipulations.

Research on behavioral momentum has been conducted using multiple schedules of reinforcement. As was described in Chapter 8, a multiple schedule has two or more components. Each component is identified by a distinctive stimulus and its accompanying schedule of reinforcement. Multiple schedules are popular in studies of behavioral momentum because they enable investigators to compare the susceptibility of behavior to disruption under two different conditions in the same session and the same subject. One may be interested, for example, in whether adding free reinforcers to a schedule of reinforcement makes behavior more resistant to change. The question can be answered by using a multiple schedule in which each component has the same VI schedule but one of the components also includes extra reinforcers that are delivered independent of responding (Podlesnik & Shahan, 2008).

A number of different sources of disruption have been examined in studies of behavioral momentum. These have included providing extra food before the experimental session, providing extra food during intervals between components of the multiple schedule, and terminating reinforcement (extinction). Most of the experiments have been conducted with pigeons and rats (e.g., Bell, Gomez, & Kessler, 2008; Odum, Shahan, & Nevin, 2005). However, there is increasing interest in exploring the implications of behavioral momentum in applied behavior analysis, because most applications of behavioral principles involve efforts to change behavior in some manner. (For an analysis of women's basketball games in terms of behavioral momentum, see Roane, Kelley, Trosclair, & Hauer, 2004.)

Studies of behavioral momentum have encouraged two major conclusions. The first is that *behavioral momentum is directly related to the rate of reinforcement* (see Nevin & Grace, 2000). A higher the rate of reinforcement produces behavior that has greater momentum and is less susceptible to disruption. Another common (but not universal) finding is that behavioral momentum is unrelated to response rate. Thus, two behaviors that occur at similar rates do not necessarily have similar degrees behavioral momentum (e.g., Nevin, Mandell, & Atak, 1983). The emphasis has been on reinforcement rate rather than response rate as the primary determinant of behavioral momentum (Nevin & Grace, 2000). This conclusion is further confirmed by studies that show that schedules that provide similar rates of reinforcement but different rates of responding produce similar momentum and resistance to change (e.g., Fath, Fields, Malott, & Grossett, 1983).

The primacy of reinforcement rate rather than response rate as the determinant of behavioral momentum has encouraged Nevin and Grace (2000) to attribute behavioral momentum primarily to Pavlovian conditioning or S-O associations (e.g., McLean, Campbell-Tie, & Nevin, 1996). An interesting corollary to this conclusion is that behavioral momentum should be increased by adding reinforcers to a component of a multiple schedule even if those reinforcers are not contingent on responding. This prediction was confirmed in a study with pigeons that I alluded to earlier (Podlesnik & Shahan, 2008) as well as in studies with children with developmental disabilities (Ahearn et al., 2003).

The effects of reinforcer rate on behavioral momentum are illustrated by a study conducted with 10 students with developmental disabilities who were between 7 and 19 years old (Dube, McIlvane, Mazzitelli, & McNamara, 2003). A variation of a video game was used that involved catching a moving icon or sprite by touching the screen with a finger or clicking on the sprite with a joy stick. Two different sprites (1 and 2) were used during baseline training, each presented on separate trials. Thus, each sprite represented a component of a multiple schedule. Correct responses were reinforced with tokens, points, or money for different participants. In the presence of each sprite, a variable interval 12-second schedule of reinforcement was in effect. To increase the rate of reinforcement in one of the components of the multiple schedule, free reinforcers were added to the VI 12-second schedule at variable times averaging six seconds (VT 6 sec). No responses were required to obtain the extra reinforcers. Thus, one sprite was associated with a higher rate of reinforcement (VI 12 sec + VT 6 sec) than the other sprite (VI 12 sec). Responding was also trained up in the presence of a third sprite, reinforced on a VI eight-second schedule. The third sprite was used at the end of the experiment to test for resistance to change.

After responding was well established to all of the sprites, tests of behavioral momentum were conducted. During each of these tests, Sprite 1 or Sprite 2 was presented by itself as usual. However, during the tests the third sprite also appeared as a distracter. The question was how much of a disruption this would cause in responding to sprites 1 and 2, and whether the degree of disruption would be different depending on the rate of reinforcement that was associated with each of the first two sprites.

The results of the experiment are summarized separately for each participant in Figure 9.11. The data are presented as proportion of responding that occurred during the momentum test (when Sprite 3 appeared as a distracter) as a proportion of baseline responding (when sprites 1 and 2 appeared alone). A score of 1.0 indicates no disruption by Sprite 3. Some disruption occurred

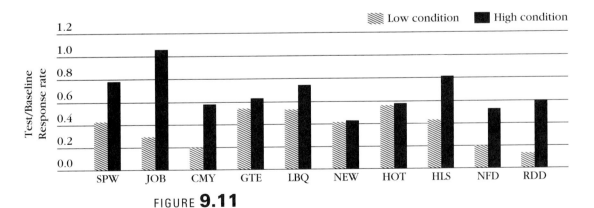

FIGURE **9.11**

Relative rate of responding during two components of a multiple schedule that involved either a low or high rate of reinforcement during a test for behavioral momentum for 10 students identified by the letters on the horizontal axis. (From Dube et al., 2003. Figure 1, page 139.)

in all of the participants. However, the major finding was that responding was less disrupted in the presence of the sprite that was associated with the higher reinforcement rate. This effect, which was predicted by the behavioral momentum hypothesis, was clear in nine of the 10 participants.

CONCLUDING COMMENTS

Extinction is one of the most active areas of contemporary research in behavior theory. Although the phenomenon was identified by Pavlov more than a hundred years ago, much of what we know about extinction has been discovered in the last 20 years. A great deal of work was done earlier on the partial reinforcement extinction effect. That line of work, and its contemporary counterpart in studies of behavioral momentum, was focused on factors that contribute to persistence in responding. In contrast, the emphasis in most other studies of extinction has been on conditions that promote the decline in conditioned responding and circumstances under which responding recovers. These issues are of great interest for translational research because of their implications for exposure therapy and relapse. Unfortunately, there are no simple answers. As Bouton and Wood (2008) commented, "extinction is a highly complex phenomenon, even when analyzed at a purely behavioral level" (p. 166).

SAMPLE QUESTIONS

1. Describe the basic behavioral and emotional consequences of extinction.
2. Describe the various ways in which control of behavior by contextual cues is relevant to the behavioral effects of extinction.
3. Describe how compounding stimuli in extinction may enhance extinction.
4. Describe evidence that identifies the development of inhibitory S-R associations in extinction.
5. Describe the partial reinforcement extinction effect and major explanations of the phenomenon.
6. Describe the concept of behavioral momentum. What are the advantages and disadvantages of the concept?

KEY TERMS

behavioral momentum The susceptibility of responding to disruption by manipulations such as pre-session feeding, delivery of free food, or a change in the schedule of reinforcement.

consolidation The establishment of a memory in relatively permanent form so that it is available for retrieval a long time after original acquisition.

continuous reinforcement A schedule of reinforcement in which every occurrence of the instrumental response produces the reinforcer. Abbreviated CRF.

discrimination hypothesis An explanation of the partial reinforcement extinction effect according to which extinction is slower after partial reinforcement than continuous reinforcement because the onset of extinction is more difficult to detect following partial reinforcement.

extinction (in classical conditioning) Reduction of a learned response that occurs because the conditioned stimulus is no longer paired with the unconditioned stimulus. Also, the procedure of repeatedly presenting a conditioned stimulus without the unconditioned stimulus.

extinction (in instrumental conditioning) Reduction of the instrumental response that occurs because the response is no longer followed by the reinforcer. Also, the procedure of no longer reinforcing the instrumental response.

forgetting A reduction of a learned response that occurs because of the passage of time, not because of particular experiences.

frustration An aversive emotional reaction that results from the unexpected absence of reinforcement.

frustration theory A theory of the partial reinforcement extinction effect, according to which extinction is retarded after partial reinforcement because the instrumental response becomes conditioned to the anticipation of frustrative nonreward.

intermittent reinforcement A schedule of reinforcement in which only some of the occurrences of the instrumental response are reinforced. The instrumental response is reinforced occasionally, or intermittently. Also called *partial reinforcement.*

overtraining extinction effect Less persistence of instrumental behavior in extinction following extensive training with reinforcement (overtraining) than following only moderate levels of reinforcement training. The effect is most prominent with continuous reinforcement.

magnitude reinforcement extinction effect Less persistence of instrumental behavior in extinction following training with a large reinforcer than following training with a small or moderate reinforcer. The effect is most prominent with continuous reinforcement.

partial reinforcement extinction effect (PREE) The term used to describe greater persistence in instrumental responding in extinction after partial (or intermittent) reinforcement training than after continuous reinforcement training.

reinstatement Recovery of excitatory responding to an extinguished stimulus produced by exposure to the unconditioned stimulus.

renewal Recovery of excitatory responding to an extinguished stimulus produced by a shift away from the contextual cues that were present during extinction.

sequential theory A theory of the partial reinforcement extinction effect according to which extinction is retarded after partial reinforcement because the instrumental response becomes conditioned to the memory of nonreward.

10

Aversive Control: Avoidance and Punishment

Avoidance Behavior

Origins of the Study of Avoidance Behavior

The Discriminated Avoidance Procedure

Two-Process Theory of Avoidance

Experimental Analysis of Avoidance Behavior

Alternative Theoretical Accounts of Avoidance Behavior

The Avoidance Puzzle: Concluding Comments

Punishment

Experimental Analysis of Punishment

Theories of Punishment

Punishment Outside the Laboratory

SAMPLE QUESTIONS

KEY TERMS

CHAPTER PREVIEW

This chapter deals with how behavior can be controlled by aversive stimulation. The discussion focuses on two types of instrumental conditioning: avoidance and punishment. Avoidance conditioning increases the performance of a target behavior, and punishment decreases the target response. However, in both cases individuals learn to minimize their exposure to aversive stimulation. Because of this similarity, theoretical analyses of avoidance and punishment share some of the same concepts. Nevertheless, for the most part, experimental analyses of avoidance and punishment have proceeded independently of each other. I will describe the major theoretical puzzles and empirical findings in both areas of research.

Fear, pain, and disappointment are an inevitable part of life. It is not surprising, therefore, that we should be interested in how behavior is controlled by aversive stimuli. Two procedures have been extensively investigated in studies of aversive control: avoidance and punishment. In an **avoidance** procedure, the individual has to make a specific response to prevent an aversive stimulus from occurring. For example, you might grab a handrail to avoid slipping, or take an umbrella to avoid getting rained on. An avoidance procedure involves a negative contingency between an instrumental response and the aversive stimulus. If the response occurs, the aversive stimulus is omitted. By contrast, **punishment** involves a positive contingency: the target response produces the aversive outcome. If you touch a hot stove, you will get burned.

Avoidance procedures increase the occurrence of instrumental behavior, whereas punishment procedures suppress instrumental responding. However, with both procedures, the final result is less contact with the aversive stimulus. Thus, both procedures involve increasing periods of safety. In one case, that is achieved by doing something. Hence avoidance conditioning is sometimes referred to as *active avoidance*. In the case of punishment, increased safety is achieved by not doing something. Hence, punishment is sometimes called *passive avoidance*.

Despite the similarities between them, avoidance and punishment have been studied using different investigative approaches. Research on avoidance behavior has focused primarily on theoretical issues. Investigators have been working hard to determine what mechanisms are responsible for behavior whose primary consequence is the absence of aversive stimulation. By contrast, scientists interested in punishment have focused on practical and ethical considerations, such as what procedures are effective in suppressing behavior, and under what circumstances is it justified to use those procedures.

AVOIDANCE BEHAVIOR

Avoidance learning has been studied for nearly 100 years. Most of the experiments have involved laboratory rats responding to avoid shock. However, numerous studies have been also conducted with human participants, and a variety of aversive stimuli have been tested including monetary losses, point losses, and time out from positive reinforcement (e.g., Declercq & De Houwer, 2008; DeFulio & Hackenberg, 2007; Molet, Leconte, & Rosas, 2006).

Origins of the Study of Avoidance Behavior

One cannot understand the study of avoidance behavior without understanding its historical roots. Experimental investigations of avoidance originated in studies of classical conditioning. The first avoidance experiments were conducted by the Russian psychologist Vladimir Bechterev (1913) as an extension of Pavlov's research. Unlike Pavlov, however, Bechterev was interested in studying associative learning in human subjects. In one situation, participants were instructed to place a finger on a metal plate. A warning stimulus (the CS) was then presented, followed by a brief shock (the US) through the metal plate. As you might predict, the participants quickly lifted their finger when they were shocked. After a few trials, they also learned to lift their finger in response to the warning stimulus.

At first Bechterev's experiment was incorrectly viewed as a standard example of classical conditioning. However, in Bechterev's method the participants determined whether or not they were exposed to the US. If they lifted their finger in response to the CS, they did not get the shock delivered through the metal plate on that trial. This aspect of the procedure constitutes a significant departure from Pavlov's methods because in standard classical conditioning making the conditioned response does not cancel (or change) the presentation of the US.

The fact that Bechterev did not use a standard classical conditioning procedure went unnoticed for many years. However, starting in the 1930s, several investigations started examining the difference between a standard classical conditioning procedure and a procedure that had an instrumental avoidance component added (e.g., Schlosberg, 1934, 1936). One of the most influential of these studies was performed by Brogden, Lipman, and Culler (1938).

Brogden et al. tested two groups of guinea pigs in a rotating wheel apparatus (see Figure 10.1). A tone served as the CS, and shock served as the US. The shock made the guinea pigs run and rotate the wheel. For the classical conditioning group, the shock was always presented two seconds after the beginning of the tone. For the avoidance conditioning group, the shock also followed the tone when the animals did not make the conditioned response (a small movement of the wheel). However, if the avoidance animals moved the wheel during the tone CS before the shock occurred, the scheduled shock was omitted. Figure 10.2 shows the percentage of trials on which each group made the conditioned response. The avoidance group quickly learned to make the conditioned response and was responding on 100% of the trials within eight days of training. In contrast, the classical conditioning group never achieved this high level of performance.

FIGURE **10.1**

Modern running wheel for rodents.

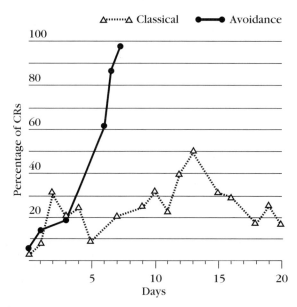

FIGURE **10.2**

Percentage of trials with a conditioned response on successive days of training. The conditioned response prevented shock delivery for the avoidance group but not for the classical group. (From "The Role of Incentive in Conditioning and Extinction" by W. J. Brogden, E. A. Lipman, and E. Culler, 1938. *American Journal of Psychology, 51,* pp. 109–117.)

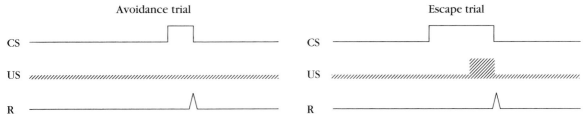

FIGURE **10.3**

Diagram of the discriminated, or signaled, avoidance procedure. *Avoidance trial:* If the participant makes the response required for avoidance during the CS (the signal) but before the US (e.g., shock) is scheduled, the CS is turned off, and the US is omitted on that trial. *Escape trial:* If the participant fails to make the required response during the CS-US interval, the scheduled shock is presented and remains on until the response occurs, whereupon both the CS and the US are terminated.

The results obtained by Brogden and his collaborators proved that avoidance conditioning is different from standard classical conditioning and ushered in years of research on avoidance learning that continues to this day.

The Discriminated Avoidance Procedure

Although avoidance behavior is not just another case of classical conditioning, the classical conditioning heritage of the study of avoidance behavior has greatly influenced its experimental and theoretical analysis to the present day. Investigators have been concerned with the importance of the warning signal in avoidance procedures and the relation of such warning signals to the US and the instrumental response. Experimental questions of this type have been extensively investigated with procedures similar to that used by Brogden and his colleagues. This method is called **discriminated**, or **signaled, avoidance.** The standard features of the discriminated avoidance procedure are diagrammed in Figure 10.3.

The first thing to note about the discriminated avoidance procedure is that it involves discrete trials. Each trial is initiated by the warning stimulus or CS. The events that occur after that depend on what the participant does. If the subject makes the target response before the shock is delivered, the CS is turned off and the US is omitted on that trial. This is a successful **avoidance trial.** If the subject fails to make the required response during the CS-US interval, the scheduled shock appears and remains on until the response occurs, whereupon both the CS and the US are terminated. In this case, the instrumental response results in escape from the shock; hence, this type of trial is called an **escape trial.** During early stages of training, most of the trials are escape trials, but as training progresses, avoidance trials come to predominate.

Discriminated avoidance procedures are often conducted in a shuttle box like that shown in Figure 10.4. The shuttle box consists of two compartments separated by an opening at floor level. The animal is placed on one side of the apparatus. At the start of a trial, the CS is presented (e.g., a light or a tone). If the subject crosses over to the other side before the shock occurs, no

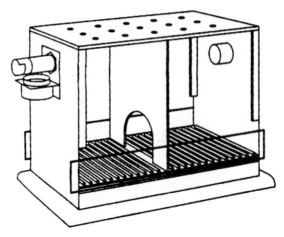

FIGURE **10.4**

A shuttle box. The box has a metal grid floor and is separated into two compartments by an archway. The instrumental response consists of crossing back and forth (shuttling) from one side of the box to the other.

shock is delivered and the CS is turned off. At the end of the intertrial interval, the next trial can be administered starting with the animal in the second compartment. With this procedure, the animal shuttles back and forth between the two sides on successive trials. That is why the response is called **shuttle avoidance.** (For a recent example of shuttle avoidance involving an inbred strain of mice, see Myers, Cohn, & Clark, 2005.)

There are two types of shuttle avoidance procedures. In the procedure just described, the animal moves from left to right on the first trial, and then back the other way on the second trial. This type of procedure is technically called *two-way shuttle avoidance,* because the animal moves in different directions on successive trials. In the second type of shuttle avoidance, the animal starts each trial on the same side of the apparatus and always moves in the same direction, to the other side. This type of procedure is called *one-way avoidance.* Generally, one-way avoidance is easier to learn than the two-way procedure.

Two-Process Theory of Avoidance

Avoidance procedures involve a negative contingency between a response and an aversive stimulus. If you make the appropriate avoidance responses, you will not fall, get rained on, or drive off the road. No particular pleasure is derived from these experiences. You simply do not get hurt. The absence of the aversive stimulus is presumably the reason that avoidance responses are made. However, how can the absence of something provide reinforcement for instrumental behavior? This is the fundamental question in the study of avoidance.

Mowrer and Lamoreaux (1942) pointed out more than a half-century ago that "not getting something can hardly, in and of itself, qualify as re-

N. E. Miller

warding" (p. 6). Since then, much intellectual effort has been devoted to figuring out what subjects "get" in avoidance conditioning procedures that might provide reinforcement for the avoidance response. In fact, the investigation of avoidance behavior has been dominated by this theoretical question. The first and most influential solution to the problem is the **two-process theory of avoidance,** proposed by Mowrer (1947) and elaborated by Miller (1951) and others.

In one form or another, two process theory has been the dominant theoretical viewpoint on avoidance learning for many years and continues to enjoy support (e.g., Levis & Brewer, 2001; McAllister & McAllister, 1995). Because other approaches deal more directly with certain findings, two-process theory is no longer viewed as a complete explanation of avoidance learning. Nevertheless, the theory remains the standard against which other explanations of avoidance behavior are always measured.

As its name implies, two-process theory assumes that two mechanisms are involved in avoidance learning. The first is a classical conditioning process activated by pairings of the warning stimulus (CS) with the aversive event (US) on trials when the organism fails to make the avoidance response. Because the US is an aversive stimulus, through classical conditioning the CS comes to elicit fear. Thus, the first component of two-process theory is the *classical conditioning of fear to the CS.* As I discussed in Chapters 3 and 9, considerable contemporary research is devoted to the mechanisms of fear conditioning and its extinction. Two-process theory treats conditioned fear as a source of motivation for avoidance learning.

Fear is an emotionally arousing unpleasant state. As I noted in Chapter 5, the termination of an unpleasant or aversive event provides negative reinforcement for instrumental behavior. The second process in two-process theory is based on such negative reinforcement. Mowrer assumed that learning of the instrumental avoidance response occurs because the response terminates the CS and thereby reduces the conditioned fear elicited by the CS. Thus, the second component in two-process theory is *instrumental reinforcement of the avoidance response through fear reduction.*

There are several noteworthy aspects of two-process theory. First, and perhaps most important, is that the classical and instrumental processes depend on each other. Instrumental reinforcement through fear reduction is not possible until fear has become conditioned to the CS. Therefore, the classical conditioning process has to occur first. That enables the reinforcement of the instrumental response through fear reduction. However, successful avoidance responses constitute extinction trials for the CS (since the US gets omitted). Thus, two-process theory predicts repeated interplay between classical and instrumental processes.

Another important aspect of two-process theory is that it explains avoidance behavior in terms of escape from conditioned fear rather than in terms of the prevention of shock. The fact that the avoidance response prevents shock is seen as an incidental by-product in two-process theory and not the primary determinant of avoidance behavior. Escape from conditioned fear is the primary causal factor. This enables the instrumental response to be reinforced by a tangible event (fear reduction) rather than merely the absence of something.

BOX **10.1**

Fear and the Amygdala

Much of what we do is motivated by fear. Because fear serves a defensive and protective function, organisms are biologically prepared to learn about stimuli that signal danger (e.g., snakes, heights). While such learning is generally adaptive, fear can grow out of proportion to the danger, producing a phobic response that undermines the person's ability to function.

Neuroscientists have discovered that a small region of the brain, the amygdala, plays a central role in fear-mediated behavior (for a recent review, see Fanselow & Poulos, 2005; Sigurdsson, Doyere, Cain, & LeDoux, 2007). The amygdala (Latin for *almond*) is part of the limbic system, a subcortical region of the brain that has been implicated in the processing of emotional stimuli. In humans, brain scans have revealed that processing fear-related stimuli (e.g., pictures of a fearful expression) activates the amygdala. Damage to the amygdala disrupts a person's ability to recognize signs of fear, and electrical stimulation of this region produces feelings of fear and apprehension.

Courtesy of Donald A. Dewsbury

M. S. Fanselow

The neural circuit that underlies conditioned fear has been explored in laboratory animals using a variety of physiological techniques, including selective lesions, localized stimulation, and physiological recording. In animals, electrical stimulation of the amygdala produces a range of behavioral and physiological responses indicative of fear, including freezing, enhanced startle to a loud acoustic stimulus, and a change in heart rate. Conversely, lesioning the amygdala produces a fearless creature that no longer avoids dangerous situations. Rats normally show signs of fear in the presence of a predator (e.g., a cat). After having the amygdala lesioned, a rat will approach a cat as if it's a long lost friend.

Lesioning the amygdala also disrupts learning about cues (CSs) that have been paired with an aversive event (e.g., a shock US) in a Pavlovian paradigm. As you have learned, animals can associate many different types of stimuli with shock. In some cases, the cue may be relatively simple, such as a discrete light or tone. In other cases, a constellation of cues, such as the environmental context in which shock occurs, may be associated with shock. In both cases, pairing the stimulus with shock produces conditioned fear, as indicated by a CS-induced increase in freezing and startle.

In fear conditioning the neural signals elicited by the CS and US converge within the amygdala (see Figure 10.5). Information about the US is provided by a number of distinct neural circuits, each of

which is sufficient to support conditioning (Lanuza, Nader, & LeDoux, 2004). Information about the CS is provided by three functionally distinct systems, each of which may represent a distinct type of stimulus quality. One CS path to the amygdala is fairly direct, a path that sacrifices stimulus detail for speed. This pathway allows for a rapid response and primes neural activity. Additional CS inputs arrive from the cortex and likely provide a slower, but more precise, representation of the features of the CS.

The third CS pathway conveys information that has been processed in the hippocampus, a structure that binds together unique sets of stimuli (Fanselow, 1999). For example, in everyday life, we associate specific events with when they occurred (e.g., what you had for breakfast yesterday). A similar type of learning is required to encode the constellation of cues that distinguishes one environmental context from another. Both types of memory are disrupted by damage to the hippocampus, a deficit that contributes to the memory dysfunction observed with Alzheimer's and Korsakoff's disease. In animal subjects, hippocampal lesions have no effect on a rat's ability to learn and remember that a discrete tone predicts shock. But this same rat is unable to associate a distinct environmental context with shock. It seems that the hippocampus plays an essential role in processing complex stimuli, packaging the components together to form a

(continued)

BOX **10.1** (continued)

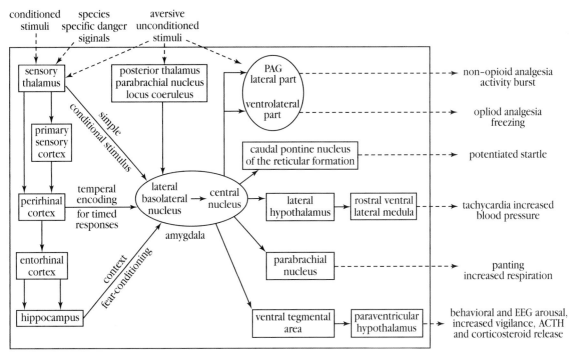

FIGURE **10.5**

A block diagram illustrating some of the neural components that mediate fear and defensive behavior. An aversive US engages parallel pathways that project to the lateral/basolateral amygdala. Information about the CS is conveyed from the sensory thalamus, the cortex, or by means of a hippocampal-dependent process. Output is channeled through the central nucleus of the amygdala, which organizes the expression of fear-mediated behavior. Distinct behavioral outcomes are produced by projections to various brain structures. (Adapted from Fendt & Fanselow, 1989.)

configural representation that can be associated with shock.

Interestingly, the role of the hippocampus changes over time. When the organism is first exposed to a complex stimulus, the hippocampus appears to be necessary to process the inter-related features of the stimulus. Over time, however, the new representation seems to be consolidated and stored elsewhere,

presumably within the cortex. Once the configural nature of a stimulus has been established, which takes about a month in rats, the new representation can function on its own without the hippocampus. As a result, lesion of the hippocampal has less effect if the lesion is administered during later stages of learning.

The neural circuits activated by the CS and US converge within the

amygdala in the lateral (towards the sides) and basal (lower) lateral region. Here, stimulus inputs may compete for association with the US, with the most predictive cues laying down a form of long-term potentiation (LTP) that helps encode the CS-US relation (Sigurdsson et al., 2007). LTP is thought to underlie information storage in other brain regions (see Box 11.1) and

(continued)

BOX **10.1** (continued)

depends on the activation of the NMDA receptor. Microinjecting a drug into the basolateral amygdala that blocks the NMDA receptor disrupts the acquisition of conditioned fear. In addition, LTP-like changes have been observed in the CS-input pathways, suggesting that multiple sources of synaptic plasticity contribute to the development of a conditioned response.

The output of the fear circuit is channeled through the central nucleus of the amygdala, which organizes the expression of conditioned fear. This structure produces a wide range of behavioral and physiological effects, the outcome of which depends on the neural system engaged. For example, enhanced startle is mediated by a neural projection to a region of the brainstem reticular formation (the pon-

tine nucleus). Slightly above this brainstem structure, in the midbrain, there is a region known as the periaqueductal gray (PAG). This structure plays a crucial role in organizing defensive behavior. The portion that lies along the upper sides (dorsolateral) organizes active defensive behaviors needed for fight and flight. These circa-strike behaviors are engaged by direct contact with a noxious, or life threatening, stimulus. The lower (ventral) portion of the PAG mediates CS-elicited freezing behavior. Rats that have lesions limited to the ventral PAG appear afraid on a variety of measures but do not freeze.

A CS that predicts shock also elicits a reduction in pain reactivity. This conditioned analgesia helps the organism cope with a painful US. The analgesia is mediated by an in-

ternally manufactured (endogenous) opioid that, like morphine, decreases behavioral reactivity to noxious stimuli. Like freezing, this physiological response depends on neurons within the ventral PAG. This conditioned analgesia could provide a form of negative feedback that decreases the effectiveness of an expected aversive US. It is well established that learning one cue predicts an aversive event can block learning about other cues. This blocking effect can be eliminated by the administration of a drug (an opioid antagonist) that prevents the opioid analgesia, providing a physiological explanation for why an expected US receives less processing (Bolles & Fanselow, 1980; Fanselow, 1998).

J. W. Grau

Experimental Analysis of Avoidance Behavior

Avoidance learning has been the subject of numerous experiments. Much of the research has been stimulated by efforts to prove or disprove two-process theory. Space does not permit reviewing all the evidence. However, I will consider several important findings that must be considered in understanding the mechanisms of avoidance behavior.

Acquired-Drive Experiments

In the typical avoidance procedure, classical conditioning of fear and instrumental reinforcement through fear reduction occur intermixed in a series of trials. However, if these two processes make separate contributions to avoidance learning, it should be possible to demonstrate their operation in a situation where the two types of conditioning are not intermixed. This is the goal of *acquired-drive experiments.*

The basic strategy is to first condition fear to a CS with a *pure* classical conditioning procedure in which the CS is paired with the US regardless of what the subject does. In the next phase of the experiment, the subjects are periodically exposed to the fear-eliciting CS and allowed to perform an instrumental response to turn off the CS (and thereby reduce fear). No shocks are scheduled in the second phase. This type of experiment was originally called an **acquired-drive** experiment because the drive to perform the instrumental response (fear) was learned through classical conditioning rather than being innate (such as hunger or thirst). More recently the procedure has been referred to as the **escape from fear (FFE) paradigm** (see Cain & LeDoux, 2007, for an extensive discussion).

Escape from fear experiments have generally upheld the predictions of two-process theory. That is, the termination of a conditioned aversive stimulus is an effective reinforcer for instrumental behavior. This result was first demonstrated in a classic experiment by Brown and Jacobs (1949). Escape from fear is attracting renewed interest in contemporary clinical work because it represents a transition from a passive fear reaction to an active coping strategy that helps to overcome fear and anxiety attendant to trauma (LeDoux & Gorman, 2001; van der Kolk, 2006). In a recent study, Esmorís-Arranz, Pardo-Vázquez, and Vázquez-Garciá (2003) compared escape from fear learning after delayed and simultaneous conditioning in a shuttle box. During the initial phase of the experiment, rats were confined to one side of the shuttle box (the *shock* side) and received 10 Pavlovian trials during each of three sessions. The CS was a 15-second audiovisual cue, and the US was 15 seconds of mild foot shock. The delayed conditioning group always got the US at the end of the CS. The simultaneous conditioning group got the US at the same time as the CS. A third group served as a control and got the CS and the US unpaired.

After the fear-conditioning phase, the barrier to the other side of the shuttle box was removed and the rats were tested for escape from fear. Each trial started with the rat place on the shock side with the CS turned on. If the rat moved to the other side within a minute, it turned off the CS and was allowed to stay on the other side for 30 seconds. The next trial was then initiated. Rats that did not move to the safe side within a minute were removed and placed in a holding box before starting their next trial. The latency to escape to the safe side is summarized in Figure 10.6. Both the delayed conditioning group and the simultaneous conditioning group showed decreased latencies to escape from the fear stimulus across trials, indicating learning to escape from fear. No systematic changes in latency to escape were evident in the unpaired control group. These results show clear escape from fear learning, as predicted by two-process theory (see also Cain and LeDoux, 2007).

Independent Measurement of Fear During Acquisition of Avoidance Behavior

Another important strategy that has been used in investigations of avoidance behavior involves independent measurement of fear and instrumental avoidance responding. This approach is based on the assumption that if fear motivates and reinforces avoidance responding, then the conditioning of fear and the conditioning of instrumental avoidance behavior should go hand in hand. Contrary to this prediction, however, conditioned fear and avoidance responding are not always highly correlated (Mineka, 1979).

Fairly early in the study of avoidance learning, Solomon and his associates noticed that dogs become less fearful as they become proficient in performing an avoidance response (Solomon, Kamin, & Wynne, 1953; Solomon & Wynne, 1953). Subsequently, more systematic measurements of fear and avoidance behavior have confirmed this observation (e.g., Kamin, Brimer, & Black, 1963; Mineka & Gino, 1980; Neuenschwander, Fabrigoule, & Mackintosh, 1987). These studies have typically used laboratory rats conditioned in a shuttle

Courtesy of Donald A. Dewsbury

S. Mineka

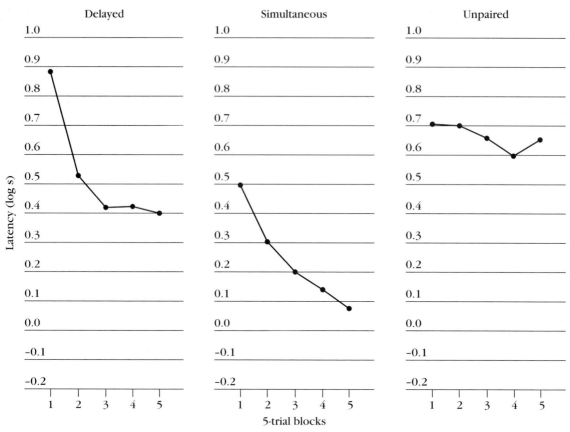

FIGURE **10.6**

Mean latencies to escape from a CS that was either conditioned using a delayed conditioning procedure, a simultaneous conditioning procedure, or was presented unpaired with the US. (Based on Esmorís-Arranz, Pardo-Vázquez, & Vázquez-Garciá, 2003.)

avoidance task, with fear measured using the conditioned suppression technique. A similar dissociation between fear and avoidance learning is observed in human subjects.

In one recent study (Lovibond, Saunders, Weidemann, & Mitchell, 2008), college students received conditioning with three different stimuli, designated as A, B, and C. The stimuli were colored blocks presented on a computer screen. The US was shock to the index finger at an intensity that was definitely uncomfortable but not painful. On trials with Stimulus A, an avoidance conditioning procedure was in effect. Stimulus A was presented for five seconds, followed by shock 10 seconds later (A+). However, if the subject pressed the correct button during the CS, shock was omitted on that trial. Stimulus B received only Pavlovian conditioning as a comparison. Each presentation of B was followed by shock (B+) without the opportunity to avoid. Stimulus C was a control cue and was never followed by shock (C–). To track the effect of these procedure, the participants were asked to rate their

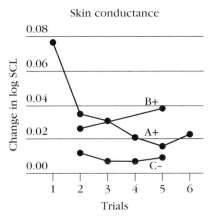
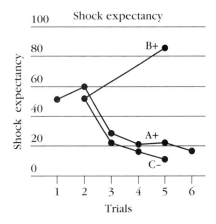

FIGURE **10.7**

Changes in skin conductance and expectancy of shock across trials for a warning stimulus in an avoidance procedure (A+), a Pavlovian CS paired with shock (B+) and a stimulus never paired with shock (C–). (Based on Lovibond et al., 2008.)

expectation that shock would occur and their skin conductance responses were recorded as an index of fear. Ratings of shock expectancy were obtained during the 10 second delay between the CS and the scheduled US.

The results of the experiment are summarized in Figure 10.7. The left graph shows changes in skin conductance as a measure of fear. Fear was always low for Stimulus C, as would be expected since C never ended in shock. Fear increased across trials for the Pavlovian Stimulus B, which ended in shock on each trial (B+). In contrast, fear decreased across trials for the avoidance stimulus (A+). The changes in fear to stimuli A and B were paralleled by changes in the expectancy of shock. Shock expectancy increased across trials for the Pavlovian Stimulus B, but decreased for the avoidance Stimulus A. Subsequent test trials indicated that the participants were not afraid of Stimulus A because they had learned to prevent shock on A trials. If their avoidance response was blocked, their fear returned, as did their expectation that shock would occur again. These findings illustrate that successful avoidance behavior is associated with low levels of fear and low expectations of danger.

The decline in fear to the CS with extended avoidance training presents a puzzle for two-process theory and has encouraged alternative formulations, some of which we will discuss below (see also discussion by Lovibond et al., 2008).

Extinction of Avoidance Behavior Through Response-Blocking and CS-Alone Exposure

If the avoidance response is effective in terminating the CS and no shocks are presented, avoidance responding can persist for a long time. For example, in an old experiment that was conducted with dogs, Solomon, Kamin, and Wynne (1953) described a subject that performed the avoidance response on 650 successive trials after only a few shocks. Given such persistence, how might avoidance behavior be extinguished? The answer to this question is very important not only for theoretical analyses of avoidance behavior, but also for the treatment of maladaptive or pathological avoidance responses.

An effective and extensively investigated extinction procedure for avoidance behavior is called **flooding,** or **response prevention** (Baum, 1970). It involves presenting the CS in the avoidance situation without the US, but with the apparatus altered in such a way that the participant is prevented from making the avoidance response. Thus, the subject is exposed to the CS without being permitted to terminate it. It is "flooded" with the CS. (For discussion of a related procedure, called *implosive therapy,* see Levis, 1995; Levis & Brewer, 2001.)

Flooding procedures have two important components. One is getting exposed to the CS without the aversive stimulus. This was clearly illustrated in a classic experiment by Schiff, Smith, and Prochaska (1972). Rats were trained to avoid shock in response to an auditory CS by going to a safe compartment. After acquisition, the safe compartment was blocked off by a barrier and the rats received various amounts of exposure to the CS without shock. Different groups received 1, 5, or 12 blocked trials, and on each of these trials the CS was presented for 1, 5, 10, 50, or 120 seconds. The barrier blocking the avoidance response was then removed and the animals were tested. At the start of each test trial, the animal was placed in the apparatus and the CS was presented until it crossed into the safe compartment. Shocks never occurred during the test trials, and each animal was tested until it took at least 120 seconds to cross into the safe compartment on three consecutive trials. The strength of the avoidance response was measured by the number of trials required to reach this extinction criterion.

The results of the experiment are summarized in Figure 10.8. As expected, blocked exposure to the CS facilitated extinction of the avoidance response. Furthermore, this effect was determined mainly by the total duration of exposure to the CS. The number of flooding trials administered (1, 5, or 12) facilitated extinction only because each trial added to the total CS exposure time. Increases in the total duration of blocked exposure to the CS resulted in more extinction (see also Baum, 1969; Weinberger, 1965).

In addition to CS exposure time, blocking access to the avoidance response also facilitates extinction (e.g., Katzev & Berman, 1974). In the study of fear conditioning in college students by Lovibond et al. (2008) that I described earlier, fear and expectancy of shock declined with successful avoidance training, but both quickly returned during test trials when the opportunity to make the avoidance response was blocked. Procedures in which the avoidance response is blocked may be especially effective in extinguishing avoidance behavior because they permit the return of fear and thereby make fear more accessible to extinction. Response blocking in extinction also makes it clear that failure to make the avoidance response no longer results in shock and that should facilitate readjustment of previously acquired shock expectancies.

Nondiscriminated (Free-Operant) Avoidance

As I have described, two-process theory places great emphasis on the role of the warning signal, or CS, in avoidance learning. Clear warning signals are often evident in pathological avoidance behavior, as when someone shies away from intimacy after an abusive relationship. Can individuals also learn

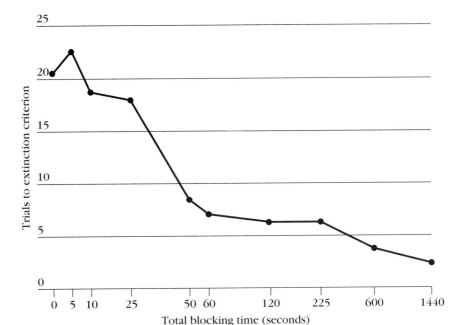

FIGURE **10.8**

Trials to an extinction criterion for independent groups of animals that previously received various durations of blocked exposure to the CS. (From "Extinction of Avoidance in Rats as a Function of Duration and Number of Blocked Trials" by R. Schiff, N. Smith, and J. Prochaska, 1972, *Journal of Comparative and Physiological Psychology, 81,* pp. 356–359. Copyright © 1972 the American Psychological Association. Reprinted by permission.)

an avoidance response if there is no external warning stimulus in the situation? Within the context of two-factor theory, this is a heretical question. However, progress in science requires posing bold questions, and Sidman (1953a, 1953b) did just that. He devised an avoidance conditioning procedure that did not involve a warning stimulus. The procedure has come to be called **nondiscriminated**, or **free-operant avoidance.**

In a free-operant avoidance procedure, the aversive stimulus (e.g., shock) is scheduled to occur periodically without warning: let's say every five seconds. Each time the participant makes the avoidance response, it obtains a period of safety: let's say 15 seconds long, during which shocks do not occur. Repetition of the avoidance response before the end of the shock-free period serves to start the safe period over again.

A free-operant avoidance procedure is constructed from two time intervals (see Figure 10.9). One of these is the interval between shocks in the absence of a response. This is called the S-S (shock-shock) **interval.** The other critical time period is the interval between the avoidance response and the next scheduled shock. This is called the R-S (response-shock) **interval.** The R-S interval is the period of safety created by each response. In our example, the S-S interval was five seconds and the R-S interval was 15 seconds. Another

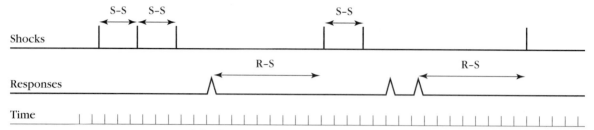

FIGURE **10.9**

Diagram of the nondiscriminated, or free-operant, avoidance procedure. Each occurrence of the response initiates a period without shock, as set by the R-S interval. In the absence of a response, the next shock occurs a fixed period after the last shock, as set by the S-S interval. Shocks are not signaled by an exteroceptive stimulus and are usually brief and inescapable.

important feature is that an avoidance response can occur at any time and will always reset the R-S interval (hence the term *free-operant avoidance*). By responding just before the end of each R-S interval, the subject can reset the R-S interval and thereby prolong its period of safety indefinitely.

Demonstrations of Free-Operant Avoidance Learning

Most of the research on free-operant avoidance learning has been conducted with laboratory rats and brief foot shock as the aversive stimulus. However, experiments have been also conducted with human participants and more "natural" aversive stimuli. For example, in one study, four college students served as the participants and exposure to carbon dioxide (CO_2) was the aversive US (Lejuez et al., 1998). CO_2 rather than shock was used because the investigators wanted to produce symptoms related to panic attacks. CO_2 inhalation produces respiratory distress, increased heart rate (tachycardia), and dizziness similar to what is experienced during a panic attack.

Potential participants for the experiment were first screened to make sure they did not have a history of respiratory problems. During the experiment, the students were asked to wear a mask that usually provided room air. To deliver the aversive stimulus the room air was switched to 20% CO_2 for 25 seconds. Each CO_2 delivery was followed by a 65-second rest period to permit resumption of normal breathing. The instrumental response was operating a plunger. Three seconds after the rest period, a hit of CO_2 was provided without warning if the participant did not pull the plunger (S-S interval = three seconds). Following a response, the next CO_2 delivery was scheduled 10 seconds later (R-S interval = 10 seconds). In addition, each occurrence of the avoidance response reset the R-S interval. If the participants never responded, they could get as many as 22 CO_2 deliveries in each session. By responding before the end of the first S-S interval and then before the end of each subsequent R-S interval, they could avoid all CO_2 deliveries. Sessions during which the avoidance contingency was in effect were alternated with control sessions during which responding had no effect and the participants received a CO_2 delivery on average every six minutes.

The results of the experiment are summarized in Figure 10.10. The left side of the figure shows the response rates of the four students during the

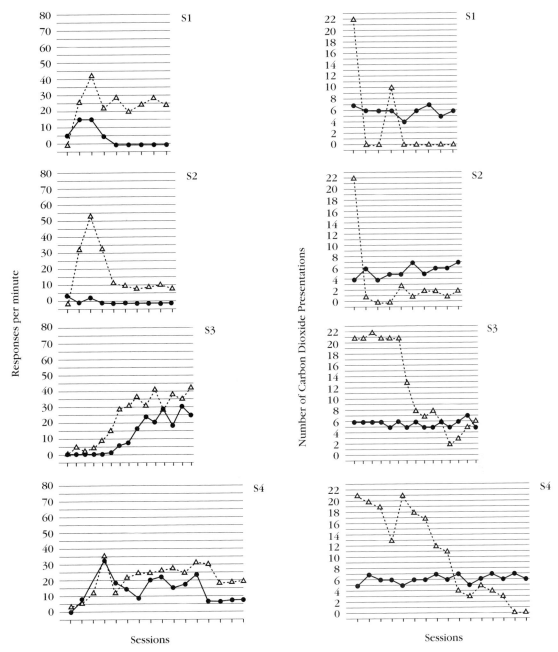

FIGURE **10.10**

Rate of responding and rate of CO_2 presentations for four college students in a study of free-operant avoidance. Open symbols represent data obtained during sessions when the avoidance contingency was in effect. Closed symbols represent data obtained during control sessions when the avoidance response was not effective and the subjects received a CO_2 delivery every six minutes. (From C. W. Lejuez, et al. (1998). Avoidance of 20% carbon dioxide-enriched air within humans. *Journal of the Experimental Analysis of Behavior, 70,* pp. 79–86. Copyright © 1998 by the Society for the Experimental Analysis of Behavior, Inc. Reprinted with permission.)

avoidance and control sessions. The right side of the figure shows the number of CO_2 deliveries the subjects received during the two types of sessions. Notice that response rates were higher during the avoidance sessions than during the control sessions. Furthermore, as the students acquired the avoidance response, the number of CO_2 presentations they received declined. These behavior changes (and consequences) occurred even though the CO_2 presentations were not signaled by an explicit warning stimulus.

No explicit instructions were provided at the beginning of the experiment concerning the response plunger. Students S1 and S2 discovered the avoidance contingency without much difficulty on their own. In contrast, students S3 and S4 had a bit of trouble at first and were given a hint before their 6th and 7th sessions, respectively. The hint was, "The only thing that you can do by pulling the plunger is sometimes change the number of times you receive carbon-dioxide-enriched air. It is even possible for you to sometimes receive no deliveries of carbon dioxide." This hint was enough to get S3 and S4 to respond effectively during subsequent avoidance sessions. However, notice that the instructions did not provide clues about the difference between the avoidance and control sessions. Nevertheless, S3 and S4 responded more vigorously during the avoidance sessions than during the control sessions by the end of the experiment. Thus, the difference in response levels (and CO_2 presentations) that occurred during avoidance versus control sessions cannot be attributed to following instructions for any of the students. They all had to discover when the avoidance contingency was in effect and when it was not in effect without help.

Free-operant avoidance behavior has been investigated in numerous other studies primarily with laboratory rats serving as subjects and brief shock as the aversive stimulus (see Hineline, 1977; Sidman, 1966). Because nonverbal subjects were used, one does not have to worry about the possible role of instructions. These experiments have shown that the rate of responding is controlled by the length of the S-S and R-S intervals. The more frequently shocks are scheduled in the absence of responding (the S-S interval), the more likely the subject is to learn the avoidance response. Increasing the periods of safety produced by the response (the R-S interval) also promotes the avoidance behavior. In addition, the relative value of the S-S and R-S intervals is important. The safe period produced by each response (R-S interval) has to be longer than the interval between shocks that would occur without responding (S-S interval).

Courtesy of Donald A. Dewsbury

P. N. Hineline

Free-Operant Avoidance and Two-Process Theory

Free-operant avoidance behavior presents a challenge for two-process theory because there is no explicit CS to elicit conditioned fear, and it is not clear how the avoidance response reduces fear. However, two-process theory has not been entirely abandoned in attempts to explain free operant avoidance (see Anger, 1963). The S-S and R-S intervals used in effective procedures are usually rather short (less than one minute). Furthermore, they remain fixed during an experiment, so that the intervals are highly predictable. Therefore, the animals can learn to respond to the passage of time as a signal for shock. (I will have more to say about learning about time in Chapter 12.)

The assumption of temporal conditioning permits application of the mechanisms of two-process theory to free-operant avoidance procedures. Since the passage of time is a reliable predictor of the next shock, temporal cues can become conditioned to elicit fear. Since the timing for the next shock starts over again with each avoidance response, each response effectively removes the fear-eliciting temporal cues. This can then reinforce the avoidance response through fear reduction. Thus, temporal cues that predict shock can have the same role in free-operant avoidance procedures as the explicit CS has in discriminative avoidance.

The preceding analysis predicts that organisms will not distribute their responses randomly in a free-operant avoidance procedure. Rather, they will concentrate their responses at the end of the R-S interval because it is here that the temporal cues presumably elicit the greatest amount of fear (and responding produces the most fear reduction). Results consistent with this prediction have been obtained. However, many animals successfully avoid a great many shocks without distributing their responses in the manner predicted by two-process theory (Sidman, 1966). Furthermore, avoidance behavior has been successfully conditioned with the use of free operant procedures in which the S-S and R-S intervals are varied throughout the experiment (for example, Herrnstein & Hineline, 1966). Making the S-S and R-S intervals unpredictable makes it more difficult to use the passage of time as a signal for shock. Results from these procedures have discouraged some investigators from accepting two-process theory as an explanation of free-operant avoidance learning (see Herrnstein, 1969; Hineline, 1977, 1981).

Alternative Theoretical Accounts of Avoidance Behavior

In two-process theory, reinforcement for the avoidance response is assumed to be provided by the reduction of fear. This is a case of negative reinforcement: reinforcement due to removal of an aversive stimulus. Several subsequent theoretical treatments have proposed that avoidance procedures also provide for positive reinforcement of the avoidance response, whereas others have suggested that neither negative nor positive reinforcement is important in avoidance learning.

Positive Reinforcement Through Conditioned Inhibition of Fear or Conditioned Safety Signals

Performance of an avoidance response always results in distinctive feedback stimuli, such as spatial cues involved in going from one side to the other in a shuttle box or tactile and other external stimuli involved in pressing a response lever. Because the avoidance response produces a period of safety in all avoidance conditioning procedures, response feedback stimuli may acquire conditioned inhibitory properties and become signals for the absence of aversive stimulation. Such stimuli are called **safety signals.** According to the *safety-signal hypothesis*, the safety signals that accompany avoidance responses may provide positive reinforcement for avoidance behavior.

In most avoidance experiments, no special cues are introduced as response feedback cues that could acquire safety signal functions. Rather, spatial, tactile, and proprioceptive stimuli that inevitably accompany the avoidance response become safety signals (Dinsmoor, 2001b). However, any avoidance procedure can be easily modified to include a distinctive stimulus (a brief light or tone) after each occurrence of the avoidance response. The safety-signal hypothesis predicts that introducing an explicit feedback stimulus will facilitate the learning of an avoidance response. Numerous experiments have found this to be true (e.g., Bolles & Grossen, 1969; Cándido, Maldonado, & Vila, 1991; D'Amato, Fazzaro, & Etkin, 1968; Keehn & Nakkash, 1959).

Other studies have shown that, during the course of avoidance training, a response feedback stimulus becomes a conditioned inhibitor of fear (e.g., Cándido, González, & de Brugada, 2004; Morris, 1974; Rescorla, 1968). Furthermore, there is also direct evidence that a feedback stimulus that has been conditioned to inhibit fear during avoidance training is an effective positive reinforcer for new responses (Morris, 1975; Weisman & Litner, 1972). Thus, there is considerable evidence for safety signals as sources of positive reinforcement in avoidance learning (see Dinsmoor, 2001b, and ensuing commentary).

The safety-signal hypothesis is particularly well suited to explain free-operant avoidance behavior. Participants often experience numerous unsignaled shocks during the initial stages of free-operant avoidance training. This makes it highly likely that the experimental context becomes conditioned to elicit fear. Because shocks never occur for the duration of the R-S interval after a response is made, the proprioceptive and tactile stimuli that accompany the response can become conditioned inhibitors of fear. Thus, response-associated feedback cues can come to provide positive reinforcement for the free-operant avoidance response (Dinsmoor, 1977, 2001a, b; Rescorla, 1968).

Reinforcement of Avoidance Through Reduction of Shock Frequency

Positive reinforcement through conditioned inhibition can occur alongside of the negative reinforcement mechanism of two-process theory. In contrast, another reinforcement mechanism, **shock-frequency reduction**, has been proposed as a radical alternative to two-process theory (deVilliers, 1974; Herrnstein, 1969; Herrnstein & Hineline, 1966; Hineline, 1981). By definition, avoidance responses prevent the delivery of shock and thereby reduce the frequency of shocks an organism receives. The theories of avoidance we have discussed so far have viewed the reduction of shocks as a secondary by-product rather than as a primary cause of avoidance behavior. By contrast, the shock-frequency reduction hypothesis views the reduction of shocks to be critical to the reinforcement of avoidance behavior.

Shock-frequency reduction as the cause of avoidance behavior was first entertained by Sidman (1962) and was later encouraged by evidence of learning in a free-operant avoidance procedure specifically designed to minimize the role of fear-conditioned temporal cues (Herrnstein & Hineline, 1966). However, several experiments have shown that animals can learn to make an avoidance response even if the response does not reduce the frequency of shocks delivered (Gardner & Lewis, 1976; see also Hineline, 1981). Responding in these studies delayed the onset of the next scheduled shock but did not prevent its delivery. Thus, overall shock frequency was unchanged. This evidence suggests that shock-frequency reduction is not necessary for avoidance learning. However, it may be a contributing factor.

Avoidance and Species-Specific Defense Reactions (SSDRs)

In the theories discussed so far, the emphasis was on how the events that precede and follow the avoidance response, control avoidance behavior. The exact nature or form of the response itself was not of concern. In addition, the reinforcement mechanisms assumed by the theories all required some time to develop. Before fear reduction can be an effective reinforcer, fear first must be conditioned to the CS; before response feedback cues can come to serve as reinforcers, they must become signals for the absence of shock; and before shock-frequency reduction can work, organisms must experience enough shocks to be able to calculate shock frequencies. Therefore, these theories tell us little about the organism's behavior during the first few trials of avoidance training.

Lack of concern with what an organism does during the first few trials of avoidance conditioning is a serious weakness of any theory. For an avoidance mechanism to be useful under natural conditions, the mechanism has to generate successful avoidance responses quickly. Consider, for example, a mouse trying to avoid being caught by a hawk. An avoidance mechanism that requires numerous training trials is of no use in this case. If the mouse fails to avoid attack by the hawk during its initial encounter, it may not survive for future training trials. Bolles (1970, 1971) recognized this problem and focused on what controls an organism's behavior during the early stages of avoidance training.

Courtesy of Donald A. Dewsbury

R. C. Bolles

Bolles assumed that aversive stimuli and situations elicit strong unconditioned, or innate, responses. These innate responses are assumed to have evolved because they are successful in defense against pain and injury. Therefore, Bolles called these **species-specific defense reactions (SSDRs)**. In rats, for example, prominent species-specific defense reactions include flight (running), freezing (remaining vigilant but motionless, except for breathing), and defensive fighting. Other reactions to danger include thigmotaxis (approaching walls), defensive burying (covering up the source of aversive stimulation), and seeking out dark areas.

Bolles proposed that the configuration of the environment determines which particular SSDR occurs. For example, flight may predominate when an obvious escape route is available and freezing may predominate if there is no way out of the situation. This is indeed the case (Blanchard, 1997; Sigmundi, 1997). Defensive fighting, for example, is not possible without an opponent, and defensive burying is not possible if something like sand is not available for burying the source of danger. Even freezing, a response that one might think does not require stimulus support, only occurs in relatively safe places (near a wall or in a corner) rather than in the middle of an arena. If a rat finds itself in the middle of an arena when it encounters danger, it will move to a wall or a corner before freezing.

A major prediction of the SSDR theory is that some responses will be more easily learned in avoidance experiments than others. Consistent with this prediction, Bolles (1969) found that rats can rapidly learn to run in a running wheel to avoid shock. By contrast, their performance of a rearing response (standing on the hind legs) did not improve much during the course of avoidance training. Presumably, running was learned faster because it was closer to the rat's SSDRs in the running wheel. (For a related finding in escape from fear learning, see Cain and LeDoux, 2007.)

Predatory Imminence and Defensive and Recuperative Behaviors

By focusing on ecological and evolutionary influences on defensive behavior, SSDR theory significantly advanced our thinking about fear and avoidance learning. The role of ecological and evolutionary factors was developed further by Fanselow and his associates who formulated the concept of a *predatory imminence continuum* (Fanselow & Lester, 1988; Fanselow, 1997; Rau & Fanselow, 2007). According to the **predatory imminence** continuum, different defensive responses occur depending on the level of danger faced by an animal.

Consider, for example, a small rodent (e.g., a rat) that is a potential source of food for cats, coyotes, snakes, and other predators. The rat is presumably safest in its nest in a burrow, but it has to go out periodically to forage for food. When it is out foraging, it is not in much danger as long as no cats or snakes are around. When a snake appears, the rat's level of danger increases, but not by much if the snake is far away. However, as the snake gets closer, the level of danger rises. The situation is very dangerous when the snake is close by and is about to strike, and danger is at its peak when the strike actually occurs. This progression of increasing levels of danger is the predatory imminence continuum and is illustrated in Figure 10.11.

Different species typical defense responses are assumed to occur at different levels of predatory imminence. If a rat is forced to forage for food in a location where it periodically encounters snakes, it is likely to leave its burrow to get food less often but eat larger meals during each excursion (Fanselow, Lester, & Helmstetter, 1988). Thus, the response to a low level of predatory imminence is an adjustment in meal patterns. When a snake appears but is not yet about to strike, the rat's defensive behavior is likely to change to freezing. Freezing will reduce the chance that a predator will see or hear the rat. Many predators will strike only at moving prey. Freezing by the prey also may result in the predator shifting its attention to something else (Suarez & Gallup, 1981).

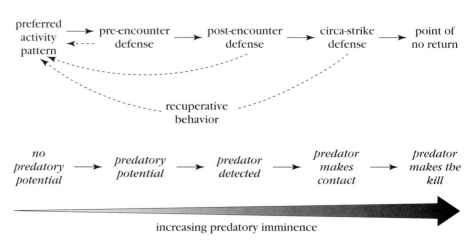

FIGURE **10.11**

The predatory-imminence continuum. (From "Neurobiological and neuroethological perspectives on fear and anxiety" by V. Rau and M. S. Fanselow, in L. J. Kirmayer, R. Lemelson, and M. Barad (Eds.), *Understanding trauma: Integrating biological, clinical, and cultural perspectives.* (pp. 27–40). Copyright © 2007 by Cambridge University Press. Reprinted by permission.)

When the snake actually touches the rat, the rat is likely to leap into the air. It is as if the rat's prior freezing behavior prepares it to explode into the air when it is touched. This is called the *circa strike response*. If the rat does not successfully escape the predator at this point, it is likely to engage in defensive aggression. If the defensive behavior is successful and the rat manages to get away from the snake, it will gradually shift to recuperative responses (such as grooming) that promote healing from injuries.

Like SSDR theory, the predatory-imminence hypothesis assumes that defensive behavior initially occurs as unconditioned responding. Defensive responses can also come to be elicited by a conditioned stimulus if that CS becomes associated with an aversive event. Which defensive response occurs to the CS will depend on the temporal relation of the CS to the unconditioned aversive stimulus. If the CS precedes the US (as in delayed conditioning), the defensive behavior will be one level lower on the predatory-imminence scale than the response elicited by the US. Thus, if the US elicits a circa strike response, the CS is likely to elicit freezing behavior. In contrast, if the CS and US are presented at the same time (as in simultaneous conditioning), the defensive response will be more similar to the response to the US (Esmorís-Arranz et al., 2003).

Differences in the behavioral manifestations of different degrees of predatory imminence are associated with a corresponding cascade of neurobiological states (Rau & Fanselow, 2007). Evolution has created powerful and specialized behavioral and neurobiological processes that enable us and other animals to deal effectively with different levels of danger. These processes were no doubt essential to survival during our ancestral history. However, they can go awry and be inappropriately activated, resulting in post-traumatic stress disorder and other disorders of stress and coping (Kirmayer, Lemelson, and Barad, 2007).

The predatory imminence formulation does not include an instrumental conditioning component, and was not intended to explain the diverse array of experimental findings that scientists have accumulated in their many decades of research on avoidance learning. However, predatory imminence is important to consider in all aversive conditioning situations because it reflects the innate coping mechanisms that come into play whenever the defensive behavior system is activated.

Given the roots of defensive behavior (and its neurobiological substrates) in our evolutionary past, the predatory imminence concept can be also used to analyze human reactions to danger. Consistent with this idea, Craske (1999) characterized human fear and anxiety reactions in terms of the imminence of the perceived danger. The lowest level of perceived danger leads to worry. The next higher level leads to fear and vigilance (like freezing in rats). The highest level of perceived threat leads to panic (which is analogous to the circa strike response). Interestingly, men and women respond differently to the stress of perceived danger. Whereas men have a flight-or-fight response, women have a tend-and-befriend response (Taylor et al., 2000). When stressed, women are more likely to protect and care for their offspring and seek out social support.

The Avoidance Puzzle: Concluding Comments

We have learned a great deal about avoidance behavior since Mowrer and Lamoreaux (1942) puzzled about how *not getting something* can motivate avoidance responses. As we saw, numerous creative answers to this puzzle have been offered. Two-process theory, conditioned inhibition reinforcement, and shock-frequency-reduction reinforcement all provide different views of what happens after an avoidance response to reinforce it. By contrast, the SSDR account focuses on unconditioned aspects of defensive behavior, which is further elaborated through the concept of predatory imminence.

None of the major theories can explain everything that occurs in aversive conditioning situations. However, each provides ideas that are useful for understanding various aspects of avoidance behavior. For example, two-process theory is uniquely suited to explain the results of the escape from fear experiments. The safety-signal theory is particularly useful in explaining free-operant avoidance learning and the role of response feedback stimuli in avoidance conditioning. Finally, the concept of predatory imminence provides the most useful account of what happens during early stages of avoidance training. Given the complexities of the various avoidance learning paradigms, we should not be surprised that several conceptual frameworks are needed to explain all of the available data.

PUNISHMENT

Courtesy of N. H. Azrin

N. H. Azrin

Although most of us engage in all sorts of avoidance responses every day, as a society, we are not particularly concerned about what is involved in avoidance behavior. This may be because procedures that generate active avoidance are rarely used in organized efforts to change or control someone's behavior. By contrast, punishment has always been in the public eye (see Repp & Singh, 1990). As a society, we use punishment as a form of retribution for egregious criminal acts. Punishment is also used to encourage adherence to religious and civil codes of conduct. Many institutions and rules have evolved to ensure that punishment is administered in ways that are ethical and just. What constitutes acceptable punishment in the criminal justice system, in childrearing, or in the treatment of individuals with developmental disabilities is a matter of continual debate.

Despite long-standing societal concerns about punishment, for many years experimental psychologists did not devote much attention to the topic. On the basis of a few experiments, Thorndike (1932) and Skinner (1938, 1953) concluded that punishment was not an effective method for controlling behavior and had only temporary effects (see also Estes, 1944). This claim was not seriously challenged until the 1960s, when punishment began to be more extensively investigated (Azrin & Holz, 1966; Campbell & Church, 1969; Church, 1963; Solomon, 1964). We now know that punishment can be a highly effective technique for modifying behavior (Dinsmoor, 1998; Lerman & Vorndran, 2002). With appropriate procedural parameters, responding can be totally suppressed in just one or two trials. Under other circumstances, the suppression of behavior may be incomplete, and responding may recover.

Consider, for example, a child who accidentally sticks a metal fork in an electric outlet. The resultant shock is likely to discourage repetition of that response for the rest of the child's life. Contrast that with getting a ticket for driving 10 miles above the speed limit. Will that produce the same dramatic suppression of the punished response? Not likely. Systematic laboratory experiments have taught us a great deal about the circumstances under which punishment does and does not work. However, numerous questions remain to be answered in efforts to translate this knowledge to therapeutic interventions (Lerman & Vorndran, 2002).

Experimental Analysis of Punishment

The basic punishment procedure is simple: An aversive stimulus is presented after a target instrumental response. If the procedure is effective, the target response becomes suppressed. Because punishment involves the suppression of behavior, it can be observed only with responses that are likely to occur in the first place. This prerequisite is easily met in therapeutic situations where the target of punishment is a harmful activity that occurs more often than one would like. Vorndran and Lerman (2006), for example, documented the effectiveness of punishment in two participants with developmental disabilities. One of the participants engaged in frequent hyperventilation and the other engaged in self-injurious mouthing of his hand (Vorndran & Lerman, 2006). The target responses were suppressed by punishment in both cases.

Laboratory studies of punishment usually begin with a preliminary phase in which the target response is first established with positive reinforcement. A pigeon, for example, may be reinforced with food for pecking a response key. A punishment procedure is then superimposed on the schedule of positive reinforcement. This sets up a conflict between responding to obtain positive reinforcement and withholding responding to avoid punishment. The degree of response suppression that occurs is determined both by variables related to presentation of the aversive stimulus and by variables related to the availability of positive reinforcement. The interplay of these two factors can be complicated and can make it difficult to predict what will happen.

Characteristics of the Aversive Stimulus and Its Method of Introduction

A great variety of aversive stimuli have been used in punishment experiments, including electric shock, a sudden burst of air, loud noise, verbal reprimands, a physical slap, a squirt of lemon juice in the mouth, and a cue previously conditioned with shock (Azrin, 1958; Hake & Azrin, 1965; Reed & Yoshino, 2008; Hall et al., 1971; Masserman, 1946; Sajwaj, Libet, & Agras, 1974; Skinner, 1938). Other response-suppression procedures have involved the loss of positive reinforcement, time out from positive reinforcement, overcorrection, and manual restraint (Foxx & Azrin, 1973; Lerman, Iwata, Shore, & DeLeon, 1997; Thomas, 1968; Trenholme & Baron, 1975).

Time out refers to removal of the opportunity to obtain positive reinforcement. Time out is often used to punish children, as when a child is told to sit in a time-out chair in the back of a classroom. Sitting in a chair is not inherently aversive. A time-out chair suppresses behavior because it prevents the child from doing other things that he or she may enjoy more. **Overcorrection** involves requiring a person not only to rectify what was done badly, but to overcorrect for the mistake. For example, a child who has placed an object in his mouth may be asked to remove the object and also to wash out his mouth with an antiseptic solution.

A convenient aversive stimulus in human studies of punishment is point loss. For example, in one study (O'Donnell, Crosbie, Williams, & Saunders, 2000), college students pressed a response lever to obtain points that could be exchanged for money at the end of the experiment. Two discriminative stimuli (lines of different lengths) were used. During the baseline phase, only one of the lines (the S^D) was presented, and responses were reinforced on a variable interval schedule. After that, the S^D was alternated with the other discriminative stimulus, which served as the S^D_P. Responding continued to be reinforced according to the VI schedule during the S^D_P, but now a point-loss punishment contingency was also in effect. With each response, points were subtracted from the total the subject had obtained.

The results of the experiment are summarized in Figure 10.12. Responding was well maintained during S^D in the baseline phase. In the subsequent punishment phase, responding continued at substantial levels during S^D but was suppressed during S^D_P. (For an analogue to point loss in a study of punishment in pigeons, see Raiff, Bullock, & Hackenberg, 2008.)

The response suppression produced by punishment depends in part on features of the aversive stimulus. The effects of various characteristics of the aversive event have been most extensively investigated in studies with laboratory rats and pigeons. Shock is usually employed as the aversive stimulus in these experiments because the duration and intensity of shock can be precisely controlled. As one might predict, more intense and longer shocks are more effective in punishing responding (see reviews by Azrin & Holz, 1966; Church, 1969; Walters & Grusec, 1977). Low-intensity punishment produces only moderate suppression of behavior. Even more problematic is the fact that responding often recovers with continued punishment with mild shock (e.g., Azrin, 1960). Thus, subjects habituate to the punishment procedure. By contrast, if the aversive stimulus is of high intensity, responding will be completely suppressed for a long time. In one experiment, for example, high-intensity punishment completely suppressed the instrumental response for six days (Azrin, 1960).

Another very important factor in punishment is how the aversive stimulus is introduced. If a high intensity of shock is used from the outset of punishment, the instrumental response will be severely suppressed. However, if the high intensity punishment is reached only after a slow escalation of punishment, much less suppression of behavior will occur (Azrin, Holz, & Hake, 1963; Miller, 1960; see also Banks, 1976). This is a very important finding. It shows that exposure to low intensity of punishment builds resistance and makes the subject immune to the effects of more severe punishment. Spending two weeks in jail is not a disturbing experience for someone who has become accustomed to shorter periods of incarceration.

The preceding findings suggest that how organisms respond during their *initial exposure* to punishment determines how they will respond to punishment subsequently (Church, 1969). This idea has an interesting implication. Suppose an individual is first exposed to intense shock that results in a very low level of responding. If the shock intensity is subsequently reduced, the severe suppression of behavior should persist. Thus, after exposure to intense shock, mild shock should be more effective in suppressing behavior than if the mild shock had been used from the beginning. Such findings have been obtained by Raymond (reported in Church, 1969). Taken together, the evidence indicates that initial exposure to mild aversive stimulation that does not disrupt behavior reduces the effects of later intense punishment. By con-

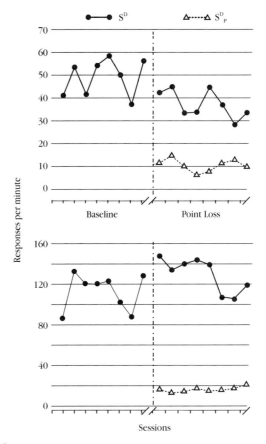

FIGURE **10.12**

Lever-press responding of college students reinforced on a variable interval schedule with points that could be exchanged for money at the end of the experiment. During the baseline phase only the reinforced discriminative stimulus (S^D) was presented. During the next phase, the S^D was presented in alternation with a punishment stimulus (S^D_P), during which the VI schedule remained in effect but each response was also punished by point loss. Each panel presents data from a different subject. (From J. O'Donnell, et al. (2000). Stimulus control and generalization of point-loss punishment with humans. *Journal of the Experimental Analysis of Behavior, 73,* Figure 1, p. 266. Copyright 2000 by the Society for the Experimental Analysis of Behavior, Inc. Reprinted with permission.)

trast, initial exposure to intense aversive stimulation increases the suppressive effects of later mild punishment (see Figure 10.13).

Response-Contingent versus Response-Independent Aversive Stimulation

Another important variable that determines the effectiveness of punishment is whether the aversive stimulus is presented contingent on the target response or

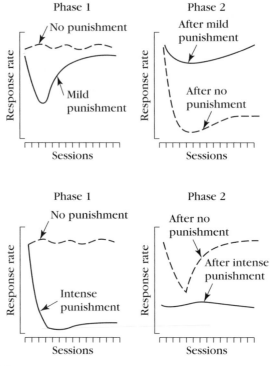

FIGURE **10.13**

Top panel: Effects of a history of mild punishment (Phase 1) on later responding during intense punishment (Phase 2). Bottom panel: Effects of a history of intense punishment (Phase 1) on later responding to mild punishment (Phase 2). (Hypothetical data.) (From M. Domjan *Essentials of conditioning and learning.* (Cengage, 3rd edition), Figures 11.1 and 11.2, p. 178.)

independently of behavior. Response-independent aversive stimulation can result in some suppression of instrumental behavior. (We saw that to be the case in the conditioned suppression effect, described in Chapter 3.) However, significantly more suppression of behavior occurs if the aversive stimulus is triggered by the instrumental response (e.g., Azrin, 1956; Bolles, Holtz, Dunn, & Hill, 1980; Camp, Raymond, & Church, 1967; Frankel, 1975).

One study of the importance of the response contingency in punishment (Goodall, 1984) compared lever-press responding in rats in the presence of two different stimuli (a tone and a light). One of the stimuli was used with a punishment procedure (the PUN cue), and the other stimulus was used with a conditioned suppression procedure (the CER cue). Lever-pressing was always reinforced on a VI 60-second food-reinforcement schedule. Once baseline responding was well established, the PUN cue and the CER cue were presented periodically. During the PUN cue, the rats received a brief shock after every third lever-press. Thus, punishment was delivered on an FR 3 schedule. Each CER trial was yoked to the preceding punishment trial, so that the rats received the same number and distribution of shocks during the CER cue as they got

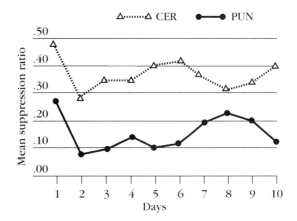

FIGURE **10.14**

Suppression of lever-pressing during punishment and CER stimuli during 10 successive sessions. During the punishment cue, lever-pressing was punished on an FR 3 schedule. During the CER cue, the same number and distribution of shocks was delivered independent of behavior. (From "Learning Due to the Response-Shock Contingency in Signaled Punishment" by G. Goodall, 1984, *The Quarterly Journal of Experimental Psychology, 36B*, pp. 259–279. Copyright © 1984 by Lawrence Erlbaum Associates. Reprinted by permission.)

during the immediately preceding PUN cue. However, shocks during the CER cue were always delivered independent of the lever-press behavior.

The results of the experiment are presented in Figure 10.14 in terms of suppression of lever-pressing during the CER and punishment cues. Given the brief and mild shocks that were used (0.5 mA, 0.5 seconds), not much suppression of behavior was evident during the CER stimulus. By contrast, the same number and distribution of shocks substantially suppressed responding during the punishment stimulus. This difference illustrates that delivering shocks contingent on an instrumental response is more effective in suppressing that response than delivering the aversive stimulus independent of behavior.

Effects of Delay of Punishment

Another critical factor in punishment is the interval between the target response and the aversive stimulus. Increasing the delay of punishment results in less suppression of behavior (e.g., Baron, 1965; Camp et al., 1967). This relation is particularly important in practical applications of punishment. Inadvertent delays can occur if the undesired response is not detected right away, if it takes time to investigate who is actually at fault for an error, or if preparing the aversive stimulus requires time. Such delays can make punishment totally ineffective. If you cannot punish the target response right away, you might as well not punish it at all.

Effects of Schedules of Punishment

Just as positive reinforcement does not have to be provided for each occurrence of the instrumental response, as we saw in the experiment by Goodall, punishment may also be delivered only intermittently. In the Goodall study, punishment was delivered on an FR 3 schedule. More systematic studies

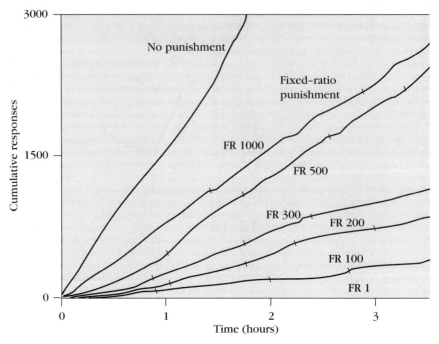

FIGURE **10.15**

Cumulative record of pecking by a pigeon when the response was not punished and when the response was punished according to various fixed-ratio schedules of punishment. The oblique slashes indicate the delivery of punishment. Responding was reinforced on a variable-interval three-minute schedule. (From "Fixed-Ratio Punishment" by N. H. Azrin, W. C. Holz, and D. R. Hake, 1963, *Journal of the Experimental Analysis of Behavior, 6*, pp. 141–148.)

have shown that the degree of response suppression produced by punishment depends on the proportion of responses that are punished.

In a study of fixed-ratio punishment by Azrin and his colleagues (1963), pigeons were first reinforced with food on a variable interval schedule for pecking a response key. Punishment was then introduced. Various fixed-ratio punishment procedures were tested while the VI reinforcement schedule remained in effect. The results are summarized in Figure 10.15. When every response was shocked (FR 1 punishment), key pecking ceased entirely. With the other punishment schedules, the rate of responding depended on how intermittent the punishment was. Higher fixed-ratio schedules allowed more responses to go unpunished. Not surprisingly, therefore, higher rates of responding occurred when higher fixed-ratio punishment schedules were used. Remarkably, however, some suppression of behavior was observed even when only every thousandth response was followed by shock.

Types and Schedules of Positive Reinforcement

In most punishment situations the target response is simultaneously maintained by a schedule of positive reinforcement. A high school student who is punished for violating the school's dress code is being simultaneously reinforced for breaking the rules by social approval from her peers. In this case the alternative source of reinforcement is obvious. In other instances, such as self-injurious behavior in a person with developmental disabilities, the target response may be maintained by intrinsic reinforcement. No matter what the alternative source of reinforcement is, the effects of punishment depend a great deal on the reinforcer that maintains the target response. This relationship is dramatic in the case of drug reinforcers. One of the hallmarks of severe drug addiction is that the individual continues to seek and take the drug even if the addiction causes the person to lose his or her job, family, house, and health.

Only recently have scientists succeeded in developing a satisfactory animal model of drug addiction that incorporates the resistance of drug seeking behavior to punishment. Pelloux, Everitt, and Dickinson (2007) trained rats to obtain a hit of cocaine using a two-lever task. The first lever was the drug-seeking lever and the second one was the drug-taking lever. At the beginning of each trial, the seeking lever was extended into the experimental chamber. Responding on this lever on a VI 120-second schedule resulted in the appearance of the taking lever. One response on the taking lever produced a hit of cocaine (delivered intravenously). Rats received either a moderate amount of training on this task (about eight sessions) or extensive training (an additional 14 sessions). Punishment was then introduced. On half of the trials, responding on the seeking lever ended in a brief shock and no cocaine was delivered. On the rest of the trials, there was no shock and cocaine was available as usual. (A control group continued being trained without punishment.)

The results of the baseline and punishment phase of the experiment are summarized in the left panel of Figure 10.16. During the baseline phase, the subjects made 200–250 seeking responses per session. Responding continued at this level for the rats that were not punished. The introduction of punishment produced a decrement in behavior. However, the decrement depended on the extent of training on the drug-reinforcement task. Punishment was highly effective for the moderately-trained rats. The results were mixed for the rats that got extensive training on cocaine self administration. Some of the extended-cocaine rats behaved just like the moderately-trained rats. Punishment suppressed their drug seeking behavior. In contrast, some of the rats in this group (five out of 21) were resistant to the effects of punishment. These punishment-resistant rats showed an initial drop in responding when punishment was introduced but their drug-seeking behavior subsequently recovered in the face of continued punishment.

Ordinarily scientists are discouraged when they find that a manipulation is effective in only a subset of their subjects. However, in this instance the fact that punishment did not work for a subset of the extended-cocaine rats is good news because that makes this a better model of human addiction. Only a subset of people who try drugs or use drugs on a regular basis develop the kind of severe addiction that leads them to continue their addictive behaviors at the expense of their marriage, job, or house. Other investigators have shown that in rats with an extensive history of cocaine self administration, resistance to punishment, persistence in drug-seeking behavior in extinction, and motivation to obtain the drug (as measured by a progressive ratio schedule) are all correlated with drug-induced relapse (Deroche-Gamonet, Belin, & Piazza, 2004).

However, there is a major remaining question: Is the resistance to punishment a consequence of the use of cocaine as the reinforcer, or are such effects

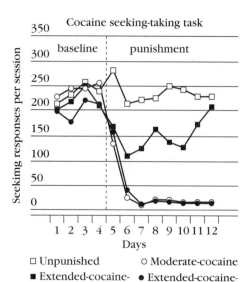
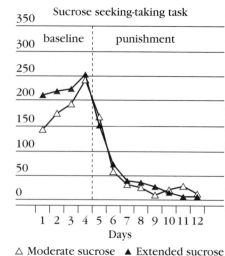

□ Unpunished ○ Moderate-cocaine
■ Extended-cocaine-
resistant ● Extended-cocaine-
sensitive

△ Moderate sucrose ▲ Extended sucrose

FIGURE **10.16**

Rate of responding to seek cocaine (left panel) or sucrose (right panel) during a baseline period and during a period when punishment occurred on half the trials. Different groups of rats received either moderate or extended training. Subjects receiving extended training with cocaine were further segregated depending on whether they were sensitive or resistant to the effects of punishment. A control group with cocaine reinforcement was tested without punishment. (After Pelloux, Everitt, & Dickinson, 2007.)

also observed following extensive training with other reinforcers? Pelloux et al. (2007) addressed that question by training rats with sucrose as the reinforcer, using procedures identical to what was used with the cocaine-reinforced subjects. The results of punishing sucrose-seeking behavior are summarized in the right panel of Figure 10.16. Sucrose seeking was suppressed by punishment whether subjects received moderate or extensive training. None of the sucrose rats showed evidence of being so addicted to sucrose that they became resistant to punishment. Only cocaine produced that result.

The results of the Pelloux et al. (2007) study show that the effects of punishment depend on what serves to reinforce the target behavior. The schedule of reinforcement used for the target response is also important. When behavior is maintained by either a fixed or a variable-interval schedule of positive reinforcement, punishment produces a decrease in the overall rate of responding. However, the temporal distribution of the behavior is not disturbed. That is, during the punishment procedure, variable interval positive reinforcement produces a suppressed but stable rate of responding (see Figure 10.15), whereas fixed-interval positive reinforcement produces the typical scalloped pattern of responding (e.g., Azrin & Holz, 1961).

The outcome is different if the behavior is maintained by a fixed-ratio schedule of positive reinforcement. As we noted in Chapter 6, fixed-ratio schedules produce a pause in responding just after reinforcement (the postreinforcement pause), followed by a high and steady rate of responding to complete the number of responses necessary for the next reinforcer (the ratio run). Punishment usually increases the length of the postreinforcement pause but has little effect on the ratio run (Azrin, 1959; see also Church, 1969; Dardano & Sauerbrunn, 1964).

Availability of Alternative Sources of Positive Reinforcement

Punishment has dramatically different outcomes depending on whether the subject is able to obtain reinforcement by engaging in some other activity. This is very important in practical applications of punishment. If the punished response is the only activity available to the subject for obtaining reinforcement, punishment will be much less effective than if an alternative source of reinforcement is provided along with punishment.

The importance of alternative sources of reinforcement was demonstrated by an early study of adult male smokers conducted by Herman and Azrin (1964). The subjects were seated facing two response levers. Pressing either lever was reinforced with a cigarette on a variable-interval schedule. After the behavior was occurring at a stable rate, responding on one of the levers was punished by a brief obnoxious noise. In one experimental condition, only one response lever was available during the punishment phase. In another condition, both response levers were available, but responding on one of the levers was punished with the loud noise. Figure 10.17 shows the results. When the punished response was the only way to obtain cigarettes, punishment produced a moderate suppression of behavior. By contrast, when the alternative response lever was available,

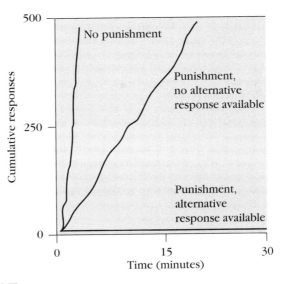

FIGURE **10.17**

Cumulative record of responding when responses were not punished, when responses were punished and there was no alternative source of reinforcement, and when responses were punished but an alternative reinforced response was available. (From "Fixed-Ratio Punishment" by N. H. Azrin and W. C. Holz, in W. K. Honig (Ed.), 1966, Operant Behavior. Copyright © 1966 by Prentice Hall.)

responding on the punished lever ceased altogether. Thus, the availability of an alternative response for obtaining positive reinforcement greatly increased the suppressive effects of punishment. Similar results have been obtained in other situations. For example, children punished for playing with certain toys are much less likely to play with these if they are allowed to play with other toys instead (Perry & Parke, 1975). Reinforcement for alternative behavior also increases the effectiveness of mild punishment in suppressing self-injurious behavior in individuals with severe developmental disabilities (Thompson, Iwata, Conners, & Roscoe, 1999).

Effects of a Discriminative Stimulus for Punishment

As we saw in Chapter 8, if positive reinforcement is available for responding in the presence of a distinctive stimulus but is not available in its absence, the organism will learn to respond only when the stimulus is present. The suppressive effects of punishment can also be brought under stimulus control. This occurs if responding is punished in the presence of a discriminative stimulus but, is not punished when the stimulus is absent. Such a procedure is called **discriminative punishment.** With discriminative punishment training, the suppressive effects of punishment will come to be limited to the presence of the discriminative stimulus (Dinsmoor, 1952).

Discriminative punishment was used in the study whose results were summarized in Figure 10.12. The college students who served in this experiment could earn points for responding during one discriminative stimulus, the S^D. In the presence of another discriminative stimulus, the S^D_P, responding was also punished by loss of points. As Figure 10.12 illustrates, the suppressive effects of punishment were largely limited to the S^D_P.

The fact that the suppressive effects of punishment can be limited to the presence of a discriminative stimulus is often problematic in applications of punishment. In many situations, the person who administers the punishment also serves as a discriminative stimulus for punishment, with the result that the undesired behavior is suppressed only as long as the monitor is present. For example, children learn which teachers are strict about discipline and learn to suppress their rambunctious behavior with those teachers more than with other teachers. A highway patrol car is a discriminative stimulus for punishment for speeding. Drivers are more likely to stay at or below the speed limit where they see patrol cars than in unpatrolled stretches of highway.

Punishment as a Signal for the Availability of Positive Reinforcement

Under certain circumstances people seem to seek out punishment. How can that be? Isn't punishment supposed to suppress behavior? Experimental evidence suggests that conventional behavioral mechanisms may lead to preference for punishment. Punishment seeking can result if positive reinforcement is available only when the instrumental response is also punished. In such circumstances, punishment may become a signal, or discriminative stimulus, for the availability of positive reinforcement. If this occurs, punishment will increase rather than suppress responding.

In one demonstration of the discriminative stimulus properties of punishment, pigeons were first trained to peck a response key for food reinforcement on a variable-interval schedule (Holz & Azrin, 1961). Each response was then punished by a mild shock sufficient to reduce the response rate by about 50%. In the next phase of the experiment, periods in which the punishment procedure was in effect were alternated with periods in which punishment was not scheduled. In addition, the pecking response was reinforced with food only during the punishment periods. The punishment and safe periods were not signaled by an environmental stimulus, such as a light or a tone. The only way for the pigeons to tell whether reinforcement was available was to see whether they were punished for pecking. Under these circumstances higher rates of pecking occurred during punishment periods than during safe periods. Punishment became a discriminative stimulus for food reinforcement. (For other examples of punishment-seeking behavior, see Brown, 1969; Brown & Cunningham, 1981; Dean & Pittman, 1991; and Melvin, 1971.)

Theories of Punishment

In contrast to the study of avoidance behavior, investigations of punishment, by and large, have not been motivated by theoretical considerations. Most of the evidence available about the effects of punishment has been the product of empirical curiosity. Investigators were interested in finding out how punishment is influenced by various manipulations rather than in testing specific theoretical formulations. In fact, there are few systematic theories of punishment, and most of these were formulated some time ago (see Spradlin, 2002). I will describe three of the most prominent theories.

The Conditioned Emotional Response Theory of Punishment

One of the first theories of punishment was proposed by Estes (1944) and is based on the observation by Estes and Skinner (1941) that a conditioned stimulus that has been paired with shock will suppress the performance of food-reinforced instrumental behavior. We discussed this conditioned suppression, or conditioned emotional response, procedure earlier in this chapter as well as in Chapters 3. Conditioned suppression involves a suppression of ongoing behavior elicited by a stimulus that has been associated with aversive stimulation. The behavioral suppression occurs primarily because a fear-conditioned stimulus elicits freezing, which then interferes with other activities.

Estes (1944) proposed that punishment suppresses behavior through the same mechanism that produces response suppression to a fear-conditioned stimulus (see also Estes, 1969). In contrast to the usual conditioned suppression experiment, however, punishment procedures usually do not involve an explicit CS that signals the impending delivery of an aversive stimulus. Estes suggested that the various stimuli an individual experiences just before making the punished response serve this function. Consider for example, how an invisible fence works to keep a dog in its yard. An invisible or electronic fence detects when the dog goes to the edge of its yard and administers a brief shock to the dog through a remote sensing collar if the dog crosses this boundary. The punished response (going too far) is associated with various cues of the boundary of the yard. When the dog is punished, the visual and other spatial cues of the yard boundary become paired with shock. With repetition of the punishment episode, the boundary stimuli become strongly conditioned by the shock. According to the conditioned emotional response

BOX **10.2**

When Punishment Doesn't Work

Sometimes children are brought to a therapist because their behavior is out of control. A child may be unruly and unresponsive to the disciplinary practices of parents or teachers. Punishment may be tried as a last resort, but without much success. The parents or teachers may note that punishing the child only makes the behavior worse. It is not uncommon for children with a severe problem of this type to be diagnosed as hyperactive or emotionally disturbed. These labels suggest there is something fundamentally wrong with the child. Behavior therapists, however, have found that in some cases the problem may be nothing more than the result of mismanaged discipline. The parents or teachers may have inadvertently established punishment as a discriminative stimulus for positive reinforcement. Instead of decreasing some undesirable behavior, punishment increases it. How can this happen?

Let us take the hypothetical situation of Johnny, who lives in a home with two busy parents. Johnny, like most children, is rather active. If he is quietly playing in his room, the parents are likely to ignore him and engage in activities of their own. By contrast, if Johnny behaves badly or makes demands, the parents are forced to pay attention to him. The parents may be giving Johnny attention only when he is misbehaving or making demands. Any time he is not being a problem, the parents may be thankfully relieved to have a moment's peace. Thus, rather than reinforcing cooperative or peaceful behavior, the parents may be ignoring Johnny at these times. What we have then is a vicious circle. The more Johnny misbehaves, the less attention he is given for nondisruptive behavior, because the parents increasingly come to cherish quiet moments as a chance to do something on their own. Misbehavior

becomes Johnny's main means of obtaining attention. The punishments and reprimands that go with the behavior signal to him that his parents are caring and attending.

In actuality, the therapist does not have the opportunity to observe how behavior problems of this type originate. The explanation in terms of the *discriminative value of punishment* is supported by the outcome of attempts to change the situation. The hypothesis suggests that if one changes the attention patterns of the parents, the behavior problem can be alleviated. Indeed, clinical psychologists often show parents how to attend to appropriate and constructive activities and how to administer punishment with a minimum of attention directed toward the child. In many cases dramatic improvement ensues when parents are able to positively reinforce cooperative behavior with their attentions and ignore disruptive activities as much as possible.

theory, as these cues acquire conditioned aversive properties, they will come to elicit freezing, which is incompatible with the punished behavior. Thus, the punished response will become suppressed.

The conditioned emotional response theory can explain many punishment effects. For example, the fact that more intense and longer duration shocks produce more response suppression can be explained by assuming that the stimuli conditioned by these aversive events elicit more vigorous conditioned emotional responses. The theory can also explain why response-contingent aversive stimulation produces more response suppression than response-independent delivery of shock. If shock is produced by the instrumental response, the stimuli that become conditioned by the shock are more likely to be closely related to performance of this behavior. Therefore, the conditioned emotional responses are more likely to interfere with the punished response.

The Avoidance Theory of Punishment

An alternative to the conditioned emotional response theory regards punishment as a form of avoidance behavior. This theory is most closely associated with Dinsmoor (1954, 1977, 1998) and follows the tradition of two-process theory of avoidance. Dinsmoor accepted the idea that the stimuli that accompany the instrumental response acquire aversive properties when the response is punished. Dinsmoor went on to propose that organisms learn to escape from the conditioned aversive stimuli related to the punished response by engaging in some other behavior that is incompatible with the punished activity. Performance of the alternative activity results in suppression of the punished behavior. Thus, the avoidance theory explains punishment in terms of the acquisition of incompatible avoidance responses.

The avoidance theory of punishment is an ingenious proposal. It suggests that all changes produced by aversive instrumental conditioning, be they an increase or a decrease in the likelihood of a response, can be explained by the same avoidance learning mechanisms. Suppression of behavior is not viewed as reflecting the weakening of the punished response. Rather, it is explained in terms of the strengthening of competing avoidance responses.

Despite its cleverness and parsimony, the avoidance theory of punishment has been controversial. Because it explains punishment in terms of avoidance mechanisms, all the theoretical problems that have burdened the analysis of avoidance behavior become problems in the analysis of punishment. Another challenge for the theory is that its critical elements are not stated in a way that makes them easy to prove or disprove (Rachlin & Herrnstein, 1969; Schuster & Rachlin, 1968). The stimuli that are assumed to acquire conditioned aversive properties are not under the direct control of the experimenter. Rather, they are events that an organism is assumed to experience when it is about to make the punished response. The avoidance responses that are presumably acquired are also ill specified. The theory cannot predict what these responses will be or how we might identify or measure them.

Punishment and the Negative Law of Effect

The third and last explanation of punishment that I will describe is also the oldest. Thorndike (1911) originally proposed that positive reinforcement and punishment involve symmetrically opposite processes. Just as positive reinforcement strengthens behavior, so punishment weakens it. In later years Thorndike abandoned the idea that punishment weakens behavior (Thorndike, 1932), but the belief that there is a negative law of effect that is comparable but opposite of a positive law of effect has been retained by other investigators (e.g., Azrin & Holz, 1966; Rachlin & Herrnstein, 1969).

One approach to the negative law of effect was initiated by Premack and his colleagues. As I discussed in Chapter 7, Premack proposed that positive reinforcement occurs when the opportunity to engage in a highly valued activity is made to depend on the prior performance of an activity of lower value. According to Premack, the punishment contingency reverses this relation. In punishment, a low valued activity occurs contingent on the performance of a higher valued behavior. Exposing oneself to shock, for example, has a much lower probability than pressing a lever for food. Hence, shock can punish lever pressing. (For further discussion, see Burkhard, Rachlin, & Schrader, 1978; Premack, 1971a.)

Contemporary research related to a possible negative law of effect has employed concurrent schedules of reinforcement in which one component includes a punishment contingency (e.g., Critchfield, Paletz, MacAleese, & Newland, 2003). As I described in Chapter 6, a concurrent schedule is one in which subjects have two responses available at the same time, and each is reinforced on a different schedule. The results of such experiments are typically analyzed using the generalized matching law that characterizes how the relative rate of responding on one alternative is related to the relative rate of reinforcement on that alternative. As I noted in Chapter 6, the generalized matching law includes parameters for response bias and sensitivity to relative rates of reinforcement (see page 202). Punishment can change these parameters.

In a recent study, Rasmussen and Newland (2008) were interested in figuring out whether a punisher and a reinforcer have equal but opposite effects (for a related study with children with ADHD, see Carlson & Tamm, 2000). To answer this question, the magnitudes of the punisher and the reinforcer have to be equated. But, that is hard to do with outcomes such as shock and food. What intensity and duration of shock is equivalent to a pellet of food? Rasmussen and Newland (2008) sidestepped this question by using monetary gains and losses as the outcomes. College students worked on a concurrent schedule that involved clicking on moving targets on a computer screen. Two different targets were available concurrently, and clicking on each was reinforced according to a different variable interval schedule. The reinforcer was gaining 4 ¢ and the punisher was losing 4 ¢. After responding stabilized on a concurrent schedule that involved only reinforcement in each component, a punishment contingency was added to one of the components. Punishment was also provided on a VI schedule. Each participant was tested on nine variations of the concurrent schedules, and the results were analyzed using the generalized matching law, with special emphasis on the bias and sensitivity parameters.

One might not predict that gaining and losing 4 ¢ would motivate much behavior among college students, but the results were dramatic. Imposing a punishment procedure in one component of the concurrent schedule created a large bias in favor of responding on the non-punished alternative. In addition, the punishment contingency caused a reduction in sensitivity to relative reinforcement rates. Most interestingly, punishment was three times more effective than reinforcement. Rasmussen and Newland concluded that "losing a penny is three times more punishing than earning that same penny is reinforcing" (p. 165).

Punishment Outside the Laboratory

As we have seen, punishment can be a highly effective procedure for rapidly suppressing behavior and can cause a major shift in favor of alternative responses that are reinforced. However, the effectiveness of punishment in laboratory studies is not sufficient to justify its application outside the laboratory. Punishment procedures are easily misused. Even if the procedures are administered appropriately, there are serious ethical constraints on their application and they can have troublesome side effects.

Punishment is typically not applied in an effective manner. Often punishment is first introduced at low intensities (e.g., a reprimand for the first offense). The aversive stimulus may not be administered rapidly after the target response but delayed until it is convenient to administer it ("Wait until I tell your parents about this"). Punishment is usually administered on an intermittent schedule, and the chances of getting caught may not be high. (How often do drivers who exceed the speed limit get a ticket?) Punishment is rarely accompanied by alternative sources of reinforcement because it is much easier to react to transgressions than it is to make sure that appropriate behavior is reinforced. Often there are clear discriminative stimuli for punishment. The undesired behavior may be monitored only at particular times or by a particular person, making it likely that the punished response will be suppressed only at those times. Finally, punishment may be the only source of attention for someone, making punishment a discriminative stimulus for positive reinforcement.

The preceding problems with the use of punishment outside the laboratory can be overcome. However, it is difficult to guard against these pitfalls in common interpersonal interactions. When you yell at your child or hang up on your girlfriend, you are likely doing so out of frustration and anger. A frustrative act of punishment is likely to violate many of the guidelines for the effective use of punishment. Punishing someone in an act of anger and frustration is a form of abuse, not a form of systematic training.

The use of punishment in parenting has been the subject of extensive research. Consistent with the implications of laboratory research, a review of the literature on parental corporal punishment concluded that punishment is strongly associated with increased immediate compliance on the part of a child (Gershoff, 2002). However, the same analysis showed that corporal punishment is also associated with unintended consequences, such as children's aggression, problems in child mental health, and parent-child relationship difficulties. In addition, parental punishment is associated with delinquent and antisocial behavior, and increased incidence of aggressive behavior in adulthood. However, it is difficult to isolate the causal role of parental punishment in these effects because most of the evidence is based on correlational data. Parents who are apt to use punishment may be cold and aloof in their relationship with their children and less likely to reward them for good behavior. Or, they may be harsh and punitive in a variety of ways, only one of which is corporal punishment.

Parental use of corporal punishment has been outlawed in a number of countries (Austria, Croatia, Cyprus, Denmark, Finland, Germany, Israel, Italy, Latvia, Norway, and Sweden). Although corporal punishment by parents is not against the law in the United States, more than half the states have adopted laws limiting the use of corporal punishment by teachers and guardians. However, punishment can be justified and may be even imperative if the target response is likely to be injurious and the behavior has to be suppressed immediately (Lerman & Vorndran, 2002). If a child is about to chase a ball into a busy street, there is no time for shaping and positive reinforcement of appropriate behavior. Punishment is sometimes also advisable for controlling self-injurious behavior in persons with developmental disabilities.

In one study, for example, punishment was used to suppress recurrent vomiting by a nine month old infant (Linscheid & Cunningham, 1977). The recurrent vomiting had resulted in excessive weight loss and malnutrition. Without treatment, the infant risked potentially fatal medical complications. Brief (0.5 second) shocks sufficient to elicit a startle response, but not sufficient to elicit crying, were used as the aversive stimulus. Within three days, vomiting was nearly totally suppressed by the punishment procedure. The suppression of vomiting persisted after discharge from the hospital. The infant started gaining weight again and was soon within normal range.

The above example demonstrates that punishment can be a useful treatment procedure and sometimes it is the only available option. But, if it is used, it is has to be a part of a well planned and systematic treatment program so as to avoid the deleterious side-effects of punishment.

SAMPLE QUESTIONS

1. What is the fundamental problem in the analysis of avoidance behavior, and how is this problem resolved by two-process theory?
2. Compare and contrast discriminated and free-operant avoidance procedures.
3. How can the concept of a safety signal be used to explain free-operant avoidance learning?
4. What are species specific defense reactions and why is it important to consider them in avoidance and punishment situations?
5. Describe factors that enhance the effectiveness of punishment in suppressing behavior.
6. In what ways is punishment similar to positive reinforcement; in what ways is it different?

KEY TERMS

acquired-drive A source of motivation for instrumental behavior caused by the presentation of a stimulus that was previously conditioned with a primary, or unconditioned, reinforcer.

avoidance An instrumental conditioning procedure in which the participant's behavior prevents the delivery of an aversive stimulus.

avoidance trial A trial in a discriminated avoidance procedure in which an avoidance response is made and prevents the delivery of the aversive stimulus.

discriminated avoidance An avoidance conditioning procedure in which occurrences of the aversive stimulus are signaled by a conditioned stimulus. Responding during the conditioned stimulus terminates the CS and prevents the delivery of the aversive unconditioned stimulus. Also called *signaled avoidance*.

discriminative punishment A procedure in which responding is punished in the presence of a particular stimulus and not punished in the absence of that stimulus.

escape trial A trial during discriminated avoidance training in which the required avoidance response is not made and the aversive unconditioned stimulus is presented. Performance of the instrumental response during the aversive stimulus results in termination of the aversive stimulus. Thus, the organism is able to escape from the aversive stimulus.

escape from fear (EFF) procedure Situation in which subjects can learn an instrumental response to escape from or terminate a stimulus that elicits fear. Escape from fear provides a coping mechanism for individuals suffering from excessive fear.

flooding A procedure for extinguishing avoidance behavior in which the conditioned stimulus is presented while the participant is prevented from making the avoidance response.

free-operant avoidance Same as *nondiscriminated avoidance.*

nondiscriminated avoidance An avoidance conditioning procedure in which occurrences of the aversive stimulus are not signaled by an external stimulus. In the absence of avoidance responding, the aversive stimulus is presented periodically, as set by the S-S interval. Each occurrence of the avoidance response creates (or resets) a period of safety determined by the S-R interval during which the aversive stimulus is not presented. Also called *free-operant avoidance;* originally called *Sidman avoidance.*

overcorrection A procedure for discouraging behavior in which the participant is not only required to correct or rectify a mistake but is also required to go beyond that by, for example, extensively practicing the correct response alternative.

predatory imminence The perceived likelihood of being attacked by a predator. Different species typical defense responses occur in the face of different degrees of predatory imminence.

punishment An instrumental conditioning procedure in which there is a positive contingency between the instrumental response and an aversive stimulus. If the participant performs the instrumental response, it receives the aversive stimulus; if the participant does not perform the instrumental response, it does not receive the aversive stimulus.

R-S interval The interval between the occurrence of an avoidance response and the next scheduled presentation of the aversive stimulus in a nondiscriminated avoidance procedure. Thus, the R-S interval sets the duration of safety created by each avoidance response in a nondiscriminated avoidance procedure.

response prevention Blocking the opportunity to make the avoidance response so that the subject is exposed to a fear stimulus without being able to escape from it. Usually used in connection with *flooding.*

safety signal A stimulus that signals the absence of an aversive event.

shock-frequency reduction A hypothesis according to which reduction in the frequency of shock serves to reinforce avoidance behavior.

shuttle avoidance A type of avoidance conditioning procedure in which the required instrumental response consists of real going back and forth (shuttling) between two sides of an experimental apparatus.

signaled avoidance Same as *discriminated avoidance.*

species-specific defense reactions Species typical responses animals perform in an aversive situation. The responses may involve freezing, fleeing, or fighting.

S-S interval The interval between successive presentations of the aversive stimulus in a nondiscriminated avoidance procedure when the avoidance response is not performed.

time out A period during which the opportunity to obtain positive reinforcement is removed. This may involve removal of the participant from the situation where reinforcers may be obtained.

two-process theory of avoidance A theory originally developed to explain discriminated avoidance learning that presumes the operation of two mechanisms: classical conditioning of fear to the warning signal or CS, and instrumental reinforcement of the avoidance response through termination of the warning signal and consequent fear reduction.

11

Comparative Cognition I: Memory Mechanisms

CHAPTER PREVIEW

The study of comparative cognition dates back to Darwin's writings about the evolution of intelligence and subsequent research on learning in nonhuman animals. However, the best research on comparative cognition has been done in the past 40 years. Chapter 11 begins with a definition of comparative cognition and a brief discussion of some cognitive effects I already described in earlier sections of this book. The rest of the chapter is devoted to memory, one of the most important cognitive processes related to learning. I start by describing the relationship between learning and memory and the distinction between working memory and reference memory. I then discuss several prominent paradigms for the study of working memory in nonhuman animals. The next section describes research relevant to three different stages of memory: acquisition, retention, and retrieval. The chapter ends with a discussion of different sources of memory failure and the phenomenon of retrograde amnesia.

––––––––––––––

As I noted in Chapter 1, interest in comparative cognition dates back to the founding of the field of animal learning in the second half of the nineteenth century. Early experimental efforts to study comparative cognition employed animal learning paradigms. However, studies of animal learning soon came to have a life of their own. Through much of the twentieth century, learning was investigated in animals for what it told us about behavior in general, rather than for what it told us about comparative cognition or animal intelligence. However, the past 40 years have witnessed a resurgence of interest in comparative cognition and animal intelligence (e.g., Griffin, 1976; Hulse, Fowler, & Honig, 1978; Ristau, 1991; Shettleworth, 1998; Spear & Riccio, 1994; Wasserman & Zentall, 2006a).

The renewed interest in comparative cognition was part of the *cognitive revolution* that swept many areas of psychology. These developments have stimulated considerable theoretical debate (e.g., Amsel, 1989; Heyes, 2003; Hintzman, 1991; Wasserman & Zentall, 2006b). Regardless of that debate, an important consequence of contemporary interest in comparative cognition has been the extension of the study of animal learning to numerous new situations. These extensions have raised many novel and interesting questions: questions that were not explored in conventional studies of classical and instrumental conditioning. I will describe some of these developments in this chapter and in Chapter 12.

In addition to providing important new information about learning and memory, studies of comparative cognition address the kind of theoretical questions about the evolution of intelligence that captivated Darwin. Exploring the cognitive skills of animals tells us about the uniqueness of various human cognitive skills, just as exploring other planets can reveal the uniqueness of our terrestrial habitat. As Wasserman (1993) put it, "comparing the intelligence of many species of animals may help us know better what it means to be human" (p. 211). Studies of comparative cognition are also important because they provide model systems for the investigation of the neurophysiological bases of cognitive functions. Memory enhancing drugs, for example, cannot be developed without first developing animal model systems for the study of memory mechanisms (e.g., Gold, 2008). Studies of the mechanisms of cognition in animals may also help us in designing intelligent machines and robots (e.g., Gnadt & Grossberg, 2007; Schaal, et al., 2004; Roitblat & Meyer, 1995).

WHAT IS COMPARATIVE COGNITION?

The word cognition comes from the Latin meaning *knowledge* or *thinking*, and is commonly used to refer to thought processes. In casual discourse, we regard thinking as voluntary, deliberate, and conscious reflection on some topic, usually involving language. Another characteristic of thinking that is more important for comparative cognition is that it can lead to actions that cannot be explained on the basis of the external stimuli an individual experiences at the time. For example, on your way to work, you may start thinking that you did not lock the door to your apartment when you left home. This idea may stimulate you to return home to check whether the door is locked. Your returning cannot be explained by the external stimuli you encountered on your way to work. You come across those stimuli every day without going back to check the door. Rather, your behavior is attributed to the thought that you might have left your apartment unlocked.

There is some controversy about what the domain of comparative cognition should be. Advocates of **cognitive ethology** claim that animals are capable of conscious thought and intentionality (Griffin, 1992; Ristau, 1991). According to cognitive ethologists, comparative cognition should encompass the full range of issues that are included in considerations of human cognition. The claim that nonhuman animals are capable of consciousness and intentionality is based on the complexity, flexibility, and cleverness of various examples of animal behavior. The argument is that conscious intent is the likely source of such clever and flexible behavior. This is basically an argument from design, an argument that has been debated and rejected by philosophers for centuries (Blumberg & Wasserman, 1995). In addition to such philosophical arguments, it is also important to consider recent studies showing the limitations of conscious intent as an adequate explanation of human behavior (Bargh & Morsella, 2008; Wegner, 2002). If conscious intent cannot adequately characterize important features of human behavior, why should we assume that the concept will be useful in explaining the behavior of nonhuman organisms?

In contrast to cognitive ethologists, experimental psychologists use the term *comparative cognition* in a more restricted sense. They follow H. S. Jennings (1904/1976) who argued a century ago that "objective evidence cannot give a demonstration either of the existence or of the non-existence of consciousness, for consciousness is precisely that which cannot be perceived objectively." Jennings went on to say that "no statement concerning consciousness in animals is open to refutation by observation and experiment" (p. 335–336). Contemporary experimental psychologists tie cognitive mechanisms closely to behavioral predictions. That way, cognitive inferences can be refuted by experimental evidence. Experimental psychologists make inferences about the internal or cognitive machinery that mediates behavior in cases where simple S-R or reflex mechanisms are insufficient. However, they are careful to accept only those hypothesized cognitive processes that lead to unambiguous behavioral predictions (Zentall, 2001). Thus, for experimental psychologists, comparative cognition does not imply anything about awareness, consciousness, or verbal reasoning. Rather **comparative cognition** refers to theoretical constructs and models used to explain aspects of behavior that cannot be readily characterized in terms of simple S-R or reflex mechanisms.

A critical feature of comparative cognition is that it employs the simplest possible explanations that are consistent with the data. Consider the following description of behavior:

> "At first, the allure is weak; there is a vague yearning and a mild agitation. Ultimately, the strength of desire grows irresistible; its head turns sharply and it skitters across the uneven floor to caress the objects of its affection with consummate rapture." (Wasserman & Zentall, 2006b, p. 3)

Whose behavior is being described here? As it turns out, this is a poetic description of a coin being drawn to a magnet. We now regard such descriptions as preposterous when applied to a coin because we have come to accept that physical objects like a coin don't have an essence that is capable of rich emotional experience. Unfortunately, adopting a similar dispassionate scientific perspective towards the behavior of nonhuman animals is much more difficult because we have been raised on Disney cartoons and other animated films whose entertainment value is based on attributing a rich mental life to ordinary and fictitious animals. When we make casual inferences about the rich mental life of a bird or squirrel, we are projecting our own thoughts, emotions, and intentions on them. Such projections hamper knowledge of comparative cognition because they are impossible to prove and they prejudge the conclusions that we may arrive at through more systematic observations. These pitfalls of overinterpreting animal behavior were pointed out more than a century ago by C. Lloyd Morgan (1894), but are just as relevant today.

Cognitive mechanisms involve an internal representation or "mental" record of something, and rules for manipulating that mental record. Internal representations may encode various types of information, such as particular features of stimuli or relations between stimuli. Internal representations and their manipulations cannot be investigated directly by looking into the brain. Rather, they have to be inferred from behavior. Thus, a cognitive mechanism is a theoretical construct inferred from behavior, just as magnetic force is a theoretical construct inferred from the behavior of objects that are attracted to each other.

Research on comparative cognition is concerned with questions like how representations are formed, what aspects of experience they encode, how the information is stored, and how it is used later to guide behavior. I have already discussed research relevant to such questions in analyses of classical and instrumental conditioning. For example, I noted in Chapter 4 that classical conditioning involves the learning of an association between a CS and a

US. As a result of this association, presentation of the CS activates a representation (*mental image,* if you will) of the US, and conditioned responding reflects the status of this representation. If the US representation is changed through US devaluation, there is a corresponding change in the conditioned response. I described similar mechanisms in Chapter 7 involving S-O and R-O associations.

ANIMAL MEMORY PARADIGMS

One of the largest areas of comparative cognition is the study of memory (e.g., Spear & Riccio, 1994; Urcelay & Miller, 2008). The term **memory** is commonly used to refer to the ability to respond on the basis of information that was acquired earlier. We are said to remember what happened in our childhood if we talk about our childhood experiences, and we are said to remember someone's name if we call that person by the correct name. Unfortunately, such tests of memory are impractical with nonhuman animals. We cannot ask a pigeon to tell us what it did last week. Instead, we have to use the bird's nonverbal responses as clues to its memory.

If your cat goes out of the house but finds its way back, you might conclude that it remembered where you live. If your dog greets you with unusual exuberance after a long vacation, you might conclude that it remembered you. These and similar examples illustrate that the existence of memory in animals is identified by the fact that *their current behavior is based on some aspect of their earlier experiences.* Any time an animal's behavior is determined by past events, we can conclude that some type of memory is involved.

You may notice that this definition of memory is very similar to the definition of learning stated in Chapter 1. There, learning was defined as an enduring change in responding to a particular situation as a result of prior experience with that type of situation. Thus, evidence of learning is also identified on the basis of changes in behavior due to earlier experiences. Indeed, learning is not possible without memory.

How, then, are studies of memory to be distinguished from studies of learning? The differences may be clarified by considering the components that are common to both learning and memory experiments (see Table 11.1). The first thing that happens in both types of experiments is that the

TABLE **11.1**
Comparison of Learning and Memory Experiments

Phase	Studies of Learning	Studies of Memory
Acquisition	Varied	Constant
Retention	Constant (long)	Varied (short and long)
Retrieval	Constant	Varied

participants are exposed to certain kinds of stimuli or information. This phase is termed **acquisition.** The information that was acquired is then retained for some time, a period called the **retention interval.** At the end of the retention interval, the participants are tested for their memory of the original experience, which requires **retrieval** or reactivation of the information encountered during acquisition. Thus, studies of learning and studies of memory all involve basically three phases: acquisition, retention, and retrieval.

Consider, for example, riding a bicycle. To be a skilled bicyclist, you first have to be trained to balance, pedal, and steer the bike (acquisition). You then have to remember those training experiences (retention). And, when you get on a bicycle again, you have to reactivate the knowledge of bike riding (retrieval).

In studies of learning, the focus is on the acquisition phase. Learning experiments deal with the kind of information we acquire and the ways in which we acquire it. Thus, *learning experiments involve manipulations of the conditions of acquisition.* The retention interval typically is not varied in learning experiments and is always fairly long (a day or longer), because short-term changes in behavior are not considered to be instances of learning. Because the emphasis is on the conditions of acquisition, the conditions of retrieval are also kept constant. All participants in a given experiment are tested for what they learned using the same test procedures.

In contrast, *studies of memory focus on the retention and retrieval phases.* Acquisition is of interest only to the extent that it is relevant to retention and retrieval. The retention interval is often varied to determine how the availability of the acquired information changes with time. Unlike studies of learning, which employ only long retention intervals, studies of memory can employ retention intervals of any duration. In fact, many studies of animal memory evaluate performance at several retention intervals.

Studies of memory also focus on the circumstances of retrieval. Consider, for example, taking a vocabulary test on a set of technical terms in a college course. You may miss many items if the test consists of a series of fill-in-the-blank questions for which you have to provide the technical terms. In contrast, you are likely to do better if you are provided with a list of the technical terms and are merely required to match each term with its definition. These different forms of the test involve different conditions of retrieval.

Memory mechanisms have been classified in various ways depending on what is remembered (the contents of memory), how long the memory lasts (the retention interval), and the mechanisms involved in the memory. Schachter and Tulving (1994), for example, identified five types of human learning and memory: procedural memory, perceptual memory, semantic memory, primary or working memory, and episodic or declarative memory. Not all these forms of memory have their counterparts in research with nonhuman subjects.

Much of the research on classical and instrumental conditioning that I described in earlier chapters involves **procedural memory.** Procedural memory reflects knowledge about relationships among features of the environment and mediates the learning of behavioral and cognitive skills that are performed automatically, without the requirement of conscious control. Studies of comparative cognition have also examined **episodic memory,** or the memory for specific events. I will have more to say about that in Chapter 12. Another distinction that has been important in comparative cognition is the distinction between working and reference memory.

Working and Reference Memory

One of the earliest experimental investigations of animal memory was conducted by the American psychologist Walter S. Hunter (1913). Hunter tested rats, dogs, and raccoons in a simple memory task. The apparatus consisted of a start area from which the animals could enter any one of three goal boxes. Only one of the goal boxes was baited with a piece of food on each trial, and the baited goal box was marked by turning on a light above it at the start of the trial. Which goal box was baited (and marked by the light) was varied from trial to trial.

After the animals learned to always choose the goal box whose light was turned on, Hunter made the task a bit more difficult. Now the light marking the baited goal box remained on for only a short time. After the signal was turned off, the animal was detained in the start area for various lengths of time before being allowed to make its choice. Therefore, the animal had to somehow remember which light had been on in order to find the food. The longer the animals were delayed, the more likely they were to make a mistake. The maximum delay rats could handle was about 10 seconds. Raccoons performed well up to about a 25-second delay. The performance of dogs did not deteriorate until the delay interval was extended past five minutes.

The species also differed in what they did during the delay interval. Rats and dogs were observed to maintain a postural orientation toward the correct goal box during the delay interval. No such postural orientations were observed in the raccoons. Since the raccoons did not maintain a postural orientation during the delay interval, their behavior required some type of internal memory mechanism.

With the delay procedure, the animals had to remember which goal box had been illuminated at the start of that trial. However, once the trial was finished, this information was no longer useful because the food could be in any of the three goal boxes on the next trial. Thus, memory for which goal box was recently illuminated was useful only on that trial. This type of memory is called **working memory.**

Working memory is operative when information has to be retained only long enough to complete a particular task, after which the information is best discarded because it is not needed or (as in Hunter's experiment) because it may interfere with successful completion of the next trial. A mechanic changing the oil and lubricating a car has to remember which steps of the job he already finished, but only as long as that particular car is being serviced. In cooking a good stew, you have to remember which spices you have already put in before adding others, but once the stew is finished, you can forget this information. These are all examples of working memory.

Working memory is often short lasting. In Hunter's experiment, the memory lasted for only 10 seconds in rats, and for 25 seconds in raccoons. However, as we will see in some situations, working memory may last for several hours.

Examples of working memory illustrate the retention, for a limited duration, of recently acquired information. However, such information is useful only in the context of more enduring knowledge. In Hunter's experiment, for example, remembering which compartment had been illuminated at the start of a trial was not enough to obtain food. This information was useful only in the context of the knowledge that the light marked the baited compartment. Information about the relation between the light and food had to be remembered on all trials. Such memory is called **reference memory** (Honig, 1978).

Reference memory is *long-term retention of information necessary for the successful use of incoming and recently acquired information.* Information about what a mechanic has done recently is useful only in the context of general knowledge about cars and lubrication procedures. Knowing which spices you have already added to a stew is useful only if you know the basics of cooking and flavoring food. All successful uses of working memory require appropriate reference memories.

Since Hunter's research, increasingly sophisticated techniques have been developed for the study of working memory. I will describe several of these. The first procedure, delayed matching to sample, is a laboratory procedure that was developed without much regard for the behavioral predispositions of animals and can be adapted to the study of how animals remember a variety of different events. The other techniques that were developed to test spatial memory or memory for particular locations take advantage of species specific behavioral specializations.

Delayed Matching to Sample

The **delayed-matching-to-sample procedure** is perhaps the most versatile technique available for the study of working memory. It is a substantial refinement of Hunter's original procedure. As in Hunter's procedure, the participant is exposed to a cue that identifies the correct response on a particular trial. This stimulus is then removed before the animal is permitted to perform the designated behavior. Figure 11.1 shows stimuli that were used in a study of memory in individuals with first-episode schizophrenia (Lencz et al., 2003). The stimuli consisted of complex patterns of dark and light voxels. The test stimulus was presented for 500 milliseconds, followed by the choice alternatives. Responding to the choice stimulus that was the same as the sample was the correct response. The correct choice alternative could appear on the left or the right. Therefore, the location of a choice alternative could not be used as a basis for making the correct choice.

During the first phase of training, the test stimuli appeared immediately after the sample and remained available until the subject made a choice. Once the subjects learned to select the matching choice alternative more than 80% of the time, a four or eight second delay was introduced between the sample and choice stimuli, as a test of memory. The experiment was also carried out with a nonclinical sample of individuals for comparison. The two groups performed equally well when the matching task did not involve a delay. However, participants with schizophrenia showed a deficit in performance when trials included a four or eight second delay between the sample stimulus and the choice alternatives. The fact that performance differed between the two groups only in the delay conditions indicates that schizophrenia includes a deficit in working memory. (For other studies of delayed matching to sample with human participants, see Koller et al., 2003; Mehta, Goodyer, & Sahakian, 2004.)

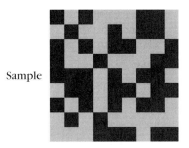

Sample

Choice
Alternatives

FIGURE **11.1**

Example of stimuli used in a matching to sample procedure with human subjects. The sample stimulus is presented initially, followed by the choice alternatives. Response to the choice alternative that is the same as the sample is reinforced. Delays introduced between exposure to the sample and presentation of the choice alternatives provide a test of memory. (Based on Lencz et al., 2003.)

The delayed-matching-to-sample procedure was initially developed for use with pigeons (Blough, 1959; Wright & Delius, 1994). Since then, species used in studies of matching to sample have included rats, monkeys, chimpanzees, dolphins, sea lions, the harbor seal, and goldfish (D'Amato, 1973; D'Amato & Colombo, 1985; Forestell & Herman, 1988; Iversen, 1993; Kastak & Schusterman, 1994; Matsuno, Kawai, & Matsuzawa, 2004; Mauk & Dehnhardt, 2005; Steinert, Fallon, & Wallace, 1976). In addition, the procedure has been adapted to investigate how animals remember a variety of stimuli, including visual shapes, numbers of responses performed, presence or absence of reward, the spatial location of stimuli, the order of two successively presented events, or which particular response the subject recently performed (e.g., D'Amato, 1973; Maki, Moe, & Bierley, 1977; MacDonald, 1993; Mercado et al., 1998; Wilkie & Summers, 1982).

Matching to sample is also useful to address questions that extend beyond memory mechanisms. For example, Izumi and Kojima (2004) asked whether chimpanzees can identify a vocalization based on just visual features of a chimp making that sound. Humans are capable of reading lips or associating a vocalization with the speaker's lip and facial movements. To see if chimpanzees can also do this, a distinctive vocalization was presented as the sample stimulus, and two video clips of chimps vocalizing served as the choice stimuli. The correct response was selecting the video clip that showed a chimp making the sound that was the sample for that trial. Using this methodology, Izumi and Kojima were able to conclude that like people, chimpanzees can read lips.

Procedural Determinants of Delayed Matching to Sample

Several aspects of the matching-to-sample procedure are critical in determining the accuracy of performance. One of these is the nature of the stimulus that serves as the sample. Some types of stimuli are more effective than others (e.g., Wilkie & Summers, 1982). Other important factors are the duration of exposure to the sample stimulus at the start of the trial and the delay interval after the sample. In a classic study, for example, Grant (1976) tested pigeons in a Skinner box that had three pecking keys in a row on one wall above a food hopper (like the box in Figure 1.7). The stimuli were colors (red, green, blue, and yellow) which could be projected on the pecking keys. At the start of each trial, the center key was illuminated with a white light, to signal the start of the trial. The pigeon was required to peck the start cue to make sure it was facing the response keys. After the pigeon pecked the start cue, the sample color for that trial was presented on the center key for 1, 4, 8, or 14 seconds. This was followed by delay intervals of 0, 20, 40, or 60 seconds, after which the two side keys were illuminated, one with the sample-matching color and the other with an alternative color. After the bird made its choice, all the keys were turned off for a 2-minute intertrial interval.

D. S. Grant

The results of the experiment are summarized in Figure 11.2. If pigeons had pecked the choice keys randomly, they would have been correct 50% of the time. Better-than-chance performance indicates the use of working memory. For each sample duration, the accuracy of matching decreased as longer delays were introduced between exposure to the sample and opportunity to make the choice response. In fact, if the sample was presented for only 1 second, and the opportunity to make a choice was delayed 40 seconds or more, the pigeons responded at chance level. Performance improved if the birds were exposed to the sample for longer periods. When the sample was presented for 4, 8, or 14 seconds, the birds performed above chance levels even at the longest delay interval (60 seconds). Thus, accuracy in the delayed-matching-to-sample procedure decreased as a function of the delay interval and increased as a function of the duration of exposure to the sample stimulus.

Results like those in Figure 11.2 can be explained by the **trace decay hypothesis,** the oldest and simplest account of memory (and memory loss) (Roberts & Grant, 1976). This hypothesis assumes that presentation of a stimulus produces changes in the nervous system that gradually dissipate, or decay, after the stimulus is turned off. The initial strength of the stimulus trace is assumed to reflect the physical energy of the stimulus. Thus, longer or more intense stimuli are presumed to produce stronger stimulus traces. However, no matter what the initial strength of the trace, it is assumed to decay at the same rate after the stimulus ends.

According to the trace decay hypothesis, the extent to which the memory of an event controls behavior depends on the strength of the stimulus trace at that moment. The stronger the trace, the stronger is the effect of the past stimulus on the organism's behavior. The trace decay model predicts results exactly like those summarized in Figure 11.2. Increasing the delay interval in

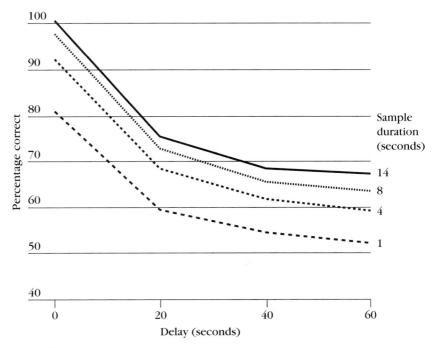

FIGURE **11.2**

Percentage of correct responses in a delayed-matching-to-sample task as a function of the duration of the sample stimulus (1–14 seconds) and the delay between the sample and the choice stimuli (0–60 seconds). (From "Effect of Sample Presentation Time on Long Delay Matching in the Pigeon" by D. S. Grant, 1976, *Learning and Motivation, 7,* pp. 580–590. Copyright © 1976 by Academic Press. Reprinted by permission.)

the matching-to-sample procedure reduces the accuracy of performance, presumably because the trace of the sample stimulus is weaker after longer delays. By contrast, increasing the duration of exposure to the sample improves performance, presumably because longer stimulus exposures establish stronger stimulus traces.

The trace decay hypothesis assumes that forgetting functions like those presented in Figure 11.2 reflect fairly directly the strength of memory for the sample stimulus at different delay intervals. Unfortunately, no behavioral test permits a *direct* readout of the strength of memory. Performance on memory tests also depends a great deal on the conditions of training. This was demonstrated by a provocative experiment conducted by Sargisson and White (2001), which I will describe next.

Investigators who employ the delayed matching to sample task typically begin training with no delay between the sample and the choice stimuli on each trial. That is what was done in the experiment whose results are summarized in Figure 11.2. Presenting the choice alternatives without a delay makes the task a bit easier and facilitates learning. After the participants have mastered the task with no delay, memory trials are conducted in which various delays are introduced between the sample and the choice alternatives.

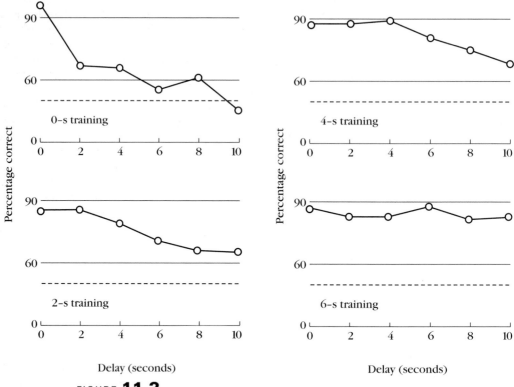

FIGURE **11.3**

Accuracy of matching to sample performance as a function of delay between the sample and choice stimuli for independent groups of pigeons that were previously trained with delays of 0, 2, 4, or 6 seconds. (From "Forgetting Functions," by R. J. Sargisson & K. G. White, 2001, *Animal Learning & Behavior, 29*, pp. 193–207. Copyright 2001 Psychonomic Society, Inc. Reprinted with permission.

Sargisson and White departed from this standard method by introducing different delay intervals from the outset, to see if better memory could be trained by using longer delay intervals from the beginning of training.

For one group of pigeons, the delay between the sample and choice stimuli was always 2 seconds during training. For other groups, this delay was 4 seconds or 6 seconds. For comparison, a control group was trained with the usual procedure of presenting the choice alternatives immediately after the sample. Training was continued until each group performed correctly on at least 80% of the trials. All of the birds were then tested with delays ranging from 0 to 10 seconds, to determine their forgetting functions. The results of these tests are presented in Figure 11.3.

The control group that had been trained with a 0-second sample-choice delay showed the standard forgetting function. Their rate of errors increased as the delay between the sample and choice stimuli was increased from 0 to 10 seconds. In contrast, no such decline was evident in pigeons, which had been trained with a 6-second delay between the sample and choice stimuli. These birds performed equally well at all test delays. The other groups showed results between these

M. Spetch

two extremes. Importantly, for all groups the most accurate performance occurred when the delay used in the test was the same as the delay that they received during training. These results clearly show that forgetting functions do not directly reflect the decay or fading of memory for the sample stimulus as a function of time. Rather, test performance depends on the similarity between the conditions of testing and the conditions of training (see also Spetch, 1987). The common finding that memory gets worse with the passage of time may simply reflect the fact that participants do not have practice with longer delay intervals.

The delay interval used in training is just one training variable that influences delayed matching to sample performance. Matching is basically instrumental-choice behavior motivated by the reinforcer provided at the end of the trial. Therefore, it should not be surprising that various factors that influence choice behavior (such as the relative rate of reinforcement for different alternatives) are also relevant in the analysis of matching to sample performance (e.g., Brown & White, 2005; Jones, 2003; Zentall, Singer, & Miller, 2008).

Response Strategies in Matching to Sample

The matching-to-sample procedure is analogous to a discrimination problem in that the participant has to respond to the correct stimulus and refrain from responding to the incorrect one to get reinforced. As I described in discussions of what is learned in discrimination training in Chapter 8, such a two-alternative task can be solved in several ways. The participant can make the correct choice by focusing on the correct stimulus, by inhibiting behavior to the incorrect stimulus, or by using both these response strategies. In discrimination learning (which establishes a reference memory), participants appear to use the combined response strategy. By contrast, participants in matching to sample appear to focus primarily on the correct choice.

One interesting experiment supporting this conclusion used a three-key apparatus for pigeons that was specially constructed so that the stimulus projected on a response key was visible only if the pigeon was standing directly in front of that key (Wright & Sands, 1981). This apparatus enabled the experimenters to determine which response key the pigeon looked at before making its choice. The results showed that the birds focused on the correct alternative. If they saw the matching stimulus, they pecked it without bothering to check what stimulus was presented on the other choice key (see also Roitblat, Penner, & Nachtigall, 1990; Wright, 1990, 1992; Zentall, Edwards, Moore, & Hogan, 1981).

A. A. Wright

General versus Specific Rule Learning

The evidence just reviewed indicates that animals focus on the correct choice in matching to sample. What leads them to identify a stimulus as correct? One possibility is that they learn a general *same-as* rule. The rule may be, "Choose the choice stimulus which is the same as the sample." Another possibility is that the animals learn a series of specific rules or stimulus-response relations. In the experiment by Grant (1976), for example, there were just four possible sample stimuli. Therefore, the pigeons may have learned a series of specific stimulus-response relations: "Select red after exposure to red," "Select green after exposure to green," and so on. Most matching-to-sample procedures can be solved either by learning a general *same-as* rule, or by learning a series of specific stimulus-response relations.

The two alternative strategies can be evaluated by testing transfer of matching performance to new stimuli. After training with one set of stimuli, another matching problem is presented with new sample and choice stimuli. Specific stimulus-response learning should not facilitate performance with new stimuli, because the required stimulus-response association has not been learned yet the first time subjects are presented with a novel sample stimulus. By contrast, general rule learning predicts considerable positive carryover, because the general *same-as* rule can be used to solve any matching-to-sample problem. Thus, in tests of transfer from one matching-to-sample problem to another, general-rule learning should produce better performance than specific-rule learning.

In a study with infant chimpanzees, Oden, Thompson, and Premack (1988) first provided training on a matching-to-sample task with just one pair of stimulus objects, a stainless steel measuring cup and a brass bolt lock. One of the objects was presented at the start of the trial, followed by a choice of both objects. If the chimp selected the matching object, it was reinforced with effusive praise, tickling, cuddling, or an edible treat, depending on its preference. After the animals learned the task with the two training stimuli, they were tested with a variety of other stimulus objects. Remarkably, with most of the test objects, the transfer performance was better than 80% accurate. Thus, the chimps seemed to have learned a general *same-as* rule with just two training stimuli.

Chimpanzees are more likely to show evidence of generalized matching than pigeons and other species. However, the preponderance of evidence suggests that both general rule learning and specific stimulus-response learning can occur as a result of matching-to-sample training in a variety of species. Which type of learning predominates appears to be related to the size of the stimulus set used in the matching-to-sample procedure. A study like Grant's (1976), in which only four different colors served as samples, is likely to favor the learning of specific stimulus-response relations. By contrast, procedures that employ a couple of hundred possible samples are likely to favor the learning of a general rule (e.g., Bodily, Katz, & Wright, 2008; Wright, Shyan, & Jitsumori, 1990).

The greatest variation in possible samples occurs in what is called a **trials-unique procedure.** In a trials-unique procedure, a different stimulus serves as the sample on each trial and is paired with another stimulus during the choice phase. Because a given sample stimulus is not presented on more than one trial, accurate performance with a trials-unique procedure is possible only if the participant learns to respond on the basis of a general *same-as* rule. (For other approaches to learning the *same-as* concept, see Brooks & Wasserman, 2008; Cook & Wasserman, 2007; and Katz & Wright, 2006.)

Spatial Memory in Mazes

The matching-to-sample procedure can be adapted to investigate how animals and people remember a variety of stimuli. The next technique I will describe has more limited applicability, but focuses on a very important type of memory: memory for places. One of the major frustrations of being in a new place is that you don't know where things are. We get around comfortably in our home town because we have learned how the streets are laid out. In addition, as we go from one place to another, we can remember where we have been and which streets we still have to take to get to our destination.

The Morris Water Maze

One common procedure that has been popular in neuroscience research on spatial memory is the Morris water maze, named after its inventor (Morris,

1981; Vorhees & Williams, 2006). The water maze is typically used with laboratory rats or mice. It consists of a circular tank, about 1–2 meters in diameter (smaller for mice), filled with water high enough to force the subjects to swim. A platform is submerged somewhere in the tank, just below the surface of the water. Rats and mice don't like to swim. Therefore, they are motivated to find the platform. The water is colored (by adding nontoxic paint or milk) so that the platform is not visible as the subjects swim around. This forces them to use spatial cues.

The first time the subjects are placed in the water tank, they swim around until they find the platform and are then allowed to remain there for 15–20 seconds so that they can learn where the platform is located in relation to the various spatial cues of the room. On subsequent trials, the subjects will have to find the platform just on the basis of these spatial cues because the platform is not visible above the surface of the water. Training trials begin with the subject placed in the water near the edge of the tank. The start position is randomly varied across trials so that the platform cannot be found by always swimming in the same direction (e.g., left of the start point). If the subject does not find the platform in 60 seconds, it is gently guided to it to end the trial.

The results of a study conducted with laboratory rats are summarized in Figure 11.4. The subjects received four trials per day. Learning progressed fairly rapidly. As they learned the task, the subjects took less time to find the platform and took more direct routes to the platform. The largest improvements in performance occurred from the first to the second day of training (Blokland, Geraerts, & Been, 2004).

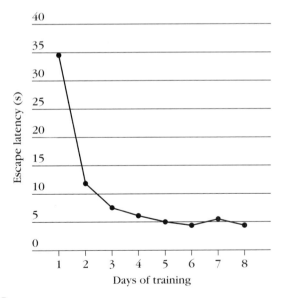

FIGURE **11.4**

Time required to find a submerged platform in the Morris water maze as a function of days of training. Subjects received four trials each day. (Based on Blokland, Geraerts, & Been, 2004.)

The Radial Arm Maze

The Morris water maze has been a useful technique for the study of the neural bases of spatial memory, but it is not a task that rats or mice are likely to encounter in their natural environment. A self-respecting rat or mouse that finds itself in a pool of water will quickly learn to avoid falling into the water again. Therefore, it is not likely to have to remember information about the location of a submerged platform. A more ecologically valid laboratory technique for the study of spatial memory is the radial arm maze, which takes advantage of evolved strategies for finding food in an animal's environment. (For a comparison of the water maze and radial arm maze techniques, see Hodges, 1996.)

In many environments, once food has been eaten at one location, it is not available there again for some time until it is replenished. Therefore, animals have to remember where they last obtained food and avoid that location until the food there is replenished. For example, the amakihi (*Loxops virens*), a species of Hawaiian honeycreeper, feeds on the nectar of mamane flowers (Kamil, 1978). After feeding on a cluster of flowers, these birds have to avoid returning to the same flowers for about an hour. By delaying their return to clusters they have recently visited, the birds increase the chance that they will find nectar in the flowers they search. They appear to remember the spatial location of recently visited flower clusters (see also Healy & Hurly, 1995).

The radial arm maze was developed to test memory for places where an animal recently obtained food and depleted that food source. Although the procedure was originally designed for use with laboratory rats (see Figure 11.5),

Courtesy of Catherine Green, from Patricia Sharp Lab, Department of Psychology, Yale University

FIGURE **11.5**

Rat foraging on an elevated radial maze.

analogous procedures have been developed for other species, including pigeons (Roberts & Van Veldhuizen, 1985) and college students (Kesner & DeSpain, 1988). There is even a report of radial maze performance in the tortoise (*Geochelone carbonaria*). The tortoise navigated the maze rather slowly but showed evidence of spatial learning (Wilkinson, Chan, & Hall, 2007).

A radial arm maze typically has eight arms radiating from a central choice area, and there is a food cup at the end of each arm (Olton & Samuelson, 1976). Before the start of each trial, a pellet of food is placed in each food cup. The rat is then placed in the center of the maze and allowed to go from one arm to another and pick up all the food. Once a food pellet has been consumed, that arm of the maze remains empty for the rest of the trial. Given this contingency, the most efficient way for a rat to get all eight pellets is to enter only those arms of the maze that it had not yet visited. That is, in fact, what rats do.

The results of an experiment conducted by Olton (the originator of this technique) are summarized in Figure 11.6. Entering an arm that had not been visited previously was considered to be a correct choice. Figure 11.6 summarizes the number of correct choices the rats made during the first eight choices of successive tests. During the first five test runs after familiarization with the maze, the rats made a mean of nearly seven correct choices during each test. With continued practice, the mean number of correct

D. S. Olton

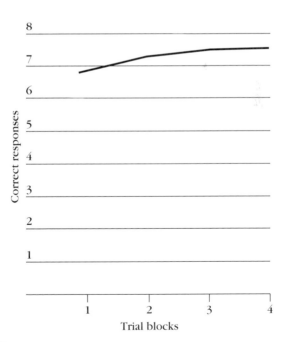

FIGURE **11.6**

Mean number of correct responses rats made in the first eight choices during blocks of five test trials in the eight-arm radial maze. (Adapted from D. S. Olton, 1978.)

choices was consistently above seven, indicating that the animals rarely entered an arm they had previously chosen on that trial (see also Olton & Samuelson, 1976).

Rats do not require much training to perform efficiently in the radial maze. The radial maze task takes advantage of foraging tactics that rats acquired through their evolutionary history. Rats live in burrows, and outings to find food are followed by return to the home burrow. While out foraging, they follow preexisting trails and move about without returning to recently visited places. In fact, their tendency to avoid recently visited places is so strong that they don't return to recently visited arms in a maze whether or not the maze arms are baited with food at the start of the trial (FitzGerald et al., 1985; Timberlake & White, 1990). These results suggest that radial maze performance has deep evolutionary roots. (For additional experiments on the ecological basis of radial arm maze performance, see Brown, Farley, & Lorek, 2007; Hoffman, Timberlake, Leffel, & Gont 1999; Timberlake, Leffel, & Hoffman, 1999.)

There are several mechanisms by which rats could choose to enter only previously un-selected arms of a maze without necessarily remembering which arms they had already visited. They could mark each arm they visit with a drop of urine, and then avoid maze arms that had this odor marker. Alternatively, they could select arms in a fixed sequence, such as always entering successive arms in a clockwise order. However, they do not appear to use either of these tactics. Various procedures have convincingly ruled out the use of odor cues and response sequences in the selection of maze arms (e.g., Olton & Samuelson, 1976; Zoladek & Roberts, 1978).

Rats appear to use distinctive features of the environment, such as a window, door, corner of the room, or poster on the wall as landmarks, and locate maze arms relative to these landmarks. Movement of landmarks relative to the maze causes the rats to treat the maze arms as being in new locations (Suzuki, Augerinos, & Black, 1980). Thus, under ordinary circumstances, spatial location is identified relative to distal room cues, not to local stimuli inside the maze. (Similar spatial cues are involved in guiding successful performance in the Morris water maze.)

Because radial maze performance usually depends on memory for recently visited locations, the radial maze procedure has become a popular technique for the study of memory processes, both at the behavioral and physiological level. The memory capacity revealed by the technique is impressive. By adding more arms to the end of a radial maze, investigators have explored the limits of working memory. These and other spatial memory tests have indicated that rats are able to remember 16 to 24 spatial locations in a food-depletion working memory task (Cole & Chappell-Stephenson, 2003). This is far more than the classic claim that human working memory has a capacity for 7 items ± 2 (Miller, 1956).

The duration of spatial working memory is also remarkable. To determine how long rats could remember where they have been, Beatty and Shavalia (1980) allowed rats to make four choices in the eight-arm radial maze in the usual manner. The subjects were then detained in their home cages for

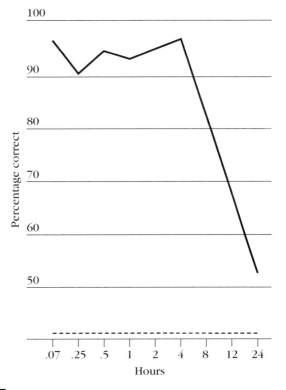

FIGURE **11.7**

Percentage correct responses on choices 5–8 in an eight-arm radial maze. Between choices 4 and 5 the animals were returned to their home cages for varying intervals ranging from 0.07 to 24 hours. The dashed line indicates chance performance (41%). (From "Spatial Memory in Rats: Time course of working memory and effects of anesthetics" by W. W. Beatty and D. A. Shavalia, 1980, *Behavioral and Neural Biology*, 28, pp. 454–462.)

various periods up to 24 hours. After the delay interval, they were returned to the maze and allowed to make the remaining four choices (choices 5–8). As usual, an entry into an alley they had not previously visited was considered a correct choice.

Figure 11.7 shows the percentage of correct choices as a function of the delay interval between the first four and last four choices. Delays of up to four hours after the first four choices did not disrupt performance. Longer periods of confinement in the home cage produced progressively more errors. These data show that spatial memory is not permanent. However, the memory can last for several hours (see also Maki et al., 1984; Strijkstra & Bolhuis, 1987).

BOX **11.1**

Learning as Synaptic Plasticity: Long-Term Potentiation (LTP) and Long-Term Depression (LTD)

It is estimated that your brain contains more than a 100 billion neurons. Each neuron may be coupled through a chemical synapse to thousands of other neurons, forming a complex neural network. If we assume that each of these connections can store just one bit of information, your brain can hold the computer equivalent of 100,000 gigs!

How can experience bring about a change within this network? Many assume that experience modifies the strength of the synaptic connections. If this is true, when are the connections modified, and what are the molecular mechanisms that mediate this synaptic plasticity?

An answer to the first question was suggested by Donald Hebb more than half a century ago (Hebb, 1949). He argued that neural connections are strengthened when two cells are active at the same time, an idea that is sometimes summarized with the mnemonic "cells that fire together wire together." Modern theorists have extended this notion to address decreases in synaptic strength, arguing that this will occur when cellular activity is uncorrelated.

In a classic experiment, Bliss and Lomo (1973) provided neural evidence for Hebb's hypothesis. They examined how neural activity within the hippocampus alters the strength of synaptic connections. To induce neural activity, they lowered an electrode into a bundle of neurons known as the perforant path and applied an electrical current (see Figure 11.8). The cells that form the perforant path synapse on

neurons called mossy fibers. By recording neural activity through electrodes placed near the mossy fiber cell bodies, Bliss and Lomo obtained a measure of synaptic strength. As we would expect, applying a moderate electrical stimulus to the perforant path elicited moderate neural activity in the mossy fibers and this response changed little over time. But if a strong input was provided, one that caused a very strong response in the mossy fibers, subsequent inputs produced a much larger response. This phenomenon is called **long-term potentiation (LTP)**. It appears that a strong input can effectively strengthen synaptic connections. A converse phenomenon, **long-term depression (LTD)**, has also been discovered that can weaken synaptic connections. Both LTP and LTD can last for days to weeks. The enduring feature of LTP and LTD has encouraged researchers to suggest that these phenomenon may represent a kind of neurobiological memory: a way in which cells can store the consequences of experience (for a recent review, see Lynch, 2004).

Cells communicate at a synapse through the release of neurotransmitters that engage a response in the adjoining (postsynaptic) neuron by activating specialized receptors. A strong input could alter the strength of a chemical synapse by increasing either the amount of transmitter released or by increasing the responsiveness of the postsynaptic cell. Research suggests that LTP is largely due to the second of these possibilities. One of the most important ways in which a postsyn-

aptic cell can become more responsive involves specialized receptors (NMDA receptors) that lie on the surface of the cell. NMDA receptors act as coincidence detectors. Their activation depends on both the release of transmitter and a strong response in the postsynaptic cell. If these two conditions are met, the NMDA receptors initiate a biochemical cascade that awakens silent AMPA receptors. The AMPA receptors mediate the propagation of the neural signal from one neuron to the next. Awakening more of these receptors increases the magnitude of the response elicited in the postsynaptic cell. As a result, the postsynaptic cell exhibits a stronger response even though the amount of neurotransmitter released has not changed.

LTP has a number of properties that suggest it plays a role in learning and memory. The most obvious is *its enduring nature*. Another important quality is *input specificity*: the modification is limited to those synapses that are concurrently active. LTP also exhibits a kind of *cooperativity*. The induction of LTP requires a strong response in the postsynaptic cell. This strong response does not have to come from just one input. Rather, a number of inputs can work together to drive the postsynaptic cell to the threshold for learning. Moreover, all the contributing inputs can benefit. A variation of this cooperativity yields the final, and most interesting property: *associativity* (Figure 11.8). If a weak input is paired with a strong input, the latter will be sufficient to engage LTP at both

(continued)

BOX **11.1** (continued)

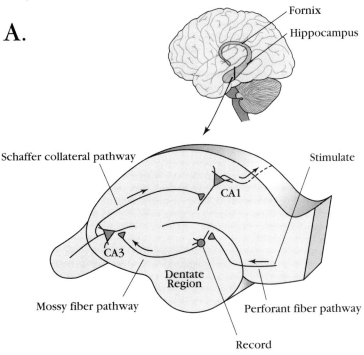

A.

Fornix

Hippocampus

Schaffer collateral pathway

Stimulate

CA1

CA3

Dentate Region

Mossy fiber pathway

Perforant fiber pathway

Record

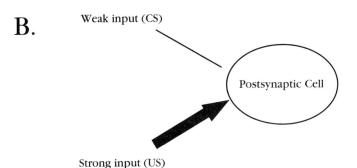

B.

Weak input (CS)

Postsynaptic Cell

Strong input (US)

FIGURE **11.8**

(A) A slice of the hippocampus. Bliss & Lomo (1973) stimulated the axons of the perforant path and recorded the response observed in the mossy fibers. They found that a strong input produced a long-lasting increase in the response elicited in the cells of the mossy fiber pathway. (B) A schematic of the neural relations that could support associativity. One cell has weak input (the CS) while another has a strong connection (the US). The weak connection can be strengthened through paired presentation of both the weak and strong inputs. (Adapted from Kandel, Schwartz, & Jessel, 2000.)

connections. As a result, the weak input will acquire the capacity to drive a response in the post synaptic cell, in much the same way that a CS acquires the ability to generate a CR as a result of being paired with a US.

To explore whether hippocampal LTP plays a role in learning and memory, researchers have used a

(continued)

BOX **11.1** (continued)

number of behavioral tasks that are known to depend on the hippocampus. One of the most popular involves the Morris water maze which contains a small hidden platform (see pages 388–389). Normally, rats quickly learn to swim to the location of the platform (see Figure 11.4). However, rats with lesions of the hippocampus do not remember where they last found the hidden platform and take far longer to find it. Lesioned rats do not have any problem swimming to a platform that is tall enough to be visible above the surface of the water. This indicates that their sensory and motor functions are not impaired. Hippocampal lesions produce a selective deficit that interferes with the capacity to learn about spatial cues.

Developing a behavioral assay that is sensitive to hippocampal lesions gives us a tool to explore whether synaptic modification (NMDA-mediated plasticity) is involved in learning. To explore this issue, researchers have tested the impact of drugs that disrupt NMDA receptor activity (e.g., APV and MK-801). These drugs bind to the NMDA receptor and prevent it from working normally. Physiological studies have shown that pretreatment with an NMDA antagonist blocks the induction of LTP. Significantly, the same drug also disrupts spatial learning in the water maze (Morris, Anderson, Lynch, & Baudry, 1986). Experiments have shown that synaptic plasticity mediated by the NMDA receptor is not limited to spatial learning. For example, en-

coding the cues that represent a context, a new object, or a new conspecific (a form of social learning), all depend on the hippocampus, and each of these forms of learning depends on NMDA-mediated plasticity (Martin et al., 2000).

Researchers have also shown that LTP occurs in many other regions of the brain. Even neurons within the spinal cord exhibit LTP. When you get a sunburn, neurons within the spinal cord become sensitized (Ji, Kohno, Moore, & Woolf, 2003; Willis, 2001). This increases the level of pain you feel when the skin is stimulated. This heightened pain appears to reflect a form of LTP, a cellular memory within the spinal cord that heightens the pain signal sent to the brain.

J. W. Grau

MEMORY MECHANISMS

The preceding section provided descriptions of several prominent techniques for the study of memory processes in animals and some of the results of that research. Next, I turn to a discussion of factors that determine what we remember and how well we remember it. As I noted earlier, memory processes involve three phases: acquisition, retention, and retrieval (see Table 11.1). What we remember and how well we remember it, depends on all three of these phases, often in combination with each other. In this part of the chapter, I will discuss research with nonhuman animals relevant to each of the three phases of memory processes.

Acquisition and the Problem of Stimulus Coding

Obviously, we cannot remember something (e.g., the winning play in a championship game) if we were not exposed to it in the first place. Memory depends on our having experienced an event and having made some kind of record of that experience. However, even when our memory is excellent, it is not because we retain a perfect or literal record of the earlier experience.

Experiences cannot be recorded in a literal sense, even by machines. A digital camera can do an excellent job recording the winning play in a championship game, but even that is not a literal record. Digital cameras create a record of an event in the form of a series of zeros and ones, or digital bits of information. The coded record bears no resemblance to the actual event. In a similar sense, we do not have a literal record of our past experiences in memory. Rather, our experiences are coded in the nervous system in some way for the purposes of retention. What we recall later depends on how an experience was coded and how that code is retrieved at a later time. Thus, **stimulus coding** is a critical feature of the acquisition phase of memory.

Investigators have been interested in several aspects of the problem of coding. Consider, for example, rats foraging for food in a radial maze (see Figure 11.5). The animals have to enter the various arms of the maze to obtain the food located at the end of each arm. So as not to waste effort, they have to select only the arms they have not yet tried that day. As we have seen, rats rely on their memory to do this. But, what do they keep in mind? How is memory coded?

Cognitive Maps and Other Navigational Codes

One possibility is that the animals make a serial list of the maze arms they visit, adding an item to the list with each new arm visited. Given the excellent performance of rats on mazes with 16 or more arms (Cole & Chappell-Stephenson, 2003), this would involve a rather long list. Such extensive list learning seems unlikely, since even humans have difficulty maintaining that many items in working memory at one time. Another possibility is that the animals form a mental map or mental representation of how the maze and the food cups are arranged. They then use this cognitive map to decide which arm of the maze to enter next (e.g., O'Keefe & Nadel, 1978; Jacobs & Schenk, 2003).

The idea that animals form a *cognitive map* which then guides their spatial navigation has been a prominent hypothesis for many years, but it calls for further specification. Potentially, maps can represent a variety of different types of information (distance, height or topography, presence of particular landmarks, compass direction, etc.). To claim that animals form a *cognitive map* does not tell us precisely what information is contained in such a map and how animals use that information. Such questions have led investigators to focus on more specific mechanisms that enable subjects to find a particular location in space. A number of mechanisms have been examined (see reviews by Roberts, 1998; Shettleworth, 1998; Spetch & Kelly, 2006). Some of these are illustrated in Figure 11.9.

In Figure 11.9, the goal (a patch of food) is located near a large rock. There is a tree to the right of the rock and a bush to the left. The tree and the bush are both closer to the rabbit than the rock. A rabbit could find the patch of food by looking at the rock and aiming straight for it. That would be *beacon following*. The rock serves as a beacon that marks the location of the goal object. Beacon following is a fairly simple navigational tactic, requiring little more than the formation of an association between the beacon and the goal object. Sign-tracking behavior described in Chapter 3 is an example of beacon following (see especially Figure 3.5). (For a recent studies of the use of beacons, see Shettleworth & Sutton, 2005; and Timberlake, Sinning, & Leffel, 2007.)

Given the cues present in Figure 11.9, the rabbit could also find the food patch by going past and to the right of the bush. In this case, it would be using the bush as a landmark to guide its navigation. A *landmark* is a distinctive stimulus that is not at the goal location, but has a fixed relation to the goal (e.g., the goal is northeast of the bush). Subjects can also find the goal location by using information derived from several landmarks. In our example, the patch of food is located between, but past, both the bush and the tree. A path could be calculated using both landmarks. (For recent studies of landmark use, see Chamizo, Rodrigo, & Mackintosh, 2006; and Fiset, 2007.)

Food Patch

FIGURE **11.9**

Diagram of a spatial task in which the goal (a patch of food) is located near rock. A tree is located on the right and a bush on the left, both closer to the rabbit. The rabbit can get to the food using a variety of spatial cues, as discussed in the text.

Notice that the bush, rock, and tree in Figure 11.9 outline the shape of a triangle. The patch of food is near the apex of the triangle. *Geometric features* such as those that constitute a triangle provide additional cues for spatial localization (e.g., Chang & Newcombe, 2005). However, the geometric arrangements that are typically studied in the laboratory are on a much smaller scale than in Figure 11.9. Another source of spatial information that can be used to locate a goal object is the distance cues that indicate how far away an object is. Distance cues provide a *spatial gradient*, with objects farther away being smaller, less bright, and less distinct.

The dominant issue in contemporary research on the coding of spatial information is how information from beacons, landmarks, geometric features, and spatial gradients is integrated into a coherent cognitive map. Investigators are examining how learning about one feature affects learning about other spatial features (e.g., Gibson & Shettleworth, 2003; Timberlake, Sinning, & Leffel, 2007), how learning about separate features may be integrated (e.g., Chamizo, Rodrigo, & Mackintosh, 2006), and how these interactions should be characterized theoretically (e.g., Chang & Newcombe, 2005; Miller & Shettleworth, 2007).

Retrospective and Prospective Coding

So far I have discussed the kinds of spatial information animals may use in finding particular food locations. Another interesting question is which food locations are encoded as rats go about foraging on a radial-arm maze. Perhaps the most obvious possibility is that the animals keep in mind where they have already been. This is called **retrospective coding.** An equally effective memory strategy is for the animals to keep in mind which maze arms they have yet to visit. This strategy is called **prospective coding.** Because animal memory paradigms typically have a limited range of outcomes, they can all be solved successfully either by remembering a past event (**retrospection**) or by remembering a plan for future action (**prospection**).

T. Zentall

The distinction between retrospective and prospective coding has become a focus of interest in comparative cognition because it is relevant to the question of time travel in animals (Roberts, 2006; Zentall, 2005). People are clearly capable of time travel, in the sense that they can re-experience past events or contemplate future ones. In fact, often it is the contemplation of past injuries and possible future problems that causes us the greatest distress. Keeping in mind or remembering a plan for future action is the essence of prospective coding. Whether people maintain this capability as they age or start to have symptoms of Alzheimer's disease is of great concern in research on human memory (e.g., Ellis, & Kvavilashvili, 2000). Are nonhuman species also capable of prospective coding, or are they stuck in time? How would you obtain evidence of prospective coding in nonverbal species?

Consider going shopping at a mall. Let's assume that to complete your shopping, you have to visit six stores: a shoe store, a record store, a bookstore, a bakery, a clothing store, and a pharmacy. Let's also assume that you have to rely entirely on your memory to visit the six stores. You cannot keep notes or look at what you have already purchased when deciding where to go next. What memory strategy could you use to avoid going to the same place twice? One possibility would be to form a memory code for each store after visiting that store. This would be a retrospective code. You could then decide whether to enter the next store on the list based on whether or not you remembered already having gone there. With such a retrospective strategy, the contents of your working memory would increase by one item with each store you visit. Thus, how much you have to keep in mind (your memory load) would increase as you progressed through the task (see Figure 11.10).

An alternative would be to memorize the list of all the stores you intended to visit before you start your trip. Such memory would involve *prospection,* because it would be memory for what you intended to do. After visiting a particular store, you could delete that item from your memory. Thus, in this scheme, a visit to a store would be *recorded* by having that store removed from the prospective memory list. Because you would be keeping in mind only which stores you still had to visit, the memory load would decrease as you progressed through your shopping, as shown in Figure 11.10.

Numerous ingenious experiments have been conducted to determine whether animals use retrospective or prospective coding for memory. Many

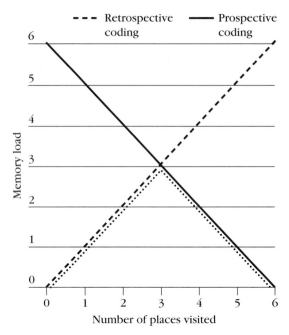

FIGURE **11.10**

Memory load following different numbers of places visited, out of a possible total of six, given retrospective and prospective coding strategies. The dashed line represents memory load when the coding strategy is changed from retrospection to prospection halfway through the task.

of these experiments have involved variations of the matching-to-sample procedure with pigeons. The experiments have demonstrated that animals use both retrospective and prospective coding, but under different circumstances. Such experiments illustrate that coding strategies are flexible, with different strategies adopted in response to different task demands (e.g., Clement & Zentall, 2000; Ducharme & Santi, 1993; Grant, 1991, 1993; Zentall, Jagielo, Jackson-Smith, & Urcuioli 1987).

To illustrate how coding strategies might change as a function of task demands, let us return to the example of having to shop in six different stores in a mall. As I have noted, with a retrospective coding strategy the demands on working memory increase as you progress through the shopping trip. In contrast, with a prospective coding strategy the demands on working memory decrease as you progress through the six stores (see Figure 11.10). How might you minimize the demands on your memory? Is there a way to keep the demands on working memory to three items or fewer throughout the shopping trip? There is, if you change your memory strategy halfway through the task.

At the start of the shopping trip, memory load is least if you use a retrospective strategy. Therefore, you should start with retrospective coding. Remembering where you have been works well for the first three stores you visit. After that, the memory load for retrospection begins to exceed the memory load for prospection (see Figure 11.10). Therefore, after having visited three stores, you should switch to a prospective code and keep in mind only which stores remain to be visited. By switching coding strategies halfway through, you minimize how much you have to remember at any one time. If you use retrospection followed by prospection, memory load will at first increase and then decrease as you complete the task, as illustrated by the dashed line in Figure 11.10.

Do animals (including people) use coding strategies flexibly, and if so how could we prove that? Several experiments have been performed indicating that coding strategies change from retrospection to prospection as one goes through a list of places or items. Early in the list, individuals keep in mind what has already happened. Later, they remember what remains to be done (e.g., Cook, Brown, & Riley, 1985; see also Brown, Wheeler, & Riley, 1989).

In one study, Kesner and DeSpain (1988) compared the coding strategies of rats and college students in spatial memory tasks. If individuals switch from retrospection to prospection in the course of remembering a series of places, memory load should first increase and then decrease. Memory load was estimated from the rate of errors the participants made on a test that was conducted after the participants had visited different numbers of places. (For a recent study of this problem in pigeons, see DiGian & Zentall, 2007.)

The rats in Kesner and DeSpain's study were first trained to forage for food on a 12-arm radial maze in the standard manner. Once they had become proficient at obtaining food by going to each maze arm, a series of test trials was conducted. On each test trial, the rats were allowed to make a certain number of arm entries. They were then removed from the maze for 15 minutes. At the end of the delay, they were returned to the maze and allowed to enter one of two alleys selected by the experimenter. One was an alley they had entered earlier; the other was a previously un-chosen alley. Selecting the new alley was judged to be the correct response. The rate of errors the rats made during the test phase is presented in the left graph of Figure 11.11. As the number of visited locations before the test increased from two to eight arms of the maze, the error rate increased. This finding is consistent with the hypothesis that the rats were using a retrospective coding strategy during the first eight arm entries. Interestingly, however, when the rats were tested after having entered 10 arms, they made fewer errors. This improvement in performance towards the end of the series suggests that the animals switched to a prospective coding strategy.

The college students in the study were presented with a grid containing 16 squares (corresponding to 16 places in a maze). During the course of a trial, the symbol X traveled from one square to another in an irregular order, simulating movement from one place to another in a maze. After the X had been presented at various locations, a delay of five seconds was introduced, followed by presentation of two test locations. One test location was a place where the X had been; the other was a new square. The participants had to identify which was the new square.

The rate of errors for the college students is presented in the right graph of Figure 11.11 as a function of the number of places where the X had appeared before the test. The results were strikingly similar to the pattern of errors obtained with the rats. The error rate initially increased, consistent with a retrospective coding strategy. After the target stimulus had been in eight places, however, the error rate decreased, consistent with a prospective coding strategy.

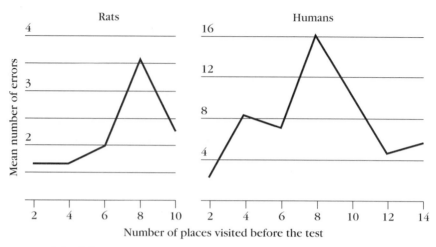

FIGURE **11.11**

Error rate of rats (left) and college students (right) on spatial memory tasks requiring identification of a new place after a delay. The delay was imposed after the participants had visited various numbers of locations. (From "Correspondence Between Rats and Humans in the Utilization of Retrospective and Prospective Codes" by R. P. Kesner and M.J. DeSpain, 1988, *Animal Learning and Behavior, 16*, pp. 299–302. Copyright © 1988 by the Psychonomic Society. Reprinted by permission.)

These results suggest that memory performance is a function of coding strategies and that coding strategies may vary as a function of task demands. Given alternative possible coding strategies, participants switch from one to another so as to reduce memory load and thereby improve response accuracy.

Retention and the Problem of Rehearsal

The second phase of memory processes is retention. With working-memory tasks, a prominent issue involving retention is **rehearsal.** Rehearsal refers to keeping information in an active state, readily available for use. If someone tells you a phone number, you may rehearse the number by repeating it to yourself over and over until you get to a phone. If someone is giving you directions to the post office, you may try to create a mental image of the route and imagine yourself following the route a number of times. Such rehearsal strategies facilitate keeping newly acquired information readily at hand, available to guide behavior.

Rehearsal processes were first investigated in animal memory as they relate to the learning of new associations. Models of learning and memory typically assume that associations are formed between two events (e.g., a CS and a US) provided that the two events are rehearsed at the same time (e.g., Wagner, 1976, 1981). Given this assumption, learning should be disrupted by manipulations that disrupt rehearsal. Early studies of rehearsal processes in animal memory focused on such manipulations and their effects on the learning of new associations (e.g., Wagner, Rudy, & Whitlow, 1973). More recently, the focus of research has been on the role of rehearsal in working memory paradigms. An important line of evidence for rehearsal processes in working memory comes from studies of **directed forgetting.**

Studies of human memory have shown that the accuracy of recall can be modified by cues or instructions indicating that something should (or should not) be remembered (e.g., Bjork, 1972; Hourlhan & Taylor, 2006; Johnson, 1994). In this research, participants are first exposed to a list of items. Some of the items are accompanied by a remember cue (R-cue), indicating that the item will appear later in a test of memory. Other items are accompanied by a forget cue (F-cue) indicating that the item will not be included in the memory test. Probe trials are occasionally included in which memory is tested for an item that was accompanied by the F-cue. The results of these probe trials indicate that memory is disrupted by forget cues.

Demonstrations of directed forgetting are important because they provide evidence that memory is an active process that can be brought under stimulus control. Research on directed forgetting in people has sparked interest in finding analogous effects with nonhuman animals. How might we devise a procedure to study directed forgetting in animals?

Directed forgetting has been examined in numerous studies with pigeons employing variations of the delayed matching to sample procedure. The procedure used in a recent study by Milmine, Watanabe, and Colombo (2008) is outlined in Figure 11.12. The experimental chamber had three pecking keys arranged in a row. The center key was used to display the sample stimulus (a red or white light), and the two side keys were used during tests of memory, which involved a choice between the sample and the alternate color. Five different types of trials could take place. On R-cue trials, the sample was followed by a two-second high pitched tone, followed by a three-second silent period and the choice test. If the pigeon pecked the matching choice stimulus, it was reinforced with food. On F-cue trials, presentation of the sample was followed by a low-pitched tone and a delay period, but then the trial ended. Thus, subjects did not have to keep anything in mind during the delay period.

The third type of trial was a free-reward trial, which also ended without a choice test, but on free-reward trials, the subjects received food at the end of the delay interval. The free-reward trials were included because previous studies had found that the anticipation of reinforcement at the end of the trial can serve to encourage memory for the sample stimulus. Free-reward trials were signaled by a pulsing auditory cue of intermediate pitch presented after the sample stimulus.

The first three trial types served to establish the functions of the R-cue, F-cue, and free-reward cue. How effective were these cues in actually controlling memory? Memory was assessed on each R-cue trial because all R-cue trials ended with the choice test. To assess memory on F-cue and free-reward trials, a choice test was included as a probe on some of those trials as well. These probe trials are outlined as the last two trial types in Figure 11.12.

Two pigeons served in the experiment. The results provided by each bird are presented in Figure 11.13. Most accurate matching performance occurred

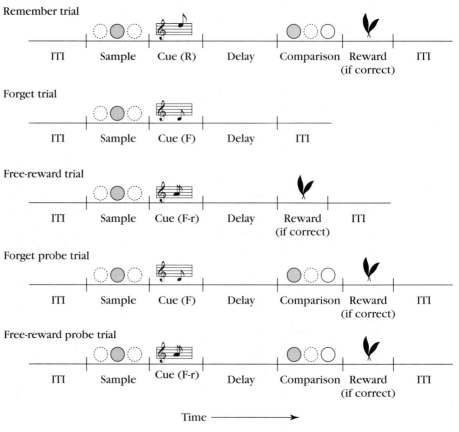

FIGURE **11.12**

Outline of types of trials used in a recent study of directed forgetting in pigeons. Each trial started with a sample stimulus presented on the center key. This was followed by different auditory cues that served as the R-cue, F-cue, or free-reward cue. Probe trials evaluated the impact of the F-cue and free-reward cue on memory. (From "Neural correlates of directed forgetting in the avian prefrontal cortex," by M. Milmine, A. Watanabe, and M. Colombo, 2008, *Behavioral Neuroscience, 122,* 199–209.)

on R-cue trials. As expected, the pigeons did poorly on the F-cue trials, indicating that the F-cue disrupted memory. Notice that because the forget instruction was provided after the sample stimulus, one cannot argue that the F-cue disrupted attention to the sample. Rather, the F-cue altered memory mechanisms (rehearsal) during the delay interval.

Memory was also good on free-reward probe trials, indicating that the anticipation of reward can also serve to facilitate memory. This is a very interesting outcome. One would expect that animals would keep in mind a signal for reward. But, in this case the free-reward cue was not the sample stimulus. Just like the R-cue and the F-cue, the free-reward cue was pre-

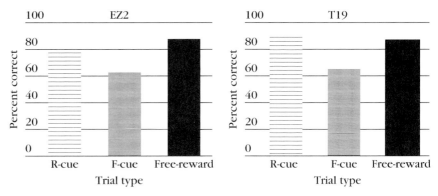

FIGURE **11.13**

Accuracy in delayed matching to sample in pigeons EZ2 and T19 on R-cue, F-cue, and free-reward trials. (From "Neural correlates of directed forgetting in the avian prefrontal cortex," by M. Milmine, A. Watanabe, and M. Colombo, 2008, *Behavioral Neuroscience, 122*, 199–209.)

sented after the sample stimulus. Nevertheless, it facilitated memory for the sample. Evidently, the anticipation of reward helps to keep recently experienced events in memory.

Milmine et al. (2008) also measured the activity of individual neurons in a part of the pigeon brain that is analogous to the mammalian prefrontal cortex, because of suggestions that directed forgetting involves executive control. Consistent with that hypothesis, they found sustained increased single-cell activity during the delay interval on R-cue trials, and suppressed activity during F-cue trials. Neuronal activity during the delay interval on free-reward trials was similar to the activity on R-cue trials. Thus, the single-cell neuronal activity in the avian analogue of the prefrontal cortex corresponded to the behavioral data, suggesting that these neurons are involved in the control of memory processes.

In the experiment by Milmine et al. (2008), the forget cue was correlated with nonreinforcement during training because the choice test was omitted on F-cue training trials. As it turns out, this is not critical. Forget cues can be trained even if the procedure includes reinforcement on F-cue trials (Roper, Kaiser, & Zentall, 1995; Kaiser, Sherburne, & Zentall, 1997). The key factor is to omit a test for memory on F-cue training trials.

Once trained, forget cues can have broad impact. For example, a recent study demonstrated that a forget cue trained in one matching-to-sample problem can control memory in a different matching problem (Roper, Chaponis, & Blaisdell, 2005). These experiments demonstrate the phylogenetic generality of directed forgetting and provide laboratory paradigms for studying the neural mechanisms of how we are able to control our memory processes.

Retrieval

In the third phase of memory processes, retrieval, stored information is recovered so that it can be used to guide behavior. Whereas problems of coding and rehearsal are primarily being investigated in working-memory paradigms, research on retrieval has focused on reference memory and, more specifically, on memory for learned associations. Retrieval processes are of special interest because many instances of memory failure reflect deficits in the recovery of information—**retrieval failure**—rather than loss of the information from the memory store (Urcelay & Miller, 2008).

During the course of our daily lives, we learn many things, all of which are somehow stored in the brain. Which aspect of our extensive knowledge we think of at a particular time depends on which pieces of information are retrieved from our long-term memory store. At any moment, we recall only a tiny proportion of what we know. Retrieval processes are triggered by reminders, or **retrieval cues.** If you are discussing summer camp experiences with your friends, the things they say will serve as retrieval cues to remind you of things you did at summer camp.

Retrieval cues are effective in reminding you of a past experience because they are associated with the memory for that experience. A song may remind you of the concert you attended on your first date. Balancing on a bicycle will remind you of what you have to do to ride a bicycle. The sensations of sinking in a swimming pool will remind you of what you learned about swimming, and the voice of a friend you have not seen for a long time will stimulate retrieval of memories for the things you used to do together.

Retrieval Cues and Memory for Instrumental Behavior in Human Infants

Courtesy of C. Rovee-Collier

C. Rovee-Collier

Various stimuli that are present during acquisition of a memory can come to serve as retrieval cues for that memory. Borovsky and Rovee-Collier (1990), for example, investigated retrieval of the memory for instrumental conditioning in six-month-old infants. The infants were trained in their own homes, in playpens whose sides were covered with a cloth liner. Some of these liners were striped and others had a square pattern. The investigators were interested in whether the cloth liner might serve as a retrieval cue for the instrumental response.

A mobile was mounted above the playpen. Each infant was seated in the playpen in a reclining baby seat so that he or she could see the mobile. One end of a satin ribbon was looped around the infant's ankle and the other end was attached to the stand that supported the mobile. With this arrangement, each kick by the infant made the mobile move. The instrumental response was kicking the leg, and the reinforcer was movement of the mobile. The kicking response first was conditioned in two short training sessions. The infants then received a test session 24 hours later.

The cues present during the test session were varied for different groups of infants. Some of the babies were tested in a crib with the same cloth liner that had been present during the training sessions (Group Same). Others were tested with the alternate cloth liner that was new to them (Group Diff). For a third group, the alternate cloth liner was familiar, but it had not been present during the training trials (Group Diff-Fam). Finally, a fourth group of babies was tested without a liner and could look around their familiar playroom (None-Fam).

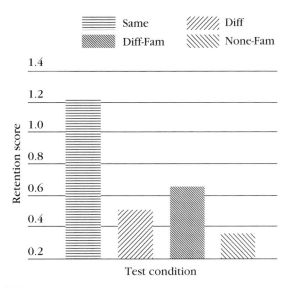

FIGURE **11.14**

Retention scores of six-month-old infants in a test of instrumental conditioning. Group Same was tested in a playpen with the same cloth liner that had been present during conditioning. Group Diff was tested with a new cloth liner. Group Diff-Fam was tested with a familiar cloth liner that was different from the one in the playpen during conditioning. Group None-Fam was tested without a cloth liner but in a familiar playpen in a familiar room. (From "Contextual Constraints on Memory Retrieval at Six Months" by D. Borovsky and C. Rovee-Collier, 1990, *Child Development,* 61, pp. 1569–1583. Copyright © 1990 by University of Chicago Press. Reprinted by permission.)

The results of the experiment are summarized in Figure 11.14. The best retention performance was evident in the group that was tested with the same playpen liner that had been present during conditioning. Each of the other groups showed significantly poorer memory performance. Infants tested with a novel liner (Group Diff) may have shown poor performance because novelty somehow disrupted their behavior (Thomas & Empedocles, 1992). However, the poor performance of group Diff-Fam indicates that novelty was not entirely responsible for the disruptions of memory that occurred. A change in the crib liner from conditioning to testing resulted in poor performance even if the liner used during testing was familiar. The inferior performance of Group Diff-Fam as compared to Group Same provides strong evidence that the cloth liner served as a retrieval cue for the instrumental kicking behavior. (For related research, see Daman-Wasserman et al., 2006; Rovee-Collier, Hayne, & Colombo, 2001.)

Contextual Cues and the Retrieval of Conflicting Memories

Changing the cloth pattern on the playpen liner changed the contextual cues of the playpen. Thus, the study by Borovsky and Rovee-Collier was a study of the role of contextual cues in memory retrieval. I previously described other examples of contextual cues in memory retrieval in the discussion of contextual stimulus control in Chapter 8 and in connection with extinction, in Chapter 9. A particularly striking example was presented in Figure 8.13, which showed data from an experiment by Thomas, McKelvie, and Mah (1985). Pigeons in this experiment first learned to peck when a vertical line (S+ = 90°) was projected on the response key and to not peck when a horizontal line (S– = 0°) appeared. The contextual cues were then changed (by altering the sounds and lighting in the chamber), and the pigeons were trained on the reversal of the original discrimination. Now, the horizontal line (0°) was S+ and the vertical line (90°) was S–.

Subsequent generalization tests in each context indicated that responding to the vertical and horizontal lines depended on the context in which the lines were tested. In one context, the vertical line produced the highest level of responding; in the other context, the horizontal line produced the most responding. The study illustrates that organisms can retain memories of diametrically opposing response tendencies, each associated with a different retrieval cue. (For other examples of involving the retrieval of conflicting memories, see Bouton, 1993, 1994; Dekeyne & Deweer, 1990 and Haggbloom & Morris, 1994.)

The Generality of Reminder Treatments

Courtesy of N. E. Spear

N. E. Spear

We now know a great deal about the facilitation of memory retrieval by reminder treatments (see Gordon, 1981; Spear & Riccio, 1994). As we have seen, contextual cues are especially effective in stimulating memory retrieval (Gordon & Klein, 1994; Hitchcock & Rovee-Collier, 1996; Zhou & Riccio, 1996). In addition, various other reminder procedures have been found to facilitate recall, including exposure to the *unconditioned stimulus* (Hunt, 1997; MacArdy & Riccio, 1995), exposure to the *reinforced conditioned stimulus* (CS+) (Gisquet-Verrier & Alexinsky, 1990; Gordon & Mowrer, 1980), and even exposure to a *nonreinforced conditioned stimulus* (CS–) that was present during training (Campbell & Randall, 1976; Miller, Jagielo, & Spear, 1992).

Furthermore, reminder treatments can be used to reverse many instances of memory loss (see Miller, Kasprow, & Schachtman, 1986; Urcelay & Miller, 2008). For example, reminder treatments have been used to facilitate memory retrieval from short-term memory (Feldman & Gordon, 1979; Kasprow, 1987). They can remind older animals (and babies) of forgotten early-life experiences (e.g., Galluccio & Rovee-Collier, 1999; Richardson, Riccio, & Jonke, 1983). Reminder treatments can counteract stimulus-generalization decrements that occur when learned behavior is tested in a new context (Millin & Riccio, 2004; Mowrer & Gordon, 1983). Reminder treatments also have been observed to increase the low levels of conditioned responding that typically occur in latent inhibition, overshadowing, and blocking procedures (Kasprow, Cacheiro, Balaz, & Miller, 1982; Kasprow, Catterson, Schachtman, & Miller, 1984; Miller, Jagielo, & Spear, 1990; Schachtman, Gee, Kasprow, & Miller, 1983; see also Gordon, McGinnis, & Weaver, 1985).

BOX **11.2**

Genes and Learning

The nervous system is composed of billions of neurons interconnected by chemical connections called synapses. In Box 11.1, I described how learning can alter behavior by producing a change in the way a synapse operates. In some cases, learning may bring about a lasting increase in synaptic strength, yielding a form of long-term potentiation (LTP). In other cases, experience will result in a down regulation known as long-term depression (LTD).

The mechanisms that mediate changes in synaptic strength operate in phases. Initially, local molecular mechanisms produce short-term and rapid changes in synaptic strength. Additional processes are then activated that result in lasting memories. Establishing a long-term memory depends on the activation of genes that manufacture new protein products that produce a lasting change in how a synapse works.

Using drugs that block protein synthesis, researchers demonstrated many years ago that the manufacture of new proteins contributes to the formation of long-term memories (Davis & Squire, 1984; see Box 9.1). More recently, it has been established that the same is true for the lasting forms of LTP and LTD (Mayford & Kandel, 1999). Even learning in the invertebrate *Aplysia* (see Box 2.2) depends on gene expression (Hawkins, Kandel, & Bailey, 2006).

Modern molecular biology has given us a host of new techniques that allow researchers to uncover the genes involved in learning. These studies have revealed that a variety of learning mechanisms depend on the induction of common genetic codes, genes that encode

some biological universals that have been well conserved through evolution. Just as the mechanisms that underlie the generation of a neural signal (the action potential) are well conserved across species, so too may be the mechanisms that underlie synaptic plasticity.

Modern genetics has also given us new tools for studying the role of gene expression in learning. We can read the genetic code, identify the locus of the relevant genes, and experimentally manipulate how those genes operate. If we believe that a particular protein plays an essential role in learning, we can test this by using mice in which the relevant gene has been knocked out. This provides a new and unique window into the molecular mechanisms that underlie learning (Nakajima & Tang, 2005).

Silva and his colleagues were among the first to use this approach to study learning, creating genetically-engineered mice that exhibit specific deficits in the way they learn and remember (Silva & Giese, 1998). Early studies addressed this issue by manipulating a protein known as CaMKII. One way a synapse can be strengthened is by allowing calcium (Ca^{++}) into the cell. Ca^{++} is an electrically charged particle that normally has a higher concentration outside of the neuron than inside. When Ca^{++} is allowed into the neuron by the NMDA receptor (see 11.15), it engages CaMKII which enhances synaptic efficacy by activating the AMPA receptors that mediate the neural signal. Silva created mice that lacked the gene that underlies the production of CaMKII within the

hippocampus. From other studies, Silva knew that the hippocampus plays a critical role in learning about spatial relations. He reasoned that if CaMKII is critical for learning, then knockout mice that lack this gene should have difficulty remembering where a hidden platform is in a Morris water maze. That is precisely what occurred, providing a link between learning and a particular protein product.

A difficulty with studies of knockout mice is that the mice may not develop normally. When a gene is missing, other biochemical mechanisms can be enlisted that help the organism compensate for its deficiency. This could yield a brain that differs in a variety of ways from a normal brain. The abnormal neural environment may make it difficult to interpret the consequences of the genetic manipulation. Neuroscientists are solving this problem by making mice in which the expression of a gene can be experimentally controlled. An interesting application of this technology involves the creation of a transgenic mouse. Instead of losing a gene (a knockout), the transgenic mouse has an extra gene that makes a new protein product.

In one example, mice were engineered that made a mutant version of CaMKII that did not work properly. These mice did not exhibit normal LTP and exhibited a learning deficit in the Morris water maze (Mayford, Bach, Huang, Wang, Hawkins, & Kandel, 1996). The expression of the added gene in these mice was controlled by a molecular switch. This switch, which had been added by the researchers, was controlled by a novel chemical

(continued)

BOX **11.2** (continued)

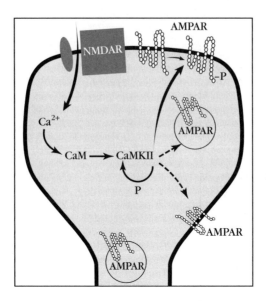

FIGURE **11.15**

The molecular mechanisms that underlie long-term potentiation. The NMDA receptor allows CA++ to enter the cell which engages an enzyme, CaMKII. CaMKII play a critical role in strengthening the synaptic response. It does so, in part, by awakening silent AMPA receptors. (Adapted from Malenka & Nicoll, 1999.)

(doxycycline). To turn the switch off, and stop production of the mutant CaMKII, all the researchers had to do was add some doxycycline to the diet of the mice. When this was done, the mice once again exhibited normal LTP. They also recovered their ability to learn and remember spatial locations. As long as doxycycline was present, their brains worked normally. Only when this chemical was removed, and the mutant gene was expressed, was LTP and learning disrupted.

All of the genetic manipulations I described so far produced deficits in memory. Researchers are also exploring the possibility that modifying gene expression might improve memory. A good example is provided by a genetically engineered mouse named Doogie, after the fictitious TV boy genius, Doogie

Howser. As I discussed in Box 11.1, the induction of LTP depends on the NMDA receptor. This receptor is formed from components (subunits), one of which changes with development. Early in development, animals have a subunit called NR2B which appears to promote the induction of LTP. In adults, this subunit is replaced by an alternative form (NR2A) that down regulates LTP. The change from the juvenile form (NR2B) to the adult form (NR2A) could make it more difficult for an adult animal to learn about new environmental relations. To explore this possibility, Tsein and his colleagues created mice that continued to make the juvenile form of the subunit (NR2B) into adulthood (Tang et al., 1999; reviewed in Tsien, 2000). As expected, these mice showed stronger LTP as

adults. The mice also exhibited enhanced learning on an object recognition task and improved spatial memory in the Morris water Maze. Across a range of tests, Doogie mice seemed smarter.

If the juvenile form of the NMDA receptor works better, why would nature replace it with one that undermines learning and memory? The answer is still being debated. Perhaps this change helps to protect some early memories that are crucial to survival. For example, once we have learned the words of our language, this information should not be readily unlearned. By enabling learning early in development, nature may open a critical window, only to close it later in life to help protect what was learned.

J. W. Grau

FORGETTING

Forgetting is the flip side of memory. We are said to exhibit **forgetting** when memory fails and we don't respond in accordance with past experience or learning. However, as Kraemer and Golding (1997) have argued, forgetting should not be viewed simply as the absence of remembering. Rather, forgetting should be considered an important phenomenon in its own right (see also White, 2001). Forgetting can be adaptive because it increases behavioral variability. That behavioral variability is not a welcome experience when you cannot remember something on a test. However, it can be useful when you move to a new job or a new city and have to learn new skills. Forgetting can also reduce the context specificity of learning and thereby permit learned behavior to occur in a broader range of situations (Riccio, Rabinowitz, & Axelrod, 1994).

The common experience is that failures of memory become more likely as time passes after a learning episode. However, it is not informative to view time as a *cause* of forgetting. As Piaget is reputed to have said, "Time is not a cause but a vehicle of causes." And, there may be a variety of causes of forgetting. As I have described, many things determine whether you perform well on a memory test. Some of these concern coding and the acquisition of information. Others involve rehearsal and the retention of information. Still others involve processes of retrieval. Things can go wrong at any point along the way. Therefore, failures of memory, or forgetting, can occur for a variety of reasons.

Forgetting has been extensively investigated in the context of two types of phenomena: interference effects and retrograde amnesia. In the concluding sections of this chapter, I will describe these phenomena in turn.

Proactive and Retroactive Interference

The most common sources of memory disruption arise from exposure to prominent stimuli either before or after the event that you are trying to remember. Consider meeting people at a party, for example. If the only new person you meet is Alice, chances are you will not have much trouble remembering her name. However, if you are introduced to a number of new people before and/or after meeting Alice, you may find it much harder to recall her name.

There are numerous well documented and analyzed situations in which memory for something is disrupted by earlier exposure to other information. In these cases the interfering information acts forward to disrupt the memory of a future target event. Therefore, the disruption of memory is called **proactive interference**. In other cases, memory for something is disrupted by subsequent exposure to competing information. In these situations the interfering stimulus acts backward to disrupt the memory of a preceding target event. Therefore, the disruption of memory is called **retroactive interference**.

The mechanisms of proactive and retroactive interference have been extensively investigated in studies of human memory (Postman, 1971; Slamecka & Ceraso, 1960; Underwood, 1957). Proactive and retroactive interference have also been investigated in various animal memory paradigms. (For examples of proactive interference, see Grant, 1982, 2000; White, Parkinson, Brown, & Wixted, 2004; and Edhouse & White, 1988a, 1988b. For examples of retroactive interference, see Escobar & Miller, 2003; Harper & Garry, 2000; and

Killeen, 2001. For a recent study of both types of interference in memory for spatial locations, see Lewis & Kamil, 2006.)

Retrograde Amnesia

Sadly, a frequent source of memory failure is severe head injury. For example, people who receive a concussion in a car accident often suffer memory loss. However, the amnesia is likely to be selective. They may forget how the injury occurred, which car crashed into them, or whether the traffic light was green or amber. But, they will continue to remember their name and address, where they grew up, and what they prefer to eat for dessert. Thus, there is a gradient of memory loss, with forgetting limited to events that occurred close to the accident. This phenomenon is called **retrograde amnesia** (Russell & Nathan, 1946). The farther back you go from the time of injury, the better the memory. (For a discussion of the human literature on retrograde amnesia, see Squire, 2006.)

The clinical significance of retrograde amnesia resulting from closed-head injury received in traffic and sports accidents has encouraged investigators to developed techniques to study this phenomenon in laboratory animals. This research has demonstrated that retrograde amnesia can be produced by many different disturbances of the nervous system in addition to closed-head injury. Other sources of retrograde amnesia include electroconvulsive shock, anesthesia, temporary cooling of the body, or injection of drugs that inhibit protein synthesis (for reviews, see McGaugh & Herz, 1972; Spear & Riccio, 1994; Riccio, Millin, & Bogart, 2006).

Why do various neural insults produce a graded loss of memory? The traditional explanation involves the concept of **memory consolidation** (see McGaugh & Herz, 1972). According to the memory-consolidation hypothesis, when a stimulus is first encountered, it enters a short-term, or temporary, memory store. While in short-term memory, the information is vulnerable and can be lost because of interfering stimuli or neurophysiological disturbances. However, if the proper conditions are met, the information gradually becomes consolidated into a relatively permanent form.

Memory consolidation is assumed to be a physiological process by which information is gradually transformed into a long-term or permanent state. Neurophysiological disturbances such as electroconvulsive shock, anesthesia, and body cooling are assumed to interfere with the consolidation process and thereby disrupt the transfer of information to long-term memory. Amnesic agents presumably lead to loss of memory for only recently experienced events because only the recent events are in short-term memory, and are thus susceptible to disruptions of consolidation.

Courtesy of D. C. Riccio

D. C. Riccio

Retrograde Amnesia for Extinction

Most of the research on memory consolidation has been done with recently learned information. As we saw in Chapter 9, extinction is a form of new learning. If that is true, then extinction should also be susceptible to retrograde amnesia. This prediction was recently tested by Briggs and Riccio (2007) in a fear-conditioning paradigm, with cooling of the body, or hypothermia, serving as the amnesic agent. Laboratory rats were conditioned in a shuttle box that had a white and a black compartment separated by a door.

Conditioning was accomplished in a single trial. The rats were placed in the white compartment and the door to the back compartment was then opened. As soon as the rats walked into the black compartment the door behind them closed and they got two inescapable shocks. This single-punishment episode made the rats reluctant to enter the black compartment again, and that was used as the measure of conditioning.

Extinction was conducted the day after conditioning and consisted of putting the rats in the black compartment without shock for 12 minutes. Following the extinction procedure, some of the rats were immersed in cold water to substantially reduce their body temperature. This hypothermia treatment was provided either immediately after the extinction treatment (when it would disrupt consolidation of the extinction experience), or 30 or 60 minutes after extinction. The next day the rats were put back into the white compartment to see how long they would take to enter the black compartment (which had been paired with shock). The test was terminated after 600 seconds if the rat did not enter the black compartment.

The results of the experiment are summarized in Figure 11.16. The first bar in the figure is for a group of rats that received the conditioning proce-

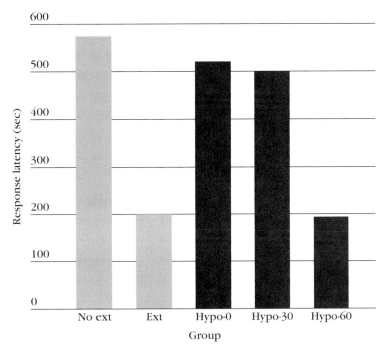

FIGURE **11.16**

Time for rats to enter the black compartment of a shuttle box after having been shocked there. The first group received only fear conditioning. The second group received extinction after the conditioning trial. Groups Hypo-0, Hypo-30, and Hypo-60 received hypothermia to induce amnesia 0, 30, or 60 minutes after the extinction procedure. (Based on Briggs & Riccio, 2007, Figure 1, p. 134.)

dure but not the extinction treatment. These rats spent nearly 600 seconds in the white side of the shuttle box, indicating strong fear of the black compartment. The second bar is for a group of rats that received the extinction procedure, but was not subjected to hypothermia. They lost their fear of the black compartment, entering it after about 200 seconds. The next three bars were from rats that received the hypothermia treatment immediately (Hypo-0), or 30 or 60 minutes after extinction (Hypo-30 and Hypo-60). Notice that rats in the Hypo-0 group behaved as if they never got extinction. They took more than 500 seconds to enter the black compartment. Similar results were obtained with the rats in the Hypo-30 group. Thus, these two groups showed retrograde amnesia for the extinction treatment. However, delaying the hypothermia 60 minutes after extinction did not produce the amnesic effect. Rats in the Hypo-60 group responded like those in the normal extinction group, entering the black compartment in about 200 seconds.

Consolidation Failure versus Retrieval Failure

Disruptions of performance caused by amnesic agents were originally explained in terms of disruptions of consolidation of the memories. A major alternative interpretation is that amnesic agents cause a failure to retrieve information that was experienced close in time to the neurophysiological disturbance (Miller & Matzel, 2006; Miller & Springer, 1973; Riccio & Richardson, 1984). This explanation is called *the retrieval failure hypothesis*. The retrieval failure hypothesis assumes that an amnesic agent alters the coding of new memories so as to make subsequent recovery of the information difficult. The information surrounding an amnesic episode is assumed to be acquired and retained in memory, but in a form that makes it difficult to access. This retrieval failure is responsible for the amnesia that is observed.

What kinds of evidence would help decide between the memory-consolidation and retrieval-failure interpretations? If information is lost because of a failure of consolidation, it cannot ever be recovered. By contrast, the retrieval-failure view assumes that amnesia can be reversed if the proper procedure is found to reactivate the memory. Thus, to decide between the alternatives, we have to find techniques that can reverse the effects of amnesic agents. Contextual cues of acquisition and unpaired presentations of the US are good potential candidates to reactivate memories.

Numerous experiments have shown that the memory deficits that characterize retrograde amnesia can be overcome by reminder treatments (e.g., Gordon, 1981; Riccio & Richardson, 1984; Spear & Riccio, 1994; Urcelay & Miller, 2008). Consider, for example, the experiment I described earlier on retrograde amnesia for extinction that was produced by hypothermia (see Figure 11.16). These rats received the hypothermia treatment after extinction. Therefore, their memory of extinction may have been encoded in the context of a low body temperature. If that is true, then the memory of extinction should be reactivated if the rats again receive the hypothermia treatment.

Briggs and Riccio (2007) repeated the experiment I described earlier, but this time they added three groups whose body temperatures were re-cooled for the memory test. The results for these groups are summarized in Figure 11.17. Recall that the subjects were first conditioned to avoid stepping into the black compartment. They then received a session of extinction followed

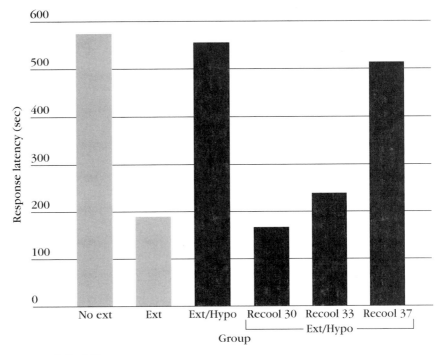

FIGURE **11.17**

Time for rats to enter the black compartment of a shuttle box after having been shocked there. The first group received only conditioning. The second group received extinction after the conditioning trial. The remaining groups received a hypothermia treatment right after extinction and were tested the next day. Group Exp/Hypo was tested without being re-cooled. Groups Re-cool 30, Re-cool 33, and Re-cool 37 were re-cooled before the memory test and were allowed to warm up to body temperatures of 30, 33, and 37 degrees (Celsius) for the test session. (Based on Briggs & Riccio, 2007, Figure 2, p. 136.)

by a memory test the next day. The first two groups in Figure 11.17 (No Ext and Ext) received the same procedures as in the first experiment without hypothermia and yielded the same results: great reluctance to enter the black compartment in the No Ext group, and more rapid entry in the Ext group. All of the other groups received hypothermia right after the extinction treatment, which should have caused amnesia for extinction. That was the outcome in the Ext/Hypo group, which was tested the day after hypothermia at normal body temperature.

The next three groups in Figure 11.17 were given the same hypothermia treatment just before the memory test that they received after the extinction, and were then tested at different points as their bodies warmed up. The normal body temperature for a rat is $37°$ C. The first of the re-cooled groups (Re-cool 30) was tested when its body temperature was $30°$ C, which is still pretty cold. This reactivated the memory of extinction, and these rats showed rapid entry into the black compartment. The next group (Re-cool 33) was allowed to warm up to $33°$ C after re-cooling and also showed some evidence of extinction. The final group (Re-cool 37) was allowed to warm up to normal body temperature (37° C) after re-cooling. This group showed no evidence of the memory of extinction.

These results show that amnesia caused by hypothermia can be reversed by returning the subjects to the body temperature they had right after the extinction procedure. Thus, hypothermia did not disrupt consolidation of the memory of extinction, but made that memory difficult to retrieve when the rats were at normal temperature. The implication of this type of experiment is that one's memory for the details of a car accident could be restored by re-enacting many of the elements of the accident.

Reconsolidation

Interest in the consolidation hypothesis has been rekindled by experiments showing that when a well-established memory is reactivated, the memory becomes unstable and is again susceptible to disruptions by amnesic agents just like newly learned memories (Nadel, Schafe, & LeDoux, 2000). These results raise the possibility that memories have to be reconsolidated after each time they are activated (see Box 9.1). If true, this would make long-term memories open to all sorts of modifications.

Reconsolidation has been the subject of extensive research in the last decade at both the level of behavior and the level of synaptic and cellular mechanisms (e.g., Dudai, 2004) and has generated considerable debate (e.g., Nader & Wang, 2006; Riccio, Millin, & Bogart, 2006). One major question is whether the neurobiological mechanisms responsible for reconsolidation are similar to the mechanisms of original consolidation. The answer to that question seems to be *yes* and *no*. There are some similarities in the neurobiological mechanisms of reconsolidation and original consolidation, but there are also differences (Miller & Sweatt, 2006). Another major issue is whether memory failures observed in reconsolidation experiments represent failures of consolidation or failures of retrieval. It is unlikely that these issues will be resolved soon. However, the debate has elevated the level of sophistication of models of memory.

Instead of considering consolidation to be a unitary process, investigators have recognized several different types of consolidation (e.g., Dudai, 2004) that operate on different time scales. Some operate on a very short time scale (on the order of seconds or minutes) whereas others operate over a much longer period, on the order of hours or even days. Miller and Matzel (2006), for example, suggested that consolidation operating on the order of milliseconds involves synaptic changes in neurons that are not susceptible to disruption by amnesic agents. In contrast, consolidation occurring over longer periods involves neural circuits and networks that prepare the memory for recall. Reminder treatments that produce recovery from retrograde amnesia presumably operate through these neural circuits.

CONCLUDING COMMENTS

The study of memory processes is central to the understanding of comparative cognition. Memory processes involve 1) acquisition and coding of information, 2) rehearsal and retention, and 3) retrieval. Difficulties in any of these phases, or problems involving interactions among them, can result in failures of memory, or forgetting. Several ingenious techniques for the study of memory processes in animals have been developed in the past 40 years. These techniques have told us much about the coding of information, rehearsal processes, and retrieval processes. This information has, in turn, allowed us to better understand failures of memory that occur in interference paradigms and in retrograde amnesia.

SAMPLE QUESTIONS

1. Compare and contrast working and reference memory.
2. Describe the delayed matching-to-sample procedure and alternative strategies that can be used to respond accurately in such a procedure. How can these response strategies be distinguished experimentally?
3. Describe spatial learning tasks and mechanisms that have been used to explain efficient performance in this situation.
4. Describe how retrospective and prospective coding can be differentiated experimentally.
5. Describe the phenomenon of directed forgetting and what it tells us about memory processes.
6. Describe the memory consolidation and retrieval failure explanations of retrograde amnesia and what evidence can be used to support one or the other hypothesis.

KEY TERMS

acquisition The initial stage of learning.

amnesia Loss of memory. (See also *retrograde amnesia.*)

cognitive ethology A branch of ethology that assumes that consciousness, awareness, and intentionality can be inferred from the complexity, flexibility, and cleverness of certain forms of behavior.

comparative cognition Theoretical constructs and models used to explain aspects of behavior that cannot be readily characterized in terms of simple S-R or reflex mechanisms. These mechanisms do not presume consciousness, awareness, or intentionality.

delayed-matching-to-sample procedure A procedure in which participants are reinforced for responding to a test stimulus that is the same as a sample stimulus that was presented some time earlier.

directed forgetting Forgetting that occurs because of a stimulus (a forget cue) that indicates that working memory will not be tested on that trial. Directed forgetting is an example of the stimulus control of memory.

Episodic memory Memory for a specific event or episode that includes information about what occurred and when and where it took place, as contrasted with memory for general facts or ways of doing things.

forgetting Failure to remember previously acquired information.

memory A term used to characterize instances in which an organism's current behavior is determined by some aspect of its previous experience.

memory consolidation The establishment of a memory in relatively permanent form, or the transfer of information from short-term to long-term memory.

proactive interference Disruption of memory caused by exposure to stimuli before the event to be remembered.

procedural memory Memory for learned behavioral and cognitive skills that are performed automatically, without the requirement of conscious control, often reflecting knowledge about invariant relationships in the environment, such as CS-US contiguity (classical conditioning) or response-reinforcer contiguity (instrumental conditioning).

prospection Same as *prospective coding*.

prospective coding Memory for an expected future event or response.

reconsolidation The process of stabilizing or consolidating a reactivated memory. Presumably the disruption of this reconsolidation leads to modification or forgetting of the original memory.

reference memory Long-term retention of background information necessary for successful use of incoming and recently acquired information. (Compare with *working memory*.)

rehearsal Maintaining information in an active state, available to influence behavior and/or the processing of other information.

retention interval The time between acquisition of information and a test of memory for that information.

retrieval The recovery of information from a memory store.

retrieval cues Stimuli related to an experience that facilitates the recall of other information related to that experience.

retrieval failure A deficit in recovering information from a memory store.

retroactive interference Disruption of memory caused by exposure to stimuli following the event to be remembered.

retrograde amnesia A gradient of memory loss going back in time from the occurrence of a major injury or physiological disturbance. Amnesia is greatest for events that took place closest to the time of injury and less for events experienced earlier.

retrospection Same as *retrospective coding*.

retrospective coding Memory for a previously experienced event or response. Also called *retrospection*.

stimulus coding How a stimulus is represented in memory.

trace decay hypothesis The theoretical idea that exposure to a stimulus produces changes in the nervous system that gradually and automatically decrease after the stimulus has been terminated.

trials-unique procedure A matching-to-sample procedure in which different sample and comparison stimuli are used on each trial.

working memory Temporary retention of information that is needed for successful responding on the task at hand but not on subsequent (or previous) similar tasks. (Compare with *reference memory*.)

12

Comparative Cognition II: Special Topics

CHAPTER PREVIEW

The final chapter explores a diversity of contemporary research areas in comparative cognition. In each of these areas, it is important to consider basic conditioning mechanisms before accepting more complex cognitive interpretations of the behavior. We begin with research on the remarkable ability of some bird species to retrieve food that they previously stored in various locations. Studies of food caching are a major source of information about spatial memory and episodic memory in nonhuman species. We next turn to how behavior can become organized in time, a ubiquitous feature of the environment, and how organisms learn about the serial order of stimuli, which is a pre-requisite for numerical skill. Research on categorization and concept learning in nonhuman species is described next. This rich area of research ranges from studies of perceptual concepts to studies of higher-level and abstract concepts, all which are required for language. The next section describes research on tool use, with emphasis on recent research on tool use in New Caledonian crows. The chapter concludes with what may be the most complex of cognitive behaviors, language. As we will see, language is actually a collection of cognitive skills, some of which are clearly evident in a number of nonhuman species.

———————————

The various aspects of behavior discussed in this chapter are not all reflections of a common underlying mechanism, nor are they all involved in the solution of a common behavioral problem or challenge to survival. Rather, they all involve major contemporary areas of research in animal cognition that have stimulated a great deal of interest. Until recently, the cognitive processes involved in these phenomena were considered to be characteristic primarily of human behavior. In addition, each of these areas of research has stimulated considerable controversy.

The controversies have centered on whether complex cognitive processes had to be postulated to explain the various behaviors that were observed. Opponents of cognitive interpretations have argued that the phenomena could be explained by traditional learning principles. By contrast, proponents of cognitive interpretations have argued that cognitive mechanisms provide simpler explanations for the phenomena and are more productive in stimulating new research. The work in this area has amply borne out this latter justification. Without a cognitive perspective, much of the research I will describe in this chapter would never have been done and many of the phenomena would never have been discovered.

FOOD CACHING AND RECOVERY

We begin the discussion of complex cognition with research on food caching and recovery. Numerous avian and mammalian species store food in various places during times of plenty, and visit these caches later to recover the stored food items (e.g., for reviews see De Kort et al., 2006; Kamil & Gould, 2008; Sherry, 1985). One remarkable example of cache recovery is provided by the Clark's nutcracker (*Nucifraga columbiana*) (Balda & Turek, 1984; Kamil & Balda, 1990). These birds live in alpine areas of the Western United States and harvest seeds from pine cones in late summer and early autumn. They hide the seeds in underground caches and recover them months later in the winter and spring when other food sources are scarce. A nutcracker may store as many as 33,000 seeds in caches of four or five seeds each and recover several thousand of these during the next winter.

Caching behavior varies considerably among species, within different populations of the same species, and is related to ecological factors. Pravosudov and Clayton (2002), for example, compared food caching and recovery in two populations of black-capped chickadees (*Poecile atricapilla*): those living in Colorado and those living in Alaska. Although both environments have harsh winters, the weather in Alaska is more challenging. Chickadees from both populations were brought into the laboratory and tested under common conditions. The Alaska chickadees stored more food items and were more efficient in their cache recovery. They also performed better on a non-caching spatial memory task, but were not better than the Colorado chickadees on a nonspatial learning task.

Food caching and recovery potentially involves many different factors. First, you have to decide what food items to cache. Storing perishable foods is not useful unless you intend to recover them soon. Nonperishables don't have to be recovered as quickly. There are also decisions about where to store food, since the location has to be recalled at the time of recovery. Caching also involves a social component: storing food is only useful if you, rather than a competitor, get to eat what you stored. The decision of whether or not to cache can be influenced by the presence of an observer who might steal the food (Dally, Emery, & Clayton, 2006). The cache location chosen may also depend on how easy that location is for competitors to find. Similar issues arise at the time of recovery. You have to decide where to look for stored food, whether to look in the presence of a competitor, which foods to retrieve first, and whether to eat or re-store what you recovered. Given the species differences that exist in food-caching behavior and the complexity of the processes involved in caching and recovery, many different types of questions can be examined using this behavior system. Therefore, food caching and recovery has become a rich source of information about comparative cognition (De Kort et al., 2006; Kamil & Gould, 2008).

Spatial Memory in Food Caching and Recovery

Laboratory studies of cache recovery are typically designed to isolate one or two variables to permit close examination of how those variables contribute to food caching and recovery. Numerous studies have focused on questions related to spatial memory and the spatial learning and memory that is involved (see Kamil & Gould, 2008, for a recent review). The theoretical ideas and experimental controls required to study spatial memory in food caching and recovery are similar to those I discussed in Chapter 11 for other forms of spatial memory. Before one can accept the conclusion that memory for specific spatial locations is involved, other possibilities have to be ruled out. One possibility is that birds find caches by searching randomly among possible cache sites. Another possibility is that they store food only in particular types of locations and then go around to these favored places to recover the food items without specifically remembering that they had put food there. They may also mark food-storage sites somehow and then look for these marks when it comes time to recover the food. Yet another possibility is that they are able to smell or see the stored food and identify caches in that way.

Ruling out nonmemory interpretations has required carefully controlled laboratory experiments (e.g., Kamil & Balda, 1990; Sherry, 1984; Sherry, Krebs, & Cowie, 1981; Shettleworth & Krebs, 1986). In one such laboratory study, for example, Kamil and Balda (1985) tested nutcrackers in a room that had a special floor with 180 recessed cups of sand (see left panel of Figure 12.1). After habituation to the experimental situation and while they were hungry, the birds were given three sessions during which they could store pinyon pine seeds in the sand cups. During each caching session, only 18 cups were available; the rest of the cups were covered with lids. This procedure forced the birds to store food in cups selected by the experimenter rather than in cups or locations the birds might have found especially attractive.

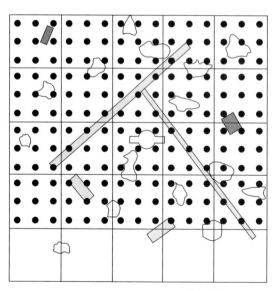
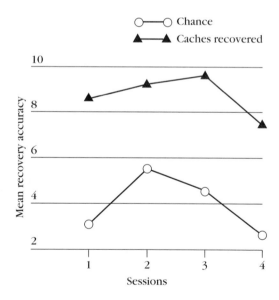

FIGURE **12.1**

Left panel: Floor plan of the apparatus used by Kamil and Balda (1985) to test the spatial memory of Clark's nutcrackers. Filled circles represent sand cups. Other symbols represent rocks, logs, and a feeder in the middle. Right panel: Recovery accuracy, compared to chance, during four successive recovery sessions started 10 days after the birds stored pine seeds. (After Kamil & Balda, 1985.)

Starting 10 days after the seeds had been stored by the nutcrackers, four recovery sessions were conducted on successive days. During recovery sessions none of the 180 sand cups was covered with a lid, but seeds were located only in the cups where the birds had previously stored seeds. The results are summarized on the right side of Figure 12.1. Notice that on average, the birds performed much better than chance in going to the cups where they had previously stored food. The correct locations could not be identified by disturbed sand because the experimenters raked the sand smooth at the start of each recovery session. Other tests showed that the correct locations were not identified by the smell of the seeds buried in the sand because the birds visited places where they had previously stored food even if the food was removed before the test session. These control studies indicate that cache recovery reflects spatial memory. In other experiments, Balda and Kamil (1992) found that memory of nutcrackers for the spatial location of cached food lasts as long as 285 days (the longest retention interval tested).

Episodic Memory in Food Caching and Recovery

Courtesy of N. S. Clayton

N. S. Clayton

The food caching and recovery paradigm has also attracted a great deal of attention in recent years as a paradigm for studying episodic memory in nonhuman species (Clayton, Bussey, & Dickinson, 2003; Salwiczek, Dickinson, & Clayton, 2008). **Episodic memory** is memory for a specific event or episode, as contrasted with memory for general facts or ways of doing things. Many of us can remember walking across the stage during graduation, or attending the wedding of a good friend. We also have memories for more common episodes, like meeting a college roommate for the first time or going on a first date with someone. Episodic memories can be rich in detail. You can recall *what* happened, *where* it happened, and *when* it happed. It is like reliving the past experience but you are aware that it was in the past and that you are remembering it. This is the phenomenological component of episodic memory.

The study of episodic memory in animals has been encouraged by claims that episodic memory is a uniquely human trait (e.g., Tulving, 1983). Starting with Darwin, the claim that something is uniquely human has been a *call to arms* for scientists studying comparative cognition, or at least it has been a call to examine the claim with ingenious experiments with nonhuman species. It is unlikely that scientists will ever find ways to establish that nonhuman species experience the phenomenological components of episodic memory (the feelings of remembering). However, science can establish whether nonhuman species exhibit the other features of episodic memory. What are those other features?

Clayton, Bussey, and Dickinson (2003) have argued that episodic memory in nonhuman species has to have certain *content*. More specifically, the memory has to include information about *what* happened, *when* it happened, and *where* it happened. Furthermore, the what, when, and where information has to be *integrated* into a coherent representation rather than being independent bits of information. Finally, this integrated representation of the past episode has to be available for *flexible use* in dealing with new problems. Given the complexity of these issues, it is not surprising that there have been debates about the criteria for episodic memory and whether any of the available

A. Dickinson

evidence satisfactorily meets these criteria (e.g., Roberts, 2002; Zentall, 2005). However, studies employing the food caching and recovery paradigm provide some of the best evidence to date on episodic memory in nonhuman species (Salwiczek, Dickinson, & Clayton, 2008). (For related studies with rats and rhesus monkeys, see Babb & Crystal, 2006; and Hampton, Hampstead, & Murray, 2005.)

The Western scrub jay is an ideal species for studying questions related to episodic memory because it caches both perishable and nonperishable food, engages in caching behavior all year round, and readily performs these activities in the laboratory. How might one take advantage of these traits to study episodic memory? If you store several different food items in a number of places, why should you care about which type of food is stored where? If you find all of the food items equally acceptable, then there is no reason to keep track of where specific foods were stored. However, if you prefer one food over another, then knowing the location of each type of food will be useful because you can retrieve the more preferred food first. Thus, by varying the palatability of the food, one can examine memory for *what* was stored *where*. Remembering *when* the food was stored becomes important if the food item is perishable because perishable foods are not worth retrieving if a long time has passed because they will not be good to eat.

Western scrub jays prefer to eat worms over peanuts. However, worms are perishable and deteriorate if they are stored a long time. Clayton and Dickinson (1999) first gave jays practice trials in which they were allowed to store worms and peanuts in the compartments of an ice cube tray (see Figure 12.2). A different tray was used for each type of food. The trays were made distinctive by placing different objects around them. To permit hiding the foods, the compartments of each ice tray were filled with sand. Each trial consisted of two storage or caching episodes (one for peanuts and the other for worms, in a counterbalanced order). A recovery period was then conducted four hours or 124 hours later with both food trays

FIGURE **12.2**

Food caching by a Western scrub jay. Food items were cached in compartments of an ice cube tray filled with sand. One tray was used for caching worms; another was used to cache peanuts. To make the trays distinctive, each tray was located near a distinctive set of Legos.

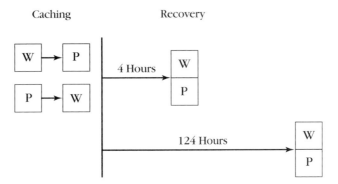

FIGURE **12.3**

Procedure used to train scrub jays to remember what, where, and when they stored worms and peanuts. (Based on Clayton & Dickinson, 1999.)

available (see Figure 12.3). On training trials with a four-hour retention interval, neither food deteriorated by the time the recovery or choice test occurred. In contrast, on trials with the 124-hour retention interval, the worms were in pretty bad shape by the time of recovery.

As training progressed, the birds learned to select the worms during the recovery period if recovery was scheduled four hours after caching. If recovery occurred 124 hours after caching, the birds selected the peanuts instead. However, this behavior could have been cued by the sight or smell of the peanut and worm caches during the recovery period. To prevent responding on the basis of visual or olfactory cues, test trials were conducted at the end of the experiment during which fresh sand was put in the trays and all food was removed. The results of those test trials are summarized in Figure 12.4. Data for the scrub jays that learned that worms deteriorate if stored for 124 hours are presented in the left panel. (This was the *deteriorate* group.) As expected, these birds searched more in the worm tray than the peanut tray if the choice test occurred four hours after caching of the worms. In contrast, they searched more in the peanut tray than in the worm tray if the worms had been stored 124 hours earlier.

The right panel shows the results for a second group of jays (*replenish*) that received a different training history. For the *replenish* group, fresh worms were always provided during the recovery or choice periods during training. Therefore, these birds did not get a chance to learn that worms deteriorate with time. Consistent with their training history, the *replenish* group showed a preference for worms whether the worms had been stored four hours or 124 hours before the recovery or choice period.

The scrub jays in the Clayton and Dickinson study could not have returned to the compartments in which food had been stored if they did not remember *where* they had stored the foods. The fact that the birds distinguished between the worm and peanut storage sites indicates that they remembered *what* type of food was stored in each site. The fact that the *deteriorate* group changed its choice depending on how long ago the worms had been stored indicates that they also remember *when* the food had been stored. Thus, these

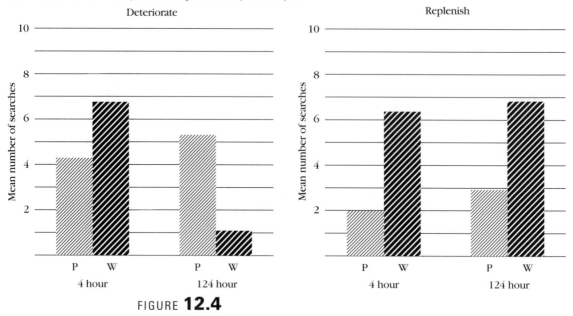

FIGURE **12.4**

Searching for worms versus peanuts in scrub jays that previously learned that worms deteriorate with time (*deteriorate* group, left panel) and scrub jays for which worms were always replenished (*replenish* group, right panel). The choice tests were conducted 4 hours or 124 hours after the caching of worms. (Based on Clayton & Dickinson, 1999.)

results indicate that scrub jays are able to remember *what, where,* and *when* they stored particular food items.

Some have argued that loss of preference for the cached worms following a 124-hour retention interval in the *deteriorate* group reflects decay of memory for the worms rather than knowledge of *when* the caching took place. To answer this criticism, de Kort, Dickinson, and Clayton (2005) conducted an experiment in which the quality of the worms improved as a function of time. This is analogous to fruit ripening and getting better with longer retention intervals. The jays in this experiment received training trials involving caching worms and peanuts, followed by retrieval opportunities after four or 28 hours later. The quality of the peanuts remained the same regardless of the retention interval, but the experimenters put better worms in the cache sites at the 28-hour retention interval than at the four-hour retention interval. Under these circumstances, the jays preferred peanuts at the short retention interval and worms at the longer interval. (For other studies of the structure and flexibility of memory for caching episodes, see Salwiczek, Dickinson, & Clayton, 2008.)

Studies with food storing birds have provided a great deal of information about episodic-like features of memory in a nonhuman species. It is unlikely that all of these results reflect specializations of the food caching and recovery system. However, the extent to which other species can be demonstrated to remember the what, when, and where of a past event in an integrated and flexible fashion remains to be seen. We can also look forward to continued spirited debate about the extent to which episodic-like features of memory in nonhuman species are the same as human episodic memory.

TIMING

Cache recovery is a highly specialized type of behavior, exhibited by a limited number of species. The next topic we turn to, timing, is universally relevant. Everything occurs across time. Some events occur closely together; others are separated by longer intervals. In either case, the effects of stimuli are determined by their durations and distribution in time.

We previously encountered numerous aspects of conditioning and learning that reflect the timing of events. Habituation, sensitization, and spontaneous recovery from habituation (Chapter 2) are all time-dependent effects. Pavlovian conditioning critically depends on the temporal relation between conditioned and unconditioned stimuli (Chapter 3), instrumental conditioning depends on the temporal relation between response and reinforcer (Chapter 5), and some schedules of reinforcement involve important temporal factors (Chapter 6). There are also important time-dependent effects in extinction (Chapter 9), avoidance and punishment (Chapter 10) and memory (Chapter 11).

In the past 35 years, behavioral and cognitive mechanisms responsible for the temporal control of behavior have been the subject of vigorous empirical research and theoretical debate (Church, 2006; Crystal, 2006; Josefowiez & Staddon, 2008; Lejeune & Wearden, 2006; Meck, 2003). Investigators are also working on identifying the neural circuits involved in timing and are studying how temporal control of behavior is influenced by neurotransmitter systems and pharmacological agents (see Buhusi & Meck, 2005; Meck, 2003; Odum, Lieving, & Schaal, 2002).

Time intervals that are significant for biological systems vary a great deal in scale. The 24-hour day-night cycle is one of the most important time cycles for biological systems. Other important time intervals operate on the order of fractions of a second (e.g., different components of the heartbeat). Intervals in the range of seconds (and occasionally minutes) are important in conditioning procedures. Timing on this order, referred to as *interval timing*, has been the focus of learning investigators. (For contrast, see Pizzo & Crystal, 2007, for a study of rats learning to time a two-day interval.)

A critical methodological requirement in studies of timing is to make sure that the passage of time is not correlated with an external stimulus, such as the noise of a clock ticking or the gradual increase in light that occurs as the sun comes up in the morning. Experimental situations have to be set up carefully to eliminate time-related external stimuli that might inadvertently tip off the organism and permit accurate responding without the use of an internal timing process. This methodological requirement is similar to what we encountered in tests for memory. Like tests for memory, tests for timing have to be designed to be sure that the behavior is mediated by the internal cognitive process of interest rather than external cues or signals.

Techniques for Studying the Temporal Control of Behavior

Various powerful techniques have been developed to investigate timing in human and nonhuman animals. Some tasks involve **duration estimation.** A duration estimation task is basically a discrimination procedure in which the discriminative stimulus is the duration of an event. One study (Fetterman, 1995), for example, employed a modified matching-to-sample procedure. Pigeons were trained in an experimental chamber that had three pecking keys arranged in a row. The sample stimulus at the start of the trial was an amber light presented on the center key for either two seconds or 10 seconds. The sample was followed by illumination of one side key with a red light and the other side key with a green light. If the sample was short (the two-second stimulus), pecks on the red key were reinforced. If the sample was long (the 10-second stimulus), pecks on the green key were reinforced. Pigeons, rats, and humans can learn to perform accurately in such tasks without too much difficulty. Once the temporal discrimination is well established, one can examine the limits of the discrimination by testing the subjects with sample durations that are more similar than the training durations (e.g., Church, Getty, & Lerner, 1976; Ferrara, Lejeune, & Wearden, 1997; Wasserman, DeLong, & Larew, 1984).

Another major technique for the study of timing, the **peak procedure,** involves duration production instead of duration estimation. Each trial begins with the presentation of a discriminative stimulus, a noise or a light. After a specified time interval, a food pellet is set up, or made ready for delivery. Once the food pellet has been set up, the subject can obtain it by performing a designated instrumental response. Thus, the peak procedure is a discrete-trial variation of a fixed-interval schedule. (Fixed-interval schedules were introduced in Chapter 6.)

A study by Roberts (1981) nicely illustrates use of the peak procedure to investigate timing in laboratory rats. The subjects were tested in a standard lever-press chamber housed in a sound-attenuating enclosure to minimize extraneous stimuli. Some trials began with a light; other trials began with a noise. In the presence of the light, food was set up after 20 seconds; in the presence of the noise, food was set up after 40 seconds. Most of the trials ended when the rats responded and obtained the food pellet. However, some of the trials were designated as test trials and continued for 80 seconds or more and ended without food reward. These extra-long trials were included to see how the subjects would respond after the usual time of reinforcement had passed.

Figure 12.5 summarizes the results of the experiment in terms of rates of responding at various points during the test trials. The figure shows that during the 20-second signal, the highest rate of responding occurred around 20 seconds into the trial. By contrast, during the 40-second signal, the highest rate of responding occurred around 40 seconds into the trial. The results were remarkably orderly. The peak response rates occurred near the times that food became available during training, with lower response rates evident before and after that point. These features make the peak procedure especially useful in animal studies of timing. However, it should be noted that results like those shown in Figure 12.5 emerge only after extensive training that includes numerous nonreinforced test trials that extend beyond the time when the reinforcer is usually set up.

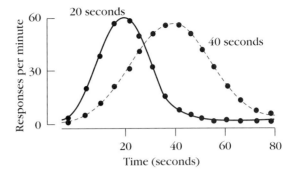

FIGURE **12.5**

Rate of responding at various times during nonreinforced test trials. During training, food became available for delivery after 20 seconds in the presence of one stimulus (solid line) and after 40 seconds in the presence of another stimulus (dashed line). (From "Isolation of an Internal Clock" by S. Roberts, 1981, *Journal of Experimental Psychology: Animal Behavior Processes, 7,* pp. 242–268. Copyright © 1981 by the American Psychological Association. Reprinted by permission.)

A variation of the peak procedure that involves less training has become popular in recent years. In this procedure, free food is delivered into a food cup at a fixed time (e.g., 40 seconds) after the start of each trial. The subject learns this predictable interval and checks the food cup with increasing frequency as the time for the next food delivery gets closer. Temporal control of behavior is evident in the frequency of head pokes into the food cup rather than lever presses reinforced with food (e.g., Kirkpatrick & Church, 2003). Peak responding again occurs near the time of food delivery.

Properties of Temporally Controlled Behavior

Numerous interesting questions have been examined in efforts to better understand the temporal control of behavior. One important question is whether organisms respond to time intervals in terms of their absolute or relative durations. Consider, for example distinguishing between three seconds and nine seconds. If we treated the intervals in terms of their absolute values, we would consider nine seconds to be six seconds longer than three seconds. In contrast, if we treated the intervals in terms of their relative values, we would consider nine seconds to be three times as long as three seconds. Numerous studies have shown that organisms respond to the relative values of time intervals. Thus, a discrimination between three and nine seconds is equivalent to a discrimination between nine and 27 seconds. If the relative value of the time intervals is preserved, the tasks are equivalent. The units of a time scale are invariant as long as each unit is the same proportion of the interval being measured. This property is called **scalar invariance.** (For a review of scalar invariance, see Lejeune & Wearden, 2006.)

Let us consider again the results presented in Figure 12.5. As I noted earlier, during one stimulus, responding was reinforced 20 seconds into the trial, whereas during the other stimulus, responding was reinforced at 40 seconds. Scalar invariance emphasizes the proportional relation between the 20 and 40 second stimuli. Because the longer stimulus was twice the value of the

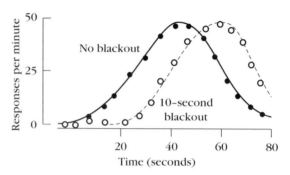

FIGURE **12.6**

Rate of responding as a function of time during a signal in the presence of which food was set up after 40 seconds. On some trials, the signal was interrupted for a 10-second blackout period (dashed line). On other trials, no blackout occurred (solid line). (From "Isolation of an Internal Clock" by S. Roberts, 1981, *Journal of Experimental Psychology: Animal Behavior Processes, 7*, pp. 242–268. Copyright © 1981 by the American Psychological Association. Reprinted by permission.)

shorter one, the peak responding occurred at approximately twice the duration for the longer stimulus. In examining Figure 12.5, you will also notice that the 40-second curve was about twice as wide as the 20-second curve. That is another manifestation of scalar invariance. The variability in response rates is proportional to the value of the reinforced interval.

Another question investigators have been interested in is what happens when a temporal interval is interrupted. Does the timing process continue during the interruption or is it also interrupted? Roberts (1981) conducted an experiment to answer this question (see also Roberts & Church, 1978). The experimental chamber used was ordinarily dark. Each trial started with the presentation of a light, and food was set up 40 seconds after the start of the trial. On special test trials without food reinforcement, the light was turned off for 10 seconds, starting 10 seconds after the start of the trial. Roberts was interested in how the interruption influenced when the rats showed their peak responding.

Figure 12.6 shows the resulting distributions of response rates at various times during trials with and without the 10-second break. Introducing the 10-second break shifted the peak response rate to the right by a bit more than 10 seconds (13.3 seconds, to be exact). These results suggest that the timing process was interrupted when the break was introduced. Some information about elapsed time was lost during the break, but when the light was turned back on, the timing process continued from where it had left off (see also de Vaca, Brown, & Hemmes, 1994). If the break had reset the timing process to zero, the peak responding would have been shifted to the right by 20 seconds on trials with the break.

Models of Timing

What might be the details of a mechanism that permits organisms to respond on the basis of temporal information? This has been one of the thorniest theoretical questions in behavior theory. The question has been vigorously examined and debated for more than 30 years, with little hint of resolution (e.g., Cheng & Crystal, 2008; Jozefowiez & Staddon, 2008). Time is not a physical reality. It is a human invention that helps us characterize certain aspects of our environment. One cannot see a time interval; one can only see the events that start and end the interval. Given that time itself is a conceptual abstraction, models of timing also tend to be fairly abstract.

Scalar Expectancy Theory (SET)

R. M. Church

The first and most influential account of timing is an information processing model proposed by Gibbon and Church (1984) known as *scalar expectancy theory (SET)* (see Church, 2003, for a recent summary). Different components of the model are diagrammed in Figure 12.7, but the model is formally stated in mathematical rather than conceptual terms and incorporates the property of scalar invariance. As Figure 12.7 illustrates, the model considers temporally controlled behavior to be the result of three independent processes: a clock process, a memory process, and a decision process.

The clock process provides information about the duration of elapsed time. A key component of the clock process is a pacemaker that generates pulses at a certain rate (something like the beeps of a metronome). The pacemaker pulses are fed to a switch, which is opened at the start of the interval to be timed. Opening the switch allows the pacemaker pulses to go to an accumulator that counts the number of pulses that comes through. When the interval to be timed ends, the switch closes, thereby blocking any further accumulations of pacemaker pulses. Thus, the accumulator adds up the number of pulses that

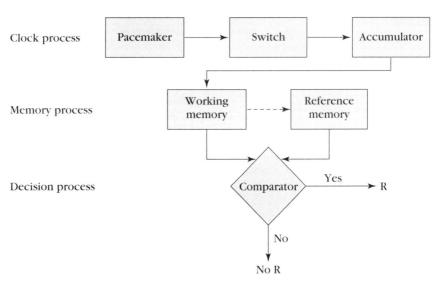

FIGURE **12.7**

Diagram of scalar expectancy theory of timing. (From "Sources of Variance in an Information Processing Theory of Timing" by J. Gibbon and R. M. Church, in H. L. Roitblat, T. G. Bever, & H. S. Terrace (Eds.), 1984, *Animal Cognition.* Copyright © 1984 Lawrence Erlbaum Associates. Reprinted by permission.)

occurred during the timed interval. The greater the number of accumulated pulses, the longer the interval. The pacemaker/accumulator operates like an hourglass. When the hourglass is turned over, particles of sand pass to the bottom bowl, and the number of sand particles that accumulate there is a measure of elapsed time.

The number of accumulated pulses is then relayed to the memory process. The memory process thereby obtains information about the duration of the current stimulus. This information is stored in working memory. The memory process is also assumed to have information about the duration of similar stimuli in reference memory from past training. The contents of working and reference memory are then compared in the decision process, and this comparison provides the basis for the individual's response. For example, in the peak procedure, if the time information in working memory matches the information in reference memory concerning availability of reinforcement, the decision is to respond. If information in working and reference memory does not match closely enough, the decision is to not respond. This mechanism produces a peak response rate close to the time when reinforcement is set up.

Scalar expectancy theory has been highly successful in stimulating research and guiding analyses of fine-grained details of timing behavior (see Church, Meck, & Gibbon, 1994; Gibbon & Church, 1984). The model has also guided investigations of the neural mechanisms of timing (Buhusi & Meck, 2005) and has been the stepping stone for pocket theory which spells out in greater detail how the cognitive mechanisms of timing generate specific patterns of responding (Kirkpatrick, 2002; Kirkpatrik & Church, 2003). However, the theory has not been without its critics, and efforts continue to formulate alternatives. Some of these alternatives emphasize behavioral mechanisms that avoid the elaborate cognitive processes of SET (clock, memory, and decision processes). Others strive to model timing behavior without using pacemaker/accumulator mechanisms. Investigators are examining whether the temporal control of behavior requires a pacemaker, or can be generated using biological decay or growth processes or oscillators that do not require accumulating pulses.

Behavioral Theory of Timing

Courtesy of P. R. Killeen

P. R. Killeen

A prominent alternative to the Gibbon-Church information processing model was offered by Killeen and Fetterman (1988, 1993; Killeen, Fetterman, & Bizo, 1997; see also Machado, 1997; Machado & Pata, 2005) who characterized the timing process in more behavioral terms. This behavioral theory of timing (BET) follows the Gibbon-Church model in postulating the existence of a pacemaker. However, the role of the pacemaker in BET is quite different. BET also characterizes the memory and decision processes differently (see Machado, 1997).

The behavioral theory of timing is based on the observation that systematic time-related behaviors emerge in situations where the primary basis for the delivery of a reinforcer is the passage of time. These activities are akin to the pacing or finger tapping that people engage in during periods of forced waiting. In experimental situations these activities have been called **adjunctive behaviors** because they are not specifically required to pass the time but seem to emerge automatically when organisms are forced to wait for something important.

Clear examples of adjunctive behavior are evident in situations in which food is presented periodically at predictable intervals, say every 15 seconds. As I described in Chapter 5 (see discussion of *Skinner's superstition experiment*, pp. 170–174), the feeding system (and its accompanying foraging responses) are activated in food-deprived animals that are given small portions of food at fixed intervals. Behavior under these circumstances reflects pre-organized species-typical foraging and feeding activities (Silva & Timberlake, 1998; Timberlake, 2000). Different behaviors occur depending on when food was last delivered and when food is going to occur again. Just after the delivery of food, the organism is assumed to display *post-food focal search* responses that involve activities near the food cup. In the middle of the interval between food deliveries (when the subjects are least likely to get food), *general search* responses are evident that take the subject away from the food cup. As time for the next food delivery approaches, subjects exhibit *pre-food focal search* responses that bring the subject back to the food cup.

The behavioral theory of timing focuses on the successive behavioral states that are activated by periodic presentations of food. Because different responses emerge at different intervals in a forced waiting period, these contrasting responses can be used to tell time. The successive adjunctive responses are assumed to reflect a pacemaker, or clock process. According to the behavioral theory of timing, participants in a timing experiment learn to use their adjunctive responses as discriminative stimuli for the experimentally required timing responses. Thus, instead of reading an internal clock, participants are assumed to "read" their adjunctive behavior to tell time.

Another behavioral model of timing (Dragoi et al., 2003) is also based on the fact that different responses occur at various time points depending on the likelihood of obtaining food, but does not employ a pacemaker/accumulator mechanism. According to this theory, temporally organized behavior emerges from the modulation of competing responses by the memory of recent reinforcement and overall arousal level related to reinforcement rate.

Oscillators Instead of Pacemakers

A second major alternative approach to SET is based on the idea that temporally organized behavior is mediated by oscillators rather than pacemakers (Crystal, 2006; Cheng & Crystal, 2008). An oscillator is like a pendulum rather than an hourglass. An oscillator cycles through a predictable sequence of events, over and over again. It goes through repeated cycles that have a fixed period. Different time points are associated with different points in the cycle. Oscillators can operate over a long time scale, such as the rotations of the earth around its axis, which have a periodicity of 24 hours, or the trajectory of the earth around the sun, which has a periodicity of a year. Oscillators can also operate over a short time scale, such as the bouncing of a weight on a spring, which can have a periodicity on the order of a second or less.

Most species show daily variations in activity and body temperature. These are referred to as circadian rhythms. Humans are diurnal and are more active during the day than at night. In contrast, rats are nocturnal and are more active at night than during the day. Such circadian rhythms have been explained using the concept of an oscillator that has the periodicity of about a day. Evidence for such an oscillator is provided by results showing

J. D. Crystal

that circadian rhythms of activity and body temperature persist even if individuals are put in a constant-light environment. Using this strategy, Crystal and Baramidze (2007) recently demonstrated that the periodicity of food-cup entries generated by delivering food at fixed intervals (e.g., every 48 seconds) persists after the food is no longer provided. Such results are not predicted by SET and suggest that short interval timing is based at least in part on the entrainment of a self-sustaining endogenous oscillator. This raises the possibility that theories of timing employing oscillators can be formulated that will provide an integrated account of timing over a broad range of time intervals (Cheng & Crystal, 2008).

SERIAL LIST LEARNING

Time is one ubiquitous characteristic of events in the environment. Another is serial order. Stimuli rarely occur randomly or independently of each other. Rather, many aspects of the environment involve orderly sequences of events. One thing leads to the next in a predictable fashion. Stimuli are arranged in orderly sequences as you walk from one end of a street to the other, as you work to open a package, or as you eat dinner, from the appetizer to the dessert. Stimulus order is also very important in language. "The hunters ate the bear" is very different from "The bear ate the hunters." It is also important in dialing phone numbers, entering your pin number at an ATM machine, or using a keyboard for text messaging. Investigators of comparative cognition have been interested in whether animals can learn the order of a series of stimuli, how animals form representations of serial order, and how they use those representations in dealing with new situations.

Possible Bases of Serial List Behavior

There are several possible ways in which to respond to a series of stimuli. By way of illustration, consider playing through a six-hole miniature golf course, a schematic of which is shown to the left in Figure 12.8. Each hole involves a unique set of stimuli and may be represented by letters of the alphabet: A, B, C, D, E, and F. Each hole also requires a unique response, a unique way in

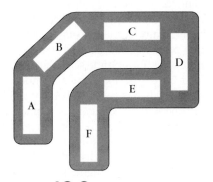 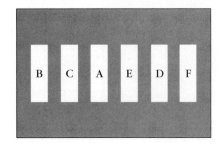

FIGURE **12.8**

Two possible layouts of a six-hole miniature golf course. A sequential arrangement is shown on the left, and a simultaneous arrangement is shown on the right.

which the ball must be hit to get it into the hole. Let's label the responses R1, R2, ..., R6. In playing the course, you have to go in order from the first to the last hole, A→F. In addition, you have to make the correct response on each hole: R1 on hole A, R2 on B, and so on.

How might you learn to play the course successfully? The simplest way would be to learn which response goes with which stimulus. In the presence of A, you would automatically make R1, which would get you to stimulus B; in the presence of B, you would automatically make R2, which would get you to C, and so on. This would be learning a set of S-R associations: A-R1, B-R2, ..., F-R6. Such a mechanism is called a **response chain.** In a response chain, each response produces the stimulus for the next response in the sequence, and correct responses occur because the organism has learned a series of S-R associations.

Although a response chain can result in responding appropriately to a series of stimuli, it does not require actually learning the stimulus sequence or forming a mental representation of the order in which the stimuli or responses occur. Response chains do not require cognitive mechanisms any more complex than S-R associations. A response-chain strategy works perfectly well on the usual miniature golf course, because the successive holes are laid out so that one is forced to go through them in the correct sequence, A→F.

Now, let us consider a course with a different layout, as shown on the right of Figure 12.8. The rules are the same; you again have to play in order from A to F. However, with this course layout you are not forced to go in order from A to F. After having played Hole A, for example, your movement would not be restricted to Hole B. You could go to any other hole next. To earn points, however, you would still have to play B after having finished with A, and then go to C, then D, etc. Learning a series of S-R associations (A-R1, B-R2, and so on) would not be enough to succeed on such a course. Even if someone got you started at A, after playing Hole A, you would not know where to go next because you would be confronted with the full array of possibilities, not just Hole B.

What would you have to learn to respond in the correct sequence with a simultaneous stimulus array? This time, you would be forced to learn something about the order of the stimuli. You could get by with just knowing the order of successive pairs of stimuli. You could learn that A is followed by B, B is followed by C, and so forth. These would be a set of independent S-S associations (A-B, B-C, C-D, and so on). This type of mechanism is called **paired-associate learning.** Once you know the correct independent paired associates, having played Hole A, you would know to go to B; having played B, you would know to go to C; and so on until you had completed the course.

Obviously, learning more than just the order of successive pairs of stimuli would also enable you to perform the task accurately. At the extreme, you might form a mental representation of the entire sequence: A-B-C-D-E-F. This alternative is called **serial-representation learning.** A serial representation can be formed in different ways. One possibility is to string together a series of paired associates, such that A activates the representation of B, which in turn activates the representation of C, and so forth (Treichler, Raghanti, & Van Tilburg, 2003, 2007). Alternatively, you could learn the particular ordinal position of each stimulus. This would involve learning that Stimulus A is in position 1, B is in position 2, and so forth.

How might we decide among possible mechanisms of serial list behavior? An especially powerful technique involves presenting carefully constructed test trials after training. Returning to our simultaneous layout of the miniature golf course (right side of Figure 12.8), consider being given a choice between holes C and E after having learned to respond to the entire sequence, A→F, in the correct order. In a choice between C and E, which hole would you play first? If you had learned a representation of the entire stimulus sequence, you could respond without difficulty because you would know that C occurs before E in the sequence. Other possible mechanisms would create errors. For example, if you had learned a response chain in which one response leads to the next stimulus, you would be in trouble because the response preceding C is not available in a choice of only C and E. You would also be in trouble if you had learned just the order of successive pairs of stimuli because C and E do not form a successive pair.

Tests with Subsets after Training with a Simultaneous Stimulus Array

Courtesy of S. B. Fountain

S. B. Fountain

Several different techniques have been developed to study the learning of serial representations in animals (for a recent review, see Fountain, 2006). Straub and Terrace (1981) introduced the simultaneous chain procedure which consists of presenting a set of stimuli all at the same time, but requiring subjects to respond to the stimuli in a prescribed order. After subjects have learned the task, they are tested with subsets of stimuli, to determine what controls their performance. Although this technique was originally developed for use with pigeons, it has been adopted for use with other species as well, including monkeys (e.g., D'Amato and Colombo, 1988; Terrace, 2006), the ring-tailed lemur, which diverged from other primates 63 million years ago (Merritt et al., 2007), and college students (Colombo & Frost, 2001). The learning and representation of serial order turns out to be remarkably similar across this broad range of species.

In an effort to specifically compare the performance of college students on a simultaneous chain procedure with that of monkeys, Colombo and Frost (2001) designed their procedures based on the previous studies with cebus monkeys by D'Amato and Colombo (1988). The research participants had to learn a five-stimulus sequence. The stimuli were icons presented on a touch screen. The icons were either representational or abstract, but that did not influence the results (see Figure 12.9). All five icons were presented at the same time at the start of a trial but the participants had to press them in a set order (A→B→C→D→E→F). The position of each icon on the screen changed randomly from trial to trial. Therefore, the subjects could not perform the task by learning a sequence of spatial positions. The task was like having the numbers on your phone replaced by pictures, and having the position of each picture change each time you went to dial a new phone number. It turns out that college students and monkeys can learn this task with sufficient training.

Courtesy of M. Colombo

M. Colombo

The next question is how do college students and monkeys represent the stimulus order that they learned? To answer this question, investigators typically examine how subjects respond to subsets of stimuli. Following training with the five-element array, Colombo and Frost (2001) tested subjects with subsets consisting of just two or three elements. Consider, for example, a sub-

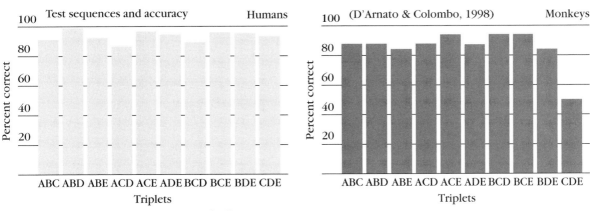

Training sequences

$A \rightarrow B \rightarrow C \rightarrow D \rightarrow E$

FIGURE **12.9**

Examples of stimuli used in training college students to respond on a five-element simultaneous chain, and test data for subsets of three stimuli for college students and cebus monkeys. Chance responding would have resulted in about 10% correct responses. (From "Representation of serial order in humans: A comparison to the findings with monkeys (*Cebus apella*)," by M. Colombo and N. Frost, 2001, *Psychonomic Bulletin & Review, 8,* 262–269.)

set consisting of elements B, D, and E. Keep in mind that these could appear in any position on the screen. If the subjects formed a representation of the order of the original five-element series, they would respond to B first, D next, and E last. That would count as a correct response to the subset.

Figure 12.9 shows the results of tests with all possible three-element subsets of the five-element serial order task. Both college students and monkeys responded with a high degree of accuracy on nearly all of the subsets, and responding was always well above chance. This indicates that the subjects were not responding on the basis of a chain of S-R associations. S-R associations would have left the subjects in the dark with any subset that did not include Stimulus A, or had adjacent elements missing.

Further evidence for the learning of a representation of serial order was provided by examining the latency of the first response to three-element subsets (see Figure 12.10). If the three-element subset included Stimulus A, the subjects responded very quickly. Their latency to make the first response was longer if the triplet started with B (BCD, BDE, or BCE), and the longest latencies occurred if the triplet started with C (CDE). Why take longer to get started with triples starting with B or C? Presumably when the subjects were tested with a triplet like BDE, they started through the full sequence (ABCDE) mentally and made their first response when they came to B. Their first response was delayed

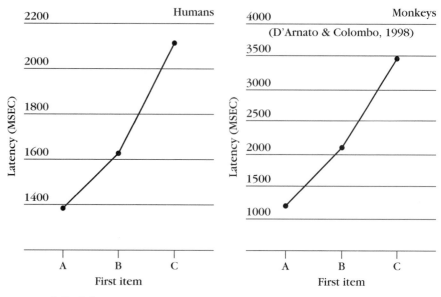

FIGURE **12.10**

Latency to respond to the first item of a three-item test, when the first item was A, B, or C, in college students and cebus monkeys. (From "Representation of serial order in humans: A comparison to the findings with monkeys (*Cebus apella*)," by M. Colombo and N. Frost, 2001, *Psychonomic Bulletin & Review, 8*, 262–269.)

further when they were tested with CDE because it took them longer to get to C mentally. Thus, these latency data are predicted by the assumption that the subjects formed a mental representation of the five-element sequence that they rehearsed when they were tested with the three-element subsets.

Another interesting line of evidence is provided by looking at the latency of the second response to three-element subsets. With some triplets, the second item could be adjacent to the first, as in ABD and BCD. In other cases, the second item could follow one missing item, as in ACD, and BDE. Finally, the second item could follow two missing items, as in ADE. If the subject was going through the full five-element sequence mentally, the latency of its second response would be greatest with the greatest number of missing items. This is exactly what was found with both college students and cebus monkeys (see Figure 12.11), providing further evidence that subjects learned a representation of the five-element series.

The simultaneous chain procedure has turned out to be a powerful technique for the study of complex cognition in nonverbal organisms. Terrace, Son, and Brannon (2003), for example, taught monkeys to respond to four different seven-element simultaneous chains. These might be represented as A1→A2→A3...→A7, B1→B2→B3...→B7, C1→C2→C3...→C7, and D1→D2→D3...→D7. After the monkeys were responding with high levels of accuracy on each seven-element series, tests with various pairs of stimuli were introduced. As one would expect, performance was highly accurate

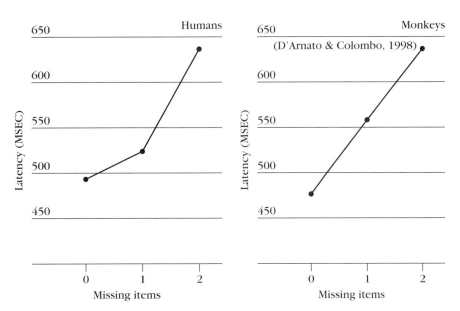

FIGURE **12.11**

Latency to respond to the second item of a three-item test in college students and cebus monkeys as a function of the number of items missing between the first and second item. (From "Representation of serial order in humans: A comparison to the findings with monkeys (*Cebus apella*)," by M. Colombo and N. Frost, 2001, *Psychonomic Bulletin & Review, 8*, 262-269.)

when the two stimuli of a pair come from the same list (e.g., A3A5, or C2C6). Remarkably, the monkeys also responded with about 90% accuracy when the two stimuli of a test pair came from different lists. Consider for example test pairs made up of A5C6. The correct response here would be to select A5 first and C6 next. To respond so well on cross-list pairs, the monkeys had to have learned the position of each element in each list and then integrated that knowledge across lists.

Study of serial list learning is not only telling us about learning and memory for lists of items. It is also opening the window to studying the cognitive foundations of arithmetic (Terrace, 2006). Arithmetic knowledge is built on an abstract serial order that puts one before two, which is before three, and so on. When the monkeys were responding to a specific icon as the 5th in a series, they were essentially telling us that they knew the order of the icons. Those icons could just as well have been Arabic numerals, and the monkeys would have been counting from one to five. Arithmetic involves more than establishing a serial order of arbitrary symbols. Those symbols also refer to different quantities. Investigators are using the simultaneous chain procedure to examine the learning of the serial order of stimuli based on quantitative information (e.g., Brannon, Cantlon, & Terrace, 2006; Judge, Evans, & Vyas, 2005).

H. S. Terrace

CATEGORIZATION AND CONCEPT LEARNING

Organisms experience a great variety of stimuli during their lifetime. In fact, in the natural environment, no stimulus ever occurs the same way twice. Fortunately, we do not have to respond to stimuli as independent and isolated events. Serial pattern learning represents one type of cognitive organization. An even more basic form of cognitive organization involves perceptual concept learning. Stimuli that vary in their physical properties can be grouped together through categorization or concept learning. Consider, for example, your favorite chair in the living room. Each time you see the chair, the sensory input you get varies depending on the amount of lighting in the room, whether you are seeing the chair from the front or the back, and how far away it is. Additional variations are provided by whether you are looking at the chair or sitting in it and feeling its firmness and shape. Instead of treating each unique view of the chair as a separate entity, we form a perceptual category that includes all of the different views and treat them as equivalent in identifying a particular chair.

The above example illustrates a basic-level perceptual category. Basic-level perceptual categorization is essential for us to navigate efficiency in our world. It permits us to recognize our car as the same vehicle regardless of our angle of view or how dirty the car might be. It also allows us to recognize an individual person as being the same individual whether we see him or her from the front or the side. However, perceptual categorization is just one way that we categorize or sort the numerous stimuli that we encounter. A specific chair can be categorized into a broader category of chairs of all sizes, shapes, and designs. Chairs can also be categorized into a higher level category of all things that are furniture or all things that are human made. These higher level categories are more abstract and involve less similarity among the members of the category. People also form more abstract categories such as *same* versus *different*. One of the major issues in comparative cognition has been whether nonhuman species are also capable of categorization and concept learning, and whether they are capable of learning abstract categories that are not based on the similarity of different members of the category.

Perceptual Concept Learning

Much of the comparative research on categorization has involved demonstrations of perceptual concept learning and explorations of the mechanisms of such learning (for a recent review, see Lazareva & Wasserman, 2008). What constitutes evidence that a nonverbal organism has learned a perceptual concept? Perceptual categorization represents a balance between stimulus discrimination and stimulus generalization. You recognize your cat as the same animal even though strictly speaking, the visual image the cat projects on your retina is different every time you see it. However, you distinguish your cat from your neighbor's cat and from your parakeet. As this example illustrates, perceptual concepts have two important and complementary characteristics, *generalization within a category* or sets of stimuli and *discrimination between categories* or sets of stimuli.

Early comparative studies of perceptual concept learning employed go/no go discrimination procedures. For example, Herrnstein, Loveland, and Cable (1976) presented color slides of various scenes as stimuli in a discrimination procedure with pigeons. If the scene included a tree or some part of a tree, the pigeons were reinforced with food for pecking the response key. If the picture did not include a tree or any part of one, pecking was not reinforced. Each experimental session consisted of 80 slide presentations, about 40 of which included a tree. The stimuli for any given training session were selected from 500–700 pictures depicting various scenes from all four seasons of the year in New England. The pigeons learned the task without much difficulty and pecked at a much higher rate in the presence of pictures that included a tree or part of a tree than in the presence of pictures without trees.

Did this discrimination performance reflect the learning of a perceptual concept? An alternative interpretation is that the pigeons memorized what the reinforced and nonreinforced pictures looked like without paying particular attention to the presence or absence of trees. Although this may seem unlikely, pigeons are capable of memorizing more than 800 pictures (Cook et al., 2005; see also Vaughan & Greene, 1984). A common tactic for ruling out the role of memorization of the training stimuli is to test for transfer of performance to stimuli that did not appear during training. Herrnstein et al. (1976) did this by presenting a new set of photos at the end of the experiment. The pigeons performed nearly as accurately on the new pictures as on those used during prior training. Such evidence of *generalization to novel exemplars* is critical for demonstrations of perceptual concept learning.

The Herrnstein et al. (1976) experiment involved a go/no-go discrimination in which subjects learned to distinguish stimuli that belonged to a particular category from stimuli that did not belong to that category. When children are taught perceptual categories, the procedure usually involves teaching them to sort stimuli into several different categories at the same time. Instead of being told "this is a dog, and that is not a dog," they are told "this is a dog, and that is a cat." Thus, the cat and dog categories are taught at the same time. Similar tactics can be used with pigeons. In one study, for example, the experimental chamber had four pecking keys, each assigned to a different category (Lazareva, Freiburger, & Wasserman, 2006). Pictures from four different categories were presented one at a time (chairs, flowers, cars, and people). The pigeon was reinforced for pecking the response key associated with the category for the picture on that trial. Using such procedures, pigeons can learn up to 16 categories concurrently.

A great deal of research has been done on the learning of perceptual concepts since this area of research was initiated by Herrnstein and his associates more than 40 years ago. In the tradition set by Herrnstein, much of the research has been done with pigeons categorizing complex visual stimuli. However, various primates and other species have been also tested. A variety of different stimulus categories have been examined. For example, pigeons have been trained to categorize the presence versus absence of water in various forms (lakes, oceans, puddles, and so on), the presence or absence of a particular person (in various types of clothing, in various situations, and engaged in various activities), pictures of male versus female human faces, or pictures of individual pigeons taken from various perspectives (for recent examples, see Aust & Huber, 2001, 2003; Loidolt et al., 2003; Loidolt et al., 2006; Nakamura, Croft, & Westbrook, 2003). Pigeons can also categorize stimuli based on their speed and direction of movement (Herbranson, Fremouw, & Shimp, 2002).

In all of these cases, the participants learned to respond similarly to stimuli belonging to the category in question even though members of the category differed in numerous respects. Perceptual concept learning is a form of stimulus equivalence learning (see Chapter 8, pp. 286–288). Because responding to various examples of the category has the same (or equivalent) reinforcing consequence, physically different stimuli come to be treated in the same manner (or equivalently) by the subject. Stimulus equivalence training promotes generalization within a set of stimuli (Astley & Wasserman, 1998, 1999).

Mechanisms of Perceptual Concept Learning

Perceptual concept learning is a well established phenomenon. How animals manage to do this, however, remains a lively topic of debate (Lazareva & Wasserman, 2008). The issue is complex because of the complexity of the stimuli that are involved. The pictures that included a tree or a part of a tree in the Herrnstein et al. (1976) experiment differed in numerous respects. What aspect(s) of the tree photographs led the pigeons to classify those photographs differently from the non-tree photographs? Were there specific colors, shapes, or textures in the photographs that were critical or was it the overall brightness or sharpness of the pictures? It was hard to tell by examining the pictures.

Progress in categorization research was stymied by the stimulus problem for nearly a quarter century. However, this obstacle is finally becoming overcome by advances in computer image analysis and image production. Investigators are examining perceptual categorization using natural images as well as computer-generated artificial images. Features of the stimuli are systematically altered using computer graphics, to determine how a particular stimulus dimension contributes to the perceptual categorization that is observed.

Aust and Huber (2003), for example, trained pigeons to discriminate between photographs that included a person and ones that did not have anyone in the scene. The pictures were of a wide range of settings, and if they included people, the people could be of either sex or any race, age, size, and could appear anywhere in the picture. After the pigeons learned to categorize the stimuli as including a person (or not), they were tested with specially altered photos in which the body parts of the people were rearranged in various ways. The types of rearrangements tested are presented schematically in Figure 12.12.

The pigeons responded at a bit less to the rearranged people photos than to photos that showed a person in a normal configuration. However, their responses to these rearranged figures were considerably higher than their response to photos that did not include a person. These findings indicate that the pigeons used the normal relative position of body parts to judge whether an image was that of a person. When the normal relative position of body parts was disturbed, responding declined. However, the pigeons also used smaller visual features, which remained intact under the various body rearrangements. Attending to those smaller visual features allowed the birds to respond more to the rearranged photos than to photos that did not include a person (see also Austin & Huber, 2001).

According to feature theory, participants use visual features common to members of a category to accurately categorize a set of complex images.

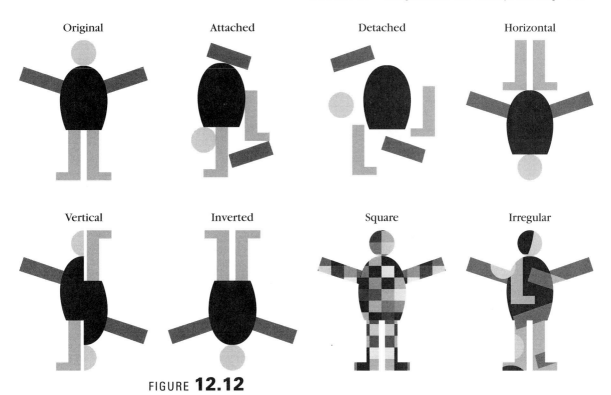

FIGURE **12.12**

Schematic representation of human figures used in a study of people-present/people-absent perceptual concept learning in pigeons (Aust & Huber, 2003). *Original* represents the normal images used in training. All of the other cartoons represent rearrangements of a normal image used in testing.

These visual features can be a small part of the image (a curve in a line or a patch of color) or more global aspects of the scene (overall brightness or contrast). Early investigators of perceptual concept learning rejected feature theory because they had difficulty identifying the critical features or combination of features in the photos of natural scenes that their subjects relied on. However, feature theories of categorization are making a comeback, encouraged by results from experiments that use carefully designed test stimuli that have preset statistical properties or stimulus features that have been altered using image morphing, blurring, or other manipulations (e.g., Jitsumori, 2006; Herbranson, Fremouw, & Shimp, 2002; Martin-Malivel et al., 2006).

According to the contemporary approach to feature theory, perceptual categorization reflects the flexible use of both local and global stimulus features common to members of a category. These cues can be used as independent inputs to a categorization decision or in combination with one another in an additive or configural fashion. Different strategies can be employed depending on different stages of training, different ways of defining the stimuli that are members of the category, or how often a particular feature appears in the stimulus set (Cook & Smith, 2006; Fremouw, Herbranson, & Shimp, 2002; Huber & Aust, 2006; Jitsumori, 2006; Shimp et al., 2006).

Learning Higher-Level Concepts

So far we have discussed basic-level perceptual categories that correspond to the naming of objects such as chairs and flowers. Chairs and flowers also may be categorized in terms of a higher-level concept: artificial versus natural. Studies with pigeons and other animals have also demonstrated higher-level categorization (e.g., Roberts & Mazmanian, 1988). In fact, animals can learn to categorize stimuli at both a basic and super-ordinate level at the same time.

In a recent study (Lazareva, Freiburger, & Wasserman, 2004), for example, pigeons were trained with pictures of cars, flowers, persons, and chairs. On some trials, four reporting keys were available (one at each corner of the display screen), and each reporting key was assigned to one of the basic level categories. Responding on the key assigned to cars was reinforced if the picture on the trial was of a car, responding on the chair key was reinforced if the picture on that trial was of a chair, and so on.

The basic-level categorization trials were intermixed with super-ordinate categorization trials. During super-ordinate training trials, two new reporting keys were available (to the left or right of the display screen). Responding on one reporting key was reinforced if the picture on that trial was an artificial object (cars or chairs), and responding on the other key was reinforced if the picture on that trial was of a natural object (a person or a flower).

The pigeons readily learned both the basic and super-ordinate categories, though learning the super-ordinate category *artificial* took a bit longer than learning the category *natural*. The pigeons were also able to correctly categorize pictures of cars, flowers, persons, or chairs that they had never seen before at both the basic and super-ordinate levels. However, their performance on the novel stimulus trials was a bit lower than with the training stimuli. The conclusion that emerges is that concept learning is a dynamic process shaped by contingencies of reinforcement that can reflect both basic and higher level categorization that generates focused behavioral output in the face of the great variations that exist in the physical stimulus inputs we receive from the environment.

Learning Abstract Concepts

Superordinate categories like *natural* versus *artificial* are fairly abstract but refer to objects in the real world. We also have concepts that are entirely cognitive. They exist only in our minds and have no referents in the physical world. Consider, for example, the concept of *same* versus *different*. These are not attributes of objects in the real world. A chair cannot be described as same or different. These terms refer to a judgment we make in comparing two objects or images. Are nonhuman species capable of learning such abstract concepts?

A great deal of research has been done on how pigeons, various primate species, and other animals learn the concepts same and different. Several different

Same Trial   Different Trial

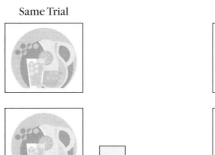

FIGURE **12.13**

Diagram of procedure for training a same/different discrimination. On *same* trials, two of the pictures in the stimulus panels are the same and subjects are reinforced for touching or pecking the lower panel. On *different* trials, the pictures are different and subjects are reinforced for touching or pecking the response button to the right of the pictures. (Photographs rather than drawings were used in the study by Wright and Katz, 2007.)

approaches have been taken to this problem (see Cook & Wasserman, 2006). In one approach (e.g., Wright & Katz, 2007), pigeons, and rhesus and cebus monkeys were presented with two pictures on each trial (see Figure 12.13). If the two pictures were the same, the subjects had to touch or peck the lower picture to obtain food reinforcement. If the two pictures were different, they had to touch or peck a reporting key to the side of the pictures to get reinforced. Training started with a set of eight pictures, but the stimulus set was doubled each time the subjects were responding correctly about 80% of the time. Learning of the same/different concept was evaluated by testing subjects with novel stimuli.

Performance on the transfer trials improved with increases in the number of pictures used in training. The number of trials required to reach criterion performance also decreased with larger sets of training stimuli. These results strongly suggest that the subjects learned the abstract concept same/different as training progressed. (For the learning of more complex abstract concepts in pigeons, see Herbranson & Shimp, 2003; Lazareva & Wasserman, 2008.)

TOOL USE IN NONHUMAN ANIMALS

In this section and the next, we turn to two of the most controversial topics in comparative cognition, tool use and language learning in nonhuman animals. Ever since Köhler (1927) observed a chimpanzee putting one box on top of another to reach a piece of food, scientists interested in comparative cognition have been fascinated with tool use in animals. Numerous species have been observed to use tools in various ways and some have been observed to make tools (e.g., Beck, 1980). Much of the research on nonhuman tool use has involved chimpanzees and other primates (e.g., Visalberghi & Fragaszy, 2006). Given all of what we have learned about the cognitive abilities of these species, the fact that they use tools does not greatly challenge our view of them. More provocative are recent reports of extensive tool use and tool fabrication by crows that live on the island of New Caledonia in the Western Pacific (*Corvus moneduloides*).

New Caledonian crows modify twigs, leaves, cardboard, and feathers to use as tools to obtain food from crevices and other places they cannot reach with their beak. To study tool use in this species more systematically, a colony of these birds was established at Oxford University by Alex Kacelnik and his colleagues. The availability of the birds for laboratory investigation has facilitated the documentation of a number of remarkable features of tool use by these birds (for reviews, see Bluff et al., 2007; Kacelnik et al., 2006). In one experiment, for example, two wild-caught crows were given access to food placed in a clear horizontal plastic tube that had one end open. The food was positioned at different distances from the opening of the tube, and twigs of different lengths were available for the birds to use to poke out the food (Chappell & Kacelnik, 2002). The crows readily used the twigs that were provided (see Figure 12.14). More importantly, they selected twigs of the appropriate length on each trial at a rate that far exceeded chance (see also, Hunt, Rutledge, & Gray, 2006).

In another study (Weir & Kacelnik, 2006), Betty, one of the wild-caught crows, was tested with food placed in a miniature bucket that was lowered into a clear plastic tube. To get the food, Betty had to fashion a hook out of a piece of metal and use that to grab the handle of the bucket so that the bucket could be

Behavioural Ecology Research Group, Oxford University.

FIGURE **12.14**

Betty, a New Caledonian crow, selecting a stick of the appropriate length to get food out of a long tube in a study by Chappell & Kacelnik, 2002.

Behavioural Ecology Research Group, Oxford University.

FIGURE **12.15**

Betty, a New Caledonian crow, pulling up a bucket with food after fashioning a hook to use as a tool.

pulled up to provide the food (see Figure 12.15). Betty was given metal strips of different shapes and had to modify each one in a unique fashion to serve as an effective hook. Betty achieved this without much difficulty.

Tool use in nonhuman species has been theoretically provocative because it appears to be very clever, and many have regarded tool use to be a defining feature of advanced intelligence. An alternative interpretation is that tool fabrication and use is a form of instrumental behavior, reinforced by food items that are obtained using the tools. The fact that there is variation in the form of the behavior is consistent with studies showing that response variability can be a basis for instrumental reinforcement (see Chapter 5). It is not easy to decide between an instrumental conditioning interpretation and explanations that emphasize extensive cognitive planning and *intelligence*. A critical issue is how the tool use behavior is acquired and how flexible the behavior is in dealing with novel situations.

Information about how wild-caught crows learned to use tools is unavailable, but Kacelnik and his colleagues have started studying the acquisition of tool use in crows that they hand-reared in captivity (Kenward et al., 2005; Kenward et al., 2006). Many have assumed that tool use in the wild is learned by imitating other crows that already had the skill. Studies with hand-reared crows have shown that modeling tool use facilitates learning but is not necessary. Crows can figure out on their own that they can obtain pieces of food by using twigs to prod out the food. However, this type of tool use is preceded by other behaviors involving manipulating twigs. Evidently, New Caledonian crows have a predisposition to pick up non-food objects and handle them in various ways. Such manipulatory behavior then makes it possible for them to learn to use the objects as tools.

LANGUAGE LEARNING IN NONHUMAN ANIMALS

Perhaps the most complex cognitive skill is linguistic competence. In fact, historically, the dominant view was that linguistic skill is so complex and specialized that it is uniquely human. According to this view, the ability to use language depends on certain innate processes that have evolved only in our own species (e.g., Chomsky, 1972; Lennenberg, 1967). By contrast, others have proposed that human beings are able to use language because they are especially intelligent and have experiences that permit language acquisition. This second view suggests that nonhuman organisms may also acquire language skills if they are sufficiently intelligent and encounter the requisite experiences. Encouraged by this possibility, investigators have tried to teach language skills to various species (e.g., Hillix & Rumbaugh, 2004).

Early language-training efforts attempted to determine whether nonhuman animals are capable of language. However, it has become evident that this is not an answerable question (Roitblat, Harley, & Helweg, 1993). Language is not a unitary entity that one either does or does not have. Rather, it consists of component skills. A human infant's language abilities, for example, improve gradually as the infant acquires and integrates increasingly sophisticated language skills. In this developmental sequence, there is no one point at which the young child graduates from not having language to having it.

If the goal is no longer to demonstrate human-like linguistic competence in nonhuman species, what is the goal of this type of research? There are several goals. One is to use language training as a vehicle to study the cognitive abilities of nonhuman species. This is the basic objective of the program of work directed by Irene Pepperberg (1999), who has been studying the cognitive abilities of a Grey parrot, Alex, since 1977. A related sentiment is expressed by Louis Herman, who directed language studies in dolphins: "The animal language work can help us to identify with more surety those processes in humans that may derive from general cognitive structures rather than from language-specific structures" (Herman & Uyeyama, 1999, p.22). Research on language learning in nonhuman species can also tell us about the cognitive prerequisites and components of language competence and provide information about how best to teach linguistic skills. This information can then be put to good use in language instruction for persons with cognitive disabilities (Sevcik, Romski, & Wilkenson, 1991).

Early Attempts at Language Training

Most efforts to teach animals language have involved chimpanzees because chimpanzees have many characteristics in common with human beings. Despite these similarities, however, chimpanzees do not learn to speak when they are given the same types of experiences that children have as they learn to speak. Cathy and Keith Hayes, for example, raised a chimpanzee named Viki with the explicit intent of teaching her to talk (Hayes & Hayes, 1951). Despite several years of training, Viki learned to say only three words: mama, papa, and cup. The search for linguistic competence in chimpanzees did not get underway seriously until the innovative work of Allen and Beatrice Gardner and their students (Gardner & Gardner, 1969, 1975, 1978) who decided to teach their chimpanzee, Washoe, American Sign Language rather than vocal speech.

American Sign Language uses manual gestures for words. Although chimpanzees make a number of distinct vocalizations that have linguistic properties (e.g., Taglialatela, Savage-Rumbaugh, & Baker, 2003), they can make a much broader range of hand movements and gestures. Washoe was a good student. She learned to sign well over 100 words. Washoe's success suggested that earlier efforts to teach speech to chimpanzees may have failed not because of

I. M. Pepperberg,
with Alex

the inability of the chimpanzee to learn linguistic skills, but because an inappropriate response medium (vocalization) was used. The success of the Gardners with Washoe encouraged other language-training efforts with chimpanzees, as well as with other species. These included a gorilla (Patterson, 1978), dolphins (Herman, 1987), sea lions (Gisiner & Schusterman, 1992; Schusterman & Gisiner, 1988), and African Grey parrots (Pepperberg, 1990).

Language Training Procedures

A variety of procedures have been employed to train language skills. For example, in the program of research on African Grey parrots directed by Irene Pepperberg (1990, 1993, 1999), an observational learning procedure known as the **model-rival technique** is used. In this technique, one research assistant acts as a trainer and the other acts as a rival student who competes with the parrot for the attention of the trainer. The trainer may present an object of interest to the parrot and ask what color it is. The person acting as the student then responds, sometimes correctly and sometimes incorrectly. An incorrect response results in a reprimand from the trainer and temporary removal of the object. A correct response results in praise and a chance to manipulate the object. The parrot observes these interactions and attempts to gain the attention of the trainer (and obtain the object) by responding correctly before the rival human student does so.

In the dolphin and sea lion language training projects, more conventional stimulus-discrimination procedures have been used (e.g., Herman, Pack, & Morrel-Samuels, 1993; Schusterman & Krieger, 1986). The instructional stimuli were provided by a person making a particular gesture (e.g., arms crossed against the chest) at the edge of the pool. The correct response on the part of the marine mammal to the gesture was reinforced with food; incorrect responses were not reinforced.

With chimpanzees, sign language training was usually conducted within the context of an established social relationship between the trainers and the chimpanzees. The chimpanzees lived in a rich home-like environment and were cared for by a small number of people throughout the day, each of whom was adept in sign language. Every effort was made to engage the chimpanzees in active conversation (through signing) during their waking hours. New signs were learned during games, in the course of getting dressed, or in going from place to place. The intent was to teach language to the chimpanzees in the way that children presumably learn to talk during the normal course of interacting with parents and other children.

Although a naturalistic context for teaching sign language may facilitate learning, the informality of the approach makes it difficult to document the course of language acquisition in detail. Other investigators developed artificial languages for use with chimpanzees. One artificial language developed by Duane Rumbaugh and his colleagues at the Language Research Center at Georgia State University, used simple designs of various shapes and colors to represent words (Rumbaugh, 1977; see also Savage-Rumbaugh, 1986). These symbols, called lexigrams, are presented on a board (see Figure 12.16). The chimpanzee can select a word by pointing to or pressing the corresponding lexigram on the board. Computer records of these lexigram responses provide detailed information about the linguistic performance of the research participant.

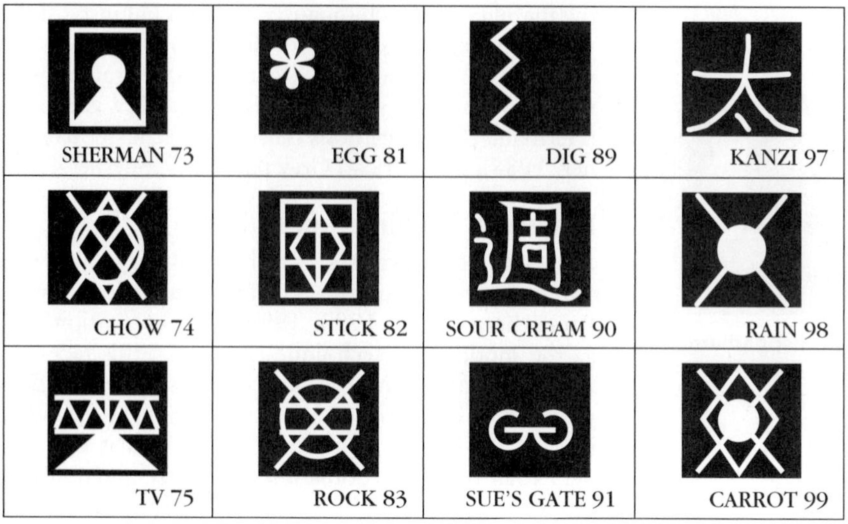

Courtesy of Duane Rumbaugh, Language Research Center, Georgia State University

FIGURE **12.16**

Examples of lexigrams used at the Language Research Center of Georgia State University.

The most sophisticated demonstrations of language competence have been obtained with bonobos (*Pan paniscus*) (Savage-Rumbaugh et al., 1993; Savage-Rumbaugh et al., 1990). Bonobos are more similar to human beings than chimpanzees, but they are rare both in the wild and in captivity. Perhaps the most famous language-trained bonobo is Kanzi. During the first 2.5 years of his life, Kanzi lived with his mother, Matata, who was born in the wild and started language training at the Language Research Center of Georgia State University when Kanzi was six months old. Matata was trained with standard procedures in which she had to indicate the lexigram names of food objects to obtain those foods. For several years, Kanzi observed these training sessions but did not participate in them. Matata was then removed for a period for breeding purposes. During this separation Kanzi began to interact with the lexigram board spontaneously. The investigators took advantage of this spontaneous use of the lexigram board and allowed Kanzi to continue to use it in addition to communicating with manual gestures. They also allowed Kanzi to continue to learn language skills by listening to spoken English and observing humans communicating with gestures and lexigrams.

Every effort was made to provide Kanzi with as rich and as natural an environment as possible. He was allowed to go on excursions in a 50-acre wooded area adjacent to the laboratory. The woods were provisioned with food stations at fixed locations. Excursions in the woods provided numerous opportunities for conversation concerning which food site to visit, what to take along, and so on. Kanzi was also allowed to visit various areas of the laboratory, including areas in which other apes were housed, and periodically he was taken on car rides.

Spoken and lexical language were incorporated into Kanzi's daily activities, such as diaper changes, food preparation, and various games. The hope

FIGURE **12.17**

Kanzi working with a lexigram board.

was that Kanzi would acquire language incidentally during his normal daily activities, as children do. No explicit language training sessions were conducted, and Kanzi's use of language was not explicitly reinforced with food. However, the reinforcement contingencies inherent in social interactions were probably important in Kanzi's language learning (Sundberg, 1996).

In addition to spontaneously learning lexigrams, Kanzi also seemed to have learned to recognize spoken English words. Kanzi, as other chimpanzees, could not produce the sounds of English words, but he appeared to know their meaning. Savage-Rumbaugh decided to evaluate this comprehension in several systematic tests. In one test (Savage-Rumbaugh et al., 1986), English words were spoken by a speech synthesizer to make sure Kanzi was not responding to the intonation of a specific individual. After each word, Kanzi was asked to select the lexical symbol for that word from a selection of three lexigrams (see Figure 12.18). The experimenter did not see the possible choices, and thus could not inadvertently prompt Kanzi. Each of 66 words was presented three times. Kanzi responded correctly each time 51 of the words was presented. In a similar test with spoken human speech, Kanzi only erred on one of the 66 words. Thus, synthesized speech was more difficult for Kanzi to comprehend, as it is for human listeners sometimes.

Evidence of "Grammar" in Great Apes

Although it is generally agreed that great apes (and Grey parrots, dolphins, and sea lions) can learn a vocabulary, language is more than just a collection of words. Language also involves arrangement of words into sequences according

Courtesy of Duane Rumbaugh, Language Research Center, Georgia State University

FIGURE **12.18**

The bonobo chimpanzee Kanzi participating in a test of English comprehension. Words were presented to him through the earphones, and he had to respond by pressing lexigrams on the panel in the background.

to certain rules set forth by the grammar or syntax of the language. Hence, a major issue in language research has been whether the subjects display evidence of using grammatical rules. There has been considerable debate about this and the debate is ongoing (e.g., Kako, 1999; Roitblat, 2007).

Early detailed studies of language production in the chimpanzee failed to provide convincing evidence of responding on the basis of some kind of grammar or set of rules for word combinations (Terrace, 1979; Terrace et al., 1979). The chimpanzee, Nim, who was taught sign language by Terrace and his associates, performed sequences of signs, but these appeared to be imitations of the trainer and included meaningless repetitions. For example, Nim's most common four-sign combination was *eat-drink-eat-drink*. More convincing evidence of the development of grammatical word sequences was obtained in studies with Kanzi (Greenfield & Lyn, 2007; Greenfield & Savage-Rumbaugh, 1990; see also Savage-Rumbaugh et al., 1990).

Data for the analysis of the possible existence of grammatical structure in Kanzi's language production were first obtained when Kanzi was 5.5 years old (Greenfield & Savage-Rumbaugh, 1990). Over a five-month period of observations, Kanzi communicated 13,691 "words." Of these, about 10% contained more than one element or word. The analysis of word sequences was limited to spontaneous communications. Thus, responses to directed questions were excluded from the analyses, as were responses that Kanzi performed to obtain something that was otherwise withheld, or responses that

TABLE **12.1**
Frequency of Various Two-Element Communications by Kanzi (lexigram responses are indicated by small capital letters)

Word Order	Frequency	Example of Dominant Order
Action → Agent	119	CARRY — gesture to Phil, who agrees
Agent → Action	13	to carry Kanzi
Action → Object	39	KEEP AWAY BALLOON — wanting to tease
Object → Action	15	Bill with a balloon and start a fight
Goal → Action	46	COKE CHASE — researcher chases Kanzi to
Action → Goal	10	place in woods where Coke is kept

Source: Adapted from Greenfield and Savage-Rumbaugh, 1990.

involved some degree of imitation. Unlike Nim, Kanzi rarely repeated himself or combined words that did not make sense together. Analyses of the multiple-word communications revealed a structure indicative of rules for word order.

Kanzi's word combinations could be categorized according to the types of words that were involved. By way of example, Table 12.1 summarizes data from three different types of two-word combinations. The first type involves a word for an action and a word for an agent. A total of 132 such action/ agent combinations were observed. Of these, in 119 instances the action word preceded the agent word. In only 13 of the 132 cases, did the word for the agent precede the word for the action. A similar bias in favor of a particular word order is evident with the other types of two-word combinations, action/object and goal/action. Notice that the "grammatical" rule is not a simple one. One of the words in all three of these types of two-word combinations involved an action. However, the action word did not come first predominantly in all three types of two-word combinations. When talking about an action and a goal, Kanzi tended to state the goal first.

Evidence for grammatical structure has been also obtained in analyses of Kanzi's language comprehension rather than language production. Comprehension precedes the ability to speak a language in human language learning. Individuals learning a second language, for example, can often understand more of that language than they are able to speak. This raises the possibility that studies of language comprehension may reveal sophisticated aspects of linguistic competence that are not evident in language production (for example, Brakke & Savage-Rumbaugh, 1995; Savage-Rumbaugh et al., 1993).

In addition to learning lexigrams, Kanzi spontaneously learned to recognize the sounds of English spoken by his trainers and companions. Savage-Rumbaugh et al. (1993) conducted detailed evaluations of the language comprehension of Kanzi when he was eight years old and compared his performance to that of a two-year-old child, Alia. Alia's mother, Jeannine Murphy, was one of Kanzi's caretakers. Alia participated in games and other activities similar to those that were used with Kanzi and received similar exposure to lexigrams and spoken English.

The test sentences involved instructions to manipulate various objects that were familiar and available to Kanzi and Alia. Kanzi had access to 12 objects, and Alia was given up to eight. In the critical test phase, the sentences were spoken by an experimenter hidden by a one-way mirror so that the experimenter could not make gestures that might prompt the correct response. All trials were recorded on video tape. Usually two or three other people were present in the room so that sentences involving interactions with these people could be included in the test. However, the additional individuals wore headphones that played loud music so that they could not hear the instructions given to Kanzi or Alia. To further preclude inadvertent influences on the data, the results of tests with Kanzi were not known to the person conducting the tests with Alia, and vice versa.

Kanzi was tested with 415 sentences and Alia was tested with 407. The sentences were distributed among seven different types. Some were fairly simple, such as "Put object X in object Y," "Give object X to person A," "Do action A on object X," and "Take object X to location Y." Others were more complicated, such as "Make pretend animate A do action A on recipient Y" (e.g., "Make the [toy] doggie bite the [toy] snake"). Both Kanzi and Alia did remarkably well. Each responded correctly more than 50% of the time on all but one sentence type. Overall, Kanzi did a bit better than Alia. Kanzi responded correctly on 74% of the trials, and Alia responded correctly on 65% of the trials.

Kanzi's performance provides the best evidence available so far that a nonhuman mammal can acquire sophisticated linguistic skills. Kanzi acquired a substantial vocabulary and also showed evidence of syntax in language production. In addition, he mastered some of the flexibility of language. He could understand differences in meaning created by different word orders and new messages created by combining familiar words in unfamiliar sentences. The language sophistication of Kanzi proves that many important linguistic skills are not uniquely human attributes. Thus, these findings vindicate Darwin's belief that seemingly unique human abilities and skills do not reflect a discontinuity in the animal kingdom. (For a discussion of the broader philosophical implications of this research, see Savage-Rumbaugh, Shanker, & Taylor, 1998.)

SAMPLE QUESTIONS

1. Describe food caching behavior and what factors experimenters have to rule out before concluding that the behavior is mediated by working memory.
2. Describe how the behavior of food storing birds can be used to provide evidence of episodic memory.
3. Describe the peak procedure and how results obtained with the peak procedure may be explained by scalar expectancy theory.
4. Compare and contrast the scalar expectancy model of timing and the behavioral theory of timing.
5. Explain why tests with subsets of items from a simultaneous array are useful in assessing the mechanisms of serial pattern learning.

6. Compare and contrast perceptual and abstract concept learning.
7. Describe how responsiveness to word order may be evaluated in the language comprehension of chimpanzees and children.

KEY TERMS

adjunctive behaviors Systematic activities or responses that occur when reinforcers are delivered at fixed intervals.

duration estimation A discrimination procedure in which the discriminative stimulus is the duration of an event.

model-rival technique An observational learning procedure in which the participant observes a trainer teaching a student and tries to compete with that student for the trainer's attention.

paired-associate learning Learning of associations between successive pairs of an ordered list of stimuli.

peak procedure A discrete-trial variation of a fixed interval schedule used to study timing in animals.

response chain A consecutively ordered series of responses in which each response produces the cue for the next response in the sequence.

scalar invariance A property of the temporal control of behavior that emphasizes that participants respond to time intervals in terms of their relative or proportional durations rather than their absolute durations.

serial representation learning The learning of a mental representation of the order of an entire list or series of stimuli.

Abramson, L. Y., Metalsky, G. I., & Alloy, L. B. (1989). Hopelessness depression: A theory-based subtype of depression. *Psychological Review, 96,* 358–372.

Adkins-Regan, E., & MacKillop, E. A., (2003). Japanese quail (*Coturnix japonica*) inseminations are more likely to fertilize eggs in a context predicting mating opportunities. *Proceedings of the Royal Society of London, Series B, 270,* 1685–1689.

Ahearn, W. H., Clark, K. M., Gardenier, N. C., Chung, B. I., & Dube, W. V. (2003). Persistence of stereotypic behavior: Examining the effects of external reinforcers. *Journal of Applied Behavior Analysis, 36,* 439–448.

Akins, C. K. (1998). Context excitation and modulation of conditioned sexual behavior. *Animal Learning & Behavior, 26,* 416–426.

Akins, C. K. (2000). Effects of species-specific cues and the CS-US interval on the topography of the sexually conditioned response. *Learning and Motivation, 31,* 211–235.

Akins, C. K. (2004). The role of Pavlovian conditioning in sexual behavior: A comparative analysis of human and nonhuman animals. *International Journal of Comparative Psychology, 17,* 241–262.

Akins, C. K., & Domjan, M. (1996). The topography of sexually conditioned behaviour: Effects of a trace interval. *Quarterly Journal of Experimental Psychology, 49B,* 346–356.

Albert, M., & Ayres, J. J. B. (1997). One-trial simultaneous and backward excitatory fear conditioning in rats: Lick suppression, freezing, and rearing to CS compounds and their elements. *Animal Learning & Behavior, 25,* 210–220.

Allan, L. G. (2005). Learning of contingent relationships. Special Issue of *Learning & Behavior, 33,* 127–130, with additional articles from pp. 131–263.

Allan, R. W., & Zeigler, H. P. (1994). Autoshaping the pigeon's gape response: Acquisition and topography as a function of reinforcer type and magnitude. *Journal of the Experimental Analysis of Behavior, 62,* 201–223.

Allison, J. (1983). *Behavioral economics.* New York: Praeger.

Allison, J. (1989). The nature of reinforcement. In S. B. Klein & R. R. Mowrer (Eds.), *Contemporary learning theories: Instrumental conditioning and the impact of biological constraints on learning,* 13–39. Hillsdale, NJ: Erlbaum.

Allison, J. (1993). Response deprivation, reinforcement, and economics. *Journal of the Experimental Analysis of Behavior, 60,* 129–140.

Allison, J., Buxton, A., & Moore, K. E. (1987). Bliss points, stop lines, and performance under schedule constraint. *Journal of Experimental Psychology: Animal Behavior Processes, 13,* 331–340.

Alvarez, V. A., & Sabatini, B. L. (2007). Anatomical and physiological plasticity of dendritic spines. *Annual Review of Neuroscience, 30,* 79–87.

Amsel, A. (1958). The role of frustrative nonreward in noncontinuous reward situations. *Psychological Bulletin, 55,* 102–119.

Amsel, A. (1962). Frustrative nonreward in partial reinforcement and discrimination learning. *Psychological Review, 69,* 306–328.

Amsel, A. (1967). Partial reinforcement effects on vigor and persistence. In K. W. Spence & J. T. Spence (Eds.), *The psychology of learning and motivation* (Vol. 1). New York: Academic Press.

Amsel, A. (1989). *Behaviorism, neobehaviorism, and cognitivism in learning theory.* Hillsdale, NJ: Erlbaum.

Amsel, A. (1992). *Frustration theory.* Cambridge, England: Cambridge University Press.

Amundson, J. C., & Miller, R. R. (2008). CS-US temporal relations in blocking. *Learning & Behavior, 36,* 92–103.

Anderson, J. R. (2005) *Cognitive psychology and its implications* (6th ed.). New York: Worth.

Anderson, M. C., & Shettleworth, S. J. (1977). Behavioral adaptation to fixed-interval and fixed-time food delivery in golden hamsters. *Journal of the Experimental Analysis of Behavior, 25,* 33–49.

Andrzejewski, M. E., Cardinal, C. D., Field, D. P., Flannery, B. A., Johnson, M., Bailey, K., & Hineline, P. N. (2005). Pigeons' choices between fixed-interval and random-interval schedules: Utility of variability? *Journal of the Experimental Analysis of Behavior, 83,* 129–145.

Andrzejewski, M. E., Ryals, C. D., Higgins, S., Sulkowski, J., Doney, J., Kelley, A. E., & Bersh, P. J. (2007). Is extinction the hallmark of operant discrimination?: Reinforcement and S$^\Delta$ effects. *Behavioural Processes, 74,* 49–63.

Anger, D. (1963). The role of temporal discrimination in the reinforcement of Sidman avoidance behavior. *Journal of the Experimental Analysis of Behavior, 6,* 477–506.

Arcediano, F., Matute, H., & Miller, R. R. (1997). Blocking of Pavlovian conditioning in humans. *Learning and Motivation, 28,* 188–199.

Arcediano, F., Ortega, N., & Matute, H. (1996). A behavioural preparation for the study of human Pavlovian conditioning. *Quarterly Journal of Experimental Psychology, 49B,* 270–283.

Astley, S. L., & Wasserman, E. A. (1998). Novelty and functional equivalence in superordinate categorization by pigeons. *Animal Learning & Behavior, 26,* 125–138.

Astley, S. L., & Wasserman, E. A. (1999). Superordinate category formation in pigeons: Association with a common delay or probability of food reinforcement makes perceptually dissimilar stimuli functionally equivalent. *Journal of Experimental Psychology: Animal Behavior Processes, 25,* 415–432.

Ator, N. A., & Griffiths, R. R. (2003). Principles of drug abuse liability assessment in laboratory animals. *Drug and Alcohol Dependence, 70,* S55–S72.

Aust, U., & Huber, L. (2001). The role of item- and category-specific information in the discrimination of people versus nonpeople images by pigeons. *Animal Learning & Behavior, 29,* 107–119.

Aust, U., & Huber, L. (2003). Elemental versus configural perception in a people-present/people-absent discrimination task by pigeons. *Learning & Behavior, 31,* 213–234.

Ayres, J. J. B. (1998). Fear conditioning and avoidance. In W. O'Donohue (Ed.), *Learning and behavior therapy.* (pp. 122–145). Boston: Allyn Bacon.

Ayres, J. J. B., Haddad, C., & Albert, M. (1987). One-trial excitatory backward conditioning as assessed by suppression of licking in rats: Concurrent observations of lick suppression and defensive behaviors. *Animal Learning & Behavior, 15,* 212–217.

Azorlosa, J. L., & Cicala, G. A. (1986). Blocking of conditioned suppression with 1 or 10 compound trials. *Animal Learning & Behavior, 14,* 163–167.

Azrin, N. H. (1956). Some effects of two intermittent schedules of immediate and non-immediate punishment. *Journal of Psychology, 42,* 3–21.

Azrin, N. H. (1958). Some effects of noise on human behavior. *Journal of the Experimental Analysis of Behavior, 1,* 183–200.

Azrin, N. H. (1959). Punishment and recovery during fixed ratio performance. *Journal of the Experimental Analysis of Behavior, 2,* 301–305.

Azrin, N. H. (1960). Effects of punishment intensity during variable-interval reinforcement. *Journal of the Experimental Analysis of Behavior, 3,* 123–142.

Azrin, N. H., & Holz, W. C. (1961). Punishment during fixed-interval reinforcement. *Journal of the Experimental Analysis of Behavior, 4,* 343–347.

Azrin, N. H., & Holz, W. C. (1966). Punishment. In W. K. Honig (Ed.), *Operant behavior: Areas of research and application* (pp. 380–447). New York: Appleton-Century-Crofts.

Azrin, N. H., Holz, W. C., & Hake, D. F. (1963). Fixed-ratio punishment. *Journal of the Experimental Analysis of Behavior, 6,* 141–148.

Azrin, N. H., Hutchinson, R. R., & Hake, D. F. (1966). Extinction-induced aggression. *Journal of the Experimental Analysis of Behavior, 9,* 191–204.

Babb, S. J., & Crystal, J. D. (2006). Discrimination of what, when, and where is not based on time of day. *Learning & Behavior, 34,* 124–130.

Babkin, B. P. (1949). Pavlov: A biography. Chicago: University of Chicago Press.

Baer, D. M., & Wolf, M. M. (1970). The entry into natural communities of reinforcement. In R. Ulrich, T stachnik, & J. Mabry (Eds.) *Control of human behavior* (Vol. 2 pp. 319–324). Glenview, IL: Scott Foresman.

Baerends, G. P. (1988). Ethology. In R. C. Atkinson, R. J. Herrnstein, G. Lindzey, & R. D. Luce (Eds.), *Stevens' handbook of experimental psychology* (Vol. 1, pp. 765–830). New York: Wiley.

Bailey, G. K., & Westbrook, R. F. (2008). Extinction and latent inhibition of within-event learning are context specific. *Journal of Experimental Psychology: Animal Behavior Processes, 34,* 106–118.

Baillargeon, R. (2008). Innate ideas revisited. *Perspectives in psychological science, 3,* 2–13.

Baker, T. B., & Tiffany, S. T. (1985). Morphine tolerance as habituation. *Psychological Review, 92,* 78–108.

Baker, T. B., Brandon, T. H., & Chassin, L. (2004). Motivational influences on cigarette smoking. *Annual Review of Psychology, 55,* 463–491.

Baker, T. B., Piper, M. E., McCarthy, D. E., Majeskie, M. R., & Fiore, M. C. (2004). Addiction motivation reformulated: An affective processing model of negative reinforcement. *Psychological Review, 111,* 33–51.

Balaz, M. A., Kasprow, W. J., & Miller, R. R. (1982). Blocking with a single compound trial. *Animal Learning & Behavior, 10,* 271–276.

Balda, R. P., & Turek, R. J. (1984). The cache-recovery system as an example of memory capabilities in Clark's nutcracker. In H. L. Roitblat, T. G. Bever, & H. S. Terrace (Eds.), *Animal cognition.* (pp. 513–532). Hillsdale, NJ: Erlbaum.

Balleine, B. W., & Ostlund, S. B. (2007). Still at the choice point.

Annals of the New York Academy of Sciences, 1104, 147–171.

Balsam, P. D. (1985). The functions of context in learning and performance. In P. D. Balsam & A. Tomie (Eds.), *Context and learning* (pp. 1–21). Hillsdale, NJ: Erlbaum.

Balsam, P. D. (1988). Selection, representation, and equivalence of controlling stimuli. In R. C. Atkinson, R. J. Herrnstein, G. Lindzey, & R. D. Luce (Eds.), *Stevens' handbook of experimental psychology.* (Vol. 2.) Learning and cognition (pp. 111–166). New York: Wiley.

Balsam, P. D., & Gallistel, C. R. (2009). Temporal maps and informativeness in associative learning. *Trends in Neuroscience.* In press.

Balsam, P. D., & Tomie, A. (Eds.). (1985). *Context and learning.* Hillsdale, NJ: Erlbaum.

Balsam, P. D., Deich, J. D., Ohyama, T., & Stokes, P. D. (1998). Origins of new behavior. In W. O'Donohue (Ed.) *Learning and behavior therapy.* (pp. 403–420). Boston: Allyn and Bacon.

Balsam, P. D., Drew, M. R., & Yang, C. (2001). Timing at the start of associative learning. *Learning and Motivation, 33,* 141–155.

Balsam, P. D., Fairhurst, S., & Gallistel, C. R. (2006). Pavlovian contingencies and temporal information. *Journal of Experimental Psychology: Animal Behavior Processes, 32,* 284–294.

Banks, R. K. (1976). Resistance to punishment as a function of intensity and frequency of prior punishment experience. *Learning and Motivation, 7,* 551–558.

Barad, M. (2006). Anatomical, molecular, and cellular substrates of fear extinction. In M. G. Craske, D. Hermans, and D. Vansteenwegen (Eds.), *Fear and learning.* (pp. 157–173). Washington, DC: American Psychological Association.

Barad, M., & Cain, C. K. (2007). Mechanisms of fear extinction: Toward improved treatment for anxiety. In L. J. Kirmayer, R. Lemelson, and M. Barad (Eds.), *Understanding trauma: Integrating biological, clinical, and cultural perspectives.* (pp. 78–97). Cambridge, England: Cambridge University Press.

Bargh, J. A., & Chartrand, T. L. (1999). The unbearable automaticity of being. *American Psyhchologist, 54,* 462–479.

Bargh, J. A., & Morsella, E. (2008). The unconscious mind. *Perspectives in psychological science, 3,* 73–79.

Barlow, (1988). *Anxiety and its disorders.* New York: Guilford Press.

Barnet, R. C., & Miller, R. R. (1996). Second-order excitation mediated by a backward conditioned inhibitor. *Journal of Experimental Psychology: Animal Behavior Processes, 22,* 279–296.

Barnet, R. C., Cole, R. P., & Miller, R. R. (1997). Temporal integration in second-order conditioning and sensory preconditioning. *Animal Learning & Behavior, 25,* 221–233.

Baron, A. (1965). Delayed punishment of a runway response. *Journal of Comparative and Physiological Psychology, 60,* 131–134.

Baron, A., & Herpolsheimer, L. R. (1999). Averaging effects in the study of fixed ratio response patterns. *Journal of the Experimental Analysis of Behavior, 71,* 145–153.

Barry, R. J. (2004). Stimulus significance effects in habituation of the phasic and tonic orienting reflex. *Integrative Physiological & Behavioral Science, 39,* 166–179.

Bashinski, H., Werner, J., & Rudy, J. (1985). Determinants of infant visual attention: Evidence for a two-process theory. *Journal of Experimental Child Psychology, 39,* 580–598.

Batsell, W. R., & Paschall, G. Y. (2008). Mechanisms of overshadowing and potentiation in flavor-aversion conditioning. In S. Reilly and T. R. Schachtman, (Eds.), *Conditioned taste aversion: Behavioral and neural processes.* (pp. 179–195). New York: Oxford University Press.

Batsell, W. R., Jr., Paschall, G. Y., Gleason, D. I., & Batson, J. D. (2001). Taste preconditioning augments odor-aversion learning. *Journal of Experimental Psychology: Animal Behavior Processes, 27,* 30–47.

Batson, J. D., & Batsell, W. R., Jr. (2000). Augmentation, not blocking, in an A+/AX+ flavor-conditioning procedure. *Psychonomic Bulletin & Review, 7,* 466–471.

Baum, M. (1969). Extinction of avoidance response following response prevention: Some parametric investigations. *Canadian Journal of Psychology, 23,* 1–10.

Baum, M. (1970). Extinction of avoidance responding through response prevention (flooding). *Psychological Bulletin, 74,* 276–284.

Baum, W. M. (1974). On two types of deviation from the matching law: Bias and undermatching. *Journal of the Experimental Analysis of Behavior, 22,* 231–242.

Baum, W. M. (1979). Matching, undermatching, and overmatching in studies of choice. *Journal of the Experimental Analysis of Behavior, 32,* 269–281.

Baum, W. M. (1993). Performances on ratio and interval schedules of reinforcement: Data and theory. *Journal of the Experimental Analysis of Behavior, 59,* 245–264.

Baum, W. M. (2002). From molecular to molar: A paradigm shift in behavior analysis. *Journal of the Experimental Analysis of Behavior, 78,* 95–116.

Baum, W. M., & Aparicio, C. F. (1999). Optimality and concurrent variable-interval variable-ratio schedules. *Journal of the Experimental Analysis of Behavior, 71,* 75–89.

Beatty, W. W., & Shavalia, D. A. (1980). Spatial memory in rats: Time course of working memory and effects of anesthetics. *Behavioral and Neural Biology, 28,* 454–462.

Bechterev, V. M. (1913). *La psychologie objective.* Paris: Alcan.

Beck, B. B. (1980). *Animal tool behavior.* New York: Garland Press.

Beck, C. D. O., & Rankin, C. H. (1997). Long-term habituation is produced by distributed training at long ISIs and not by massed training or short ISIs in *Caenorhabditis elegans. Animal Learning & Behavior, 25,* 446–457.

Bee, M. A. (2001). Habituation and sensitization of aggression in bullfrogs (*Rana catesbeiana*): Testing the dual-porcess theory of habituation. *Journal of Comparative Psychology, 115,* 307–316.

Begley, S. (2001, Feb. 12). How it all starts inside your brain. *Newsweek, 137*(7), 40–42.

Belke, T. W., & Hancock, S. D. (2003). Responding for sucrose and wheel-running reinforcement: Effects of sucrose concentration and wheel-running reinforcer duration. *Journal of the Experimental Analysis of Behavior, 79,* 243–265.

Bell, M. C., Gomez, B. E., & Kessler, K. (2008). Signals, resistance to change, and conditioned reinforcement in a multiple schedule. *Behavioural Processes, 78,* 158–164.

Berg, M. E., & Grace, R. C. (2006). Initial-link duration and acquisition of preference in concurrent chain. *Learning & Behavior, 34,* 50–60.

Bernstein, I. L. (1978). Learned taste aversions in children receiving chemotherapy. *Science, 200,* 1302–1303.

Bernstein, I. L. (1991). Aversion conditioning in response to cancer and cancer treatment. *Clinical Psychology Review, 11,* 185–191.

Bernstein, I. L., & Borson, S. (1986). Learned food aversion: A component of anorexia syndromes. *Psychological Review, 93,* 462–472.

Bernstein, I. L., & Webster, M. M. (1980). Learned taste aversions in humans. *Physiology and Behavior, 25,* 363–366.

Berridge, K. C., & Robinson, T. E. (2003). Parsing reward. *Trends in Neuroscience, 26,* 507–513.

Berridge, K. C., & Schulkin, J. (1989). Palatability shift of a salt-associated incentive during sodium depletion. *Quarterly Journal of Experimental Psychology, 41B,* 121–138.

Best, M. R., Dunn, D. P., Batson, J. D., Meachum, C. L., & Nash, S. M. (1985). Extinguishing conditioned inhibition in flavour-aversion learning: Effects of repeated testing and extinction of the excitatory element. *Quarterly Journal of Experimental Psychology, 37B,* 359–378.

Bevins, R. A., McPhee, J. E., Rauhut, A. S., & Ayres, J. J. B. (1997). Converging evidence for one-trial context fear conditioning with an immediate shock: Importance of shock potency. *Journal of Experimental Psychology: Animal Behavior Processes, 23,* 312–324.

Bickel, W. K., Green, L., & Vuchinich, R. E. (1995). Behavioral economics. *Journal of the Experimental Analysis of Behavior, 64,* 257–262.

Bitterman, M. E. (1964). Classical conditioning in the goldfish as a function of the CS-US interval. *Journal of Comparative and Physiological Psychology, 58,* 359–366.

Bitterman, M. E. (1988). Vertebrate-invertebrate comparisons. In H. J. Jerison & I. Jerison (Eds.) *Intelligence and evolutionary biology*

(NATO ASI Series, Vol. G17, pp. 251–276). Berlin: Springer.

Bitterman, M. E. (1996). Comparative analysis of learning in honeybees. *Animal Learning & Behavior, 24,* 123–141.

Bizo, L. A., & Killeen, P. R. (1997). Models of ratio schedule performance. *Journal of Experimental Psychology: Animal Behavior Processes, 23,* 351–367.

Bizo, L. A., & McMahon, C. V. (2007). Temporal generalization and peak shift in humans. *Learning & Behavior, 35,* 123–130.

Bjork, R. A. (1972). The updating of human memory. In G. H. Bower (Ed.), *The psychology of learning and motivation* (Vol. 12, pp. 235–259). New York: Academic Press.

Blackman, D. (1977). Conditioned suppression and the effects of classical conditioning on operant behavior. In W. K. Honig & J. E. R. Staddon (Eds.), *Handbook of operant behavior.* (pp. 340–363). Englewood Cliffs, NJ: Prentice Hall.

Blackmore, T. L., Foster, T. M., Sumpter, C. E., & Temple, W. (2008). An investigation of colour discrimination with horses (*Equus caballus*). *Behavioural Processes, 78,* 387–396.

Blaisdell, A. P., Gunther, L. M., & Miller, R. R. (1999). Recovery from blocking through deflation of the blocking stimulus. *Animal Learning & Behavior, 27,* 63–76.

Blakely, E., & Schlinger, H. (1988). Determinants of pausing under variable-ratio schedules: Reinforcer magnitude, ratio size, and schedule configuration. *Journal of the Experimental Analysis of Behavior, 50,* 65–73.

Blakemore, C., & Cooper, G. F. (1970). Development of the brain depends on visual environment. *Science, 228,* 477–478.

Blanchard, D. C. (1997). Stimulus, environmental, and pharmacological control of defensive behaviors. In M. E. Bouton and M. S. Fanselow (Eds.), *Learning, motivation, and cognition.* (pp. 283–303). Washington, DC: American Psychological Association.

Blass, E. M., Ganchrow, J. R., & Steiner, J. E. (1984). Classical conditioning in newborn humans 2–48 hours of age. *Infant Behavior and Development, 7,* 223–235.

Bliss, T. V. P, & Lomo, T. (1973). Long-lasting potentiation of synaptic transmission in the dentate area of the anesthetized rabbit following stimulation of the perforant path. *Journal of Physiology, 232,* 331–356.

Blokland, A., Geraerts, E., & Been, M. (2004). A detailed analysis of rats' spatial memory in a probe trial of a Morris task. *Behavioural Brain Research, 154,* 71–75.

Blough, D. S. (1959). Delayed matching in the pigeon. *Journal of the Experimental Analysis of Behavior, 2,* 151–160.

Bluff, L. A., Weir, A. A. S., Rutz, C., Wimpenny, J. H., & Kacelnik, A. (2007). Tool-related cognition in New Caledonian Crows. *Comparative Cognition & Behavior Reviews, 2,* 1–25.

Blumberg, M. S., & Wasserman, E. A. (1995). Animal mind and the argument from design. *American Psychologist, 50,* 133–144.

Boakes, R. A. (1984). From Darwin to behaviourism. Cambridge: Cambridge University Press.

Boakes, R. A., & Halliday, M. S. (Eds.). (1972). Inhibition and learning. London: Academic Press.

Bodily, K. D., Katz, J. S., & Wright, A. A. (2008). Matching-to-sample abstract concept learning by pigeons. *Journal of Experimental Psychology: Animal Behavior Processes, 34,* 178–184.

Boice, R. (1973). Domestication. *Psychological Bulletin, 80,* 215–230.

Boice, R. (1977). Burrows of wild and albino rats: Effects of domestication, outdoor raising, age, experience, and maternal state. *Journal of Comparative and Physiological Psychology, 91,* 649–661.

Boice, R. (1981). Behavioral comparability of wild and domesticated rats. *Behavior Genetics, 11,* 545–553.

Bolles, R. C. (1969). Avoidance and escape learning: Simultaneous acquisition of different responses. *Journal of Comparative and Physiological Psychology, 68,* 355–358.

Bolles, R. C. (1970). Species-specific defense reactions and avoidance learning. *Psychological Review, 71,* 32–48.

Bolles, R. C. (1971). Species-specific defense reaction. In F. R. Brush (Ed.), *Aversive conditioning and learning* (pp. 183–233). New York: Academic Press.

Bolles, R. C. (1972). Reinforcement, expectancy, and learning. *Psychological Review, 79,* 394–409.

Bolles, R. C., & Fanselow, M. S. (1980). A perceptual defensive-recuperative model of fear and pain. *Behavioral and Brain Sciences, 3,* 291–323.

Bolles, R. C., & Grossen, N. E. (1969). Effects of an informational stimulus on the acquisition of avoidance behavior in rats. *Journal of Comparative and Physiological Psychology, 68,* 90–99.

Bolles, R. C., Holtz, R., Dunn, T., & Hill, W. (1980). Comparisons of stimulus learning and response learning in a punishment situation. *Learning and Motivation, 11,* 78–96.

Borovsky, D., & Rovee-Collier, C. (1990). Contextual constraints on memory retrieval at six months. *Child Development, 61,* 1569–1583.

Borrero, J. C., Crisolo, S. S., Tu, Q., Rieland, W. A., Ross, N. A., Francisco, M. T., & Yamamoto, K. Y. (2007). An application of the matching law to social dynamics. *Journal of Applied Behavior Analysis, 40,* 589–601.

Borszcz, G. S., Cranney, J., & Leaton, R. N. (1989). Influence of long-term sensitization on long-term habituation of the acoustic startle response in rats: Central gray lesions, preexposure, and extinction. *Journal of Experimental Psychology: Animal Behavior Processes, 15,* 54–64.

Bouton, M. E. (1984). Differential control by context in the inflation and reinstatement paradigms. *Journal of Experimental Psychology: Animal Behavior Processes, 10,* 56–74.

Bouton, M. E. (1993). Context, time, and memory retrieval in the interference paradigms of Pavlovian learning. *Psychological Bulletin, 114,* 80–99.

Bouton, M. E. (1994). Conditioning, remembering, and forgetting. *Journal of Experimental Psychology: Animal Behavior Processes, 20,* 219–231.

Bouton, M. E. (2001). Classical conditioning and clinical psychology. In N. J. Smelser and P. B. Baltes (Eds.), *Encyclopedia of the Social and Behavioral Sciences.* Elsevier Science.

Bouton, M. E., & Bolles, R. C. (1980). Conditioned fear assessed by freezing and by the suppression of three different baselines. *Animal Learning & Behavior, 8,* 429–434.

Bouton, M. E., & King, D. A. (1983). Contextual control of the extinction of conditioned fear: Tests for the associative value of the context. *Journal of Experimental Psychology: Animal Behavior Processes, 9,* 248–265.

Bouton, M. E., & Nelson, J. B. (1998). The role of context in classical conditioning: Some implications for behavior therapy. In O'Donohue, W. (Ed.), *Learning and behavior therapy.* (pp. 59–84). Boston: Allyn and Bacon.

Bouton, M. E., & Ricker, S. T. (1994). Renewal of extinguished responding in a second context. *Animal Learning & Behavior, 22,* 317–324.

Bouton, M. E., & Swartzentruber, D. (1986). Analysis of the associative and occasion-setting properties of contexts participating in a Pavlovian discrimination. *Journal of Experimental Psychology: Animal Behavior Processes, 12,* 333–350.

Bouton, M. E., & Woods, A. M. (2008). Extinction: Behavioral mechanisms and their implications. In R. Menzel (Ed.), *Learning theory and behavior.* In J. Byrne (Ed.), *Learning and Memory: A comprehensive reference* (Vol. 1, pp. 151–172). Oxford: Elsevier.

Bouton, M. E., Kenney, F. A., & Rosengard, C. (1990). State-dependent fear extinction with two benzodiazepine tranquilizers. *Behavioral Neuroscience, 104,* 44–55.

Bouton, M. E., Mineka, S., & Barlow, D. H. (2001). A modern learning theory perspective on the etiology of panic disorder. *Psychological Review, 108,* 4–32.

Bouton, M. E., Woods, A. M., Moody, E. W., Sunsay, C., & Garcia-Gutiérrez, A. (2006). Counteracting the context-dependence of extinction: Relapse and tests of some relapse prevention methods. In M. G. Craske, D. Hermans, and D. Vansteenwegen (Eds.), *Fear and learning.* (pp. 175–196). Washington, DC: American Psychological Association.

Bowe, C. A., Miller, J. D., & Green, L. (1987). Qualities and locations of stimuli and responses affecting discrimination learning of chinchillas (*Chinchilla laniger*) and pigeons (*Columbia livia*). *Journal of Comparative Psychology, 101,* 132–138.

Bradfield, L., & McNally, G. P. (2008). *Journal of Experimental Psychology: Animal Behavior Processes, 34,* 256–265.

Bradley, M. M., Moulder, B., & Lang, P. J. (2005). When good things go bad: The reflex physiology of defense. *Psychological Science, 16,* 468–473.

Brakke, K. E., & Savage-Rumbaugh, E. S. (1995). The development of language skills in bonobo and chimpanzee. I. Comprehension. *Language & Communication, 15,* 121–148.

Branch, M. N., & Hackenberg, T. D. (1998). Humans are animals, too: Connecting animal research to human behavior and cognition. In W. O'Donohue (Ed.), *Learning and behavior therapy* (pp. 15–35). Boston: Allyn and Bacon.

Brannon, E. M., Cantlon, J. F., & Terrace, H. S. (2006). The role of reference points in ordinal numerical comparisons by rhesus macaques (*Macaca mulatta*). *Journal of Experimental Psychology: Animal Behavior Processes, 32,* 120–134.

Breland, K., & Breland, M. (1961). The misbehavior of organisms. *American Psychologist, 16,* 681–684.

Briggs, J. F., & Riccio, D. C. (2007). Retrograde amnesia for extinction: Similarities with amnesia for original acquisition memories. *Learning & Behavior, 35,* 131–140.

Brogden, W. J., Lipman, E. A., & Culler, E. (1938). The role of incentive in conditioning and extinction. *American Journal of Psychology, 51,* 109–117.

Brooks, D. C. (2000). Recent and remote extinction cues reduce spontaneous recovery. *Quarterly Journal of Experimental Psychology, 53B,* 25–58.

Brooks, D. C., & Bouton, M. E. (1993). A retrieval cue for extinction attenuates spontaneous recovery. *Journal of Experimental Psychology: Animal Behavior Processes, 19,* 77–89.

Brooks, D. C., & Bouton, M. E. (1994). A retrieval cue for extinction attenuates response recovery caused by a return to the conditioning context. *Journal of Experimental Psychology: Animal Behavior Processes, 20,* 366–379.

Brooks, D. C., Bowker, J. L., Anderson, J. E., & Palmatier, M. I. (2003). Impact of brief or extended extinction of a taste aversion in inhibitory associations: Evidence from summation, retardation, and preference tests. *Learning & Behavior, 31,* 69–84.

Brooks, D. C., Palmatier, M. I., Garcia, E. O., & Johnson, J. L. (1999). An extinction cue reduces spontaneous recovery of a conditioned taste aversion. *Animal Learning & Behavior, 27,* 77–88.

Brooks, D. I., Wasserman, E. A. (2008). Same/different discrimination learning with trial-unique stimuli. *Psychonomic Bulletin & Review, 15,* 644–650.

Brown, B. L., Hemmes, N. S., & de Vaca, S. C. (1997). Timing of the CS-US interval by pigeons in trace and delay autoshaping. *Quarterly Journal of Experimental Psychology, 50B,* 40–53.

Brown, G. S., & White, K. G. (2005). On the effects of signaling reinforcer probability and magnitude in delayed matching to sample. *Journal of the Experimental Analysis of Behavior, 83,* 119–128.

Brown, J. S. (1969). Factors affecting self-punitive behavior. In B. Campbell & R. M. Church (Eds.), *Punishment and aversive behavior.* New York: Appleton-Century-Crofts.

Brown, J. S., & Cunningham, C. L. (1981). The paradox of persisting self-punitive behavior. *Neuroscience & Biobehavioral Reviews, 5,* 343–354.

Brown, J. S., & Jacobs, A. (1949). The role of fear in the motivation and acquisition of responses. *Journal of Experimental Psychology, 39,* 747–759.

Brown, M. F., Farley, R. F., & Lorek, E. J. (2007). Remembrance of places you passed: Social spatial working memory in rats. *Journal of Experimental Psychology: Animal Behavior Processes, 33,* 213–224.

Brown, M. F., Wheeler, E. A., & Riley, D. A. (1989). Evidence for a shift in the choice criterion of rats in a 12–arm radial maze. *Animal Learning & Behavior, 17,* 12–20.

Brown, P. L., & Jenkins, H. M. (1968). Auto-shaping the pigeon's key peck. *Journal of the Experimental Analysis of Behavior, 11,* 1–8.

Budzynski, C. A., & Bingman, V. P. (1999). Time-of-day discriminative learning in homing pigeons, *Columba livia. Animal Learning & Behavior, 27,* 295–302.

Buhusi, C. V., & Meck, W. H. (2005) What makes us tick? Functional and neural mechanisms of interval timing. *Nature Reviews Neuroscience, 6,* 755–765.

Bulow, P. J., & Meller, P. J. (1998). Predicting teenage girls' sexual activity and contraception use: An application of matching law. *Journal of Community Psychology, 26,* 581–596.

Burkhard, B., Rachlin, H., & Schrader, S. (1978). Reinforcement and punishment in a closed system. *Learning and Motivation, 9,* 392–410.

Burns, M., & Domjan, M. (1996). Sign tracking versus goal tracking in the sexual conditioning of male Japanese quail (*Coturnix japonica*). *Journal of Experimental Psychology: Animal Behavior Processes, 22,* 297–306.

Burns, M., & Domjan, M. (2000). Sign tracking in domesticated quail with one trial a day: Generality across CS and US parameters. *Animal Learning & Behavior, 28,* 109–119.

Burns, M., & Domjan, M. (2001). Topography of spatially directed conditioned responding: Effects of context and trial duratin. *Journal of Experimental Psychology: Animal Behavior Processes, 27,* 269–278.

Byrne, J. H. (Ed.) (2008). *Learning and Memory: A comprehensive Reference.* (Vols. 1–4). Oxford: Elsevier.

Cadieu, N., El Ghadraoui, L., & Cadieu, J.-C. (2000). Egg-laying preference for ethanol involving learning has adaptive significance in *Drosophila melanogaster. Animal Learning & Behavior, 28,* 187–194.

Cain, C. K., & LeDoux, J. E. (2007). Escape from fear: A detailed behavioral analysis of two atypical responses reinforced by CS termination. *Journal of Experimental Psychology: Animal Behavior Processes, 33,* 451–463.

Cain, C. K., Blouin, A. M., & Barad, M. (2003). Temporally massed CS presentations generate more fear extinction than spaced presentations. *Journal of Experimental Psychology: Animal Behavior Processes, 29,* 323–333.

Cameron, J., & Pierce, W. D. (1994). Reinforcement, reward, and intrinsic motivation: A meta-analysis. *Review of Educational Research, 64,* 363–423.

Cameron, J., Banko, K. M., & Pierce, W. D. (2001). Pervasive negative effects of rewards on intrinsic motivation: The myth continues. *The Behavior Analyst, 24,* 1–44.

Camhi, J. M. (1984). *Neuroethology.* Sunderland, MA: Sinauer.

Camp, D. S., Raymond, G. A., & Church, R. M. (1967). Temporal relationship between response and punishment. *Journal of Experimental Psychology, 74,* 114–123.

Campbell, B. A., & Church, R. M. (Eds.). (1969). Punishment and aversive behavior. New York: Appleton-Century-Crofts.

Campbell, B. A., & Randall, P. K. (1976). The effect of reinstatement stimulus conditions on the maintenance of long-term memory. *Developmental Psychobiology, 9,* 325–333.

Campolattaro, M. M., Schnitker, K. M., & Freeman, J. H. (2008). Changes in inhibition during differential eyeblink conditioning with increased training. *Learning & Behavior, 36,* 159–165.

Cándido, A., González, F., & de Brugada, I. (2004). Safety signals from avoidance learning but not from yoked classical conditioning training pass both summation and retardation tests of inhibition. *Behavioural Processes, 66,* 153–160.

Cándido, A., Maldonado, A., & Vila, J. (1991). Effects of duration of feedback on signaled avoidance. *Animal Learning & Behavior, 19,* 81–87.

Capaldi, E. D., Hunter, M. J., & Lyn, S. A. (1997). Conditioning with taste as the CS in conditioned flavor preference learning. *Animal Learning & Behavior, 25,* 427–436.

Capaldi, E. J. (1967). A sequential hypothesis of instrumental learning. In K. W. Spence & J. T. Spence (Eds.), *The psychology of learning and motivation* (Vol. 1, pp. 67–156). New York: Academic Press.

Capaldi, E. J. (1971). Memory and learning: A sequential viewpoint. In W. K. Honig & P. H. R. James (Eds.), *Animal memory* (pp. 115–154). New York: Academic Press.

Capaldi, E. J., Alptekin, S., & Birmingham, K. M. (1996). Instrumental performance and time between reinforcements: Intimate relation to learning or memory retrieval? *Animal Learning & Behavior, 24,* 211–220.

Capaldi, E. J., Alptekin, S., Miller, D. J., & Barry, K. (1992). The role of instrumental responses in memory retrieval in a T-maze. *Quarterly Journal of Experimental Psychology, 45B,* 65–76.

Carew, T. J., Hawkins, R. D., & Kandel, E. R. (1983). Differential classical conditioning of a defensive withdrawal reflex in Aplysia californica. *Science, 219,* 397–400.

Carlson, C. L., & Tamm, L. (2000). Responsiveness of children with attention deficit-hyperactivity disorder to reward and response cost: Differential impact on performance and motivation. *Journal of Consulting and Clinical Psychology, 68,* 73–83.

Carr, D., & Blackman, D. E. (2001). Relations among equivalence, naming, and conflicting baseline control. *Journal of the Experimental Analysis of Behavior, 75,* 55–76.

Carr, D., Wilkinson, K. M., Blackman, D., & McIlvane, W. J. (2000). Equivalence classes in individuals with minimal verbal repertoires. *Journal of the Experimental Analysis of Behavior, 74,* 101–114.

Carrell, L. E., Cannon, D. S., Best, M. R., & Stone, M. J. (1986). Nausea and radiation-induced taste aversions in cancer patients. *Appetite, 7,* 203–208.

Carroll, M. E., & Overmier, J. B. (Eds.) (2001). *Animal research and human health.* Washington, DC: American Psychological Association.

Carter, M. M., Hollon, S. D., Carson, R., & Shelton, R. C. (1995). Effects of a safe person on induced distress following a biological challenge in panic disorder with agoraphobics. *Journal of Abnormal Psychology, 104,* 156–163.

Catania, A. C. (1999). Thorndike's legacy: Learning, selection, and the law of effect. *Journal of the Experimental Analysis of Behavior, 72,* 425–428.

Chance, P. (1999). Thorndike's puzzle boxes and the origins of the experimental analysis of behavior. *Journal of the Experimental Analysis of Behavior, 72,* 433–440.

Chamizo, V. D., Rodrigo, T., Mackintosh, N. J. (2006). Spatial integration with rats. *Learning & Behavior, 34,* 348–354.

Chang, R. C. Blaisdell, A. P., & Miller, R. R. (2003). Backward conditioning: Mediation by context. *Journal of Experimental Psychology: Animal Behavior Processes, 29,* 171–183.

Chappell, J., & Kacelnik, A. (2002). Tool selectivity in a non-primate, the New Caledonian crow (*Corvus moneduloides*). *Animal Cognition, 5,* 71–78.

Charlop, M. H., Kurtz, P. F., & Casey, F. G. (1990). Using aberrant behaviors as reinforcers for autistic children. *Journal of Applied Behavior Analysis, 23,* 163–181.

Chase, A. R. (2001). Music discrimination by carp (*Cyprinus carpio*). *Animal Learning & Behavior, 29,* 336–353.

Chelonis, J. J., Calton, J. L., Hart, J. A., & Schachtman, T. R. (1999). Attenuation of the renewal effect by extinction in multiple contexts. *Learning and Motivation, 30,* 1–14.

Chen, J.-S., & Amsel, A. (1980). Learned persistence at 11–12 but not at 10–11 days in infant rats. *Developmental Psychobiology, 13,* 481–491.

Cheng, K., & Crystal, J. D. (2008). Learning to time intervals. In R. Menzel (Ed.), *Learning theory and behavior.* Vol. 1 of J. Byrne (Ed.), *Learning and Memory: A comprehensive reference.* (pp. 341–364). Oxford: Elsevier.

Cheng, K., & Newcombe, N. S. (2005). Is there a geometric module for spatial orientation? Squaring theory and evidence. *Psychonomic Bulletin & Review, 12,* 1–23.

Cheng, K., & Spetch, M. L. (1995). Stimulus control in the use of landmarks by pigeons in a touch-screen task. *Journal of the Experimental Analysis of Behavior, 63,* 187–201.

Cheng, K., & Spetch, M. L. (2002). Spatial generalization and peak shift in humans. *Learning and Motivation, 33,* 358–389.

Chomsky, N. (1972). *Language and mind.* New York: Harcourt Brace Jovanovich.

Church, R. M. (1963). The varied effects of punishment on behavior. *Psychological Review, 70,* 369–402.

Church, R. M. (1969). Response suppression. In B. A. Campbell & R. M. Church (Eds.), *Punishment and aversive behavior* (pp. 111–156). New York: Appleton Century-Crofts.

Church, R. M. (2003). A concise introduction to scalar timing theory. In W. H. Meck (Ed.) *Functional and neural mechanisms of interval timing* (pp. 2–21). Boca Raton, FL: CRC Press.

Church, R. M. (2006). Behavioristic, cognitive, biological, and quantitative explanations of timing. In E. A. Wasserman and T. R. Zentall (Eds.) *Comparative cognition* (pp. 249–269). Oxford, UK: Oxford University Press.

Church, R. M., Getty, D. J., & Lerner, N. D. (1976). Duration discrimination by rats. *Journal of Experimental Psychology: Animal Behavior Processes, 2,* 303–312.

Church, R. M., Meck, W. H., & Gibbon, J. (1994). Application of scalar timing theory to individual trials. *Journal of Experimental Psychology: Animal Behavior Processes, 20,* 135–155.

Clark, R. E., & Squire, L. R. (1998). Classical conditioning and brain systems: The role of awareness. *Science, 280,* 77–81.

Clayton, N. S., & Dickinson, A. (1999). Scrub jays (*Aphelocoma coerulescens*) remember the relative time of caching as well as the location and content of their caches. *Journal of Comparative Psychology, 113,* 403–416.

Clayton, N. S., Bussey, T. J., & Dickinson, A. (2003). Can animals recall the past and plan for the future? *Nature Reviews Neuroscience, 4,* 685–691.

Cleland, G. G., & Davey, G. C. L. (1982). The effects of satiation and reinforcer devaluation on signal centered behavior in the rat. *Learning and Motivation, 13,* 343–360.

Cleland, G. G., & Davey, G. C. L. (1983). Autoshaping in the rat: The effects of localizable visual and auditory signals for food. *Journal of the Experimental Analysis of Behavior, 40,* 47–56.

Clement, T. S., & Zentall, T. R. (2000). Development of a single-code/default coding strategy in pigeons. *Psychological Science, 11,* 261–264.

Cole, M. R. (1994). Response-rate differences in variable-interval and variable-ratio schedules: An old problem revisited. *Journal of the Experimental Analysis of Behavior, 61,* 441–451.

Cole, M. R. (1999). Molar and molecular control in variable-interval and variable-ratio schedules. *Journal of the Experimental Analysis of Behavior, 71,* 319–328.

Cole, M. R., & Chappell-Stephenson, R. (2003). Exploring the limits of spatial memory in rats, using very large mazes. *Learning & Behavior, 31,* 349–368.

Cole, R. P., Barnet, R. C., & Miller, R. R. (1995). Temporal encoding in trace conditioning. *Animal Learning & Behavior, 23,* 144–153.

Cole, R. P., Barnet, R. C., & Miller, R. R. (1997). An evaluation of conditioned inhibition as defined by Rescorla's two-test strategy. *Learning and Motivation, 28,* 323–341.

Colombo, M., & Frost, N. (2001). Representation of serial order in humans: A comparison to the findings with monkeys (*Cebus apella*). *Psychonomic Bulletin & Review, 8,* 262–269.

Colwill, R. M., & Delamater, B. A. (1995). An associative analysis of instrumental biconditional discrimination learning. *Animal Learning & Behavior, 23,* 218–233.

Colwill, R. M., & Motzkin, D. K. (1994). Encoding of the unconditioned stimulus in Pavlovian conditioning. *Animal Learning & Behavior, 22,* 384–394.

Colwill, R. M., & Rescorla, R. A. (1986). Associative structures in instrumental learning. In G. H. Bower (Ed.), *The psychology of learning and motivation* (Vol. 20, pp. 55–104). Orlando, FL: Academic Press.

Colwill, R. M., & Rescorla, R. A. (1990). Evidence for the hierarchical structure of instrumental learning. *Animal Learning & Behavior, 18,* 71–82.

Colwill, R. M., Goodrum, K., & Martin, A. (1997). Pavlovian appetitive discriminative conditioning in *Aplysia californica. Animal Learning & Behavior, 25,* 268–276.

Conklin, C. A., & Tiffany, S. T. (2002). Applying extinction research and theory to cue-exposure addiction treatments. *Addiction, 97,* 155–167.

Conn, P. M., & Parker, J. (1998). Animal rights: Reaching the public. *Science, 282,* 1417.

Cook, R. G., & Wasserman, E. A. (2006). Relational discrimination learning in pigeons. In E. A. Wasserman and T. R. Zentall (Eds.) *Comparative cognition* (pp. 307–324). Oxford, UK: Oxford University Press.

Cook, R. G., & Wasserman, E. A. (2007). Learning and transfer of relational matching-to-sample. *Psychonomic Bulletin & Review, 14,* 1107–1114.

Cook, R. G., Brown, M. F., & Riley, D. A. (1985). Flexible memory processing by rats: Use of prospective and retrospective information in the radial maze. *Journal of Experimental Psychology: Animal Behavior Processes, 11,* 453–469.

Cook, R. G., Levison, D. G., Gillett, S. R., Blaisdell, A. P. (2005). Capacity and limits of associative memory in pigeons. *Psychonomic Bulletin & Review, 12,* 350–358.

Courville, A. C., Daw, N. D., & Touretzky, D. S., (2006). Bayesian theories of conditioning in a changing world. *Trends in Cognitive Sciences, 10,* 294–300.

Craig, W. (1918). Appetites and aversions as constituents of instinct. *Biological Bulletin, 34,* 91–107.

Craske, M. G. (1999). *Anxiety disorders: Psychological approaches to theory and treatment.* Boulder, CO: Westview Press.

Craske, M. G., & Mystkowski, J. L. (2006). Exposure therapy and extinction: Clinical studies. In M. G. Craske, D. Hermans, and D. Vansteenwegen (Eds.), *Fear and learning* (pp. 217–233). Washington, DC: American Psychological Association.

Craske, M. G., & Waters, A. M. (2005). Panic disorder, phobias, and generalized anxiety disorder. *Annual Review of Clinical Psychology, 1,* 197–225.

Craske, M. G., Glover, D., & DeCola, J. (1995). Predicted versus unpredicted panic attacks: Acute versus general distress. *Journal of Abnormal Psychology, 104,* 214–223.

Craske, M. G., Hermans, D., & Vansteenwegen, D. (Eds.) (2006). *Fear and learning.* Washington, DC: American Psychological Association.

Crespi, L. P. (1942). Quantitative variation in incentive and performance in the white rat. *American Journal of Psychology, 55,* 467–517.

Critchfield, T. S., & Kollins, S. H. (2001). Temporal discounting: Basic research and the analysis of socially important behavior. *Journal of Applied Behavior Analysis, 34,* 101–122.

Critchfield, T. S., & Lattal, K. A. (1993). Acquisition of a spatially defined operant with delayed reinforcement. *Journal of the Experimental Analysis of Behavior, 59,* 373–387.

Critchfield, T. S., Paletz, E. M., MacAleese, K. R., & Newland, M. C. (2003). Punishment in human choice: Direct or competitive suppression? *Journal of the Experimental Analysis of Behavior, 80,* 1–27.

Critchfield, T. S., Haley, R., Sabo, B., Colbert, J., & Macropoulis, G. (2003). A half century of scalloping in the work habits of the United States Congress. *Journal of Applied Behavior Analysis, 36,* 465–486.

Cronin, P. B. (1980). Reinstatement of post response stimuli prior to reward in delayed-reward discrimination learning by pigeons. *Animal Learning & Behavior, 8,* 352–358.

Crookes, A. E., & Moran, P. M. (2003). An investigation into age and gender differences in human Kamin blocking, using a computerized task. *Developmental Neuropsychology, 24,* 461–477.

Crossman, E. K., Bonem, E. J., & Phelps, B. J. (1987). A comparison of response patterns on fixed-, variable-, and random-ratio schedules. *Journal of the Experimental Analysis of Behavior, 48,* 395–406.

Crown, E. D., & Grau, J. W. (2001). Preserving and restoring behavioral potential within the spinal cord using an instrumental training paradigm. *Journal of Neurophysiology, 86,* 845–855.

Crystal, J. D. (2006). Sensitivity to time: Implications for the representation of time. In E. A. Wasserman and T. R. Zentall (Eds.) *Comparative cognition* (pp. 270–284). Oxford, UK: Oxford University Press.

Crystal, J. D., & Baramidze, G. T. (2007). Endogenous oscillations in short-interval timing. *Behavioural Processes, 74,* 152–158.

Cumming, W. W. (1999). A review of Geraldine Jončič's *The sane positivist: A biography of Edward L. Thorndike. Journal of the Experimental Analysis of Behavior, 72,* 429–432.

Cunningham, C. L. (1979). Alcohol as a cue for extinction: State dependency produced by conditioned inhibition. *Animal Learning & Behavior, 7,* 45–52.

Cusato, B., & Domjan, M. (1998). Special efficacy of sexual conditioned stimuli that include species typical cues: Tests with a CS preexposure design. *Learning and Motivation, 29,* 152–167.

Cusato, B., & Domjan, M. (2000). Facilitation of appetitive conditioning with naturalistic conditioned stimuli: CS and US factors. *Animal Learning and Behavior, 28,* 247–256.

Dallery, J., Soto, P. L., & McDowell, J. J. (2005). A test of the formal and modern theories of matching. *Jour-*

nal of the Experimental Analysis of Behavior, 84, 129–145.

Dally, J. M., Emery, N. J., & Clayton, N. S. (2006). Food caching Western scrub-jays keep track of who was watching when. Science, 312, 1662–1665.

Daman-Wasserman, M., Brennan, B., Radcliffe, F., Prigot, J., & Fagen, J. (2006). Auditory-visual context and memory retrieval in 3–month-old infants. Infancy, 10, 201–220.

D'Amato, M. R. (1973). Delayed matching and short-term memory in monkeys. In G. H. Bower (Ed.), The psychology of learning and motivation (Vol. 7, pp. 227–269). New York: Academic Press.

D'Amato, M. R., & Colombo, M. (1985). Auditory matching-to-sample in monkeys (Cebus apella). Animal Learning & Behavior, 13, 375–382.

D'Amato, M. R., & Colombo, M. (1988). Representation of serial order in monkeys (Cebus apella). Journal of Experimental Psychology: Animal Behavior Processes, 14, 131–139.

D'Amato, M. R., & Salmon, D. P. (1982). Tune discrimination in monkeys (Cebus apella) and in rats. Animal Learning & Behavior, 10, 126–134.

D'Amato, M. R., Fazzaro, J., & Etkin, M. (1968). Anticipatory responding and avoidance discrimination as factors in avoidance conditioning. Journal of Comparative and Physiological Psychology, 77, 41–47.

Dardano, J. F., & Sauerbrunn, D. (1964). An aversive stimulus as a correlated block counter in FR performance. Journal of the Experimental Analysis of Behavior, 7, 37–43.

Darwin, C. (1897). The descent of man and selection in relation to sex. New York: Appleton-Century-Crofts.

Davey, G. C. L., & Cleland, G. G. (1982). Topography of signal-centered behavior in the rat: Effects of deprivation state and reinforcer type. Journal of the Experimental Analysis of Behavior, 38, 291–304.

Davey, G. C. L., Phillips, S., & Cleland, G. G. (1981). The topography of signal-centered behaviour in the rat: The effects of solid and liquid food reinforcers. Behaviour Analysis Letters, 1, 331–337.

Davidson, T. L., Aparicio, J., & Rescorla, R. A. (1988). Transfer between Pavlovian facilitators and

instrumental discriminative stimuli. Animal Learning & Behavior, 16, 285–291.

Davidson, T. L., Flynn, F. W., & Jarrard, L. E. (1992). Potency of food deprivation intensity cues as discriminative stimuli. Journal of Experimental Psychology: Animal Behavior Processes, 18, 174–181.

Davis, E. R., & Platt, J. R. (1983). Contiguity and contingency in the acquisition and maintenance of an operant. Learning and Motivation, 14, 487–512.

Davis, H. (1968). Conditioned suppression: A survey of the literature. Psychonomic Monograph Supplements, 2 (14, Whole No. 30), 283–291.

Davis, M. (1974). Sensitization of the rat startle response by noise. Journal of Comparative and Physiological Psychology, 87, 571–581.

Davis, M. (1989). Sensitization of the acoustic startle reflex by footshock. Behavioral Neuroscience, 103, 495–503.

Davis, M. (1997). The neurophysiological basis of acoustic startle modulation: Research on fear motivation and sensory gating. In P. J. Lang, R. F. Simons, and M. T. Balaban (Eds.) Attention and orienting: Sensory and motivational processes (pp. 69–96). Mahwah, NJ: Erlbaum.

Davis, H. P., & Squire, L. R. (1984). Protein synthesis and memory: A review. Psychological Bulletin, 96, 518–559.

Davis, M., Myers, K. M., Ressler, K. J., & Rothbaum, B. O. (2005). Facilitation of extinction of conditioned fear by D-cycloserine. Current Directions in Pschological Science, 14, 214–219.

Davis, R. L. (1996). Physiology and biochemistry of Drosophila learning mutants. American Physiological Society, 76, 299–317.

Davison, M., & Baum, W. M. (2003). Every reinforcer counts: Reinforcer magnitude and local preference. Journal of the Experimental Analysis of Behavior, 80, 95–129.

Davison, M., & McCarthy, D. (1988). The matching law: A research review. Hillsdale, NJ: Erlbaum.

Davison, M., & Nevin, J. A. (1999). Stimuli, reinforcers, and behavior: An integration. Journal of the Experimental Analysis of Behavior, 71, 439–482.

De Houwer, J., Thomas, S., & Baeyens, F. (2001). Associative learning of

likes and dislikes: A review of 25 years of research on human evaluative conditioning. Psychological Bulletin, 127, 853–869.

de Kort, S. R., Dickinson, A., & Clayton, N. S. (2005). Retrospective cognition by food-caching Western scrub-jays. Learning and Motivation, 36, 159–176.

de Kort, S. R., Tebbich, S., Dally, J. M., Emery, N. J., & Clayton, N. S. (2006). The comparative cognition of caching. In E. A. Wasserman and T. R. Zentall (Eds.) Comparative cognition (pp. 602–615). Oxford, UK: Oxford University Press.

Dean, S. J., & Pittman, C. M. (1991). Self-punitive behavior: A revised analysis. In M. R. Denny (Ed.), Fear, avoidance and phobias (pp. 259–284). Hillsdale, NJ: Erlbaum.

DeCarlo, L. T. (1985). Matching and maximizing with variable-time schedules. Journal of the Experimental Analysis of Behavior, 43, 75–81.

Declercq, M., & De Houwer, J. (2008). On the role of US expectancies in avoidance behavior. Psychonomic Bulletin & Review, 15, 99–102.

DeCola, J. P., & Rosellini, R. A. (1990). Unpredictable/ uncontrollable stress proactively interferes with appetitive Pavlovian conditioning. Learning and Motivation, 21, 137–152.

DeFulio, A., & Hackenberg, T. D. (2007). Discriminated timeout avoidance in pigeons: The roles of added stimuli. Journal of the Experimental Analysis of Behavior, 88, 51–71.

DeGrandpre, R. J., Bickel, W. K., Rizvi, S. A. T., & Hughes, J. R. (1993). Effect of income on drug choice in humans. Journal of the Experimental Analysis of Behavior, 59, 483–500.

Deich, J. D., Allan, R. W., & Zeigler, H. P. (1988). Conjunctive differentiation of gape during food-reinforced keypecking in the pigeon. Animal Learning & Behavior, 16, 268–276.

DeKeyne, A., & Deweer, B. (1990). Interaction between conflicting memories in the rat: Contextual pretest cuing reverses control of behavior by testing context. Animal Learning & Behavior, 18, 1–12.

Delamater, A. R. (2004). Experimental extinction in Pavlovian conditioning: Behavioural and neuroscience perspectives. Quarterly Journal *of Experimental Psychology, 57B,* 97–132.

Delamater, A. R. (1996). Effects of several extinction treatments upon the integrity of Pavlovian stimulus–outcome associations. *Animal Learning & Behavior, 24,* 437–449.

Delamater, A. R., Campese, V., LoLordo, V. M., & Sclafani, A. (2006). Unconditioned stimulus devaluation effects in nutrient-conditioned flavor preferences. *Journal of Experimental Psychology: Animal Behavior Processes, 32,* 295–306.

Delameter, A. R., & Holland, P. C. (2008). The influence of CS-US interval on several different indices of learning in appetitive conditioning. *Journal of Experimental Psychology: Animal Behavior Processes, 34,* 202–222.

Delgado, M. R., Olsson, A., & Phelps, E. A. (2006). Extending animal models of fear conditioning to humans. *Biological Psychiatry, 73,* 39–48.

Delius, J. D., Jitsumori, M., & Siemann, M. (2000). Stimulus equivalencies through discrimination reversals. In C. Heyes and L. Huber (Eds.) *The evolution of cognition* (pp. 103–122). Cambridge, MA: Bradford/MIT Press.

Denniston, J. C., Blaisdell, A. P., & Miller, R. R. (2004). Temporal coding in conditioned inhibtion: Analysis of associative structure of inhibition. *Journal of Experimental Psychology: Animal Behavior Processes, 30,* 190–202.

Denniston, J. C., Savastano, H. I., & Miller, R. R. (2001). The extended comparator hypothesis: Learning by contiguity, responding by relative strength. In R. R. Mowrer and S. B. Klein (Eds.). *Handbook of contemporary learning theories* (pp. 65–117). Mahwah, NJ: Erlbaum.

Deroche-Gamonet, V., Belin, D., & Piazza, P. V. (2004). Evidence for addiction-like behavior in the rat. *Science, 305,* 1014–1017.

de Vaca, S. C., Brown, B. L., & Hemmes, N. S. (1994). Internal clock and memory processes in animal timing. *Journal of Experimental Psychology: Animal Behavior Processes, 20,* 184–198.

deVilliers, P. A. (1974). The law of effect and avoidance: A quantitative relationship between response rate and shock-frequency reduction.

Journal of the Experimental Analysis of Behavior, 21, 223–235.

DeVito, P. L., & Fowler, H. (1987). Enhancement of conditioned inhibition via an extinction treatment. *Animal Learning & Behavior, 15,* 448–454.

Dewsbury, D. A. (1998). Celebrating E. L. Thorndike a century after *Animal intelligence. American Psychologist, 53,* 1121–1124.

Dickinson, A., & Balleine, B. (1994). Motivational control of goal-directed behavior. *Animal Learning & Behavior, 22,* 1–18.

Dickinson, A., & Brown, K. J. (2007). Flavor-evaluative conditioning is unaffected by contingency knowledge during training with color-flavor compounds. *Learning & Behavior, 35,* 36–42.

Dickinson, A., Balleine, B., Watt, A., Gonzalez, F., & Boakes, R. A. (1995). Motivational control after extended instrumental training. *Animal Learning & Behavior, 23,* 197–206.

Dickinson, A., Nicholas, D. J., & Macintosh, N. J. (1983). A re-examination of one-trial blocking in conditioned suppression. *Quarterly Journal of Experimental Psychology, 35,* 67–79.

Dickinson, A., Watt, A., & Griffiths, W. J. H. (1992). Free-operant acquisition with delayed reinforcement. *The Quarterly Journal of Experimental Psychology, 45B,* 241–258.

Didden, R., Prinsen, H., & Sigafoos, J. (2000). The blocking effect of pictorial prompts on sight-word reading. *Journal of Applied Behavior Analysis, 33,* 317–320.

DiGian, K. A., & Zentall, T. R. (2007). Pigeons may not use dual coding in the radial maze analog task. *Journal of Experimental Psychology: Animal Behavior Processes, 33,* 262–272.

Dinsmoor, J. A. (1952). A discrimination based on punishment. *Quarterly Journal of Experimental Psychology, 4,* 27–45.

Dinsmoor, J. A. (1954). Punishment: I. The avoidance hypothesis. *Psychological Review, 61,* 34–46.

Dinsmoor, J. A. (1977). Escape, avoidance, punishment: Where do we stand? *Journal of the Experimental Analysis of Behavior, 28,* 83–95.

Dinsmoor, J. A. (1998). Punishment. In W. O'Donohue (Ed.), *Learning and*

behavior therapy (pp. 188–204). Boston: Allyn Bacon.

Dinsmoor, J. A. (2001a). Still no evidence for temporally extended shock-frequency reduction as a reinforcer. *Journal of the Experimental Analysis of Behavior, 75,* 367–378.

Dinsmoor, J. A. (2001b). Stimuli inevitably generated by behavior that avoids electric shock are inherently reinforcing. *Journal of the Experimental Analysis of Behavior, 75,* 311–333.

Dobrzecka, C., Szwejkowska, G., & Konorski, J. (1966). Qualitative versus directional cues in two forms of differentiation. *Science, 153,* 87–89.

Dollard, J., Miller, N. E., Doob, L. W., Mowrer, O. H., & Sears, R. R. (1939). *Frustration and aggression.* New Haven, CT: Yale University Press.

Domjan, M. (1980). Ingestional aversion learning: Unique and general processes. In J. S. Rosenblatt, R. A. Hinde, C. Beer, & M. Busnel (Eds.), *Advances in the study of behavior* (Vol. 11). New York: Academic Press.

Domjan, M. (1983). Biological constraints on instrumental and classical conditioning: Implications for general process theory. In G. H. Bower (Ed.), *The psychology of learning and motivation* (Vol. 17). New York: Academic Press.

Domjan, M. (1987). Animal learning comes of age. *American Psychologist, 42,* 556–564.

Domjan, M. (1997). Behavior systems and the demise of equipotentiality: Historical antecedents and evidence from sexual conditioning. In M. E. Bouton and M. S. Fanselow (Eds.), *Learning, motivation, and cognition* (pp. 31–51). Washington, DC: American Psychological Association.

Domjan, M. (1998). Going wild in the laboratory: Learning about species typical cues. In D. L. Medin (Ed.), *The Psychology of Learning and Motivation* (Vol. 38, pp. 155–186). San Diego: Academic Press.

Domjan, M. (2003). Stepping out of the box in considering the C/T ratio. *Behavioural Processes, 62,* 103–114.

Domjan, M. (2005). Pavlovian conditioning: A functional perspective. *Annual Review of Psychology, 56,* 179–206.

Domjan, M. (2008). Adaptive specializations and generality of the laws of classical and instrumental conditioning. In R. Menzel (Ed.), *Learning theory and behavior.* Vol. 1 of J. Byrne (Ed.), *Learning and Memory: A comprehensive reference* (pp. 327–340). Oxford: Elsevier.

Domjan, M., Blesbois, E., & Williams, J. (1998). The adaptive significance of sexual conditioning: Pavlovian control of sperm release. *Psychological Science, 9,* 411–415.

Domjan, M., Cusato, B., & Krause, M. (2004). Learning with arbitrary versus ecological conditioned stimuli: Evidence from sexual conditioning. *Psychonomic Bulletin & Review, 11,* 232–246.

Domjan, M., Cusato, B., & Villarreal, R. (2000). Pavlovian Feed-Forward Mechanisms in the Control of Social Behavior. *Behavioral and Brain Sciences, 23,* 235–249.

Doyere, V., Debiec, J., Monfils, M.-H., Schafe, G. E., & LeDoux, J. E. (2007). Synapse-specific reconsolidation of distinct fear memories in the lateral amygdala. *Nature Neuroscience, 10,* 414–416.

Dragoi, V., Staddon, J. E. R., Palmer, R. G., & Buhusi, C. V. (2003). Interval timing as an emergent learning property. *Psychological Review, 110,* 126–144.

Dube, W. V., & McIlvane, W. J. (2001). Behavioral momentum in computer-presented discriminations in individuals with severe mental retardation. *Journal of the Experimental Analysis of Behavior, 75,* 15–23.

Dube, W. V., McIlvane, W. J., Mazzitelli, K., & McNamara, B. (2003). Reinforcer rate effects and behavioral momentum in individuals with developmental disabilities. *American Journal on Mental Retardation, 108,* 134–143.

Ducharme, M. J., & Santi, A. (1993). Alterations in the memory code for temporal events induced by differential outcome expectancies in pigeons. *Animal Learning & Behavior, 21,* 73–81.

Dudai, Y. (1989). The neurobiology of memory: Concepts, findings, trends. Oxford University Press: Oxford.

Dudai, Y. (2004). The neurobiology of consolidation, or, how stable is the engram? *Annual Review of Psychology, 55,* 51–86.

Dudley, R. T., & Papini, M. R. (1995). Pavlovian performance of rats following unexpected reward omissions. *Learning and Motivation, 26,* 63–82.

Dudley, R. T., & Papini, M. R. (1997). Amsel's frustration effect: A Pavlovian replication with control for frequency and distribution of rewards. *Physiology & Behavior, 61,* 627–629.

Dweck, C. S., & Wagner, A. R. (1970). Situational cues and correlation between conditioned stimulus and unconditioned stimulus as determinants of the conditioned emotional response. *Psychonomic Science, 18,* 145–147.

Dworkin, B. R. (1993). *Learning and physiological regulation.* Chicago and London: University of Chicago Press.

Dwyer, D. M. (2005). Reinforcer devaluation in palatability-based learned flavor preferences. *Journal of Experimental Psychology: Animal Behavior Processes, 31,* 487–492.

Edgerton, V. R., Tillakaratne, N. J. K., Bigbee, A. J., de Leon, R. D., & Roy, R. R. (2004). Plasticity of the spinal neural circuitry after injury. *Annual Review of Neuroscience, 27,* 145–167.

Edhouse, W. V., & White, K. G. (1988a). Cumulative proactive interference in animal memory. *Animal Learning & Behavior, 16,* 461–467.

Edhouse, W. V., & White, K. G. (1988b). Sources of proactive interference in animal memory. *Journal of Experimental Psychology: Animal Behavior Processes, 14,* 56–70.

Ehrman, R. N., Robbins, S. J., Childress, A. R., & O'Brien, C. P. (1992). Conditioned responses to cocaine-related stimuli in cocaine abuse patients. *Psychopharmacology, 107,* 523–529.

Eisenberger, R., & Adornetto, M. (1986). Generalized self-control of delay and effort. *Journal of Personality and Social Psychology, 51,* 1020–1031.

Eisenberger, R., & Cameron, J. (1996). Detrimental effects of reward: Reality or Myth? *American Psychologist, 51,* 1153–1166.

Eisenberger, R., & Shanock, L. (2003). Rewards, intrinsic motivation, and creativity: A case study of conceptual and methodological isolation. *Creativity Research Journal, 15,* 121–130.

Eisenberger, R., Karpman, M., & Trattner, J. (1967). What is the necessary and sufficient condition for reinforcement in the contingency situation? *Journal of Experimental Psychology, 74,* 342–350.

Ellins, S. R., Cramer, R. E., & Martin, G. C. (1982). Discrimination reversal learning in newts. *Animal Learning & Behavior, 10,* 301–304.

Ellis, J., & Kvavilashvili, L. (2000). Prospective memory in 2000: Past, present, and future directions. *Applied Cognitive Psychology, 14,* S1–S9.

Ellison, G. D. (1964). Differential salivary conditioning to traces. *Journal of Comparative and Physiological Psychology, 57,* 373–380.

Emmerton, J., & Renner, J. C. (2006). Scalar effects in the visual discrimination of numerosity by pigeons. *Learning & Behavior, 34,* 176–192.

Epstein, L. H., Handley, E. A., Dearing, K. K., Cho, D. D, Roemmich, J. N., Paluch, R. A., Raja, S., Pak, Y., & Spring, B. (2006). Purchases of food in youth. *Psychological Science, 17,* 82–89.

Epstein, L. H., Leddy, J. J., Temple, J. L., & Faith, M. S. (2007). Food reinforcement and eating: A multilevel analysis. *Psychological Bulletin, 133,* 884–906.

Epstein, L. H., Robinson, J. L., Temple, J. L., Roemmich, J. N., Marusewski, A., & Nadbrzuch, R. (2008). Sensitization and habituation of motivated behavior in overweight and non-overweight children. *Learning and Motivation, 39,* 243–255.

Epstein, L. H., Rodefer, J. S., Wisniewski, L., & Caggiula, A. R. (1992). Habituation and dishabituation of human salivary response. *Physiology & Behavior, 51,* 945–950.

Epstein, L. H., Saad, F. G., Giacomelli, A. M., & Roemmich, J. N. (2005). Effects of allocation of attention on habituation to olfactory and visual food stimuli in children. *Physiology & Behavior, 84,* 313–319.

Epstein, L. H., Saad, F. G., Handley, E. A., Roemmich, J. N., Hawk, L. W., & McSweeney, F. K. (2003). Habituation of salivation and motivated responding for food in children. *Appetite, 41,* 283–289.

Escobar, M., & Miller, R. R. (2003). Timing in retroactive interference. *Learning & Behavior, 31,* 257–272.

Escobar, M., Matute, H., & Miller, R. R. (2001). Cues trained apart compete for behavioral control in rats: Convergence with the associative interference literature. *Journal of Experimental Psychology: General, 130,* 97–115.

Esmorís-Arranz, F. J., Pardo-Vázquez, J. L., & Vázquez-Garcia, G. A. (2003). Differential effects of forward or simultaneous conditioned stimulus-unconditioned stimulus intervals on the defensive behavior system of the Norway rat (*Rattus Norvegicus*). *Journal of Experimental Psychology: Animal Behavior Processes, 29,* 334–340.

Estes, W. K. (1943). Discriminative conditioning: I. A discriminative property of conditioned anticipation. *Journal of Experimental Psychology, 32,* 150–155.

Estes, W. K. (1944). An experimental study of punishment. *Psychological Monographs, 57* (3, Whole No. 263).

Estes, W. K. (1948). Discriminative conditioning: II. Effects of a Pavlovian conditioned stimulus upon a subsequently established operant response. *Journal of Experimental Psychology, 38,* 173–177.

Estes, W. K. (1969). Outline of a theory of punishment. In B. A. Campbell & R. M. Church (Eds.), *Punishment and aversive behavior* (pp. 57–82). New York: Appleton-Century-Crofts.

Estes, W. K., & Skinner, B. F. (1941). Some quantitative properties of anxiety. *Journal of Experimental Psychology, 29,* 390–400.

Estévez, A. F., Fuentes, L. J., Mari-Beffa, P., González, C., & Alvarez, D. (2001). The differential outcome effect as a useful tool to improve conditional discrimination learning in children. *Learning and Motivation, 32,* 48–64.

Ettenberg, A. (2004). Opponent process properties of self-administered cocaine. *Neuroscience and Biobehavioral Reviews, 27,* 721–728.

Everitt, B. J., & Robbins, T. W. (2005). Neural systems of reinforcement for drug addiction: From actions to habits to compulsion. *Nature Neuroscience, 8,* 1481–1489.

Falls, W. A., & Davis, M. (1994). Fear-potentiated startle using three conditioned stimulus modalities. *Animal Learning & Behavior, 22,* 379–383.

Fanselow, M. S. (1997). Species-specific defense reactions: Retrospect and prospect. In M. E. Bouton and M. S. Fanselow (Eds.), *Learning, motivation, and cognition* (pp. 321–341). Washington, DC: American Psychological Association.

Fanselow, M. S. (1998). Pavlovian conditioning, negative feedback, and blocking: Mechanisms that regulate association formation. *Neuron, 20,* 625–627.

Fanselow, M. S. (1999). Learning theory and neuropsychology: Configuring their disparate elements in the hippocampus. *Journal of Experimental Psychology: Animal Behavior Processes, 25,* 275–283.

Fanselow, M. S., & Lester, L. S. (1988). A functional behavioristic approach to aversively motivated behavior: Predatory imminence as a determinant of the topography of defensive behavior. In R. C. Bolles & M. D. Beecher (Eds.), *Evolution and learning* (pp. 185–212). Hillsdale, NJ: Erlbaum.

Fanselow, M. S., & Poulos, A. M. (2005). The neuroscience of mammalian associative learning. *Annual Review of Psychology, 56,* 207–234

Fanselow, M. S., Lester, L. S., & Helmstetter, F. J. (1988). Changes in feeding and foraging patterns as an antipredator defensive strategy: A laboratory simulation using aversive stimulation in a closed economy. *Journal of the Experimental Analysis of Behavior, 50,* 361–374.

Farley, J., & Alkon, D. L. (1980). Neural organization predicts stimulus specificity for a retained associative behavioral change. *Science, 210,* 1373–1375.

Farmer-Dougan, V. (1998). A disequilibrium analysis of incidental teaching determining reinforcement effects. *Behavior Modification, 22,* 78–95.

Fath, S. J., Fields, L., Malott, M. K., & Grossett, D. (1983). Response rate, latency, and resistance to change. *Journal of the Experimental Analysis of Behavior, 39,* 267–274.

Feldman, D. T., & Gordon, W. C. (1979). The alleviation of short-term retention decrements with reactivation. *Learning and Motivation, 10,* 198–210.

Felton, M., & Lyon, D. O. (1966). The post-reinforcement pause. *Journal of the Experimental Analysis of Behavior, 9,* 131–134.

Fendt, M., & Fanselow, M. (1999). The neuroanatomical and neurochemical basis of conditioned fear.

Neuroscience and biobehavioral reviews, 23, 743–760.

Ferrara, A., Lejeune, H., & Wearden, J. H. (1997). Changing sensitivity to duration in human scalar timing: An experiment, a review, and some possible explanations. *Quarterly Journal of Experimental Psychology, 50B,* 227–237.

Ferster, C. B., & Skinner, B. F. (1957). *Schedules of Reinforcement.* New York: Appleton-Century-Crofts.

Fetterman, J. G. (1995). The psychophysics of remembered duration. *Animal Learning & Behavior, 23,* 49–62.

Fetterman, J. G. (1996). Dimensions of stimulus complexity. *Journal of Experimental Psychology: Animal Behavior Processes, 22,* 3–18.

Fetsko, L. A., Stebbins, H. E., Gallagher, K. K., & Colwill, R. M. (2005). Acquisition and extinction of facilitation in the C57BL/6J mouse. *Learning & Behavior, 33,* 479–500.

Field, D. P., Tonneau, F., Ahearn, W., & Hineline, P. N. (1996). Preference between variable-ratio and fixed-ratio schedules: Local and extended relations. *Journal of the Experimental Analysis of Behavior, 66,* 283–295.

Fiset, S. (2007). Landmark-based search memory in the domesticated dog (*Canis familiaris*). *Journal of Comparative Psychology, 121,* 345–353.

FitzGerald, R. E., Isler, R., Rosenberg, E., Oettinger, R., & Battig, K. (1985). Maze patrolling by rats with and without food reward. *Animal Learning & Behavior, 13,* 451–462.

Flagel, S. B., Akil, H., & Robinson, T. E. (2008). Individual differences in the attribution of incentive salience to reward-related cues: Implications for addiction, *Neuropharmacology,* in press.

Flaherty, C. F. (1996). *Incentive relativity.* Cambridge, UK: Cambridge University Press.

Flaten, M. A., & Blumenthal, T. D. (1999). Caffeine-associated stimuli elicit conditioned responses: An experimental model of the placebo effect. *Psychopharmacology, 145,* 105–112.

Foa, E. B., Zinbarg, R., & Rothbaum, B. O. (1992). Uncontrollability and unpredictability in post-traumatic stress disorder: An animal model. *Psychological Review, 112,* 218–238.

Foltin, R. W. (1991). An economic analysis of "demand" for food in baboons.

Journal of the Experimental Analysis of Behavior, 56, 445–454.

Foltin, R. W. (1994). Does package size matter? A unit-price analysis of "demand" for food in baboons. *Journal of the Experimental Analysis of Behavior, 62,* 293–306.

Foltin, R. W. (1999). Food and cocaine self-administration by baboons: Effects of alternatives. *Journal of the Experimental Analysis of Behavior, 72,* 215–234.

Foree, D. D., & LoLordo, V. M. (1973). Attention in the pigeon: The differential effects of food-getting vs. shock avoidance procedures. *Journal of Comparative and Physiological Psychology, 85,* 551–558.

Forestell, P. H., & Herman, L. M. (1988). Delayed matching of visual materials by a bottlenosed dolphin aided by auditory symbols. *Animal Learning & Behavior, 16,* 137–146.

Fountain, S. B. (2006). The structure of sequential behavior. In E. A. Wasserman and T. R. Zentall (Eds.) *Comparative cognition* (pp. 439–458). Oxford, UK: Oxford University Press.

Fowler, H., Lysle, D. T., & DeVito, P. L. (1991). Conditioned excitation and conditioned inhibition of fear: Asymmetrical processes as evident in extinction. In M. R. Denny (Ed.), *Fear, avoidance and phobias* (pp. 317–362). Hillsdale, NJ: Erlbaum.

Foxx, R. M., & Azrin, N. H. (1973). The elimination of aubstic self-stimulatory behavior by overcorrection. *Journal of Applied Behavioral Analysis, 6,* 1–14.

France, K. G., & Hudson, S. M. (1990). Behavior management of infant sleep disturbance. *Journal of Applied Behavior Analysis, 23,* 91–98.

Frankel, F. D. (1975). The role of response-punishment contingency in the suppression of a positively reinforced operant. *Learning and Motivation, 6,* 385–403.

Frankland, P. W., & Yeomans, J. S. (1995). Fear-potentiated startle and electrically evoked startle mediated by synapses in rostrolateral midbrain. *Behavioral Neuroscience, 109,* 669–680.

Freeman, J. H., & Nicholson, D. A. (2004). Developmental changes in the neural mechanisms of eyeblink conditioning. *Behavioral and Cognitive Neuroscience Reviews, 3,* 3–13.

Fremouw, T., Herbranson, W. T., & Shimp, C. P. (2002). Dynamic shifts of avian local/global attention. *Animal Cognition, 5,* 233–243.

Friedman, B. X., Blaisdell, A. P., Escobar, M., & Miller, R. R. (1998). Comparator mechanisms and conditioned inhibition: Conditioned stimulus preexposure disrupts Pavlovian conditioned inhibition but not explicitly unpaired inhibition. *Journal of Experimental Psychology: Animal Behavior Processes, 24,* 453–466.

Frisher, M., & Beckett, H. (2006). Drug use desistance. *Criminology and criminal justice, 6,* 127–145.

Gallistel, C. R., & Gibbon, J. (2000). Time, rate, and conditioning. *Psychological Review, 107,* 289–344.

Gallistel, C. R., & Gibbon, J. (2001). Computational versus associative models of simple conditioning. *Current Directions in Psychological Science, 10,* 146–150.

Galluccio, L., & Rovee-Collier, C. (1999). Reinstatement effects on retention at 3 months of age. *Learning and Motivation, 30,* 296–316.

Gallup, G. G., Jr., & Suarez, S. D. (1985). Alternatives to the use of animals in psychological research. *American Psychologist, 40,* 1104–1111.

Gamzu, E. R., & Williams, D. R. (1971). Classical conditioning of a complex skeletal act. *Science, 171,* 923–925.

Gamzu, E. R., & Williams, D. R. (1973). Associative factors underlying the pigeon's key pecking in autoshaping procedures. *Journal of the Experimental Analysis of Behavior, 19,* 225–232.

Gantt, W. H. (1966). Conditional or conditioned, reflex or response? *Conditioned Reflex, 1,* 69–74.

Garber, J., & Seligman, M. E. P. (Eds.). (1980). *Human helplessness: Theory and application.* New York: Academic Press.

Garcia, J., & Koelling, R. A. (1966). Relation of cue to consequence in avoidance learning. *Psychonomic Science, 4,* 123–124.

Garcia, J., Ervin, F. R., & Koelling, R. A. (1966). Learning with prolonged delay of reinforcement. *Psychonomic Science, 5,* 121–122.

Gardner, E. T., & Lewis, P. (1976). Negative reinforcement with shock-frequency increase. *Journal of the Experimental Analysis of Behavior, 25,* 3–14.

Gardner, R. A., & Gardner, B. T. (1969). Teaching sign language to a chimpanzee. *Science, 165,* 664–672.

Gardner, R. A., & Gardner, B. T. (1975). Early signs of language in child and chimpanzee. *Science, 187,* 752–753.

Gardner, R. A., & Gardner, B. T. (1978). Comparative psychology and language acquisition. *Annals of the New York Academy of Science, 309,* 37–76.

Gemberling, G. A., & Domjan, M. (1982). Selective association in one-day-old rats: Taste-toxicosis and textureshock aversion learning. *Journal of Comparative and Physiological Psychology, 96,* 105–113.

Gershoff, E. T. (2002). Parental corporal punishment and associated child behaviors and experiences: A meta-analytic and theoretical review. *Psychological Bulletin, 128,* 539–579.

Gewirtz, J. C., Brandon, S. E., & Wagner, A. R. (1998). Modulation of the acquisition of the rabbit eyeblink conditioned response by conditioned contextual stimuli. *Journal of Experimental Psychology: Animal Behavior Processes, 24,* 106–117.

Gharib, A., Derby, S., & Roberts, S. (2001). Timing and the control of variation. *Journal of Experimental Psychology: Animal Behavior Processes, 27,* 165–178.

Ghirlanda, S., & Enquist, M. (2003). A century of generalization. *Animal Behaviour, 66,* 15–36.

Gibbon, J., & Balsam, P. (1981). Spreading association in time. In C. M. Locurto, H. S. Terrace, & J. Gibbon (Eds.), *Autoshaping and conditioning theory* (pp. 219–253). New York: Academic Press.

Gibbon, J., & Church, R. M. (1984). Sources of variance in an information processing theory of timing. In H. L. Roitblat, T. G. Bever, & H. S. Terrace (Eds.), *Animal cognition.* Hillsdale, NJ: Erlbaum.

Gibson, B. M., & Shettleworth, S. J. (2003). Competition among spatial cues in a naturalistic food-carrying task. *Learning & Behavior, 31,* 143–159.

Gilbert, D. (2006). *Stumbling on happiness.* New York: Afred A. Knopf.

Gillan, D. J., & Domjan, M. (1977). Taste-aversion conditioning with expected versus unexpected drug treatment. *Journal of Experimental*

Psychology: Animal Behavior Processes, 3, 297–309.

Gisiner, R., & Schusterman, R. J. (1992). Sequence, syntax, and semantics: Responses of a language-trained sea lion (*Zalophus californianus*) to novel sign combinations. *Journal of Comparative Psychology, 106,* 78–91.

Gisquet-Verrier, P., & Alexinsky, T. (1990). Facilitative effect of a pretest exposure to the CS: Analysis and implications for the memory trace. *Animal Learning & Behavior, 18,* 323–331.

Glanzman, D. L. (2006). The cellular mechanisms of learning in Aplysia: Of blind men and elephants. *Biological Bulletin, 210,* 271–279.

Gnadt, W., & Grossberg, S. (2007). SOVEREIGN: An autonomous neural system for incrementally learning planned action sequences to navigate toward a rewarded goal. *Neural Networks, 21,* 699–758.

Godsil, B. P., & Fanselow, M. S. (2004). Light stimulus change evokes an activity response in the rat. *Learning & Behavior, 32,* 299–310.

Gold, P. (2008). Memory enhancing drugs. In H. Eichenbaum (Ed.), *Learning and memory: A comprehensive reference. Vol. 3: Memory systems.* (pp.555–576). Oxford: Elsevier.

Goldshmidt, J. N., Lattal, K. M., & Fantino, E. (1998). Context effects on choice. *Journal of the Experimental Analysis of Behavior, 70,* 301–320.

Goodall, G. (1984). Learning due to the response-shock contingency in signalled punishment. *Quarterly Journal of Experimental Psychology, 36B,* 259–279.

Goodall, G., & Mackintosh, N. J. (1987). Analysis of the Pavlovian properties of signals for punishment. *Quarterly Journal of Experimental Psychology, 39B,* 1–21.

Gordon, W. C. (1981). Mechanisms for cue-induced retention enhancement. In N. E. Spear & R. R. Miller (Eds.), *Information processing in animals: Memory mechanisms.* Hillsdale, NJ: Erlbaum.

Gordon, W. C., & Klein, R. L. (1994). Animal memory: The effects of context change on retention performance. In N. J. Mackintosh (Ed.), *Animal learning and cognition* (pp. 255–279). San Diego: Academic Press.

Gordon, W. C., & Mowrer, R. R. (1980). An extinction trial as a reminder treatment following electro-convulsive shock. *Animal Learning & Behavior, 8,* 363–367.

Gordon, W. C., McGinnis, C. M., & Weaver, M. S. (1985). The effect of cuing after backward conditioning trials. *Learning and Motivation, 16,* 444–463.

Gormezano, I. (1966). Classical conditioning. In J. B. Sidowski (Ed.), *Experimental methods and instrumentation in psychology.* New York: McGraw-Hill.

Gormezano, I., Kehoe, E. J., & Marshall, B. S. (1983). Twenty years of classical conditioning research with the rabbit. In J. M. Prague & A. N. Epstein (Eds.), *Progress in psychobiology and physiological psychology* (Vol. 10). New York: Academic Press.

Gosling, S. D. (2001). From mice to men: What can we learn about personality from animal research? *Psychological Bulletin, 127,* 45–86.

Gosling, S. D., John, O. P., Craik, K. H., & Robins, R. W. (1998). Do people know how they behave? Self-reported act frequencies compared with on-line codings by observers. *Journal of Personality and Social Psychology, 74,* 1337–1349.

Gottlieb, D. A. (2004). Acquisition with partial and continuous reinforcement in pigeon autoshaping. *Learning & Behavior, 32,* 321–334.

Gottlieb, D. A. (2008). Is the number of trials a primary determinant of conditioned responding? *Journal of Experimental Psychology: Animal Behavior Processes, 34,* 185–201.

Grace, R. C. (1999). The matching law and amount-dependent exponential discounting as accounts of self-control choice. *Journal of the Experimental Analysis of Behavior, 71,* 27–44.

Grace, R. C., & Nevin, J. A. (2004). Behavioral momentum and Pavlovian conditioning. *Behavioral and Brain Sciences, 27,* 695–697.

Graham, J. M., & Desjardins, C. (1980). Classical conditioning: Induction of luteinizing hormone and testosterone secretion in anticipation of sexual activity. *Science, 210,* 1039–1041.

Grant, D. S. (1976). Effect of sample presentation time on long-delay matching in the pigeon. *Learning and Motivation, 7,* 580–590.

Grant, D. S. (1982). Intratrial proactive interference in pigeon short-term memory: Manipulation of stimulus dimension and dimensional similarity. *Learning and Motivation, 13,* 417–433.

Grant, D. S. (1991). Symmetrical and asymmetrical coding of food and no-food samples in delayed matching in pigeons. *Journal of Experimental Psychology: Animal Behavior Processes, 17,* 186–193.

Grant, D. S. (1993). Coding processes in pigeons. In T. R. Zentall (Ed.). *Animal cognition* (pp. 193–216). Hillsdale, NJ: Erlbaum.

Grant, D. S. (2000). Influence of intertrial interval duration on the intertrial agreement effect in delayed matching-to-sample with pigeons. *Animal Learning & Behavior, 28,* 288–297.

Grau, J. W., Crown, E. D., Ferguson, A. R., Washburn, S. N., Hook, M.A., & Miranda, R. C. (2006). Instrumental learning within the spinal cord: Underlying mechanisms and implications for recovery after injury. *Behavioral and Cognitive Neuroscience Reviews, 5,* 1–48.

Grau, J. W., & Joynes, R. L. (2001). Spinal cord injury: From animal research to human therapy. In M. E. Carroll & J. B. Overmier (Eds.), *Animal research and human health: Advancing human welfare through behavioral science* (pp. 209–226). Washington, DC: American Psychological Association.

Grau, J. W., & Joynes, R. L. (2005). A neural-functionalist approach to learning. *International Journal of Comparative Psychology, 18,* 1–22.

Green, L., & Estle, S. J. (2003). Preference reversals with food and water reinforcers in rats. *Journal of the Experimental Analysis of Behavior, 79,* 233–242.

Green, L., & Freed, D. E. (1998). Behavioral economics. In O'Donohue (Ed.), *Learning and behavior therapy* (pp. 274–300). Boston: Allyn and Bacon.

Greenfield, P. M., & Savage-Rumbaugh, E. S. (1990). Grammatical combination in Pan paniscus: Processes of learning and invention in the evolution and development of language. In S. T. Parker & K. R. Gibson (Eds.), *Language and intelligence in monkeys and apes* (pp. 540–578). Cambridge: Cambridge University Press.

Greenfield, P., & Lyn, H. (2007). Symbol combination in *Pan*: Language, Action, and Culture. In D. A. Washburn (Ed.), *Primate* perspectives on behavior and cognition (pp. 255–267). Washington, DC: American Psychological Association.

Grice, G. R. (1948). The relation of secondary reinforcement to delayed reward in visual discrimination learning. *Journal of Experimental Psychology, 38,* 1–16.

Griffin, D. R. (1976). *The question of animal awareness.* New York: Rockefeller University Press.

Griffin, D. R. (1992). *Animal minds.* Chicago: University of Chicago Press.

Grigson, P. S., Twining, R. C., Freet, C. S., Wheeler, R. A., & Geddes, R. I. (2008). Drug-induced suppression of CS intake: Reward, aversion, and addiction. In Reilly, S., & Schachtman, T. R. (Eds.), (2008). *Conditioned taste aversion: Behavioral and neural processes* (pp. 74–91). New York: Oxford University Press.

Groves, P. M., & Thompson, R. F. (1970). Habituation: A dual-process theory. *Psychological Review, 77,* 419–450.

Groves, P. M., Lee, D., & Thompson, R. F. (1969). Effects of stimulus frequency and intensity on habituation and sensitization in acute spinal cat. *Physiology and Behavior, 4,* 383–388.

Gunther, L. M., Denniston, J. C., & Miller, R. R. (1998). Conducting exposure treatment in multiple contexts can prevent relapse. *Behaviour Research and Therapy, 36,* 75–91.

Gunther, M. (1961). Infant behavior at the breast. In B. Foss (Ed.), *Determinants of infant behavior.* London: Wiley.

Gutiérrez, G., & Domjan, M. (1996). Learning and male-male sexual competition in Japanese quail (*Coturnix japonica*). *Journal of Comparative Psychology, 110,* 170–175.

Guttman, N., & Kalish, H. I. (1956). Discriminability and stimulus generalization. *Journal of Experimental Psychology, 51,* 79–88.

Hackenberg, T. D., & Vaidya, M. (2003). Determinants of pigeons' choices in token-based self-control procedures. *Journal of the Experimental Analysis of Behavior, 79,* 207–218.

Haggbloom, S. J., & Morris, K. M. (1994). Contextual cues and the retrieval of competing memories of goal events. *Animal Learning & Behavior, 22,* 165–172.

Haggbloom, S. J., Lovelace, L., Brewer, V. R., Levins, S. M., Owens, J. D. (1990). Replacement of event-generated memories of nonreinforcement with signal-generated memories of reinforcement during partial reinforcement training: Effects on resistance to extinction. *Animal Learning & Behavior, 18,* 315–322.

Hailman, J. P. (1967). The ontogeny of an instinct. *Behaviour Supplements, 15,* 1–159.

Hake, D. F., & Azrin, N. H. (1965). Conditioned punishment. *Journal of the Experimental Analysis of Behavior, 8,* 279–293.

Hall, G. (1991). *Perceptual and associative learning.* Oxford, England: Clarendon Press.

Hall, G. (2008). Preexposure to the US in nausea-based aversion learning. In S. Reilly and T. R. Schachtman, (Eds.), *Conditioned taste aversion: Behavioral and neural processes* (pp. 58–73). New York: Oxford University Press.

Hall, G., & Honey, R. C. (1989). Contextual effects in conditioning, latent inhibition, and habituation: Associative and retrieval functions of contextual cues. *Journal of Experimental Psychology: Animal Behavior Processes, 15,* 232–241.

Hall, G., Kaye, H., & Pearce, J. M. (1985). Attention and conditioned inhibition. In R. R. Miller & N. E. Spear (Eds.), *Information processing in animals: Conditioned inhibition.* Hillsdale, NJ: Erlbaum.

Hall, R. V., Axelrod, S., Foundopoulos, M., Shellman, J., Campbell, R. A., & Cranston, S. S. (1971). The effective use of punishment to modify behavior in the classroom. *Educational Technology, 11* (4), 24–26.

Hallam, S. C., Grahame, N. J., Harris, K., & Miller, R. R. (1992). Associative structures underlying enhanced negative summation following operational extinction of a Pavlovian inhibitor. *Learning and Motivation, 23,* 43–62.

Hampton, R. R., Hampstead, B. M., & Murray, E. A. (2005). Rhesus monkeys (*Macacamulatta*) demonstrate robust memory for what and where, but not when, in an open-field test of memory. *Learning and Motivation, 36,* 245–259.

Han, C. J., O'Tuathaigh, C. M., van Trigt, L., Quinn, J. J., Fanselow, M.S., Mongeau, R., Koch, C., & Anderson, D. J. (2003) Trace but not delay fear conditioning requires attention and the anterior cingulate cortex *Proceedings of the National Academy of Sciences, USA., 100,* 13087–13092.

Hanley, G. P., Iwata, B. A., Thompson, R. H., & Lindberg, J. S. (2000). A component analysis of "stereotypy as reinforcement" for alternative behavior. *Journal of Applied Behavioral Analysis, 33,* 285–297.

Hanson, H. M. (1959). Effects of discrimination training on stimulus generalization. *Journal of Experimental Psychology, 58,* 321–333.

Hanson, S. J., & Timberlake, W. (1983). Regulation during challenge: A general model of learned performance under schedule constraint. *Psychological Review, 90,* 261–282.

Harris, J. A., Jones, M. L., Bailey, G. K., & Westbrook, R. F. (2000). Contextual control over conditioned responding in an extinction paradigm. *Journal of Experimental Psychology: Animal Behavior Processes, 26,* 174–185.

Harlow, H. F. (1969). Age-mate or peer affectional system. In D. S. Lehrman, R. H. Hinde, & E. Shaw (Eds.), *Advances in the study of behavior* (Vol. 2). New York: Academic Press.

Harper, D. N., & Garry, M. (2000). Postevent cues bias recognition performance in pigeons. *Animal Learning & Behavior, 28,* 59–67.

Hart, B. L. (1973). Reflexive behavior. In G. Bermant (Ed.), *Perspectives in animal behavior.* Glenview, IL: Scott Foresman.

Harvey, L., Inglis, S. J., & Espie, C. A. (2002). Insomniac's reported use of CBT components and relationship to long-term clinical outcome. *Behavioural Research and Therapy, 40,* 75–83.

Haselgrove, M., Aydin, A., Pearce, J. M. (2004). A partial reinforcement extinction effect despite equal rates of reinforcement during Pavlovian conditioning. *Journal of Experimental Psychology: Animal Behavior Processes, 30,* 240–250.

Hastjarjo, T., & Silberberg, A. (1992). Effects of reinforcer delays on choice as a function of income level.

Journal of the Experimental Analysis of Behavior, 57, 119–125.

Haug, M., & Whalen, R. E. (Eds.) (1999). *Animal models of human emotion and cognition.* Washington, DC: American Psychological Association.

Hawkins, R. D., & Kandel, E. R. (1984). Is there a cell-biological alphabet for simple forms of learning? *Psychological Review, 91*, 375–391.

Hawkins, R. D., Kandel, E. R., & Bailey, C. H. (2006). Molecular mecahnisms of memory storage in *Aplysia. Biological Bulletin, 210*, 174–191.

Hayden, A., Bhatt, R. S., Joseph, J. E., & Tanaka, J. W. (2007). The other-race effect in infancy: Evidence using a morphing technique. *Infancy, 12*, 95–104.

Hayes, K. J., & Hayes, C. (1951). The intellectual development of a home-raised chimpanzee. *Proceedings of the American Philosophical Society, 95*, 105–109.

Healy, S. D., & Hurly, R. A. (1995). Spatial memory in rufous hummingbirds (*Selasphorus rufus*): A field test. *Animal Learning & Behavior, 23*, 63–68.

Hearst, E. (1968). Discrimination learning as the summation of excitation and inhibition. *Science, 162*, 1303–1306.

Hearst, E. (1969). Excitation, inhibition, and discrimination learning. In N. J. Mackintosh & W. K. Honig (Eds.), *Fundamental issues in associative learning.* Halifax: Dalhousie University Press.

Hearst, E. (1975). Pavlovian conditioning and directed movements. In G. Bower (Ed.), *The psychology of learning and motivation* (Vol. 9). New York: Academic Press.

Hearst, E., & Jenkins, H. M. (1974). *Sign-tracking: The stimulus-reinforcer relation and directed action.* Austin, TX: Psychonomic Society.

Hebb, D. O. (1949). *The Organization of Behavior.* New York: Wiley.

Heffner, H. E. (1998). Auditory awareness. *Applied Animal Behavioural Science, 57*, 259–268.

Henkel, V., Bussfeld, P., Möller, H. J., & Hegerl, U. (2002). Cognitive-behavioural theories of helplessness/hopelessness: Valid models of depression? *European Archives of Psychiatry and Clinical Neuroscience, 252*, 240–249.

Herbranson, W. T., & Shimp, C. P. (2003). Artificial grammar learning in pigeons: A preliminary analysis. *Learning & Behavior, 31*, 98–106.

Herbranson, W. T., Fremouw, T., & Shimp, C. P. (2002). Categorizing a moving target in terms of its speed and direction. *Journal of the Experimental Analysis of Behavior, 78*, 249–270.

Herman, L. M. (1987). Receptive competencies of language-trained animals. In J. S. Rosenblatt, C. Beer, M.-C. Busnel, & P. J. B. Slater (Eds.), *Advances in the study of behavior* (Vol. 17, pp. 1–60). Orlando, FL: Academic Press.

Herman, L. M., & Uyeyama, R. K. (1999). The dolphin's grammatical competency: Comments on Kako (1999). *Animal Learning & Behavior, 27*, 18–23.

Herman, L. M., Pack, A. A., & Morrel-Samuels, P. (1993). Representational and conceptual skills of dolphins. In Roitblat, H. L., Herman, L. M., & Nachtigall, P. E. (Eds.), *Language and communication: Comparative perspectives* (pp. 403–442). Hillsdale, NJ: Erlbaum.

Herman, R. L., & Azrin, N. H. (1964). Punishment by noise in an alternative response situation. *Journal of the Experimental Analysis of Behavior, 7*, 185–188.

Hernandez, P. J., & Abel, T. (2008). The role of protein synthesis in memory consolidation: Progress amid decades of debate. *Neurobiology of Learning and Memory, 89*, 293–311.

Herrnstein, R. J. (1961). Relative and absolute strength of response as a function of frequency of reinforcement. *Journal of the Experimental Analysis of Behavior, 4*, 267–272.

Herrnstein, R. J. (1969). Method and theory in the study of avoidance. *Psychological Review, 76*, 49–69.

Herrnstein, R. J. (1970). On the law of effect. *Journal of the Experimental Analysis of Behavior, 13*, 243–266.

Herrnstein, R. J. (1997). *The matching law.* (H. Rachlin and D. I. Laibson, Eds.) New York: Russell Sage; and Cambridge: Harvard University Press.

Herrnstein, R. J., & Hineline, P. N. (1966). Negative reinforcement as shock-frequency reduction. *Journal of the Experimental Analysis of Behavior, 9*, 421–430.

Herrnstein, R. J., & Vaughan, W., Jr. (1980). Melioration and behavioral allocation. In J. E. R. Staddon (Ed.), *Limits to action.* New York: Academic Press.

Herrnstein, R. J., Loveland, D. H., & Cable, C. (1976). Natural concepts in pigeons. *Journal of Experimental Psychology: Animal Behavior Processes, 2*, 285–301.

Herzog, H. A., Jr. (1988). The moral status of mice. *American Psychologist, 43*, 473–474.

Heyes, C. (2003). Four routes of cognitive evolution. *Psychological Review, 110*, 713–727.

Heyman, G. M., & Herrnstein, R. J. (1986). More on concurrent interval-ratio schedules: A replication and review. *Journal of the Experimental Analysis of Behavior, 46*, 331–351.

Higgins, S. T., Heil, S. H., & Lussier, J. P. (2004). Clinical implications of reinforcement as a determinant of substance use disorders. *Annual Review of Psychology, 55*, 431–461.

Higgins, S. T., Silverman, K., & Heil, S. H. (2008). *Contingency management in substance abuse treatment.* New York: Guilford Press.

Hilgard, E. R., & Marquis, D. G. (1940). *Conditioning and learning.* New York: Appleton.

Hilliard, S. H., Domjan, M., Nguyen, M., & Cusato, B. (1998). Dissociation of conditioned appetitive and consummatory sexual behavior: Satiation and extinction tests. *Animal Learning & Behavior, 26*, 20–33.

Hillix, W. A., & Rumbaugh, D. (2004). *Animal bodies, human minds: Ape, dolphin, and parrot language skills.* New York: Kluwer academic/Plenum.

Hineline, P. N. (1977). Negative reinforcement and avoidance. In W. K. Honig & J. E. R. Staddon (Eds.), *Handbook of operant behavior.* Englewood Cliffs. NJ: Prentice-Hall.

Hineline, P. N. (1981). The several roles of stimuli in negative reinforcement. In P. Harzem & M. D. Zeiler (Eds.), *Predictability, correlation, and contiguity.* Chichester, England: Wiley.

Hinson, J. M., & Staddon, J. E. R. (1983a). Hill-climbing by pigeons. *Journal of the Experimental Analysis of Behavior, 39*, 25–47.

Hinson, J. M., & Staddon, J. E. R. (1983b). Matching, maximizing, and hill-climbing. *Journal of the*

Experimental Analysis of Behavior, 40, 321–331.

Hintzman, D. L. (1991). Twenty-five years of learning and memory: Was the cognitive revolution a mistake? In D.E. Meyer & S. Kornblum (Eds.), *Attention and performance XIVP.* Hillsdale, NJ: Erlbaum.

Hitchcock, D. F. A., & Rovee-Collier, C. (1996). The effect of repeated reactivations on memory specificity in infancy. *Journal of Experimental Child Psychology, 62,* 378–400.

Hodges, H. (1996). Maze procedures: The radial-arm and water maze compared. *Cognitive Brain Research, 3,* 167–181.

Hoffman, C. M., Timberlake, W., Leffel, J., & Gont, R. (1999). How is radial arm maze behavior in rats related to locomotor search tactics? *Animal Learning & Behavior, 27,* 426–444.

Hoffman, H. S., & Fleshler, M. (1964). An apparatus for the measurement of the startle-response in the rat. *American Journal of Psychology, 77,* 307–308.

Holland, P. C. (1984). Origins of behavior in Pavlovian conditioning. In G. H. Bower (Ed.), *The psychology of learning and motivation* (Vol. 18, pp. 129–174). Orlando, FL: Academic Press.

Holland, P. C. (1985). The nature of conditioned inhibition in serial and simultaneous feature negative discriminations. In R. R. Miller & N. E. Spear (Eds.), *Information processing in animals: Conditioned inhibition.* Hillsdale, NJ: Erlbaum.

Holland, P. C. (1986). Temporal determinants of occasion setting in feature-positive discriminations. *Animal Learning and Behavior, 14,* 111–120.

Holland, P. C. (1989a). Feature extinction enhances transfer of occasion setting. *Animal Learning & Behavior, 17,* 269–279.

Holland, P. C. (1991). Acquisition and transfer of occasion setting in operant feature positive and feature negative discriminations. *Learning and Motivation, 22,* 366–387.

Holland, P. C. (1992). Occasion setting in Pavlovian conditioning. In D. L. Medin (Ed.), *The psychology of learning and motivation* (Vol. 28, pp. 69–125). San Diego, CA: Academic Press.

Holland, P. C. (2000). Trial and inter-trial durations in appetitive condi-

tioning in rats. *Animal Learning & Behavior, 28,* 121–135.

Holland, P. C. (2004). Relations between Pavlovian-instrumental transfer and reinforcer devaluation. *Journal of Experimental Psychology: Animal Behavior Processes, 30,* 104–117.

Holland, P. C., & Kenmuir, C. (2005). Variations in unconditioned stimulus processing in unblocking. *Journal of Experimental Psychology: Animal Behavior Processes, 31,* 155–171.

Holland, P. C., & Rescorla, R. A. (1975). The effect of two ways of devaluing the unconditioned stimulus after first- and second-order appetitive conditioning. *Journal of Experimental Psychology: Animal Behavior Processes, 1,* 355–363.

Holliday, M., & Hirsch, J. (1986). Excitatory conditioning of individual Drosophila melanogaster. *Journal of Experimental Psychology: Animal Behavior Processes, 12,* 131–42.

Hollis, K. L. (1997). Contemporary research on Pavlovian conditioning: A "new" functional analysis. *American Psychologist, 52,* 956–965.

Hollis, K. L., Cadieux, E. L., & Colbert, M. M. (1989). The biological function of Pavlovian conditioning: A mechanism for mating success in the blue gourami (*Trichogaster trichopterus*). *Journal of Comparative Psychology, 103,* 115–121.

Hollis, K. L., Pharr, V. L., Dumas, M. J., Britton, G. B., & Field, J. (1997). Classical conditioning provides paternity advantage for territorial male blue gouramis (*Trichogaster trichopterus*). *Journal of Comparative Psychology, 111,* 219–225.

Holman, J. G., & Mackintosh, N. J. (1981). The control of appetitive instrumental responding does not depend on classical conditioning to the discriminative stimulus. *Quarterly Journal of Experimental Psychology, 33B,* 21–31.

Holz, W. C., & Azrin, N. H. (1961). Discriminative properties of punishment. *Journal of the Experimental Analysis of Behavior, 4,* 225–232.

Honey, R. C., & Hall, G. (1989). Acquired equivalence and distinctiveness of cues. *Journal of Experimental Psychology: Animal Behavior Processes, 15,* 338–346.

Honey, R. C., Willis, A., & Hall, G. (1990). Context specificity in pigeon autoshaping. *Learning and Motivation, 21,* 125–136.

Honig, W. K. (1978). Studies of working memory in the pigeon. In S. H. Hulse, H. Fowler, & W. K. Honig (Eds.), *Cognitive processes in animal behavior.* Hillsdale, NJ: Erlbaum.

Honig, W. K., & Urcuioli, P. J. (1981). The legacy of Guttman and Kalish (1956): 25 years of research on stimulus generalization. *Journal of the Experimental Analysis of Behavior, 36,* 405–445.

Horgen, K. B., & Brownell, K. D. (2002). Comparison of price change and health message interventions in promoting healthy food choices. *Health Psychology, 21,* 505–512.

Hourlhan, K. L., & Taylor, T. L. (2006). Case remembering: Control processes in directed forgetting. *Journal of Experimental Psychology: Human Perception and Performance, 32*(6), 1354–1365.

Hu, C. J., O'Tuathaigh, C. M., van Trigt, L., Quinn, J. J., Fanselow, M. S., Mongeau, R., Koch, C., & Anderson, D. J. (2003). Trace but not delay fear conditioning requires attention and the anterior cingulate cortex. *Proceedings of the National Academy of Sciences, 100,* 13087–13092.

Huber, L., & Aust, U. (2006). A modified feature theory as an account of pigeon visual categorization. In E. A. Wasserman and T. R. Zentall (Eds.), *Comparative cognition* (pp. 325–342). Oxford, UK: Oxford University Press.

Huber, L., Apfalter, W., Steurer, M., & Prosssinger, H. (2005). A new learning paradigm elicits fast visual discrimination in pigeons. *Journal of Experimental Psychology: Animal Behavior Processes, 31,* 237–246.

Hull, C. L. (1930). Knowledge and purpose as habit mechanisms. *Psychological Review, 30,* 511–525.

Hull, C. L. (1931). Goal attraction and directing ideas conceived as habit phenomena. *Psychological Review, 38,* 487–506.

Hulse, S. H. (1958). Amount and percentage of reinforcement and duration of goal confinement in conditioning and extinction. *Journal of Experimental Psychology, 56,* 48–57.

Hulse, S. H., Fowler, H., & Honig, W. K. (Eds.). (1978). *Cognitive processes in animal behavior*. Hillsdale, NJ: Erlbaum.

Hulse, S. H., Page, S. C., & Braaten, R. F. (1990). Frequency range size and the frequency range constraint in auditory perception by European starlings (*sturnus vulgaris*). *Animal Learning & Behavior, 18*, 238–245.

Hunt, G. R., Rutledge, R. B., & Gray, R. D. (2006). The right tool for the job: What stratetgies do wild New Caledonian crows use? *Animal Cognition, 9*, 307–316.

Hunt, P. S. (1997). Retention of conditioned autonomic and behavioral responses in preweanling rats: Forgetting and reinstatement. *Animal Learning & Behavior, 25*, 301–311.

Hunter, W. S. (1913). The delayed reaction in animals and children. *Behavior Monographs, 2*, serial #6.

Hursh, S. R., & Silberberg, A. (2008). Economic demand and essential value. *Psychological Review, 115*, 186–198.

Hursh, S. R., Raslear, T. G., Shurtleff, D., Bauman, R., & Simmons, L. (1988). A cost-benefit analysis of demand for food. *Journal of the Experimental Analysis of Behavior, 50*, 419–440.

Hyman, S. E. (2005). Addiction: A disease of learning and memory. *American Journal of Psychiatry, 162*, 1414–1422.

Hyman, S. E., Malenka, R. C., & Nestler, E. J. (2006). Neural mechanisms of addiction: The role of reward-related learning and memory. *Annual Review of Neuroscience, 29*, 565–598.

Innis, N. K., Simmelhag-Grant, V. L., & Staddon, J. E. R. (1983). Behavior induced by periodic food delivery: The effects of interfood interval. *Journal of the Experimental Analysis of Behavior, 39*, 309–322.

Irwin, M. R., Cole, J. C., & Nicassio, P. M. (2006). Comparative meta-analysis of behavioral interventions for insomnia and their efficacy in middle-aged adults and in older adults 55+ years of age. *Health Psychology, 25*, 3–14.

Ishida, M., & Papini, M. R. (1997). Massed-trial overtraining effects on extinction and reversal performance in turtles (*Geoclemys reevesii*). *Quarterly Journal of Experimental Psychology, 50B*, 1–16.

Iversen, I. H. (1993). Acquisition of matching-to-sample performance in rats using visual stimuli on nose keys. *Journal of the Experimental Analysis of Behavior, 59*, 471–482.

Ivkovich, D., Collins, K. L., Eckerman, C. O., Krasnegor, N. A., & Stanton, M. E. (1999). Classical delay eyeblink conditioning in 4- and 5-month-old human infants. *Psychological Science, 10*, 4–8.

Izumi, A., & Kojima, S. (2004). Matching vocalizations to vocalizing faces in a chimpanzee (*Pan troglodytes*). *Animal Cognition, 7*, 179–184.

Jackson, R. L., & Minor, T. R. (1988). Effects of signaling inescapable shock on subsequent escape learning: Implications for theories of coping and "learned helplessness." *Journal of Experimental Psychology: Animal Behavior Processes, 14*, 390–400.

Jackson, R. L., Alexander, J. H., & Maier, S. F. (1980). Learned helplessness, inactivity, and associative deficits: Effects of inescapable shock on response choice escape learning. *Journal of Experimental Psychology: Animal Behavior Processes, 6*, 1–20.

Jacobs, L. F., & Schenk, F. (2003). Unpacking the cognitive map: The parallel map theory of hippocampal function. *Psychological Review, 110*, 285–315.

Jenkins, H. M. (1962). Resistance to extinction when partial reinforcement is followed by regular reinforcement. *Journal of Experimental Psychology, 64*, 441–450.

Jenkins, H. M. (1977). Sensitivity of different response systems to stimulus-reinforcer and response-reinforcer relations. In H. Davis & H. M. B. Hurwitz (Eds.), *Operant-Pavlovian interactions* (pp. 47–62). Hillsdale, NJ: Erlbaum.

Jenkins, H. M., & Harrison, R. H. (1960). Effects of discrimination training on auditory generalization. *Journal of Experimental Psychology, 59*, 246–253.

Jenkins, H. M., & Harrison, R. H. (1962). Generalization gradients of inhibition following auditory discrimination learning. *Journal of the Experimental Analysis of Behavior, 5*, 435–441.

Jenkins, H. M., & Moore, B. R. (1973). The form of the auto-shaped response with food or water reinforcers. *Journal of the Experimental Analysis of Behavior, 20*, 163–181.

Jenkins, H. M., Barnes, R. A., & Barrera, F. J. (1981). Why auto-shaping depends on trial spacing. In C. M. Locurto, H. S. Terrace, & J. Gibbon (Eds.), *Autoshaping and conditioning theory* (pp. 255–284). New York: Academic Press.

Jennings, D. J., Bonardi, C., & Kirkpatrick, K. (2007). Overshadowing and stimulus duration. *Journal of Experimental Psychology: Animal Behavior Processes, 33*, 464–475.

Jennings, H. E. (1976). *Behavior of lower organisms*. Bloomington, IN: Indiana University Press. (Originally published 1904.)

Jiao, C., Knight, P. K., Weerakoon, P., & Turman, A. B. (2007). Effects of visual erotic stimulation on vibrotactile detection thresholds in men. *Archives of Sexual Behavior, 36*, 787–792.

Ji, R-R., Kohno, T., Moore, K. A., & Woolf, C. J. (2003). Central sensitization and LTP: do pain and memory share similar mechanisms? *Trends in Neuroscience, 26*, 696–705.

Jitsumori, M. (2006). Category structure and typicality effects. In E. A. Wasserman and T. R. Zentall (Eds.), *Comparative cognition* (pp. 343–362). Oxford, UK: Oxford University Press.

Jitsumori, M., Shimada, N., & Inoue, S. (2006). Family resemblance facilitates formation and expansion of functional equivalence classes in pigeons. *Learning & Behavior, 34*, 162–175.

Job, R. F. S. (2002). The effects of uncontrollable, unpredictable aversive and appetitive events: Similar effects warrant similar, but not identical, explanations? *Integrative Psychological and Behavioral Science, 37*, 59–81.

Johnson, H. M. (1994). Processes of successful intentional forgetting. *Psychological Bulltin, 116*, 274–292.

Johnson, J. W., Munk, D. D., van Laarhoven, T., Repp, A. C., Dahlquist, C. M. (2003). Classroom applications of the disequilibrium model of reinforcement. *Behavioral Interventions, 18*, 63–85.

Johnson, M. W., & Bickel, W. K. (2006). Replacing relative reinforcing efficacy with behavioral economic demand curves. *Journal of the Experimental Analysis of Behavior, 85,* 73–93.

Jones, B. M. (2003). Quantitative analyses of matching-to-sample performance. *Journal of the Experimental Analysis of Behavior, 79,* 323–350.

Jostad, C. M., Miltenberger, R. G, Kelso, P., & Knudson, P. (2008). Peer tutoring to prevent firearm play: Acquisition, generalization, and long-term maintenance of safety skills. *Journal of Applied Behavior Analysis, 41,* 117–123.

Jozefowiez, J., & Staddon, J. E. R. (2008). Operant behavior. In R. Menzel (Ed.), *Learning theory and behavior.* Vol. 1 of J. Byrne (Ed.), *Learning and Memory: A comprehensive reference.* (pp. 75–102). Oxford: Elsevier.

Judge, P. G., Evans, T. A., & Vyas, D. K. (2005). Ordinal representation of numeric quantities by brown capuchin monkeys (*Cebus apella*). *Journal of Experimental Psychology: Animal Behavior Processes, 31,* 79–94.

Kacelnik, A., Chappell, J., Kenward, B., & Weir, A. A. S. (2006). Cognitive adaptations for tool-related behavior in New Caledonian crows. In E. A. Wasserman and T. R. Zentall (Eds.), *Comparative cognition* (pp. 515–528). Oxford, UK: Oxford University Press.

Kaiser, D. H., Sherburne, L. M., & Zentall, T. R. (1997). Directed forgetting in pigeons resulting from reallocation of memory-maintaining processes on forget-cue trials. *Psychonomic Bulletin & Review, 4,* 559–565.

Kaiser, L., & De Jong, R. (1995). Induction of odor preference in a specialist insect parasitoid. *Animal Learning & Behavior, 23,* 17–21.

Kako, E. (1999). Elements of syntax in the systems of three language-trained animals. *Animal Learning & Behavior, 27,* 1–14.

Kalmbach, B. E., Ohyama, T., Kreider, J. C., Riusech, F., & Mauk, M. D. (2009). Interactions between prefrontal cortex and cerebellum revealed by trace eyelid conditioning. *Learning and Memory, in press.*

Kamil, A. C. (1978). Systematic foraging by a nectarfeeding bird, the amakihi (*Loxops virens*). *Journal of Comparative and Physiological Psychology, 92,* 388–396.

Kamil, A. C., & Balda, R. P. (1985). Cache recovery and spatial memory in Clark's nutcrackers (*Nucifraga columbiana*). *Journal of Experimental Psychology: Animal Behavior Processes, 11,* 95–111.

Kamil, A. C., & Balda, R. P. (1990). Spatial memory in seed-caching corvids. In G. H. Bower (Ed.), *The psychology of learning and motivation* (Vol. 26, pp. 1–25). San Diego: Academic Press.

Kamil, A. C., & Gould, K. L. (2008). Memory in food caching animals. In R. Menzel (Ed.), *Learning theory and behavior.* Vol. 1 of J. Byrne (Ed.), *Learning and Memory: A comprehensive reference* (pp. 419–440). Oxford: Elsevier.

Kamin, L. J, Brimer, C. J., & Black, A. H. (1963). Conditioned suppression as a monitor of fear of the CS in the course of avoidance training. *Journal of Comparative and Physiological Psychology, 56,* 497–501.

Kamin, L. J. (1965). Temporal and intensity characteristics of the conditioned stimulus. In W. F. Prokasy (Ed.), *Classical conditioning.* New York: Appleton-CenturyCrofts.

Kamin, L. J. (1968). "Attention-like" processes in classical conditioning. In M. R. Jones (Ed.), *Miami Symposium on the Prediction of Behavior: Aversive stimulation* (pp. 9–31). Miami: University of Miami Press.

Kamin, L. J. (1969). Predictability, surprise, attention, and conditioning. In B. A. Campbell & R. M. Church (Eds.), *Punishment and aversive behavior* (pp. 279–296). New York: Appleton-Century-Crofts.

Kandel, E. R., & Schwartz, J. H. (1982). Molecular biology of learning: Modulation of transmitter release. *Science, 218,* 433–443.

Kandel, E. R., Schwartz, J. H., & Jessell, T. M. (2000). *Principles of neural science.* New York: McGraw-Hill.

Kaplan, P. S., & Hearst, E. (1982). Bridging temporal gaps between CS and US in autoshaping: Insertion of other stimuli before, during, and after the CS. *Journal of Experimental Psychology: Animal Behavior Processes, 8,* 187–203.

Kaplan, P. S., Werner, J. S., & Rudy, J. W. (1990). Habituation, sensitization, and infant visual attention. In C. Rovee-Collier & L. P. Lipsitt (Eds.), *Advances in infancy research* (Vol. 6, pp. 61–109). Norwood, Nl: Ablex.

Karpicke, J. (1978). Directed approach responses and positive conditioned suppression in the rat. *Animal Learning & Behavior, 6,* 216–224.

Kasprow, W. J. (1987). Enhancement of short-term retention by appetitive-reinforcer reminder treatment. *Animal Learning & Behavior, 15,* 412–416.

Kasprow, W. J., Cacheiro, H., Balaz, M. A., & Miller, R. R. (1982). Reminder-induced recovery of associations to an overshadowed stimulus. *Learning and Motivation, 13,* 155–166.

Kasprow, W. J., Catterson, D., Schachtman, T. R., & Miller, R. R. (1984). Attenuation of latent inhibition by post-acquisition reminder. *Quarterly Journal of Experimental Psychology, 36B,* 53–63.

Kastak, D., & Schusterman, R. J. (1994). Transfer of visual identity matching-to-sample in two California sea lions (*Zatophus californianus*). *Animal Learning & Behavior, 22,* 427–435.

Kastak, D., & Schusterman, R. J. (1998). Low-frequency amphibious hearing in pinnipeds: Methods, measurement, noise, and ecology. *Journal of the Acoustical Society of America, 103,* 2216–2228.

Kastak, D., Schusterman, R. J., Southall, B. L., & Reichmuth, C. J. (1999). Underwater temporary threshold shift induced by octave-band noise in three species of pinniped. *Journal of the Acoustical Society of America, 106,* 1142–1148.

Katz, J. S. & Wright, A. A. (2006). Same/Different abstract-concept learning by pigeons. *Journal of Experimental Psychology: Animal Behavior Processes, 32,* 80–86.

Katzev, R. D., & Berman, J. S. (1974). Effect of exposure to conditioned stimulus and control of its termination in the extinction of avoidance behavior. *Journal of Comparative and Physiological Psychology, 87,* 347–353.

Kaufman, L. W., & Collier, G. (1983). Cost and meal pattern in wild-caught rats. *Physiology and Behavior, 30,* 445–449.

Keehn, J. D., & Nakkash, S. (1959). Effect of a signal contingent upon an avoidance response. *Nature, 184*, 566–568.

Kehoe, E. J. (2008). Discrimination and generalization. In R. Menzel (Ed.), *Learning theory and behavior*. Vol 1 of J. Byrne (Ed.), *Learning and Memory: A comprehensive reference.* (pp. 123–150). Oxford: Elsevier.

Kehoe, E. J., & White, N. E. (2004). Overexpectation: Response loss during sustained stimulus compounding in the rabbit nictitating membrane response. *Learning & Memory, 11*, 476–483.

Kehoe, E. J., Cool, V., & Gormezano, I. (1991). Trace conditioning of the rabbit's nictitating membrane response as a function of CS-US interstimulus interval and trials per session. *Learning and Motivation, 22*, 269–290.

Kelber, A., Vorobyev, M., & Osorio, D. (2003). Animal colour vision: Behavioural tests and physiological concepts. *Biological Reviews, 78*, 81–118.

Kelley, M. J. (1986). Selective attention and stimulus reinforcer interactions in the pigeon. *Quarterly Journal of Experimental Psychology, 38B*, 97–110.

Kelling, A. S, Snyder, R. J., Marr, M. J., Bloomsmith, M. A., Gardner, W., & Maple, T. L. (2006). Color vision in the gian panda (*Ailuropoda melanoleuca*). *Learning & Behavior, 34*, 154–161.

Kenward, B., Rutz, C., Weir, A. A. S., & Kacelnik, A. (2006). Development of tool use in New Caedonian crows: Inherited action patterns and social influences. *Animal Behaviour, 72*, 1329–1343.

Kenward, B., Weir, A. A. S., Rutz, C., & Kacelnik, A. (2005). Tool manufacture by naïve juvenile crows. *Nature, 433*, 121.

Kesner, R. P., & DeSpain, M. J. (1988). Correspondence between rats and humans in the utilization of retrospective and prospective codes. *Animal Learning & Behavior, 16*, 299–302.

Kessler, R. C., McGonagle, K. A., Zhao, S., Nelson, C. B., Hughes, M., Eshleman, S., Wittchen, H.-U., & Kendler, K. S. (1994). Lifetime and 12–month prevalence of DSM-III-R psychiatric disorders in the United States: Results from the National Comorbidity Survey. *Archives of General Psychiatry, 51*, 8–19.

Khallad, Y., & Moore, J. (1996). Blocking, unblocking, and overexpectation in autoshaping with pigeons. *Journal of the Experimental Analysis of Behavior, 65*, 575–591.

Killeen, P. R. (1995). Economics, ecologics, and mechanics: The dynamics of responding under conditions of varying motivation. *Journal of the Experimental Analysis of Behavior, 64*, 405–431.

Killeen, P. R. (2001). Writing and overwriting short-term memory. *Psychonomic Bulletin & Review, 8*, 18–43.

Killeen, P. R., & Fetterman, J. G. (1988). A behavioral theory of timing. *Psychological Review, 95*, 274–295.

Killeen, P. R., & Fetterman, J. G. (1993). The behavioral theory of timing: Transition analyses. *Journal of the Experimental Analysis of Behavior, 59*, 411–422.

Killeen, P. R., Fetterman, J. G., & Bizo, L. A. (1997). Time's causes. In C. M. Bradshaw and E. Szabadi (Eds.), *Time and behaviour: Psychological and neurobiological analyses* (pp. 79–239). Amsterdam: Elsevier Science.

Kim, J. J., Krupa, D. J. et al. (1998). Inhibitory cerebello-olivary projections and blocking effect in classical conditioning. *Science, 279*, 570–573.

Kim, S. D., Rivers, S., Bevins, R. A., Ayres, J. J. B. (1996). Conditioned stimulus determinants of conditioned response form in Pavlovian fear conditioning. *Journal of Experimental Psychology: Animal Behavior Processes, 22*, 87–104.

Kimble, G. A. (1961). *Hilgard and Marquis' conditioning and learning* (2nd ed.). New York: Appleton.

Kirkpatrick, K. (2002). Packet theory of conditioning and timing. *Behavioural Processes, 57*, 89–106.

Kirkpatrick, K., & Church, R. M. (2000). Independent effects of stimulus and cycle duration in conditioning: The role of timing processes. *Animal Learning & Behavior, 28*, 373–388.

Kirkpatrick, K., & Church, R. M. (2003). Tracking of the expected time to reinforcement in temporal conditioning procedures. *Learning & Behavior, 31*, 3–21.

Kirkpatrick, K., & Church, R. M. (2004). Temporal learning in random control procedures. *Journal of Experimental Psychology: Animal Behavior Processes, 30*, 213–228.

Kirmayer, L. J., Lemelson, R., & Barad, M. (Eds.). (2007). *Understanding trauma: Integrating biological, clinical, and cultural perspectives*. New York: Cambridge University Press.

Klein, B. G., LaMon, B., & Zeigler, H. P. (1983). Drinking in the pigeon (*Columba livia*): Topography and spatiotemporal organization. *Journal of Comparative Psychology, 97*, 178–181.

Klein, M., & Rilling, M. (1974). Generalization of free operant avoidance behavior in pigeons. *Journal of the Experimental Analysis of Behavior, 21*, 75–88.

Köhler, W. (1927). *The mentality of apes*. London: Routledge & Kegan Paul.

Köhler, W. (1939). Simple structural functions in the chimpanzee and in the chicken. In W. D. Ellis (Ed.), *A source book of Gestalt psychology* (pp. 217–227). New York: Harcourt Brace Jovanovich.

Koller, G., Satzger, W., Adam, M., Wagner, M., Kathmann, N., Soyka, M., & Engel, R. (2003). Effects of scopolamine on matching to sample paradigm and related tests in human subjects. *Neuropsychobiology, 48*(2), 87–94.

Koob, G. F. (1999). Drug reward and addiction. *In Fundamental Neuroscience* (by L. S. Squire, F. E. Bloom, S. K. McConnell, J. L. Roberts, N. C. Spitzer, & M. J. Zigmond). New York: Academic Press.

Koob, G. F., & Le Moal, M. (2008). Addiction and the brain antireward system. *Annual Review of Psychology, 59*, 29–53.

Koob, G. F. Caine, S. B., Parsons, L., Markou, A., & Weiss, F. (1997). Opponent-process model and psychostimulant addiction. *Pharmacology Biochemistry and Behavior, 57*, 531–521.

Kraemer, P. J., & Golding, J. M. (1997). Adaptive forgetting in animals. *Psychonomic Bulletin & Review, 4*, 480–491.

Kraemer, P. J., & Roberts, W. A. (1985). Short-term memory for simultaneously presented visual and auditory signals in the pigeon. *Journal of Experimental Psychology: Animal Behavior Processes, 11*, 13–39.

Kraemer, P. J., Hoffmann, H., Randall, C. K., & Spear, N. E. (1992). Devaluation of Pavlovian conditioning in the 10–day-old rat. *Animal Learning & Behavior, 20,* 219–222.

Krägeloh, C. U., Davison, M., & Elliffee, D. M. (2005). Local preference in concurrent schedules: The effects of reinforcer sequences. *Journal of the Experimental Analysis of Behavior, 84,* 37–64.

Krieckhaus, E. E., & Wolf, G. (1968). Acquisition of sodium by rats: Interaction of innate and latent learning. *Journal of Comparative and Physiological Psychology, 65,* 197–201.

Kruschke, J. K., Kappenman, E. S., & Hetrick, W. P. (2005). Eye gaze and individual differences consistent with learned attention in associative blocking and highlighting. *Journal of Experimental Psychology: Learning, Memory, and Cognition, 31,* 830–845.

Kruse, J. M., Overmier, J. B., Konz, W. A., & Rokke, E. (1983). Pavlovian conditioned stimulus effects upon instrumental choice behavior are reinforcer specific. *Learning and Motivation, 14,* 165–181.

Kyonka, E. G. E. & Grace, R.C. (2008). Rapid acquisition of preference in concurrent chains when alternatives differ on multiple dimensions of reinforcement. *Journal of the Experimental Analysis of Behavior, 89,* 49–69.

LaBar, K. S., & Phelps, E. A. (2005). Reinstatement of conditioned fear in humans is context dependent and impaired in amnesia. *Behavioral Neuroscience, 119,* 677–686.

Lansdell, H. (1988). Laboratory animals need only humane treatment: Animal "rights" may debase human rights. *International Journal of Neuroscience, 42,* 169–178.

Lanuza, E., Nader, K., & LeDoux, J. E. (2004). Unconditioned stimulus pathways to the amygdala: Effects of posterior thalamic and cortical lesions on fear conditioning. *Neuroscience, 125,* 305–315.

Lashley, K. S., & Wade, M. (1946). The Pavlovian theory of generalization. *Psychological Review, 53,* 72–87.

Lattal, K. A. (1998). A century of effect: Legacies of E. L. Thorndike's *Animal intelligence* monograph. *Journal of the Experimental Analysis of Behavior, 70,* 325–336.

Lattal, K. A., & Gleeson, S. (1990). Response acquisition with delayed reinforcement. *Journal of Experimental Psychology: Animal Behavior Processes, 16,* 27–39.

Lattal, K. A., & Neef, N. A. (1996). Recent reinforcement-schedule research and applied behavior analysis. *Journal of Applied Behavior Analysis, 29,* 213–230.

Lattal, K. A., Metzger, B. (1994). Response acquisition by Siamese fighting fish (*Betta spendens*) with delayed visual reinforcement. *Journal of the Experimental Analysis of Behavior, 61,* 35–44.

Lattal, K. M. (1999). Trial and intertrial durations in Pavlovian conditioning: Issues of learning and performance. *Journal of Experimental Psychology: Animal Behavior Processes, 25,* 433–450.

Lattal, K. M., & Nakajima, S. (1998). Overexpectation in appetitive Pavlovian and instrumental conditioning. *Animal Learning & Behavior, 26,* 351–360.

Lazareva, O. F., & Wasserman, E. A. (2008). Categories and concepts in animals. In R. Menzel (Ed.), *Learning theory and behavior.* Vol. 1 of J. Byrne (Ed.), *Learning and Memory: A comprehensive reference.* (pp. 197–226). Oxford: Elsevier.

Lazareva, O. F., Freiburger, K. L., & Wasserman, E. A. (2004). Pigeons concurrently categorize photographs at both basic and superordinate levels. *Psychonomic Bulletin & Review, 11,* 1111–1117.

Lazareva, O. F., Freiburger, K. L., & Wasserman, E. A. (2006). Effects of stimulus manipulations on visual categorization in pigeons. *Behavioural Processes, 72,* 224–233.

Lazareva, O. F., Miner, M., Wasserman, E. A., & Young, M. E. (2008). Multiple-pair training enhances transposition in pigeons. *Learning & Behavior, 36,* 174–187.

Lea, S. E. G. (1978). The psychology and economics of demand. *Psychological Bulletin, 85,* 441–466.

Lea, S. E. G., & Wills, A. J. (2008). Use of multiple dimensions in learned discriminations. *Comparative Cognition & Behavior Reviews, 3,* 115–133.

Leaf, R. C., & Muller, S. A. (1965). A simple method for CER conditioning and measurement. *Psychological Reports, 17,* 211–215.

Leaton, R. N. (1976). Long-term retention of the habituation of lick suppression and startle response produced by a single auditory stimulus. *Journal of Experimental Psychology: Animal Behavior Processes, 2,* 248–259.

LeDoux, J. E., & Gorman, J. M. (2001). A call to action: Overcoming anxiety through active coping. *American Journal of Psychiatry 158,* 1953–1955.

Leising, K. J., Sawa, K., & Blaisdell, A. P. (2007). Temporal integration in Pavlovian appetitive conditioning in rats. *Learning & Behavior, 35,* 11–18.

Lejeune, H., & Wearden, J. H. (2006). Scalar properties in animal timing: Conformity and violations. *Quarterly Journal of Experimental Psychology, 59,* 1875–1908.

Lejuez, C. W., O'Donnell, J., Wirth, O., Zvolensky, M. J., & Eifert, G. H. (1998). Avoidance of 20% carbon dioxide-enriched air with humans. *Journal of the Experimental Analysis of Behavior, 70,* 79–86.

Lencz, T., Bilder, R. M., Turkel, E., Goldman, R. S., Robinson, D., Kane, J. M., & Lieberman, J. A. (2003). Impairments in perceptual competency and maintenance on a visual delayed match-to-sample test in first-episode schizophrenia. *Archives of General Psychiatry, 60,* 238–243.

Lennenberg, E. H. (1967). *Biological foundations of language.* New York: Wiley.

Lerman, D. C., & Vorndran, C. M. (2002). On the status of knowledge for using punishment: Implications for treating behavior disorders. *Journal of Applied Behavior Analysis, 35,* 431–464.

Lerman, D. C., Iwata, B. A., Shore, B. A., & DeLeon, I. G. (1997). Effects of intermittent punishment on self-injurious behavior: An evaluation of schedule thinning. *Journal of Applied Behavioral Analysis. 30,* 187–201.

Lerman, D. C., Iwata. B. A., & Wallace, M. D. (1999). Side effects of extinction: Prevalence of bursting and aggression during the treatment of self-injurious behavior. *Journal of Applied Behavior Analysis, 32,* 1–8.

Leslie, A. M. (2001). Learning: Association or computation? Introduction to special section. *Psychological Science, 10,* 124–127.

Leung, H. T., Bailey, G. K., Laurent, V., Westbrook, R. F. (2007). Rapid reacquisition of fear to a completely extinguished context is replaced by transient impairment with additional extinction training. *Journal of Experimental Psychology: Animal Behavior Processes, 33,* 299–313.

Levenson, D. H., & Schusterman, R. J. (1999). Dark adaptation and visual sensitivity in shallow and deep-diving pinnipeds. *Marine Mammal Science, 15,* 1303–1313.

Levis, D. J. (1995). Decoding traumatic memory: Implosive theory of psychopathology. In W. O'Donohue and L. Krasner (Eds.), *Theories of behavior therapy* (pp. 173–207). Washington, DC: American Psychological Association.

Levis, D. J., & Brewer, K. E. (2001). The neurotic paradox: Attempts by two-factor fear theory and alternative avoidance models to resolve the issues associated with sustained avoidance responding in extinction. In R. R. Mowrer and S. B. Klein (Eds.), *Handbook of contemporary learning theories* (pp. 561–597). Mahwah, NJ: Erlbaum.

Lewis, J. L., & Kamil, A. C. (2006). Interference effects in the memory for serially presented locations in Clark's nutcracker, *Nucifraga columbiana. Journal of Experimental Psychology: Animal Behavior Processes, 32,* 407–418.

Lewis, M., Alessandri, S. M., & Sullivan, M. W. (1990). Violation of expectancy, loss of control, and anger expression in young infants. *Developmental Psychology, 125,* 745–751.

Lieberman, D. A., & Thomas, G. V. (1986). Marking, memory and superstition in the pigeon. *Quarterly Journal of Experimental Psychology, 38B,* 449–459.

Lieberman, D. A., Davidson, F. H., & Thomas, G. V. (1985). Marking in pigeons: The role of memory in delayed reinforcement. *Journal of Experimental Psychology: Animal Behavior Processes, 11,* 611–624.

Lieberman, D. A., McIntosh, D. C., & Thomas, G. V. (1979). Learning when reward is delayed: A marking hypothesis. *Journal of Experimental Psychology: Animal Behavior Processes, 5,* 224–242.

Lieberman, D. A., Sunnucks, W. L., & Kirk, J. D. J. (1998). Reinforcement without awareness: I. Voice level. *Quarterly Journal of Experimental Psychology, 51B,* 301–316.

Lindberg, J. S., Iwata, B. A., Kahng, S. W., DeLeon, I. G. (1999). DRO contingencies: An analysis of variable-momentary schedules. *Journal of Applied Behavior Analysis, 32,* 123–136.

Linscheid, T. R., & Cunningham, C. E. (1977). A controlled demonstration of the effectiveness of electric shock in the elimination of chronic infant rumination. *Journal of Applied Behavior Analysis, 10,* 500.

Lipp, O. V., Sheridan, J., & Siddle, D. A. T. (1994). Human blink startle during aversive and nonaversive Pavlovian conditioning. *Journal of Experimental Psychology: Animal Behavior Processes, 20,* 380–389.

LoBue, V., & DeLoache, J. S. (2008). Detecting the snake in the grass: Attention to fear-relevant stimuli by adults and young children. *Psychological Science, 19,* 284–289.

Lockard, R. B. (1968). The albino rat: A defensible choice or a bad habit? *American Psychologist, 23,* 734–742.

Locurto, C. M., Terrace, H. S., & Gibbon, J. (Eds.). (1981). *Autoshaping and conditioning theory.* New York: Academic Press.

Loeb, J. (1900). *Comparative physiology of the brain and comparative psychology.* New York: G. P. Putman.

Logue, A. W. (1985). Conditioned food aversion learning in humans. *Annals of the New York Academy of Sciences.*

Logue, A. W. (1988). A comparison of taste aversion learning in humans and other vertebrates: Evolutionary pressures in common. In R. C. Bolles & M. D. Beecher (Eds.), *Evolution and learning* (pp. 97–116). Hillsdale, NJ: Erlbaum.

Logue, A. W. (1995). *Self-control: Waiting until tomorrow for what you want today.* Englewood Cliffs, NJ: Prentice-Hall.

Logue, A. W. (1998a). Laboratory research on self-control: Applications to administration. *Review of General Psychology, 2,* 221–238.

Logue, A. W. (1998b). Self-control. In W. O'Donohue (Ed.), *Learning and behavior therapy* (pp. 252–273). Boston: Allyn and Bacon.

Logue, A. W., Ophir, I., & Strauss, K. E. (1981). The acquisition of taste aversions in humans. *Behaviour Research and Therapy, 19,* 319–333.

Loidolt, M., Aust, U., Meran, I., & Huber, L. (2003). Pigeons use item-specific and category-level information in the identification and categorization of human faces. *Journal of Experimental Psychology: Animal Behavior Processes, 29,* 261–276.

Loidolt, M., Aust, U., Steurer, M., Troje, N. F., & Huber, L. (2006). Limits of dynamic object perception in pigeons: Dynamic stimulus presentation does not enhance perception and discrimination of complex shape. *Learning & Behavior, 34,* 71–85.

LoLordo, V. M. (1971). Facilitation of food-reinforced responding by a signal for response-independent food. *Journal of the Experimental Analysis of Behavior, 15,* 49–55.

LoLordo, V. M. (1979). Selective associations. In A. Dickinson & R. A. Boakes (Eds.), *Mechanisms of learning and motivation* (pp. 367–398). Hillsdale, NJ: Erlbaum.

LoLordo, V. M., & Fairless, J. L. (1985). Pavlovian conditioned inhibition: The literature since 1969. In R. R. Miller & N. E. Spear (Eds.), *Information processing in animals: Conditioned inhibition.* Hillsdale, NJ: Erlbaum.

LoLordo, V. M., & Taylor, T. L. (2001). Effects of uncontrollable aversive events: Some unsolved puzzles. In R. R. Mowrer and S. B. Klein (Eds.), *Handbook of contemporary learning theories* (pp. 469–504). Mahwah, NJ: Erlbaum

LoLordo, V. M., Jacobs, W. J., & Foree, D. D. (1982). Failure to block control by a relevant stimulus. *Animal Learning & Behavior, 10,* 183–193.

LoLordo, V. M., McMillan, J. C., & Riley, A. L. (1974). The effects upon food-reinforced pecking and treadle-pressing of auditory and visual signals for response-independent food. *Learning and Motivation, 5,* 24–41.

Losey, G. S., & Sevenster, P. (1995). Can three-spined sticklebacks learn when to display? Rewarded displays. *Animal Behaviour, 49,* 137–150.

Lovibond, P. F. (1983). Facilitation of instrumental behavior by a Pavlovian appetitive conditioned stimulus. *Journal of Experimental Psychology: Animal Behavior Processes, 9,* 225–247.

Lovibond, P. F., Saunders, J. C., Weidemann, G., & Mitchell, C. J. (2008). Evidence for expectancy as a mediator of avoidance and anxiety in a laboratory model of human avoidance learning. *Quarterly Journal of Experimental Psychology, 61,* 1199–1216.

Lubow, R. E. (1989). *Latent inhibition and conditioned attention theory.* Cambridge, England: Cambridge University Press.

Lubow, R. E., & Gewirtz, J. C. (1995). Latent inhibition in humans: Data, theory, and implications for schizophrenia. *Psychological Bulletin, 117,* 87–103.

Lubow, R. E., & Kaplan, O. (2005). The visual search analogue of latent inhibition: Implications for theories of irrelevant stimulus processing in normal and schizophrenic groups. *Psychonomic Bulletin & Review, 12,* 224–243.

Lubow, R. E., & Moore, A. U. (1959). Latent inhibition: the effect of nonreinforced preexposure to the conditioned stimulus. *Journal of Comparative and Physiological Psychology, 52,* 415–419.

Lussier, J. P., Heil, S. H., Mongeon, J. A., Badget, G. J., & Higgins, S. T. (2006). A meta-analysis of voucher-based reinforcement therapy for substance abuse disorder. *Addiction, 101,* 192–203.

Lynch, M. A. (2004). Long-term potentiation and memory. *Physiological Reviews, 125,* 87–136.

Lyon, D. O. (1968). Conditioned suppression: Operant variables and aversive control. *Psychological Record, 18,* 317–338.

Lysle, D. T., & Fowler, H. (1985). Inhibition as a "slave" process: Deactivation of conditioned inhibition through extinction of conditioned excitation. *Journal of Experimental Psychology: Animal Behavior Processes, 11,* 71–94.

MacArdy, E. A., & Riccio, D. C. (1995). Time-dependent changes in the effectiveness of a noncontingent footshock reminder. *Learning and Motivation, 26,* 29–42.

MacDonald, S. E. (1993). Delayed matching-to-successive-samples in pigeons: Short-term memory for item and order information. *Animal Learning & Behavior, 21,* 59–67.

MacDonall, J. S. (1999). A local model of concurrent performance. *Journal of the Experimental Analysis of Behavior, 71,* 57–74.

MacDonall, J. S. (2000). Synthesizing concurrent interval performances. *Journal of the Experimental Analysis of Behavior, 74,* 189–206.

MacDonall, J. S. (2005). Earning and obtaining reinforcers under concurrent interval scheduling. *Journal of the Experimental Analysis of Behavior, 84,* 167–183.

Machado, A. (1989). Operant conditioning of behavioral variability using a percentile reinforcement schedule. *Journal of the Experimental Analysis of Behavior, 52,* 155–166.

Machado, A. (1992). Behavioral variability and frequency-dependent selection. *Journal of the Experimental Analysis of Behavior, 58,* 241–263.

Machado, A. (1994). Polymorphic response patterns under frequency-dependent selection. *Animal Learning & Behavior, 22,* 53–71.

Machado, A., & Cevik, M. (1998). Acquisition and extinction under periodic reinforcement. *Behavioural Processes, 44,* 237–262.

Mackintosh, N. J. (1974). *The psychology of animal learning.* London: Academic Press.

Mackintosh, N. J. (1975). A theory of attention: Variations in the associability of stimuli with reinforcement. *Psychological Review, 82,* 276–298.

Mackintosh, N. J., & Dickinson, A. (1979). Instrumental (Type II) conditioning. In A. Dickinson & R. A. Boakes (Eds.), *Mechanisms of learning and motivation* (pp. 143–169). Hillsdale, NJ: Erlbaum.

Mackintosh, N. J., Bygrave, D. J., & Picton, B. M. B. (1977). Locus of the effect of a surprising reinforcer in the attenuation of blocking. *Quarterly Journal of Experimental Psychology, 29,* 327–336.

Madden, G. J., & Bickel, W. K. (1999). Abstinence and price effects on demand for cigarettes: A behavioral-economic analysis. *Addiction, 94,* 577–588.

Madden, G. J., Bickel, W. K., & Jacobs, E. A. (2000). Three predictions of the economic concept of unit price in a choice context. *Journal of the Experimental Analysis of Behavior, 73,* 45–64.

Madden, G. J., Peden, B. F., & Yamaguchi, T. (2002). Human group choice: Discrete-trial and free-operant tests of the ideal free distribution. *Journal of the Experimental Analysis of Behavior, 78,* 1–15.

Madden, G. J., Petry, N. M., Badger, G. J., & Bickel, W. K. (1997). Impulsive and self-control choices in opioid-dependent patients and non-drug-using control participants: Drug and monetary rewards. *Experimental and Clinical Psychopharmacology, 5,* 256–262.

Maes, J. H. R. (2003). Response stability and variability induced in humans by different feedback contingencies. *Learning & Behavior, 31,* 332–348.

Mahometa, M. J., & Domjan, M. (2005). Classical conditioning increases reproductive success in Japanese quail, *Coturnix japonica. Animal Behaviour, 69,* 983–989.

Maier, S. F., & Jackson, R. L. (1979). Learned helplessness: All of us were right (and wrong): Inescapable shock has multiple effects. In G. H. Bower (Ed.), *The psychology of learning and motivation* (Vol. 13). New York: Academic Press.

Maier, S. F., & Seligman, M. E. P. (1976). Learned helplessness: Theory and evidence. *Journal of Experimental Psychology: General, 105,* 3–46.

Maier, S. F., Rapaport, P., & Wheatley, K. L. (1976). Conditioned inhibition and the UCS-CS interval. *Animal Learning and Behavior, 4,* 217–220.

Maier, S. F., Seligman, M. E. P., & Solomon, R. L. (1969). Pavlovian fear conditioning and learned helplessness. In B. A. Campbell & R. M. Church (Eds.), *Punishment and aversive behavior.* New York: Appleton-CenturyCrofts.

Maki, W. S., Beatty, W. W., Hoffman, N., Bierley, R. A., & Clouse, B. A. (1984). Spatial memory over long retention intervals: Nonmemorial factors are not necessary for accurate performance on the radial arm maze by rats. *Behavioral and Neural Biology, 41,* 1–6.

Maki, W. S., Moe, J. C., & Bierley, C. M. (1977). Short-term memory for stimuli, responses, and reinforcers. *Journal of Experimental Psychology: Animal Behavior Processes, 3,* 156–177.

Malenka, R. C., & Nicoll, R. A. (1999). Long-term potentiation—A decade of progress? *Science, 285,* 1870–1874.

Marchand, A. R., & Kamper, E. (2000). Time course of cardiac conditioned responses in restrained rats as a function of the trace CS-US interval. *Journal of Experimental Psychology: Animal Behavior Processes, 26,* 385–398.

Marsh, G. (1972). Prediction of the peak shift in pigeons from gradients of excitation and inhibition. *Journal of Comparative and Physiological Psychology, 81,* 262–266.

Martin-Malivel, J., Mangini, M. C., Fagot, J., & Biederman, I. (2006). Do humans and baboons use the same information when categorizing human and baboon faces? *Psychological Science, 17,* 599–607.

Martin, S. J., Grimwood, P. D., & Morris, R. G. M. (2000). Synaptic plasticity and memory: An evaluation of the hypothesis. *Annual Review of Neuroscience, 23,* 649–711.

Marx, B. P., Heidt, J. M., & Gold, S. D. (2005). Perceived uncontrollability and unpredicatability, self-regulation, and sexual revictimization. *Review of General Psychology, 9,* 67–90.

Masserman, J. H. (1946). *Principles of dynamic psychiatry.* Philadelphia: Saunders.

Matsuno, T., Kawai, N., & Matsuzawa, T. (2004). Color classification by chimpanzees (*Pan troglodytes*). *Behavioural Brain Research, 148,* 157–165.

Matthews, R. N., Domjan, M., Ramsey, M., & Crews, D. (2007). Learning effects on sperm competition and reproductive fitness. *Psychological Science, 18,* 758–762.

Matzel, L. D., Gladstein, L., & Miller, R. R. (1988). Conditioned excitation and conditioned inhibition are not mutually exclusive. *Learning and Motivation, 19,* 99–121.

Mauk, B., & Dehnhardt, G. (2005). Identity concept formation during visual multiple-choice matching in a harbor seal (*Phoca vitulina*). *Learning & Behavior, 33,* 428–436.

Mayford, M., Bach, M. E., Huang, Y.-Y., Wang, L., Hawkins, R. D., & Kandel, E. R. (1996). Control of memory formation through regulated expression of a CaMKII transgene. *Science, 125,* 1678–1683.

Mayford, M., & Kandel, E. R. (1999). Genetic approaches to memory storage. *Trends in Genetics, 125,* 463–470.

Mazur, J. E. (1987). An adjusting procedure for studying delayed reinforcement. In M. L. Commons, J. E. Mazur, J. A. Nevin, & H. Rachlin (Eds.), *Quantitative analyses of behavior: Vol. 5. The effect of delay and intervening events on reinforcement value* (pp. 55–73). Hillsdale, NJ: Erlbaum.

Mazur, J. E. (1998). Choice with delayed and probabilistic reinforcers: Effects of prereinforcer and postreinforcer stimuli. *Journal of the Experimental Analysis of Behavior, 70,* 253–265.

Mazur, J. E. (2000). Two- versus three-alternative concurrent-chain schedules: A test of three models. *Journal of Experimental Psychology: Animal Behavior Processes, 26,* 286–293.

Mazur, J.E. (2006). Choice between single and multiple reinforcers in concurrent-chains schedules. *Journal of the Experimental Analysis of Behavior, 86,* 211–222.

McAllister, W. R., & McAllister, D. E. (1995). Two-factor fear theory: Implications for understanding anxiety-based clinical phenomena. In W. O'Donohue and L. Krasner (Eds.), *Theories of behavior therapy* (pp. 145–171). Washington, DC: American Psychological Association.

McCrink, K., & Wynn, K. (2007). Ratio abstraction by 6–month-old infants. *Psychological Science, 18,* 740–745.

McDowell, J. J. (2005). On the classic and modern theories of matching. *Journal of the Experimental Analysis of Behavior, 84,* 111–127.

McGaugh, J. L., & Herz, M. J. (1972). *Memory consolidation.* San Francisco: Albion.

McGee, G. G., Krantz, P. J., & McClannahan, L. E. (1986). An extension of incidental teaching procedures to reading instruction for autistic children. *Journal of Applied Behavior Analysis, 19,* 147–157.

McLaren, I. P. L., & Mackintosh, N. J. (2000). An elemental model of associative learning: I. Latent inhibition and perceptual learning. *Animal Learning & Behavior, 28,* 211–246.

McLean, A. P., Campbell-Tie, P., & Nevin, J. A. (1996). Resistance to change as a function of stimulus-reinforcer and location-reinforcer contingencies. *Journal of the Experimental Analysis of Behavior, 66,* 169–191.

McMillan, D. E., & Li, M. (1999). Drug discrimination under a concurrent fixed-ratio fixed-ratio schedule. *Journal of the Experimental Analysis of Behavior, 72,* 187–204.

McMillan, D. E., & Li, M. (2000). Drug discrimination under two concurrent fixed-interval fixed-interval schedules. *Journal of the Experimental Analysis of Behavior, 74,* 55–77.

McNally, G. P., & Westbrook, R. F. (2006). A short intertrial interval facilitates acquisition of context-conditioned fear and a short retention interval facilitates its expression. *Journal of Experimental Psychology: Animal Behavior Processes, 32,* 164–172.

McNish, K. A., Betts, S. L., Brandon, S. E., & Wagner, A. R. (1997). Divergence of conditioned eyeblink and conditioned fear in backward Pavlovian training. *Animal Learning & Behavior, 25,* 43–52.

McNish, K. A., Betts, S. L., Brandon, S. E., & Wagner, A. R. (1997). Divergence of conditioned eyeblink and conditioned fear in backward Pavlovian conditioning. *Animal Learning & Behavior, 25,* 43–52.

McSweeney, F. K., & Swindell, S. (1999). General-process theories of motivation revisited: The role of habituation. *Psychological Bulletin, 125,* 437–457.

McSweeney, F. K., Hinson, J. M., & Cannon, C. B. (1996). Sensitization-habituation may occur during operant conditioning. *Psychological Bulletin, 120,* 256–271.

Meck, W. H. (Ed.) (2003). *Functional and neural mechanisms of interval timing.* Boca Raton, FL: CRC Press.

Mehta, M. A., Goodyer, I. M., & Sahakian, B. J. (2004). Methylphenidate improves working memory and set-shifting in AD/HD: Relationships to baseline memory capacity. *Journal of Child Psychology and Psychiatry, 45,* 293–305.

Melchers, K.G., Shanks, D.R., Lachnit, H., 2008. Stimulus coding in human associative learning: flexible representations of parts and wholes. *Behavioural Processes, 77,* 413–427.

Mellgren, R. L. (1972). Positive and negative contrast effects using delayed reinforcement. *Learning and Motivation, 3,* 185–193.

Melvin, K. B. (1971). Vicious circle behavior. In H. D. Kimmel (Ed.),

Experimental psychopathology. New York: Academic Press.

Mercado, E. III, Murray, S. O., Uyeyama, R. K., Pack, A. A., & Herman, L. M. (1998). Memory for recent actions in the bottlenosed dolphin (*Tursiops truncates*): Repetition of arbitrary behaviors using an abstract rule. *Animal Learning & Behavior, 26,* 210–218.

Merritt, D., MacLean, E. L., Jaffe, S., & Brannon, E. M. (2007). A comparative analysis of serial order in ring-tailed lemurs (*Lemur catta*). *Journal of Comparative Psychology, 121,* 363–371.

Meyer, J.-A., Berthoz, A., Floreano, D., Roitblat, H., & Wilson, S. W. (Eds.). (2000). *From animals to animats 6.* Cambridge, MA: MIT Press.

Miller, C. A., & Sweatt, J. D. (2006). Amnesia or retrieval deficit? Implications of a molecular approach to the question of reconsolidation. *Learning and Memory, 13,* 498–505.

Miller, G. A. (1956). The magic number seven plus or minus two: Some limits on our capacity for processing information. *Psychological Review, 63,* 81–97.

Miller, J. S., Jagielo, J. A., & Spear, N. E. (1990). Alleviation of short-term forgetting: Effects of the CS– and other conditioning elements in prior cueing or as context during test. *Learning and Motivation, 21,* 96–109.

Miller, J. S., Jagielo, J. A., & Spear, N. E. (1992). The influence of the information value provided by prior-cuing treatment on the reactivation of memory in preweanling rats. *Animal Learning & Behavior, 20,* 233–239.

Miller, N. E. (1951). Learnable drives and rewards. In S. S. Stevens (Ed.), *Handbook of experimental psychology.* New York: Wiley.

Miller, N. E. (1960). Learning resistance to pain and fear: Effects of overlearning, exposure, and rewarded exposure in context. *Journal of Experimental Psychology, 60,* 137–145.

Miller, N. E., & Dollard, J. (1941). *Social learning and imitation.* New Haven, CT: Yale University Press.

Miller, N. Y., & Shettleworth, S. J. (2007). Learning about environmental geometry: An associative model. *Journal of Experimental Psychology: Animal Behavior Processes, 33,* 191–212.

Miller, R. R., & Matute, H. (1996). Animal analogues of causal judgment. *The Psychology of Learning and Motivation, 34,* 133–166.

Miller, R. R., & Matzel, L. D. (1988). The comparator hypothesis: A response rule for the expression of associations. In G. H. Bower (Ed.), *The psychology of learning and motivation* (pp. 51–92). Orlando, FL: Academic Press.

Miller, R. R., & Matzel, L. D. (2006). Retrival failure vs. memory loss in experimental amnesia: Definitions and processes. *Learning and Memory, 13,* 491–497.

Miller, R. R., & Springer, A. D. (1973). Amnesia, consolidation, and retrieval. *Psychological Review, 80,* 69–79.

Miller, R. R., Barnet, R. C., & Grahame, N. J. (1995). Assessment of the Rescorla-Wagner model. *Psychological Bulletin, 117,* 363–386.

Miller, R. R., Kasprow, W. J., & Schachtman, T. R. (1986). Retrieval variability: Sources and consequences. *American Journal of Psychology, 99,* 145–218.

Miller, V., & Domjan, M. (1981). Selective sensitization induced by lithium malaise and footshock in rats. *Behavioral and Neural Biology, 31,* 42–55.

Millin, P. M., & Riccio, D. C. (2004). Is the context shift effect a case of retrieval failure? The effects of retrieval enhancing treatments on forgetting under altered stimulus conditions in rats. *Journal of Experimental Psychology: Animal Behavior Processes, 30,* 325–334.

Milmine, M., Watanabe, A., & Colombo, M. (2008). Neural correlates of directed forgetting in the avian prefrontal cortex. *Behavioral Neuroscience, 122,* 199–209.

Mineka, S. (1979). The role of fear in theories of avoidance learning, flooding, and extinction. *Psychological Bulletin, 86,* 985–1010.

Mineka, S., & Gino, A. (1980). Dissociation between conditioned emotional response and extended avoidance performance. *Learning and Motivation, 11,* 476–502.

Mineka, S., & Henderson, R. (1985). Controllability and predictability in acquired motivation. *Annual Review of Psychology, 36,* 495–530.

Mineka, S., & Öhman, A. (2002). Phobias and preparedness: The selective, automatic, and encapsulated nature of fear. *Biological Psychiatry, 52,* 927–937.

Minor, T. R., Dess, N. K., & Overmier, J. B. (1991). Inverting the traditional view of "learned helplessness." In M. R. Denny (Ed.), *Fear, avoidance and phobias* (pp. 87–133). Hillsdale, NJ: Erlbaum.

Minor, T. R., Trauner, M. A., Lee, C.-Y., & Dess, N. K. (1990). Modeling signal features of escape response: Effects of cessation conditioning in "learned helplessness" paradigm. *Journal of Experimental Psychology: Animal Behavior Processes, 16,* 123–136.

Misanin, J. R., Miller, R. R., & Lewis, D. J. (1968). Retrograde amnesia produced by electroconvulsive shock after reactivation of a consolidated memory trace. *Science, 160,* 554–555.

Mitchell, C. J., Lovibond, P. F., Minard, E., & Lavis, Y. (2006). Forward blocking in human learning sometimes reflects the failure to encode a cue-outcome relationship. *Quarterly Journal of Experimental Psychology, 59,* 830–844.

Mitchell, W. S., & Stoffelmayr, B. E. (1973). Application of the Premack principle to the behavioral control of extremely inactive schizophrenics. *Journal of Applied Behavior Analysis, 6,* 419–423.

Molet, M., Leconte, C., & Rosas, J. M. (2006). Acquisition, extinction, and temporal discrimination in human conditioned avoidance. *Behavioural Processes, 73*(2), 199–208.

Moody, E. W., Sunsay, C., & Bouton, M. E. (2006). Priming and trial spacing in extinction: Effects on extinction performance, spontaneous recovery, and reinstatement in appetitive conditioning. *Quarterly Journal of Experimental Psychology, 59,* 809–929.

Morgan, C. L. (1894). *An introduction to comparative psychology.* London: Scott.

Morgan, C. L. (1903). *Introduction to comparative psychology* (Rev. ed.). New York: Scribner.

Morgan, L., & Neuringer, A. (1990). Behavioral variability as a function of response topography and reinforcement contingency. *Animal Learning & Behavior, 18,* 257–263.

Morris, R. G. M. (1974). Pavlovian conditioned inhibition of fear during shuttlebox avoidance behavior. *Learning and Motivation, 5,* 424–447.

Morris, R. G. M. (1975). Preconditioning of reinforcing properties to an exteroceptive feedback stimulus. *Learning and Motivation, 6,* 289–298.

Morris, R. G. M. (1981). Spatial localization does not require the presence of local cues. *Learning and Motivation, 12,* 239–260.

Morris, R. G. M., Anderson, E., Lynch, G. S., & Baudry, M. (1986). Selective impairment of learning and blockade of long-term potentiation by an N-methyl-D-aspartate receptor antagonist, AP5. *Nature, 319,* 774–776.

Mowrer, O. H. (1947). On the dual nature of learning: A reinterpretation of "conditioning" and "problem-solving." *Harvard Educational Review, 17,* 102–150.

Mowrer, O. H., & Lamoreaux, R. R. (1942). Avoidance conditioning and signal duration: A study of secondary motivation and reward. *Psychological Monographs, 54* (Whole No. 247).

Mowrer, R. R., & Gordon, W. C. (1983). Effects of cuing in an "irrelevant" context. *Animal Learning & Behavior, 11,* 401–406.

Mowrer, R. R., & Klein, S. B. (Eds.). (2001). *Handbook of contemporary learning theories.* Mahwah, NJ: Erlbaum.

Moye, T. B., & Thomas, D. R. (1982). Effects of memory reactivation treatments on postdiscrimination generalization performance in pigeons. *Animal Learning & Behavior, 10,* 159–166.

Mui, R., Haselgrove, M., McGregor, A., Futter, J., Heyes, C., & Pearce, J. M. (2007). The discrimination of natural movement by budgerigars (*Melopsittacus undulates*) and pigeons (*Columba livia*). *Journal of Experimental Psychology: Animal Behavior Processes, 33,* 371–380.

Murkerjee, M. (1997, February). Trends in animal research. *Scientific American,* 86–93.

Murphy, J. G., Correla, C. J., & Barnett, N. P. (2007). Behavioral economic approaches to reduce college student drinking. *Addictive Behaviors, 32,* 2573–2585.

Murray, J. E., & Bevins, R. A. (2007). The conditional stimulus effects of nicotine vary as a function of training dose. *Behavioral Pharmacology, 18,* 707–716.

Myers, K. M., & Davis, M. (2007). Mechanisms of fear extinction. *Molecular Psychiatry, 12,* 120–150.

Myers, K. M., Ressler, K. J., & Davis, M. (2006). Different mechanisms of fear extinction dependent on length of time since fear acquisition. *Learning and Memory, 13,* 216–223.

Myers, K. M., Vogel, E. H., Shin, J., & Wagner, A. R. (2001). A comparison of the Rescorla-Wagner and Pearce models in a negative patterning and summation problem. *Animal Learning & Behavior, 29,* 36–45.

Myers, T. M., Cohn, S. I., & Clark, M. G. (2005). Acquisition and performance of two-way shuttlebox avoidance: Effects of aversive air intensity. *Learning and Motivation, 36,* 312–321.

Mystkowski, J. L., Craske, M. G., Echiverri, A. M., & Labus, J. S (2006). Mental reinstatement of context and return of fear in spider-fearful participants. *Behaviour Therapy, 37,* 49–60.

Nadel, K., Schafe, G., & LeDoux, J. E. (2000). Reconsolidation: The labile nature of consolidation theory. *Nature Reviews Neuroscience, 1,* 216–219.

Nader, K., Schafe, G. E., & LeDoux, J. E. (2000). Fear memories require protein synthesis in the amygdala for reconsolidation after retrieval. *Nature, 406,* 722–726.

Nader, K., & Wang, S.-H. (2006). Fading in. *Learning and Memory, 13,* 530–535.

Nakajima, A., & Tang, Y.-P. (2005). Genetic approaches to the molecular/neuronal mechanisms underlying learning and memory in the mouse. *Journal of Pharmacological Sciences, 125,* 1–5.

Nakamura, T., Croft, D. B., & Westbrook, R. F. (2003). Domestic pigeons (*Columba livia*) discriminate between photographs of individual pigeons. *Learning & Behavior, 31,* 307–317.

Nakamura, T., Ito, M., Croft, D. B., & Westbrook, R. F. (2006). Domestic pigeons (*Columba livia*) discriminate between photographs of male and female pigeons. *Learning & Behavior, 34,* 327–339.

Nation, J. R., & Cooney, J. B. (1982). The time course of extinction-induced aggressive behavior in humans: Evidence for a stage model of extinction. *Learning and Motivation, 13,* 95–112.

Neef, N. A., Bicard, D. F., & Endo, S. (2001). Assessment of impulsivity and the development of self-control in students with attention deficit hyperactivity disorder. *Journal of Applied Behavior Analysis, 34,* 397–408.

Neill, J. C., & Harrison, J. M. (1987). Auditory discrimination: The Konorski quality-location effect. *Journal of the Experimental Analysis of Behavior, 48,* 81–95.

Nelson, J. B., & del Carmen Sanjuan, M. (2006). A context-specific latent inhibition effect in a human conditioned suppression task. *Quarterly Journal of Experimental Psychology, 59,* 1003–1020.

Neuenschwander, N., Fabrigoule, C., & Mackintosh, N. J. (1987). Fear of the warning signal during overtraining of avoidance. *Quarterly Journal of Experimental Psychology, 39B,* 23–33.

Neuringer, A. (2004). Reinforced variability in animals and people: Implications for adaptive action. *American Psychologist, 59,* 891–906.

Neuringer, A., Kornell, N., & Olufs, M. (2001). Stability and variability in extinction. *Journal of Experimental Psychology: Animal Behavior Processes, 27,* 79–94.

Nevin, J. A. (1979). Overall matching versus momentary maximizing: Nevin (1969) revisited. *Journal of Experimental Psychology: Animal Behavior Processes, 5,* 300–306.

Nevin, J. A. (1992). An integrative model for the study of behavioral momentum. *Journal of the Experimental Analysis of Behavior, 57,* 301–316.

Nevin, J. A., & Grace, R. C. (2000). Behavioral momentum and the law of effect. *Behavioral and Brain Sciences, 23,* 73–130.

Nevin, J. A., & Grace, R. C. (2005). Resistance to extinction in the steady state and in transition. *Journal of Experimental Psychology: Animal Behavior Processes, 31,* 199–212.

Nevin, J. A., Mandell, G., & Atak, J. R. (1983). The analysis of behavioral momentum. *Journal of the Experimental Analysis of Behavior, 39,* 49–59.

Norrholm, S. D., Jovanovic, T., Vervliet, B., Myers, K. M., Davis,

M., Rothbaum, B. O., & Duncan, E. J. (2006). Conditioned fear extinction and reinstatement in a human fear-potentiated startle paradigm. *Learning and Memory, 13*, 681–685.

O'Donnell, J., Crosbie, J., Williams, D. C., & Saunders, K. J. (2000). Stimulus control and generalization of point-loss punishment with humans. *Journal of the Experimental Analysis of Behavior, 73*, 261–274.

O'Donohue, W. (1998). Conditioning and third-generation behavior therapy. In W. O'Donohue (Ed.), *Learning and behavior therapy* (pp. 1–14). Boston: Allyn and Bacon.

O'Keefe, J., & Nadel, L. (1978). *The hippocampus as a cognitive map.* Oxford, England: Oxford University Press.

Oden, D. L., Thompson, R. K. R., & Premack, D. (1988). Spontaneous transfer of matching by infant chimpanzees (Pan troglodytes). *Journal of Experimental Psychology: Animal Behavior Processes, 14*, 140–145.

Odum, A. A., Lieving, L. M., & Schaal, D. W. (2002). Effects of d-amphetamine in a temporal discrimination procedure: Selective changes in timing or rate dependancy? *Journal of the Experimental Analysis of Behavior, 78*, 195–214.

Odum, A. L., Shahan, T. A., & Nevin, J. A. (2005). Resistance to change of forgetting functions and response rates. *Journal of the Experimental Analysis of Behavior, 84*, 65–75.

Öhman, A., & Mineka, S. (2001). Fear, phobias, and preparedness: Towards an evolved module of fear and fear learning. *Psychological Review, 108*, 483–522.

Öhman, A., & Soares, J. J. F. (1998). Emotional conditioning to masked stimuli: Expectancies for aversive outcomes following nonrecognized fear-irrelevant stimuli. *Journal of Experimental Psychology: General, 127*, 69–82.

Ohyama, T., & Mauk, M. D. (2001). Latent acquisition of timed responses in cerebellar cortex. *Journal of Neuroscience, 21*, 682–690.

Ohyama, T., Gibbon, J., Deich, J. D., & Balsam, P. (1999). Temporal control during maintenance and extinction of conditioned keypecking in ring doves. *Animal Learning & Behavior, 27*, 89–98.

Ohyama, T., Nores, W. L., Murphy, M. & Mauk, M. D. (2003). What the cerebellum computes. *Trends in Neuroscience, 26*, 222–227.

Olmstead, M. C. (2006). Animal models of drug addiction: Where do we go from here? *Quarterly Journal of Experimental Psychology, 59*, 625–653.

Olton, D. S., & Samuelson, R. J. (1976). Remembrance of places passed: Spatial memory in rats. *Journal of Experimental Psychology: Animal Behavior Processes, 2*, 97–116.

Ost, J. W. P., & Lauer, D. W. (1965). Some investigations of salivary conditioning in the dog. In W. F. Prokasy (Ed.), *Classical conditioning.* New York: Appleton-Century-Crofts.

Ostlund, S. B., & Balleine, B. W. (2007). Selective reinstatement of instrumental performance depends on the discriminative stimulus properties of the mediating outcome. *Learning & Behavior, 35*, 43–52.

Ostlund, S. B., Winterbauer, N. E., & Balleine, B. W. (2008). Theory of reward systems. In R. Menzel (Ed.), *Learning theory and behavior.* Vol 1 of J. Byrne (Ed.), *Learning and Memory: A comprehensive reference* (pp. 701–720). Oxford: Elsevier.

Overmier, J. B. (1999). On the nature of animals models of human behavioral dysfunction. In M. Haug and R. E. Whalen (Eds.), *Animal Models of human emotion and cognition* (pp. 15–24). Washington, DC: American Psychological Association.

Overmier, J. B. (2002). On learned helplessness. *Integrative Physiological and Behavioral Science, 37*, 4–8.

Overmier, J. B., & Lawry, J. A. (1979). Pavlovian conditioning and the mediation of behavior. In G. H. Bower (Ed.), *The psychology of learning and motivation* (Vol. 13). New York: Academic Press.

Overmier, J. B., & Linwick, D. (2001). Conditional choice-unique outcomes establish expectancies that mediate choice behavior. *Integrative Psychological & Behavioral Science, 36*, 173–181.

Overmier, J. B., & LoLordo, V. M. (1998). Learned helplessness. In W. O'Donohue (Ed.), *Learning and behavior therapy* (pp. 352–373). Boston: Allyn and Bacon.

Overmier, J. B., & Seligman, M. E. P. (1967). Effects of inescapable shock upon subsequent escape and avoidance learning. *Journal of Comparative and Physiological Psychology, 63*, 23–33.

Page, S., & Neuringer, A. (1985). Variability as an operant. *Journal of Experimental Psychology: Animal Behavior Processes, 11*, 429–452.

Papadouka, V., & Matthews, T. J. (1995). Motivational mechanisms and schedule-induced behavioral stereotypy. *Animal Learning & Behavior, 23*, 461–469.

Papini, M. R. (2003). Comparative psychology of surprising nonreward. *Brain, Behavior and Evolution, 62*, 83–95.

Papini, M. R. (2008). *Comparative psychology* (2nd Edition). London: Taylor Francis.

Papini, M. R., & Bitterman, M. E. (1990). The role of contingency in classical conditioning. *Psychological Review, 97*, 396–403.

Parker, L. A. (2003). Taste avoidance and taste aversion: Evidence for two different processes. *Learning & Behavior, 31*, 165–172.

Patterson, F. G. (1978). The gestures of a gorilla: Language acquisition in another pongid. *Brain and Language, 5*, 56–71.

Patterson, M. M., & Grau, J. W. (Eds.) (2001). Spinal cord plasticity: Alterations in reflex function. Boston: Kluwer Academic Publishers.

Pavlov, I. P. (1927). *Conditioned reflexes* (G. V. Anrep, trans.). London: Oxford University Press.

Pearce, J. M. (1987). A model for stimulus generalization in Pavlovian conditioning. *Psychological Review, 94*, 61–73.

Pearce, J. M. (1994). Similarity and discrimination: A selective review and a connectionistic model. *Psychological Review, 101*, 587–607.

Pearce, J. M. (2002). Evaluation and development of a connectionist theory of configural learning. *Animal Learning & Behavior, 30*, 73–95.

Pearce, J. M., & Bouton, M. E. (2001). Theories of associative learning. *Annual Review of Psychology, 52*, 111–139.

Pearce, J. M., & Hall, G. (1980). A model for Pavlovian learning: Variations in the effectiveness of conditioned but not of unconditioned stimuli. *Psychological Review, 87,* 532–552.

Pearce, J. M., Graham, M., Good, M. A., Jones, P. M., McGregor, A. (2006). Potentiation, overshadowing, and blocking of spatial learning based on the shape of the environment. *Journal of Experimental Psychology: Animal Behavior Processes, 32,* 201–214.

Pecina, S., Smith, K. S., & Berridge, K. C. (2006). Hedonic hot spots in the brain. *The Neuroscientist, 12,* 500–511.

Pedreira, M. E., Romano, A., Tomsic, D., Lozada, M., & Maldonado, H. (1998). Massed and spaced training build up different components of long-term habituation in the crab *Chasmagnathus. Animal Learning & Behavior, 26,* 34–45.

Pelchat, M. L., & Rozin, P. (1982). The special role of nausea in the acquisition of food dislikes by humans. *Appetite, 3,* 341–351.

Pelley, M. E. (2004). The role of associative history in models of associative learning: A selective review and a hybrid model. *Quarterly Journal of Experimental Psychology, 57B,* 193–243.

Pelloux, Y., Everitt, B. J., & Dickinson, A. (2007). Compulsive drug seeking by rats under punishment: effects of drug taking history. *Psychopharmacology, 194,* 127–137.

Pepperberg, I. M. (1990). Some cognitive capacities of an African grey parrot (*Psittacus erithacus*). In P. J. B. Slater, J. S. Rosenblatt, & C. Beer (Eds.), *Advances in the study of behavior* (Vol. 19, pp. 357–409). San Diego: Academic Press.

Pepperberg, I. M. (1993). Cognition and communication in an African Grey parrot (*Psittacus erithacus*): Studies on a nonhuman, nonprimate, nonmammalian subject. In Roitblat, H. L., Herman, L. M., & Nachtigall, P. E. (Eds.), *Language and communication: Comparative perspectives* (pp. 221–248). Hillsdale, NJ: Erlbaum.

Pepperberg, I. M. (1999). Rethinking syntax: A commentary on E. Kako's "Elements of syntax in the systems of three language-trained animals." *Animal Learning & Behavior, 27,* 15–17.

Pepperberg, I. M. (1999). *The Alex studies: Cognitive and communicative abilities of Grey Parrots.* Cambridge, MA: Harvard University Press.

Pérez, C., Fanizza, L. J., & Sclafani, A. (1999). Flavor preferences conditioned by intragastric nutrient infusions in rats fed chow or a cafeteria diet. *Appetite, 32,* 155–170.

Perry, D. G., & Parke, R. D. (1975). Punishment and alternative response training as determinants of response inhibition in children. *Genetic Psychology Monographs, 91,* 257–279.

Peterson, C., & Seligman, M. E. P. (1984). Causal explanations as a risk factor for depression: Theory and evidence. *Psychological Review, 91,* 347–374.

Peterson, C., Maier, S. F., & Seligman, M. E. P. (1993). *Learned helplessness: A theory for the age of personal control.* New York: Oxford University Press.

Peterson, G. B., & Trapold, M. A. (1980). Effects of altering outcome expectancies on pigeons' delayed conditional discrimination performance. *Learning and Motivation, 11,* 267–288.

Peterson, G. B., Ackil, J. E., Frommer, G. P., & Hearst, E. S. (1972). Conditioned approach and contact behavior toward signals for food and brain-stimulation reinforcement. *Science, 177,* 1009–1011.

Pfaus, J. G., Kippin. T. E., & Centeno, S. (2001). Conditioning and sexual behavior: A review. *Hormones and Behavior, 40,* 291–321.

Pilz, P. K., Schnitzler, H.-U. (1996). Habituation and sensitization of the acoustic startle response in rats: Amplitude, threshold, and latency measures. *Neurobiology of Learning and Memory, 66,* 67–79.

Pineño, O., & Miller, R. R. (2004). Signaling a change in cue-outcome relations in human associative learning. *Learning & Behavior, 32,* 360–375.

Pinker, S. (2002). *The blank slate: The modern denial of human nature.* New York: Viking.

Pisacreta, R. (1982). Some factors that influence the acquisition of complex, stereotyped, response sequences in pigeons. *Journal of the Experimental Analysis of Behavior, 37,* 359–369.

Pizzo, M. J., & Crystal, J. D. (2007). Temporal discrimination of alternative days in rats. *Learning & Behavior, 35,* 165–168.

Ploog, B. O. (2001). Effects of primary reinforcement on pigeons' initial-link responding under a concurrent-chains schedule with nondifferential terminal links. *Journal of the Experimental Analysis of Behavior, 76,* 75–94.

Ploog, B. O. (2001). Net amount of food affects autoshaped response rate, response latency, and gape amplitude in pigeons. *Learning and Motivation, 32,* 383–400.

Ploog, B. O., & Zeigler, H. P. (1996). Effects of food-pellet size on rate, latency, and topography of autoshaped key pecks and gapes in pigeons. *Journal of the Experimental Analysis of Behavior, 65,* 21–35.

Pockett, S., Banks, W. P., & Gallagher, S. (Eds.). (2006). *Does consciousness cause behavior?* Cambridge, Mass: MIT Press.

Podlesnik, C. A., & Shahan, T. A. (2008). Response-reinforcer relations and resistance to change. *Behavioural Processes, 77,* 109–125.

Poling, A., Nickel, M., & Alling, K. (1990). Free birds aren't fat: Weight gain in captured wild pigeons maintained under laboratory conditions. *Journal of the Experimental Analysis of Behavior, 53,* 423–424.

Postman, L. (1971). Transfer, interference, and forgetting. In J. W. Kling & L. A. Riggs (Eds.), *Woodworth and Schlosberg's experimental psychology* (3rd ed.). New York: Holt, Rinehart and Winston.

Poulos, C. X., & Cappell, H. (1991). Homeostatic theory of drug tolerance: A general model of physiological adaptation. *Psychological Review, 98,* 390–408.

Prados, J., Manteiga, R. D., & Sansa, J. (2003). Recovery effects after extinction in the Morris swimming pool navigation task. *Learning & Behavior, 31,* 299–304.

Pravosudov, V. V., & Clayton, N. S. (2002). A test of the adaptive specialization hyothesis: Population differences in caching, memory, and the hippocampus in black-capped chickadees (*Poecile atricapilla*). *Behavioral Neuroscience, 116,* 515–522.

Premack, D. (1965). Reinforcement theory. In D. Levine (Ed.), *Nebraska Symposium on Motivation* (Vol. 13, pp. 123–180). Lincoln: University of Nebraska Press.

Premack, D. (1971a). Catching up with common sense, or two sides of a generalization: Reinforcement and punishment. In R. Glaser (Ed),

The nature of reinforcement. New York: Academic Press.

Premack, D. (1971b). Language in chimpanzee? *Science, 172*, 808–822.

Premack, D. (1976). *Intelligence in ape and man*. Hillsdale, NJ: Erlbaum.

Prescott, T. J., Bryson, J. J., & Seth, A. K. (2007). Modelling natural action selection. *Philosophical Transactions of the Royal Society 362B*, 1521–1529.

Preston, K. L., Umbricht, A., Wong, C. J., & Epstein, D. H. (2001). Shaping cocaine abstinence by successive approximations. *Journal of Consulting and Clinical Psychology, 69*, 43–654.

Puente, G. P., Cannon, D. S., Best, M. R., & Carrell, L. E. (1988). Occasion setting of fluid ingestion by contextual cues. *Learning and Motivation, 19*, 239–253.

Quinn, J. J., & Fanselow, M. (2006). Defenses and memories: Functional neural circuitry of fear and conditional responding. In M. G. Craske, D. Vansteenwegen, and D. Hermans (Eds.), *Fear and learning: From basic processes to clinical implictions* (pp. 55–74). Washington, DC: American Psychological Association.

Quirk, G. J., Milad, M. R., Santini, E., & Lebrón, K. (2007). Learning not to fear: A neural systems approach. In L. J. Kirmayer, R. Lemelson, and M. Barad (Eds), *Understanding trauma: Integrating biological, clinical, and cultural perspectives* (pp. 60–77). Cambridge, England: Cambridge University Press.

Quirk, G. J. & Mueller, D. (2008). Neural mechanisms of extinction learning and retrieval. *Neuropsychopharmacology, 33*, 56–72.

Rachlin, H. (1995). Behavioral economics without anomalies. *Journal of the Experimental Analysis of Behavior, 64*, 397–404.

Rachlin, H. (1976). *Behavior and learning*. New York (?): W. H. Freeman.

Rachlin, H. (1989). *Judgement, decision, and choice*. New York: Freeman.

Rachlin, H. (2000). *The science of self-control*. Cambridge, Massachusetts: Harvard University Press.

Rachlin, H. (2006). Notes on discounting. *Journal of the Experimental Analysis of Behavior, 85*, 425–435.

Rachlin, H. C., & Green, L. (1972). Commitment, choice, and self-control. *Journal of the Experimental Analysis of Behavior, 17*, 15–22.

Rachlin, H. C., & Herrnstein, R. L. (1969). Hedonism revisited: On the negative law of effect. In B. A. Campbell & R. M. Church (Eds.), *Punishment and aversive behavior*. New York: Appleton Century-Crofts.

Raia, C. P., Shillingford, S. W., Miller, H. L., Jr., & Baier, P. S. (2000). *Journal of the Experimental Analysis of Behavior, 74*, 265–281.

Raiff, B. R., Bullock, C. E., & Hackenberg, T. D. (2008). Response-cost punishment with pigeons: Further evidence of response suppression via token loss. *Learning & Behavior, 36*, 29–41.

Ramirez, I. (1997). Carbohydrate-induced stimulation of saccharin intake: Yoked controls. *Animal Learning & Behavior, 25*, 347–356.

Randell, T., & Remington, B. (1999). Equivalence relations between visual stimuli: The functional role of naming. *Journal of the Experimental Analysis of Behavior, 71*, 395–415.

Randich, A., & LoLordo, V. M. (1979). Associative and non-associative theories of the UCS preexposure phenomenon: Implications for Pavlovian conditioning. *Psychological Bulletin, 86*, 523–548.

Rasmussen, E. B., & Newland, M. C. (2008). Asymmetry of reinforcement and punishment in human choice. *Journal of the Experimental Analysis of Behavior, 89*, 157–167.

Rau, V., & Fanselow, M. S. (2007). Neurobiological and neuroethological prespectives on fear and anxiety. In L. J. Kirmayer, R. Lemelson, and M. Barad (Eds), *Understanding trauma: Integrating biological, clinical, and cultural perspectives* (pp. 27–40). Cambridge, England: Cambridge University Press.

Rauhut, A. S., Thomas, B. L., & Ayres, J. J. B. (2001). Treatments that weaken Pavlovian conditioned fear and thwart its renewal in rats: Implications for treating human phobias. *Journal of Experimental Psychology: Animal Behavior Processes, 27*, 99–114.

Raymond, J. L., Lisberger, S. G., & Mauk, M. D. (1996). The cerebellum: A neuronal learning machine? *Science, 272*, 1126–1131.

Reberg, D. (1972). Compound tests for excitation in early acquisition and after prolonged extinction of conditioned suppression. *Learning and Motivation, 3*, 246–258.

Reberg, D., Innis, N. K., Mann, B., & Eizenga, C. (1978). "Superstitious" behavior resulting from periodic response-independent presentations of food or water. *Animal Behaviour, 26*, 506–519.

Reed, D. D., Critchfield, T. S., & Martins, B. K. (2006). The generalized matching law in elite sport competition: Football play calling as operant choice. *Journal of Applied Behavior Analysis, 39*, 281–297.

Reed, P. (2007a). Human sensitivity to reinforcement feedback functions. *Psychonomic Bulletin & Review, 14*, 653–657.

Reed, P. (2007b). Response rate and sensitivity to the molar feedback function relating response and reinforcement rate on VI+ schedules of reinforcement. *Journal of Experimental Psychology: Animal Behavior Processes, 33*, 428–439.

Reed, P., & Yoshino, T. (2008). Effect of contingent auditory stimuli on concurrent schedule performance: An alternative punisher to electric shock. *Behavioural Processes, 78*, 421–428.

Reid, A. K., Chadwick, C. Z., Dunham, M., & Miller, A. (2001). The development of functional response units: The role of demarcating stimuli. *Journal of the Experimental Analysis of Behavior, 72*, 81–96.

Reilly, S., & Schachtman, T. R. (Eds.), (2008). *Conditioned taste aversion: Behavioral and neural processes*. New York: Oxford University Press.

Repp, A. C., & Singh, N. N. (Eds.). (1990). *Perspectives on the use of nonaversive and aversive interventions for persons with developmental disabilities*. Sycamore, IL: Sycamore.

Rescorla, R. A. (1967a). Inhibition of delay in Pavlovian fear conditioning. *Journal of Comparative and Physiological Psychology, 64*, 114–120.

Rescorla, R. A. (1967b). Pavlovian conditioning and its proper control procedures. *Psychological Review, 74*, 71–80.

Rescorla, R. A. (1968). Pavlovian conditioned fear in Sidman avoidance learning. *Journal of Comparative and Physiological Psychology, 65*, 55–60.

Rescorla, R. A. (1969a). Conditioned inhibition of fear resulting from negative CS-US contingencies. *Journal of Comparative and Physiological Psychology, 67,* 504–509.

Rescorla, R. A. (1969b). Pavlovian conditioned inhibition. *Psychological Bulletin, 72,* 77–94.

Rescorla, R. A. (1980). *Pavlovian second-order conditioning.* Hillsdale, NJ: Erlbaum.

Rescorla, R. A. (1982). Effect of a stimulus intervening between CS and US in autoshaping. *Journal of Experimental Psychology: Animal Behavior Processes, 8,* 131–141.

Rescorla, R. A. (1985). Conditioned inhibition and facilitation. In R. R. Miller & N. E. Spear (Eds.), *Information processing in animals: Conditioned inhibition.* Hillsdale, NJ: Erlbaum.

Rescorla, R. A. (1986). Extinction of facilitation. *Journal of Experimental Psychology: Animal Behavior Processes, 12,* 16–24.

Rescorla, R. A. (1987). Facilitation and inhibition. *Journal of Experimental Psychology: Animal Behavior Processes, 13,* 250–259.

Rescorla, R. A. (1988). Facilitation based on inhibition. *Animal Learning & Behavior, 16,* 169–176.

Rescorla, R. A. (1990a). Evidence for an association between the discriminative stimulus and the response-outcome association in instrumental learning. *Journal of Experimental Psychology: Animal Behavior Processes, 16,* 326–334

Rescorla, R. A. (1990b). The role of information about the response-outcome relation in instrumental discrimination learning. *Journal of Experimental Psychology: Animal Behavior Processes, 16,* 262–270.

Rescorla, R. A. (1992). Association between an instrumental discriminative stimulus and multiple outcomes. *Journal of Experimental Psychology: Animal Behavior Processes, 18,* 95–104.

Rescorla, R. A. (1993a). Inhibitory associations between S and R in extinction. *Animal Learning & Behavior, 21,* 327–336.

Rescorla, R. A. (1993b). Preservation of response-outcome associations through extinction. *Animal Learning & Behavior, 21,* 238–245.

Rescorla, R. A. (1996a). Preservation of Pavlovian associations through extinction. *Quarterly Journal of Experimental Psychology, 49B,* 245–258.

Rescorla, R. A. (1996b). Response-outcome associations remain functional through interference treatments. *Animal Learning & Behavior, 24,* 450–458.

Rescorla, R. A. (1997). Response-inhibition in extinction. *Quarterly Journal of Experimental Psychology, 50B,* 238–252.

Rescorla, R. A. (1997a). Spontaneous recovery after Pavlovian conditioning with multiple outcomes. *Animal Learning & Behavior, 25,* 99–107.

Rescorla, R. A. (1997b). Spontaneous recovery of instrumental discriminative responding. *Animal Learning & Behavior, 27,* 485–497.

Rescorla, R. A. (1997c). Summation: Assessment of a configural theory. *Animal Learning Behavior, 25,* 200–209.

Rescorla, R. A. (1999a). Associative changes in elements and compounds when the other is reinforced. *Journal of Experimental Psychology: Animal Behavior Processes, 25,* 247–255.

Rescorla, R. A. (1999b). Summation and overexpectation with qualitatively different outcomes. *Animal Learning & Behavior, 27,* 50–62.

Rescorla, R. A. (1999c). Within-subject partial reinforcement extinction effect in autoshaping. *Quarterly Journal of Experimental Psychology, 52B,* 75–87.

Rescorla, R. A. (2000a). Associative changes with a random CS-US relationship. *Quarterly Journal of Experimental Psychology, 53B,* 325–340.

Rescorla, R. A. (2000b). Extinction can be enhanced by a concurrent excitor. *Journal of Experimental Psychology: Animal Behavior Processes, 26,* 251–260.

Rescorla, R. A. (2001a). Experimental extinction. In R. R. Mowrer & S. B. Klein (Eds.), *Contemporary learning theories* (pp. 119–154). Mahwah, NJ: Erlbaum.

Rescorla, R. A. (2001b). Retraining of extinguished Pavlovian stimuli. *Journal of Experimental Psychology: Animal Behavior Processes, 27,* 115–124.

Rescorla, R. A. (2003). Protection from extinction. *Learning & Behavior, 31,* 124–132.

Rescorla, R. A. (2004a). Spontaneous recovery. *Learning and Memory, 11,* 501–509.

Rescorla, R. A. (2004b). Spontaneous recovery varies inversely with the training-extinction interval. *Learning & Behavior, 32,* 401–408.

Rescorla, R. A. (2006a). Deepened extinction from compound stimulus presentation. *Journal of Experimental Psychology: Animal Behavior Processes, 32,* 135–144.

Rescorla, R. A. (2006b). Spontaneous recovery from overexpectation. *Learning & Behavior, 34,* 13–20.

Rescorla, R. A. (2006c). Stimulus generalization of excitation and inhibition. *Quarterly Journal of Experimental Psychology, 59,* 53–67.

Rescorla, R. A. (2007a). Renewal after overexpectation. *Learning & Behavior, 35,* 19–26.

Rescorla, R. A. (2007b). Spontaneous recovery after reversal and partial reinforcement. *Learning & Behavior, 35,* 191–200.

Rescorla, R. A. (2008). Evaluating conditioning of related and unrelated stimuli using a compound test. *Learning & Behavior, 36,* 67–74.

Rescorla, R. A., & Furrow, D. R. (1977). Stimulus similarity as a determinant of Pavlovian conditioning. *Journal of Experimental Psychology: Animal Behavior Processes, 3,* 203–215.

Rescorla, R. A., & Heth, C. D. (1975). Reinstatement of fear to an extinguished conditioned stimulus. *Journal of Experimental Psychology: Animal Behavior Processes, 104,* 88–96.

Rescorla, R. A., & Solomon, R. L. (1967). Two-process learning theory: Relationships between Pavlovian conditioning and instrumental learning. *Psychological Review, 74,* 151–182.

Rescorla, R. A., & Wagner, A. R. (1972). A theory of Pavlovian conditioning: Variations in the effectiveness of reinforcement and nonreinforcement. In A. H. Black & W. F. Prokasy (Eds.), *Classical conditioning II: Current research and theory* (pp. 64–99). New York: Appleton-Century-Crofts.

Rescorla, R. A., Durlach, P. J., & Grau, J. W. (1985). Contextual learning in Pavlovian conditioning. In P. Balsam & A. Tomie (Eds.), *Context and learning* (pp. 23–56). Hillsdale, NJ: Erlbaum.

Revusky, S. H., & Garcia, J. (1970). Learned associations over long delays. In G. H. Bower & J. T. Spence (Eds.), *The psychology of learning and motivation* (Vol. 4). New York: Academic Press.

Reynolds, G. S. (1961). Attention in the pigeon. *Journal of the Experimental Analysis of Behavior, 4,* 203–208.

Reynolds, G. S. (1975). *A primer of operant conditioning.* Glenview, IL: Scott Foresman.

Riccio, D. C., & Richardson, R. (1984). The status of memory following experimentally induced amnesias: Gone, but not forgotten. *Physiological Psychology, 12,* 59–72.

Riccio, D. C., MacArdy, E. A., & Kissinger, S. C. (1991). Associative processes in adaptation to repeated cold exposure in rats. *Behavioral Neuroscience, 105,* 599–602.

Riccio, D. C., Millin, P. M., & Bogart, A. R. (2006). Reconsolidation: A brief history, a retrieval view, and some recent issues. *Learning and Memory, 13,* 536–544.

Riccio, D. C., Rabinowitz, V. C., & Axelrod, S. (1994). Memory: When less is more. *American Psychologist, 49,* 917–926.

Richardson, R., Ledgerwood, L., & Cranney, J. (2004). Facilitation of fear extinction by D-cycloserine: Theoretical and clinical implications. *Learning and Memory, 11,* 510–516.

Richardson, R., Riccio, D. C., & Jonke, T. (1983). Alleviation of infantile amnesia in rats by means of a pharmacological contextual state. *Developmental Psychobiology, 16,* 511–518.

Riley, A. L., & Freeman, K. B. (2008). *Conditioned taste aversion: An annotated bibliography.* American University. www.ctalearning.com.

Ristau, C. A. (Ed.). (1991). *Cognitive ethology.* Hillsdale, NJ: Erlbaum.

Robbins, S. J. (1990). Mechanisms underlying spontaneous recovery in autoshaping. *Journal of Experimental Psychology: Animal Behavior Processes, 16,* 235–249.

Roberts, S. (1981). Isolation of an internal clock. *Journal of Experimental Psychology: Animal Behavior Processes, 7,* 242–268.

Roberts, S., & Church, R. M. (1978). Control of an internal clock. *Journal of Experimental Psychology: Animal Behavior Processes, 4,* 318–337.

Roberts, W. A. (1998). *Animal cognition.* Boston: McGraw-Hill.

Roberts, W. A. (2006). The questions of temporal and spatial displacement in animal cognition. In E. A. Wasserman and T. R. Zentall (Eds.) *Comparative cognition* (pp. 145–163). Oxford, UK: Oxford University Press.

Roberts, W. A., & Grant, D. S. (1976). Studies of short-term memory in the pigeon using the delayed matching to sample procedure. In D. L. Medin, W. A. Roberts, & R. T. Davis (Eds.), *Processes of animal memory.* Hillsdale, NJ: Erlbaum.

Roberts, W. A., & Grant, D. S. (1978). An analysis of light-induced retroactive inhibition in pigeon short term memory. *Journal of Experimental Psychology: Animal Behavior Processes, 4,* 219–236.

Roberts, W. A., & Van Veldhuizen, N. (1985). Spatial memory in pigeons on a radial maze. *Journal of Experimental Psychology: Animal Behavior Processes, 11,* 241–260.

Roberts, W. A., & Veldhuizen, N. V. (1985). Spatial memory in pigeons on the radial maze. *Journal of Experimental Psychology: Animal Behavior Processes, 11,* 241–260.

Roberts, W.A. (2002). Are animals stuck in time? *Psychological Bulletin, 128,* 473–489.

Robinson, T. E., & Berridge, K. C. (2003). Addiction. *Annual Review of Psychology, 54,* 25–53.

Rogers, R. F., Schiller, K. M., & Matzel, L. D. (1996). Chemosensory-based contextual conditioning in *Hermissenda crassicornis. Animal Learning & Behavior, 24,* 28–37.

Roitblat, H. L. (2007). A comparative psychologist looks at language. In D. A. Washburn (Ed.), *Primate perspectives on behavior and cognition* (pp. 235–242). Washington, DC: American Psychological Association.

Roitblat, H. L., & Meyer, J.-A. (Eds.). (1995). *Comparative approaches to cognitive science.* Cambridge, MA: MIT Press.

Roitblat, H. L., Harley, H. E., & Helweg, D. A. (1993). Cognitive processing in artificial language research. In Roitblat, H. L., Herman, L. M., & Nachtigall, P. E. (Eds.), *Language and communication: Comparative perspectives* (pp. 1–23). Hillsdale, NJ: Erlbaum.

Roitblat, H. L., Penner, R. H., & Nachtigall, P. E. (1990). Matching-to-sample by an echo locating dolphin (*Tursiops truncatus*). *Journal of Experimental Psychology: Animal Behavior Processes, 16,* 85–95.

Roll, J. M., & Newton, T. (2008). Methamphetamines. In S. T. Higgins, K. Silverman, & S. H. Heil (2008). *Contingency management in substance abuse treatment* (pp. 80–98). New York: Guilford Press.

Romanes, G. J. (1882). *Animal intelligence.* New York: Appleton.

Romaniuk, C. B., & Williams, D. A. (2000). Conditioning across the duration of a backward conditioned stimulus. *Journal of Experimental Psychology: Animal Behavior Processes, 26,* 454–461.

Roper, K. L., Chaponis, D. M., & Blaisdell, A. P. (2005). Transfer of directed-forgetting cues across discrimination tasks with pigeons. *Psychonomic Bulletin & Review, 12,* 1005–1010.

Roper, K. L., Kaiser, D. H., & Zentall, T. R. (1995). True directed forgetting in pigeons may occur only when alternative working memory is required on forget-cue trials. *Animal Learning & Behavior, 23,* 280–285.

Rosellini, R. A., & DeCola, J. P. (1981). Inescapable shock interferes with the acquisition of a low-activity response in an appetitive context. *Animal Learning & Behavior, 9,* 487–490.

Rosellini, R. A., DeCola, J. P., & Shapiro, N. R. (1982). Cross-motivational effects of inescapable shock are associative in nature. *Journal of Experimental Psychology: Animal Behavior Processes, 8,* 376–388.

Rosellini, R. A., DeCola, J. P., Plonsky, M., Warren, D. A., & Stilman, A. J. (1984). Uncontrollable shock proactively increases sensitivity to response-reinforcer independence in rats. *Journal of Experimental Psychology: Animal Behavior Processes, 10,* 346–359.

Ross, R. T., & Holland, P. C. (1981). Conditioning of simultaneous and serial feature-positive discriminations. *Animal Learning & Behavior, 9,* 293–303.

Rothbaum, B. O., Hodges, L., Smith, S., Lee, J.H., & Price, L. (2000). A controlled study of virtual reality exposure therapy for the fear of flying. *Journal of Consulting and Clinical Psychology, 68,* 1020–1026.

Rothbaum, B. O., Hodges, L. F., Ready, D., Graap, K., & Alarcon, R.D. (2001). Virtual reality exposure therapy for Vietnam veterans with post–traumatic stress disorder. *Jouranal of Clinical Psychiatry, 62,* 617–622.

Routtenberg, A. (2008). The substrate for long-lasting memory: If not protein synthesis, then what? *Neurobiology of Learning and Memory, 89,* 225–233.

Rovee-Collier, C., Hayne, H., & Colombo, M. (2001). *The development of implicit and explicit memory.* Philadelphia: John Benjamins.

Rozin, P., & Zellner, D. (1985). The role of Pavlovian conditioning in the acquisition of food likes and dislikes. *Annals of the New York Academy of Sciences, 443,* 189–202.

Rudy, J. W. (2008). Is there a baby in the bathwater? Maybe: Some methodological issues for the de novo protein synthesis hypothesis. *Neurobiology of Learning and Memory, 89,* 219–224.

Rumbaugh, D. M. (Ed.). (1977). *Language learning by a chimpanzee: The Lana project.* New York: Academic Press .

Russell, M. S., & Burch, R. L. (1959). *The principles of humane experimental technique.* London: Methuen.

Russell, W. R., & Nathan, P. W. (1946). Traumatic amnesia. *Brain, 69,* 280–300.

Russella, R., & Kirkpatrick, K. (2007). The role of temporal generalization in a temporal discrimination task. *Behavioural Processes, 74,* 115–125.

Sahley, C., Rudy, J. W., & Gelperin, A. (1981). An analysis of associative learning in a terrestrial mollusc: I. Higher-order conditioning, blocking, and a transient US-pre-exposure effect. *Journal of Comparative Physiology-A, 144,* 1–8.

Sajwaj, T., Libet, J., & Agras, S. (1974). Lemon-juice therapy: The control of life-threatening rumination in a six-month-old infant. *Journal of Applied Behavior Analysis, 7,* 557–563.

Saladin, M. E., Brady, K. T., Graap, K., & Rothbaum, B. O. (2004). A preliminary report on the use of virtual reality technology to elicit craving and cue reactivity in cocaine dependent individuals. *Addictive Behaviors, 31,* 1881–1894.

Saladin, M. E., Have, W. N., Saper, Z. L., Labinsky, J. S., & Tait, R. W. (1989). Retardation of rabbit nictitating membrane conditioning following US preexposures depends on the distribution and numbers of US presentations. *Animal Learning & Behavior, 17,* 179–187.

Salwiczek, L. H., Dickinson, A., & Clayton, N. S. (2008). What do animals remember about their past? In R. Menzel (Ed.), *Learning theory and behavior.* Vol. 1 of J. Byrne (Ed.), *Learning and Memory: A comprehensive reference* (pp. 441–460). Oxford: Elsevier.

Sanabria, F., Sitomer, M. T., & Killeen, P. R. (2006). Negative automaintenance omission training is effective. *Journal of the Experimental Analysis of Behavior, 86,* 1–10.

Sargisson, R. J., & White, K. G. (2001). Generalization of delayed matching to sample following training at different delays. *Journal of the Experimental Analysis of Behavior, 75,* 1–14.

Savage-Rumbaugh, E. S. (1986). *Ape language.* New York: Columbia University Press.

Savage-Rumbaugh, E. S., McDonald, K., Sevcik, R. A., Hopkins, W. D., & Rubert, E. (1986). Spontaneous symbol acquisition and communicative use by pigmy chimpanzees (*Pan paniscus*). *Journal of Experimental Psychology: General, 115,* 211–235.

Savage-Rumbaugh, E. S., Murphy, J., Sevcik, R. A., Brakke, K. E., Williams, S. L., & Rumbaugh, D. M. (1993). Language comprehension in ape and child. *Monographs of the Society for Research in Child Development* (Vol. 58, Nos. 3–4, Serial No. 233).

Savage-Rumbaugh, E. S., Sevcik, R. A., Brakke, K. E., & Rumbaugh, D. M. (1990). Symbols: Their communicative use, comprehension, and combination by bonobos (*Pan paniscus*). In C. Rovee-Collier & L. P. Lipsitt (Eds.), *Advances in infancy research* (Vol. 6, pp. 221–278). Norwood, NJ: Ablex.

Savage-Rumbaugh, S., Shanker, S. G., & Taylor, T. J. (1998). *Apes, language, and the human mind.* New York: Oxford University Press.

Savastano, H. I., & Fantino, E. (1996). Differences in delay, not ratios, control choice in concurrent chains. *Journal of the Experimental Analysis of Behavior, 66,* 97–116.

Savastano, H. I., & Miller, R. R. (1998). Time as content in Pavlovian conditioning. *Behavioural Processes, 44,* 147–162.

Savastano, H. I., Arcediano, F., Stout, S. C., & Miller, R. R. (2003). Interaction between preexposure and overshadowing: Further analysis of the extended comparator hypothesis. *Quarterly Journal of Experimental Psychology, 56B,* 371–395.

Savastano, H. I., Cole, R. P., Barnet, R. C., & Miller, R. R. (1999). Reconsidering conditioned inhibition. *Learning and Motivation, 30,* 101–127.

Savastano, H., & Fantino, E. (1994). Human choice in concurrent ratio-interval schedules of reinforcement. *Journal of the Experimental Analysis of Behavior, 61,* 453–463.

Sawa, K., Nakajima, S., & Imada, H. (1999). Facilitation of sodium aversion learning in sodium-deprived rats. *Learning and Motivation, 30,* 281–295.

Scalera, G. (2002). Effects of conditioned food aversions on nutritional behavior in humans. *Nutritional Neuroscience, 5,* 159–188.

Scalera, G., & Bavieri, M. (2008). Role of conditioned taste aversion on the side effects of chemotherapy in cancer patients. In S. Reilly, & T. R. Schachtman (Eds.), *Conditioned taste aversion: Behavioral and neural processes* (pp. 513–542). New York: Oxford University Press.

Scavio, M. J., Jr., & Gormezano, I. (1974). CS intensity effects on rabbit nictitating membrane conditioning, extinction and generalization. *Pavlovian Journal of Biological Science, 9,* 25–34.

Schaal, S. et al. (2004). *From animals to animats 8.* Cambridge, MA: MIT Press.

Schachter, D. L., & Tulving, E. (1994). What are the memory systems of 1994? In D. L. Schachter and E. Tulving (Eds.), *Memory systems 1994* (pp. 1–38). Cambridge, MA: MIT Press.

Schachtman, T. R., Brown, A. M., & Miller, R. R. (1985). Reinstatement-induced recovery of a taste-LiCl association following extinction.

Animal Learning & Behavior, 13, 223–227.

Schachtman, T. R., Gee, J.-L., Kasprow, W. J., & Miller, R. R. (1983). Reminder-induced recovery from blocking as a function of the number of compound trials. *Learning and Motivation, 14,* 154–164.

Schafe, G. E., & LeDoux, J. E. (2000). Memory consolidation of auditory Pavlovian fear conditioning requires protein synthesis and protein kinase A in the amygdala. *Journal of Neuroscience, 20:* RC96, 1–5.

Schiff, R., Smith, N., & Prochaska, J. (1972). Extinction of avoidance in rats as a function of duration and number of blocked trials. *Journal of Comparative and Physiological Psychology, 81,* 356–359.

Schindler, C. W., & Weiss, S. J. (1982). The influence of positive and negative reinforcement on selective attention in the rat. *Learning and Motivation, 13,* 304–323.

Schlinger, H., Blakely, E., & Kaczor, T. (1990). Pausing under variable-ratio schedules: Interaction of reinforcer magnitude, variable-ratio size, and lowest ratio. *Journal of the Experimental Analysis of Behavior, 53,* 133–139.

Schlosberg, H. (1934). Conditioned responses in the white rat. *Journal of Genetic Psychology, 45,* 303–335.

Schlosberg, H. (1936). Conditioned responses in the white rat: II. Conditioned responses based upon shock to the foreleg. *Journal of Genetic Psychology, 49,* 107–138.

Schmajuk, N. A., & Holland, P. C. (Eds.). (1998). *Occasion setting: Associative learning and cognition in animals.* Washington, DC: American Psychological Association.

Schmajuk, N. A., & Holland, P. C. (Eds.). (1998). *Occasion setting.* Washington, DC: American Psychological Association.

Schmajuk, N. A., & Larrauri, J. A. (2006). Experimental challenges to theories of classical conditioning: Application of an attentional model of storage and retrieval. *Journal of Experimental Psychology: Animal Behavior Processes, 32,* 1–20.

Schmidt, N. B., Anthony, R. J., Maner, J. K., & Woolaway-Bickel, K. (2006). Differential effects of safety in extinction of anxious responding to a CO_2 challenge in patients with panic disorder. *Journal of Abnormal Psychology, 115,* 341–350.

Schneiderman, N., & Gormezano, I. (1964). Conditioning of the nictitating membrane of the rabbit as a function of CS-US interval. *Journal of Comparative and Physiological Psychology, 57,* 188–195.

Schöner, G., & Thelen, E. (2006). Using dynamic field theory to rethink infant habituation. *Psychological Review, 113,* 273–299.

Schreibman, L., Koegel, R. L., Charlop, M. H., & Egel, A. L. (1990). Infantile autism. In A. S. Bellack, M. Hersen, & A. E. Kazdin (Eds.), *International handbook of behavior modification and therapy.* (pp. 763–789). New York: Plenum.

Schreurs, B. G. (1998). Long-term memory and extinction of rabbit nictitating membrane trace conditioning. *Learning and Motivation, 29,* 68–82.

Schultz, W. (2006). Behavioral theories and the neurophysiology of reward. *Annual Review of Psychology, 57,* 87–115.

Schultz, W., Dayan, P., & Montaque, P. R. (1997). A neural substrate of prediction and reward. *Science, 275,* 1593–1599.

Schuster, C. R. (1999). Foreword. In S. T. Higgins & K. Silverman (Eds.), *Motivating behavior change among illicit-drug abusers.* Washington, DC: American Psychological Association. (p. xiii).

Schuster, R. H., & Rachlin, H. (1968). Indifference between punishment and free shock: Evidence for the negative law of effect. *Journal of the Experimental Analysis of Behavior, 11,* 777–786.

Schusterman, R. J., & Gisiner, R. (1988). Artificial language comprehension in dolphins and sea lions: The essential cognitive skills. *Psychological Record, 38,* 311–348.

Schwartz, B. (1976). Positive and negative conditioned suppression in the pigeon: Effects of the locus and modality of the CS. *Learning and Motivation, 7,* 86–100.

Schwartz, B. (1980). Development of complex, stereotyped behavior in pigeons. *Journal of the Experimental Analysis of Behavior, 33,* 153–166.

Schwartz, B. (1981). Reinforcement creates behavioral units. *Behavioural Analysis Letters, 1,* 33–41.

Schwartz, B. (1985). On the organization of stereotyped response sequences. *Animal Learning & Behavior, 13,* 261–268.

Schwartz, B. (1988). The experimental synthesis of behavior: Reinforcement, behavioral stereotypy, and problem solving. In G. H. Bower(Ed.), *The psychology of learning and motivation* (Vol. 22, pp. 93–138). Orlando, FL: Academic Press.

Schweitzer, J. B., & Sulzer-Azaroff, B. (1988). Self-control: Teaching tolerance for delay in impulsive children. *Journal of the Experimental Analysis of Behavior, 50,* 173–186.

Sclafani, A. (1997). Learned controls of ingestive behaviour. *Appetite, 29,* 153–158.

Seligman, M. E. P., & Maier, S. F. (1967). Failure to escape traumatic shock. *Journal of Experimental Psychology, 74,* 1–9.

Senkowski, P. C. (1978). Variables affecting the overtraining extinction effect in discrete-trial lever pressing. *Journal of Experimental Psychology: Animal Behavior Processes, 4,* 131–143.

Sevcik, R. A., Romski, M. A., & Wilkenson, K. (1991). Roles of graphic symbols in the language acquisition process for persons with severe cognitive disabilities. *Journal of Augmentative and Alternative Communication, 7,* 161–170.

Sevenster, P. (1973). Incompatibility of response and reward. In R. A. Hinde & J. Stevenson-Hinde (Eds.), *Constraints on learning.* London: Academic Press.

Sheffield, F. D., Roby, T. B., & Campbell, B. A. (1954). Drive reduction versus consummatory behavior as determinants of reinforcement. *Journal of Comparative and Physiological Psychology, 47,* 349–354.

Sherry, D. F. (1984). Food storage by black-capped chickadees: Memory for the location and contents of caches. *Animal Behaviour, 32,* 451–464.

Sherry, D. F. (1985). Food storage by birds and mammals. *Advances in the study of behavior, 15,* 153–188.

Sherry, D. F., Krebs, J. R., & Cowie, R. J. (1981). Memory for the location of stored food in marsh tits. *Animal Behaviour, 29,* 1260–1266.

Shettleworth, S. J. (1975). Reinforcement and the organization of behavior in golden hamsters: Hunger, environment, and food reinforcement. *Journal of Experimental Psychology: Animal Behavior Processes, 1,* 56–87.

Shettleworth, S. J. (1998). *Cognition, evolution, and behavior.* New York: Oxford University Press.

Shettleworth, S. J., & Krebs, J. R. (1986). Stored and encountered seeds: A comparison of two spatial memory tasks in marsh tits and chickadees. *Journal of Experimental Psychology: Animal Behavior Processes, 12,* 248–257.

Shettleworth, S. J., & Sutton, J. E. (2005). Multiple systems for spatial learning: Dead reckoning and beacon homing in rats. *Journal of Experimental Psychology: Animal Behavior Processes, 31,* 125–141.

Shimp, C. P. (1966). Probabilistically reinforced choice behavior in pigeons. *Journal of the Experimental Analysis of Behavior, 9,* 443–455.

Shimp, C. P. (1969). Optimum behavior in free-operant experiments. *Psychological Review, 76,* 97–112.

Shimp, C. P., Herbranson, W. T., Fremouw, T., & Froehlich, A. L. (2006). Rule learning, memorization strategies, switching attention between local and global levels of perception, and optimality in avian visual categorization. In E. A. Wasserman and T. R. Zentall (Eds.) *Comparative cognition.* (pp. 388–404). Oxford, UK: Oxford University Press.

Shors, T. J. (2006). Stressful experience and learning across the lifespan. *Annual Review of Psychology, 57,* 55–85.

Shuwairi, S. M., Albert, M. K., & Johnson, S. P. (2007). Discrimination of possible and impossible objects in infancy. *Psychological Science, 18,* 303–307.

Sidman, M. & Tailby, W. (1982). Conditional discrimination vs. matching to sample: An expansion of the testing paradigm. *Journal of the Experimental Analysis of Behavior, 37,* 5–22.

Sidman, M. (1953a). Avoidance conditioning with brief shock and no exteroceptive warning signal. *Science, 118,* 157–158.

Sidman, M. (1953b). Two temporal parameters of the maintenance of avoidance behavior by the white rat. *Journal of Comparative and Physiological Psychology, 46,* 253–261.

Sidman, M. (1960). *Tactics of scientific research.* New York: Basic Books.

Sidman, M. (1962). Reduction of shock frequency as reinforcement for avoidance behavior. *Journal of the Experimental Analysis of Behavior, 5,* 247–257.

Sidman, M. (1966). Avoidance behavior. In W. K. Honig (Ed.), *Operant behavior.* New York: Appleton-Century-Crofts.

Sidman, M. (1990). Equivalence relations: Where do they come from? In D. E. Blackman & H. Lejeune (Eds.), *Behavioral analysis in theory and practice: Contributions and controversies* (pp. 93–114). Hillsdale, NJ: Erlbaum.

Sidman, M. (1994). *Equivalence relations and behavior: A research story.* Boston: Authors Cooperative.

Sidman, M. (2000). Equivalence relations and the reinforcement contingency. *Journal of the Experimental Analysis of Behavior, 74,* 127–146.

Siegel, S. (1984). Pavlovian conditioning and heroin overdose: Reports by overdose victims. *Bulletin of the Psychonomic Society, 22,* 428–430.

Siegel, S. (1999). Drug anticipation and drug addiction. The 1998 H. David Archibald lecture. *Addiction, 94,* 1113–1124.

Siegel, S. (2005). Drug tolerance, drug addiction, and drug anticipation. *Current Directions in Psychological Science, 14,* 296–300.

Siegel, S. (2008). Learning and the wisdom of the body. *Learning & Behavior, 36,* 242–252.

Siegel, S., & Allen, L. G. (1996). The widespread influence of the Rescorla-Wagner model. *Psychonomic Bulletin & Review, 3,* 314–321.

Siegel, S., & Allan, L. G. (1998). Learning and homeostasis: Drug addiction and the McCollough effect. *Psychological Bulletin, 124,* 230–239.

Siegel, S., & Domjan, M. (1971). Backward conditioning as an inhibitory procedure. *Learning and Motivation, 2,* 1–11.

Siegel, S., & Ramos, B. M. C. (2002). Applying laboratory research: Drug anticipation and the treatment of drug addiction. *Experimental and Clinical Psychopharmacology, 10,* 162–183.

Siegel, S., Baptista, M. A. S., Kim, J. A., McDonald, R. V., & Weise-Kelly, L. (2000). Pavlovian psychopharmacology: The associative basis of tolerance. *Experimental and Clinical Psychopharmacology, 8,* 276–293.

Siegel, S., Hinson, R. E., Krank, M. D., & McCully, J. (1982). Heroin "overdose" death: Contribution of drug associated environmental cues. *Science, 216,* 436–437.

Sigurdsson, T., Doyere, V., Cain, C. K., & LeDoux, J. E. (2007). Long-term potentiation in the amygdala: A cellular mechanism of fear learning and memory. *Neuropharmacology, 125,* 215–227.

Sigmundi, R. A. (1997). Performance rules for problem-specific defense reactions. In M. E. Bouton and M. S. Fanselow (Eds.), *Learning, motivation, and cognition* (pp. 305–319). Washington, DC: American Psychological Association.

Sigmundi, R. A., & Bolles, R. C. (1983). CS modality, context conditioning, and conditioned freezing. *Animal Learning & Behavior, 11,* 205–212.

Sigurdsson, T., Doyere, V., Cain, C. K., & LeDoux, J. E. (2007). Long-term potentiation in the amygdala: A cellular mechanism of fear learning and memory. *Neuropharmacology, 52,* 215–227.

Silberberg, A., Warren-Boulton, F. R., & Asano, T. (1987). Inferior-good and Giffen-good effects in monkey choice behavior. *Journal of Experimental Psychology: Animal Behavior Processes, 13,* 292–301.

Silva, A. J., & Giese, K. P. (1998). Gene tageting: A novel window into the biology of learning and memory. In J. L. Martinez & R. P. Kesner (Eds.), *Neurobiology of learning and memory* (pp. 89–142). San Diego: Academic Press.

Silva, K. M., & Timberlake, W. (1997). A behavior systems view of conditioned states during long and short CS-US intervals. *Learning and Motivation, 28,* 465–490.

Silva, K. M., & Timberlake, W. (1998). The organization and temporal properties of appetitive behavior in rats. *Animal Learning & Behavior, 26,* 182–195.

Simons, R. C. (1996). *Boo! Culture, experience, and the startle reflex.* New York: Oxford University Press.

Singh, N. N., & Solman, R. T. (1990). A stimulus control analysis of the picture-word problem in children who are mentally retarded: The blocking effect. *Journal of Applied Behavior Analysis, 23,* 525–532.

Skinner, B. F. (1938). *The behavior of organisms.* New York: Appleton-Century-Crofts.

Skinner, B. F. (1948). "Superstition" in the pigeon. *Journal of Experimental Psychology, 38,* 168–172.

Skinner, B. F. (1953). *Science and human behavior.* New York: Macmillan.

Slamecka, N. J., & Ceraso, J. (1960). Retroactive and proactive inhibition of verbal learning. *Psychological Bulletin, 57,* 449–475.

Small, W. S. (1899). An experimental study of the mental processes of the rat: 1. *American Journal of Psychology, 11,* 133–164.

Small, W. S. (1900). An experimental study of the mental processes of the rat: 11. *American Journal of Psychology, 12,* 206–239.

Smeets, P. M., & Barnes-Holmes, D. (2005). Establishing equivalence classes in preschool children with one-to-many and many-to-one training protocols. *Behavioural Processes, 69,* 281–293.

Smith, C. N., Clark, R. E., Manns, J. R., & Squire, L. R. (2005). Acquisition of differential delay eyeblink classical conditioning is independent of awareness. *Behavioral Neuroscience, 119,* 78–86.

Smith, J. C., & Roll, D. L. (1967). Trace conditioning with X-rays as an aversive stimulus. *Psychonomic Science, 9,* 11–12.

Smith, M. C., Coleman, S. R., & Gormezano, I. (1969). Classical conditioning of the rabbit's nicti-tating membrane response at backward, simultaneous, and forward CS-US intervals. *Journal of Comparative and Physiological Psychology, 69,* 226–231.

Smith, M. T., Perlis, M. L., Park, A., Smith, M. S., Pennington, J., Giles, D. E., & Buysse, D. J. (2002). Comparative meta-analysis of pharmacotherapy and behavior therapy for persistent insomnia. *American Journal of Psychiatry, 159,* 5–11.

Snodgrass, S. H., & McMillan, D. E. (1996). Drug discrimination under a concurrent schedule. *Journal of the Experimental Analysis of Behavior, 65,* 495–512.

Solomon, R. L. (1964). Punishment. *American Psychologist, 19,* 239–253.

Solomon, R. L., & Corbit, J. D. (1973). An opponent-process theory of motivation: II. Cigarette addiction. *Journal of Abnormal Psychology, 81,* 158–171.

Solomon, R. L., & Corbit, J. D. (1974). An opponent-process theory of motivation: I. The temporal dynamics of affect. *Psychological Review, 81,* 119–145.

Solomon, R. L., & Wynne, L. C. (1953). Traumatic avoidance learning: Acquisition in normal dogs. *Psychological Monographs, 125* (Whole No. 354).

Solomon, R. L., Kamin, L. J., & Wynne, L. C. (1953). Traumatic avoidance learning: The outcomes of several extinction procedures with dogs. *Journal of Abnormal and Social Psychology, 48,* 291–302.

Spear, N. E., & Riccio, D. C. (1994). *Memory: Phenomena and principles.* Boston: Allyn and Bacon.

Spence, K. W. (1936). The nature of discrimination learning in animals. *Psychological Review, 43,* 427–449.

Spence, K. W. (1937). The differential response in animals to stimuli varying within a single dimension. *Psychological Review, 44,* 430–444.

Spence, K. W. (1956). *Behavior theory and conditioning.* New Haven, CT: Yale University Press.

Spetch, M. L. (1987). Systematic errors in pigeons' memory for event duration: Interaction between training and test delays. *Animal Learning & Behavior, 15,* 1–5.

Spetch, M. L., & Kelly, D. M. (2006). Comparative spatial cognition: Processes in landmark- and surface-based place finding. In In E. A. Wasserman and T. R. Zentall (Eds.) *Comparative cognition* (pp. 210–228). Oxford, UK: Oxford University Press.

Spetch, M. L., Cheng, K., & Clifford, C. W. G. (2004). Peak shift but not range effects in recognition of faces. *Learning and Motivation, 35,* 221–241.

Spetch, M. L., Wilkie, D. M., & Pinel, J. P. J. (1981). Backward conditioning: A reevaluation of the empirical evidence. *Psychological Bulletin, 89,* 163–175.

Spetch, M. L., Wilkie, D. M., & Skelton, R. W. (1981). Control of pigeons' keypecking topography by a schedule of alternating food and water reward. *Animal Learning & Behavior, 9,* 223–229.

Spradlin, J. E. (2002). Punishment: A primary process? *Journal of Applied Behavior Analysis, 35,* 457–477.

Squire, L. R. (2006). Lost forever or temporarily misplaced? The long debate about the nature of memory impairment. *Learning and Memory, 13,* 522–529.

Staddon, J. (2001). *The new behaviorism: Mind, Mechanism, and Society.* Philadelphia: Taylor Fracis, Psychology Press.

Staddon, J. E. R. (1983/2003). *Adaptive behavior and learning.* Cambridge: Cambridge University Press.

Staddon, J. E. R. (1988). Quasi-dynamic choice models: Melioration and ratio invariance. *Journal of the Experimental Analysis of Behavior, 49,* 303–320.

Staddon, J. E. R. (2001). *Adaptive dynamics.* Cambridge, Massachusetts: MIT Press.

Staddon, J. E. R., & Cerutti, D. T. (2003). Operant conditioning. *Annual Review of Psychology, 54,* 115–144.

Staddon, J. E. R., & Higa, J. (1996). Multiple time scales in simple habituation. *Psychological Review, 203,* 720–733.

Staddon, J. E. R., & Simmelhag, V. L. (1971). The "superstition" experiment: A reexamination of its implications for the principles of adaptive behavior. *Psychological Review, 78,* 3–43.

Stafford, D., & Branch, M. N. (1998). Effects of step size and break point criterion on progressive-ratio performance. *Journal of the Experimental Analysis of Behavior, 70,* 123–138.

Stanhope, K. J. (1992). The representation of the reinforcer and the force of the pigeon's keypeck in first- and second-order conditioning. *The Quarterly Journal of Experimental Psychology, 44B,* 137–158.

Stasiak, M., & Masterton, R. B. (1996). Auditory quality cues are more effective than auditory location cues in a R-no R (go-no go) differentiation: The extension of the rule to primitive mammals (American opossum *Didelphis virginiana*). *Acta Neurobiologica Experimentalis, 56,* 949–953.

Steinert, P., Fallon, D., & Wallace, J. (1976). Matching to sample in gold-fish (*Carassuis auratus*). *Bulletin of the Psychonomic Society, 8,* 265.

Steinmetz, J. E., Gluck, M. A., & Solomon, P. R. (2001). Model Systems and the Neurobiology of Associative Learning: A Festschrift in Honor of Richard F. Thompson. Erlbaum: Hillsdale, NJ.

Steinmetz, J. E., Tracy, J. A., & Green, J. T. (2001). Classical eyeblink conditioning: Clinical models and applications. *Integrative Physiological and Behavioral Science, 36,* 220–238.

Stephenson, D., & Siddle, D. (1983). Theories of habituation. In D. Siddle (Ed.), *Orienting and habituation: Perspectives in human research.* Chichester, England: Wiley.

Stevens, S. S. (1951). Mathematics, measurement and psychophysics. In S. S. Stevens (Ed.), *Handbook of experimental psychology* (pp. 1–49). New York: Wiley.

Stewart, J., & Eikelboom, R. (1987). Conditioned drug effects. In L. L. Iversen, S. D. Iversen, & S. H. Snyder (Eds.), *Handbook of psychopharmacology* (Vol. 19, pp. 1–57). New York: Plenum.

Stewart, J., & Wise, R. A. (1992). Reinstatement of heroin self-administration habits: Morphine prompts and naltrexone discourages renewed responding after extinction. *Psychopharmacology, 108,* 79–84.

Stokes, P. D. (2006). *Creativity from constraints.* New York: Springer.

Stokes, P. D., Mechner, F., & Balsam, P. D. (1999). Effects of different acquisition procedures on response variability. *Animal Learning & Behavior, 27,* 28–41.

Stokes, T. F., & Baer, D. M. (1977). An implicit technology of generalization. *Journal of Applied Behavior Analysis, 10,* 349–367.

Stone, A. A., Turkkan, J. S., Bachrach, C. A., Jobe, J. B., Kurtzman, H. S., Cain, V. S. (Eds.). (2000). *The science of self-report.* Mahwah, NJ: Erlbaum.

Stout, S, Escobar, M., & Miller, R. R. (2004). Trial number and compound stimuli temporal relationships as joint determinants of second-order conditioning and conditioned inhibition. *Learning & Behavior, 32,* 230–239.

Stout, S. C., & Miller, R. R. (2007). Sometimes-competing retrieval (SOCR): A formalization of the comparator hypothesis. *Psychological Review, 114,* 759–783. Correc-

tion published in 2008, *Psychological Review, 115,* 82.

Straub, R. O., & Terrace, H. S. (1981). Generalization of serial learning in the pigeon. *Animal Learning & Behavior, 9,* 454–468.

Strijkstra, A. M., & Bolhuis, J. J. (1987). Memory persistence of rats in a radial maze vanes with training procedure. *Behavioral and Neural Biology, 47,* 158–166.

Suarez, S. D., & Gallup, G. G. (1981). An ethological analysis of open-field behavior in rats and mice. *Learning and Motivation, 12,* 342–363.

Sumpter, C. E., Temple, W., & Foster, T. M. (1998). Response form, force, and number: Effects on concurrent-schedule performance. *Journal of the Experimental Analysis of Behavior, 70,* 45–68.

Sumpter, C. E., Temple, W., & Foster, T. M. (2004). Comparing demand functions when different price manipulations are used: Does unit price help? *Learning & Behavior, 32,* 202–212.

Sundberg, M. L. (1996). Toward granting linguistic competence to apes: A review of Savage-Rumbaugh et al.'s *Language comprehension in ape and child. Journal of the Experimental Analysis of Behavior, 65,* 477–492.

Sunsay, C., & Bouton, M. E. (2008). Analysis of the trial-spacing effect with relatively long intertrial intervals. *Learning & Behavior, 36,* 104–115.

Susswein, A. J., & Schwarz, M. (1983). A learned change of response to inedible food in Aplysia. *Behavioral and Neural Biology, 39,* 1–6.

Sutherland, A. (2008). *What Shamu taught me about life, love, and marriage.* New York: Random House.

Sutphin, G., Byrne, T., & Poling, A. (1998). Response acquisition with delayed reinforcement: A comparison of two-lever procedures. *Journal of the Experimental Analysis of Behavior, 69,* 17–28.

Sutton, R. S., & Barto, A. G. (1998). *Reinforcement learning: An Introduction.* Cambridge, Mass: MIT Press.

Suzuki, S., Augerinos, G., & Black, A. H. (1980). Stimulus control of spatial behavior on the eight-arm maze in rats. *Learning and Motivation, 11,* 1–18.

Svartdal, F. (2000). Persistence during extinction: Conventional and re-

versed PREE under multiple schedules. *Learning and Motivation, 31,* 21–40.

Swartzentruber, D. (1993). Transfer of contextual control across similarly trained conditioned stimuli. *Animal Learning & Behavior, 21,* 14–22.

Swartzentruber, D. (1995). Modulatory mechanisms in Pavlovian conditioning. *Animal Learning & Behavior, 23,* 123–143.

Swartzentruber, D. (1997). Modulation by the stimulus properties of excitation. *Journal of Experimental Psychology: Animal Behavior Processes, 23,* 434–440.

Taglialatela, J. P., Savage-Rumbaugh, S., & Baker, L. A. (2003). Vocal production by a language-competent *Pan paniscus. International Journal of Primatology, 24,* 1–15.

Tait, R. W., & Saladin, M. E. (1986). Concurrent development of excitatory and inhibitory associations during backward conditioning. *Animal Learning & Behavior, 14,* 133–137.

Takeuchi, S. A. (2006). On the matching phenomenon in courtship: A probability matching theory of mate selection. *Marriage & Family Review, 40,* 25–51.

Tang, Y.-P., Shimizu, E., Dube, G. R., Rampon, C., Kerchner, G. A., Zhuo, M., Liu, G., & Tsien, J. Z. (1999). Genetic enhancement of learning and memory in mice. *Nature, 401,* 63–69.

Tindell, A. J., Smith, K. S., Pecina, S., Berridge, K. C., & Aldridge, J. W. (2006). Ventral pallidum firing codes hedonic reward: when a bad taste turns good. *Journal of Neurophysiology, 96,* 2399–2409.

Tsien, Joe Z. Building a brainier mouse. *Scientific American, 282,* 62–69.

Tanno, T. & Sakagami, T. (2008). On the primacy of molecular processes in determining response rates under variable-ratio and variable-interval schedules. *Journal of the Experimental Analysis of Behavior, 89,* 5–14.

Taylor, K. M., Joseph, V. T., Balsam, P. D., & Bitterman, M. E. (2008). Target-absent controls in blocking experiments with rats. *Learning & Behavior, 36,* 145–148.

Taylor, S. E., Klein, L. C., Lewis, B. P., Gruenewald, T. L., Gurung, R. A. R., & Updegraff, J. A. (2000). Biobehavioral responses to stress in females: Tend-and-befriend, not fight-or-flight. *Psychological Review, 107,* 411–429.

Terrace, H. (2006). The simultaneous chain: A new look at serially organized behavior. In E. A. Wasserman and T. R. Zentall (Eds.), *Comparative cognition* (pp. 481–511). Oxford, UK: Oxford University Press.

Terrace, H. S. (1979). *Nim.* New York: Knopf.

Terrace, H. S., Petitto, L. A., Sanders, R. J., & Bever, T. G. (1979). Can an ape create a sentence? *Science, 206,* 891–1201.

Terrace, H. S., Son, L. K., & Brannon, E. M. (2003). Serial expertise of rhesus macaques. *Psychological Science, 14,* 66–73.

Theios, J. (1962). The partial reinforcement effect sustained through blocks of continuous reinforcement. *Journal of Experimental Psychology, 64,* 1–6.

Theios, J., & Brelsford, J. (1964). Overlearning-extinction effect as an incentive phenomena. *Journal of Experimental Psychology, 67,* 463–467.

Thomas, B. L., & Ayres, J. J. B. (2004). Use of the ABA fear renewal paradigm to assess the effects of extinction with co-present fear inhibitors or excitors: Implications for theories of extinction and for treating human fears and phobias. *Learning and Motivation, 35,* 22–52.

Thomas, B. L., & Papini, M. R. (2001). Adrenalectomy eliminates the extinction spike inn autoshaping with rats. *Physiology & Behavior, 72,* 543–547.

Thomas, D. R. (1993). A model for adaptation-level effects on stimulus generalization. *Psychological Review, 100,* 658–673.

Thomas, D. R., & Empedocles, S. (1992). Novelty vs. retrieval cue value in the study of long-term memory in pigeons. *Journal of Experimental Psychology: Animal Behavior Processes, 18,* 22–23.

Thomas, D. R., McKelvie, A. R., & Mah, W. L. (1985). Context as a conditional cue in operant discrimination reversal learning. *Journal of Experimental Psychology: Animal Behavior Processes, 11,* 317–330.

Thomas, G. V., & Lieberman, D. A. (1990). Commentary: Determinants of success and failure in experiments on marking. *Learning and Motivation, 21,* 110–124.

Thomas, J. R. (1968). Fixed ratio punishment by timeout of concurrent variable-interval behavior. *Journal of the Experimental Analysis of Behavior, 11,* 609–616.

Thompson, R. F. (1986). The neurobiology of learning and memory. *Science, 233,* 941–947.

Thompson, R. F. (1993). The brain: A neuroscience primer. W. H. Freeman: New York.

Thompson, R. F. (2005). In search of memory traces. *Annual Review of Psychology, 56,* 1–23.

Thompson, R. F., & Spencer, W. A. (1966). Habituation: A model phenomenon for the study of neuronal substrates of behavior. *Psychological Review, 73,* 16–43.

Thompson, R. F., Groves, P. M., Teyler, T. J., & Roemer, R. A. (1973). A dual-process theory of habituation: Theory and behavior. In H. V. S. Peeke & M. J. Herz (Eds.), *Habituation.* New York: Academic Press.

Thompson, R. H., Iwata, B. A., Conners, J., & Roscoe, E. M. (1999). Effects of reinforcement for alternative behavior during punishment of self-injury. *Journal of Applied Behavior Analysis, 32,* 317–328.

Thorndike, E. L. (1898). Animal intelligence: An experimental study of the association processes in animals. *Psychological Review Monograph, 2* (Whole No. 8).

Thorndike, E. L. (1911). *Animal intelligence: Experimental studies.* New York: Macmillan.

Thorndike, E. L. (1932). The *fundamentals of learning.* New York: Teachers College, Columbia University.

Tierney, K. J. (1995). Molar regulatory theory and behavior therapy. In W. O'Donohue and L. Krasnerr (Eds.), *Theories of behavior therapy* (pp. 97–128). Washington, DC: American Psychological Association.

Tierney, K. J., & Bracken, M. (1998). Stimulus equivalence and behavior therapy. In W. O'Donohue (Ed.), *Learning and behavior therapy* (pp. 392–402). Boston: Allyn and Bacon.

Timberlake, W. (1980). A molar equilibrium theory of learned performance. In G. H. Bower (Ed.), *The psychology of learning and motivation* (Vol. 14). New York: Academic Press.

Timberlake, W. (1983). Rats' responses to a moving object related to food or water: A behavior-systems analysis. *Animal Learning & Behavior, 11,* 309–320.

Timberlake, W. (1984). Behavior regulation and learned performance: Some misapprehensions and disagreements. *Journal of the Experimental Analysis of Behavior, 41,* 355–375.

Timberlake, W. (1990). Natural learning in laboratory paradigms. In D. A. Dewsbury (Ed.), *Contemporary issues in comparative psychology* (pp. 31–54). Sunderland, MA: Sinauer.

Timberlake, W. (1994). Behavior systems, associations, and Pavlovian conditioning. *Psychonomic Bulletin & Review, 1,* 405–420.

Timberlake, W. (1995). Reconceptualizing reinforcement: A causal-system approach to reinforcement and behavior change. In W. O'Donohue and L. Krasnerr (Eds.), *Theories of behavior therapy* (pp. 59–96). Washington, DC: American Psychological Association.

Timberlake, W. (2001). Motivational modes in behavior systems. In R. R. Mowrer and S. B. Klein (Eds.), *Handbook of contemporary learning theories* (pp. 155–209). Mahwah, NJ: Erlbaum.

Timberlake, W., & Allison, J. (1974). Response deprivation: An empirical approach to instrumental performance. *Psychological Review, 81,* 146–164.

Timberlake, W., & Farmer- Dougan, V. A. (1991). Reinforcement in applied settings: Figuring out ahead of time what will work. *Psychological Bulletin, 110,* 379–391.

Timberlake, W., & Grant, D. S. (1975). Auto-shaping in rats to the presentation of another rat predicting food. *Science, 190,* 690–692.

Timberlake, W., & Lucas, G. A. (1985). The basis of superstitious behavior: Chance contingency, stimulus substitution, or appetitive behavior? *Journal of the Experimental Analysis of Behavior, 44,* 279–299.

Timberlake, W., & Lucas, G. A. (1989). Behavior systems and learning: From misbehavior to general principles. In S. B. Klein & R. R. Mowrer (Eds.),

Contemporary learning theories: Instrumental conditioning and the impact of biological constraints on learning (pp. 237–275). Hillsdale, NJ: Erlbaum.

Timberlake, W., & Lucas, G. A. (1991). Period water, interwater interval, and adjunctive behavior in a 24–hour multiresponse environment. *Animal Learning & Behavior, 19,* 369–380.

Timberlake, W., & White, W. (1990). Winning isn't everything: Rats need only food deprivation and not food reward to efficiently traverse a radial arm maze. *Learning and Motivation, 21,* 153–163.

Timberlake, W., Leffel, J., & Hoffman, C. M. (1999). Stimulus control and function of arm and wall travel by rats on a radial arm floor maze. *Animal Learning & Behavior, 27,* 445–460.

Timberlake, W., Sinning, S. A., & Leffel, J. K. (2007). Beacon training in a water maze can facilitate and compete with subsequent room cue learning in rats. *Journal of Experimental Psychology: Animal Behavior Processes, 33,* 225–243.

Timberlake, W., Wahl, G., & King, D. (1982). Stimulus and response contingencies in the misbehavior of rats. *Journal of Experimental Psychology: Animal Behavior Processes, 8,* 62–85.

Tinbergen, N. (1951). *The study of instinct.* Oxford: Oxford University Press, Clarendon Press.

Tinbergen, N., & Perdeck, A. C. (1950). On the stimulus situation releasing the begging response in the newly hatched herring gull chick (*Larus argentatus argentatus Pont*). *Behaviour, 3,* 1–39.

Todes, D. P. (1997). From the machine to the ghost within: Pavlov's transition from digestive physiology to conditioned reflexes. *American Psychologist, 52,* 947–955.

Tomie, A., Brooks, W., & Zito, B. (1989). Sign-tracking: The search for reward. In S. B. Klein & R. R. Mowrer (Eds.), *Contemporary learning theories: Pavlovian conditioning and the status of learning theory* (pp. 191–223). Hillsdale, NJ: Erlbaum.

Tomie, A., Carelli, R., & Wagner, G. C. (1993). Negative correlation between tone (S-) and water increases target biting during S- in rats. *Animal Learning & Behavior, 21,* 355–359.

Treichler, F. R., Rhaganti, M. A., & Van Tilburg, D. N. (2003). Linking of serially ordered lists by macaque monkeys (*Macaca mulatta*): List position influences. *Journal of Experimental Psychology: Animal Behavior Processes, 29,* 211–221.

Treichler, F. R., Rhaganti, M. A., & Van Tilburg, D. N. (2007). Serial list linking by macaque monkeys (*Macaca mulatta*): List property limitations. *Journal of Comparative Psychology, 121,* 250–259.

Trenholme, I. A., & Baron, A. (1975). Immediate and delayed punishment of human behavior by loss of reinforcement. *Learning and Motivation, 6,* 62–79.

Trosclair- Lasserre, N. M., Lerman, D. C., Call, N. A., Addison, L. R., & Kodak, T. (2008). Reinforcement magnitude: An evaluation of preference and reinforcer efficacy. *Journal of Applied Behavior Analysis, 41,* 203–220.

Tulving, E. (1983). *Elements of Episodic Memory.* New York: Clarendon Press.

Turkkan, J. S. (1989). Classical conditioning: The new hegemony. *The Behavioral and Brain Sciences, 12,* 121–179.

Twitmyer, E. B. (1974). A study of the knee jerk. *Journal of Experimental Psychology, 103,* 1047–1066.

Tzschentke, T. M. (2007). Measuring reward with the conditioned place preference (CPP) paradigm: Update of the last decade. *Addictive Biology, 12,* 227–262.

Underwood, B. J. (1957). Interference and forgetting. *Psychological Review, 64,* 49–60.

Ungless, M. A. (1998). A Pavlovian analysis of food-attraction conditioning in the snail *Helix aspersa*. *Animal Learning & Behavior, 26,* 15–19.

Üngör, M., & Lachnit, H. (2006). Contextual control in discrimination reversal learning. *Journal of Experimental Psychology: Animal Behavior Processes, 32,* 441–453.

Urcelay, G. P., & Miller, R. R. (2006). A comparator view of Pavlovian and differential inhibition. *Journal of Experimental Psychology: Animal Behavior Processes, 32,* 271–283.

Urcelay, G. P., & Miller, R. R. (2008a). Counteraction between two kinds of conditioned inhibition training. *Psychonomic Bulletin & Review, 15,* 103–107.

Urcelay, G. P., & Miller, R. R. (2008b). Retrieval from memory. In R. Menzel (Ed.), *Learning theory and behavior.* Vol 1 of J. Byrne (Ed.), *Learning and Memory: A comprehensive reference* (pp. 53–74). Oxford: Elsevier.

Urcuioli, P. J. (2005). Behavioral and associative effects of differential outcomes in discrimination learning. *Learning & Behavior, 33,* 1–21.

Urcuioli, P. J. (2006). Responses and acquired equivalence classes. In E. A. Wasserman and T. R. Zentall (Eds.), *Comarative cognition* (pp. 405–421). New York: Oxford University Press.

Urcuioli, P. J. (2008). The nature of the response in Simon discriminations by pigeons. *Learning & Behavior, 36,* 200–209.

Urcuioli, P. J., & Kasprow, W. J. (1988). Long-delay learning in the T-maze: Effects of marking and delay-interval location. *Learning and Motivation, 19,* 66–86.

van der Kolk, B. A. (2006). Clinical implications of neuroscience research in PTSD. *Annals of the New York Academy of Sciences, 1071,* 277–293.

Vansteenwegen, D., Dirikx, T., Hermans, D., Vervliet, B., & Eelen, P. (2006). Renewal and reinstatement of fear: Evidence from human conditioning research. In M. G. Craske, D. Hermans, and D. Vansteenwegen (Eds.), *Fear and learning* (pp. 197–215). Washington, DC: American Psychological Association.

Vansteenwegen, D., Vervliet, B., Iberico, C., Baeyens, F., Van den Bergh, O., & Hermans, D. (2007). The repeated confrontation with videotapes of spiders in multiple contexts attenuates renewal of fear in spider-anxious students. *Behaviour Research and Therapy, 45,* 1169–1179.

Vaughan, W., Jr. (1981). Melioration, matching, and maximizing. Journal of the Experimental *Analysis of Behavior, 36,* 141–149.

Vaughan, W., Jr. (1985). Choice: A local analysis. *Journal of the Experimental Analysis of Behavior, 43,* 383–405.

Vaughan, W., Jr., & Greene, S. L. (1984). Pigeon visual memory capacity. *Journal of Experimental*

Psychology: Animal Behavior Processes, 10, 256–271.

Vicken, R. J., & McFall, R. M. (1994). Paradox lost: Implications of contemporary reinforcement theory for behavior therapy. *Current Directions in Psychological Science, 4,* 121–125.

Visalberghi, E., & Fragaszy, D. (2006). What is challenging about tool use? The capuchin's perspective. In E. A. Wasserman and T. R. Zentall (Eds.), *Comparative cognition* (pp. 529–552). Oxford, UK: Oxford University Press.

Vogel, E. H., Castro, M. E., & Saavedra, M. A. (2004). Quantitative models of Pavlovian conditioning. *Brain Research Bulletin, 63,* 173–202.

Vollmer, T. R., & Bourret, J. (2000). An application of the matching law to evaluate the allocation of two- and three-point shots by college basketball players. *Journal of Applied Behavior Analysis, 33,* 137–150.

Vorhees, C. V., & Williams, M. T. (2006). Morris water maze: Procedures for assessing spatial and related forms of learning and memory. *Nature Protocols, 1,* 848–858.

Vorndran, C. M., & Lerman, D. C. (2006) Establishing and maintaining treatment effects with less intrusive consequences via a pairing procedure. *Journal of Applied Behavior Analysis, 39,* 35–48.

Vuchinich, R. E., & Tucker, J. A. (2006). Behavioral economic concepts in the analysis of substance abuse. In F. Rotgers, J. Morgenstern, & S. T. Walters (Eds.) *Treating substance abuse: Theory and technique* (pp. 217–247). New York: Guilford Press.

Waddell, J., Morris, R. W., & Bouton, M. E. (2006). Effects of bed nucleus of the stria terminalis lesions conditioned anxiety: Conditioning with long-duration conditional stimuli and reinstatement of extinguished fear. *Behavioral Neuroscience, 120,* 324–336.

Wade-Galuska, T., Perone, M., & Wirth, O. (2005). Effects of past and upcoming response-force requirements on fixed-ratio pausing. *Behavioural Processes, 68,* 91–95.

Wagner, A. R. (1961). Effects of amount and percentage of reinforcement and number of acquisition trials on conditioning and extinction. *Journal of Experimental Psychology, 62,* 234–242.

Wagner, A. R. (1976). Priming in STM: An information processing mechanism for self-generated or retrieval generated depression in performance. In T. J. Tighe & R. N. Leaton (Eds.), *Habituation: Perspectives from child development, animal behavior, and neurophysiology.* Hillsdale, NJ: Erlbaum.

Wagner, A. R. (1981). SOP: A model of automatic memory processing in animal behavior. In N. E. Spear & R. R. Miller (Eds.), *Information processing in animals: Memory mechanisms* (pp. 5–47). Hillsdale, NJ: Erlbaum.

Wagner, A. R. (2003). Context-sensitive elemental theory. *Quarterly Journal of Experimental Psychology, 56B,* 7–29.

Wagner, A. R. (2008a). Evolution of an elemental theory of Pavlovian conditioning. *Learning & Behavior, 36,* 253–265.

Wagner, A. R. (2008b). Some observations and remembrances of Kenneth W. Spence. *Learning & Behavior, 36,* 169–173.

Wagner, A. R., & Rescorla, R. A. (1972). Inhibition in Pavlovian conditioning: Application of a theory. In R. A Boakes & M. S. Halliday (Eds.), *Inhibition and learning.* London: Academic Press.

Wagner, A. R., & Vogel, E. H. (2008). Configural and elemental processing in associative learning: Commentary on Melchers, Shanks, and Lachnit. *Behavioural Processes, 77,* 446–450.

Wagner, A. R., Rudy, J. W., & Whitlow, J. W. (1973). Rehearsal in animal conditioning. *Journal of Experimental Psychology, 97,* 407–426.

Wagner, K., & Neuringer, A. (2006). Operant variability when reinforcement is delayed. *Learning & Behavior, 34,* 111–123.

Walters, E. T. (1994). Injury related behavior and neuronal plasticity: An evolutionary perspective on sensitization, hyperalgesia, and analgesia. *International Review of Neurobiology, 36,* 325–427.

Walters, G. C., & Grusec, J. F. (1977). *Punishment.* San Francisco: W. H. Freeman.

Ward-Robinson, J., & Hall, G. (1996). Backward sensory preconditioning. *Journal of Experimental Psychol-*

ogy: Animal Behavior Processes, 22, 395–404.

Ward-Robinson, J., & Hall, G. (1998). Backward sensory preconditioning when reinforcement is delayed. *Quarterly Journal of Experimental Psychology, 51,* 349–362.

Wasserman, E. A. (1993). Comparative cognition: Beginning the second century of the study of animal intelligence. *Psychological Bulletin, 113,* 211–228.

Wasserman, E. A., & Miller, R. R. (1997). What's elementary about associative learning? *Annual Review of Psychology, 48,* 573–607.

Wasserman, E. A., & Zentall, T. R. (Eds.) (2006a). *Comparative cognition.* Oxford: Oxford University Press.

Wasserman, E. A., & Zentall, T. R. (2006b). Comparative cognition: A natural science approach to the study of animal intelligence. In E. A. Wasserman and T. R. Zentall (Eds.), *Comparative cognition* (pp. 3–11). Oxford, England: Oxford University Press.

Wasserman, E. A., DeLong, R. E., & Larew, M. B. (1984). Temporal order and duration: Their discrimination and retention by pigeons. *Annals of the New York Academy of Sciences, 423,* 103–115.

Watanabe, S., Sakamoto, J., & Wakita, M. (1995). Pigeons' discrimination of paintings by Monet and Picasso. *Journal of the Experimental Analysis of Behavior, 63,* 165–174.

Watson, J. B., & Rayner, R. (1920). Conditioned emotional reactions. *Journal of Experimental Psychology, 3,* 1–14. Reprinted in 2000 *American Psychologist, 55,* 313–317.

Wegner, D. M. (2002). *The illusion of conscious will.* Cambridge, Mass: MIT Press.

Weidemann, G., & Kehoe, E. J. (2003). Savings in classical conditioning in the rabbit as a function of extended extinction. *Learning & Behavior, 31,* 49–68.

Weinberger, N. (1965). Effect of detainment on extinction of avoidance responses. *Journal of Comparative and Physiological Psychology, 60,* 135–138.

Weir, A. A. S, & Kacelnik, A. (2006). A New Caledonian crow (*Corvus moneduloides*) creatively re-designs tools by bending or unbending aluminium strips. *Animal Cognition, 9,* 317–334.

Weisman, R. G., & Litner, J. S. (1972). The role of Pavlovian events in avoidance training. In R. A. Boakes & M. S. Halliday (Eds.), *Inhibition and learning*. London: Academic Press.

Weiss, S. J., Kearns, D. N., Cohn, S. I., Schindler, C. W., & Panlilio, L. V. (2003). Stimulus control of cocaine self-administration. *Journal of the Experimental Analysis of Behavior, 79,* 111–135.

Weiss, S. J., Panlilio, L. V., & Schindler, C. W. (1993a). Selective associations produced solely with appetitive contingencies: The stimulus-reinforcer interaction revisited. *Journal of the Experimental Analysis of Behavior, 59,* 309–322.

Weiss, S. J., Panlilio, L. V., & Schindler, C. W. (1993b). Single-incentive selective associations produced solely as a function of compound-stimulus conditioning context. *Journal of Experimental Psychology: Animal Behavior Processes, 19,* 284–294.

Wernig, A., Muller, S., Nanassy, A., & Cagol, E. (1995). Laufband therapy based on "rules of spinal locomotion" is effective in spinal cord injured persons. *European Journal of Neuroscience, 7,* 823–829.

Wheeler, D. S., Sherwood, A., & Holland, P. C. (2008). Excitatory and inhibitory learning with absent stimuli. *Journal of Experimental Psychology: Animal Behavior Processes, 34,* 247–255.

White, K. G. (2001). Forgetting functions. *Animal Learning & Behavior, 29,* 193–207.

White, K. G., Parkinson, A. E., Brown, G. S., & Wixted, J. T. (2004). Local proactive interference in delayed matching to sample: The role of reinforcement. *Journal of Experimental Psychology: Animal Behavior Processes, 30,* 83–95.

Wiers, R. W., & Stacy, A. W. (2006). Implicit cognition and addiction. *Current directions in psychological science, 15,* 292–296.

Wilkie, D. M., & Summers, R. J. (1982). Pigeons' spatial memory: Factors affecting delayed matching of key location. *Journal of the Experimental Analysis of Behavior, 37,* 45–56.

Wilkinson, A., Chan, H.-M., & Hall, G. (2007). Spatial learning and memory in the tortoise (*Geochelone carbonaria*). *Journal of Comparative Psychology, 121,* 412–418.

William, B. A. (1991). Choice as a function of local versus molar contingencies of reinforcement. *Journal of the Experimental Analysis of Behavior, 56,* 455–473.

William, B. A. (1994). Reinforcement and choice. In N. J. Mackintosh (Ed.), *Animal learning and cognition* (pp. 81–108). San Diego: Academic Press.

Williams, A. M., & Lattal, K. A. (1999). The role of the response-reinforcer relation in delay-of-reinforcement effects. *Journal of the Experimental Analysis of Behavior, 71,* 187–194.

Williams, B. A. (1991). Marking and bridging versus conditioned reinforcement. *Animal Learning & Behavior, 19,* 264–269.

Williams, B. A. (1992). Inverse relations between preference and contrast. *Journal of the Experimental Analysis of Behavior, 58,* 303–312.

Williams, B. A. (1997). Conditioned reinforcement dynamics in three-link chained schedules. *Journal of the Experimental Analysis of Behavior, 67,* 145–159.

Williams, B. A. (2001). The critical dimensions of the response-reinforcer contingency. *Behavioural Processes, 54,* 111–126.

Williams, B. A. (1999). Blocking the response-reinforcer association: theoretical implications. *Psychonomic Bulletin & Review, 6,* 618–623.

Williams, D. A., & Hurlburt, J. L. (2000). Mechanisms of second-order conditioning with a backward conditioned stimulus. *Journal of Experimental Psychology: Animal Behavior Processes, 26,* 340–351.

Williams, D. A., & Overmier, J. B. (1988). Some types of conditioned inhibitors carry collateral excitatory associations. *Learning and Motivation, 19,* 345–368.

Williams, D. A., Johns, K. W., & Brindas, M. (2008). Timing during inhibitory conditioning. *Journal of Experimental Psychology: Animal Behavior Processes, 34,* 237–246.

Williams, D. A., Lawson, C., Cook, R., & Johns, K. W. (2008). Timed excitatory conditioning under zero and negative contingencies. *Journal of Experimental Psychology: Animal Behavior Processes, 34,* 94–105.

Williams, D. A., Overmier, J. B., & LoLordo, V. M. (1992). A reevaluation of Rescorla's early dictums about Pavlovian conditioned inhibition. *Psychological Bulletin, 111,* 275–290.

Williams, D. C., Saunders, K. J., & Perone, M. (2008). Extended pausing in human subjects on multiple fixed-ratio schedules with varied reinforcer magnitude and response requirements. *Journal of Experimental Analysis of Behavior.*

Willis, W. D. (2001). Mechanisms of central sensitization of nociceptive dorsal horn neurons. In M. M. Patterson and J. W. Grau (Eds.), *Spinal cord plasticity: Alterations in reflex function* (pp. 127–161). Boston: Kluwer Academic Publishers.

Winter, J., & Perkins, C. C. (1982). Immediate reinforcement in delayed reward learning in pigeons. *Journal of the Experimental Analysis of Behavior, 38,* 169–179.

Winterbauer, N. E., & Balleine, B. W. (2005). Motivational control of second-order conditioning. *Journal of Experimental Psychology: Animal Behavior Processes, 31,* 334–340.

Witcher, E. S., & Ayres, J. J. B. (1984). A test of two methods for extinguishing Pavlovian conditioned inhibition. *Animal Learning & Behavior, 12,* 149–156.

Wolpe, J. (1990). *The practice of behavior therapy.* (4th ed.). New York: Pergamon.

Wood, W., & Neal, D. T. (2007). A new look at habits and the habit-goal interface. *Psychological Review, 114,* 843–863.

Woodruff-Pak, D. S. (2001). Eyeblink classical conditioning differentiates normal aging from Alzheimer's disease. *Integrative Physiological and Behavioral Science, 36,* 87–108.

Woodruff-Pak, D. S., Seta, S., Roker, L. A., & Lehr, M. A. (2007). Effects of age and inter-stimulus interval in delay and trace eyeblink classical conditioning in rabbits. *Learning & Memory, 14,* 287–294.

Woodson, J. C. (2002). Including "learned sexuality" in the organization of sexual behavior. *Neuroscience & Biobehavioral Reviews, 26,* 69–80.

Wright, A. A. (1990). Markov choice processes in simultaneous matching-to-sample at different levels of discriminability. *Animal Learning & Behavior, 18,* 277–286.

Wright, A. A. (1992). Learning mechanisms in matching to sample. *Journal of Experimental Psychology: Animal Behavior Processes, 18,* 67–79.

Wright, A. A., & Delius, J. D. (1994). Scratch and match: Pigeons learn matching and oddity with gravel stimuli. *Journal of Experimental Psychology: Animal Behavior Processes, 20,* 108–112.

Wright, A. A., & Katz, J. S. (2007). Generalization hypothesis of abstract-concept learning: Learning strategies and related issues in *Macaca mulatta, Cebus apella,* and *Columbia livia. Journal of Comparative Psychology, 121,* 387–397.

Wright, A. A., & Sands, S. F. (1981). A model of detection and decision processes during matching to sample by pigeons: Performance with 88 different wavelengths in delayed and simultaneous matching tasks. *Journal of Experimental Psychology: Animal Behavior Processes, 7,* 191–216.

Wright, A. A., Shyan, M. R., & Jitsumori, M. (1990). Auditory same/different concept learning by monkeys. *Animal Learning & Behavior, 18,* 287–294.

Yeomans, M. R., Durlach, P. J., & Tinley, E. M. (2005). Flavour liking and preference conditioned by caffeine in humans. *Quartely Journal of Experimental Psychology, 58B,* 47–58.

Yerkes, R. M., & Morgulis, S. (1909). The method of Pavlov in animal psychology. *Psychological Bulletin, 6,* 257–273.

Yin, H., Barnet, R. C., & Miller, R. R. (1994). Second-order conditioning and Pavlovian conditioned inhibition: Operational similarities and differences. *Journal of Experimental Psychology: Animal Behavior Processes, 20,* 419–428.

Zamble, E., Hadad, G. M., Mitchell, J. B., & Cutmore, T. R. H. (1985). Pavlovian conditioning of sexual arousal: First- and second-order effects. *Journal of Experimental Psychology: Animal Behavior Processes, 11,* 598–610.

Zarcone, T. J., & Ator, N. A. (2000). Drug discrimination: stimulus control during repeated testing in extinction. *Journal of the Experimental Analysis of Behavior, 74,* 283–294.

Zeiler, M. D. (1984). The sleeping giant: Reinforcement schedules. *Journal of the Experimental Analysis of Behavior, 42,* 485–493.

Zentall, T. R. (2001). The case for a cognitive approach to animal learning and behavior. *Behavioural Processes, 54,* 65–78.

Zentall, T. R. (2005). Animals may not be stuck in time. *Learning and Motivation, 36,* 208–225.

Zentall, T. R., & Smeets, P. M. (Eds.). (1996). *Stimulus class formation in humans and animals. Advances in Psychology* (Vol. 117). New York: North-Holland (Elsevier Science).

Zentall, T. R., Edwards, C. A., Moore, B. S., & Hogan, D. E. (1981). Identity: The basis for both matching and oddity learning in pigeons. *Journal of Experimental Psychology: Animal Behavior Processes, 7,* 70–86.

Zentall, T. R., Jagielo, J. A., Jackson-Smith, P. & Urcuioli, P. J. (1987). Memory codes in pigeon short-term memory: Effects of varying the number of sample and comparison stimuli. *Learning and Motivation, 18,* 21–33.

Zentall, T. R., Singer, R. A., & Miler, H. C. (2008). Matching-to-sample by pigeons: The dissociation of comparison choice frequency from the probability of reinforcement. *Behavioural Processes, 78,* 185–190.

Zhou, Y., & Riccio, D. C. (1995). Concussion-induced retrograde amnesia in rats. *Physiology & Behavior, 57,* 1107–1115.

Zhou, Y., & Riccio, D. C. (1996). Manipulation of components of context: The context shift effect and forgetting of stimulus attributes. *Learning and Motivation, 27,* 400–407.

Zimmer- Hart, C. L., & Rescorla, R. A. (1974). Extinction of Pavlovian conditioned inhibition. *Journal of Comparative and Physiological Psychology, 86,* 837–845.

Zoladek, L., & Roberts, W. A. (1978). The sensory basis of spatial memory in the rat. *Animal Learning & Behavior, 6,* 77–81.

Workbook for Michael Domjan's The Principles of Learning and Behavior, 6th edition

Mark A. Krause
Southern Oregon University

Table of Contents

Preface

Your course on learning will be full of terminology, concepts, and theories that have developed over the long history of this discipline. Organizing and making sense of the material is challenging. But you will reap the rewards that go with understanding the complex process of learning. This workbook is designed to help you enhance and solidify your knowledge of the psychology of learning.

Students who are working to grasp the basic foundations of the field find it challenging to organize the vast amount of information that is standard for most courses in learning. The learning course you are taking probably involves lectures from your professor, discussions and demonstrations done in class, assignments using Sniffy the Virtual Rat, and, for some, an actual laboratory opportunity. This workbook will provide you with another active, hands-on approach to studying learning.

As you encounter the terminology and concepts of learning it is important that you are actively engaged with the material. This workbook facilitates hands-on, active learning and has a chapter that coincides with the material from each chapter of your text, *The Principles of Learning and Behavior* (6th edition) by Michael Domjan. The workbook is not a condensed alternative to the text. I do not recommend that you attempt to work through any of the exercises *before* reading the corresponding text chapter. I recommend that you first carefully read each textbook chapter before attempting the corresponding workbook exercises. I do not devote much time and space to reiterating background information from the text. However, once you have read the text the terminology and concepts in the exercises will be familiar. I frequently refer you to textbook pages to refresh your memory of specific topics we cover. For this workbook, it was not possible to cover *all* terms and concepts in your textbook. This does not imply that some of the material in your textbook is not important.

The problems in the chapters that follow take a variety of forms. Many are designed to reflect how learning is studied. For example, research on learning involves frequent experimentation on human and nonhuman subjects. Thus, many of the exercises ask you to design experiments. You will also work with some small data sets from actual and hypothetical experiments. I frequently ask you to use graphs to illustrate and summarize results from experiments. This allows you to more clearly picture the concepts you are learning about, and encourages you to think carefully about the material.

Some of the exercises in this workbook ask you to apply concepts to your own experiences. For example, the terminology from classical conditioning is often confusing to students, so I have provided exercises that will allow you to apply these terms to new situations. Many of the problems in the workbook involve exercises. In addition, I have included something called "concept questions." These questions typically ask you to elaborate and apply ideas and theories presented in your text.

Your professor may have required you to use Sniffy the Virtual Rat (Pro version 2.0). Throughout the workbook I include an icon

SNIFFY APPLICATION

that refers to exercises and corresponding page numbers from your Sniffy manual. The purpose of this is to coordinate the Sniffy exercises with your textbook and workbook.

Studying the psychology of learning is a highly rewarding undertaking. Theories of learning are foundational to the field of psychology and apply to its many sub-disciplines. There are numerous practical applications of learning as well, from educational to therapeutic settings. One thing we know, as both psychologists and students, is that learning involves *doing*. Sometimes this means going beyond your textbook to get information. Thus, it is my hope that you find the exercises in this workbook helpful and that they facilitate your learning about learning.

Finally, I would like to thank your textbook author, Michael Domjan, for inviting me to write this and for helping to develop many of the exercises.

Mark A. Krause
Southern Oregon University

1 Introduction

The first chapter of your text serves to orient you toward the basic questions that psychologists ask about learning, and the theoretical perspectives that contemporary researchers in learning adopt. We will start this workbook with several exercises based on **chapter 1** of your text. First, we ask you some concept questions about topics including associationism, functional neurology, and model systems (**section 1-1**). Following this series of questions are exercises that serve to clarify our definition of learning (**section 1-2**). Our knowledge of learning is almost exclusively derived from carefully designed experiments. Familiarity with terminology and concepts associated with experimental methodology is essential to understanding the text material. **Sections 1-3** and **1-4** help you brush up on your knowledge of common experimental concepts and with graphing and interpreting results.

After completing these exercises you should be able to:

- Describe the concept of *association* and apply it to examples
- Understand the role of functional neurology in the study of learning
- Distinguish between changes in behavior due to learning and other processes such as fatigue, maturation, and motivation
- Identify and apply basic terminology associated with the experimental method
- Read and create clear, interpretable graphs

1-1 Historical Viewpoints

Concept Questions

1) Describe an example of an association you have made between two stimuli from your daily experience. What is the triggering stimulus? What memory is activated by the stimulus? Is this association based on learning? What is your evidence for this?

2) What were Aristotle's laws of association? Using your example of an association described above, which of Aristotle's laws apply? How?

3) What is functional neurology? Why are studies of learning relevant to it?

4) What are the critical features of a model system (**page 14**) that is designed to represent other species or situations?

1-2 Defining Learning

One of the defining features of learning is that behavior changes as a result of experience. However, this feature alone does not distinguish learned behaviors from changes resulting from other processes such as fatigue, maturation, or motivational and physiological states. It may be helpful to review **pages 17-19** of your text before completing this exercise. First, we should reiterate the definition of learning from your text:

….an enduring change in the mechanisms of behavior involving specific stimuli and/or responses that results from prior experience with those or similar stimuli and responses (**p. 17**)

Concept Questions

1) How does the definition of learning quoted above distinguish between learning and fatigue or motivational changes?

2) How does the definition distinguish between learning and maturation?

3) What is performance? How does the definition of learning distinguish between learning and performance?

4) What aspect of the definition makes learning a causal mechanism?

1-2.2 Applying the definition. Below are descriptions of 10 different behaviors that involve change. Your task will be to identify the situations in which learning, as opposed to some other process, has occurred. Circle the option you choose and explain your choice. Some alternative processes could include maturation and physical growth, motivational influences, genetic change, or insightful problem solving.

1) A rat is placed in a T-maze. The left arm of the maze is lighted and the right arm of the maze is dark. The dark portion of the maze has food at the end of it. On the first 20 trials, the rat enters the dark portion on 10 of the trials. On the next set of 20 trials, the rat enters the dark portion on all 20 trials. Is the change in behavior between the first 20 trials and the second 20 trials due to learning?

a. Yes   b. No   c. Maybe

Why did you choose this answer?

2) Infants rely on the rooting reflex to initiate breast feeding. When infants are weaned and stop rooting, is the loss of the reflex due to learning?

a. Yes   b. No   c. Maybe

Why did you choose this answer?

3) One set of cats observed their mothers killing mice from an early age and subsequently killed mice when given the chance. Other cats did not observe their mothers killing mice and were much less likely to become mouse killers. Do cats *learn* the "killing instinct"?

a. Yes   b. No   c. Maybe

Why did you choose this answer?

4) An infant makes the transition between crawling and walking. Is the transition due to learning?

a. Yes   b. No   c. Maybe

Why did you choose this answer?

5) You compete against a computer at a video game. During an initial 20 games the computer responds to your moves in a random fashion. During the final 20 games the computer responds to your moves using information based on the first 20 games. Did the computer learn?

a. Yes   b. No   c. Maybe

Why did you choose this answer?

6) Jeb sits in his cubicle typing reports at an average of 20 words per minute. As the day progresses, his productivity increases to 45 words per minute until he completes his assigned work. Is the increase in productivity due to learning how to type faster?

a. Yes   b. No   c. Maybe

Why did you choose this answer?

7) A plant orients the surfaces of its leaves toward sunlight to facilitate photosynthesis. Did the plant learn?

a. Yes   b. No   c. Maybe

Why did you choose this answer?

8) A chimpanzee sits in its enclosure with a long stick and a wooden crate. A banana is placed out of the chimpanzee's reach. After an hour of staring at the banana, the crate, and the stick, the chimpanzee places the crate beneath the banana, stands on it, and knocks the banana into the enclosure with the pole. Assuming the chimpanzee has not used a long stick or crate of this sort before, is this an example of learning?

a. Yes   b. No   c. Maybe

Why did you choose this answer?

9) George works overtime the night before taking the Graduate Record Examination. His combined verbal-quantitative score is 950 out of 1600. George retakes the GRE the following week after a full night of sleep and scores 1190. Is the rise in his score due to learning?

a. Yes   b. No   c. Maybe

Why did you choose this answer?

10) The sound of a toilet flushing signaled a major change in shower water temperature in an old apartment building where John was living. The result was that John would jump at the sound of the toilet flushing after only a few times that he took a shower in that apartment. A plumber fixed the problem and the jumping response declined over the course of two weeks. Was the jumping response learned?

a. Yes   b. No   c. Maybe

Why did you choose this answer?

Concept Questions

---

1) On **page 21** your author states that learning can only be understood by conducting experiments. Why does the study of learning require experimentation?

2) Describe an instance of learning from your personal experience. How can you be sure that it is an example of learning and not some other process?

1-3 Experimental Terminology

Throughout your textbook you will read about the details of key experiments that relate to the theories and concepts of conditioning and learning. The purpose of this section is to refresh your memory of some of the terminology and concepts associated with experiments. Box 1-3 lists some of these terms.

Box 1-3. Key terms in experimental methods.

Independent variable (IV): The variable(s) controlled and manipulated by the experimenter.

Dependent variable (DV): The response measured by an experimenter to determine whether the independent variable was effective.

Extraneous or confounding variable: Uncontrolled variable that causes systematic changes in the dependent variable.

Experimental group: The group exposed to the independent variable.

Control group: The group compared with the experimental group that is not exposed to the independent variable.

1-3.1 In each example below, identify the IV and DV in the study described. Identify some possible extraneous variables that may need to be controlled. (Note: a study can have more than one IV and more than one DV).

---

1) A psychologist examined how different amounts of food reward affected the frequency of bar pressing by rats.

IV:

DV:

Possible extraneous variables to control?

2) A behavioral neuroscientist examined the effects of a drug on maze running performance in 10 female rats that came from strain of animals bred for efficient spatial learning and memory.

IV:

DV:

Possible extraneous variables to control?

3) An applied psychologist tested whether different computer screen displays influenced productivity in office workers.

IV:

DV:

Possible extraneous variables to control?

1-4 How to Read and Create Graphs

Throughout your text you will find numerous figures that consist of graphs reporting key experimental results. Experiments in learning often involve dependent variables that yield numerical values such as time or frequency. Graphing is an effective way of revealing the effects of an independent variable(s) on a dependent variable(s). Many of the exercises in this workbook ask that you graph and interpret data. The purpose of this section is to provide you with some practice with reading, interpreting, and creating graphs.

1-4.1 Reading graphs. Consider a straightforward example from some early research in learning done by Tolman and Honzik (1930). Two groups of rats ran through a maze in order to receive food. The dependent variable was the number of times the rats made errors, such as entering wrong alleys of the maze. The independent variable was food deprivation. One group of rats was food deprived at the onset of the experiment and another was fed prior to the experiment and therefore was not hungry. Below are hypothetical data generated by the two groups of rats. The numbers in the cells represent the number of errors made while traveling through the maze.

Trial	Fed group	Food deprived group
1	200	205
2	194	200
3	188	185
4	180	165
5	179	156
6	175	130
7	170	100
8	160	75
9	161	60
10	165	45
Total averages	177.2	132.1

The averages for the two groups suggest that the food deprived group made fewer errors in this experiment. However, often in research on learning we are interested in examining the *pattern* of the results in addition to overall effects. Thus, we should plot the results using a line graph:

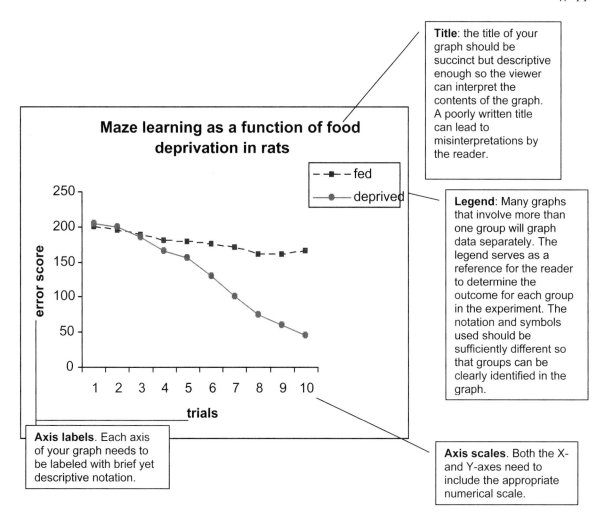

Title: the title of your graph should be succinct but descriptive enough so the viewer can interpret the contents of the graph. A poorly written title can lead to misinterpretations by the reader.

Legend: Many graphs that involve more than one group will graph data separately. The legend serves as a reference for the reader to determine the outcome for each group in the experiment. The notation and symbols used should be sufficiently different so that groups can be clearly identified in the graph.

Axis labels. Each axis of your graph needs to be labeled with brief yet descriptive notation.

Axis scales. Both the X- and Y-axes need to include the appropriate numerical scale.

There are many other ways of graphing data, including bar graphs, which will be used in subsequent chapters. The same general guidelines mentioned in the graph above still apply. Graphs are an important feature of a research report. Additionally, your interpretation of the graph is important. Your interpretation is written out in the body of the text and should include statements about how the independent variable affected the dependent variable. For example:

Food deprivation influenced the rate at which maze learning occurred. Rats that were deprived of food made fewer maze running errors over the course of 10 trials than did rats that were fed.

1-4.2 Creating graphs. Here we will practice creating a graph with the elements listed above. Imagine that two chimpanzees were taught to use American Sign Language using different methods. One chimpanzee was encouraged to imitate a human who formed the signs in her presence (Imitate). A second chimpanzee learned signs with the assistance of a human who molded the chimp's hands into the correct shape and moved them in the appropriate fashion (Molding). Below are data summarizing the cumulative number of signs learned by each chimp over the course of 8 weeks.

Week	Imitate	Molding
1	2	3
2	5	6
3	6	8
4	8	11
5	12	19
6	14	23
7	15	27
8	19	31

1) Plot these data on the axes below.
2) Be sure to scale and label the axes and include a title at the top.
3) Write out an interpretation below your graph.

Title:

Interpretation:

2 Elicited Behavior, Habituation, and Sensitization

This chapter introduces you to some basic categories of behavior, including reflexes and simple processes for changing behavior called habituation and sensitization. **Section 2-1** elaborates on the concept of a modal action pattern (MAP) described on **page 36** of your text. Following this are exercises that are designed to help you identify some factors that influence rates of habituation and sensitization (**section 2-2**). We conclude with a practice exercise in which you will apply the opponent process theory of emotion and motivation to your own experiences (**section 2-3**).

After completing these exercises you should be able to:
- Identify examples of modal action patterns
- Apply concepts of ethology to various examples of behavior
- Define and apply the concepts of appetitive and consummatory responding
- Recognize several factors that influence the extent to which responses habituate and sensitize
- Visualize how dual-process theory works
- Apply the opponent-process theory of motivation and emotion

2-1 Modal Action Patterns

Your text discusses the concept of a modal action pattern (MAP). On **page 36** several examples of MAPs in animal behavior are described. For example, herring gulls use their bills to return eggs that have gone astray from their nests using a relatively stereotyped series of movements. This response has adaptive value. Clearly, *not* engaging in this behavior compromises the reproductive fitness of the birds. The concept of a MAP comes from the discipline of ethology, which focuses on the biological and evolutionary significance of behavior. One of ethology's major proponents, Niko Tinbergen (1963), identified four fundamental approaches that ethologists take when studying behavior. The four approaches are:
- Adaptation (survival value): focuses on how behavior influences survival and reproductive success. Research in this area typically searches for a direct link between a behavior and how it impacts survival of individuals and their offspring.
- Causation: focuses on the neurological and physiological processes that underlie and control behavior.
- Development (ontogeny): focuses on behavioral changes due to processes such as maturation, early experience, and learning.

- Evolution: examines similarities and differences in behavior between species.

Each of these four approaches can be found in the material from your textbook. The following exercise will help you differentiate them.

2-1.1 Using the descriptions of the four ethological issues above, identify which of the four is being applied to each of the following examples based on published research:

---

1) Peter Marler studied how young birds acquire their songs by listening to members of their own species. **Answer:**_____

2) Konrad Lorenz studied the different cues that hatchling geese respond to as they imprint upon their mothers (or upon Lorenz himself, as he discovered during his work with these birds).
   Answer:_____

3) Esther Cullen compared nesting and social behavior of kittiwakes (*Rissa tridactyla*) that nest on cliffs with other sea dwelling gulls (*Larus argentatus*) that nest on open beaches. **Answer:**_____

4) Martha McClintock demonstrated that co-habitation by women in college dormitories results in menstrual synchrony, probably mediated by an olfactory cue. **Answer:**_____

5) Karl von Frisch described and experimented on the "language" that bees use to direct other bees in the hive toward food sources. Von Frisch examined the different movements the bees made that indicated the direction, distance, and quality of the food source so that hive-mates watching these movements could locate the food.
   Answer:_____

6) Howard Evans compared various prey carrying strategies in different species of wasps. **Answer:**_____

7) Harry Harlow examined the effects of maternal deprivation on infant attachment and social behavior. **Answer:**_____

8) Erich von Holst examined how different regions of the brain control peripheral organs. **Answer:**_____

9) Robert Provine studied the specific facial features that elicit contagious yawning, a modal action pattern. **Answer:**_____

10) Niko Tinbergen demonstrated that gulls remove opened eggshells, which are highly visible to predators, from their nests, increasing survival rates in their young. **Answer:**_____

2-1.2 Sequential organization of behavior. Many behavioral scientists make a distinction between appetitive and consummatory responses (see **page 39**). First, review these concepts in your text. Then consider the sequence of behaviors required for a rattlesnake to find its prey. For each phase of the sequence below identify whether the behavior is of the appetitive or consummatory variety.

---

1) The rattlesnake moves 30 feet to a location where food has been previously discovered. *Circle one: Appetitive Consummatory*

2) Snake crawls over fallen logs where last meal had been discovered. *Appetitive Consummatory*

3) Snake begins searching for prey by flicking its tongue. *Appetitive Consummatory*

4) Snake crawls into burrow in search of prey and finds none. *Appetitive Consummatory*

5) Snake coils up on top of a mat of leaves in a shady area.

   Appetitive   *Consummatory*

6) Snake strikes and injects venom into rodent passing by.

   Appetitive   *Consummatory*

7) Snake moves about while tongue flicking to locate the dying rodent 10 feet away. *Appetitive*   *Consummatory*

8) Snake opens jaws and maneuvers rodent for swallowing.

   Appetitive   *Consummatory*

9) Snake swallows rodent. *Appetitive*   *Consummatory*

10) Snake extends neck and stomach region to force rodent into digestive tract. *Appetitive*   *Consummatory*

2-2 Habituation and Sensitization

Exposure to a stimulus can cause habituation, which is a decrease in responding, or sensitization, an increase in responding. Starting on **page 40** of your text the basic processes of habituation and sensitization are described. It would be helpful to review these pages before working on the exercises below. In these exercises we will explore some factors that influence whether habituation or sensitization occur. Below is a figure that depicts a decrease in startle responses across 10 trials.

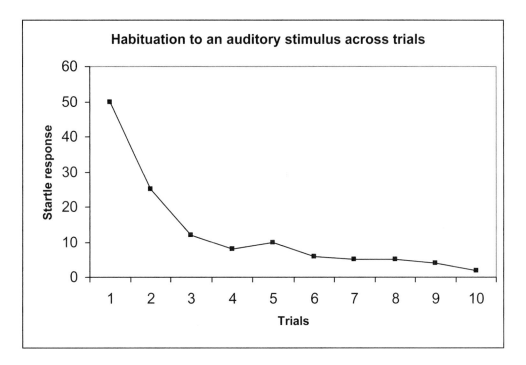

2-2.1 Factor #1: The inter-stimulus interval. One factor influencing the degree to which habituation occurs is the amount of time that passes between one presentation of the stimulus and the next. As a general rule, a longer interval between stimulus presentations results in slower rates of habituation. For example, if you listen to a new song five times in succession in one day, habituation will be more pronounced than if you listen to the song once daily for five days. With this in mind, view the habituation curves below. Imagine that a habituation experiment was conducted with three groups:

Group 1: Exposed to novel stimulus for 5 seconds, once per minute
Group 2: Exposed to novel stimulus for 5 seconds, once per hour
Group 3: Exposed to novel stimulus for 5 seconds, once per day

The graph below shows hypothetical data for the three groups across the ten stimulus presentation trials. Specify in the graph below which curve represents the likely result for each of the three groups.

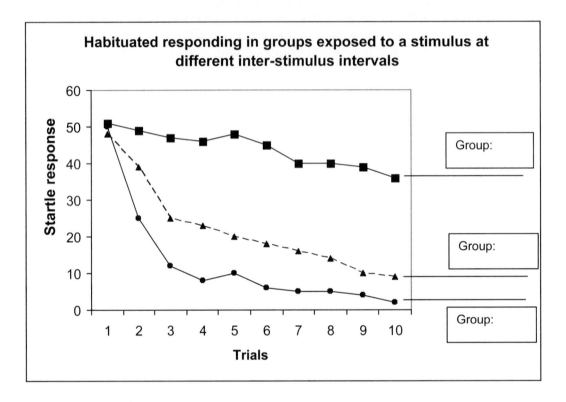

2-2.2 Factor #2: Stimulus duration. Another factor influencing levels of habituation and sensitization is the duration of the stimulus. For example, habituation to a 10 second stimulus will be slower than habituation to a 30 second stimulus. Now imagine a study with three groups treated as follows:

Group 1: Exposed to a novel stimulus for 1 minute each time for 10 trials
Group 2: Exposed to a novel stimulus for 2 minutes each time for 10 trials
Group 3: Exposed to a novel stimulus for 10 minutes each time for 10 trials

In the graph on the next page, draw your own curves representing habituation in these three groups. Be sure to label the lines representing each group and give your graph a title.

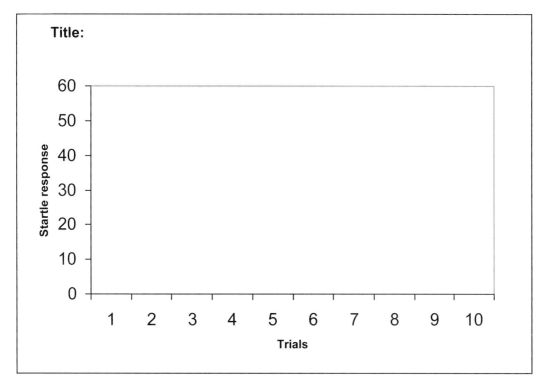

Title:

Startle response (y-axis): 0, 10, 20, 30, 40, 50, 60

Trials (x-axis): 1 2 3 4 5 6 7 8 9 10

2-2.3 Factor #3: Stimulus specificity. Habituation tends to be stimulus specific (see **page 55**), meaning that responding rebounds if the stimulus is changed. For example, imagine you have an ice cream cone with two scoops of differing flavors. As you work your way through the first scoop you may habituate to its flavor. Assuming you are sufficiently hungry, when you reach the second scoop you are likely to find that you are no longer habituated to the ice cream. Your interest in the ice cream will be renewed by the switch to the second flavor.

An example of stimulus specificity of habituation can be found in the alarm calls of vervet monkeys. These monkeys have three distinct sounding calls they emit when they spot a leopard, an eagle, or a snake. When they emit these calls other group members stop and scan either the sky or the ground for the predator. Curious researchers, including Cheney and Seyfarth (1990), have played pre-recorded vocalizations back to monkeys to examine their responses. For example, a leopard call could be played back repeatedly from a recording of a single monkey. Habituation to the leopard call coming from *this* monkey should occur, as evidenced by group members ignoring it. However, playing a leopard call from a different monkey results in strong responses from group members.

In the blank graph on the next page:
1) Draw a curve that indicates habituation to a leopard call after repeated presentations from Monkey A.
2) Indicate with a single data point how responding would occur to a single playback of Monkey B's leopard vocalization following habituation to Monkey A.

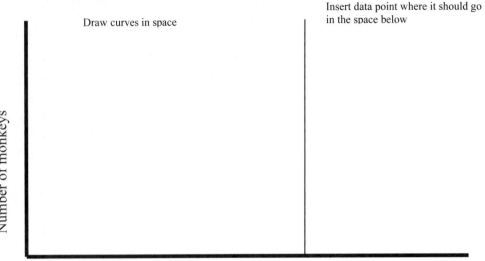

Draw curves in space

Insert data point where it should go in the space below

Number of monkeys

Number of times call is played

Remember that these monkeys are able to use three different types of alarm calls. Now imagine that you have played Monkey A's leopard calls repeatedly, but this time you complete your experiment by presenting Monkey A's eagle and snake alarm calls. Given what you know about stimulus specificity and habituation, in the graph below draw a habituation curve for the leopard call and then add two data points indicating responses to the eagle and snake calls.

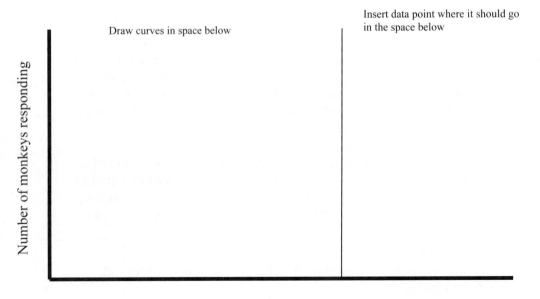

Draw curves in space below

Insert data point where it should go in the space below

Number of monkeys responding

Number of times call is played back

2.2-4 Habituation, adaptation and fatigue. This exercise will help you distinguish between three processes that can account for a decline in responding. Be sure to review **pages 52-53** of your text before completing this exercise.

Identify and describe a personally relevant example of how a response may be reduced because of:

habituation

adaptation

fatigue

How do you know the responses belong to their respective categories?

2-2.5 Dual-Process Theory. Page 53 of your text introduces the dual-process theory of habituation and sensitization. This theory suggests that the net response to a stimulus reflects the simultaneous buildup of habituation and sensitization processes. The exercises below provide you with practice visualizing how this theory works.

In the graph below, draw curves that reflect a net response increase of 15 by the 10th trial. There should be 3 curves in total. One curve indicating habituation over 10 trials, one indicating sensitization, and a hypothetical curve representing net responding across the 10 trials. Be sure to label each of your three curves.

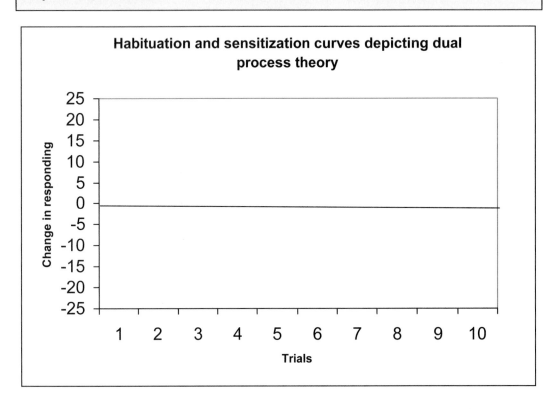

Next, in the graph below draw habituation, sensitization, and net responding curves that reflect a net response decrease of -10 by trial 10. Be sure to label each of your three curves.

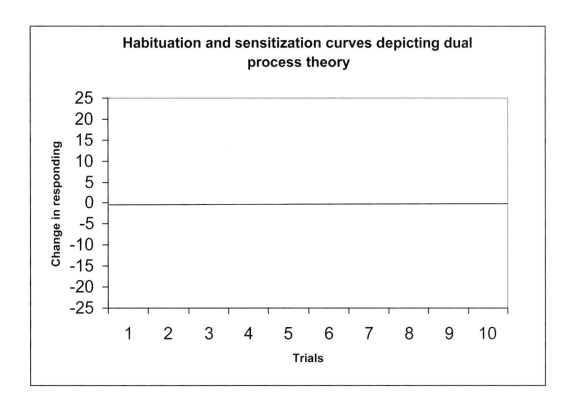

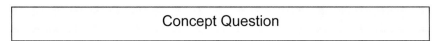

Concept Question

1) With regard to habituation and sensitization, what is an *S-R system* and what is a *state system*?

2-3 Opponent Process Theory of Motivation

The opponent-process theory of motivation (**pp. 60-63** of your text) also involves two processes. However, the two processes here are called the primary and opponent processes. In addition, the opponent process theory is typically applied to complex emotional responses, such as happiness or sadness, rather than reflex responses. The exercise below asks you to apply opponent-process theory to your own experiences.

> Try to recall an event that first elicited a strong emotional reaction, followed by a decreased reaction after repeated exposure. Describe the event, the emotions it elicited, and how your reaction changed over time.

What was the primary, or *a*, process?_____

What was the secondary, or *b*, process?_____

3 Classical Conditioning: Foundations

This chapter will familiarize you with the terminology, concepts, and theories of classical conditioning. We will continue to build upon some of the material from **chapter 2**, including graphing and interpreting data, and using the terminology of experiments. In **section 3-1** we will cover some terminology and applications of classical conditioning, and how to use suppression ratios. You are also asked to apply concepts of classical conditioning to personal examples. Following this are exercises that focus on the procedures of excitatory conditioning (**section 3-2**). **Section 3-3** focuses on inhibitory conditioning and the notation and procedures that are involved in designing experiments in classical conditioning.

After completing these exercises you should be able to:
- Apply the terminology of classical conditioning
- Calculate and interpret suppression ratios
- Apply concepts and terminology of classical conditioning to personal examples
- Compare and contrast the different excitatory conditioning procedures
- Describe the relative effectiveness of the different excitatory procedures
- Become familiar with notation and procedures for diagramming experiments in classical conditioning
- Apply some different methods for studying conditioned inhibition

3-1 Terminology and the Classical Conditioning Paradigm

Terminology is often a challenge for students learning about classical conditioning. Confusion over what is conditioned, what is unconditioned, what is a stimulus and what constitutes a response is common. The best way to meet this challenge is to practice. Before starting with the exercises I recommend that you review some of the key terms listed below. You may also refer to your text for definitions of these terms.

Key terms in Classical conditioning

Unconditional stimulus (US): A stimulus that elicits a response without the necessity of prior training.

Unconditional response (UR): A response that occurs to a stimulus without prior training.

Conditional stimulus (CS): A stimulus that does not elicit a particular response initially, but comes to do so as a result of becoming associated with an unconditioned stimulus.

Conditional response (CR): The response that occurs to the conditional stimulus as a result of classical conditioning.

Test trial: A trial in which a CR is measured in response to a CS (usually without the US present) to determine the strength of conditional responding.

Acquisition: The learning of a CR as a result of pairing the CS and US.

Your textbook describes some of the early history of classical conditioning, including Ivan Pavlov's familiar examination of the conditioned salivary reflexes in dogs. The salivary reflex (the UR) occurs naturally in response to food cues such as taste and smell. We do not learn to salivate in response to food; we do so without conditioning (as do dogs). However, if a stimulus such as a smell (a CS) occurs in conjunction with food (the US), the smell can then also elicit salivation (a CR). The conditional eye blink response in rabbits, described in **chapter 3** of your text (**page 75**) involves the same type of learning. To review some key terms in classical conditioning, let's look at this example a little more closely in the schematic below.

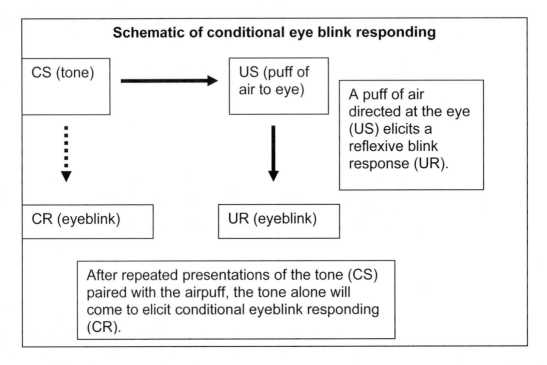

Schematic of conditional eye blink responding

CS (tone) → US (puff of air to eye)

A puff of air directed at the eye (US) elicits a reflexive blink response (UR).

CR (eyeblink)   UR (eyeblink)

After repeated presentations of the tone (CS) paired with the airpuff, the tone alone will come to elicit conditional eyeblink responding (CR).

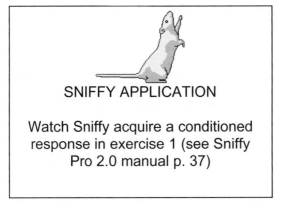

SNIFFY APPLICATION

Watch Sniffy acquire a conditioned response in exercise 1 (see Sniffy Pro 2.0 manual p. 37)

3-1.1 Applying terms and concepts. Now let's practice applying the terms and concepts reviewed above. Following are some examples of classical conditioning. Think about what is happening in each and identify the US, CS, UR, and CR in the spaces provided.

1) A nursing mother responds to the crying of her infant by putting the infant to her breast, which stimulates the delivery of milk. After this has occurred several times the sound of the baby crying stimulates the milk letdown reflex.
US_____, UR_____, CS_____,

CR_____

2) A child has a routine of having his teddy bear with him when his parents comfortably tuck him in. When his parents are away, the teddy bear comforts him.
US_____, UR_____, CS_____,

CR_____

3) A song continues to evoke arousal and nervousness in a person who heard the song during her first kiss with a person to whom she was wildly attracted.
US_____, UR_____, CS_____,

CR_____

4) A stuntman has a terrible accident causing immense pain while performing a stunt on a motorcycle. Thereafter, motorcycles elicit fear.
US_____, UR_____, CS_____,

CR_____

5) A cyclist was attacked by a dog while riding down "country road 5." On subsequent trips down that road, the cyclist's heart pumps extra fast and he experiences heightened anxiety.
US_____, UR_____, CS_____,

CR_____

3-1.2 Conditioned suppression and suppression ratios. Suppression ratios are often used as indicators of conditioned fear or anxiety (see **p. 73** of text). What is suppressed is normal, ongoing behavior such as eating or drinking. Think of when you are extremely stressed. At such times, you are not likely to eat or drink. We can use this decrease in eating and drinking as an index of your stress level.

The suppression ratio is calculated as follows:

$$\text{Suppression ratio} = \frac{CS_{responding}}{CS_{responding} + \text{pre-}CS_{responding}}$$

Where $CS_{responding}$ is the measure of responding during the test trial (e.g., amount of time spent moving), and pre-$CS_{responding}$ is a measure of the response *before* the CS is presented (also referred to as a "baseline" measure). So imagine that the day before an exam you spend 60 minutes at the breakfast table enjoying a large, leisurely breakfast. The following day you are stressed and food is therefore less appetizing so you spend only 15 minutes at the table. Your suppression ratio would be:

$$\frac{15}{15+60} = 0.20$$

> **Question**

Now imagine that your roommate is also taking the exam, but she is completely relaxed about it. If your roommate spends an hour eating on both days, what is her suppression ratio?

We will use rats as a way of further examining suppression ratios. Imagine the CS in this study is a 60 second presentation of white noise at a standard (dB) level. The US is a brief (1 second) shock presented immediately afterward. The conditional response is suppression of drinking activity. We measure drinking activity one minute prior to the onset of the CS (the pre-CS responding phase) and during a one minute CS presentation (the CS responding phase). Two groups of subjects were used. The experimental group experienced the CS and US together, while the control group experienced the CS and US one minute apart.

Below are sample data (in seconds) after five conditioning trials for six subjects (Ss), three in each group. These data come from the final test trial of the experiment.

- Calculate suppression ratios for each rat in the study, and then the average suppression ratio for each group.
- Graph the average suppression ratios for both groups with a bar graph below and write an interpretation.

	rat	Pre-CS period	CS period	Pre-CS + CS period	Suppression ratio
Experimental group	1	20	1		
	2	17	2		
	3	19	5		
	Average suppression ratio =				

	rat				
Control group	4	22	20		
	5	20	11		
	6	23	24		
	Average suppression ratio =				

Title:

Interpretation:

3-1.3 Personal application: Conditioned fear and taste aversion. Your text describes the phenomena of conditioned fear and taste aversions. Apply these two concepts to your own experiences. If no examples come to mind, ask a friend to share their experiences. In the space below, describe each scenario. Using the format shown on page 26 above diagram each (be sure to specify the CS, US, CR and UR and link them up appropriately with arrows).

Conditioned fear

Description:

Diagram:

Conditioned taste aversion

Description:

Diagram:

3-2 Excitatory Conditioning Procedures

As you have learned from your textbook, classical conditioning is not always a simple matter of pairing a CS with a US. There are many other factors at work here. Numerous variables influence whether classical conditioning occurs. These include the arrangement in time between the CS and US, the number of CS-US pairings, the amount of experience one has had with the CS, and more. In this section we will focus on how various factors influence excitatory conditioning.

3-2.1 Excitatory conditioning procedures. The timing, or *temporal relationship*, between the CS and the US influences the extent to which a response is conditioned (**pp. 84-85**). There are four general ways to characterize the temporal characteristics of conditioning procedures: trace, delay, simultaneous, and backward conditioning (see **figure 3-7** reprinted from **p. 84** of your text below).

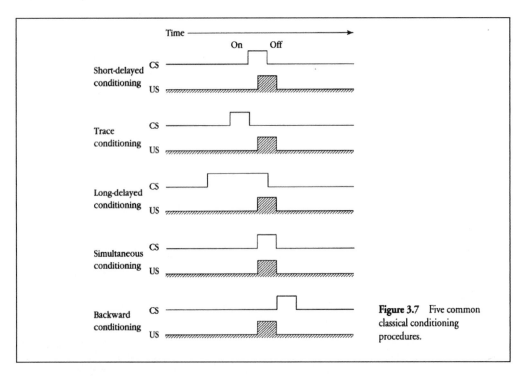

Figure 3.7 Five common classical conditioning procedures.

To visualize how the relationship between the CS and US affects conditioning, plot the following data in line graph format on the axes below and write out an interpretation of the patterns. The numbers below each type of conditioning (e.g., trace: 1, 5, 10, ...) represent the magnitude of the CR over the course of four conditioning trials. (You should have four separate lines, one for each type of conditioning, and four points per line representing each trial.)

Trials	Trace	Delay	Backward	Simultaneous
1	1	0	1	0
2	5	8	3	2
3	10	15	4	3
4	15	19	5	4

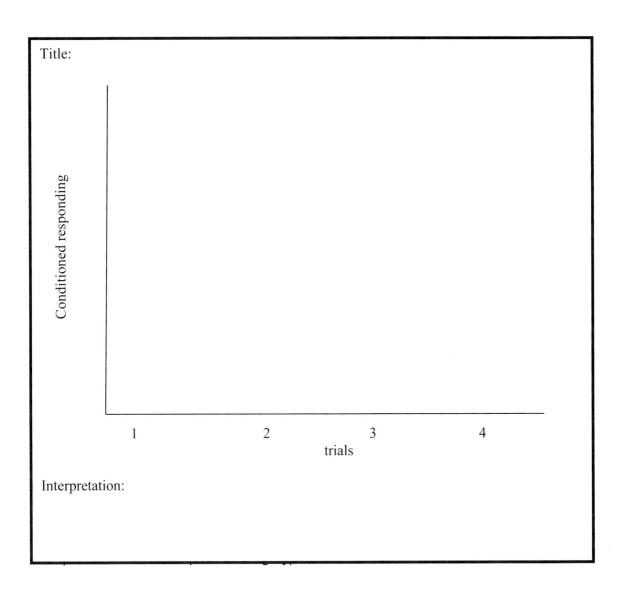

Title:

Conditioned responding

1   2   3   4

trials

Interpretation:

3-2.2 Measuring excitatory responses. Conditioned responding can be measured in a variety of ways. Some common types of measure include.
  1) *Magnitude*
  2) *Probability*
  3) *Latency*

The application of these measures is described on **page 85** of your text. Below are some examples of conditioned responding. Circle the option that best applies to each example.

1) Number of drops of saliva to the CS. *magnitude   probability   latency*

2) Time taken to approach a light. *magnitude probability   latency*

3) Percentage of trials in which eye blinking occurs.

   magnitude   probability   latency

4) Level of anxiety as measured by galvanic skin responding.

   magnitude   probability   latency

5) Supression of drinking as a measure of a conditioned taste aversion.

   magnitude   probability   latency

6) Time taken to reach ½ of maximum heart rate on a particular trial?

   magnitude   probability   latency

7) Percentage of times in which a leg withdrawal reflex occurs to a CS.

   magnitude   probability   latency

8) Amount of testosterone secreted in response to a CS.

   magnitude   probability   latency

3-3 Diagramming and Designing Experiments in Classical Conditioning: Applications to the Measurement of Conditioned Inhibition

Our understanding of the mechanisms of classical conditioning is largely derived from carefully controlled laboratory experiments. One useful skill we recommend you develop is the ability to identify and use some of the symbols and strategies for diagramming experiments. Your professor may use some abbreviations and shorthand for diagramming experiments in class. Below are some recommended abbreviations, but keep in mind that people vary in how they communicate this information, so you will probably encounter some minor differences.

- **Paired CS and US**: To indicate that two events are paired in time use an arrow: →, as in CS →US. This notation is also used to indicate that a stimulus is eliciting a response, as in US→UR.

- **Unpaired CS and US**: To indicate that two events are unpaired between the CS and US, use a forward slash: "/," as in CS/US. (note: Be aware, the "/" may also be used to indicate that two CSs occur together, such as CS+/CS-.)

- **Phase** of an experiment. Some experiments, such as those involving retardation of acquisition as a measure of conditioned inhibition, involve more than one phase (e.g., Phase 1 = inhibitory training, Phase 2 = excitatory conditioning).

- **Positive (+) and negative (-) signs**. In classical conditioning these typically mean that a CS signals a US (CS+) or that a CS signals the absence of a US (CS-). This is the most common use of the + and – notation. However, note that in some experiments there are trials where the US is present (US+) or absent (US-).

For example, if you are designing an experiment on conditioned inhibition you might see something like this:

> Phase 1 establishes a CR after CS-US pairings

Phase 1:

 Group 1: CS+→US
 Group 2: CS+→US

Phase 2:

 Group 1 (control): CS+→US, [CS+ and CS-] → US (indicates alternating trials of both types)
 Group 2 (experimental): CS+→US, [CS+ and CS-] / US

Test: Group 1: CS-
   Group 2: CS-

> A test procedure is conducted after phase 2 to determine whether the CS- is a conditioned inhibitor.

> Phase 2 conditions the inhibitory response to the CS-. For Group 1 (control) the CS+ and CS- are always paired with a US. For Group 2 (experimental) the CS+ is paired with a US on some trials but the CS- is never paired with the US.

Concept Questions

---

1) Why was phase 1 necessary?

2) What was the purpose of treating Group 2 differently from Group 1 during Phase 2?

3) Which group should show stronger inhibition to the CS-?

3-3.2 Inhibition procedures. Your text describes some common procedures for studies of conditioned inhibition (**pp. 91-96**). One involves bidirectional response systems, another involves doing a compound-stimulus, or summation, test, and the third involves the retardation-of-acquisition test. Before completing this exercise you should carefully review these pages.

Concept Question

---

1) What is a bidirectional response system and what is one limitation of using this type of system for a conditioned inhibition study?

Diagram a conditioned inhibition experiment that uses the retardation-of-acquisition procedure. Be sure to identify the different phases of the experiment and include control groups. In addition, be sure to indicate which groups receive paired and unpaired stimulus presentations in the different phases.

The figure below is a reprinted version of **figure 3.12** in your text (**p. 95**). The figure summarizes results from an experiment on conditioned inhibition that used a compound-stimulus test procedure. Review the details of this experiment and **figure 3.12** below and answer the concept questions that follow.

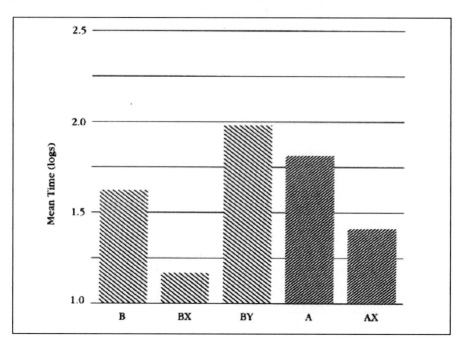

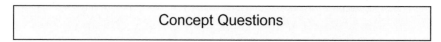

Concept Questions

1) What was the purpose of conditioning to both CSA and CSB?

2) Why were the mean times to complete 5 seconds of interrupted drinking comparatively short for the BX and AX tests?

3) What was the purpose of testing BY?

SNIFFY APPLICATION

Experiment with inhibitory
conditioning procedures in exercises
10 and 11 (pp. 78, 83)

4 Classical Conditioning: Mechanisms

Chapter 4 brings together many important concepts of classical conditioning. After reading this chapter you can probably appreciate that classical conditioning is not a simple matter of a CS being paired with a US. Conditioning depends on a variety of factors such as the novelty of the CS and US, their intensity, and their relevance to each other. **Section 4-1** provides exercises that allow you to examine how each of these affects the strength of conditioning. In addition, the *form* of a conditioned response is determined by several factors, such as the CS, the US, and the CS-US interval. How this occurs is examined by several thought questions that are posed in **section 4-2**. In **section 4-3** we consider some of the mechanisms that underlie CS-US relationships.

After completing these exercises you should be able to:
- Evaluate different ways that the CS affects conditioning
- Evaluate different ways that the US affects conditioning
- Describe how conditioning can occur with multiple CSs
- Describe how different aspects of the CS determine whether conditioning occurs
- Explain different mechanisms that underlie classical conditioning

4-1 Effectiveness of the CS and US

Conditioning is not always a simple matter of pairing a CS with a US and looking for a CR. Numerous variables influence whether conditioning occurs and to what degree. Here we explore several of these factors.

4-1.1 CS and US factors. The development of a CR depends on a variety of factors. These include the type of CS, the type of US, and the degree to which the CS and US are related. **Pages 104-109** of your text describe several properties of CSs and USs that determine their effectiveness. You will need to review these pages prior to completing the exercises below.

Below are graphs showing results from four experiments that examined variables that influence classical conditioning. Study each graph carefully and identify which variable was examined. Possible answers include:
1) Initial responses to the stimuli
2) Novelty of the CS or US
3) CS and US intensity/salience
4) CS-US relevance

Be sure to pay close attention to the variables studied, the values of the axes, and how the groups were affected by the treatments.

---

1) Variable examined:_____

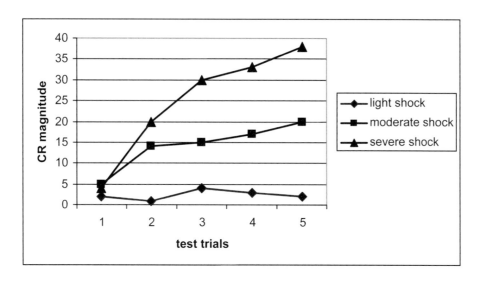

2) Variable examined:_____

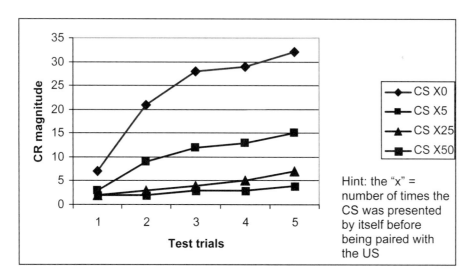

3) Variable examined:_____

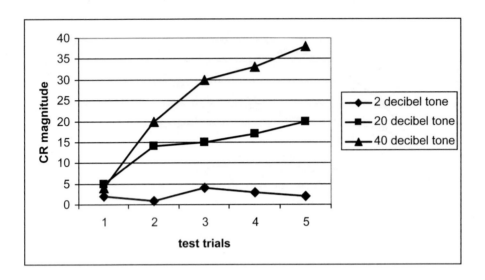

4) Variable examined:_____

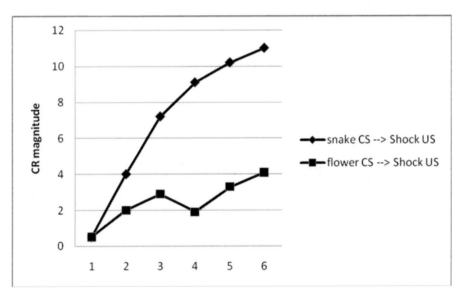

5) Which of the determinants listed above applies to the results in the figure reprinted from your text (**figure 4.3, page 109**) below? Explain your answer by referring to the results found for each group reported in the figure.

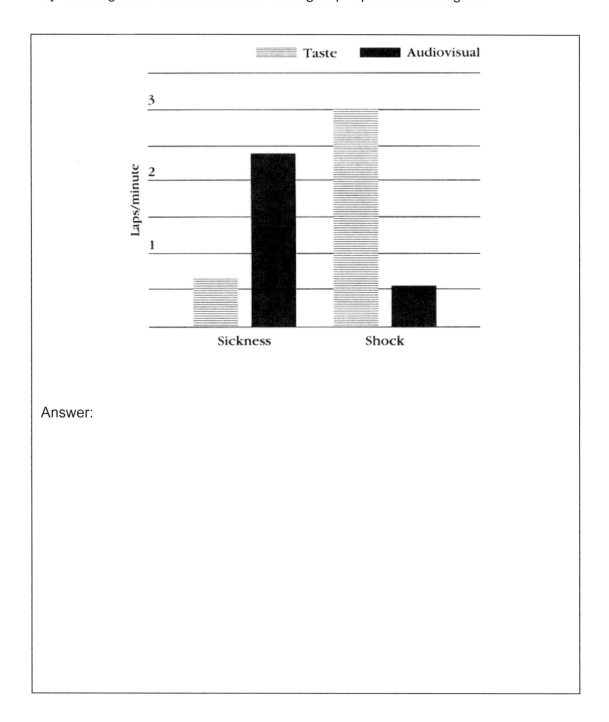

Answer:

SNIFFY APPLICATION

Test the effects of CS and US strength/intensity on conditioning Sniffy in exercises 4 and 5 (p. 45, 53)

4-1.2 Biological strength: Conditioning with multiple CSs. Students frequently have trouble differentiating higher-order conditioning and sensory preconditioning. The two are very similar in that both involve the pairing of at least two CSs at some point in the process, but they are in fact quite different phenomena (see **pp. 110-112** of your text). It may be helpful to review your text before completing this exercise.

In the space below, diagram an example of higher-order conditioning and sensory preconditioning. Be sure to include actual examples of CSs and USs in your diagrams and make them plausible situations. Avoid using examples you already have seen in your text. After completing your diagrams answer the question that follow.

Higher-order conditioning:

Sensory preconditioning:

SNIFFY APPLICATION

Experiment with sensory-preconditioning and higher-order conditioning in exercises 12 and 13 (pp. 88, 94)

Concept Question

1) Describe the key procedural difference between higher-order conditioning and sensory preconditioning.

4-1.3 Latent inhibition. Your text describes an interesting phenomenon called latent inhibition (**p. 105**), which refers to the retardation of conditioning if a CS is experienced repeatedly prior to being paired with a US. For example, if a tone is heard several hundred times before being paired with a puff of air to the eye, conditioning of the tone may take longer than if the tone is not heard so frequently before being paired with the air puff US.

Let's consider an experiment conducted by Westbrook and colleagues (2000). In this experiment, conducted with rats, a 30 second clicking noise was used as the CS and the US was a mild shock to the feet. The researchers wanted to determine whether repeated exposure to the clicking noise without any shock would subsequently slow down the acquisition of conditioned fear responses. Rats are known to freeze when frightened, and CSs that predict the onset of foot shock elicit freezing behavior. Thus, the dependent variable was freezing behavior. Before continuing, think about how you would design this experiment. What would your independent variable be and how would you manipulate it?

The experiment can be summarized as follows:

Groups			
Pre-exposed		Not pre-exposed	
Paired	Unpaired	Paired	Unpaired

The independent variables involve exposure to the CS (pre-exposed or not pre-exposed) and pairings of the CS with the US (paired vs. unpaired). The experimenters decided to use four groups, summarized above, and note that there are two unpaired control groups, one for each level of the preexposure variable.

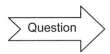 Question

> *Before proceeding,* state a hypothesis about what you predict for each of the four groups. (Which group(s) will show a high percentage of freezing behavior?)

Below are sample data based on the experiment. The numbers represent the mean percentage of freezing to the CS. Please graph and interpret the data below.

	Groups			
	Pre-exposed		Not pre-exposed	
	Paired	Unpaired	Paired	Unpaired
Mean % freezing	23%	25%	97%	39%

Title:

Interpretation:

SNIFFY APPLICATION

Test the effects of CS and US pre-exposure in Sniffy in exercises 19, 20, and 21 (pp. 123, 127, 129)

4-2   Determinants of the Conditioned Response

On **pages 112-122** of your text, some factors that determine the form of the conditioned response are described. After reading these sections, answer the following concept questions.

Concept Questions

1) Does the stimulus substitution model apply to salivary conditioning? Why or why not?

2) What are conditioned homeostatic responses and how are they relevant to drug tolerance?

3) What was the CS in Timberlake and Grant's (1975) study (see **page 118**)? What type of CR did this CS elicit? Why was this of theoretical interest?

4) What are general and focal search behaviors? Give an example of each. What is a consummatory response? Provide an example.

5) How is the form of the CR determined by the CS-US interval? (Hint: review the Akins 2000 study described on **pages 120-121** of your text.)

4-2.2   S-R and S-S learning

Your text describes the important distinction between S-R and S-S learning. Review these pages carefully and answer the questions that follow.

1) Review Pavlov's basic salivary conditioning procedure. According to S-R theory, what did the dogs learn? What did they learn according to S-S theory? Why is the distinction important?

2) How can one devalue the US after a CS-US association has been formed?

3) How would US devaluation affect the CR if the behavior is mediated by S-R mechanisms, and how would it affect the CR with S-S mechanisms?

4) Provide a concrete example involving classical conditioning (identifying the CS, the US, and the CR) and describe how changing US value would address the questions above.

SNIFFY APPLICATION

Test S-R and S-S theories with Sniffy
in the exercises from Chapter 7 of
your Sniffy Pro manual

4-3 Mechanisms of Associating CSs and USs

4-3.1 The Rescorla-Wagner Model. The Rescorla-Wagner model (**pages 126-132**) is one of the most influential models of learning that has been proposed in recent times. Its basic assumption is that the increment in learning that is produced by a conditioning trial depends on how surprising the outcome of the trial is. Furthermore, how surprising something is depends on all of the cues present during a conditioning trial.

One stimulus that is always present in an experiment is the experimental chamber or context in which the conditioning trials are conducted. In the following examples, explain how the conditioning context might influence learning about a discrete tone that is paired with food. Use the Rescorla-Wagner model as the basis for your predictions.

---

1) Subjects are first habituated to an experimental chamber. Then, a series of conditioning trials are conducted in which a tone is paired with food.

2) Subjects first receive several sessions in which food is presented periodically without warning in the experimental chamber. Then, a series of conditioning trials is conducted in which a tone is paired with food.

3) Subjects first receive several sessions in which food is presented periodically without warning in the experimental chamber. In the next phase of the experiment, the subjects are placed in the experimental chamber repeatedly for a week without getting food or any other US there. Then, a series of conditioning trials is conducted in which a tone is paired with food.

4) Subjects receive the tone paired with food 10 times during each experimental session. In addition, food is presented at random times between trials 10 times per day.

5) Subjects receive food presented 10 times at random intervals during each experimental session. A tone is also presented periodically, but any food presentations that might have occurred during a 2-min period after each tone are cancelled.

The basic Rescorla-Wagner equation is $\Delta V = k(\lambda - V)$. In this equation, V is the associative value of all of the cues present on a conditioning trial; λ is the asymptote of learning possible with the stimulus outcome (US or no US) that ends each trial; ΔV is the change in associative value, or what is learned, as a result of a conditioning trial; and the parameter k represents a constant related to the salience of the CS and the US. The following questions provide practice in interpreting how various manipulations are represented in the equation.

1) At the beginning of training, what is the value of V?

2) In a typical learning experiment, subjects show large improvements early in training. However, as training progresses, the improvement that results from each conditioning trial gets smaller and smaller. Which term in the equation represents the size of the improvement that occurs with each trial? How does this term change as training progresses? What term on the right side of the equation causes this change?

3) Assume that after three sessions of training a CS has been conditioned to asymptote, and the CS is the only cue in this situation. What will be the value of V at the end of the three sessions?

4) Assuming the scenario described in the preceding question, what will be the value of ΔV if conditioning is continued past the asymptote of learning?

5) In extinction, each presentation of the CS ends without a US. Which term of the equation represents this stimulus outcome? What is the value of this term in extinction?

6) Assume that one group of subjects is conditioned with a US that consists of one pellet of food and another is conditioned with a US that consists of 4 pellets of food? Which term of the equation represents these differences in the magnitude of the US? How does the value of this term change with the increase from 1 to 4 food pellets?

SNIFFY APPLICATION

Experiment with the blocking effect in Exercise 7 (p. 64)

5 Instrumental Conditioning: Foundations

Chapter 5 of your text opens with some descriptions and examples of procedures used to study instrumental conditioning. For example, Edward Thorndike's research on trial and error learning with cats escaping from puzzle boxes was described. Since Thorndike's early experiments, we have learned a lot about the details of what is called *instrumental conditioning*, or *operant learning*. The exercises below serve to familiarize you with the foundational terms and concepts that comprise instrumental conditioning. We start with an exercise designed to help you make the distinction between instrumental and classical conditioning (**section 5-1**). The differences between two general procedures for studying learning, discrete-trial and free-operant procedures, are explored in **section 5-2**. Exercises designed to help you apply the procedures of shaping are in **section 5-3**. Students first encountering the concepts of positive and negative reinforcement and punishment often find it challenging to apply these terms to new situations, and **section 5-4** has exercises to help you develop skills in doing this. **Section 5.5** focuses on how contingency and contiguity affect instrumental conditioning.

After completing these exercises you should be able to:
- Distinguish instrumental and classical conditioning
- Identify situations that used discrete-trial and free-operant procedures
- Identify target behaviors and devise methods for shaping them
- Successfully apply the concepts of positive and negative reinforcement, punishment, and omission training
- Appreciate the importance of behavioral variability in shaping target behaviors
- Distinguish the effects of contingency and contiguity on instrumental conditioning

5-1 Instrumental and Classical Conditioning Compared

These exercises are designed to help you distinguish between instrumental and classical conditioning. The two are often confused, so it is important to recognize some of the differences. The most important distinguishing characteristic is that with instrumental learning, there is a contingency between a response and a stimulus, and in classical conditioning there is a contingency between two stimuli (the CS and US), and no response is required for a stimulus to be presented.

Below are descriptions that summarize published experiments on either classical or instrumental conditioning. Based on the distinctions between the two types of learning that are described above and in your text, review the following examples of conditioning, indicate which type of learning (instrumental or classical) has occurred, and explain your choice.

1) Rats learned that they can escape through a hole when a particular visual stimulus is presented. The rats were placed in an arena that had an escape hole leading to their home cages on one side. The home cage contained a drop of condensed milk, a rat favorite (Rossier et al., 2000).

Instrumental or Classical (circle one)

Explanation:

2) Rats were transported from their home cages to a test box and were then shocked. The researchers then examined freezing behavior in response to both the test box and the procedures used to transport the rats to it. (Bevins, et al. 2000).

Instrumental or Classical

Explanation:

3) Rats were given intracranial stimulation to a reward center in the brain whenever they pressed a bar. The authors examined the relationship between the amount of pressing and the amount of brain stimulation provided. (Leon & Gallistel, 1998).

Instrumental or Classical

Explanation:

4) Rats were given food when (and only when) they directed an appropriate amount of force upon a bar. (Slifkin & Brener, 1998).

Instrumental or Classical (circle one)

Explanation:

5) In a bar pressing task, rats were given food for making the discrimination between a drug (pentobarbital) and a control substance (saline). (McMillan & Hardwick, 2000).

Instrumental or Classical (circle one)

Explanation:

6) Wallabies, a small marsupial species, were exposed to a model of a fox (a predator species) in conjunction with a human who acted as though he/she was going to capture the wallabies (a threatening event). Wallabies were then tested for their avoidance responses toward the model fox alone. (Griffin et al., 2001).

Instrumental or Classical (circle one)

Explanation:

5-2 Discrete Trial and Free Operant Procedures

Pages 148-151 of your text describe the differences between discrete-trial and free operant procedures and it may be helpful to review these pages before proceeding.

Remember that:

- In discrete trial procedures the behavior of the subject terminates the trial and the timing of successive trials (or repetitions of the response) is determined by the experimenter.

- In free operant procedures, the behavior of interest may be repeated any number of times. Thus, the timing of successive repetitions of the response is determined by the subject.

Read the following examples and indicate whether each one involves a discrete-trial or a free-operant procedure (circle the correct option) and explain your choice.

---

1) A rat presses a lever that turns off a shock delivered to its feet.

discrete trials or free operant

Why?

---

2) A rat presses a lever 10 times and turns off a shock delivered to its feet.

discrete trials or free operant

Why?

3) Children are given as many crayons and sheets of paper they want and are rewarded with praise for each drawing they complete.

discrete trials or free operant

Why?

4) A kitten is rewarded with treats each time it successfully uses a litter box.

discrete trials or free operant

Why?

5) A pigeon is placed in an operant chamber and receives reinforcement for every ten times it pecks a key.

discrete trials or free operant

Why?

6) An assembly line worker is paid $1 for every 5 widgets assembled during an 8 hour shift.

discrete trials or free operant

Why?

7) An assembly line worker is paid $100 for each 8 hour shift completed.

discrete trials or free operant

Why?

8) A person logs in and checks email repeatedly until a message is received.

discrete trials or free operant

Why?

9) A runner's progress in completing a marathon in under five hours is monitored over a 12 month period.

discrete trials or free operant

Why?

10) A child is rewarded with a story for inhibiting bedtime tantrums.

discrete trials or free operant

Why?

5-3 Shaping

In instrumental conditioning a subject either makes an appropriate response or avoids making an inappropriate response in order to receive reinforcement. A rat may need to press a lever to receive reinforcement. A child needs to try speaking in order to benefit from speech therapy. Without a response there is nothing to reinforce. As you know from material starting on **page 151,** shaping procedures can be used to bring about the target response. The following exercises are designed to familiarize you with some procedures and details involved in shaping.

5-3.1 Basic procedures

Identify a target behavior. Be creative. Choose a behavior that might not occur spontaneously but could be shaped. After identifying the target behavior list the successive approximations to that behavior below.

Target Behavior:_____

Successive approximations (note: there is no set number of successive approximations you need to come up with. Try to break down the response into several individual behaviors):

Your text describes some variables that influence successful shaping. Prior to completing the exercise below you should review these pages. As you will see, effective shaping requires you to create a good balance between reinforcement and non-reinforcement.

Concept Questions

Imagine you are attempting to train a tiger to offer its shoulder to the side of its cage so that a veterinarian can take a blood sample. Shaping this behavior would require several steps (e.g., getting the tiger to move to the desired side of the cage, presenting the correct side of the body, pressing its shoulder to the cage, holding still while the procedure is completed).

1) Identify beginning, intermediate, and final target behaviors.

2) How could providing too much reinforcement for one of intermediate behaviors hinder reaching the final target response?

3) How could providing too much non-reinforcement of an intermediate response hinder reaching the final target response?

SNIFFY APPLICATION
Practice with magazine training and shaping Sniffy by completing exercises 22 and 23 (p. 147-148). The exercises will also familiarize you with cumulative recordings. More detail on cumulative recordings will be encountered in chapter 6 of your text. You may also want to try some of the more advanced shaping exercises in chapter 14 of your Sniffy Pro manual.

5-4 Procedures of Instrumental Conditioning

The terminology that describes the different procedures of instrumental learning is relatively straightforward. Terms such as positive reinforcement and punishment are easy enough to define. However, it can be challenging to apply these terms to various scenarios in which instrumental learning occurs. **Table 5.1**, reprinted from your text, lists the procedures of instrumental conditioning, the response-outcome contingency, and their effects on responding. Take a few moments to review the contents of **table 5.1**.

TABLE **5.1**
Types of Instrumental Conditioning Procedures

Name of Procedure	Response-Outcome Contingency	Result of Procedure
Positive Reinforcement	*Positive:* Response produces an appetitive stimulus	*Reinforcement* or increase in response rate
Punishment (Positive Punishment)	*Positive:* Response produces an aversive stimulus	*Punishment* or decrease in response rate
Negative Reinforcement (Escape or Avoidance)	*Negative:* Response eliminates or prevents the occurrence of an aversive stimulus	*Reinforcement* or increase in response rate
Omission Training (DRO)	*Negative:* Response eliminates or prevents the occurrence of an appetitive stimulus	*Punishment* or decrease in response rate

It is helpful to practice applying these four outcomes to actual situations. On the next pages are brief descriptions of common behaviors that can change as a result of instrumental conditioning. Read through each one and think about the behavior described, the consequence, and the likely effect of the consequence on behavior. For each example, **1)** identify the behavior, **2)** the response-outcome contingency (positive or negative), and **3)** the name of the procedure listed on the left-hand column of **table 5.1** (positive reinforcement, punishment, negative reinforcement, omission training).

1) Amy drove 70mph every day in a posted 45mph zone until she received a speeding ticket and fine for $500.

Behavior:_____

Response-outcome contingency:_____

Procedure:_____

2) Rachel's English 101 professor compliments her on her writing ability and she subsequently takes several composition classes.

Behavior:_____

Response-outcome contingency:_____

Procedure:_____

3) Geoff is expelled from school for cheating. (Assume in this example he wants to return to school)

Behavior:_____

Response-outcome contingency:_____

Procedure:_____

4) Cory works out at the health club and pushes himself so hard he becomes ill.

Behavior:_____

Response-outcome contingency:_____

Procedure:_____

5) Stephanie buys Eric a candy bar so that he will discontinue his public temper tantrum. From Stephanie's perspective, what is she learning, what is the response-outcome contingency, and what is the procedure?

Behavior:_____

Response-outcome contingency:_____

Procedure:_____

6) A person with a heroin addiction begins feeling withdrawal symptoms and injects another dose to get rid of the unpleasant feelings.

Behavior:_____

Response-outcome contingency:_____

Procedure:_____

7) Laura complains to her fellow students about a professor she has. Her fellow students get tired of hearing it and no longer provide sympathy.

Behavior:_____

Response-outcome contingency:_____

Procedure:_____

8) Marty notices an improvement in his cardiovascular fitness when his buildings elevator breaks down and he has to climb 6 flights of stairs several times per day. After the elevator is fixed, Marty continues taking the stairs.

Behavior:_____

Response-outcome contingency:_____

Procedure:_____

5-5   Response and Reinforcer Relations

5-5.1 Response variability and shaping. Imagine that you have shaped four pigeons to reliably peck a disc. However, now you want the pigeons to peck the disc with their beaks open. This example is based on a study conducted by Deich, Allan, and Zeigler (1988). Below are frequency distributions representing hypothetical data from your pigeons. The graphs show the number of times each pigeon opened its beak at various widths while pecking during a 1 hour baseline session (0 millimeters = beak closed, 25 millimeters = beak wide open). For example, pigeon 1 opened its beak 15mm 25% of the time. The pattern of results varies from pigeon to pigeon, which represents a challenge to you in your task.

Study each graph below and answer the questions that follow.

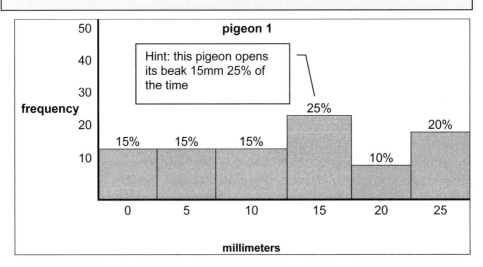

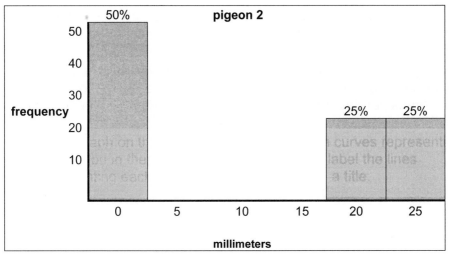

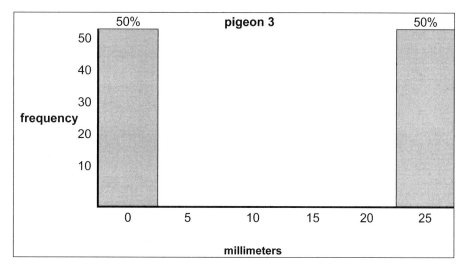

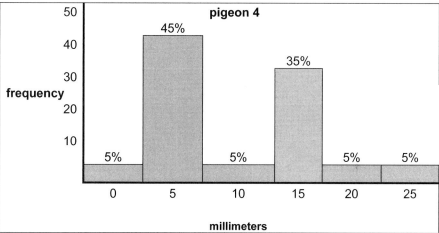

Note: These data are hypothetical and are designed to illustrate concepts rather than replicate the findings of Deich et al.

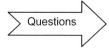

a) Which pigeon showed the greatest variability in responding during the baseline phase? Why did you conclude this?

b) Which showed the least variability? Why did you conclude this?

Remember that these data represent baseline levels of responding. With these same four pigeons you now want to attempt to shape the actual topography of their pecking behavior.

c) Which pigeon could you shape to peck with a 25mm gap most quickly? Why?

d) Which pigeon could you shape to peck with a 10mm gap most quickly? Why?

e) Which pigeon could you shape to peck with a 0mm gap most quickly? Why?

Starting on **page 168** of your text there is a detailed discussion on how responses and reinforcers are related. For example, contiguity and contingency between the response and reinforcer are important determinants of instrumental learning. The exercises below will help you to better see how contiguity and contingency have different roles in conditioning. In addition, there are exercises that focus on the learned-helplessness effect.

5-5.2 Contiguity and contingency.

For each of the following indicate whether there is contiguity between response and outcome, contingency between response and outcome, both, or neither. Examples of contiguity should indicate that the timing between responding and a reinforcer is a critical factor in learning. Examples of contingency should indicate that the causal relation between a response and its consequence is critical in influencing the behavior.

1) John makes a left turn as he walks to the store and just then it starts raining.

Answer:

2) Mary buys a scratch-off lottery ticket and wins $20.

Answer:

3) Peter, a budding poet, tries to get his poems published and continues to submit them to magazines even though one has yet to be accepted.

Answer:

4) Toby wakes up feeling sad. In an effort to feel better, he goes jogging. This gradually gets him out of his funk.

Answer:

5) Joe enjoys bowling and always wears a special shirt for important games.

Answer:

5-5.3   Learned helplessness.

(See page 177 for review) Describe a situation in which you have no control over an aversive stimulus. How could you reduce the detrimental effects of this experience?

6 Schedules of Reinforcement and Choice Behavior

Chapter 6 covers a very important topic in operant learning. Schedules of reinforcement and their impact on rates of responding is a critical area of interest to psychologists. There are numerous types of schedules that are described in your text. The exercises below are designed to give you practice with identifying the schedules and to help you understand how each schedule influences responding. We will also examine some applications of research on schedules of reinforcement, such as choice behavior. Exercises in **section 6-1** provide an overview of some general features of cumulative records. **Section 6-2** serves to familiarize you with the differences between intermittent schedules of reinforcement, namely, how intermittent schedules influence rates of responding. **Section 6-3** has exercises that will help you see how choice behavior is modeled using the matching law. **Section 6-4** covers the topics of self-control and value discounting.

After completing these exercises you should be able to:
- Differentiate between cumulative responding and response rates
- Interpret cumulative records generated by different schedules of reinforcement
- Describe, compare, and contrast the different types of intermittent schedules of reinforcement
- Apply the different schedules of reinforcement to real-world scenarios
- Describe and apply the matching law
- Apply the concepts of self-control and value discounting

6-1 Cumulative Response Recordings

Cumulative records were introduced on **page 188** of your text. Here we will be dealing with cumulative records in much more detail, so first we will practice using and interpreting them.

6-1.1 Plotting data: Response rates vs. cumulative responding. Below are data on free operant responding over a 60-minute period for two subjects.

minute	responses of subject *a* in 10-min blocks	cumulative responses for subject *a*	responses of subject *b* in 10-min blocks	cumulative responses for subject *b*
0	0	0	1	
10	2	2	4	
20	3	5	6	
30	6		11	
40	14		14	
50	18		23	
60	20		30	

In the blank graph below, plot the number of responses for each 10 minute period for both subjects. Be sure to clearly label the two lines separately on your graph.

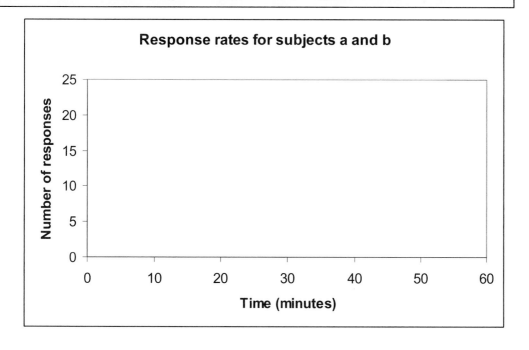

Response rates for subjects a and b

Number of responses / Time (minutes)

To the right of each subject's data above are blank cells for entering cumulative responses over time. Fill in these cells. Using these data plot the cumulative responses of subjects *a* and *b* in the blank graph below.

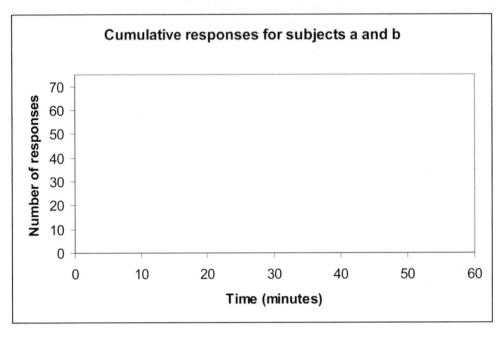

Cumulative responses for subjects a and b

Questions

a) What was the average overall response rate at the end of 10 minutes for:

Subject *a* _____

Subject *b* _____

b) View your cumulative record graph above, assuming both subjects were on the same schedule of reinforcement, which subject may have been given a higher quality reinforcer? Why did you choose this answer?

6-2 Simple Schedules of Intermittent Reinforcement

      Simple schedules of reinforcement include continuous reinforcement (CRF), fixed ratio (FR) and variable ratio (VR) schedules, and fixed interval (FI) and variable interval (VI) schedules. In this exercise we will focus on the intermittent schedules of reinforcement; the FR, VR, FI, and VI schedules. **Figure 6-2** from your text is reprinted below because we will be referring to it several times in the coming exercises. Please review this figure and read the caption before proceeding.

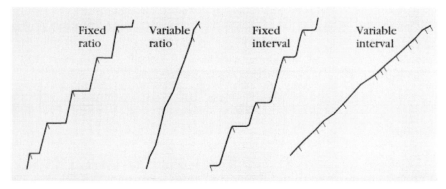

FIGURE **6.2**

Sample cumulative records of different pigeons pecking a response key on four simple schedules of food reinforcement: fixe ratio 120, variable ratio 360, fixed interval 4 minute, and variable interval 2 minute. (From *Schedules of Reinforcement*, by C.B. Ferster and B. F. Skinner, 1957, Appleton-Century-Crofts.)

Questions

6-2.1 Fixed ratio (FR) and variable ratio (VR) schedules.

a) How does increasing the ratio requirement (e.g., from an FR20 to an FR 50) affect responding on FR schedules? (hint: See **p. 190** of your text)

b) Review the FR cumulative response curve from **figure 6-2** above. In the blank figure below fill in a likely cumulative response curve for a subject on a FR20 schedule and subject on a FR40 schedule. Be sure to include post reinforcement pauses and ticks where reinforcement has occurred.

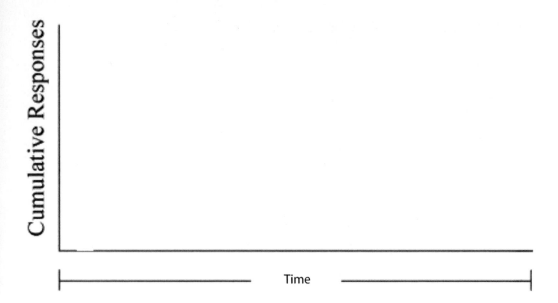

Cumulative Responses

Time

c) Why do VR schedules tend to maintain steady rates of responding?

d) Imagine you have two subjects that were reinforced on two different VR schedules. Subject 1 was reinforced after making the following number of responses: 4, 6, 4, 7, 2, 1, 4. Subject 2 was reinforced after 10, 10, 15, 20, 15, 12, 16 responses. What type of VR schedules were these two subjects on?

Subject 1 _____

Subject 2 _____

e) What is meant by "ratio strain," and describe how you would increase a ratio from a CRF schedule to an FR50.

6-2.2 Fixed interval (FI) and variable interval (VI) schedules

Question

a) Study the FI and VI cumulative records in **figure 6-2** above. Explain why the cumulative record of the subject with the FI schedule differs from that of the subject on the VI schedule.

b) Imagine you are taking two classes in which each of your professors plans to give 10 quizzes over the course the semester. One professor gives pop quizzes and the other professor gives scheduled quizzes. In the blank graphs below, plot two plausible cumulative response curves representing your study efforts for the two classes. Be sure to identify which line corresponds to which class (pop vs. scheduled quizzes).

Cumulative Responses

Time

6-2.3 Applications of schedules of reinforcement. Students generally find the definitions of each schedule of reinforcement to be straightforward. However, actually applying these schedules can be a bit more challenging. In this exercise you can gain practice with applying schedules of reinforcement. In the left column are different scenarios describing different schedules. Answer the questions posed in each scenario in the right column. Note that not all answers require a number for an answer. You may need to write out an explanation to address a question.

Scenario	Answer
1) How many reinforcers can be earned in an hour for a subject on an FR 5 schedule?	
2) What is the maximum number of reinforcers available per hour on a VI 2 min schedule?	
3) What is the maximum number of reinforcers per hour on a VR 2 schedule?	
4) Why do #2 and #3 above differ?	
5) A subject receives 20 reinforcers on a VI 3 min schedule (in an hour). How many reinforcers will it get if it doubles its response rate?	

> Below is a list of examples in which reinforcement is being delivered on a type of schedule that was described in **pages 187-194** of your text. Identify the reinforcement schedule illustrated in these examples using the following abbreviations (Fixed ratio = **FR**, Variable ratio = **VR**, Fixed interval = **FI**, Variable interval = **VI**).

Remember,
- "Ratio" refers to schedules in which reinforcement is delivered based on how many times a subject responds.
- "Interval" refers to the amount of time that must pass before reinforcement is available following the last reinforcer.
- Keep in mind these schedules are based on laboratory experimental procedures. They apply to real world situations but sometimes you have to be a bit flexible in making the application.

1) A young child is allowed to go outside alone to play with friends, under the condition that she checks in with her mother every 30 minutes. Reinforcement in the form of praise is given each time she checks in at the agreed upon time. **Answer:**_____

2) Pop quizzes are a common motivator professors use to encourage studying material on a regular basis and for attending class. Which of the four schedules are being used by professors who give their students pop quizzes? **Answer:** _____

3) Playing slot machines at gambling casinos provide payoffs on occasion, as long as a person is performing the operant response of putting money in the machine and pulling the lever. **Answer:** _____

4) Checking your voicemail to see if any new messages have arrived. **Answer:** _____

5) A factory worker paid on piecework (e.g., having to assemble a certain number of units to receive money). **Answer:** _____

6) In contrast to fishing from the comfort of your boat, fly fishing involves frequent casting and reeling back before catching fish. Which type of schedule is a fly fisher on (hint: the more you cast the better your chances)? **Answer:** _____

7) What type of schedule does a salesperson paid solely on commission experience? **Answer:** _____

8) A radio station announces a free concert ticket giveaway to the 10th person to call if and when a particular song is played between 9 and 10am. **Answer:** _____

9) An executive's contract specifies salary increases to be negotiated every 6 months. **Answer:** _____

10) A custodian takes a break after each floor cleaned. **Answer:**_____

SNIFFFY APPLICATION

Practice conditioning under various schedules of reinforcement with exercises 31-35 (pp. 181-185)

6-3 Schedules, Choice, and the Matching Law

Thus far our examples of schedules of reinforcement comprise of situations in which a subject was responding to one schedule. However, after reading about choice behavior in your text (**starting on p. 198**) you should have come to appreciate that we often encounter several different schedules at once. Furthermore, we can make choices about how we respond to different schedules and the degree to which we respond is proportional to the degree to which we find reinforcement. The matching law summarizes the relationship between effort and reinforcement using a simple equation that is repeated here:

$$B_L/B_R = r_L/r_R$$

Where B_L and B_R are responses or behaviors and r_L and r_R are corresponding rates of reinforcement.

Remember that the matching law states that the relative rate of each behavior is equal to the relative rate of reinforcement that is provided for that behavior. Therefore, if we know the relative rates of reinforcement, then we should be able to predict relative rates of responding on those schedules. The following exercises will give you some practice with using the matching law.

6-3.1 Using the matching law equations. Imagine playing a video game in which you can press buttons to make things happen on the screen. There are two buttons (Left, R_A, and Right, R_B) that can be pressed and the consequences on the screen (reinforcers) are programmed on two different schedules of reinforcement. Based on this:

a) Fill in the missing value to satisfy the matching law in both scenarios below.

Responses to left (B_L)	Responses to right (B_R)
Responses to left (B_L) 25	Responses to right (B_R) 20
Reinforcers to left (r_L) 100	Reinforcers to right (r_R)

Responses to left (B_L)	Responses to right (B_R) 80
Reinforcers to left (r_L) 12	Reinforcers to right (r_R) 96

 Questions

Now let's assume that responding is reinforced on an FI5" schedule on side LEFT and on an FI20" schedule on side RIGHT. Based on the matching law, what percentage of the total amount of time should be devoted to LEFT and RIGHT?

FI5": _____%

FI20": _____%

b) Let's say we have two concurrent schedules and reinforcers are distributed as r_L = 65%, and r_R = 35%. Given this, what value(s) would we have for B_L and B_R if a total of 200 responses occurred?

B_L =

B_R =

c) In the table below the number of reinforcers delivered under r_A and r_B are given. Also given is the total number of responses recorded during each one-hour session. Given this information, fill in the missing values of the table for B_L and B_R. In other words, how many responses should occur when rates of reinforcement are distributed as indicated under r_L and r_R?

B_L	B_R	r_L	r_R	Total responses recorded
		75	50	250
		1000	45	1253
		50	50	271
		12	26	50

d) Let's make some predictions about response rates based on the types of concurrent schedules we are using.

Estimate the proportion of responding you would expect a subject to devote to concurrent VI 20" and VI 30" schedules.

Questions

VI 20" _____

VI 30" _____

Assume a total of 1200 responses were made during the course of this experiment. Write out the matching equation for a concurrent VI 20" and VI 30" schedule, assuming the subject obtained all of the reinforcers that were available with each response alternative.

6-4   Self-control and Value Discounting

One application of instrumental conditioning is in self-control. We often face situations in which we must choose to be rewarded immediately, or to delay a reward. Drinking a high-calorie sweetened beverage brings immediate rewards. Drinking a glass of water has long term rewards because it is healthier choice. As you learned from chapter 6 of your text, we frequently face choices about the quantity of reinforcement. Furthermore, organisms are sensitive to the delay that intervenes between making a response and receiving reinforcement. Reinforcers tend to lose their value when a delay is imposed. A $1000 reward right this moment is perceived to be more valuable than the same amount paid in five years. Value discounting describes this phenomenon. In the exercises below you can gain some practice with the concepts of self-control and value discounting.

6-4.1 Self-control. Describe a situation in which someone might have difficulty showing self control (This can include, but is not limited to, situations involving spending money, eating, and substance use).

What are the two reinforcers in this situation? How do they differ in value?

Which reinforce occurs with a shorter delay?

What tactics might help to encourage self-control in this situation?

6-4.2 Value discounting. Value discounting refers to the fact that the perceived value of a reinforcer is less the longer you have to wait for it. Reinforcer value is discounted or reduced by waiting time or delay to the delivery of the reinforcer (see **p. 213** for review).

Consider the perceived value of getting $100 today. To illustrate this in concrete terms, in the table below indicate how valuable $100 would be for you if you got the money today, tomorrow, 30 days from now, 150 days from now, or 300 days from now. Remember, we are asking for your *perceived* value of $100.

Delay to Delivery in Days	Perceived Value of $100
0	$100
1	
30	
150	
300	

Next, plot the values that you listed in the above table on the axes provided below. Draw a line connecting your points in the format similar to what you see on **figure 6.9** on **p. 214** of your text. Note that in this graphic representation, delay to delivery of the reinforcer is plotted from right to left.

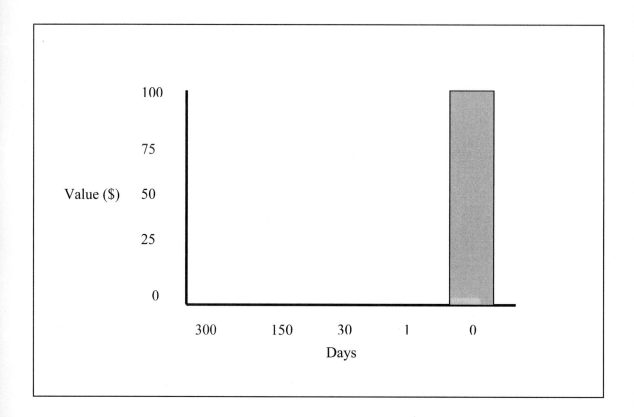

Let's assume that the value discounting function you drew is for a normally functioning individual. For certain types of individuals (heroin addicts, for example), reward value drops much faster the longer they have to wait to obtain the reward. On the graph below, indicate what a discounting function might look like for someone who is less able to appreciate the value of a delayed reinforcer.

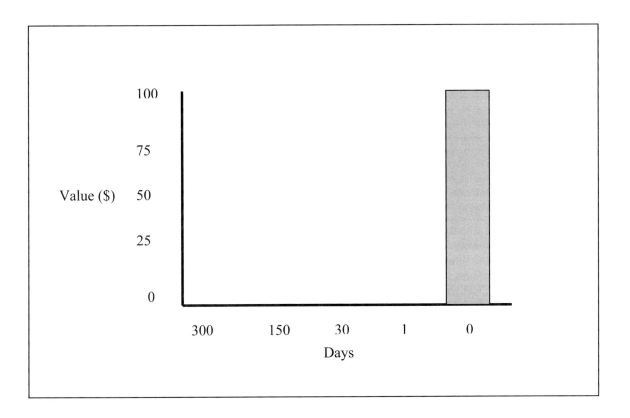

7 Instrumental Conditioning: Motivational Mechanisms

In **Chapters 5** and **6** you learned about many of the different concepts and phenomena of instrumental conditioning. Here we turn to examining the underlying mechanisms. **Chapter 7** of your text tackles two general approaches to the study of the motivational mechanisms of instrumental conditioning: *associative structure* and *behavioral regulation*. First we will explore the associative structure of instrumental conditioning. Classical conditioning can occur during the course of instrumental conditioning and helps to motivate the instrumental response. Thus, the two types of conditioning interact. In **Section 7-1** you will apply several different approaches to examining the nature of these interactions. In contrast to associative theories, theories of behavioral regulation examine instrumental learning in the context of goal-directedness and the constraints that operate on our ongoing behavioral activities. **Section 7-2** includes exercises that will help you apply the different approaches to behavioral regulation.

After completing these exercises you should be able to:
- Compare and contrast the associative structure and behavioral regulation approaches to instrumental conditioning
- Identify the differences between S-R, S-O, R-O, and S-(R-O) associations in instrumental conditioning
- Apply each of these four types of associations to new examples
- Understand and apply the Premack Principle to new examples
- Apply the concept of behavioral bliss point to your own experiences

7-1 The Associative Structure of Instrumental Learning

The exercises in this section are designed to help you identify and understand several different ways in which psychologists explain how associations underlie instrumentally learned responses. As you may recall in reading the first couple pages of the chapter, psychologists examine the motivational mechanisms of instrumental learning from two approaches: associative structure and behavioral regulation.

7-1.1 Differentiating associative structure and behavioral regulation. Most of the chapter is devoted to these two approaches so we will start by contrasting them. For this exercise you should pay close attention to the introductory paragraphs on **pages 220-221** of your text.

For each of the following, indicate whether it applies best to the *associative structure* approach or to the *behavioral regulation* approach to the analysis of instrumental conditioning, and briefly explain why.

1) It takes a more molar rather than molecular approach.

Circle one*:   associative structure   behavioral regulation*

Why?

2) It considers reinforcers to be stimuli rather than responses.

Circle one*:   associative structure   behavioral regulation*

Why?

3) It focuses only on the instrumental response that is involved in a particular instrumental conditioning procedure.

Circle one*:   associative structure   behavioral regulation*

Why?

4) It ignores the concept of optimality.

Circle one*:   associative structure   behavioral regulation*

Why?

5) It ignores the concept of reward expectancy.

Circle one*:   associative structure   behavioral regulation*

Why?

6) It ignores changes in the reinforcer response.

Circle one: *associative structure*   *behavioral regulation*

Why?

7) It ignores the effect of other available reinforcers.

Circle one: *associative structure*   *behavioral regulation*

Why?

8) It can be tested with the use of transfer of control experiments.

Circle one: *associative structure*   *behavioral regulation*

Why?

7-1.2   Associative structure and the three-term contingency. Your text goes into detailed discussion of the associative structure of instrumental conditioning. One of the main issues addressed here concerns how the parts of the three main components of an instrumental conditioning procedure (stimulus-response-outcome; S, R, O) are related. In other words, which of these three terms are associated? and how? For example:

> **S-O: Stimulus-outcome**. When a response is followed by a certain outcome (O) in the presence of a stimulus context (S), S can become associated with O. Once this occurs, S tells the organism that O will occur.
> **S-R: Stimulus-response**. The association is between the stimulus context and the response it elicits. The outcome may help create the association, but is not itself associated with either the antecedent stimulus or the response.
> **R-O: Response-outcome**. An association is formed between a response and its outcome.
> **S-(R-O): Stimulus-(response-outcome)**. The Stimulus context activates the response-outcome association. This is an association in hierarchical form.

The Law of Effect maintains that associations are of the S-R variety. However, as you saw in your text and in the list above, there are numerous other ways to conceptualize the associative nature of instrumental learning. The purpose of this exercise is to allow you to apply these different associative structures to a common example. Below are **figures 5-1** and **5-2** reprinted from your text. Recall that Edward Thorndike examined trial and error learning in cats that were attempting to escape from the boxes shown below. The learning curve below is an example of Thorndike's data. Although the experiment appears rather simple, you may want to refer back to **pages 145-147** to refresh your memory of how it worked.

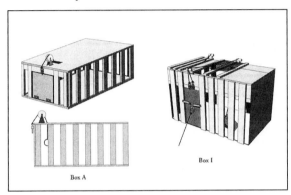

Box I

Box A

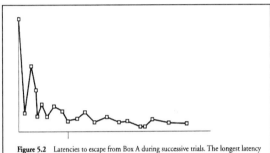

Figure 5.2 Latencies to escape from Box A during successive trials. The longest latency was 160 seconds; the shortest was 6 seconds. (Notice that the axes are not labeled, as in Thorndike's original report.)

Question

In reference to Thorndike's procedures that used box 1 of **figure 5.1** above, what was the:

Stimulus?

Response?

Outcome?

For this exercise you need to consider how each scenario of associative learning applies to the puzzle box learning example. In the spaces below, describe how S-O, S-R, R-O, and S-(R-O) learning applies to cats escaping from Thorndike's puzzle boxes. Be sure to identify what exactly is being associated and how that association develops.

S-O:

S-R:

R-O:

S-(R-O):

Concept Questions

1) What is a reason for doing a reinforcer devaluation procedure? Which type of association is this procedure most relevant to?

2) What is "reward expectancy" and why is it relevant to S-O associations?

3) According to two-process theory, how does a CS modify the rate of an instrumental response? Describe an example of how this happens.

4) How can an S-(R-O) association be involved in lever pressing for food in a Skinner box? What are the S, the R, and the O in this case?

5) Assume a rat reinforced with food for pressing a response lever only learns an R-O association. Could an R-O association alone explain lever press responding? Why or why not?

7-2 Behavioral Regulation

The behavioral regulation perspective on instrumental conditioning is quite distinct from that of the associative structure perspective you practiced above. You may recall from your text that one primary distinction is that behavioral regulation theories focus on the ways in which contingencies limit the ongoing behaviors of organisms. An early theory, called consummatory response theory, holds that the act of engaging in responses such as eating, drinking, and sex is inherently reinforcing. So in this case responses, not stimuli, are reinforcing. Theories that expanded on this perspective, such as the Premack Principle have led to modern approaches to behavioral regulation. The exercises below are designed to better acquaint you with these theories related to behavioral regulation.

7-2.1 Premack Principle. A milestone on the road to the behavioral regulation perspective on instrumental conditioning is the differential probability, or Premack principle (introduced **on pag 236**). The Premack principle maintains that response probabilities are critical features of instrumental conditioning. Recall that Premack dismissed the idea that there is a fundamental distinction between reinforcers and instrumental responses. A response itself can serve as a reinforcer. More specifically, a highly probable response can be used to reinforce a less probable response. For example, eating dessert is a more probable response than eating vegetables for many kids (and adults). Making the response of eating dessert contingent upon eating vegetables is an effective way of increasing the lower probability, vegetable eating, response.

On **page 238** of your text an experiment conducted on rats by Premack was described. The responses involved wheel running and drinking and Premack designed an experiment to test the differential probability principle with these two responses. Before proceeding with the exercise below please review this study.

Figure 7.5 of your text, reprinted below, diagrams another experiment Premack (1965) conducted with children. Below this figure is a set of blank graphs. For this exercise, first review the Premack (1965) study described on **page 237** of your text and think about his results. Next, fill in the blank graphs with probable results of the study (hint: use **figure 7.5** as a guide). Be sure to label the axes of the graphs.

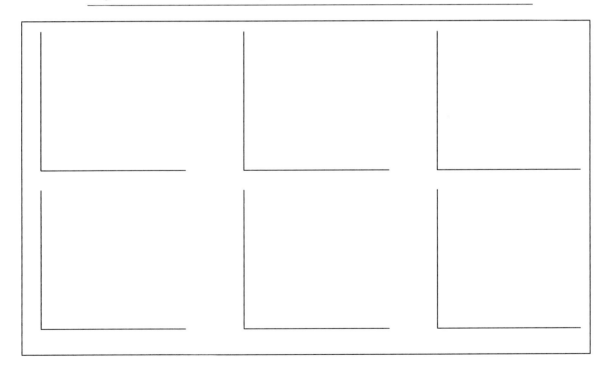

Phase 1
Free eating and pinball playing

All subjects

Ate more
candies

Played more
pinball

Phase 2
Instrumental
conditioning
procedure

Eating
reinforces
pinball playing

Pinball playing
reinforces
eating

FIGURE **7.5**

Diagram of Premack's (1965) study.

7-2.2 The behavioral bliss point. A fundamental assumption of behavioral
\regulation is the concept of the *behavioral bliss point*. **Pages 241-244** discuss
the concept of the bliss point and it will be helpful to review these pages before
doing the exercises below. You probably notice some similarities between the
behavioral bliss point and the Premack principle. Behavioral regulation theories
assume that there is an optimal distribution of activities under free baseline
conditions. When there are no constraints on the activities we may perform we
distribute our activities at our own individually-based optimum levels. However,
sometimes we have to engage in less-preferred activities more than we would
hope. This is because there are instrumental contingencies that cause deviations
from the optimal distribution of activity. Before completing the exercises below
first review **figure 7.8** reprinted below.

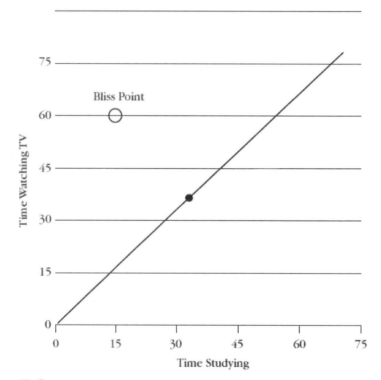

FIGURE **7.8**

Allocation of behavior between watching TV and studying. The open circle shows the
optimal allocation, or behavioral bliss point, obtained when there are no constraints on
either activity. The schedule line represents a schedule of reinforcement in which the
student is required to study for the same amount of time that she gets to watch TV.
Notice that once this schedule of reinforcement is imposed, it is no longer possible for
the student to achieve the behavioral bliss point. The schedule deprives the student of
access to the TV and forces or motivates and increase in studying.

The figure below plots the baseline bliss point (open circle) of a child who was given the opportunity to play pinball and eat candy under unconstrained conditions. As you can see, at the bliss point, the child spent 20 minutes eating candy and 10 minutes playing pinball. Thus, at the baseline or bliss point the ratio of eating to playing pinball was 2:1. The line in the graph is a contingency line that represents the ratio when an instrumental conditioning procedure is introduced that constrains the child's choices. The instrumental contingency represented by the line requires that the child change from its baseline or "bliss" level of responding to one in which she spends 10 minutes eating candy for every 40 minutes she spends playing pinball. Thus, the ratio of times spent on the two responses required by the instrumental procedure is 1:4. Draw a point on the contingency line that shows how the child will redistribute her behavior under the 1:4 contingency.

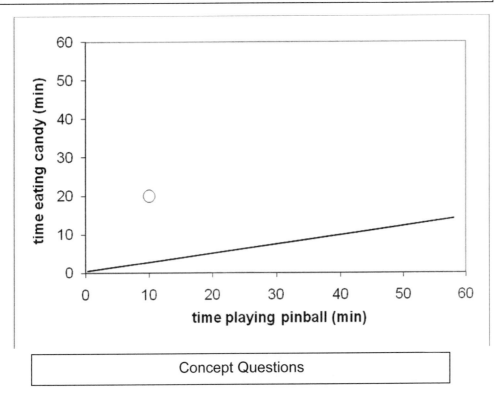

Concept Questions

1) If the child were to insist on spending as much time eating when the instrumental procedure is in effect as during the bliss point, how much time will she have to devote to playing the pinball machine?

2) If she insist on playing the pinball machine as long as she did during the bliss point, how much time will she have to devote to eating?

3) In the above example, the bliss point involves 20 minutes of eating and 10 minutes of playing pinball. According to the Premack Principle, could playing pinball reinforce eating as the instrumental response? Why or why not? Could eating reinforce playing pinball as the instrumental response? Why or why not?

4) Given the schedule line, can she return to the bliss point? If not, how will the child have to redistribute her behavior under these conditions?

According to the response deprivation hypothesis, an activity will serve as a reinforcer if access to it is restricted to less time than what the subject is likely to perform under baseline or unrestricted conditions. Given the bliss point identified in the above figure, answer the following questions using the response deprivation hypothesis.

5) How could playing pinball reinforce eating as the instrumental response?

6) How could eating reinforce playing pinball as the instrumental response?

7-2.3 Personal application. The following exercise asks you to apply the behavioral bliss point approach to your own activities. First, think about how much time you devote to different activities during a normal weekday. How much time, in minutes, do you spend in class, with friends, eating, at work, etc.? Surely the numbers vary by day of the week, timing of the semester, etc. It may be helpful to just pick one particular day of the week in which you engage in most of the activities you list. The numbers you come up with probably differ from what you would have under less constrained conditions. Perhaps the way you allocate your time during winter or spring breaks better reflects your baseline level of responding for various activities such as watching television, spending time with friends, exercising, etc. The exercise below allows you to compare your time allocation under unconstrained and constrained conditions.

> In the left hand column below, list five common activities you engage in during a 24-hour period. Under the *Actual* column indicate the estimated amount of time (in minutes) you spend on these activities during a normal weekday that includes classes, studying, working, sleeping, etc. The time you spend on *actual* activities should reflect the constraints you experience with your busy school schedule. Under the *Ideal* column estimate the amount of time (in minutes) you would spend on each activity under ideal or unconstrained conditions. List the activities under each column from most frequent to least frequent. (Note: presumably you are going to list schoolwork as an activity. If so, treat this as a general category that includes attending class, doing assignments, studying, etc.)

	Activity	Actual amount of time spent (min)	Ideal amount of time spent (min)
1			
2			
3			
4			
5			

> Of the five activities you listed above, pick two from under **Ideal** conditions. In the graph below plot the bliss point between the two activities. Be sure to label the axes of the graph and write a title. Next, plot the **Actual** point on the graph for the same two activities. Connect this point with the origin of the x- and y-axis.

Title:

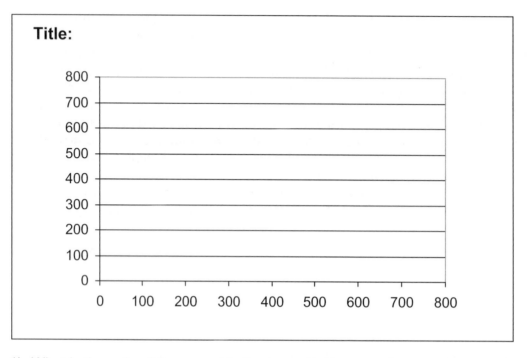

1) What is the ratio of time spent in the two activities you chose under actual conditions?

2) What is the ratio of time spent under ideal conditions (the "bliss point)?

3) Which activity is further from the bliss point under actual conditions?

4) Could you conceive of a substitute for one of the activities? What instrumental requirements are needed to gain access to this substitute? What would be the impact of having access to this substitute?

8 Stimulus Control of Behavior

Chapter 8 covers some common processes that are found in both instrumental and classical conditioning. These processes are generalization, discrimination and stimulus control, and they reflect the dynamic interactions that occur between organisms and the stimuli they experience. At this point you can probably appreciate the importance of both flexibility and selectivity when it comes to learning. The exercises below are designed to enhance your understanding of the details of how these processes are studied and how they work. First we will examine some basics of how stimulus control is measured by focusing on the processes of discrimination and generalization (**section 8-1**). Next, you will consider some of the factors that influence stimulus control, and you will be asked to apply these factors to your own experiences (**section 8-2**). The exercises in **section 8-3** are designed to familiarize you with the details of how stimulus control is studied. Most studies that you will be reading about deal with stimuli that are *discrete*, that is, they usually appear for only a brief period of time. However, many of our responses are also under the control of more general, contextual features of our environment.

After completing these exercises you should be able to:
- Differentiate the processes of generalization and discrimination
- Differentiate between stimulus control in instrumental and classically conditioned responding
- Identify the ways in which stimulus control is established
- Identify various factors that predispose organisms to stimulus control
- Describe how experience with stimuli affects stimulus control

8-1 Measuring stimulus control

Organisms must be able to determine which stimuli predict that a US or reinforcer is available. Sometimes a CS+ or S+ may be very similar to stimuli that do NOT signal a US (the CS-) or reinforcement (the S-). For example, long, long ago cell phones sounded very much alike when a call arrived. The difference between your cell phone (the S+) and someone else's (theS-) was not so great. This was before many different personalized ring options became available. Because the S+ and S- were often very similar (if not identical), it was common to see several people in a crowd reflexively fumbling for their phone when they heard someone else's phone ring. In situations such as this, we notice that over time people may develop a heightened ability to discriminate one stimulus (their own ringtone) from another very similar stimulus (someone else's ringtone).

Describe two examples in which you have had to discriminate between stimuli in order for a response to be reinforced.

Generalization occurs when an organism responds in a similar fashion to two or more stimuli. Some examples of how generalization is studied are described in your text. Based on our definition of generalization, it appears that a standard experiment on generalization requires at least two phases, a training phase and a testing phase. It is important to appreciate the importance of this. Therefore, before proceeding, answer the following question.

Generally speaking, what happens during each phase of a generalization study and why?

Let's review how generalization is depicted graphically. **Figure 8.2 is** reprinted on the next page. Notice that this particular graph refers to an instrumental response that has generalized to different colored stimuli.

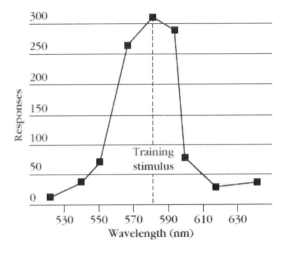

FIGURE **8.2**

Stimulus generalization gradient for pigeons that were trained to peck in the presence of a colored light of 580-nm wavelength and were then tested in the presence of other colors. (From "Discriminability and Stimulus Generalization," by N. Guttman and H. I. Kalish, 1956, *Journal of Experimental Psychology, 51*, pp. 79–88.)

In the graph below, plot generalization gradients for three people who have a fear of heights, ranging from light, moderate, to severe. Your y-axis refers to anxiety level (rated on a scale of 1-10) and the x-axis includes a measure of height. (Note: The style of this graph will be different from the one above because there is a zero point on the x-axis.)

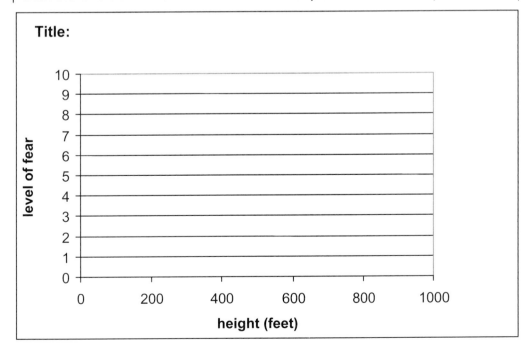

Concept Questions

1) Which of the above curves you drew shows the most stimulus generalization? Which shows the least?

2) Which shows the strongest stimulus control by the stimulus dimension of "height"? Keep in mind that the strength of stimulus control is determined by the slope of the generalization gradient. The steeper the slope, the stronger is the behavior under the control of that stimulus dimension.

SNIFFFY APPLICATION

Examine the processes of generalization, discrimination, and stimulus control in exercises 37-42 (pp. 203-209)

8-2 Stimulus and Response Factors

There are several factors that determine whether responding comes under stimulus control. Individual subjects may attend to different features of complex stimuli, and these are the features that may determine whether responding occurs (recall the experiment by Reynolds, 1961). In addition, the sensory capacities and biological predispositions of an individual or species may also determine whether stimulus control occurs. Several stimulus and response factors that influence stimulus control are discussed on **pages 265-272** of your text. For example:

- Sensory capacity and orientation
- Relative ease of conditioning various stimuli
- Type of reinforcement
- Type of instrumental response

From this list, choose two factors and describe an example of each as it applies to your own experiences. In your answer you need to identify the response that was learned, the stimulus or stimuli that controlled the response, and how that stimulus control developed.

1) Factor:_____

Description:

2) Factor:_____

Description:

8-3 Learning Factors in Stimulus Control

Discrimination training brings behavior under stimulus control. But how does this happen? Suppose we are studying color vision and want to train nonhuman primate subjects to discriminate a specific color—or light of a specific wavelength. For instance, how would we train monkeys to press a button when a color with a wavelength of 550 nm was presented? To demonstrate that pressing a button in response to a 550 nm stimulus is under stimulus control we could run an experiment with the appropriate control groups.

Imagine that during discrimination training monkeys are exposed to a screen that presents a colored stimulus measuring 550 nm. If a monkey presses a button while the stimulus is on, it receives food each time. The S+ is the 550 nm stimulus. The S- varies though. One group cannot receive food reinforcement while the screen is grey (group 1), and a second group learns that it cannot receive food when a slightly different color, a 540 nm stimulus, is presented (group 2). A third control group is not trained to discriminate. It is reinforced for all button presses, regardless of the color on the screen. The experimental design can be summarized as follows:

	Group 1	Group 2	Group 3 (control)
S+	550 nm	550 nm	No discrimination
S-	grey	540 nm	Training

After conducting several hundred trials with these different procedures, you run test trials in which you expose the monkeys to colors ranging from 500 to 600 nm. How do you think monkeys in each group will respond to colors ranging from 500-600 nm?

> In the graph on the next page, fill in three generalization gradients you would predict for the three groups and write a title and interpretation for your graph. You may want to review figure 8.2 for a reminder on how generalization gradients are drawn.

Title:

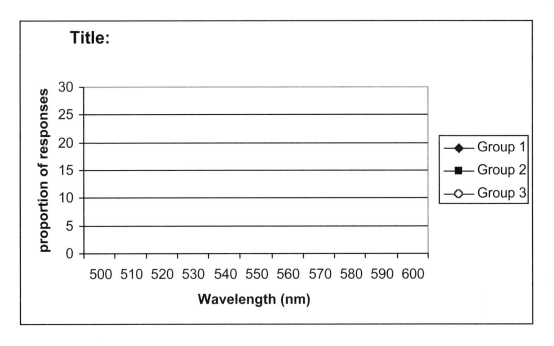

Interpretation:

> Questions

1) Why was group 3, the control group, needed when the S- for group 1 was a grey screen (with no color)?

2) State how stimulus control applies to this experiment. Which group showed the most stimulus control? Which showed the least? Why?

The discrimination learning theory of Spence has generated much research in the area of stimulus control. His theory focuses on both the excitatory and inhibitory components of learning. So far we have focused on excitatory conditioning. Discrimination training results in increased responding to the target stimulus, and less responding to stimuli that differ from the target stimulus. However, it is important to remember that during the CS- or S- phases of discrimination training an organism inhibits responding, since the US or the reinforcer is not forthcoming. So excitatory and inhibitory conditioning interact during learning; Spence's theory tells us this. Let's now examine how the interaction between the two occurs.

Imagine that you trained a pigeon to peck at a key following the onset of a 600 Hz tone. The S+ during training was the 600 Hz tone and the S- was a 400 Hz tone. During testing, the pigeon was presented with tones ranging from 200 to 1000 Hz. Below are hypothetical data that show the level of both conditioned excitation and conditioned inhibition to each frequency during the test phase of the experiment.

Hertz	conditioned excitation	Conditioned inhibition
200	0	-.50
400	.50	-.75
600	1.0	-.50
800	.50	-.25
1000	.25	0

In the graph on the next page, plot these data, using separate lines for excitatory and inhibitory responding using the symbols (● or ■) provided in the legend of the graph and write an interpretation.

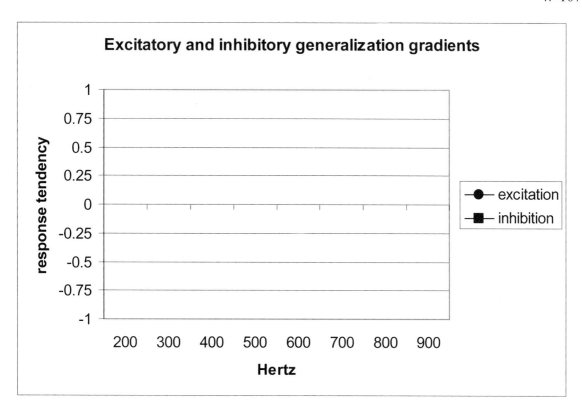

Interpretation:

One phenomenon that is important to Spence's theory is "peak shift" (**p. 282** of your text). This is a very common occurrence in studies of stimulus control. If you indicated that peak shift occurred in the color discrimination study with monkeys described above, well done! If you did not indicate peak shift, take a moment to redraw the lines with peak shift included in the figure below.

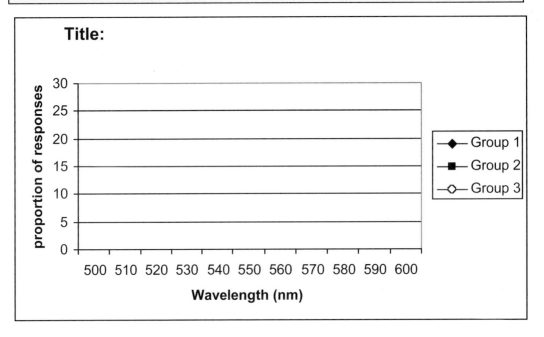

a) Compare and contrast Spence's explanation of peak shift with alternative accounts (p. 285).

b) How might peak shift be maladaptive in some cases?

9 Extinction of Conditioned Behavior

Chapter 9 focuses on the process of extinction. Extinction is a very important phenomenon that has received a lot of attention in basic and applied research. It is also a process that is found in both instrumental and classical conditioning. Thus, an entire chapter devoted to the process of extinction is justified. First, in **section 9-1** you will have a chance to visualize some basic processes involved in extinction, and to practice working with the important role of context in learning and extinction. In **section 9-2** we will see how prior learning history affects extinction.

After completing these exercises you should be able to:

- Understand the processes of extinction and spontaneous recovery of conditioned responding
- Describe the relevance of extinction to treating conditioned fear responses
- Describe the importance of context in extinction
- Distinguish between the renewal effect, reinstatement, and spontaneous recovery
- Apply different characteristics of extinction to real-world examples.
- Describe paradoxical reward effects
- Apply the phenomenon of spontaneous recovery
- Apply different methods of enhancing extinction treatments to real world situations
- Compare and contrast theories of the partial reinforcement extinction effect

9-1 Extinction and Original Learning

9-1.1 Extinction and spontaneous recovery of conditioned responding.

Two processes of classical conditioning that have generated a lot of laboratory and applied research are extinction and spontaneous recovery. In this section you can gain some familiarity with these processes. First, in the graph below indicate in each panel how the data would look if an excitatory conditioned response was acquired, extinguished, and showed spontaneous recovery.

SNIFFFY APPLICATION

Practice with the concepts of extinction and spontaneous recovery in exercises 2 and 3 (p. 41, 44) for classical conditioning and 25-27 (pp. 156-163) for instrumental conditioning.

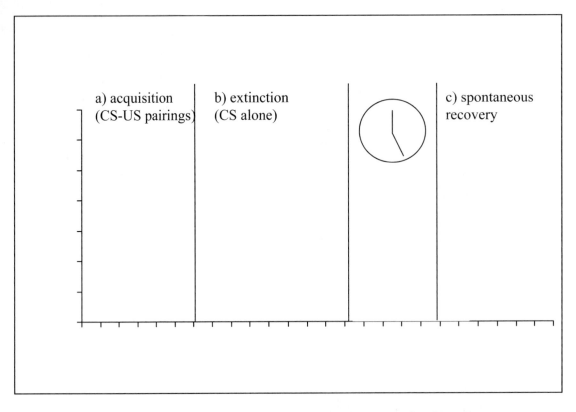

a) acquisition (CS-US pairings)   b) extinction (CS alone)   c) spontaneous recovery

     Next let's examine an actual research application to extinction of conditioned responding.

9-1.2 Phobias: Treatments, relapse prevention, and the renewal effect.

Phobias are frequently treated with behavioral therapies, but there are some limitations to the therapy if sessions are only conducted in one setting. This exercise provides you with the opportunity to practice working with some sample data based on an actual experiment[1], conducted on rats, with implications for treating phobias in humans. On **page 310** of your text, the applied, clinical significance of a phenomenon called the *renewal effect* is discussed. It will be helpful to review the text before completing this exercise. In this exercise we will consider a possible method for extinguishing conditioned phobic responses. The study examined acquisition and extinction in several different physical settings, or contexts.

     One problem with phobias is that people who suffer from them frequently experience relapses when they encounter the phobic stimulus in a context that differs from where they received treatment. Gunther et al. (1998) reasoned that exposure to phobia therapy in multiple contexts, accomplished by using extinction in each one, can provide a more robust treatment of phobias.

---

[1] This example is adopted from Gunther, Denniston, & Miller (1998).

The experimenters conditioned a fear response in groups of rats placed in one of three test chambers that differed in physical characteristics, representing the different contexts. The CS used in this study was a brief presentation of white noise, and this was followed by foot shock delivered via the floor grid of the experimental chambers. Recall that freezing behavior is a common response found in rats when an aversive event is pending, and that a standard dependent variable in studies such as this is drinking behavior. Thus, we can predict that thirsty rats would spend less time drinking if they are in a context that elicits fear. We would expect drinking to become suppressed during conditioning, and return to normal levels during extinction. Three groups of rats were needed to test whether extinction in multiple contexts generalizes to a novel context that the rats never experienced before:

1) a control group that received no extinction ("Group NE")
2) a group that received extinction in one context ("Group E1")
3) a group that received extinction in three different contexts ("Group E3")

Let's briefly return to the question of how this experiment applies to the treatment of phobias. Can you think of a real-world example that humans experience that is analogous to the rat study?

Think of how this might play out in people who want to overcome social anxieties. Imagine that several people are being treated for social phobia. You have three groups and you want to see which group, after extinction treatments, will show the least amount of anxiety while attending a large party. One group receives no extinction and is tested for anxiety at a large party. A second group receives extinction treatment at a small dinner party prior to testing. And a third group receives extinction treatment at the small dinner party, in a large classroom, and in a crowded restaurant. Which treatment group will show the least amount of anxiety at the large party?

Question

Before proceeding, what do you predict for each of the three groups of rats in the Gunther et al. experiment? (In other words, how much conditioned responding do you expect to see in each group of rats when tested in the novel context after the extinction treatments?)

NE:

E1:

E3:

The critical measure in this experiment is the amount of time it took the rats in each group to complete five cumulative seconds of drinking in the presence of the CS when placed in an experimental chamber or context they had never encountered before (the novel context). Below are hypothetical data that reflect the results of this study:

	Group		
	NE	E1	E3
Time to complete 5 seconds of drinking	30	20	5

Graph these data on the axes below and write an interpretation.

Title:

Interpretation:

Questions

The renewal effect and spontaneous recovery seem like very similar effects. People often confuse the two. How does the renewal effect differ from spontaneous recovery?

How are the renewal effect and reinstatement similar? How do the two phenomena differ?

In chapter 3 (exercise 3-1.3) you described a conditioned fear. Possibly, you have overcome the fear that you described. If you have overcome it, have you ever experienced spontaneous recovery, renewal, or reinstatement? How so?

9-2 Enhancing the Effects of Extinction

As we have seen in the exercises above, extinction is *not* necessarily forever. Conditioned responding can reappear under numerous circumstances. This is an issue of concern when it comes to using extinction in behavioral therapies. Take exposure therapy for a conditioned fear response as an example. A person who repeatedly experiences the feared CS in the absence of a US may feel less anxiety and fear about the CS. This all sounds nice and simple. However, there are numerous mechanisms by which an originally extinguished CR reappears. How can this be avoided?

9-2.1 Application of extinction enhancement strategies. Imagine that a client is visiting a behavioral therapist for help with overcoming an intense social phobia. The behavioral therapist and client decide to try exposure therapy to help this individual overcome his fear.

1) Describe in general how a therapist might use extinction treatments as exposure therapy for the client (hint: manipulating exposure to social situations might be a good place to start).

2) How would the therapist address the following issues so that extinction treatments are enhanced (hint see chapter 9 for clues)?

   a. Number and spacing of extinction trials

   b. Reduce spontaneous recovery

   c. Reduce renewal

   d. Compounding extinction stimuli (This may or may not apply, but try to provide an answer.)

9-3 What is Learned in Extinction?

It makes intuitive sense that extinction involves "unlearning" something because the conditioned response is diminished. However, extinction is not a matter of unlearning something, but rather learning something new. In this section there are two sets of exercises that focus on some special properties of extinction. We will explore how prior learning histories affect extinction rates.

9-3.1 Paradoxical reward effects. There are three rather peculiar phenomena of extinction described on **pages 322-325** of your text:
- The overtraining extinction effect
- The magnitude reinforcement extinction effect
- The partial reinforcement extinction effect

First review these effects and then complete the exercise below.

Following are some scenarios involving extinction of learned responses. Read these carefully and identify which of the three effects noted above apply. Answer the questions that follow.

---

1) Veronica answers phones for a company and is paid $2.50 per call for her work. Somehow, Derek does the same job at the same company for $1.00 per call. During a recession, **both** employees are not paid for several days without warning. Which person would you predict will be less inclined to answer the phone when it rings during this period? Which effect explains your answer?

2) Dr. Burns has two students, Jacquie and Kelcy, who repeatedly smile when she attempts to humor the class during lectures. As a result, Dr. Burns makes eye contact with these students more often than with other students. Jacquie smiles at all of Dr. Burns' jokes. Kelcy smiles at some of her jokes. Unfortunately, both students earned Fs on their first exams and subsequently stop smiling at Dr. Burns' jokes. Following the exam, which of the two students do you think Dr. Burns will try looking to more frequently after she tells a joke? Which effect explains your answer?

3) In 1985, Coca-Cola Co. switched to "New Coke", which tasted quite different from traditional Coke. This created quite a stir among beverage drinkers because people did not like the New Coke product as well as the "Classic" Coke it replaced. Based on the theme of these exercises, do you think older, more experienced Classic Coke drinkers would extinguish drinking New Coke more or less rapidly than younger drinkers? Which effect explains your answer?

4) A rat was trained to press two levers for food on two CRF schedules. A red light indicated that the lever on the right could be pressed for one food pellet. A green light indicated that the lever on the left could be pressed for two food pellets. The lights came on, one after the other, at regular intervals. After responding on the two schedules was well established the rat was placed on extinction. The red and green lights were switched on at regular intervals but no food was made available. Which lever will be pressed more frequently during extinction? Which effect explains your answer?

5) Mr. Simpson owns a lawnmower that has a starter cord that has to be pulled several times before it starts. His neighbor, Mr. Flanders, owns a mower that starts at a single pull of the cord. Neighborhood vandals stole spark plugs from both mowers one night. The next time the two go to start their mowers, which one will pull the cord more often before giving up? Which effect explains your answer?

The partial reinforcement extinction effect is of considerable interest to many researchers of learning. There are a few competing theories explaining the mechanisms of the PREE, and **pages 325-327** of your text provide some background and explanations of it. On the next page we will explore some additional details of this effect.

In the graph below, draw 3 hypothetical cumulative response records for subjects that were placed on CRF, VR5, and VR10 schedules of reinforcement until each schedule produced the same total number of lever press responses, and then indicate how the curves would look if extinction followed. Be sure your graph clearly shows how the three groups were differentially affected by the extinction procedure. Write an interpretation of your results below your graph.

Cumulative Responses

Time

Interpretation:

Questions

The discrimination hypothesis. Based on the discrimination hypothesis, which of the following schedules would produce the greatest PREE and why? FR1, FR10, VR10.

Frustration theory. Which of the following would produce the greatest level of frustration when extinction is introduced and why? FR1, FR10, VR10.

The sequential hypothesis. Assume that "R" indicates reward and "N" indicates no reward. Imagine there are three groups of subjects on intermittent reinforcement schedules that are reinforced as follows:

Subject 1: N R R N N R R N R R
Subject 2: R R R N R R N R R N
Subject 3: N N N R N R N R N R

Based on the sequential hypothesis, which subject is most likely to show the strongest evidence of the PREE? Explain your answer.

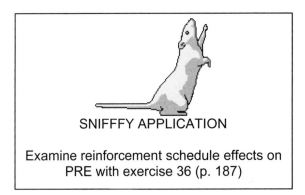

SNIFFFY APPLICATION

Examine reinforcement schedule effects on
PRE with exercise 36 (p. 187)

10 Aversive Control: Avoidance and Punishment

Our approach to studying learning changes a bit with this chapter. Here we will examine how aversive stimulation results in conditioned avoidance responding. Also we will explore the ways that punishment results in decreased instrumental responding. In our analysis of avoidance, we will approach the topic from procedural, theoretical, and applied perspectives (**section 10-1**). According to two-process theory, classical and instrumental conditioning interact during avoidance learning and we will explore how this occurs in **section 10-1**. In **section 10-2** we will turn our discussion to punishment. The exercises will cover some of the applied aspects of punishment.

After completing these exercises you should be able to:

- Distinguish the processes of avoidance and escape
- Describe how two-process theory explains aversive conditioning
- Apply two-process theory to real-world examples
- Identify various procedures for measuring avoidance learning
- Describe some alternatives to two-process theory
- Identify different factors that influence the effectiveness of punishment

10-1 Avoidance Behavior

First we will explore in detail the procedures and theories behind conditioned avoidance. The distinction between avoidance and escape will be made, followed by an exercise that tests two-process theory. Also, we will explore various experimental approaches to studying avoidance responding.

10-1.1 Avoidance, escape and two-process theory. Below are some examples of behaviors that reduce an aversive event. As you read in chapter 10 we can either use avoidance or escape to remove something aversive. Avoidance and escape differ and it will be helpful to review the distinction between the two phenomena before proceeding.

The examples below involve different situations in which an aversive stimulus is present and a response is made to remove that stimulus. Indicate below which examples are instances of avoidance and which are instances of escape.

---

1) Bringing your umbrella with you after hearing a weather report of rain before leaving home.

Circle one: *Avoidance*   *Escape*

2) A rat runs to the opposite side of a shuttle box in response to a tone that predicts shock delivery in 5 seconds.

Avoidance   Escape

3) Switching off your alarm clock just before it goes off

Avoidance   Escape

4) Turning off a noisy car alarm

Avoidance   Escape

5) Taking calcium tablets before eating a large, spicy dinner

Avoidance   Escape

10-1.2 Experimental analysis of avoidance. The exercises below provide you with some practice in differentiating different ways of analyzing avoidance behavior.

1) *Acquired drive experiments* (**p. 342**)

Figure 10.4 from your text (**p. 338**) is reprinted below. This is a standard apparatus used in experiments on avoidance conditioning.

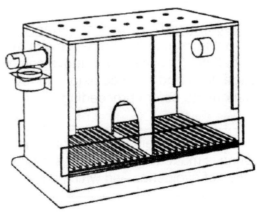

FIGURE **10.4**

A shuttle box. The box has a metal grid floor and is separated into two compartments by an archway. The instrumental response consists of crossing back and forth (shuttling) from one side of the box to the other.

I. In the space below, describe how this apparatus might be modified for use in an acquired-drive experiment. Be sure to differentiate between classical and instrumental conditioning procedures.

II. How does this procedure demonstrate an "acquired drive"?

2) *Independent measurement of fear during acquisition and avoidance behavior* (pp. 343-345)

Figure 10.7 from your text (see below) summarizes results from a study by Lovibond et al. (2008). The experiment tested whether fear and avoidance learning become dissociated in college student participants. Before answering the questions below review the figure and your text.

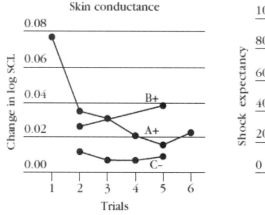 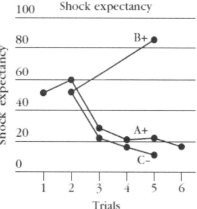

FIGURE **10.7**

Changes in skin conductance and expectancy of shock across trials for a warning stimulus in an avoidance procedure (A+), a Pavlovian CS paired with shock (B+) and a stimulus never paired with shock (C–). (Based on Lovibond et al., 2008.)

I. Why do you think there are measures of both skin conductance (SCR) and shock expectancy?

II. The decline in fear responding in group A+, and the increased responding in B+ is a particularly interesting finding. How might these data, shown in **figure 10.7** above, contradict two-process theory?

3) *Extinction of avoidance behavior through response-blocking and CS-alone exposure* (**p. 345**)

I. Imagine the following scenario.

When Emily was young she was attacked and bitten by a feisty house cat. She immediately acquired a strong fear of cats. Cats became a CS predicting pain (the US). Describe how response-blocking and CS-alone exposure could be used to help her overcome her fear of cats.

10-1.3 Alternative theories of avoidance. Two-process theory explains many phenomena of avoidance learning. However, there are alternatives to two-process theory and they are described on **pages 351-355** of your text. You may want to review these pages before answering the questions below. The alternatives/phenomena include:

1. positive reinforcement through conditioned inhibition or for conditioned safety signals
2. reinforcement of avoidance through reduction of shock frequency
3. avoidance and species-specific defense reactions
4. predatory imminence and defensive and recuperative behaviors

---

Following are statements about avoidance learning. The statements are based on observations that suggest some alternatives to two-process theory. Read each statement carefully and identify (using numbers 1-4 above) which alternative to two-process theory applies (there may be more than one answer to each).

---

1. Avoidance behavior increases in frequency in response to stimuli that signal the onset of an aversive stimulus. _____

2. External and proprioceptive stimuli that are involved in making responses that reduce the number of shocks received become conditioned inhibitors of fear. _____

3. The avoidance responses that develop during the initial learning trials are of critical importance and reflect innate defensive responses.

    _____

4. The avoidance response that is elicited by a threat is directly related to the level of danger present in a given situation. _____

5. Avoidance responses occur because they reduce the frequency of shock, irrespective of signals for shock or safety. _____

SNIFFFY APPLICATION

Examine how different types of punishment influence instrumental responding in exercises 28-30 (pp. 167-170)

10-2   Punishment

The next set of exercises deal with punishment. As you learned from your text this is a controversial topic and much of the research has been focused on identifying the effectiveness of various punishment procedures, although some theoretical issues have been also addressed. Here we will explore various factors that influence the degree to which punishment is effective.

10-2.1 Punishment and instrumental responding. The intensity of a punisher can determine the extent to which operant responding decreases. We will explore this rule in more detail, but first we need to review a method used for studying punishment.

Recall that researchers use suppression ratios to measure the effects of an aversive stimulus on responding. In Pavlovian conditioning an aversive CS suppresses ongoing activity or produces a freezing response. In instrumental conditioning an aversive stimulus also suppresses an operant response. For example, free operant bar pressing will be suppressed if responding is followed by punishers such as loud noise or shock to the feet. The exercise below is designed to illustrate how suppression ratios are used in a study on the effects of punisher intensity on operant responding.

Smoking reduction. Imagine you are conducting a study with four people who are very heavy smokers (2-5 packs per day). The four people are motivated to quit smoking but find the addiction too strong to rely on self-control (so cold turkey is not an option). At the outset you collect four $500 checks from each participant. The checks are made out to each participant's least favorite person or organization. If they fail to reduce their smoking behavior at the end of each week, a check is mailed to the payee. Each participant could lose up to $2000. Each person has a spouse or close friend who monitors the free operant responding of cigarette smoking during the study. The table below shows the number of packs each participant normally smoked (baseline) and the number of packs smoked at the end of each week of the four week study.

Participant	Baseline (packs/week)	Week 1	S.R. 1	Week 2	S.R. 2	Week 3	S.R. 3	Week 4	S.R. 4
1	35	35	0.5	35		34		8	
2	14	10	0.42	8		7		7	
3	21	14		10		6		3	
4	28	25		10		5		25	

 Questions

a) Calculate the suppression ratios (S.R. 1 – 4) for each subject at the end of each week. Write your answers in the shaded boxes to the right of the data for each week.

b) What would the suppression ratio be if each participant reduced the total number of packs smoked per week by one-half?

c) Imagine that this value is the criterion you adopted for all four weeks. Any suppression ratio **greater** than this value resulted in having the check sent for that week.

    a. How much money did subject 1 lose?_____

    b. How much money did subject 2 lose?_____

    c. How much money did subject 3 lose?_____

    d. How much money did subject 4 lose?_____

d) Do you think that altering your criterion could have had a positive effect (e.g., fewer cigarettes smoked) on your results? How so?

10-2.2 Introductory level of punishment. The effectiveness of punishment procedures depends in part on the introductory strength of the punishment. Generally, starting with a weak introductory level of punishment is less effective than starting with strong punishment.

    Imagine you are conducting a study to test this hypothesis using rats as subjects and foot shock as punishment. After training your rats to bar press for food you conduct five punishment sessions in which bar pressing results in the delivery of shock. Your design might look as follows.

Group	Introductory punishment level (volts)	Session 1 suppression ratio	Session 2 – 5 punishment level (volts)	Session 5 suppression ratio
Control	0		0	
Exp 1	50		150	
Exp 2	100		150	
Exp 3	150		150	

Assume that the food delivered is not especially tasty to the rats, and is still delivered during the punishment sessions to rats in all four groups. Your control group is not shocked throughout the duration of the study. Your three experimental groups (Exp 1-3) receive varying introductory levels of punishment. In the table above you will notice empty cells for the suppression ratios for each group.

Fill in the empty cells in the table above with likely suppression ratios for each group at Session 1 and then at Session 5 following a **standard** punishment level phase. Graph your results below with a separate line for each subject.

Title:

Interpretation:

a) What do your results reveal about introductory levels of punishment?

b) Why was food delivered throughout the duration of the punishment sessions?

c) What might the effects on suppression ratios be if you were to use a highly preferred food?

10-2.3 Contingency and contiguity. In addition to punisher intensity, you read about several other factors that influence the effectiveness of punishment. Two such factors are response and stimulus contingency and contiguity.

Contingency: Design an experiment that demonstrates the importance of contingency in punishing a response. Be sure to include a control group. Use the graph on the next page to write in hypothetical results demonstrating that your experiment worked and write an interpretation (see **pp. 359-361**) for ideas on how this might work.

Experimental design.

Title:

Interpretation:

Contiguity: Design an experiment that demonstrates the importance of temporal contiguity in punishing a response and graph and interpret the results below (see **p. 361**).

Experimental design.

Title:

Interpretation:

11 Comparative Cognition I: Memory Mechanisms

The final two chapters of your text focus on the topic of comparative cognition. This topic is different from others covered in your text in that it deals with some relatively complex forms of learning. In addition, a more focused discussion of the topic of memory is provided in **Chapter 11**. In the exercises below, you are first asked to consider a couple of concept questions that serve to help you distinguish comparative cognition from other perspectives covered in the text (**section 11-1**). Next, we will turn our discussion to the various procedures used to study memory, namely delayed matching to sample (**section 11-2**). In **section 11-3** you will be asked to apply various mechanisms of memory to actual situations. The topic of forgetting is covered in **section 11-4** and you will be asked to differentiate between proactive and retroactive interference.

After completing these exercises you should be able to:

- Distinguish comparative cognition from related fields
- Describe the differences between procedural, working, and reference memories
- Describe the delayed matching to sample procedure
- Create your own examples of how the delayed matching to sample procedure works
- Apply concepts behind different memory mechanisms to real-world examples
- Differentiate between proactive and retroactive interference

11-1 Comparative Cognition Defined

The field of *comparative cognition* is distinct from perspectives such as *animal learning* or *cognitive ethology*. The differences can be challenging to identify because there are many similarities between the perspectives. Here you are asked to consider a couple of questions that serve to help you conceptualize the field of comparative cognition.

0

Concept Questions

1) Describe a major difference between cognitive ethology and comparative cognition. How are they similar?

2) Classical conditioning is traditionally presented as a relatively mechanical process that does not require any thinking on the part of the organism. This does not mean that a cognitive interpretation of classical conditioning cannot be offered. How might you apply a cognitive interpretation to conditioned salivary responding?

3) What aspects of the analysis of instrumental learning involve cognitive processes?

11-2 Memory Paradigms

Paradigms represent the ways in which we conceptualize information, and the methods we used to study phenomena. As you have seen, in the psychology of learning there are standard methods used to study things such as blocking, sensory preconditioning, schedules of reinforcement, and many other phenomena. The study of memory relies on standardized procedures as well, such as delayed matching to sample. In this section we will deal with some basic concepts of memory and the methods used to study them.

11-2.1 Procedural memory. After reviewing **page 380** and the definition of procedural memory, list three activities you routinely engage in that utilize your procedural memory system.

1)

2)

3)

11-2.2   Working memory and reference memory. In the examples below, identify which task utilizes working memory and which task uses reference memory.

1) A server in a restaurant takes an order without writing it down. The information must be memorized until the order is placed with the cook.

Circle one: *working*   *reference*

2) A server memorizes the specials that she has to describe to each customer that evening.

   working   *reference*

3) John gets a job as a server in a new restaurant and has to familiarize himself with the standard items on the menu.

working   *reference*

4) London cabbies have to pass a test demonstrating their knowledge of the streets of London before they are allowed to operate cabs.

working   *reference*

5) A dentist doing a root canal runs into unexpected problems and decides she needs to consult a colleague before finishing the case. During the consultation, she is asked to describe what she has done so far and what she found.

working   *reference*

6) A detective is trying to retrace the steps of a suspect and interviews a cab driver who picked up the suspect shortly before the crime. The detective is interested in the route the cab driver took.

working   *reference*

7) To obtain a real estate license, Mary has to pass a test on real estate laws and procedures in her state.

working   *reference*

8) A pilot completing her pre-flight preparations has to keep in mind what aspects of the plane she has already looked at and what aspects she still has to check out.

working   *reference*

11-2.3 <u>Delayed matching to sample.</u> Pages 382-388 describe a method of measuring memory called delayed matching to sample. Review these pages and answer the following concept questions.

```
                    Concept Questions
```

1) Review figure 11.1 on **page 383** of your text. Why would keeping the choice alternatives in the same position (left/right) on each trial be problematic?

2) How might the trace decay hypothesis explain why patients with schizophrenia perform worse on delayed matching to sample tasks than do normal people?

11-3 Memory Mechanisms

On **page 397** of your text, four strategies used for navigation are described. These involve using:
- A Beacon
- A Landmark
- Geometric features
- Spatial gradients

Read the following brief scenarios below and circle the strategy for navigation that applies to each example.

1) Finding a car that was parked behind a large S.U.V. in a parking lot.

Beacon   Landmark   Geometric Features   Spatial Gradient

2) Locating the dining hall using the relative position of the library and dormitory building as two reference points.

Beacon   Landmark   Geometric Features   Spatial Gradient

3) Looking for the "Deli" sign in a grocery store to find a sandwich.

Beacon   Landmark   Geometric Features   Spatial Gradient

4) Finding a home in the country that is one mile north of a large red barn.

Beacon   Landmark   Geometric Features   Spatial Gradient

5) Paddling toward an island to find shelter.

Beacon   Landmark   Geometric Features   Spatial Gradient

6) Approaching a light that has been associated with the delivery of food.

Beacon   Landmark   Geometric Features   Spatial Gradient

7) Finding the quickest way out of a dark wooded area by approaching the brightest light you can see.

Beacon   Landmark   Geometric Features   Spatial Gradient

11-4 Forgetting

Page 411 of your text describes proactive and retroactive interference as two possible sources of forgetting. Review these and complete the exercise below.

Read the scenarios below and identify whether forgetting was due to proactive or retroactive interference (circle one).

1) Wade had two exams in a single day. His first exam was for a learning class at 8:00am. At 10:00am he then took an exam for his behavioral neuroscience class. During his neuroscience exam Wade forgot several details about the cerebellum because of what he memorized for his learning class.

    proactive   **retroactive**

2) Dan was a football player who transferred from the University of Kentucky to the University of North Carolina. Dan experienced difficulty memorizing the names for new plays he was learning at UNC, as many of them were similar to what he learned at Kentucky.

    proactive   **retroactive**

3) Each semester Dr. Matthews learns the names of her new students. Occasionally when she runs into students from previous semesters she has trouble recalling their names because of all of the new students she has met.

    proactive   **retroactive**

4) A cooking school student learns to identify the names of all the spices used in Asian cooking. She subsequently has difficultly remembering the names of some of them because of her learning about Indian cuisine.

    proactive   **retroactive**

5) Julie moved to a new city and frequently cites her previous area code when providing her new phone number.

    proactive   **retroactive**

12 Comparative Cognition II: Special Topics

Here we will explore some additional aspects of comparative cognition. Exercises in **section 12-1** deal with a specialized form of spatial memory found in birds. **Section 12-2** explores the ways in which animals process time, and **12-3** examines serial list learning. In our final set of exercises, we will further explore research that examines the language abilities of nonhuman species such as African grey parrots, chimpanzees, and bonobos (**section 12-4**).

After completing these exercises you should be able to:
- Evaluate several important variables that influence spatial memory in birds
- Apply theories of timing to real-world examples
- Compare and contrast two theories of timing
- Compare and contrast different explanations of serial learning, and identify what makes serial learning a cognitive ability.
- Evaluate different procedures used to test for language abilities in nonhuman primates

12-1   Food Caching and Recovery

The fascinating feats of memory found in food-storing birds such as Clark's nutcrackers are described at the beginning of chapter 12. Carefully controlled experiments have shown that birds rely on memory for locating food stored in thousands of separate locations. In addition to remembering *where* food was stored, these birds appear to remember the type of food stored and when the food was stored. Clayton and Dickinson (1999) tested whether birds remember food quality and duration in which food has been stored. Below are results from their experiment, which is reprinted from **figure 12.4** of your text.

Review the figure below and also the description of the study in your text and answer the questions that follow.

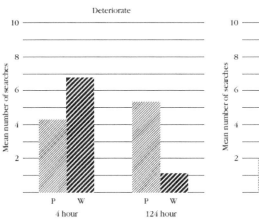
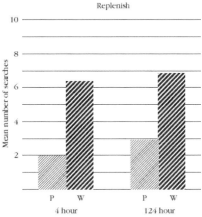

1) What do P and W represent in the figure?

2) What is the "Deteriorate" condition? How is this different from the "Replenish" condition?

3) What did the birds in the "deteriorate" condition experience?

4) What did the birds in the "replenish" condition experience?

5) What do the data of Clayton and Dickinson (1999) suggest about the variables of *what* and *when* in food storage?

6) Critics maintained that the decline in preference for worms cached for 124 hours was a result of memory decay, not episodic memory of when caching occurred. How have researchers responded to this criticism?

12-2 Timing

Now we turn to how animals respond to the passage of time. The procedures used to study timing are important to understand. In the exercises below you are asked to consider some procedural issues in the study of timing, and also consider two alternative theories to timing behavior.

Concept questions

1) If you take a class in the basement of a building with no clocks or watches present, what cues might you use to estimate the amount of time that has passed since the beginning of the class period?

2) Subjects in timing experiments are often trained to respond on a Fixed Interval schedule. This leads to increased response rates as subjects get closer to the time that the reinforcer is made available. How is an FI schedule related to the "peak procedure" used to produce evidence of timing. Where does the "peak" occur in this procedure?

3) What would happen if a "blackout" period were introduced into the peak procedure? What does this demonstrate about timing?

4) Based on studies discussed in the text, how do most organisms discriminate the difference between 12 seconds and 48 seconds (circle your choice):

    a. 48 seconds is 36 seconds more than 12 seconds

    b. 48 seconds is four times as long as 12 seconds

What principle reviewed in chapter 12 explains your choice?

12-2.2 Scalar Expectancy Theory

> Study the *information processing model of timing* depicted in **figure 12.7** below (**p. 431 of your text**). At first it might seem a bit abstract. However, carefully thinking through each step will help you see how it applies to how you process time. Review the model and answer the following questions.

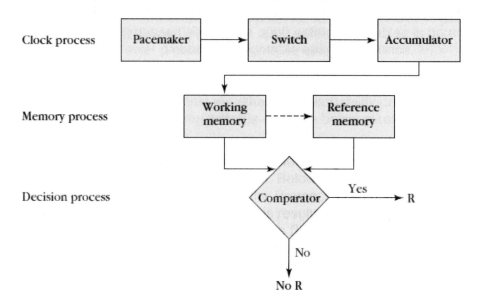

1) What does the *accumulator* accumulate?

2) How are the *switch* and *accumulator* related?

3) How are *working memory* and *reference memory* systems processing the number of accumulated pulses?

4) What is the function of the *comparator*?

Imagine the coach of a football team calls a timeout that can last no more than two minutes to avoid incurring a penalty. During the timeout period the coach has to decide on a play and announce it to his team within 90 seconds of calling the timeout. Describe below how the information processing model of timing applies to this situation.

12-2.3   Information processing versus behavioral theory.

The *information processing theory* of timing contrasts with the *behavioral theory* of timing (**pp. 432-433**). The exercise below is designed to help you apply each theory, and to identify similarities and differences between the two.

Read the following scenario and answer the questions that follow.

You have placed a takeout order at your favorite restaurant. The restaurant is as always very busy and there will be a wait before your food is ready. Based on past experience the wait could be 20 minutes or so. Assume that external cues such as a clock or watch are absent so your only cue is the passage of time that follows placing your order. Your decision to check the front counter of the restaurant to see if your food is ready is the instrumental response.

1) Based on this information, describe how the information processing model of timing applies to this example. Be sure to make reference to all components of the model (the pacemaker, switch, accumulator, working and reference memory, and comparator).

2) Describe how the behavioral theory of timing could be applied to this example. Be sure to refer to adjunctive behaviors, interim, and terminal responses.

3) How do the two theories differ? How are they similar?

12-3 Serial List Learning

The phenomenon of serial list learning is discussed on **pages 434 – 439** of your text. Serial learning involves learning the orderly sequences in which stimuli occur.

Review **figure 12.8** on **page 434** of your text and answer the questions below.

1) Contrast learning a **response chain** versus **serial representation learning**.

2) What specifically makes learning the sequence of stimuli on the right hand portion of **figure 12.8** different from learning the sequence on the left?

3) Which of the two types of learning that occur in the situation depicted on **figure 12.8** involves a cognitive component? Why did you choose your answer?

12-4 Language

Sue Savage-Rumbaugh leads a productive group of researchers examining language abilities in primates. This work is featured on **pages 449-454** of your text. Dr. Savage-Rumbaugh initiated the work with a bonobo named Kanzi while at the Language Research Center at Georgia State University. The work has continued for many years. Kanzi, as well as other language-trained apes and Dr. Savage-Rumbaugh, are currently located at the Great Ape Trust in Iowa. The work is featured at www.greatapetrust.org. As you learned in your text Kanzi communicates using an artificial language composed of lexigram symbols such as those pictured in **figure 12.16**, reprinted from your text below.

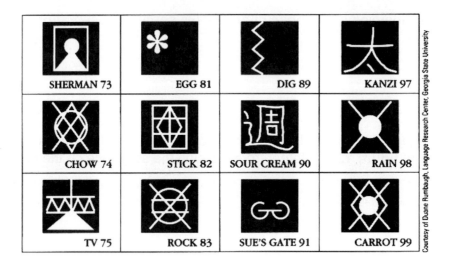

Courtesy of Duane Rumbaugh, Language Research Center, Georgia State University

These symbols represent words of the Yerkish language. The work in animal language capacities is controversial. It is also somewhat difficult to evaluate if one only reads about it. It may help to view some actual examples as suggested below.

Your text describes research on Kanzi's ability to recognize spoken English words. You can view examples at
http://www.greatapetrust.org/research/general/kanzi.php
View the clip entitled "*Kanzi understands spoken language*" and answer the questions that follow.

---

1) Why does Kanzi wear the headphones? And why does the experimenter sit behind Kanzi?

2) Based on your observations of this clip *alone*, do you think Kanzi understands the lexigrams as words?

3) Based on what you have learned about classical and instrumental conditioning, do you see how these forms of learning may apply to what Kanzi was doing in the clip you watched?

Your text describes some experiments involving language comprehension. The experiments were designed to determine if Kanzi could understand language in a flexible way. For example, Kanzi was asked to do something unusual like "Make the (toy) doggie bite the (toy) snake". You can see sample trials of this experiment at http://www.greatapetrust.org/research/general/panbanishaKanzi.php.

View the media clip entitled "Kanzi and novel sentences" and answer the questions about the clip.

1) Why did the experimenter wear the mask?

2) Why did the experimenter ask Kanzi to do things that seemed somewhat unusual?

3) Compared with the first video clip you watched, does this one demonstrate greater evidence of language ability in Kanzi? Why or why not?

References

Bevins, R., Rauhut, A. S., McPhee, J. E., & Ayers, J. J. B. (2000). One-trial context fear conditioning with immediate shock: The roles of transport and contextual cues. *Animal Learning and Behavior, 28*, 162-171.

Cheney, D. L., & Seyfarth, R. M. (1990). *How monkeys see the world.* Chicago: University of Chicago Press.

Clayton, N. S., & Dickinson, A. (1999). Scrub jays (Aphelocoma coerulescens) remember the relative time of caching as well as the location and content of their caches. *Journal of Comparative Psychology, 113*, 403-416.

Deich, J. D., Allan, R. W., & Zeigler, H. P. (1988). Conjunctive differentiation of gape during food-reinforced key pecking in the pigeon. *Animal Learning and Behavior, 16*, 268-276.

Griffin, A.S., Evans, C.S., & Blumstein, D.T. (2001). Learning specificity in acquired predator recognition. *Animal Behaviour, 62*, 577-589.

Gunther, L.M., Denniston, J. C., & Miller, R. R. (1998). Conducting exposure treatment in multiple contexts can prevent relapse. *Behaviour Research and Therapy, 36*, 75-91.

Leon, M. I. & Gallistel, C. R. (1998). Self-stimulating rats combine subjective reward magnitude and subjective reward rate multiplicatively. *Journal of Experimental Psychology: Animal Behavior Processes*, 24, 265-277.

McMillan, D. E., & Hardwick, W. C. (2000). Drug discrimination in rats under concurrent variable-interval variable-interval schedules. *Journal of the Experimental Analysis of Behavior, 73*, 103-120.

Reynolds, G. S. (1961). Attention in the pigeon. *Journal of the Experimental Analysis of Behavior, 4*, 203-208.

Rossier, J., Grobety, M-C., & Schenk, F. (2000). Spatial learning in rats across visually disconnected environments. *Animal Learning and Behavior, 28*, 16-27.

Slifkin, A. B., & Brener, J. (1998). Control of operant force production. *Journal of Experimental Psychology: Animal Behavior Processes, 24*, 1-8.

Timberlake, W., & Grant, D. S. (1975). Auto-shaping in rats to the presentation of another rat predicting food. *Science*, 190, 690-692.

Tinbergen, N. (1963). On aims and methods of ethology. *Zeitschrift für Tierpsychologie, 20*, 410-433.

Tolman, E. C., & Honzik, C. H. (1930). Degrees of hunger, reward and non-reward, and maze learning in rats. *University of California Publications in Psychology, 4,* 241-256.

Westbrook, R. F., Jones, M. L., Bailey, G. K., & Harris, J. A. (2000). Contextual control over conditioned responding in a latent inhibition paradigm. *Journal of Experimental Psychology: Animal Behavior Processes, 26,* 157-173.